Integrating Legal Compliance With Sustainable Development Goals

Farahdilah Ghazali
Universiti Putra Malaysia, Malaysia

Siti Fazilah Abdul Shukor
University of Tunku Abdul Rahman, Malaysia

IGI Global
Scientific Publishing
Publishing Tomorrow's Research Today

Vice President of Editorial	Melissa Wagner
Director of Acquisitions	Mikaela Felty
Director of Book Development	Jocelynn Hessler
Production Manager	Mike Brehm
Cover Design	Jose Rosado

Published in the United States of America by
IGI Global Scientific Publishing
701 East Chocolate Avenue
Hershey, PA, 17033, USA
Tel: 717-533-8845
Fax: 717-533-7115
Website: https://www.igi-global.com E-mail: cust@igi-global.com

Library of Congress Cataloging-in-Publication Data

Names: Ghazali, Farahdilah editor | Siti Fazilah Abdul Shukor, 1986- editor
Title: Integrating legal compliance with sustainable development goals / edited by Farahdilah Ghazali, Siti Fazilah Abdul Shukor.
Description: Hershey : IGI Global Scientific Publishing, 2026. | Includes bibliographical references and index. | Summary: "This book explores the intersection of legal compliance and sustainable development, examining how laws, policies, and regulations can support the achievement of SDGs. It seeks to address key issues such as leveraging legal systems to achieve sustainability objectives as well the challenges and opportunities for integrating compliance frameworks with SDGs"-- Provided by publisher.
Identifiers: LCCN 2025007597 (print) | LCCN 2025007598 (ebook) | ISBN 9798337317922 hardcover | ISBN 9798337317939 paperback | ISBN 9798337317946 ebook
Subjects: LCSH: Sustainable development--Law and legislation--Malaysia | Sustainable development--Law and legislation--India | Environmental law--Malaysia | Environmental law--India
Classification: LCC KNC705 .I58 2025 (print) | LCC KNC705 (ebook) | DDC 344.5404/6--dcundefined
LC record available at https://lccn.loc.gov/2025007597
LC ebook record available at https://lccn.loc.gov/2025007598
British Cataloguing in Publication Data
A Cataloguing in Publication record for this book is available from the British Library.

Table of Contents

Detailed Table of Contents

Marine spatial planning emerged around 40 years ago due to the pressing anthropogenic activities that exert degradation on marine ecosystem. Today, it is widely adopted by more than 102 countries and territories to effectively allocate users and uses in the marine space. MSP is proven as a tool to address multiple ocean issues due to its area-based characteristics. By utilising MSP to govern the ocean areas, conflicting uses, and domination of single activity in a space can be prevented while promoting ecosystem recovery. However, Malaysia as a maritime nation is lacked behind in advancing MSP to manage it waters. This chapter discusses the law and policies in Malaysia that would contribute to the adoption of MSP, thus achieving blue economy and Sustainable Development Goals. Australia, China and the Netherlands have successfully used MSP to manage their marine resources. By benchmarking these countries, Malaysia can uphold a transparent decision making and balanced top-down and bottom-up management, build a resilient ecosystem especially for the livelihood of coastal communities.

Legal tools and sustainable urban planning are involved to establish smart cities to achieve the environmental sustainability, social equity and economic stability. The smart city development is one of the elements to be analyzed by determining how legal instruments support the planning structures of the cities. Sustainable solutions through technical solutions and good administration are needed to counter urban growth and environmental challenge. Sustainable transportation, eco-friendly infrastructure bespeak of the legal tools being used in the form of zoning laws, land use regulations and environmental policies. It is also through public private partnerships that investment in projects related to the smart city grows, coupled with IoT, AI, and blockchain, which helps make things more sustainable. Business growth through the balance paid by legal frameworks of ecological conservation, disasters resilience and climate adaptation.

This chapter explores the crucial role of fish in global food security, particularly in Malaysia, where high consumption necessitates imports from neighboring countries. The aquaculture sector has emerged as a strategic solution to balance supply and demand with Asia leading global production. Over the years, advancements in biotechnology including in the aquaculture sector have enhanced aquaculture through genetic improvements, disease prevention and optimized breeding techniques. However, rapid expansion poses challenges such as environmental sustainability and regulatory oversight. The chapter examines international perspectives on transgenic fish, focusing on Norway and Australia's regulatory frameworks, biosecurity measures, and risk assessments. Malaysia's biosafety framework, including the Malaysian Biosafety Act 2007 and ASEAN Guidelines are also analyzed in this chapter to assess their effectiveness in protecting ecosystems and ensuring food security amid evolving aquaculture technologies.

Spain adopted the 2030 Agenda for Sustainable Development in 2015, making SDG 6—Clean Water and Sanitation—a national priority. Key regulations, such as Law 7/2021 on Climate Change and Royal Decree 3/2023 on water quality, strengthened water management and environmental resilience. Public water companies were required to adapt strategies, promoting clear sustainability reporting, thus fostering greater accountability and stakeholder trust. This chapter analyzes the presence and evolution of SDG 6-related information in the Sustainability Reports of public water companies in Spain. It explores how recent regulations have influenced reporting practices, and whether they have led to more comprehensive and aligned disclosures with national and international sustainability standards. The comparative analysis

Sustainable Development Goal (SDG) 16- promoting peace, justice, and strong institutions, it is key to building inclusive and accountable societies. To achieve SDG 16, this need not only systematic gap assessments and robust measures of the legal world and issue of access to justice, but also we need legal and policy innovations to bridge those gaps, as SDG 16 is demanding a whole spectrum of change. Ensuring that we have effective legal systems in place is key to upholding human rights and fighting corruption and transparency. Increasingly, we see policymakers themselves are turning to digital tools, from blockchain technology to AI-driven governance systems, to simplify legal processes, cut bureaucratic waste, and increase confidence in public institutions. Policy innovations are also essential when it comes to tackling global challenges on the rise like political instability, economic inequality, and environmental catastrophe.

Good governance is very important for improving the performance and effectiveness of higher education institutions (HEIs). This research looks examines how the application of good governance is used by interpreting the applicable principles in Malaysian HEIs. By conducting an extensive literature review and thorough analysis of relevant policy papers, this research presents key dimensions of good governance, such as accountability, transparency, autonomy, and participation from stakeholders. The results show that while Malaysian HEIs are getting better at adopting good governance practices, there still needs to be improvement, especially in the areas of institutional autonomy and stakeholder engagement. This research provides suggestions for Malaysian HEIs to make further changes to strengthen their governance structures and processes, to come into alignment with international best practices, and to ultimately improve their overall performance and responsiveness to societal needs.

The Sustainable Development Goals (SDGs) aim to end poverty, protect the planet, and promote peace and prosperity by 2030. Achieving these goals requires good governance, which depends on the legal literacy of key actors, including company officers. This study explores the legal literacy of company officers in Malaysia, focusing on their understanding of the Companies Act 2016 (Act 777). Using a qualitative approach, the study analyzed court cases, statutes, and data from in-depth semi-structured interviews with seven company officers. Thematic analysis revealed that directors often lack legal literacy, while company secretaries and auditors demonstrate moderate understanding of the Act. These gaps contribute to breaches of duties and legal actions, impacting corporate governance. The findings highlight the urgent need for improved legal awareness among company officers and offer insights for policymakers to strengthen regulatory frameworks. This research links legal literacy to SDG 16, emphasizing its role in promoting strong institutions and sustainable governance.

Preface

The Sustainable Development Goals (SDGs) are a globally agreed blueprint for achieving a more equitable, peaceful, and sustainable future. Adopted by all United Nations member states in 2015, these 17 goals address the world's most pressing challenges including poverty, hunger, education, climate change, clean water, and strong institutions by encouraging countries to work collaboratively across sectors and borders.

Their importance lies in providing a shared vision and measurable targets that guide policy, business, and civil society toward long-term development that doesn't compromise future generations. By embedding principles of justice, inclusion, environmental stewardship, and economic resilience, the SDGs help ensure that progress is not only rapid but meaningful and fair.

The 193 member states of the United Nations adopted the 2030 Agenda and committed to work collectively across 17 interconnected goals to tackle global challenges like poverty, climate change, health, education, and justice. Achieving these ambitious goals demands coordinated action across diverse sectors, with robust legal frameworks and compliance mechanisms serving as foundational pillars. Laws and regulations are crucial not only for promoting sustainable practices and protecting the environment but also for ensuring social justice and fostering resilient economic growth.

This edited volume, *Integrating Legal Compliance with Sustainable Development Goals*, delves into the vital intersection of legal compliance and sustainable development. It offers a comprehensive exploration of how laws, policies, and regulations can be harnessed to support and accelerate the realization of the SDGs. Throughout its chapters, the book examines both the opportunities and challenges of aligning legal compliance frameworks with sustainability objectives.

The contributions within this book present a rich blend of theoretical insights, empirical case studies, and pragmatic policy recommendations. Together, they bridge the gap between legal compliance and sustainable development, showcasing best practices and innovative approaches from a variety of jurisdictions and sectors.

The scope of this volume spans international legal standards such as the SDGs and the Paris Agreement as well as country-specific regulations that shape corporate sustainability and governance.

Our objectives in assembling this collection are threefold:

1. To examine how legal frameworks and compliance mechanisms can be leveraged to achieve the Sustainable Development Goals.
2. To identify challenges and propose actionable solutions for integrating legal compliance with sustainable development practices.
3. To highlight exemplary case studies and policy initiatives that demonstrate successful alignment of law and sustainability.

This volume presents a comprehensive exploration of how legal frameworks intersect with sustainability across diverse sectors, showcasing the potential of law to drive transformative change in alignment with the Sustainable Development Goals (SDGs). Chapters cover themes such as sustainable tourism, urban planning, marine spatial governance, aquaculture, and clean water management, offering case studies from Malaysia and beyond. The book also delves into innovative regulatory tools like green subsidies, carbon tariffs, AI governance, and public-private partnerships to demonstrate how legal reforms can support climate resilience, economic diversification, and environmental protection. The recognition of effective legal structures coupled with transparent reporting, stakeholder engagement, and integrated governance are key to sustainable development.

Human rights and institutional reform feature prominently, with chapters addressing legal compliance under the 2030 Agenda, the rights of prisoners and refugees, and the role of legal literacy in achieving SDG 16. The volume emphasizes the need for inclusive justice systems, social equity, and strong institutions, while also advocating for reforms in higher education governance, remote work legislation, and corporate responsibility. Drawing on both domestic and international comparisons, the book highlights practical pathways for embedding sustainability across legal, economic, and social systems, positioning law as a catalyst for regenerative development and long-term resilience.

As we conclude this comprehensive volume, it is clear that the path toward sustainable development in the 21st century is deeply intertwined with the evolution and implementation of robust legal frameworks, innovative policies, and resilient governance structures across diverse sectors and geographies. The chapters presented herein collectively underscore the indispensable role that law, regulation, and institutional capacity play in addressing some of the most pressing challenges of our time, from water security to sustainable trade, urban planning, marine resource management, and the future of work.

This book illuminates how legal systems can act both as enablers and safeguards, balancing economic growth with environmental stewardship, social equity, and human rights. It also highlights the importance of inclusivity, transparency, and cross-sector collaboration in crafting legal instruments that are adaptable to evolving technological, ecological, and socio-political realities.

Ultimately, this collection affirms that sustainable development is not merely an aspirational ideal but a practical imperative one that requires continuous legal innovation, vigilant governance, and collective action. We are hopeful that the insights and guidance offered in these pages will inspire and equip those engaged in this transformative endeavor, fostering legal and policy environments that truly support a sustainable, just, and thriving world.

Chapter 1
Sustainable Tourism Law: Advancing Regenerative Tourism and SDG Integration Through Legal Pathways

Mooi Kwong Anthony Tee
https://orcid.org/0000-0001-5754-4015
Universiti Tunku Abdul Rahman, Malaysia

Ai Na Seow
Universiti Tunku Abdul Rahman, Malaysia

ABSTRACT

This chapter explores the evolving landscape of sustainable tourism law, focusing on how legal frameworks can facilitate the transition from sustainable to regenerative tourism practices while supporting the achievement of the United Nations Sustainable Development Goals (SDGs). This study explores international, regional, and national legal instruments that support the development of sustainable tourism. It highlights best practices and innovative legal pathways that foster environmental stewardship, promote social equity, and strengthen economic resilience. By drawing on case studies and policy analysis, the chapter examines how tourism law can be effectively aligned with the Sustainable Development Goals (SDGs). Key legal challenges are addressed to uncover opportunities for reform. The chapter concludes with practical recommendations and presents a clear roadmap for policymakers, legal practitioners, and tourism stakeholders dedicated to advancing regenerative tourism.

DOI: 10.4018/979-8-3373-1792-2.ch001

INTRODUCTION

Sustainable tourism is defined by the World Tourism Organization (UNWTO) as tourism that considers its current and future economic, social, and environmental impacts. The approach focuses on meeting the needs of visitors, the tourism industry, the environment, and host communities (UNWTO, 2017). The core principles of sustainable tourism revolve around minimizing environmental impact, fostering cultural integrity, and ensuring socio-economic benefits for local communities (Hall et al., 2019). The triple bottom line approach in sustainable tourism is to balance economic viability, environmental conservation, and social equity. It is to ensure that resources are preserved for the benefit of future generations. Conversely, "regenerative tourism" incorporates the concepts of circular economy, ecosystem restoration, and community welfare (Mang & Reed, 2018). It prioritises collaborative partnerships, local empowerment, and adaptive management to restore and strengthen the natural and cultural resources essential for tourism (Fullagar & Wilson, 2020). In contrast, regenerative tourism goes beyond mere sustainability by proactively revitalising ecosystems and communities. This approach transitions the emphasis from reducing harm to generating net positive effects on the environment and society.

Transitioning from sustainable to regenerative tourism is crucial for undertaking the urgent challenges of climate change, biodiversity loss, and social inequities aggravated by traditional tourism models. While sustainable tourism plays a significant role in reducing negative impacts, it falls short of actively enhancing positive contributions. Regenerative tourism, in contrast, focuses on restoring natural systems, strengthening community resilience, and creating lasting socio-economic benefits (Sheldon, 2020). This revolution is crucial in the context of the United Nations Sustainable Development Goals (SDGs), which call for urgent action to combat climate change, protect terrestrial and marine ecosystems, and reduce inequalities (United Nations, 2015). Regenerative tourism advances these objectives by promoting practices that restore ecosystems, empower local communities, and ensure equitable distribution of tourism-related benefits. For instance, it supports SDG 13 (Climate Action) by encouraging carbon sequestration initiatives and advances SDG 15 (Life on Land) through targeted biodiversity conservation efforts. (Harris & Pappalepore, 2021). Additionally, the regenerative approach addresses the shortcomings of traditional tourism models, including over-tourism, resource depletion, and cultural and community disruption. Prioritizing regenerative practices enables destinations to build resilience against environmental and economic disruptions, ensuring long-term sustainability and well-being for all stakeholders (Boley & Johnson Gaither, 2020). The transition from sustainable to regenerative tourism drives the creation of a tourism industry that sustains and rejuvenates the ecosystems and communities. This shift tackles the global challenges of the 21st century and aligns tourism practices with the broader goals of sustainable development. The transition to regenerative tourism and the effective management of global challenges necessitate the role of law in shaping sustainable tourism practices. Legal frameworks are essential for ensuring that tourism development aligns with the principles of environmental protection, social equity, and economic resilience.

ROLE OF LAW IN SUSTAINABLE TOURISM

Legal Frameworks as Tools for Achieving SDGs

Legal frameworks actively shape and enforce sustainable tourism practices that align with the United Nations Sustainable Development Goals (SDGs). Through effective regulation, laws drive tourism development that prioritizes environmental conservation, promotes social equity, and enhances economic resilience (Gössling & Higham, 2021). For example, environmental legislation focused on emissions, waste management, and land use is vital for achieving SDG 13 (Climate Action) and SDG 15 (Life on Land). Such laws reduce the environmental footprint of tourism while promoting biodiversity conservation (Sharpley & Telfer, 2018). Additionally, legal mechanisms such as zoning regulations, environmental impact assessments, and protected area statutes are crucial for managing the impact of tourism on fragile ecosystems. These tools help balance tourism demand with the preservation of natural habitats and cultural heritage sites (Buckley, 2019). For example, environmental impact assessments for tourism projects help ensure that potential adverse effects are identified and mitigated, aligning with SDG 11 (Sustainable Cities and Communities) (Holden, 2019). Moreover, laws that encourage corporate social responsibility (CSR) in the tourism sector can foster inclusive growth and empower communities, contributing to SDG 8 (Decent Work and Economic Growth) and SDG 10 (Reduced Inequalities). Legal frameworks that mandate CSR encourage tourism businesses to adopt practices that strengthen local economies, respect cultural identities, and ensure fair labour conditions (Scheyvens & Biddulph, 2018). As such, by reinforcing ethical business practices, these laws contribute to environmental protection while simultaneously fostering socio-economic development in host communities.

Legal Pathways to Support Regenerative Practices

Sustainable tourism seeks to minimize harm, while regenerative tourism necessitates proactive legal frameworks that actively restore and elevate both ecological and social systems. Existing legal structures must evolve to support regenerative practices that transcend conservation, focusing on enhancing community well-being apart from replenishing natural resources (Higgins-Desbiolles, 2020). For example, legal incentives for regenerative agriculture and ecotourism actively restore degraded landscapes and enhance biodiversity, directly advancing SDG 12 (Responsible Consumption and Production) and SDG 15 (Life on Land). Furthermore, regenerative tourism necessitates laws that enable community participation and co-management of tourism resources. Legal frameworks should empower local communities to actively participate in tourism planning and benefit-sharing, aligning with the principles of equity and social justice at the heart of regenerative tourism (Mair, 2019). For example, legal support for community-based tourism initiatives ensures that tourism revenues are reinvested in local development, directly contributing to SDG 1 (No Poverty) and SDG 10 (Reduced Inequalities).

Legal reforms are also essential to address the evolving challenges of regenerative tourism, such as climate change adaptation, resource depletion, and socio-economic disparities. Adaptive legal frameworks that incorporate feedback loops and stakeholder consultations can foster a more resilient tourism sector capable of responding to environmental and social shifts (Horne & Venables, 2020). These legal pathways drive regenerative practices and ensure that tourism actively contributes to the broader sustainable development agenda. Law in sustainable tourism goes beyond regulation; it facilitates and empowers. By establishing supportive legal frameworks, the tourism sector leads the shift from sustainability to regeneration, playing a vital role in achieving the SDGs.

Critical Perspectives on Regenerative Tourism

Regenerative tourism remains theoretically contested, with scholars divided between viewing it as an essential evolution beyond sustainability (Mang & Reed, 2018), a rebranding of existing practices (Fletcher, 2023), or a potential source of new inequalities (Duffy et al., 2023). These debates reflect tensions in SDG implementation related to the distribution of costs and benefits. Structural challenges include corporate lobbying against regulations (CLIA, 2023), bureaucratic inertia (Bianchi, 2022), and, in developing nations, corruption diverting community funds (Akama, 2023). Even successful models, such as Costa Rica's Payment for Ecosystem Services, face replication challenges due to issues like land conflicts (Wunder, 2023). The premium pricing of regenerative tourism may exclude budget travellers, causing "green gentrification" (Viteri Mejía, 2023), while projects in Fiji have displaced traditional livelihoods (Harrison, 2023). Employment quotas often lack enforcement (ILO, 2023). The absence of standardized metrics enables "regeneration-washing" (Higgins-Desbiolles, 2023), while developing countries struggle with enforcement capacity (Nyakabwa, 2023). Effective frameworks require safeguards for equity, anti-corruption measures, and adaptive protocols. Bhutan's Gross National Happiness model demonstrates balanced regeneration (Dorji, 2023), suggesting the need for politically-engaged legal solutions.

LEGAL FOUNDATIONS FOR SUSTAINABLE TOURISM

International Legal Frameworks

United Nations Sustainable Development Goals (SDGs)

The United Nations Sustainable Development Goals (SDGs) serve as a comprehensive blueprint for global sustainable development, encompassing 17 goals and 169 targets. SDG 8 (Decent Work and Economic Growth) and SDG 12 (Responsible Consumption and Production) are particularly relevant to sustainable tourism. The SDGs highlight tourism's potential to foster economic growth while promoting environmental conservation and cultural heritage protection (United Nations, 2015).

The tourism sector drives job creation and economic growth, especially in developing countries. However, issues such as resource consumption and environmental degradation require urgent attention and action. Legal frameworks aligned with the SDGs help ensure that tourism practices contribute meaningfully to both local and global sustainability goals (Gössling & Hall, 2019). By incorporating SDG targets into national tourism policies and regulations, sustainable tourism that complements the environment and local communities can be implemented.

Paris Agreement and Its Implications for Tourism

The legal engagement with tourism has undergone a significant transformation, particularly before and after the adoption of the Sustainable Development Goals (SDGs) in 2015 and the Paris Agreement that same year. Prior to 2015, tourism governance was largely fragmented and economically driven, with minimal consideration for environmental or social impacts (Hall, 2019). Laws primarily focused on maximizing tourism's economic benefits, often leading to unchecked development and environmental degradation in coastal areas and other sensitive ecosystems (Sharpley & Telfer, 2018). Environmental protections during this period relied mainly on voluntary guidelines like the Global Code of Ethics for Tourism (UNWTO, 1999), which lacked binding enforcement mechanisms (Dredge & Jamal, 2015). Climate change considerations were notably absent from most tourism policies, despite the sector's substantial carbon footprint from aviation and hospitality operations (Gössling & Peeters, 2015).

The adoption of the Paris Agreement and SDGs in 2015 marked a turning point, integrating tourism into broader climate action and sustainability frameworks. The Paris Agreement explicitly recognized tourism's dual role as both a contributor to and victim of climate change, necessitating sector-specific mitigation strategies (Scott et al., 2019). This led to the implementation of legal mechanisms such as carbon pricing systems that now include aviation under the EU Emissions Trading Scheme (Peeters et al., 2018), and renewable energy mandates requiring tourism businesses to adopt sustainable energy sources. For example, Spain's Renewable Energy Plan (2020) compels hotels to transition to solar and wind power. Small island nations like the Maldives have developed comprehensive strategies such as their Carbon Neutrality Strategy (2020), which combines green taxes with coral reef restoration laws to align tourism with the Agreement's 1.5°C target (Ministry of Environment, Maldives, 2021).

Concurrently, the SDGs provided a holistic framework for sustainable tourism development. SDG 13 (Climate Action) has prompted countries to develop tourism-specific climate adaptation plans, while SDG 8 (Decent Work) has strengthened labour protections for tourism workers worldwide (ILO, 2023). This represents a shift from voluntary guidelines to legally binding standards, as seen in the EU's Green Claims Directive (2023) which penalizes false sustainability claims in the industry. Modern tourism laws now assess the sector's full environmental impact, including supply chain emissions (Lenzen et al., 2021), while innovative approaches like community benefit-sharing and ecosystem legal personhood are emerging in countries like Kenya and Costa Rica (Mwangi & Omwenga, 2021; Rivera-Murillo et al., 2020).

The evolution of tourism law reflects broader changes in global sustainability governance. Where pre-2015 frameworks emphasized economic growth with limited safeguards, contemporary legal instruments demonstrate a more balanced approach that integrates environmental protection, climate action and social equity. However, challenges remain in enforcement, particularly in Global South nations where resources for implementation may be limited (Zainal et al., 2020). The progression from voluntary codes to binding regulations illustrates tourism law's growing sophistication in addressing the sector's complex sustainability challenges.

Convention on Biological Diversity (CBD)

The Convention on Biological Diversity (CBD) is a key international treaty dedicated to the conservation of biological diversity. It encourages the sustainable use of its components and guarantees the fair and equitable sharing of benefits derived from genetic resources. Tourism relies heavily on natural and cultural heritage, making the CBD highly relevant to the sector (Buckley, 2019). Legal frameworks can enable tourism to contribute to biodiversity conservation by establishing protected areas, promoting sustainable land use, and regulating activities that impact biodiversity. The CBD encourages the integration of biodiversity considerations into tourism planning and development, ensuring that tourism activities protect ecological integrity (Spenceley, 2018). Legal instruments derived from the CBD, such as national biodiversity strategies and action plans, guide sustainable tourism development by safeguarding ecosystems and species essential to the tourism experience.

Regional and National Laws

Analysis of Regional Agreements

Regional agreements play a critical role in harmonizing sustainable tourism practices across countries. In the European Union (EU), directives such as the Habitats Directive and the Water Framework Directive set binding obligations for member states to protect natural habitats and water resources, which are essential for tourism (Pechlaner et al., 2020). The EU's legal framework promotes sustainable tourism through regulations on environmental protection, resource management, and regional development. For instance, the EU's Green Deal and the Circular Economy Action Plan provide legal pathways for reducing the environmental footprint of tourism by promoting sustainable resource use, waste reduction, and circular business models (European Commission, 2020). These directives ensure that tourism development is aligned with broader sustainability objectives, supporting both environmental conservation and socio-economic resilience.

Examples of National Laws Promoting Sustainable Tourism

National laws are crucial for implementing sustainable tourism practices tailored to local contexts. For example, Costa Rica's Biodiversity Law establishes a comprehensive legal framework for conserving biodiversity and promoting ecotourism. The law mandates environmental impact assessments for tourism projects and provides incentives for sustainable tourism initiatives (Honey & Krantz, 2021). Similarly, New Zealand's Resource Management Act emphasizes sustainable management of natural and physical resources, directly impacting tourism development. The Act requires local authorities to consider environmental sustainability in tourism planning and decision-making, ensuring that tourism growth does not compromise the country's natural heritage (Hall, 2019). These national legal frameworks demonstrate how tailored legal instruments can effectively promote sustainable tourism while addressing local environmental and socio-economic challenges. Having discussed legal foundations for sustainable tourism, we now turn to environmental law and sustainable tourism.

ENVIRONMENTAL LAW AND SUSTAINABLE TOURISM

Legal Mechanisms for Environmental Protection

Environmental Impact Assessments (EIA) in Tourism Projects

Environmental Impact Assessments (EIAs) are critical legal tools used to evaluate the potential environmental consequences of proposed tourism projects before they are undertaken. EIAs help ensure that tourism development is conducted in an environmentally responsible manner, mitigating adverse effects on natural ecosystems and local communities (Glasson, Therivel, & Chadwick, 2019). In the context of tourism, EIAs are mandated by various national and international legal frameworks to assess impacts on biodiversity, water resources, and cultural heritage. For example, the European Union's EIA Directive requires member states to conduct assessments for projects likely to have significant environmental effects, including tourism-related infrastructure (European Parliament, 2014). Similarly, many countries have national laws mandating EIAs for large-scale tourism projects. In Malaysia, the Environmental Quality Act 1974 requires EIAs for projects that may impact the environment, helping to prevent unchecked tourism development in sensitive areas (Zakaria & Hassan, 2020). EIAs serve as a preventative measure, ensuring that potential environmental harms are identified and mitigated before project implementation. This process promotes sustainable tourism by balancing development needs with environmental protection, fostering long-term ecological and economic benefits.

Laws Regulating Pollution, Conservation, and Resource Management

Environmental laws regulating pollution, conservation, and resource management play a pivotal role in sustainable tourism. These laws ensure that tourism activities do not degrade natural resources and ecosystems, which are often the main attractions for tourists. Pollution control laws, such as those regulating air, water, and waste management, are essential for maintaining the environmental quality of tourism destinations. For instance, the Clean Water Act in the United States regulates discharges into waterways, protecting aquatic ecosystems that are integral to tourism

(U.S. Environmental Protection Agency, 2020). Similarly, conservation laws, such as the National Parks Act in various countries, safeguard biodiversity and natural landscapes by establishing protected areas and regulating tourism activities within them (Buckley, 2018). Resource management laws, particularly those governing the sustainable use of water, energy, and land, are crucial for minimizing the ecological footprint of tourism. Legal frameworks that promote the efficient use of resources, such as water-saving regulations in hotels and resorts, contribute to the sustainability of tourism operations (Bramwell & Lane, 2018). By enforcing these laws, governments ensure that tourism development aligns with broader environmental conservation goals.

Climate Change and Tourism Law

Legal Obligations for Reducing Carbon Footprints in Tourism

Tourism is a significant contributor to global carbon emissions, primarily through transportation and energy-intensive operations. Legal obligations for reducing carbon footprints in tourism are critical to achieving climate change mitigation goals, as outlined in the Paris Agreement. Countries have implemented various legal instruments to curb carbon emissions in the tourism sector. Carbon taxes, emissions trading systems, and regulations on energy efficiency are common legal tools used to incentivize low-carbon tourism practices. For example, the European Union's Emissions Trading System (ETS) includes aviation, compelling airlines to reduce their carbon emissions or purchase allowances, thereby promoting more sustainable travel options (European Commission, 2021). National policies, such as New Zealand's Zero Carbon Act, set legally binding targets for reducing greenhouse gas emissions, impacting tourism by encouraging the adoption of renewable energy and sustainable practices (New Zealand Government, 2019). These legal obligations push tourism businesses to innovate and reduce their environmental impact, aligning with global climate goals.

Role of Renewable Energy and Sustainable Practices in Tourism Operations

The transition to renewable energy and sustainable practices in tourism operations is increasingly driven by legal mandates. Laws and regulations promoting renewable energy adoption help reduce the reliance on fossil fuels, significantly lowering the carbon footprint of tourism. Several countries have introduced legal requirements for tourism establishments to integrate renewable energy sources, such as solar and wind power, into their operations. For instance, Spain's Renewable Energy

Plan mandates the use of renewable energy in the hospitality sector, supporting the country's sustainability objectives (Ministerio para la Transición Ecológica y el Reto Demográfico, 2020). Legal frameworks also encourage sustainable practices, such as waste reduction, water conservation, and the use of eco-friendly materials. Certification schemes, often supported by legal standards, recognize tourism businesses that meet stringent sustainability criteria. These certifications not only enhance the environmental performance of tourism operations but also boost their market appeal by attracting eco-conscious travellers (Font & McCabe, 2017). By integrating renewable energy and sustainable practices, tourism businesses can comply with legal requirements while contributing to the broader goals of environmental conservation and climate change mitigation with the focus on these key areas:

- Social equity and tourism law
- Economic dimensions of sustainable tourism law
- Legal frameworks for tourism crisis management and resilience
- Legal tools for managing over tourism
- Combating greenwashing through legal mechanisms
- Co-management and Indigenous economic rights in tourism law
- Urban law, smart cities, and tourism regulation

SOCIAL EQUITY AND TOURISM LAW

Human Rights and Tourism

Legal Protections for Local Communities and Indigenous Peoples

Tourism development's impact on communities and workers requires comprehensive legal safeguards that address both formal and customary systems. International instruments like United Nations Declaration on the. Rights of Indigenous Peoples [UNDRIP] (United Nations, 2007) establish Free, Prior, and Informed Consent (FPIC) principles that are increasingly being adapted to local contexts across developing economies. In Latin America, countries like Bolivia and Ecuador have constitutionalized indigenous rights, requiring tourism projects to respect community governance structures like the Andean "Ayllu" system (Postero, 2023). Similarly, Indonesia's 2017 Village Law empowers local "Adat" communities to regulate tourism through customary laws (Warren, 2023). These protections extend to labour rights (Scheyvens & Biddulph, 2018), though implementation varies significantly across economic contexts. While Canada's impact assessment process (Government of Canada, 2021) represents a formalized approach, many developing nations rely on hybrid systems.

In Kenya, Maasai communities combine statutory law with traditional "Enkang" land tenure rules to regulate safari tourism (Kipuri, 2023). Pacific Island nations integrate customary marine tenure (e.g., Fiji's "Qoliqoli" system) with national tourism policies, protecting both fishing rights and dive tourism sites (Harrison, 2023). However, persistent gaps remain in protecting vulnerable workers (ILO, 2023). Informal sector protections are emerging through innovative approaches like Bali's "Desa Wisata" (tourism village) program that formalizes homestay operators under customary "Banjar" governance (Duffy et al., 2023), Botswana's community trusts that apply Tswana customary law to regulate safari camp employment (Mbaiwa, 2023), and Thailand's Digital Platform Labor Act (2023) that extends protections to app-based tourism workers while respecting informal work arrangements (ILO, 2023). Religious environmental norms also shape tourism regulation. In Bhutan, Buddhist principles inform zoning laws that limit mountain tourism (Dorji, 2023), while in Bali, Hindu "Tri Hita Karana" philosophy underpins resort sustainability certifications (Picard, 2023). These examples demonstrate how effective legal frameworks must bridge international standards (Colchester & Ferrari, 2021), national laws, and community-based governance systems to ensure truly inclusive tourism development.

Laws Promoting Equitable Benefit-Sharing in Tourism

Equitable benefit-sharing is a critical component of sustainable tourism, ensuring that the economic benefits derived from tourism are fairly distributed among all stakeholders, particularly local communities. Legal frameworks can facilitate this by mandating community participation and benefit-sharing mechanisms in tourism projects. Many countries have implemented laws requiring tourism operators to contribute to community development funds or engage in partnerships with local communities. For example, in Tanzania, the Wildlife Conservation Act mandates that a portion of tourism revenues from national parks and wildlife reserves be allocated to local communities for development projects (Nelson, 2017). Such laws help ensure that tourism benefits are not concentrated among a few stakeholders but are distributed in a way that promotes social equity and economic development. Moreover, legal provisions can support community-based tourism (CBT) initiatives, where local communities have direct control over tourism activities and revenue distribution. CBT models have been successful in various regions, such as the G Adventures-supported projects in Peru, where legal frameworks ensure that indigenous communities retain ownership and control over tourism resources (Zeppel, 2020).

Cultural Heritage and Tourism

Legal Frameworks for Protecting Cultural Sites and Practices

Cultural heritage is a significant driver of tourism, but it also faces threats from over-tourism, commercialization, and neglect. Legal frameworks are essential for protecting cultural sites and practices, ensuring that tourism development does not compromise their integrity. International legal instruments, such as the UNESCO World Heritage Convention, provide a framework for the protection and preservation of cultural and natural heritage sites (UNESCO, 1972). This convention obliges signatory countries to take measures to safeguard heritage sites, including regulating tourism activities to prevent damage and degradation. Countries like Italy have enacted stringent regulations to control visitor numbers and activities at cultural sites such as Venice and Pompeii, balancing tourism with heritage conservation (Cellini & Cuccia, 2019). National laws also play a crucial role in protecting cultural heritage. For instance, India's Ancient Monuments and Archaeological Sites and Remains Act provides comprehensive legal protection for its rich cultural heritage, regulating access, conservation, and management of historical sites (Basu, 2020). These legal frameworks ensure that tourism development is aligned with heritage preservation goals, promoting sustainable tourism practices.

Intellectual Property Rights and Their Role in Cultural Tourism

Intellectual property rights (IPR) are increasingly recognized as a vital component of cultural tourism, particularly in protecting traditional knowledge, cultural expressions, and indigenous art forms. Legal frameworks that recognize and enforce IPR can help prevent the unauthorized use and commercialization of cultural assets, ensuring that communities retain control over their cultural heritage. The World Intellectual Property Organization (WIPO) has developed guidelines for protecting traditional cultural expressions (TCEs) and traditional knowledge (TK) through intellectual property laws (WIPO, 2019). These guidelines encourage countries to adopt legal measures that recognize the rights of indigenous and local communities over their cultural assets, promoting equitable benefit-sharing and cultural preservation. In countries like Australia, legal frameworks have been established to protect indigenous art and cultural expressions from exploitation. The Indigenous Art Code provides legal protection for indigenous artists, ensuring that they are fairly compensated and that their cultural heritage is respected (Janke, 2020). By integrating IPR into cultural tourism strategies, these legal measures help promote sustainable and culturally sensitive tourism practices.

ECONOMIC DIMENSIONS OF SUSTAINABLE TOURISM LAW

Corporate Social Responsibility (CSR) and Governance

Legal Requirements for CSR in the Tourism Sector

Corporate Social Responsibility (CSR) has become a fundamental aspect of business operations, particularly in the tourism sector, where companies are increasingly held accountable for their environmental and social impacts. Legal frameworks in various jurisdictions have begun to mandate CSR activities, requiring companies to adopt sustainable practices. For instance, the European Union's Directive 2014/95/EU requires large companies to disclose non-financial information, including environmental, social, and governance (ESG) factors, which directly influence tourism businesses (European Commission, 2014).

In the tourism sector, CSR obligations often include commitments to environmental conservation, community engagement, and ethical labour practices. Countries like India have integrated CSR into their legal fabric, with the Companies Act, 2013, mandating certain companies to spend a percentage of their profits on CSR activities, including those promoting sustainable tourism (Ministry of Corporate Affairs, 2013). These legal requirements push tourism companies to align their operations with broader sustainability goals, thus contributing to the achievement of SDGs.

Governance Models Integrating Sustainability

Governance models that integrate sustainability are essential for ensuring long-term economic, environmental, and social benefits in tourism. Sustainable governance involves not only complying with legal requirements but also embedding sustainability into the core decision-making processes. Multi-stakeholder governance models, which include government agencies, private sector players, and community groups, have proven effective in managing sustainable tourism destinations. For example, New Zealand's sustainable tourism framework emphasizes collaborative governance involving the government, local communities, and tourism operators to promote sustainable practices and protect natural resources (Tourism New Zealand, 2020). These governance models ensure that sustainability is not an afterthought but a guiding principle in tourism development. They facilitate the implementation of integrated policies that balance economic growth with environmental protection and social equity.

Trade, Investment, and Tourism

Legal Incentives for Sustainable Tourism Investment

Legal incentives play a critical role in encouraging investment in sustainable tourism. Governments worldwide have implemented various legal mechanisms, such as tax incentives, subsidies, and grants, to promote environmentally and socially responsible tourism projects. For instance, the United States offers tax credits and deductions for businesses that invest in energy-efficient technologies and renewable energy, which are particularly relevant for eco-tourism ventures (Internal Revenue Service, 2021). Similarly, the European Union's Green Deal includes financial instruments aimed at supporting sustainable tourism projects. These legal incentives help lower the financial barriers to adopting sustainable practices, making it more attractive for investors and businesses to engage in sustainable tourism development.

Challenges in Balancing Economic Growth with Sustainability

While legal incentives are critical for promoting sustainable tourism, challenges remain in balancing economic growth with sustainability. One of the primary challenges is the potential conflict between short-term economic gains and long-term sustainability objectives. Tourism destinations often face pressure to maximize revenue through increased visitor numbers, which can lead to over-tourism and environmental degradation. Legal frameworks must address these challenges by setting clear sustainability standards and limits on resource use.

Moreover, inconsistent regulatory environments across different jurisdictions can complicate the implementation of sustainable practices. For example, while some countries have stringent environmental regulations, others may lack the necessary legal infrastructure, creating an uneven playing field for businesses operating in multiple regions (World Tourism Organization, 2019). Addressing these challenges requires harmonized legal frameworks that ensure sustainability is prioritized alongside economic development.

LEGAL FRAMEWORK FOR TOURISM CRISIS MANAGEMENT AND RESILIENCE

The COVID-19 pandemic revealed significant deficiencies in global tourism crisis management frameworks, highlighting the urgent need for comprehensive legal protections for tourists, local communities, and businesses during emergencies (UNDRR, 2021). Progressive models like New Zealand's Civil Defence and Emergency Management Act (2002) demonstrate how legislation can mandate tourism operators to develop robust resilience plans for natural disasters, while the UNDRR's Sendai Framework (2015) provides critical guidance for integrating disaster risk reduction into national tourism policies. Thailand's response exemplifies this approach, with its revised Tourism Authority Act (2020) establishing emergency funds for displaced workers and requiring business continuity plans from tourism enterprises (World Bank, 2022). These legal instruments emphasize two key pillars: preventive mechanisms such as early warning systems, and equitable recovery protocols that specifically protect vulnerable groups like informal tourism workers (ILO, 2023). However, implementation gaps persist, particularly in developing nations where resource constraints hinder effective enforcement of these protective measures.

LEGAL TOOLS FOR MANAGING OVERTOURISM

Destinations worldwide are increasingly adopting innovative legal mechanisms to address overtourism. Venice's 2024 regulations represent a groundbreaking approach, implementing daily visitor caps and introducing a tiered entry fee system (€5-10) during peak periods (Comune di Venezia, 2023). Similarly, Barcelona's Special Urban Plan for Tourist Accommodation utilizes zoning laws to restrict short-term rentals in overcrowded neighbourhoods (Ajuntament de Barcelona, 2021). Peru has taken a different tack at Machu Picchu, limiting daily visitors to 2,500 and mandating guided tours to better manage the cultural site's preservation (MINCETUR, 2022). While these tools demonstrate promising results in balancing economic benefits with ecological protection, their effectiveness varies significantly across regions, with enforcement proving particularly challenging in developing countries facing capacity constraints (Milano et al., 2023).

COMBATING GREENWASHING THROUGH LEGAL MECHANISMS

Recent years have seen governments implement stricter regulations to combat misleading environmental claims in the tourism sector. The European Union's Green Claims Directive (2023) sets a new standard by requiring businesses to provide third-party verified evidence for all eco-labels and sustainability assertions (European Commission, 2023). Australia has taken parallel action through its 2022 Consumer Law amendments, which notably penalized a major resort chain for exaggerating its coral reef conservation efforts (ACCC, 2023). These legal measures serve dual purposes: empowering consumers to make informed choices while compelling tourism businesses to adopt genuinely sustainable practices rather than superficial green marketing. The growing body of case law in this area suggests regulators are taking an increasingly stringent approach to environmental claims verification.

CO-MANAGEMENT AND INDIGENOUS ECONOMIC RIGHTS IN TOURISM LAW

Indigenous communities are transforming tourism governance through co-management models that bridge state legal systems with deeply rooted customary laws. In Canada's Gwaii Haanas National Park Reserve, the Haida Nation's "Gina 'Waadluxan KilGuhlGa" (Land-Sea-People Management Plan) integrates hereditary chief governance with federal park law, enforcing traditional harvesting bans during cultural ceremonies through both Haida oral law and Canadian statutes (Jones et al., 2023). Australia's Kakadu National Park exemplifies this synergy, where Aboriginal "Rom" law dictates seasonal closures of sacred sites through a formalized Traditional Owner Board that wields equal authority to park administrators (Altman & Jackson, 2023).

Across Africa, indigenous legal systems are shaping tourism policy. The Maasai "Enkang" land tenure system, codified in Kenya's Community Land Act (2016), requires tourism investors to obtain approval from councils of elders ("Laibon") and compensate clans through livestock rather than cash payments in some regions (Kipuri, 2023). In Botswana, San communities apply "N!ore" territorial rules through community trusts, using ancestral rainmaking ceremonies to determine acceptable tourist numbers during drought periods (Suzman, 2023).

Pacific Island nations demonstrate how religious environmental norms govern tourism. Fiji's "Vanua" framework embeds chiefly governance ("Turaga ni Koro") in resort approvals, requiring ceremonial "sevusevu" gifts and adherence to "tabu" (sacred) fishing grounds (Harrison, 2023). The Māori "tikanga" (customary law) system in New Zealand mandates that tourism operators observe "rāhui" (temporary bans) declared by local iwi to protect overvisited ecosystems (Harmsworth & Awatere, 2023).

However, tensions emerge when oral traditions confront statutory systems. In the Ecuadorian Amazon, Kichwa communities' "Sumak Kawsay" (living well) principles often conflict with state tourism concessions, leading to indigenous patrols ("guardianes") enforcing customary laws against unauthorized guides (Lu et al., 2023). The Sami "Siida" system in Scandinavia faces similar challenges, where reindeer herding laws compete with government-issued tourism permits (Pettersson, 2023).

These cases reveal a global pattern: successful models like Nepal's "Bheja" system (rotating forest stewardship) or Namibia's conservancy laws show that when states formally recognize indigenous jurisprudence, whether written or oral, tourism becomes a tool for cultural preservation rather than displacement (Xanthaki, 2023). The key lies in creating legal "interface mechanisms" that translate customary norms into enforceable regulations while preserving their spiritual essence (Sambo, 2023).

URBAN LAW, SMART CITIES, AND TOURISM REGULATION

The rapid growth of urban tourism has necessitated innovative legal frameworks that integrate smart city technologies with sustainable tourism management. Cities worldwide are adopting zoning laws, digital governance tools, and data-driven regulations to balance tourism development with urban liveability (Gretzel et al., 2021). Barcelona serves as a pioneering example, where the 2014 Special Urban Plan for Tourist Accommodation established strict zoning regulations to curb the proliferation of short-term rentals in residential areas, preserving housing affordability for local residents (Ajuntament de Barcelona, 2021). Similarly, Singapore's Smart Tourism 2025 initiative leverages artificial intelligence and IoT sensors to monitor visitor flows in real-time, enabling dynamic pricing and crowd control at key attractions like Gardens by the Bay (Singapore Tourism Board, 2023). These smart regulations are supported by urban data platforms that help policymakers optimize tourism infrastructure while minimizing neighbourhood disruptions (Neirotti et al., 2022).

Emerging legal models also address the platform economy's impact on urban tourism. Amsterdam's 2023 Platform Economy Regulation requires short-term rental platforms like Airbnb to share real-time data with municipal authorities, ensuring compliance with occupancy limits (City of Amsterdam, 2023). In Kyoto, Japan, a digital permit system restricts access to overcrowded heritage districts during peak seasons, with QR code checkpoints enforcing visitor quotas (Kyoto City Government, 2022). These examples demonstrate how urban law is evolving from static land-use rules to adaptive, technology-enabled systems that prioritize equitable access and community well-being (Maitland, 2023). However, challenges persist in data privacy and enforcement consistency, particularly where tourism platforms resist regulatory oversight (Guttentag, 2023). Key legal innovations in Smart Tourism Cities, includes Dynamic Zoning in Barcelona's neighbourhood with specific caps on tourist apartments (Colau & Martí-Costa, 2022), using predictive analytics such as AI to forecast and mitigate overtourism in Singapore (STB, 2023) and Amsterdam's API integration with rental platforms; an automated compliance (Van der Borg, 2023).

Table 1. Matrix: Legal tools, challenges, and outcomes by ecosystem type and stakeholder group

Ecosystem Type / Stakeholder Group	Legal Tools Used	Key Challenges	Outcomes Achieved
Forests & Mountains	EIAs, Protected Area Laws, Rights of Nature (e.g., Ecuador, NZ's Te Urewera Act)	Land tenure conflicts, limited enforcement, eco-gentrification	Legal personhood for nature, indigenous co-management, biodiversity conservation
Marine & Coastal Areas	Customary Tenure Laws (e.g., Qoliqoli in Fiji), Reef Protection (e.g., Rah Laws, Maldives), Climate Laws	Resource depletion, resort sprawl, enforcement deficits	Coral reef restoration, reduced reef damage, community-based marine governance
Urban Areas	Zoning Laws, Smart City Platforms, Short-Term Rental Regulations (e.g., Barcelona, Amsterdam)	Data privacy, resistance by platforms, overcrowding	Visitor caps, improved liveability, dynamic management using IoT and AI
Indigenous Communities	Customary Law Recognition, FPIC, Land Tribunal Acts (e.g., Kenya, Vanuatu, Canada)	Statutory-customary conflicts, corruption, lack of metrics	Empowered local governance, spiritual-cultural preservation, inclusive benefit-sharing
Tourism Workers (Formal & Informal)	Labor Laws, Informal Sector Protections (e.g., Digital Platform Labor Acts), CSR Laws	Weak enforcement, informal labour exclusion	Enhanced protections, formalization of informal work, equitable income access
Private Sector / Investors	Green Investment Incentives, Emission Trading, CSR Mandates (e.g., India, EU ETS)	Greenwashing, short-termism, weak compliance monitoring	Greener supply chains, ESG reporting, climate mitigation efforts

CHALLENGES IN LEGAL IMPLEMENTATION

Regulatory Gaps and Inconsistencies

Challenges Posed by Fragmented Legal Systems

Fragmented legal systems create significant barriers to implementing sustainable and regenerative tourism practices effectively. Different jurisdictions impose varying environmental regulations, zoning laws, and tourism policies, leading to inconsistencies that complicate compliance for tourism operators. For example, a tourism business operating across multiple countries faces a patchwork of regulations, with each country enforcing different environmental standards and reporting requirements.

This fragmentation hinders the development of cohesive sustainability strategies and discourages investment in sustainable tourism initiatives (Gössling & Hall, 2019).

Moreover, the lack of harmonization in legal frameworks can result in loopholes that businesses might exploit, leading to unsustainable practices that undermine global sustainability efforts. For example, while some countries have stringent regulations to protect natural resources, others may have lax enforcement, allowing harmful tourism activities to persist (Bramwell & Lane, 2018).

Case Studies of Regulatory Failures and Enforcement Issues

Case studies highlight the impact of regulatory failures and enforcement issues on sustainable tourism. One notable example is the case of over-tourism in Barcelona, Spain. Despite regulations aimed at controlling tourist numbers and preserving the city's cultural heritage, enforcement has been inconsistent, leading to overcrowding and strain on local resources (Milano et al., 2019). This case underscores the importance of robust enforcement mechanisms to ensure that regulations achieve their intended outcomes.

Another example is the failure to adequately regulate coastal tourism development in Thailand, which has led to significant environmental degradation. Weak enforcement of environmental impact assessments and building codes has resulted in unchecked construction, harming marine ecosystems and reducing the appeal of tourist destinations (Kontogeorgopoulos, 2020). These cases demonstrate the critical need for effective regulatory frameworks and enforcement to support sustainable tourism development.

Legal Barriers to Regenerative Tourism

Legal and Bureaucratic Hurdles in Adopting Regenerative Practices

Adopting regenerative tourism practices often encounters legal and bureaucratic hurdles that can stifle innovation and progress. Regulatory frameworks designed for traditional tourism models may not accommodate the unique requirements of regenerative tourism, such as the need for flexible land use policies and adaptive management approaches. For example, regenerative tourism projects often require collaboration across multiple sectors and jurisdictions, but rigid regulatory structures can impede this necessary coordination (Steiner & Posch, 2021). Additionally, bureaucratic processes, such as lengthy permitting and approval procedures, can delay or discourage the implementation of regenerative tourism initiatives. These delays can be particularly detrimental in regions where tourism is a critical economic driver, as they may result in missed opportunities for sustainable development (Dredge & Gyimóthy, 2017).

Restrictions on Innovation and Sustainable Tourism Development

Legal frameworks that fail to keep pace with emerging trends in tourism can restrict innovation and sustainable development. For instance, the slow adaptation of regulations to support eco-tourism and nature-based tourism has limited the ability of businesses to invest in these growing sectors. In many cases, outdated laws do not recognize the potential of new technologies, such as renewable energy solutions and digital platforms, to enhance sustainability in tourism operations (Higgins-Desbiolles, 2020). Furthermore, restrictions on land use and development can prevent the creation of eco-friendly tourism infrastructure. For example, regulations that limit the use of renewable energy sources or impose stringent building codes without considering sustainability can hinder the development of sustainable tourism facilities (Lew et al., 2020). Addressing these legal barriers requires a proactive approach to updating and modernizing regulatory frameworks to support innovative and regenerative tourism practices.

Comparative Implementation Challenges of Regenerative Tourism Laws

The implementation of regenerative tourism laws reveals stark disparities between Global North and Global South contexts, shaped by differing legal traditions and institutional capacities. Developed nations typically benefit from stronger governance frameworks - the EU's circular economy directives (European Commission, 2022) and New Zealand's Te Urewera Act (Kauffman & Martin, 2021) demonstrate how advanced legal systems can institutionalize regenerative principles. However, developing countries often struggle with colonial-era statutes that conflict with both modern sustainability goals and traditional governance systems (Mwangi & Omwenga, 2023). For instance, while Norway's Sami Parliament effectively co-manages tourism through indigenous legal systems (Pettersson, 2023), similar initiatives in Tanzania face challenges from outdated land laws (Nelson, 2022). The global diversity of legal systems creates complex implementation landscapes. Civil law countries like France incorporate regenerative principles through centralized codes (Dredge, 2023), whereas common law systems rely more on precedent and case law. Hybrid systems in post-colonial states must reconcile Western legal frameworks with persistent customary laws; Botswana's Community-Based Natural Resource Management program succeeds by recognizing Tswana customary courts alongside statutory law (Mbaiwa, 2023). However, this legal pluralism can backfire when poorly managed; in Peru, conflicting national and indigenous jurisdiction over Machu Picchu has created regulatory gaps exploited by unregulated tour operators (Chevalier, 2023). Corporate-driven regenerative tourism initiatives frequently create new inequalities when divorced from local contexts. In Cambodia, international eco-resorts using "regenerative" branding have displaced traditional fishing communities despite complying with national laws (Milne, 2023). Similarly, South Africa's luxury safari industry meets formal regeneration criteria while perpetuating racial inequities in employment and land ownership (Spenceley, 2023). These cases reveal how even technically sound laws can fail when they prioritize environmental metrics over social justice or ignore place-based governance systems (Whyte, 2023). The Maldives' climate-resilient tourism policies demonstrate better practice, combining international standards with local "Rah" (traditional conservation) practices in island-specific regulations (Zubair, 2023).

Political and Institutional Barriers to Implementation

The implementation of regenerative tourism laws frequently encounters systemic obstacles, including corporate lobbying against stringent regulations, as seen in the cruise industry's resistance to decarbonization mandates (CLIA, 2023). Bureaucratic inertia perpetuates outdated policies, with many governments slow to adopt adaptive legal frameworks (Bianchi, 2022). In developing nations, corruption often diverts funds meant for community-based tourism initiatives, as documented in Kenya's wildlife conservancies (Akama, 2023). These challenges are compounded when political elites prioritize short-term economic gains over sustainability, as observed in Thailand's lax enforcement of coastal development laws (Kontogeorgopoulos, 2023). Such barriers undermine even well-designed legal systems, creating gaps between policy intent and on-ground outcomes (Müller & Pforr, 2023).

INNOVATIVE LEGAL PATHWAYS FOR REGENERATIVE TOURISM

Integrative Legal Frameworks

Combining Environmental, Social, and Economic Laws for Holistic Tourism Development

The complexity of regenerative tourism demands an integrative legal approach that synthesizes environmental, social, and economic dimensions. Traditional tourism laws often compartmentalize these aspects, leading to fragmented policies that fail to address the interconnected nature of sustainability. Integrative legal frameworks, by contrast, recognize the need for synergy among these elements to foster holistic tourism development (Steiner & Posch, 2021). For instance, an integrative legal framework might combine environmental impact assessments (EIAs) with community benefit-sharing mandates. This ensures that tourism development not only minimizes environmental harm but also delivers tangible social and economic benefits to local communities. Countries like Costa Rica have pioneered such approaches by embedding environmental protection, community empowerment, and economic incentives within their tourism laws. Their Payment for Ecosystem Services (PES) program is an exemplary model, linking tourism activities to conservation funding while involving local stakeholders (Rivera-Murillo et al., 2020).

Additionally, integrative frameworks can align with international legal instruments such as the United Nations Sustainable Development Goals (SDGs), creating legal pathways that explicitly address global sustainability targets. For example, policies that incentivize carbon-neutral tourism projects contribute directly to SDG 13 (Climate Action) and SDG 8 (Decent Work and Economic Growth).

Examples of Integrated Legal Approaches

Integrated legal approaches are emerging in several jurisdictions. In New Zealand, the Te Urewera Act (2014) grants legal personhood to natural landscapes, allowing ecosystems to have standing in legal disputes. This innovative law merges ecological protection with cultural heritage preservation by recognizing the intrinsic connection of the indigenous Māori people to their environment (Kauffman & Martin, 2021). Similarly, the European Union's Tourism and Transport Package incorporates climate, environmental, and economic considerations into a single policy initiative, promoting sustainable travel while supporting local economies. By integrating multiple policy areas, these frameworks demonstrate how holistic legal approaches can advance regenerative tourism goals (European Commission, 2022)

Technology and Legal Compliance

Role of Digital Tools (Blockchain, AI) in Enhancing Legal Compliance

Digital tools like blockchain and artificial intelligence (AI) are revolutionizing legal compliance in tourism by increasing transparency, efficiency, and accountability. Blockchain technology provides an immutable record of transactions, making it ideal for tracking compliance with sustainability regulations. For instance, tourism operators can use blockchain to document their adherence to eco-certification standards, such as carbon offsets or waste reduction practices. These fosters trust among stakeholders, including regulators, investors, and consumers (Cai et al., 2020).

AI, on the other hand, enhances compliance by automating complex legal processes. Machine learning algorithms can analyse large datasets to identify potential regulatory violations, reducing the burden on enforcement agencies. For example, AI-powered tools can monitor environmental impact assessments in real-time, flagging activities that exceed permissible thresholds. This proactive approach to compliance minimizes environmental harm while streamlining regulatory oversight (Liu et al., 2021).

Technology-Driven Solutions for Monitoring and Reporting Sustainability Metrics

The adoption of technology-driven solutions for monitoring and reporting sustainability metrics is critical for advancing regenerative tourism. Geographic Information Systems (GIS), for instance, enable real-time mapping of environmental changes caused by tourism activities, such as deforestation or coastal erosion. This data can inform policy adjustments and improve the effectiveness of legal frameworks (Scholz et al., 2022). Smart tourism platforms that integrate IoT (Internet of Things) devices also play a key role. These systems collect data on energy consumption, water usage, and waste generation in tourism facilities, providing actionable insights for compliance with sustainability laws. For instance, smart meters can automatically report energy usage to regulatory bodies, ensuring that tourism operators meet renewable energy quotas. Moreover, digital reporting tools simplify compliance for businesses while enhancing transparency for regulators. Platforms like the Global Sustainable Tourism Council (GSTC) offer standardized reporting templates that align with international sustainability criteria, reducing discrepancies and improving accountability (GSTC, 2023)

CASE STUDIES

Success Stories in Sustainable Tourism Law

Analysis of Cases Where Legal Frameworks Have Successfully Promoted Sustainable and Regenerative Tourism

Costa Rica: A Model for Sustainable Tourism Legislation. Costa Rica is globally recognized for its pioneering legal framework that integrates environmental protection into tourism development. The General Tourism Law (No. 1917) emphasizes sustainable practices, mandating environmental impact assessments (EIAs) for all major tourism projects. Additionally, the country's Payment for Ecosystem Services (PES) program incentivizes conservation by linking tourism revenue to environmental restoration initiatives. This law has led to the preservation of over 25% of the nation's land area as protected reserves, boosting biodiversity and sustainable tourism (Rivera-Murillo et al., 2020). Legal frameworks that prioritize environmental conservation create long-term benefits for tourism. Financial incentives such as PES encourage private sector compliance with sustainability goals.

New Zealand: Legal Personhood for Natural Resources. New Zealand's ground-breaking Te Urewera Act (2014) granted legal personhood to Te Urewera National Park, transforming its governance. This law ensures that tourism activities respect indigenous cultural values and protect ecological integrity. A similar framework was adopted for the Whanganui River in 2017. These policies have enhanced environmental stewardship and empowered indigenous communities to co-manage tourism resources sustainably (Kauffman & Martin, 2021). Recognizing natural resources as legal entities fosters accountability, protects ecosystems from exploitation, and involves indigenous stakeholders in legal frameworks to ensure cultural preservation and equitable tourism benefits.

Overview of Global South Innovations in Sustainable Tourism Law. Across Africa, Asia, Latin America, and small island states, innovative legal frameworks are emerging that integrate traditional governance systems with modern sustainability principles. In Africa, Namibia's Nature Conservation Amendment Act (1996) has established 86 communal conservancies that generate $10 million annually through community-managed wildlife tourism while protecting biodiversity (Weaver & Skyer, 2023). Kenya's Community Land Act (2016) similarly requires tourism investors to obtain approval from Maasai Laibon (councils of elders) and share revenues through community trusts (Mwangi, 2023), demonstrating how statutory law can reinforce customary governance structures. Southeast Asian nations have pioneered the formalization of customary law in tourism governance. Bali's Desa Wisata program institutionalizes Banjar (village council) oversight of homestays under Adat customary law, protecting over 200 traditional communities from displacement (Warren, 2023). Similarly, the Philippines' Indigenous Peoples Rights Act (1997) enables Ifugao communities to apply Lapat conservation rules to manage visitor numbers at UNESCO-listed rice terraces (Dressler et al., 2023), showcasing how traditional ecological knowledge can be codified in modern legal systems. Latin American approaches emphasize rights-based frameworks. Ecuador's Constitutional Rights of Nature (2008), inspired by New Zealand's precedents, empowers indigenous groups to block unsustainable tourism projects in sacred areas (Kauffman, 2023). Mexico's Pueblos Mágicos program employs zoning laws to safeguard indigenous artisan economies from mass tourism gentrification (López-Santillán, 2023), illustrating how spatial planning tools can protect cultural heritage. Small island states face unique climate challenges that demand adaptive legal solutions. The Maldives has codified traditional Rah coral reef protection methods into national tourism regulations (Zubair, 2023), while Vanuatu's Customary Land Tribunal Act (2023) grants chiefs veto power over coastal resort developments (Harrison, 2023). These cases reveal how traditional stewardship practices can be scaled through formal legal recognition.

Three key lessons emerge from these diverse implementations. First, legal hybridity - as demonstrated by Botswana's dual court system that resolves 80% of tourism disputes through customary mechanisms (Mbaiwa, 2023) proves more effective than purely statutory approaches. Second, traditional ecological knowledge, when legally recognized (e.g., Fiji's Qoliqoli marine tenure laws that reduced reef damage by 40% post-pandemic (Vuki, 2023), enhances climate resilience. Most critically, successful frameworks combined formal recognition of customary governance, mandatory benefit-sharing mechanisms, and climate adaptation protocols, offering a replicable model for equitable regenerative tourism worldwide.

Comparative Legal Analysis

Comparison of Legal Systems and Their Effectiveness in Promoting Sustainable Tourism

European Union vs. Southeast Asia. The European Union (EU) has developed comprehensive directives such as the EU Habitats Directive and the Sustainable Tourism Strategy. These frameworks provide standardized guidelines for sustainable tourism practices, including waste management, energy efficiency, and biodiversity protection. For example, EU member states are required to integrate these directives into national laws, ensuring consistent implementation across borders (European Commission, 2022). In contrast, Southeast Asia lacks uniformity in legal approaches. Countries like Thailand and Indonesia have implemented standalone policies for sustainable tourism, such as Thailand's Green Leaf Certification Program and Indonesia's Ecotourism Guidelines. However, enforcement is often inconsistent due to limited resources and fragmented governance (Zainal et al., 2020).

Comparative Analysis of Regional Approaches to Sustainable Tourism Governance

Table 2. Comparative analysis of sustainable tourism governance

Region	Legal Framework	Strengths	Challenges	Outcomes
EU	Habitats Directive (European Commission, 2022)	Centralized enforcement	Bureaucratic complexity	High policy consistency
Southeast Asia	Ecotourism Guidelines (Zainal et al., 2020)	Localized innovation	Enforcement gaps	Uneven progress
Australia	Great Barrier Reef Act (GBRMPA, 2023)	Science-based thresholds	High compliance costs	Ecological-economic balance
Africa	Wildlife Conservation Act (Mwangi & Omwenga, 2021)	Community engagement	Development-conservation tension	Economic prioritization

Table 2 reveals distinct regional patterns in sustainable tourism governance. The European Union's centralized model enables consistent policy implementation (European Commission, 2022), though its rigidity may limit local adaptation. Southeast Asian nations demonstrate policy innovation (e.g., Thailand's Green Leaf Certification) but struggle with fragmented enforcement and resource disparities (Zainal et al., 2020). Australia's ecosystem-specific legislation, particularly the Great Barrier Reef Marine Park Act, shows how science-based regulation can balance conservation and tourism value (Great Barrier Reef Marine Park Authority, 2023). Conversely, African approaches like Kenya's Wildlife Conservation Act prioritize economic development, often resulting in environmental trade-offs (Mwangi & Omwenga, 2021). These contrasts highlight that effective governance requires either strong institutional coordination (EU/Australia) or mechanisms to overcome fragmentation (Asia/Africa).

POLICY RECOMMENDATIONS

Enhancing Legal Frameworks

Strengthening Existing Laws and Creating New Policies

To effectively promote sustainable and regenerative tourism, legal frameworks need to adapt to emerging challenges. Existing laws can be strengthened by integrating clear sustainability goals and measurable outcomes. For instance, the incorporation of mandatory Environmental Impact Assessments (EIA) into broader tourism policies has proven effective in minimizing adverse environmental effects (McLennan et al., 2021). Similarly, adaptive legislation, such as periodic reviews and updates of tourism laws, ensures responsiveness to emerging sustainability issues, including climate change and over tourism. A significant area of improvement lies in drafting policies that encourage regenerative tourism. These policies should prioritize restoring ecosystems and cultural heritage over mere conservation. Countries like New Zealand, with its *Tourism Futures Taskforce* recommendations, have demonstrated the benefits of aligning policy with long-term sustainability visions (Smith & Hall, 2022). Strategies for Policy Development:

- Mandate comprehensive stakeholder engagement during the legislative process to ensure inclusivity.
- Introduce tax incentives for tourism businesses that adopt sustainable practices and achieve certifications, such as carbon neutrality or regenerative operations.
- Develop sector-specific guidelines to address challenges unique to tourism subsectors, such as adventure tourism or ecotourism.

Recommendations for Improving Legal Enforcement and Compliance

Enforcement gaps often undermine the effectiveness of legal frameworks. Governments must prioritize capacity-building for enforcement agencies, focusing on resource allocation and staff training. Additionally, leveraging technology, such as blockchain, can enhance transparency in legal compliance. Blockchain systems can create immutable records of environmental audits, ensuring accountability among tourism operators (Khan et al., 2023). To encourage compliance, governments can adopt participatory monitoring models where local communities and civil society organizations act as watchdogs. Successful examples include Costa Rica's community-led monitoring initiatives, which ensure that tourism activities align with environmental laws (Rivera-Murillo et al., 2020).

Promoting Collaborative Governance

Role of Multi-Stakeholder Partnerships in Legal Compliance

Collaborative governance is a critical factor in advancing sustainable tourism. Partnerships involving governments, non-governmental organizations (NGOs), private sector actors, and local communities create shared accountability and facilitate effective implementation of sustainability laws. For instance, the European Union's *Smart Specialisation Strategy for Sustainable Tourism* fosters partnerships between local governments and private firms to ensure compliance with sustainability objectives (European Commission, 2023). A strong multi-stakeholder framework can also streamline legal processes by reducing redundancies and addressing conflicting interests. The inclusion of indigenous communities in tourism governance, as seen in Australia's co-management of national parks, demonstrates the benefits of shared responsibility (Davis et al., 2021). Key Recommendations:

- Institutionalize public-private dialogues to address challenges in policy implementation and enforcement.
- Create multi-stakeholder platforms that facilitate the exchange of best practices in regenerative tourism.
- Foster capacity-building initiatives for underrepresented stakeholders, ensuring equitable participation in governance structures.

Importance of Public-Private Collaboration in Advancing Regenerative Tourism

Public-private collaboration plays a pivotal role in the transition to regenerative tourism. Governments can provide the legal and institutional support necessary for private entities to innovate and adopt sustainable practices. For example, public subsidies for green infrastructure, such as renewable energy in hotels, can encourage private investment in sustainability. Collaborations can also address funding gaps for large-scale regenerative projects. Initiatives such as the Global Tourism Resilience Fund, which pools resources from public and private sectors, highlight how partnerships can facilitate transformative tourism projects (Global Tourism Resilience Council, 2022). Key Recommendations:

- Establish legal agreements that define roles and responsibilities between public and private entities to avoid accountability gaps.
- Develop joint funding mechanisms, such as sustainability-linked bonds, to support regenerative tourism projects.
- Promote knowledge-sharing platforms that showcase successful public-private collaborations, inspiring wider adoption of similar models.

CONCLUSION

Summary of Key Insights

Law has emerged as a pivotal instrument in transforming tourism from an extractive model into a regenerative force for ecosystems and societies. The integration of environmental, social, and economic legal frameworks has enabled a more holistic governance approach, one that aligns tourism with the United Nations Sustainable Development Goals (Gössling & Higham, 2021; Rivera-Murillo et al., 2020). Internationally, instruments like the Paris Agreement and the Convention on Biological Diversity have catalysed sectoral shifts, compelling nations to adopt climate mitigation measures, ecosystem protections, and community-inclusive governance (Scott et al., 2019; Buckley, 2019). Regionally, differentiated legal pathways have evolved. In the Global North, codified rights of nature, carbon pricing, and AI-enabled urban regulations exemplify systemic innovation (Kauffman & Martin, 2021; European Commission, 2023). In the Global South, hybrid models; where customary law intersects with statutory systems have proven effective in managing ecosystems, empowering Indigenous groups, and fostering benefit-sharing mechanisms (Mbaiwa, 2023; Harrison, 2023). These models demonstrate that legal hybridity and localized adaptation are not merely complementary but essential for equitable and culturally grounded tourism regulation.

Success stories such as Costa Rica's PES scheme and New Zealand's legal personhood frameworks reflect how well-designed laws can restore ecological integrity and support Indigenous sovereignty (Rivera-Murillo et al., 2020; Kauffman & Martin, 2021). Yet, persistent legal and institutional barriers remain. Fragmented regulatory environments, outdated land statutes, and weak enforcement capacity hinder effective implementation—particularly in developing contexts where resource constraints, corruption, and political inertia pose serious challenges (Zainal et al., 2020; Akama, 2023). Additionally, emerging issues like regeneration-washing and elite capture in luxury eco-tourism further complicate equity outcomes (Higgins-Desbiolles, 2023; Milne, 2023).

The evolution of tourism law must now focus on three core imperatives: (1) institutionalizing regenerative principles into binding legal frameworks, (2) leveraging technological tools for transparency and compliance, and (3) ensuring participatory governance through co-management and community-led enforcement (Horne & Venables, 2020; Khan et al., 2023). This includes scaling blockchain for sustainability verification, integrating AI into environmental monitoring, and recognizing ecosystem rights through jurisprudence (Cai et al., 2020; Harmsworth & Awatere, 2023).

Regenerative tourism laws must be responsive and inclusive. They should recognize and integrate plural legal traditions, foster multi-stakeholder partnerships, and prioritize place-based equity. Policymakers, legal practitioners, and tourism actors are urged to co-create legal architectures that are adaptive, culturally sensitive, and rooted in justice. In essence, the role of law is not only to regulate but to enable transformation. It must move beyond containment to become a catalyst for restoring ecological systems, uplifting marginalized communities, and reimagining tourism as a force for regenerative futures.

Future Outlook

Emerging Legal Trends and Their Potential Impact on Tourism

Several emerging legal trends show promise for advancing sustainability in tourism. Among these, the integration of technologies like blockchain and artificial intelligence (AI) is transforming how compliance and enforcement are managed. Blockchain systems offer enhanced transparency and accountability in sustainability reporting, while AI enables real-time monitoring of environmental and social impacts (Khan et al., 2023). Additionally, international collaboration on climate change and biodiversity protection is influencing domestic tourism laws. Agreements such as the Glasgow Climate Pact (2021) emphasize the need to embed climate resilience into national tourism strategies, signalling that robust legal measures will be essential to support this shift (United Nations, 2021).

Call to Action for Legal Practitioners, Policymakers, and Tourism Stakeholders

The future of tourism depends on the collective efforts of legal practitioners, policymakers, and stakeholders from both the public and private sectors. Legal practitioners must champion innovative legal tools and advocate for adaptive laws that address dynamic environmental and societal needs. Policymakers need to promote cross-sector collaboration, ensuring that tourism laws are inclusive and reflect the interests of diverse stakeholders. Meanwhile, tourism stakeholders, including businesses and local communities, must actively engage in co-creating legal frameworks to ensure these laws are practical and impactful. A shared commitment to sustainability and regeneration is crucial to unlocking the transformative potential of tourism as a force for good.

By prioritizing collaboration, innovation, and inclusivity, future legal frameworks can shape a tourism industry that goes beyond minimizing harm, actively driving the restoration and regeneration of ecosystems and communities. This approach will ensure that tourism becomes a true catalyst for positive environmental and social change.

Emerging Legal Paradigms in Tourism Governance

The tourism sector is witnessing transformative legal developments across three key areas. First, the recognition of ecosystem rights is accelerating globally, with 15 nations considering rights-of-nature laws for tourism sites (Kauffman & Martin, 2023), exemplified by Chile's proposed Glacier Protection Act (Valenzuela, 2023) and Brazil's protections for the Amazon (Ferrante & Fearnside, 2023). Second, climate litigation is reshaping accountability, as seen in Klimaatzaak v. TUI (2023), which mandates emission cuts, and the Pacific Island Nations' reef damage claims (FIC, 2024), driving "climate due diligence" requirements (Peeters et al., 2023). Third, AI-driven governance is emerging through Singapore's dynamic visitor management (STB, 2023), Barcelona's blockchain zoning enforcement (Ajuntament de Barcelona, 2024), and UNESCO's overtourism prediction tools (UNESCO, 2023). These trends demand adaptive legal leadership: practitioners must master ecological jurisprudence, policymakers should create regulatory sandboxes, businesses need AI ethics frameworks, and communities must co-design governance systems. The Maldives' integration of AI monitoring with traditional Rah protections (Zubair, 2023) exemplifies that hybrid approaches can achieve genuine regenerative tourism through culturally grounded, technologically enhanced legal frameworks.

REFERENCES

ACCC (Australian Competition and Consumer Commission). (2023). Guidelines on Environmental Claims. https://www.accc.gov.au

Ajuntament de Barcelona. (2024). Smart tourism regulation annual report. https://www.barcelona.cat

Akama, J. (2023). Conservation finance and community displacement in Kenyan tourism. *African Studies Review*, *66*(1), 45–67.

Akama, J. (2023). Conservation finance and corruption in African tourism. *African Studies Review*, *66*(1), 45–67.

Altman, J., & Jackson, S. (2023). Aboriginal Customary Law and National Park Management in Australia. *Journal of Legal Pluralism and Unofficial Law*, *55*(1), 112–130.

Basu, S. (2020). Cultural heritage law in India: A critical analysis of the Ancient Monuments and Archaeological Sites and Remains Act. *Journal of Heritage Tourism*, *15*(3), 258–272. DOI: 10.1080/1743873X.2020.1728957

Bianchi, R. (2022). The political economy of tourism development: A critical review. *Tourism Geographies*, *24*(4-5), 467–489.

Boley, B. B., & Johnson Gaither, C. (2020). Exploring empowerment within the framework of sustainable tourism: A multilevel analysis of the tourism empowerment scale. *Journal of Sustainable Tourism*, *28*(4), 529–549. DOI: 10.1080/09669582.2019.1707216

Bramwell, B., & Lane, B. (2018). Sustainable tourism: A global perspective. *Tourism Management*, *68*, 450–454. DOI: 10.1016/j.tourman.2018.04.014

Buckley, R. (2018). *Tourism and conservation: Science, ethics, and practice*. CABI.

Buckley, R. (2019). *Tourism and biodiversity: Concepts and issues*. Channel View Publications.

Buckley, R. (2019). Tourism development and environmental protection: Definitions, concepts, and approaches. *Tourism Geographies*, *21*(5), 685–694. DOI: 10.1080/14616688.2018.1557735

Cai, W., Richter, J., & Zhan, Y. (2020). Blockchain Technology in Sustainable Supply Chain Management: Applications and Challenges. *Journal of Cleaner Production*, *274*, 123233. DOI: 10.1016/j.jclepro.2020.123233

Cellini, R., & Cuccia, T. (2019). The economics of cultural tourism: International perspectives. *Tourism Economics, 25*(2), 245–259. DOI: 10.1177/1354816619829189

Chevalier, J. M. (2023). Legal pluralism and tourism governance at Machu Picchu. *World Development, 161*, 106132.

City of Amsterdam. (2023). Regulation of Platform-Based Short-Term Rentals. https://www.amsterdam.nl

CLIA. (2023). *Global cruise industry environmental report.* Cruise Lines International Association.

CLIA. (2023). *State of the cruise industry report.* Cruise Lines International Association.

Colau, A., & Martí-Costa, M. (2022). Urban tourism governance in Barcelona: From deregulation to recentralization. *Cities (London, England), 131*, 103998.

Colchester, M., & Ferrari, M. (2021). Indigenous peoples' rights and tourism: A legal perspective. *Journal of Sustainable Tourism, 29*(5), 731–748. DOI: 10.1080/09669582.2021.1879196

Comune di Venezia. (2023). Tourist Access Regulation. https://www.comune.venezia.it

Davis, J., Carter, R., & Collins, M. (2021). Collaborative governance in tourism: Lessons from indigenous co-management of national parks. *Journal of Sustainable Tourism, 29*(4), 567–585. DOI: 10.1080/09669582.2021.193890

Dorji, T. (2023). Bhutan's GNH-based tourism policy: Lessons for regenerative tourism. *Journal of Sustainable Tourism, 31*(2), 312–330.

Dorji, T. (2023). Buddhist ecology and tourism regulation in Bhutan. *Journal of Sustainable Tourism, 31*(2), 312–330.

Dredge, D. (2023). Comparative tourism law in civil law systems. *Annals of Tourism Research, 98*, 103525.

Dredge, D., & Gyimóthy, S. (2017). *Collaborative Economy and Tourism: Perspectives, Politics, Policies and Prospects.* Springer. DOI: 10.1007/978-3-319-51799-5

Dredge, D., & Jamal, T. (2015). Progress in tourism planning and policy: A post-structural perspective on knowledge production. *Tourism Management, 51*, 285–297. DOI: 10.1016/j.tourman.2015.06.002

Dressler, W.. (2023). Indigenous tourism governance in the Cordilleras. *Journal of Sustainable Tourism, 31*(4), 567–585.

Duffy, L. N., Kline, C., & Mowatt, R. A. (2023). Informal tourism labor and systemic exclusion in island economies. *Annals of Tourism Research, 98*, 103522. DOI: 10.1016/j.annals.2023.103522

European Commission. (2014). Directive 2014/95/EU of the European Parliament and of the Council. Retrieved from https://eur-lex.europa.eu

European Commission. (2020). A European Green Deal: Striving to be the first climate-neutral continent. Retrieved from https://ec.europa.eu/green-deal

European Commission. (2021). EU Emissions Trading System (EU ETS). Retrieved from https://ec.europa.eu/clima/policies/ets_en

European Commission. (2022). *Tourism and Transport Package: Policy Initiatives for Sustainable*

European Commission. (2022). *EU Biodiversity Strategy for 2030*. Publications Office.

European Commission. (2023). *Overview of EU Tourism Policy.*

European Commission. (2023). *Smart Specialisation Strategy for Sustainable Tourism: Policy Brief.* Retrieved from https://ec.europa.eu

European Commission. (2023). Directive on Green Claims. https://ec.europa.eu

European Parliament. (2014). Directive 2014/52/EU of the European Parliament and of the Council of 16 April 2014 amending Directive 2011/92/EU on the assessment of the effects of certain public and private projects on the environment. *Official Journal of the European Union.* Retrieved from https://eur-lex.europa.eu/legal-content/EN/TXT/?uri=CELEX%3A32014L0052

Ferrante, L., & Fearnside, P. M. (2023). Legal protection of the Amazon for tourism. *Nature Sustainability*, *6*(3), 256–269.

FIC (Foundation for International Law). (2024). Climate litigation case tracker. https://www.fil.org

Fletcher, R. (2023). Against the regenerative turn in tourism. *Annals of Tourism Research*, *98*, 103524.

Font, X., & McCabe, S. (2017). Sustainability and marketing in tourism: Its contexts, paradoxes, approaches, challenges, and potential. *Journal of Sustainable Tourism*, *25*(7), 869–883. DOI: 10.1080/09669582.2017.1301721

Fullagar, S., & Wilson, E. (2020). Slow tourism and wellbeing: The convergence of the sustainable and the restorative. *Journal of Sustainable Tourism*, *28*(6), 938–953. DOI: 10.1080/09669582.2020.1715997

Glasson, J., Therivel, R., & Chadwick, A. (2019). *Introduction to environmental impact assessment*. Routledge. DOI: 10.4324/9780429470738

Global Tourism Resilience Council. (2022). Advancing regenerative tourism through public-private collaboration. *Tourism and Development Review*, *36*(2), 112–126.

Gössling, S., & Hall, C. M. (2019). *Sustainable Tourism: A Global Perspective*. Routledge.

Gössling, S., & Higham, J. (2021). *Sustainable tourism: A global perspective*. Routledge.

Gössling, S., & Peeters, P. (2015). Assessing tourism's global environmental impact 1900-2050. *Journal of Sustainable Tourism*, *23*(5), 639–659. DOI: 10.1080/09669582.2015.1008500

Government of Canada. (2021). Impact assessment process for indigenous participation in tourism. Retrieved from https://www.canada.ca

Great Barrier Reef Marine Park Authority [GBRMPA]. (2023). Reef 2050 Long-Term Sustainability Plan.

Gretzel, U.. (2021). Smart tourism cities: Legal and governance challenges. *Journal of Sustainable Tourism*, *29*(12), 2045–2062.

GSTC. (2023). *Global Sustainable Tourism Council: Reporting Tools for Sustainable Tourism*. Retrieved from https://www.gstc.org

Guttentag, D. (2023). Regulating Airbnb: How cities adapt laws to the sharing economy. *Annals of Tourism Research*, *98*, 103521.

Hall, C. M. (2019). Tourism and sustainable development goals: The role of national tourism laws and policies. *Journal of Sustainable Tourism*, *27*(4), 492–504. DOI: 10.1080/09669582.2018.1557398

Hall, C. M., Gossling, S., & Scott, D. (2019). *Sustainable tourism: A global perspective*. Routledge.

Harmsworth, G., & Awatere, S. (2023). Māori Environmental Knowledge in Tourism Policy. *New Zealand Geographer*, *79*(2), 89–104.

Harris, E., & Pappalepore, I. (2021). Regenerative tourism: A new approach to sustainable tourism in the post-COVID-19 era. *Journal of Sustainable Tourism, 29*(9), 1499–1518. DOI: 10.1080/09669582.2021.1906503

Harrison, D. (2023). Customary marine tenure in Pacific Island tourism. *Oceania, 93*(1), 78–95.

Harrison, D. (2023). Fijian Vanua Law in Coastal Tourism Governance. *Pacific Studies, 46*(2), 45–68.

Harrison, D. (2023). Tourism and displacement in Pacific island communities. *Pacific Affairs, 96*(1), 23–45.

Higgins-Desbiolles, F. (2020). The Elusive Sustainable Tourism Model: The Risks of Caution and the Need for Boldness. *Tourism Geographies, 22*(4), 689–704.

Higgins-Desbiolles, F. (2020). The evolution of sustainable tourism: From economic growth to the well-being of all life. *Journal of Sustainable Tourism, 28*(3), 365–384. DOI: 10.1080/09669582.2019.1679823

Higgins-Desbiolles, F. (2023). Regenerative tourism: A deconstruction. *Tourism Recreation Research, 48*(3), 1–15.

Holden, A. (2019). *Environment and tourism*. Routledge.

Honey, M., & Krantz, D. (2021). *Costa Rica: A global leader in sustainable tourism.* Island Press.

Horne, R., & Venables, D. (2020). Legal frameworks for sustainable tourism: Building resilience in a changing world. *Journal of Environmental Law, 32*(2), 291–311. DOI: 10.1093/jel/eqaa006

ILO. (2023). *Decent work in island tourism economies.* International Labour Organization.

ILO. (2023). *Decent work in island tourism economies.* International Labour Organization.

Internal Revenue Service. (2021). Energy Incentives for Businesses in the American Recovery and Reinvestment Act. Retrieved from https://www.irs.gov

International Labour Organization (ILO). (2023). *Decent work in the tourism sector: Addressing informality and seasonality.* https://www.ilo.org

Janke, T. (2020). Indigenous intellectual property and tourism: Protecting indigenous art and culture. *Australian Indigenous Law Review, 23*(1), 45–62.

Jones, R.. (2022). Haida Law and Marine Tourism Governance. *Coastal Management, 50*(3), 215–233.

Jones, R.. (2023). Haida Oral Law in Park Management. *Journal of Legal Anthropology, 7*(1), 112–130.

Kauffman, C. M. (2023). Ecuador's nature rights jurisprudence. *World Development, 161*, 106132.

Kauffman, C. M., & Martin, P. L. (2021). Can Rights of Nature Make Development More Sustainable? Why Some Laws are Better than Others. *World Development, 144*, 105452. DOI: 10.1016/j.worlddev.2021.105452

Kauffman, C. M., & Martin, P. L. (2021). Rights of nature in tourism governance. *World Development, 144*, 105452.

Kauffman, C. M., & Martin, P. L. (2023). Global expansion of nature's rights. *Science, 379*(6634), 654–656.

Khan, R., Al-Ansari, T., & Saif, U. (2023). Blockchain applications for sustainability compliance in tourism. *Tourism Technology Journal, 9*(1), 45–58. DOI: 10.1016/j.ttj.2023.100184

Kipuri, N. (2023). Maasai Customary Land Systems in Kenya's Tourism Sector. *The American Journal of International Law, 34*(2), 45–67.

Kipuri, N. (2023). Maasai customary law in Kenyan tourism governance. *The American Journal of International Law, 34*(2), 45–67.

Kontogeorgopoulos, N. (2020). *Tourism and the Economy in Thailand: Challenges and Opportunities*. Oxford University Press.

Kontogeorgopoulos, N. (2023). Regulatory failure in Thai coastal tourism. *Journal of Sustainable Tourism, 31*(2), 245–263.

Kyoto City Government. (2022). Digital Tourism Access Management System. https://www.city.kyoto.lg.jp

Lenzen, M., Sun, Y.-Y., Faturay, F., Ting, Y.-P., Geschke, A., & Malik, A. (2021). The carbon footprint of global tourism. *Nature Climate Change, 8*(6), 522–528. DOI: 10.1038/s41558-018-0141-x

Lew, A. A., Ng, P. T., & Teng, Y. (2020). *Nature-Based Tourism: Ecology, Impacts, and Management*. Cambridge University Press.

Liu, Z., Zhang, J., & Wang, L. (2021). Artificial Intelligence Applications in Sustainable Tourism Management. *Sustainability, 13*(12), 6784. DOI: 10.3390/su13126784

López-Santillán, A. (2023). Cultural zoning in Mexican tourism. *Annals of Tourism Research, 98*, 103527.

Lu, F.. (2023). Indigenous Environmental Stewardship in Amazonian Tourism. *Conservation & Society, 21*(1), 12–25.

Mair, J. (2019). *Community-based tourism: Principles and practices*. Channel View Publications.

Maitland, R. (2023). *Smart Cities and Tourism: The Role of Urban Law*. Routledge.

Mang, P., & Reed, B. (2018). Designing for resilience: Regenerative tourism as a path to systemic change. *Tourism Geographies, 20*(1), 68–86. DOI: 10.1080/14616688.2017.1386968

Mbaiwa, J. (2023). Community-based tourism and customary law in Botswana. *Journal of Ecotourism, 22*(1), 45–62.

Mbaiwa, J. E. (2023). Customary law in African tourism governance. *Journal of Sustainable Tourism, 31*(3), 456–475.

McLennan, C. J., Becken, S., & Watt, M. (2021). Strengthening tourism laws for sustainability: A global review. *International Journal of Tourism Research, 23*(2), 198–213. DOI: 10.1002/jtr.2412

Milano, C., Cheer, J. M., & Novelli, M. (2019). *Overtourism: Excesses, Discontents, and Measures in Travel and Tourism*. CABI. DOI: 10.1079/9781786399823.0000

Milne, S. (2023). Neoliberal conservation and tourism displacement. *Geoforum, 138*, 103662.

Ministerio para la Transición Ecológica y el Reto Demográfico. (2020). Renewable energy plan. Retrieved from https://www.miteco.gob.es

Ministry of Corporate Affairs. (2013). The Companies Act, 2013. Retrieved from https://www.mca.gov.in

Ministry of Environment. Maldives. (2021). National Carbon Neutrality Strategy. https://www.environment.gov.mv

Müller, D., & Pforr, C. (2023). The implementation gap in tourism policy. *Annals of Tourism Research, 98*, 103530.

Mwangi, W. (2022). *Community Land Rights and Tourism in Kenya*. African Legal Review.

Mwangi, W. (2023). Maasai land rights in Kenyan tourism. African Journal of International Law.

Mwangi, W., & Omwenga, M. (2021). Legal frameworks and community-led tourism in Kenya: A pathway to sustainability. *Tourism Management Perspectives*, *40*, 100827. DOI: 10.1016/j.tmp.2021.100827

Mwangi, W., & Omwenga, M. (2023). Post-colonial legal reforms in African tourism. *Third World Quarterly*, *44*(2), 234–251.

Neirotti, P.. (2022). IoT and big data for crowd management in tourist cities. *Tourism Management*, *93*, 104608.

Nelson, F. (2017). Community conservation in Tanzania: Policies and legal frameworks. *Development Policy Review*, *35*(5), 593–615. DOI: 10.1111/dpr.12245

Nelson, F. (2022). Tourism law reform in Tanzania. *Development Policy Review*, *40*(3), 412–430.

New Zealand Government. (2019). Climate Change Response (Zero Carbon) Amendment Act. Retrieved from https://www.legislation.govt.nz

Nyakabwa, A. (2023). Enforcement challenges in African conservation tourism. *Journal of Ecotourism*, *22*(1), 78–95.

Ólafsdóttir, R., & Runnström, M. C. (2020). Managing tourism impacts on fragile ecosystems in Iceland. *Environmental Management*, *65*(3), 432–446. DOI: 10.1007/s00267-020-01282-3

Pechlaner, H., Volgger, M., & Innerhofer, E. (2020). *Sustainable tourism and regional development: The European experience*. Edward Elgar Publishing.

Peeters, P.. (2023). Climate due diligence in tourism law. *Journal of Sustainable Tourism*, *31*(8), 1789–1807.

Peeters, P., Higham, J., Kutzner, D., Cohen, S., & Gössling, S. (2018). The Paris Agreement and tourism: How can tourism contribute to the 1.5°C target? *Journal of Sustainable Tourism*, *26*(7), 1093–1107. DOI: 10.1080/09669582.2018.1428391

Pettersson, R. (2023). Sami law in Scandinavian tourism. *Arctic Review*, *14*, 1–18.

Pettersson, R. (2023). Sami Reindeer Herding Law vs. Tourism Permits. *Arctic Review*, *14*, 1–18.

Pettersson, R., & Viken, A. (2023). Sami Tourism and Legal Pluralism in Scandinavia. *Arctic Review*, *14*, 1–18.

Picard, M. (2023). Balinese Hinduism and sustainable tourism. *Asian Journal of Tourism Research*, *8*(1), 112–128.

Postero, N. (2023). Indigenous constitutionalism and tourism in Bolivia. *Latin American Politics and Society*, *65*(1), 89–107.

Rivera-Murillo, G., Porras, I., & Barton, D. N. (2020). Lessons from Costa Rica's sustainable tourism policy. *Tourism Management*, *36*(4), 378–392. DOI: 10.1016/j.tmp.2020.100738

Rivera-Murillo, G., Porras, I., & Barton, D. N. (2020). Payment for Ecosystem Services in Tourism: Lessons from Costa Rica. *Tourism Management Perspectives*, *36*, 100738. DOI: 10.1016/j.tmp.2020.100738

Sambo, W. (2023). Interface of Customary and State Law in Tourism. *Journal of Legal Pluralism and Unofficial Law*, *55*(3), 301–320.

Scheyvens, R., & Biddulph, R. (2018). Inclusive tourism development. *Tourism Geographies*, *20*(4), 589–606. DOI: 10.1080/14616688.2017.1381985

Scholz, J., Krumme, K., & Hilty, L. M. (2022). The Role of Geographic Information Systems in Sustainable Tourism. *Tourism Geographies*, *24*(4), 547–563. DOI: 10.1080/14616688.2021.1983347

Schwartzman, S.. (2023). Indigenous Justice Systems and Ecotourism in the Amazon. *Conservation & Society*, *21*(1), 12–25.

Scott, D., Hall, C. M., & Gössling, S. (2019). *Climate change and tourism: Impacts, adaptation, and mitigation*. Routledge.

Sharpley, R., & Telfer, D. J. (2018). *Tourism and development: Concepts and issues*. Channel View Publications.

Sheldon, P. J. (2020). Resilience and regenerative tourism: Facing climate change and other global challenges. *Tourism Review*, *75*(2), 243–251. DOI: 10.1108/TR-02-2020-0036

Singapore Tourism Board (STB). (2023). Smart Tourism 2025 Blueprint. https://www.stb.gov.sg

Smith, L., & Hall, C. M. (2022). Policy innovation for regenerative tourism: Lessons from New Zealand. *Tourism Management Perspectives*, *43*, 101057. DOI: 10.1016/j.tmp.2022.101057

Spenceley, A. (2018). *Sustainable tourism: A global perspective*. Routledge.

Spenceley, A. (2023). Equity in African conservation tourism. *Tourism Geographies, 25*(1), 112–130.

STB (Singapore Tourism Board). (2023). AI for sustainable visitor management. https://www.stb.gov.sg

Steiner, G., & Posch, A. (2021). *Regenerative Tourism: Challenges and Opportunities for Policy and Practice.* Springer.

Suzman, J. (2023). San N!ore Systems and Community Tourism. *Journal of Southern African Studies, 49*(4), 689–705.

Tourism New Zealand. (2020). Sustainability in Tourism. Retrieved from https://www.tourismnewzealand.com

UNDRR. (2021). Tourism Resilience Scorecard. https://www.undrr.org

UNESCO. (1972). Convention concerning the protection of the world cultural and natural heritage. Retrieved from https://whc.unesco.org

UNESCO. (2023). Machine learning in heritage tourism. https://whc.unesco.org

United Nations. (2007). United Nations Declaration on the Rights of Indigenous Peoples. Retrieved from https://www.un.org

United Nations. (2015). *Transforming our world: The 2030 Agenda for Sustainable Development.* https://sustainabledevelopment.un.org/post2015/transformingourworld

United Nations. (2015). Transforming our world: The 2030 Agenda for Sustainable Development. Retrieved from https://sustainabledevelopment.un.org/

United Nations. (2021). Glasgow Climate Pact. *UN Climate Change Conference 2021*. Retrieved from https://unfccc.int

UNWTO. (2017). *Sustainable development of tourism.* https://www.unwto.org/sustainable-development

U.S. Environmental Protection Agency. (2020). Clean Water Act (CWA). Retrieved from https://www.epa.gov/laws-regulations/summary-clean-water-act

Valenzuela, P. (2023). Glacier rights in Andean tourism. *Mountain Research and Development, 43*(1), R23–R31.

Van der Borg, J. (2023). Platform regulation in urban tourism: The Amsterdam model. *Journal of Destination Marketing, 27*, 100782.

Viteri Mejía, C. (2023). Green gentrification in Costa Rican tourism. *Latin American Perspectives, 50*(3), 112–128.

Vuki, V. (2023). Traditional marine management in Fiji. *Oceania, 93*(1), 78–95.

Warren, C. (2023). Adat law and tourism governance in Indonesia. *Pacific Affairs, 96*(2), 245–263.

Weaver, D. (2023). Certification challenges in regenerative tourism. *Journal of Sustainable Tourism, 31*(4), 889–907.

Weaver, D., & Skyer, P. (2023). Namibian conservancies. *Tourism Management, 94*, 104632.

Whyte, K. (2023). Indigenous justice in tourism development. *Environmental Ethics, 45*(1), 45–63.

WIPO. (2019). Traditional knowledge and cultural expressions: Intellectual property issues. Retrieved from https://www.wipo.int

World Tourism Organization. (2019). Sustainable Tourism Development: Guide for Policy Makers. Retrieved from https://www.unwto.org

Wunder, S. (2023). Payments for ecosystem services: Global lessons. *World Development, 161*, 106118.

Xanthaki, A. (2023). Indigenous Jurisprudence in Sustainable Tourism. *International Journal of Human Rights, 27*(3), 456–475.

Zainal, A., Radzi, S. M., & Hashim, N. (2020). Challenges in sustainable tourism enforcement in Asia-Pacific. *Journal of Tourism Research, 29*(3), 87–101.

Zakaria, Z., & Hassan, M. N. (2020). The effectiveness of environmental impact assessments in sustainable tourism planning in Malaysia. *Journal of Environmental Management, 260*, 110154. DOI: 10.1016/j.jenvman.2020.110154

Zeppel, H. (2020). Indigenous ecotourism: Sustainable development and management. *Journal of Ecotourism, 19*(3), 245–259. DOI: 10.1080/14724049.2020.1727483

Zubair, S. (2023). Maldivian traditional law and climate tourism. *Island Studies Journal, 18*(1), 89–104.

KEY TERMS AND DEFINITIONS

Sustainable Tourism Law: Legal regulations and policies designed to promote tourism that minimizes environmental impact, supports local communities, and ensures long-term economic viability.

Regenerative Tourism: A transformative approach to tourism that goes beyond sustainability, actively restoring ecosystems, empowering communities, and creating net-positive impacts.

Sustainable Development Goals (SDGs): A UN-backed set of 17 global objectives (e.g., climate action, reduced inequalities) guiding sustainable practices, including tourism.

Environmental Law: Legal frameworks governing natural resource protection, pollution control, and biodiversity conservation, applied to tourism operations.

Social Equity: Fair distribution of tourism benefits across communities, ensuring marginalized groups have access to opportunities and rights.

Economic Resilience: Policies and strategies that help tourism-dependent economies adapt to crises (e.g., pandemics, climate disasters).

Legal Frameworks: Structured systems of laws, regulations, and treaties that govern sustainable and regenerative tourism practices globally.

Chapter 2
Role of Green Subsidies and Carbon Tariffs Towards a Sustainable Future Under International Trade Law

Sheikh Inam Ul Mansoor
https://orcid.org/0000-0001-8636-4769
Dayananda Sagar University, India

ABSTRACT

This chapter examines how green subsidies and carbon tariffs help create a more sustainable future through international trade rules. These tools act through trade rules to fight climate change and help the WTO control them. This study defines how green subsidies and carbon tariffs promote innovation to decrease emissions while advancing toward a low-carbon economy. This chapter examines how practices of green subsidies and carbon tariffs affect WTO agreements like SCM and GATT and studies legal problems that could develop from their implementation. This chapter examines equity implications of green subsidies and carbon tariffs on developing countries and proposes solutions to make these policies fair overall. This chapter presents suggested trade policy changes to align international rules with environmental sustainability targets while urging systemic updates to add Green strategies to global trade methods and maintain global monetary fairness during climate efforts.

DOI: 10.4018/979-8-3373-1792-2.ch002

INTRODUCTION

Humanity faces one of the most dangerous issues of contemporary time with climate change. The problems caused by climate change damage both natural environments and touch every part of global society and government (Ripple et al., 2024). To solve climate change problems international groups formed the Paris Agreement which works to limit temperature rise while making business systems sustainable (Huang & Zhai, 2021). Climate change affects the global climate, and its impacts are realized on a global level. Behind the management of the natural environment, addressing it effectively is more than a question of managing the environment: it requires integrated protection action including in the fields of environment, economics and the social (Klingelhöfer et al., 2020). The rise of globalization depends on trade flows while making the process responsible for carbon emissions across production supply chains and distribution networks. The two functions of trade systems recommend changes to make them work better with sustainable development goals (Zhang et al., 2023). The combination of trade policy and environmental protection creates fundamental legal and policy hurdles to overcome. Free trade promotes economic growth yet hurts the environment mostly because weak environmental laws exist in certain areas (Felbermayr et al., 2024). Industrialized nations that produced most greenhouse gases today want to put in place systems that factor climate impact into international trade. Green subsidies and carbon tariffs have become significant strategies to correct the environmental problems caused by international trade. The trade policies want manufacturers to build environmentally-friendly practices while stopping carbon heavy imports to balance trade with environment protection (Böhringer et al., 2021).

Current environmental treaties cannot handle global climate change properly which shows why trade rules need sustainability integration. Successful trade policies boost environmental protection through support for renewable energy adoption and promote eco-friendly technology along with emission reduction (Droege, 2025). The goal to include sustainability approaches comes up against WTO trade rules at international standards. The WTO defends global trade regulations by banning unfair treatment while making all deals public and stopping practices that hinder trade. These rules to keep markets equal could block how nations support environmentally-friendly industries (Negi, 2020). When governments support industries with special benefits they encourage companies to switch to greener production methods. Green industry sectors like renewable energy and electric vehicles need substantial government support due to market failure problems that limit market participation (Duan et al., 2024). The benefits green subsidies deliver to the environment face important legal challenges under WTO SCM Agreement rules. Under SCM Agreement rules, the WTO prohibits subsidies used by local companies to gain unfair market benefits over foreign competitors unless they fulfil one of the agreement's specified exceptions (Charnovitz, 2014). Measuring if green subsidies create trade barriers or support environmental goals demands careful analysis of WTO rules to combine trade protection with worldwide preservation of this planet (Zhao, 2024).

Carbon tariffs act as border carbon adjustment mechanisms designed to control carbon leakage. When industries move to nations with weaker environmental rules because of strict rules in one country this pushes global emission reductions farther away (Dobranschi et al., 2024). Carbons tariffs add fees to imported goods from poor environmental performers while making domestic green companies more competitive. The adoption of carbon tariffs generates issues under GATT law because they challenge MFN rights and treatment standards (Zhou et al., 2024). To make sure carbon tariffs comply with trade guidelines companies need to practice them correctly. Even though green subsidies and carbon tariffs can boost environmental progress they face significant obstacles. They cause disagreements between developed and developing nations because the global trading rules create unfair treatment (Wang & Zhou, 2024). Developing nations generally do not have enough resources or technical knowledge to use green technology so they consider these policies as market restrictions that stop their development. The practice of placing carbon tariffs on developing country exports makes many people think the system is unfair because these nations produced far fewer total emissions over time (Hunjra et al., 2024). For equitable development, need of joint programs that teach skills plus distribute green tech and funding to nations facing economic challenges. International trade law needs to support and adjust climate protection measures. Since its trade-centred establishment the WTO must adapt to modern challenges of climate protection and sustainability (Marceau, 2016). The trade rules need to be reviewed from an environmental lens matching existing rules aimed at saving the planet. Today the WTO can justify its relevance to show how it can handle disputes over green subsidies and carbon tariffs (Felbermayr et al., 2024).

This chapter deeply studies how international trade law manages green subsidies and carbon tariffs. It tries to discover how green policies can create a better future and what political and financial barriers exist with them. This chapter uses legal documents and trade policy reports to study examples from which it presents important facts about combining trade and environmental protection aims. It suggests practical ways government officials and law professionals can handle the tough challenges of making sustainability part of global trade rules. This exploration reveals how trade policies guide the development of a sustainable low-carbon economy that benefits everyone.

GREEN SUBSIDIES: INNOVATION & SUSTAINABILITY

Modern climate policies use green subsidies to connect environmental needs with economic market systems. These financial government programs help industries switch to environmentally friendly technologies by offering them support to make the change happen (Gugler et al., 2021). Under the Paris Agreement and multilateral environmental treaties states employ green subsidies to support environmental projects and drive innovative technologies. People disagree about using these programs because they affect WTO rules that control global trade (Kalfagianni & Young, 2022). Economists need to study how green subsidies work in real life to understand their effect on achieving sustainable business practices worldwide (Benkhodja et al., 2023). Government subsidies support multiple funding methods that target specific industries to solve market problems that harm greenhouse gas reduction efforts. High expenses in environmental technology research and deployment create challenges for private investment to proceed (Song et al., 2022). Through financial bonuses green subsidies lower the investment risk and expenses of sustainable innovation. Officials use money transfers combined with tax privileges as well as additional incentives for people who use green electricity and invest in utilities for the public (Li et al., 2021). Different types of support measures target key environmental governance concerns by driving renewable energy adoption as well as enhancing energy efficiency and sustainable farming while promoting circular economy principles (Chai & Ma, 2025). They work to steer market operations toward environmentally sustainable outcomes. Feed-in tariff programs establish fixed payments that renewable energy producers receive when they put their generated electricity into the power grid. Different countries especially Europe and Asian markets use this strategy to build their renewable energy industries (Couture & Gagnon, 2010). Tax credit programs and tax deductions help private organizations invest in clean energy projects by limiting how much companies must pay when they move to low-carbon technology platforms. Money from research and development subsidies support projects that improve energy efficiency technology and decrease pollution (Shafi et al., 2023).

Many real programs demonstrate green subsidies can create powerful changes in systems. Through the Renewable Energy Sources Act in Germany (EEG) feed-in tariffs launched a global renewable energy lead that turned Germany into the world's top solar and wind producer (Selder, 2014). The scheme expanded Germany's renewable energy resources while building a strong local sector of green technology companies (Sauter et al., 2013). By providing financial support to PV solar production China built its market status as the leading supplier of solar panels worldwide. These support payments decreased how much solar electricity costs all over the world so more people could afford and use solar power (Allouhi et al., 2022). The Production Tax Credit and Investment Tax Credit from the United States federal government support both wind power and solar energy sectors. Private money enters the country to fund renewable energy projects that begin operating across multiple locations (Celsa & Xydis, 2023). Even environment-friendly financial aids face official trade law protests especially under World Trade Organization regulations. Under the SCM Agreement WTO members must follow rules to use their financial incentives with the agreement splitting these subsidies into two parts (Tamiotti, 2010). The WTO rules specifically ban subsidies that force firms to export more or prefer local over imported products. Actionable subsidies generate negative effects toward other WTO members such as harming local industries and making benefits from existing agreements harder to achieve (Laprévote & Kang, 2011).

Green subsidies qualify as actionable subsidies because they create unequal market benefits for domestic producers that affect international trade fairness. When governments offer production cost reductions for renewable energy equipment the market becomes saturated with discounted items and this hurts foreign manufacturers (Jin et al., 2025). Nations used countervailing duties to fight their trade war because China's solar panel industry repeatedly received unfair support according to U.S allegations. The legal review of environmental subsidies under SCM Agreement champions debates about the relationship between market freedom and environmental defence (Metzger, 1974). The SCM Agreement currently restricts most subsidy policies yet people compete to add green subsidies to WTO regulations because of climate goals require support (Cima, 2017). Under GATT rules and General Agreement on Tariffs and Trade (GATT) standards the relationship between green subsidies and WTO principles shows its clearest strain in the field of non-discrimination. When trade rules benefit domestic green hardware makers over foreign competitors they can be deemed against WTO's rule to treat all producers equally (Borlini & Montanaro, 2018). Article XX of the General Agreement on Tariffs and Trade permits member nations to use environmental regulations when protecting human health and life or plant and animal well-being when conserving natural resources but requires these measures to be reasonably applied (Mansoor & Chopra, 2020). Despite its legal limits many see Article XX conflicting with green subsidy practices because these measures require actual environmental objectives and protectionist avoidance to qualify (Mansoor, 2022).

Implementation of green subsidies produces legal challenges as well as substantial impact on environmental and economic outcomes. By offering these subsidies, these subsidies do a lot to radically accelerate the transition to a low carbon economy by cutting by way of the adoption of cleaner applied sciences and cutting back human reliance on fossil fuels (Li, et al., 2021). Green subsidies internalize environmental costs so that green solutions for climate goals and the planet can be pursued. They encourage investment in environmentally friendly research and production, foster the growth of new green industries, and create jobs and healthy competition in an environmentally conscious industry (Shi & Zhou, 2024). Although green subsidies help save the environment, they can create uneven economic effects. These measures create wrong market alignments that benefit particular sectors and technological areas without business merits (Benkhodja et al., 2023). Addressing these troubles gets harder when subsidies go to the wrong people who misuse them to create bad systems. Single policies become a major fiscal problem in developing countries when they use public dollars to subsidize industry. Developed nations can distribute larger green subsidies plainly, because they have stronger financial backing (Cai et al., 2023). The global imbalance in this system demands worldwide partnership between countries to manage green subsidies without worsening trade gaps.

CARBON TARIFFS: COMBATING LEAKAGE & ACCOUNTABILITY

Carbon tariffs have become a main weapon to fight climate change by handling environmental impacts during commerce while making businesses worldwide responsible for emissions (Zhou et al., 2024). As international trade meets environmental standards today these tariffs create fairness between nations by making carbon-intensive imports pay domestic carbon prices (Larch & Wanner, 2017). This approach brings governments with weak climate rules into line while blocking industry relocations and supports sustainable development in global economic system (Glass & Newig, 2019). States use carbon tariffs to unite protection of their environment with their economic aims when handling trade compliance under global rules (Böhringer et al., 2021). As Border Carbon Adjustments function as carbon tariffs they extend national climate policies to imported goods. BCAs add a carbon value to imported items that matches the price domestic production pays under carbon controls (Mehling et al., 2019). The approach uses Border Carbon Adjustments to protect environment and make businesses worldwide follow responsible carbon standards. When one nation sets strong climate rules it pushes companies to move operations to areas with weaker environmental norms making global emission cuts harder (Rocchi et al., 2018). BCAs stop climate polluters from shifting operations abroad and push low-regulation countries to use better climate-friendly technologies to reach worldwide emission targets (Mehling et al., 2017). Using carbon tariffs in trade policy creates complex legal and trade agreement problems under both GATT and WTO rules. Under GATT leadership the multilateral trading system defines rules that require equal treatment of all trading partners with its members. Under carbon tariff systems producers from other countries may face non-discriminatory treatment because these rules divide goods based on their carbon emissions levels (Veel, 2009). According to GATT, countries may take necessary protective measures for health and species under Article XX but only when these measures don't discriminate unfairly against imports (Mansoor & Chopra, 2020). Carbon tariffs can qualify for WTO Article XX provisions only when they demonstrate environmental need and show proper balance with WTO principles.

The European Union leads global discussions on carbon control with their Carbon Border Adjustment Mechanism (CBAM) implementation. The Carbon Border Adjustment Mechanism combines trade rules with climate policies to control imports that contain excessive carbon products such as steel, cement, aluminium, fertilizers, and electricity (Pan & Liu, 2024). Companies importing products must acquire carbon certificates that equal their merchandise's emissions levels plus adjustments for existing carbon policies of their suppliers' home countries (Gupta & Rakshit, 2023). The plan works together with ETS to protect EU industries but pushes foreign producers towards EU's climate goals. As the EU rolls out CBAM in stages they show their dedication to making climate progress while obeying trade rules and influencing other governments pursuing the same approach (Dechezleprêtre et al., 2023). The CBAM system faces legal obstacles that demonstrate the complexity of making environmental progress while meeting trade requirements. Those opposing CBAM say it breaks MFN principles by giving unfair treatment to products from countries without carbon price systems (Meng, 2024). The system would potentially violate CBAM's national treatment requirement if foreign producers faced more costs from CBAM than domestic producers from the ETS system. Under carbon tariff systems producers from other countries may face non-discriminatory treatment because these rules divide goods based on their carbon emissions levels (Sun et al., 2024). Carbon tariffs produce effects that stretch further than their immediate power to lower emissions. Carbon tariffs set market rules to stimulate industries that use sustainable practices and green technologies across all supply chains worldwide (Roy, 2025). Their presence shows companies want to be responsible for climate action while pushing trading partners to improve their own climate goals. Evaluation should include studying how carbon tariffs affect developing nations at economic level. Imposing these rules would further damage equal conditions across trading nations because weaker economies need more support to meet carbon standards (Yang & Yan, 2023). Carbon tariffs as a sustainability solution needs to include measures that create equal opportunities for all nations to transition fairly into a sustainable future.

EQUITY CONCERNS AND DEVELOPING COUNTRIES

International trade law needs updated policies with green subsidies and carbon tariffs because these rules affect how fairly developing and least-developed countries compete in the world economy today (Cheng et al., 2024). These methods to improve sustainability and tackle environmental stressors create severe struggle for nations that have weak resources and weak infrastructure (Ma & Xu, 2024). Rules that restrict trade can make existing global trade differences worse so nations need to build fair and inclusive rules before they start using these tools. This analysis shows how green subsidies and carbon tariffs create equity problems across nations but also explains why international groups should help vulnerable economies face these challenges (Wang & Zhou, 2024). Despite intending to fight climate change green subsidies and carbon tariffs create harmful trade imbalances that affect developing nations most (Gugler et al., 2021). Countries with advanced technology and strong financial sectors can use environmental policies without jeopardizing their industry leading position (Yunxia & Yuqing, 2025). Developing nations and Least Developed Countries with development needs and budget challenges face significant disadvantage compared to them. When the government supports clean energy industries differently in developed nations these places receive better treatment compared to other areas (Md Akhtaruzzaman et al., 2025). Green subsidies create unfair market conditions and weaken emerging producers' business potential because they lack resources to match these incentives (Fang & Zhao, 2023). The added trade costs of carbon tariffs heavily burden developing nations because their weak environmental standards and limited production technology expose them to unfair import charges (An, 2024). The plan to adjust borders based on emissions risks sanctioning small carbon producers who suffer major climate change effects first (Rocchi et al., 2018). Through CBDR-RC principles international environment law shows developed world countries must face emission history while helping developing countries adapt based on their unique abilities. Applying a single carbon tariff policy ignores these specific differences and disrupts the core fairness goals of world climate agreements (Ari & Sari, 2017).

Countries in development and underdevelopment find many obstacles when they must respond simultaneously to green subsidies and carbon tariffs. Developing countries cannot meet international standards because they lack enough money to build their green industry (Zhao, 2024). Developing nations experience severe difficulties because they must pay heavy expenses for industry conversion into low-carbon operations. Developing nations struggle to accept sustainable methods because they lack proper technology and expert assistance which makes their products less competitive globally (Wu & Wan, 2024). Countries seeking development face major challenges when addressing new trade regulations because their government agencies need improvement. To successfully use green subsidies or adjust to carbon tariffs requires countries to build strong regulation tools and clear governance systems along with efficient administrative processes which many least developed countries (LDCs) may lack (Cai, Dan, Ge, et al., 2023). The uneven systems for measuring carbon emissions and weak reporting systems in developing nations raise great challenges that increase trade problems and disputes (Sheng et al., 2025). The social and financial structure of these developing nations will undergo major changes when carbon reduction requirements affect businesses that generate power with carbon emissions (Hunjra et al., 2024).

To make green subsidies and carbon tariffs fair for everyone governments must create policies that prevent unfair treatment. Special breaks for developing countries should help them during the transition until they build industry capabilities by sharing expertise (Dossa & Miassi, 2024). Green tariff rules should give LDCs special tariff rates because they need development support with minimal emission responsibilities. The CBDR-RC principle supports treating different countries differently in these initiatives that builds their credibility among nations worldwide (Sasmal et al., 2024). Building capabilities helps developing nations fully join green trade activities. When international partners share their knowledge and money they help global markets adopt and follow sustainable trading rules (Olabi et al., 2025). Technological transfers rely on intellectual property regimes that support innovation while helping people across all regions gain fair access to new technological solutions. Developing countries can better transition to sustainable trade by gaining access to clean technologies while innovating under these initiatives (Neves et al., 2021).

International organizations play a major part in solving issues related to fairness in global trade. The World Trade Organization (WTO), the United Nations Framework Convention on Climate Change (UNFCCC) and the United Nations Conference on Trade and Development (UNCTAD) have special roles helping countries balance trade and environment while keeping global rules fair (Chakraborty & Dey, 2024). The WTO needs to resolve disputes around trade rules and climate policy while deciding if green subsidy programs and carbon tariffs harm WTO principles. Through member state discussions the WTO helps create rules that preserve environmental goals yet stay fair to all global participants (Asmelash, 2023). The UNFCCC and Paris Agreement let countries take climate steps together with fair treatment principles. These tools show governments must give financial and technical help to developing nations for climate action because their inclusion helps reach global climate objectives (Pauw et al., 2019). The Green Climate Fund lets countries weakest to climate change receive funds to take actions needed both to reduce emissions and prepare for climate impacts. Trade policies like carbon tariffs and green subsidies work better when they operate with financing and climate protection groups (Garschagen & Doshi, 2022).

The implementation of green subsidies and carbon tariffs laced with protection for the vulnerable nations can be well facilitated through trade agreements between regions and countries. Such agreements can serve to strengthen developing countries by including provisions ensuring such countries' technical capacities, institutional framework and financial support (Bellmann & van der Ven, 2020). The adjusted strategy for these measures makes them more successful and meets the essential needs of developing trade partners. When green subsidies and carbon tariffs ignore equity issues they create major damage to both the environment and economy. When these climate and trade measures benefit certain nations more than others they break international rules and cause more damage to world equality (Carattini et al., 2024). When developing countries feel their rights are not respected through international rules they stand together less to fight climate change. Resistance will show up as disagreements in trade talks and weaker support for international climate accords plus actions that undermine global trade rules (Sforna, 2019). Green subsidies and carbon regulations can help ensure that all citizens can enjoy equal access to green subsidies and carbon regulations that may help to achieve such global climate targets, while encouraging inclusive economic growth. Such measures prepare countries for the specific problems they face in development and encourage the development and innovation in international trading systems (Wei et al., 2025). Equitable policy choices strengthen international trade and climate institutions so they can lead better partnership efforts.

TRADE LAW & SUSTAINABILITY

Experts from trade law and sustainability fields must join forces to tackle international trade barriers in present climate emergency. Though the major trading systems run by the WTO helped create worldwide economic connections they do not suit the urgent environmental needs of today. National legal systems do not easily integrate with trade rules at the international level which creates problems in achieving sustainable trade goals therefore they need to be re-evaluated (Cima & Esty, 2024). An analysis of present WTO framework weaknesses shows that it lacks the tools to help green policies succeed. While WTO Agreements and GATT/SCM Agreements mention environmental protection they do not work well because of their trade-focused system limitations (Tanveer et al., 2024). Under Article XX of GATT nations can protect lifeforms through regulation however strict interpretations that favour free trade currently weaken environmental safeguards (Charnovitz, 1991). States must show strong reasons and fair treatment when building green policies because of the demand to hit these standards. WTO trade rules and climate protection aims create an unnecessary stress because WTO agreements do not clearly support climate change mitigation. History explains why these treaties do not mention climate change as they were created before global awareness increased about this issue (Kulovesi, 2013). The World Trade Organization's rules create many legal challenges to sustainability-driven initiatives such as carbon tariffs and green subsidies. Under SCM Agreement rules subsidies for renewable energy tend to breach the agreement because they provide unfair market benefits (Huang, 2021). Under GATT rules, any carbon tariff structure that does not follow the principle of non-discrimination may be seen as protectionist even if it aims to stop carbon leakage and equalize market conditions (Pan et al., 2024).

The trade rules need updates to work properly with environmental protection efforts. Trading system can better serve its purpose when changes protect trade flows and protect environment by making eco-conscious standards govern global commerce. The GATT framework needs changes to let Article XX ease trading restrictions for climate actions and strategies. This update would help countries follow environmental treaty commitments by allowing them to choose policies that match Paris Agreement demands without breaking World Trade Organization rules (Matsushita et al., 2015).

The WTO needs to create an official legal document that shows how trade and environment connections can work together. The WTO should work towards building a Trade and Sustainability Agreement to help regulatory and environmental trade welfare systems work better together (Tamiotti, 2010). This agreement must define how countries should use carbon tariffs and green subsidies alongside related trade rules as environmental standards. The platform would help solve environmental trade-related problems and create organized rules that connect trade and environmental issues (Böhringer et al., 2021). Bringing the Paris Agreement into international trade law functions as another main step towards connecting trade rules to environmental aims. The Paris Agreement enables nations to take climate action by letting them outline specific steps that suit their particular abilities and conditions (Bertram & Van Coppenolle, 2024). Trade rules in the WTO need stronger direct connections to the Paris Agreement's climate goals to achieve their support objectives effectively. Creating a joint governance system between the two regimes will connect their energy better to help international climate targets (Stranadko, 2022). The best way to bring these objectives together is by adding environmental responsibilities to trade treaty specifications. Many trade deals between regions and nations now have environment protection chapters that cover subjects like eco-energy investment and protecting land and water for future heat waves (Padhan & Bhat, 2023). Trade agreements that contain sustainability provisions can teach multilateral trade organizations how to design policies that help environmental targets instead of harming them. The WTO should work to help its members match their trade actions with the climate targets outlined in their NDCs through training and funding assistance for developing countries (Harrison, 2023).

The importance of dispute settlement systems in meeting sustainability objectives needs more examination. The WTO Dispute Settlement Body solves trade conflicts and remains mostly unaware of how actions affect the environment (Asmelash, 2023). The DSB needs to make its decision process more complex by inviting environmental specialists and thinkers to participate. To properly evaluate green policies during trade disputes specific experts in both trade law and environmental law should make up dispute settlement panels (Sharma, 2018). The WTO can better solve trade-environment conflicts by creating its own official environmental dispute resolution system. Effective capacity building and technical help programs help all nations properly use trade rules that support sustainability. Poor and least-developed states struggle to apply environmental standards due to limited resources and weak institutions plus missing technology knowledge (Mishra & Krishna, 2021). Through federal collaboration and joint action with UNEP and GCF the WTO can lead efforts to resolve these difficulties. Through funding and technology sharing and training programs the WTO supports developing nations to engage in green trade practices and meet their environmental agreements (Velázquez Gomar, 2016).

By bringing trade and environmental rules together nations can build sustainable development systems that benefit all countries. The combined problems of climate change and biodiversity loss demand an integrated approach linking trade to sustainability standards (Chakraborty & Dey, 2024). The ability to transform trade into a sustainable growth strategy depends on how legal problems would be fixed and improve organizational systems in global commerce. The global trade system needs updated rules plus new standards that match today's worldwide business evolution (Mahajan et al., 2023). States will move toward uniting trade and environmental policies only when they abandon national benefits in favor of corporate efforts. Together nations must operate through strong legal systems and shared institutions to make trade support global sustainability (Basheer et al., 2022). As the world's leading trade authority the WTO must prove its value by showing it can handle today's 21st century challenges. By matching WTO rules with environmental agreements and Paris Agreement targets the organization can show its dedication to both business expansion and environmental protection (Vieira, 2020).

Private companies benefit from joining sustainability and trade efforts by adopting greener methods and investing in sustainable technology. Businesses turn toward greener production when international trade rules include support for environmental subsidies and carbon taxes (Hegab et al., 2023). The economic shift makes companies more successful in today's global market and helps protect both the planet from climate change and nature. Officials businesses and civil society organizations can work together to move global economy toward sustainability at a faster pace.

TECH & GREEN TRADE

Technology and innovation help make green subsidies and carbon tariffs succeed as climate change solutions under international trade rules (Matos et al., 2022). Green subsidies receive recognition for eco-friendly innovation, as carbon tariffs make it hard to import if not impossible due to the charges imposed on imports (Lyu, Ma, & Arash, 2024). According to international trade law technology and innovation help make these instruments work well and follow the rules on fairness, no discrimination and sustainable use (Soete, 1987). Modern technology leads the way toward building a green economy. Through green subsidies governments support scientific exploration and market launch of new technologies including renewable energy sources and efficient product development (Han et al., 2025). Subsidies provide money to reduce technology adoption expenses so private investment can thrive despite market problems. International trade subsidies help countries with eco-transition goals especially when they compete against heavily supported industries in unregulated nation. (Song et al., 2022). To make carbon tariffs work properly, advanced clean energy solutions as basic elements are needed. The goal of border carbon adjustments is to match international imports with local environmental standards while reducing the risk of firms moving operations to places with weaker environmental rules (Pan et al., 2024). To succeed carbon tariffs need precise systems that show how much carbon each product contains when built using advanced technology. Better emission and product lifetime methods must develop to make carbon tariffs work both accurately and legally under WTO requirements (Larch & Wanner, 2017). Research and development of these measurements assist in making sure carbon tariffs respect justice and do not affect developing nations that struggle with technical reporting requirements (Zhou et al., 2024).

Technology helps countries follow WTO rules by making sure that trade happens based on transparency standards and does not discriminate between nations. The World Trade Organization's GATT rules about non-discrimination must guide to introduce carbon tariffs and green subsidies (Larch & Wanner, 2017). Green subsidies work most effectively when MRV systems use modern technologies to verify implementation against WTO regulations. MRV systems deliver verified environmental results so governments can use this data to show carbon tariff and green subsidy programs do not break WTO trade rules (Shi & Zhou, 2024). The correct measurement of products' carbon content helps ensure carbon tariffs work across all product origins through technology. Digital systems help enhance green subsidy and carbon tariff innovation thanks to their rapid adoption across many industries. Through blockchain, technology companies can track emissions across their full supply chain using an open and permanent system for data (Lee et al., 2025). These technologies help decrease trade dispute risk under WTO agreements through their abilities to prove the carbon content of goods reliably and securely. AI systems that analyse big data help to track emissions, as they happen to produce exact numbers needed for setting carbon tariffs (Huang et al., 2024). These systems make environmental data more dependable and help decision-makers base their tariff decisions on scientific research. Green subsidies and carbon tariffs mark the first steps toward sustainable world trade development but technology and innovation drive the path forward. The main challenge for policy creators today is to shield developing and least-developed nations from unequal treatment by green aid packages and carbon import taxes because they do not have the industry needed to compete in a sustainable economy (Wieczorek, 2018). A strong technology transfer and training system needs to help developing nations build their environmental technology skills. World Trade Organization and UNFCCC recognize technology transfer as essential for meeting climate action targets combined with sustainable development (Sajid *et al.*, 2024). Through technology integration into green subsidy and carbon tariff systems the world could achieve better sustainable development outcomes across rich and developing nations.

Technology and innovation are becoming more advanced and require studying how they fit within international trade law. Environmental factors now affect global trade so trade laws must adapt to keep pace with modern technological development. Under current trade conditions the WTO rules need adjustments that best serve sustainable international trade policymaking (Felbermayr et al., 2024). Technology support for green subsidies and carbon tariffs needs regular updates to trade rules that help businesses maintain sustainable methods. As carbon-pricing methods improve, the WTO must revise its rules on border carbon adjustments to stay compliant with international law while still achieving climate objectives (Yunxia & Yuqing, 2025). Innovation leads to making new green trade tools that function better than basic carbon tariffs and green subsidies. Global supply chains keep growing in complexity so need is of fresh trade policy approaches to help companies build better circular systems and eco-friendly operations (Li, Li, & Wang, 2024). Trade policies that include new technology can help better use waste reduction systems and renewable materials while making green subsidies and carbon tariffs work more effectively. New technology demands changes to trade laws that help promote innovation and stay fair for everyone.

CONCLUSION

Green subsidies and carbon tariffs are one of the very important factors that need to be examined in the international trade law because they are an important driver of climate action as well as an important factor in fostering sustainable development. Because the importance of environmental concerns has grown, these tools help include environmental rules within trade laws to tackle the problems created by climate change. Their real-world application faces multiple hurdles but also creates possibilities because both need proper examination to stay true to their economic and ecological targets. This investigation shows how green subsidies drive business innovation while developing better tech and helping industries shift to renewable energy sources. When countries receive economic assistance to buy green technologies they can switch to sustainable practices without harming their economic growth goals. The WTO's SCM Agreement of Subsidies and Countervailing Measures creates important legal issues when governments use this tool to promote sustainability. Countries need detailed analysis to separate the legitimate environmental aid from unfair trade practices with no dedicated climate policy rules in place. Using carbon tariffs highlights two important ways to prevent pollution movement across borders and make countries responsible for their climate actions. These actions charge more import duties based on product carbon emissions to create fair business conditions between nations that protect the environment and those that do not. These proposals encounter difficulties when measured against WTO rules especially General Agreement on Tariffs and Trade (GATT) discrimination requirements. For carbon tariffs to work properly and remain credible, they need to keep away from arbitrary purposes and protectionist behaviour.

In this discussion, balance is struck about how to obtain environmental goals in international trade without unfair treatment of all nations. Developed nations have the financial resources and technological capacity to put green policies in place with very little loss in terms of productivity. However, developing and least developed countries do not have enough financial resources and technological capacity to carry out the same green policies, and therefore there is needed to adapt them to specific circumstances. Crafting smart green subsidies and carbon tariffs becomes necessary since improper design would make global trade imbalance worse and hurt developing economies today. Supporting developing nations through capacity development and technology sharing plus funding will help them reduce climate impacts without losing their goal to develop further. World sees real progress through these instruments because they help countries team up and think up new ideas together. Green subsidies and carbon tariff programs drive environmental progress across industries so nations want to integrate sustainability throughout their trade and economic policies. The systems allow countries to combine their climate policies with worldwide ecosystem goals creating a smoother path to solve climate problems. Countries need to unite their efforts to solve legal and political challenges before green subsidies and carbon tariffs achieve their full potential.

To build environmentally friendly trade policies for tomorrow need is to change current trade systems to match special requirements for climatic action. The first priority needs to change WTO rules to officially back environmental programs by supporting renewable energy tax incentives and international border carbon offset programs. Recommendations would require updates to SCM and definition changes to GATT Article XX so eco-friendly subsidies receive clearer WTO approval. Creating a special WTO agreement about trade and sustainability would create a basic structure to resolve trade-environment conflicts. Green trade policies need to include everybody worldwide to work properly. The WTO and UNFCCC should unite to help developing countries access green trade participation with equal benefits through financial and technical aid. LDCs need special attention because their particular situation demands trade rules that do not harm their development yet help them build up their economies.

Nations have to work together to share information while building agreements around environmental trade standards. Multilateral discussions provide a chance for nations to debate and develop shared solutions when addressing hot button subjects including how to implement carbon tariffs. High-quality monitoring systems and enforcement methods will make sure green trade rules are followed while preventing these rules from becoming trade barriers against competitors. When carbon tariffs have open financial and operational details the practice becomes fairer and builds trust between nations. The primary job of international trade laws stands to empower transformation when it comes to addressing climate issues. The global community should make their Paris Agreement and sustainability targets part of their trade programs to make the World Trade Organization support environmental progress. A new way of thinking about trade and the environment is needed since traditional methods put economic efficiency first rather than making both nature and society more important than profit.

Technology and innovation drive the successful execution of green subsidies and carbon tariffs as the main topic. Technological progress actively supports present use of green policy tools while helping to advance these solutions further to match sustainability needs and global trade standards. The use of digital tools like AI blockchain analytics makes emission monitoring and reporting more transparent while reducing errors and boosting the speed at which carbon trade rules get followed. The scientific data base helps to make sustainable border carbon adjustments that meet WTO requirements. Advanced technology helps developing nations take part in the ecological transition path to a green economy. Building technical skills and sharing technology will make sure all world nations join climate efforts equally when markets use carbon tariffs and green economic benefits. This chapter needs to prove that worldwide cooperation between trade and technology development will make green trade agreements successful. Future green assistance and carbon taxes will succeed only when they address environmental risks without harming international trade fairness, inclusion, and equality. Policies succeed when they receive appropriate legal and institutional structures in addition to creating good policy design. The world needs joint action that links different environmental issues while using trade tools to create better outcomes.

REFERENCES

Akhtaruzzaman, M., Banerjee, A. K., & Boubaker, S. (2025). Government intervention and green innovation in renewable energy. *Energy Economics*, *108*, 108185. DOI: 10.1016/j.eneco.2025.108185

Allouhi, A., Rehman, S., Buker, M. S., & Said, Z. (2022). Up-to-date literature review on Solar PV systems: Technology progress, market status and R&D. *Journal of Cleaner Production*, *362*, 132339. DOI: 10.1016/j.jclepro.2022.132339

An, Q. (2024). Empirical analysis of trade costs and their impact on carbon emissions in RCEP countries. *Journal of Environmental Management*, *365*, 121666. DOI: 10.1016/j.jenvman.2024.121666 PMID: 38968893

Ari, I., & Sari, R. (2017). Developing CBDR-RC indices for fair allocation of emission reduction responsibilities and capabilities across countries†. *Cogent Environmental Science*, *3*(1), 1420365. Advance online publication. DOI: 10.1080/23311843.2017.1420365

Asmelash, H. (2023). The WTO dispute settlement system as a forum for climate litigation? *Review of European, Comparative & International Environmental Law*, *32*(2), 321–333. DOI: 10.1111/reel.12490

Basheer, M., Nechifor, V., Calzadilla, A., Ringler, C., Hulme, D., & Harou, J. J. (2022). Balancing national economic policy outcomes for sustainable development. *Nature Communications*, *13*(1), 5041. DOI: 10.1038/s41467-022-32415-9 PMID: 36028486

Bellmann, C., & van der Ven, C. (2020). Greening regional trade agreements on non-tariff measures through technical barriers to trade and regulatory co-operation. *OECD Trade and Environment Working Papers, No. 2020/04*. OECD Publishing. https://doi.org/DOI: 10.1787/18166881

Benkhodja, M. T., Fromentin, V., & Ma, X. (2023). Macroeconomic effects of green subsidies. *Journal of Cleaner Production*, *410*, 137166. DOI: 10.1016/j.jclepro.2023.137166

Bertram, C., & Van Coppenolle, H. (2024). Strengthening the Paris Agreement through trade? The potential and limitations of EU preferential trade agreements for climate governance. *International Environmental Agreement: Politics, Law and Economics*, *24*(4), 589–610. DOI: 10.1007/s10784-024-09653-x

Böhringer, C., Schneider, J., & Asane-Otoo, E. (2021). Trade in Carbon and Carbon Tariffs. *Environmental and Resource Economics, 78*(4), 669–708. DOI: 10.1007/s10640-021-00548-y

Borlini, L. S., & Montanaro, F. (2018). Climate change and trade: Challenges and lingering questions on the relationship between renewable energy subsidies and WTO disciplines. *China-EU Law Journal, 6*(1), 81–101. DOI: 10.1007/s12689-017-0079-x

Cai, X., Dan, W., Ge, D., Zhao, X., & Wang, Y. (2023). The impact of environmental regulations and government subsidies and their policy mix on clean technology innovation. *Environment, Development and Sustainability, 27*(1), 1987–2023. Advance online publication. DOI: 10.1007/s10668-023-03953-z

Carattini, S., Kim, G., Melkadze, G., & Pommeret, A. (2024). Carbon taxes and tariffs, financial frictions, and international spillovers. *European Economic Review, 170*, 104883. DOI: 10.1016/j.euroecorev.2024.104883

Chai, J., & Ma, Z. (2025). Energy governance systems and climate change in the world's major economies under the low carbon background. *Sustainable Energy Research, 12*(2), 2. Advance online publication. DOI: 10.1186/s40807-024-00145-9

Chakraborty, D., & Dey, O. (2024). Trade, environment and climate change. In Chakraborty, D., & Dey, O. (Eds.), *Influence of WTO and global dynamics on trade flows* (pp. 289–347). Springer., DOI: 10.1007/978-981-99-7375-0_4

Charnovitz, S. (1991). Exploring the environmental exceptions in GATT Article XX. *Journal of World Trade, 25*(5), 37–55. https://kluwerlawonline.com/journalarticle/Journal+of+World+Trade/25.5/TRAD1991028. DOI: 10.54648/TRAD1991028

Charnovitz, S. (2014). Green subsidies and the WTO. *Robert Schuman Centre for Advanced Studies Research Paper No. RSCAS 2014/93, GWU Law School Public Law Research Paper No. 2014-51, GWU Legal Studies Research Paper No. 2014-51*. Available at *SSRN*: https://ssrn.com/abstract=2498518 or http://dx.doi.org/DOI: 10.2139/ssrn.2498518

Cheng, X., Wang, W., Chen, X., Zhang, W., & Song, M. (2024). Carbon tariffs and energy subsidies: Synergy or antagonism? *Energy, 306*, 132563. DOI: 10.1016/j.energy.2024.132563

Cima, E. (2017). Caught between WTO rules and climate change: The economic rationale of 'green' subsidies. In Mathis, K., & Huber, B. (Eds.), *Environmental law and economics: Economic analysis of law in European legal scholarship* (Vol. 4, pp. 379–404). Springer., DOI: 10.1007/978-3-319-50932-7_15

Cima, E., & Esty, D. C. (2024). Making international trade work for sustainable development: Toward a new WTO framework for subsidies. *Journal of International Economic Law*, *27*(1), 1–17. DOI: 10.1093/jiel/jgae008

Couture, T., & Gagnon, Y. (2010). An analysis of feed-in tariff remuneration models: Implications for renewable energy investment. *Energy Policy*, *38*(2), 955–965. DOI: 10.1016/j.enpol.2009.10.047

Dechezleprêtre, A., Nachtigall, D., & Venmans, F. (2023). The joint impact of the European Union emissions trading system on carbon emissions and economic performance. *Journal of Environmental Economics and Management*, *118*, 102758. DOI: 10.1016/j.jeem.2022.102758

Dobranschi, M., Nerudová, D., Solilová, V., & Stadler, K. (2024). Carbon border adjustment mechanism challenges and implications: The case of Visegrád countries. *Heliyon*, *10*(10), e30976. DOI: 10.1016/j.heliyon.2024.e30976 PMID: 38770295

Dossa, K. F., & Miassi, Y. E. (2024). Impact of carbon pricing policies on economic growth and green innovation: A global analysis. *Climate Change*, 10, e5cc1031. https://doi.org/DOI: 10.1016/j.clima.2024.01.004

Droege, P. (2025). Beyond Paris: Emergency imperatives for global policy and local action. *Sustain Earth Reviews*, *8*(1), 2. DOI: 10.1186/s42055-024-00100-y

Duan, Y., Xi, B., Xu, X., & Xuan, S. (2024). The impact of government subsidies on green innovation performance in new energy enterprises: A digital transformation perspective. *International Review of Economics & Finance*, *94*, 103414. DOI: 10.1016/j.iref.2024.103414

Fang, L., & Zhao, S. (2023). On the green subsidies in a differentiated market. *International Journal of Production Economics*, *257*, 108758. DOI: 10.1016/j.ijpe.2022.108758

Felbermayr, G., Peterson, S., & Wanner, J. (2024). Trade and the environment, trade policies and environmental policies—How do they interact? *Journal of Economic Surveys*, •••, 1–37. DOI: 10.1111/joes.12628

Garschagen, M., & Doshi, D. (2022). Does funds-based adaptation finance reach the most vulnerable countries? *Global Environmental Change*, *73*, 102450. DOI: 10.1016/j.gloenvcha.2021.102450

Glass, L.-M., & Newig, J. (2019). Governance for achieving the Sustainable Development Goals: How important are participation, policy coherence, reflexivity, adaptation and democratic institutions? *Earth System Governance*, *2*, 100031. DOI: 10.1016/j.esg.2019.100031

Gugler, K., Haxhimusa, A., & Liebensteiner, M. (2021). Effectiveness of climate policies: Carbon pricing vs. subsidizing renewables. *Journal of Environmental Economics and Management, 106*, 102405. DOI: 10.1016/j.jeem.2020.102405

Gupta, H., & Rakshit, D. (2023). Assessing the demand for carbon credits from the most polluting and hard-to-abate sectors in India. *Journal of Cleaner Production, 425*, 138825. DOI: 10.1016/j.jclepro.2023.138825

Han, S., Peng, D., Guo, Y., Aslam, M. U., & Xu, R. (2025). Harnessing technological innovation and renewable energy and their impact on environmental pollution in G-20 countries. *Scientific Reports, 15*(1), 2236. DOI: 10.1038/s41598-025-85182-0 PMID: 39824979

Harrison, J. (2023). Trade agreements and sustainability: Exploring the potential of global value chain (GVC) obligations. *Journal of International Economic Law, 26*(2), 199–215. DOI: 10.1093/jiel/jgac057

Hegab, H., Shaban, I., Jamil, M., & Khanna, N. (2023). Toward sustainable future: Strategies, indicators, and challenges for implementing sustainable production systems. *Sustainable Materials and Technologies, 36*, e00617. DOI: 10.1016/j.susmat.2023.e00617

Huang, J., Chen, X., & Zhao, X. (2024). How Digital Technology Reduces Carbon Emissions: From the Perspective of Green Innovation, Industry Upgrading, and Energy Transition. *Journal of the Knowledge Economy, 15*(4), 19294–19326. Advance online publication. DOI: 10.1007/s13132-024-01895-z

Huang, M.-T., & Zhai, P.-M. (2021). Achieving Paris Agreement temperature goals requires carbon neutrality by middle century with far-reaching transitions in the whole society. *Advances in Climate Change Research, 12*(2), 281–286. DOI: 10.1016/j.accre.2021.03.004

Huang, Y. (2021). Technology innovation and sustainability: Challenges and research needs. *Clean Technologies and Environmental Policy, 23*(9), 1663–1664. DOI: 10.1007/s10098-021-02152-6 PMID: 34276276

Hunjra, A. I., Bouri, E., Azam, M., Azam, R. I., & Dai, J. (2024). Economic growth and environmental sustainability in developing economies. *Research in International Business and Finance*, 70(A), 102341. https://doi.org/DOI: 10.1016/j.ribaf.2024.102341

Jin, A., He, G., Ge, S., & Wu, S. (2025). The impact of government green subsidies on corporate green innovation. *Finance Research Letters, 71*, 106378. DOI: 10.1016/j.frl.2024.106378

Kalfagianni, A., & Young, O. R. (2022). The politics of multilateral environmental agreements: Lessons from 20 years of INEA. *International Environmental Agreement: Politics, Law and Economics*, *22*(2), 245–262. DOI: 10.1007/s10784-022-09567-6 PMID: 35228841

Klingelhöfer, D., Müller, R., Braun, M., Brüggmann, D., & Groneberg, D. A. (2020). Climate change: Does international research fulfill global demands and necessities? *Environmental Sciences Europe*, *32*(1), 137. DOI: 10.1186/s12302-020-00419-1 PMID: 33078088

Kulovesi, K. (2013). Climate change and trade: At the intersection of two international legal regimes. In E. Hollo, K. Kulovesi, & M. Mehling (Eds.), *Climate Change and the Law* (Ius Gentium: Comparative Perspectives on Law and Justice, Vol. 21, pp. 273–289). Springer, Dordrecht. https://doi.org/DOI: 10.1007/978-94-007-5440-9_16

Laprévote, F.-C., & Kang, S. (2011). Subsidies issues in the WTO – An update. *European State Aid Law Quarterly, 10*(3), 445–456. https://www.jstor.org/stable/26686640

Larch, M., & Wanner, J. (2017). Carbon tariffs: An analysis of the trade, welfare, and emission effects. *Journal of International Economics*, *109*, 195–213. DOI: 10.1016/j.jinteco.2017.09.003

Lee, C.-C., Hussain, J., & Abass, Q. (2025). An integrated analysis of AI-driven green financing, subsidies, and knowledge to enhance CO2 reduction efficiency. *Economic Analysis and Policy*, *85*, 675–693. DOI: 10.1016/j.eap.2024.12.021

Li, F., Li, J., & Wang, D. (2024). Policy instruments and green innovation: Evidence and implications for corporate performance. *Journal of Cleaner Production*, *471*, 143443. DOI: 10.1016/j.jclepro.2024.143443

Li, Z., Pan, Y., Yang, W., Ma, J., & Zhou, M. (2021). Effects of government subsidies on green technology investment and green marketing coordination of supply chain under the cap-and-trade mechanism. *Energy Economics*, *101*, 105426. DOI: 10.1016/j.eneco.2021.105426

Lyu, H., Ma, C., & Arash, F. (2024). Government innovation subsidies, green technology innovation, and carbon intensity of industrial firms. *Journal of Environmental Management*, *369*, 122274. DOI: 10.1016/j.jenvman.2024.122274 PMID: 39241599

M., & Xydis, G. (2023). The Inflation Reduction Act versus the 1.5 cent/kWh and 30% investment tax credit proposal for wind power. *SN Business & Economics, 3*, 68. https://doi.org/DOI: 10.1007/s43546-023-00448-x

Ma, J., & Xu, J. (2024). Potential economic impacts of carbon tariffs on target countries: A systematic review. *Climate Policy*, •••, 1–17. DOI: 10.1080/14693062.2024.2407830

Mahajan, N., Kaur, N., Singh, V., Gupta, A., & Garg, N. (2023). Green trade: Transition towards a sustainable economy. *IOP Conference Series. Earth and Environmental Science*, *1279*(1), 012023. DOI: 10.1088/1755-1315/1279/1/012023

Mansoor, S. I. U. (2022). International Environmental Law in Promoting Sustainable Development: A Critical Analysis. *Central University of Kashmir Law Review*, *2*, 91–111.

Mansoor, S. I. U., & Chopra, M. (2020). Article XX Of GATT: Territoriality Of Unilateral Trade Measure And Sustainable Development. *Ilkogretim Online*, *19*(4), 7784–7792.

Marceau, G. (2016). The interface between the trade rules and climate change actions. In Park, D. Y. (Ed.), *Legal issues on climate change and international trade law* (pp. 3–39). Springer., DOI: 10.1007/978-3-319-29322-6_1

Matos, S., Viardot, E., Sovacool, B. K., Geels, F. W., & Xiong, Y. (2022). Innovation and climate change: A review and introduction to the special issue. *Technovation*, *117*, 102612. DOI: 10.1016/j.technovation.2022.102612

Matsushita, M., & Associates. (2015). Environmental Protection and Trade. In *The World Trade Organization: Law, Practice, and Policy* (3rd ed.). Oxford International Law Library. https://doi.org/DOI: 10.1093/law/9780199571857.003.0020

Mehling, M., van Asselt, H., Das, K., Droege, S., & Verkuij, C. (2017). Front matter. In *Designing border carbon adjustments for enhanced climate action* (pp. 2–3). Climate Strategies., https://www.jstor.org/stable/resrep16316.1

Mehling, M. A., van Asselt, H., Das, K., Droege, S., & Verkuijl, C. (2019). Designing border carbon adjustments for enhanced climate action. *The American Journal of International Law*, *113*(3), 433–481. DOI: 10.1017/ajil.2019.22

Meng, H. (2024). Challenges and controversies to the European CBAM from a legal perspective. *Advances in Economics. Management and Political Sciences*, *81*, 201–206.

Metzger, S. D. (1974). Governmental intervention in the international competitive process: Subsidies, countervailing duties, and "voluntary" agreements restraining imports. *Antitrust Law Journal*, *43*(3), 621–630. https://www.jstor.org/stable/40842113

Mishra, R. K., & Krishna, P. S. (2021). Capacity building and technical cooperation for achieving sustainable development goals. In: Leal Filho, W., Azul, A.M., Brandli, L., Lange Salvia, A., Özuyar, P.G., Wall, T. (eds) *Peace, justice and strong institutions*. Encyclopedia of the UN Sustainable Development Goals. Springer, Cham. https://doi.org/, pp 1–11.DOI: 10.1007/978-3-319-71066-2_8-1

Negi, A. (2020). The World Trade Organization and sustainability standards. In Negi, A., Pérez-Pineda, J., & Blankenbach, J. (Eds.), *Sustainability standards and global governance* (pp. 39–59). Springer., DOI: 10.1007/978-981-15-3473-7_3

Neves, P. C., Afonso, O., Silva, D., & Sochirca, E. (2021). The link between intellectual property rights, innovation, and growth: A meta-analysis. *Economic Modelling, 97*, 196–209. DOI: 10.1016/j.econmod.2021.01.019

Olabi, A. G., Shehata, N., Issa, U. H., Mohamed, O. A., Mahmoud, M., Abdelkareem, M. A., & Abdelzaher, M. A. (2025). The role of green buildings in achieving the sustainable development goals. *International Journal of Thermofluids, 25*, 101002. DOI: 10.1016/j.ijft.2024.101002

Padhan, L., & Bhat, S. (2023). Interrelationship between trade and environment: A bibliometric analysis of published articles from the last two decades. *Environmental Science and Pollution Research International, 30*(7), 17051–17075. DOI: 10.1007/s11356-023-25168-5 PMID: 36626051

Pan, J., Cross, J. L., Zou, X., & Zhang, B. (2024). To tax or to trade? A global review of carbon emissions reduction strategies. *Energy Strategy Reviews, 55*, 101508. DOI: 10.1016/j.esr.2024.101508

Pan, X., & Liu, S. (2024). The development, changes and responses of the European Union carbon border adjustment mechanism in the context of global energy transition. *World Development Sustainability, 4*, 100148. DOI: 10.1016/j.wds.2024.100148

Pauw, P., Mbeva, K., & van Asselt, H. (2019). Subtle differentiation of countries' responsibilities under the Paris Agreement. *Palgrave Communications, 5*(1), 86. DOI: 10.1057/s41599-019-0298-6

Ripple, W. J., Wolf, C., Gregg, J. W., Rockström, J., Mann, M. E., Oreskes, N., Lenton, T. M., Rahmstorf, S., Newsome, T. M., Xu, C., Svenning, J.-C., Pereira, C. C., Law, B. E., & Crowther, T. W. (2024). The 2024 state of the climate report: Perilous times on planet Earth. *Bioscience, 74*(12), 812–824. DOI: 10.1093/biosci/biae087

Rocchi, P., Serrano, M., Roca, J., & Arto, I. (2018). Border carbon adjustments based on avoided emissions: Addressing the challenge of its design. *Ecological Economics, 145*, 126–136. DOI: 10.1016/j.ecolecon.2017.08.003

Roy, A. (2025). Does carbon tax promote green trade and comparative advantages: Evidence from Panel Difference-In-Difference (DID) causal experiment. *Environmental Economics and Policy Studies, 27*(2), 331–352. Advance online publication. DOI: 10.1007/s10018-024-00434-z

Sajid, M. J., Zhang, Y., & Janjua, L. R. (2024). Breaking barriers: Assessing technology transfer for climate-resilient development. *Environmental Technology & Innovation, 33*, 103471. DOI: 10.1016/j.eti.2023.103471

Sasmal, S., Zhang, D., Lydgate, E., & Winters, L. A. (2024). Exempting least developed countries from border carbon adjustments: Simple economically but complex legally. *World Trade Review, 23*(3), 408–431. DOI: 10.1017/S1474745624000132

Sauter, P., Witt, J., Billig, E., & Thrän, D. (2013). Impact of the Renewable Energy Sources Act in Germany on electricity produced with solid biofuels – Lessons learned by monitoring the market development. *Biomass and Bioenergy, 53*, 162–171. DOI: 10.1016/j.biombioe.2013.01.014

Selder, K. (2014). Renewable Energy Sources Act and trading of emission certificates: A national and a supranational tool to direct energy turnover to renewable electricity supply in Germany. *Energy Policy, 64*, 302–312. DOI: 10.1016/j.enpol.2013.08.030

Sforna, G. (2019). Climate change and developing countries: From background actors to protagonists of climate negotiations. *International Environmental Agreement: Politics, Law and Economics, 19*(3), 273–295. DOI: 10.1007/s10784-019-09435-w

Shafi, M., Ramos-Meza, C. S., Jain, V., Salman, A., Kamal, M., Shabbir, M. S., & Rehman, M. (2023). The dynamic relationship between green tax incentives and environmental protection. *Environmental Science and Pollution Research International, 30*(12), 32184–32192. DOI: 10.1007/s11356-023-25482-y PMID: 36723845

Sharma, D. (2018). Jurisdictional concerns in the settlement of environmental disputes under the WTO regime. *International Journal of Law Management & Humanities, 1*(5), 1-XX. ISSN: 2581-5369. Retrieved from https://www.ijlmh.com

Sheng, X., Chen, L., Liu, M., Wang, Q., Ma, Q., Zuo, J., & Yuan, X. (2025). Input-output models for carbon accounting: A multi-perspective analysis. *Renewable & Sustainable Energy Reviews, 207*, 114950. DOI: 10.1016/j.rser.2024.114950

Shi, H., & Zhou, Q. (2024). Government R&D subsidies, environmental regulation and corporate green innovation performance. *Finance Research Letters, 69*(Part B), 106088. https://doi.org/DOI: 10.1016/j.frl.2024.106088

Smith, I. D., Overland, I., & Szulecki, K. (2024). The EU's CBAM and its 'significant others': Three perspectives on the political fallout from Europe's unilateral climate policy initiative. *Journal of Common Market Studies*, *62*(3), 603–618. DOI: 10.1111/jcms.13512

Soete, L. (1987). The impact of technological innovation on international trade patterns: The evidence reconsidered. *Research Policy*, *16*(2–4), 101–130. DOI: 10.1016/0048-7333(87)90026-6

Song, Y., Sahut, J.-M., Zhang, Z., Tian, Y., & Hikkerova, L. (2022). The effects of government subsidies on the sustainable innovation of university-industry collaboration. *Technological Forecasting and Social Change*, *174*, 121233. DOI: 10.1016/j.techfore.2021.121233

Stranadko, N. (2022). Global climate governance: Rising trend of translateral cooperation. *International Environmental Agreement: Politics, Law and Economics*, *22*(4), 639–657. DOI: 10.1007/s10784-022-09575-6 PMID: 35370522

Sun, X., Mi, Z., Cheng, L., Coffman, D. M., & Liu, Y. (2024). The carbon border adjustment mechanism is inefficient in addressing carbon leakage and results in unfair welfare losses. *Fundamental Research (Beijing)*, *4*(3), 660–670. DOI: 10.1016/j.fmre.2023.02.026 PMID: 39659982

Tamiotti, L. (2010). Trade and the Environment: Fundamental Issues in International Law, WTO Law and Legal Theory by Erich Vranes. *World Trade Review*, *9*(1), 285–288. DOI: 10.1017/S147474560999022X

Tanveer, A., Zeng, S., Zaman, R., & Scagnelli, S. (2024). World Trade Organization (WTO) trade policy reviews and green technology adoption: Global evidence. *International Review of Financial Analysis*, *96*(B), 103715. https://doi.org/DOI: 10.1016/j.irfa.2024.103715

Veel, P.-E. (2009). Carbon tariffs and the WTO: An evaluation of feasible policies. *Journal of International Economic Law*, *12*(3), 749–800. DOI: 10.1093/jiel/jgp031

Velázquez Gomar, J. O. (2016). Environmental policy integration among multilateral environmental agreements: The case of biodiversity. *International Environmental Agreement: Politics, Law and Economics*, *16*(4), 525–541. DOI: 10.1007/s10784-014-9263-4

Vieira, A. C. (2020). The WTO and the Paris Agreement: A Dialogue on Climate Change Mitigation. *Beijing Law Review*, *11*(2), 399–414. DOI: 10.4236/blr.2020.112025

Wang, Y., & Zhou, R. (2024). Can carbon emission trading policies promote the withdrawal of government subsidies and the green development of enterprises? Empirical evidence from China's A-share market. *Humanities and Social Sciences Communications, 11*(1723). https://doi.org/DOI: 10.1057/s41599-024-04255-z

Wei, L., Liu, Z., Cao, P., & Zhang, H. (2025). Environmental subsidies and green innovation: The role of environmental regulation and chief executive officer green background. *Clean Technologies and Environmental Policy*, *27*(3), 389–402. DOI: 10.1007/s10098-024-02755-9

Wieczorek, A. J. (2018). Sustainability transitions in developing countries: Major insights and their implications for research and policy. *Environmental Science & Policy*, *84*, 204–216. DOI: 10.1016/j.envsci.2017.08.008

Wu, Y., & Wan, J. (2024). The race between global economic growth and carbon emissions: Based on a comparative study of developed and developing countries. *Environmental Science and Pollution Research International*, *31*(13), 19226–19243. DOI: 10.1007/s11356-024-32275-4 PMID: 38355861

Yang, C., & Yan, X. (2023). Impact of carbon tariffs on price competitiveness in the era of global value chain. *Applied Energy*, *336*, 120805. DOI: 10.1016/j.apenergy.2023.120805

Yunxia, X., & Yuqing, N. (2025). The technological advancement environmental regulations and their impact on energy efficiency and CO2 emissions. *Scientific Reports*, *15*(1), 2781. DOI: 10.1038/s41598-025-86581-z PMID: 39843519

Zhang, S., Kaikun, W., Yastrubskyi, M., & Huang, C. (2023). Carbon emissions from international trade and consumption: Assessing the role of cumulative risk for EU and Chinese economic development. *Energy Strategy Reviews*, *50*, 101219. DOI: 10.1016/j.esr.2023.101219

Zhao, R. (2024). Green trade barriers in global play: Legal challenges and strategic opportunities for developing countries. *Journal of Education. Humanities and Social Sciences*, *39*, 48–55. DOI: 10.54097/kz926p47

Zhou, X., Zhu, Q., Xu, L., Wang, K., Yin, X., & Mangla, S. K. (2024). The effect of carbon tariffs and the associated coping strategies: A global supply chain perspective. *Omega*, *122*, 102960. DOI: 10.1016/j.omega.2023.102960

KEY TERMS AND DEFINITIONS

Green Subsidies: Monetary support offered by governments to help advance renewable energy, clean ways of moving goods and people and sustainable farming. Green subsidies may be argued against in the WTO if they affect trade, but will be permitted if they are assessed as general infrastructure improvements or non-specific subsidies according to Article 1 of the SCM Agreement.

Carbon Tariffs: Goods entering the country are assigned special measures depending on how much carbon was released in their processing. They are called Border Carbon Adjustments (BCAs) and help make certain that industries following tough climate rules in the EU do not lose out to competitors from elsewhere. It is questioned whether these measures are legal under the General Agreement on Tariffs and Trade (GATT), mainly related to Articles I (Most Favoured Nation), III (National Treatment) and XX (General Exceptions).

Carbon Leakage: A situation in which businesses move to places with fewer climate rules, making no significant change to global emissions. Because carbon leakage weakens climate policies within a nation, it is one reason why carbon tariffs or border carbon adjustments are justified.

Technology Transfer: The transfer of technology from developed or private sector sources to developing or least developed countries usually takes place with help from international cooperation or similar programs. The green trade process relies on technology exchange to ensure that all countries are able to become active in green development, as WTO discussions on development mention.

Border Carbon Adjustments (BCAs): Policies that level the carbon cost difference between domestic and imported products by taxing imports the same way domestic products are taxed. BCAs need to agree with both environmental regulations and the WTO, so they must be made in a way that keeps the main GATT obligations intact.

Sustainable Development: Under international law, a concept aimed at finding a balance between the economy, nature and social wellbeing. The WTO's Preamble and Doha Development Agenda address trade policy was defining sustainable development as a main point, helping to interpret WTO rules in ways that protect the environment.

General Exceptions (Article XX of GATT): Laws in the WTO where its member nations can adapt measures that would generally disobey GATT, but are needed to protect life or health or to protect resources that cannot be renewed (Article XX(b) and Article XX(g)). Such exceptions are necessary to justify the use of green subsidies and carbon tariffs when accused of blocking trade.

Chapter 3
Implementing Marine Spatial Planning:
Is Malaysia Ready With the Existing Law and Policy?

Wei Yien Lua
https://orcid.org/0009-0006-1257-2323
Institute of Oceanography and Environment, Universiti Malaysia Terengganu, Malaysia

Nazli Aziz
https://orcid.org/0000-0002-5071-2175
Institute of Oceanography and Environment, Universiti Malaysia Terengganu, Malaysia & Faculty of Business, Economics and Social Development, Universiti Malaysia Terengganu, Malaysia & Blue Economy Research Interest Group, Universiti Malaysia Terengganu, Malaysia

ABSTRACT

Marine spatial planning emerged around 40 years ago due to the pressing anthropogenic activities that exert degradation on marine ecosystem. Today, it is widely adopted by more than 102 countries and territories to effectively allocate users and uses in the marine space. MSP is proven as a tool to address multiple ocean issues due to its area-based characteristics. By utilising MSP to govern the ocean areas, conflicting uses, and domination of single activity in a space can be prevented while promoting ecosystem recovery. However, Malaysia as a maritime nation is lacked behind in advancing MSP to manage it waters. This chapter discusses the law and policies in Malaysia that would contribute to the adoption of MSP, thus achieving blue economy and Sustainable Development Goals. Australia, China and the Netherlands have successfully used MSP to manage their marine resources. By benchmarking these countries, Malaysia can uphold a transparent decision making

DOI: 10.4018/979-8-3373-1792-2.ch003

and balanced top-down and bottom-up management, build a resilient ecosystem especially for the livelihood of coastal communities.

INTRODUCTION

Marine Spatial Planning (MSP) is an important management tool for managing ocean resources sustainably, particularly as human activities and pressures on marine habitats increase. As coastal and marine ecosystems continue to confront threats such as overfishing, ocean acidification, habitat destruction, and evolving threats from climate change, MSP provides a comprehensive framework for ensuring that maritime areas are managed efficiently and responsibly (Gissi et al., 2019; Santos et al., 2016). In Malaysia, with its extensive and diverse marine territories, MSP is critical for balancing economic growth, environmental conservation, social welfare, and integrated management (George et al., 2016). This planning process integrates several sectors, including fisheries, tourism, and maritime transport, while prioritising ecosystem health and coastal community livelihoods.

In Malaysia, the maritime sector is a key industry serving as a significant driver of economic performance and substantially boosting its growth (Malaysian Investment Development Authority, 2024). Thus, marine spatial planning is urgently needed to meet the mounting pressures on the country's marine and coastal resources. However, rising urbanisation, industrial expansion, and unsustainable practices endanger marine habitats and species, emphasising the importance of a systematic approach to managing these resources. By adopting MSP, Malaysia can protect its natural assets while also supporting its economic and development objectives.

Aligning MSP with the United Nations Sustainable Development Goals (SDGs) is critical to achieving long-term sustainability. SDG 14: Life Below Water underlines the importance of conserving and using marine resources sustainably. Integrating the SDGs into marine spatial planning enables a comprehensive approach to managing Malaysia's maritime spaces, promoting a balance between environmental preservation and economic development. However, reaching the SDGs through MSP requires collective action across various sectors, policy levels, and stakeholders.

This article aims to study the significance of marine spatial planning in relation to Malaysia's development needs, as well as its potential to help attain the SDGs. It investigates the present concerns confronting Malaysia's marine habitats and shows how successful MSP might help overcome them. This study intends to emphasise the importance of MSP as a vital approach for creating a balanced and sustainable future for Malaysia's coastal and marine ecosystems by taking into account the combination of sustainable development practices and marine management.

MARINE SPATIAL PLANNING DEFINITION

In general, the MSP definition varies based on a country's governance and legal system. Nonetheless, marine spatial planning has been prominently studied as an integrated marine and coastal management worldwide. Table 1 lists down the definitions of MSP in several publications. However, the most widely used definition is the one published by IOC UNESCO as "…a public process that is usually achieved through a political process that includes analysing and allocating the spatial and temporal distribution of human activities in marine areas, to achieve ecological, economic, and social objectives (Ehler & Douvere, 2009). This study then defines MSP as an integrated area-based management process through the allocation of marine space in balancing towards sustainable ecosystems and social developments. This type of management process is an adaptive management that evolves over time when new information is uncovered. According to Ehler & Douvere (2009), there are ten steps in developing and implementing MSP as shown in Figure 1.

Table 1. Definition of MSP by different scholars

Definition of MSP	References
Marine Spatial Planning is practically a future-oriented type of tool to reduce the problems, protect ecosystem services by providing appropriate management, and when it comes together with effective ocean zoning, it will not replace or change existing regulations. In contrast, it adds to spatial guidelines of what activities could occur areas.	Crowder et al. (2006)
Marine Spatial Planning is a practical way to establish a rational organisation for marine space uses and balance the demand for development with needs to protect the marine ecosystem.	Ehler & Douvere, (2009)
Marine Spatial Planning is considered a principal tool to implement integrated maritime policy, facilitates stakeholders and authorities to organise activities and use of resources, to balance between environmental protection and economic development.	Schaefer & Barale, (2011)
Marine Spatial Planning is considered a practical approach to implementing ecosystem-based management to sustainably manage a marine environment.	Olsen et al. (2014)
Marine Spatial Planning is a political and social process by natural and social sciences where it has been a practical approach rather than just a concept towards sustainable development in oceans.	Ehler et al. (2018)
Marine Spatial Planning is a practical way to manage the marine space and the interaction of human influence, including fisheries, shipping, tourism, and deep-sea mining.	Santos et al. (2019)

Figure 1. Ten steps in MSP development and implementation

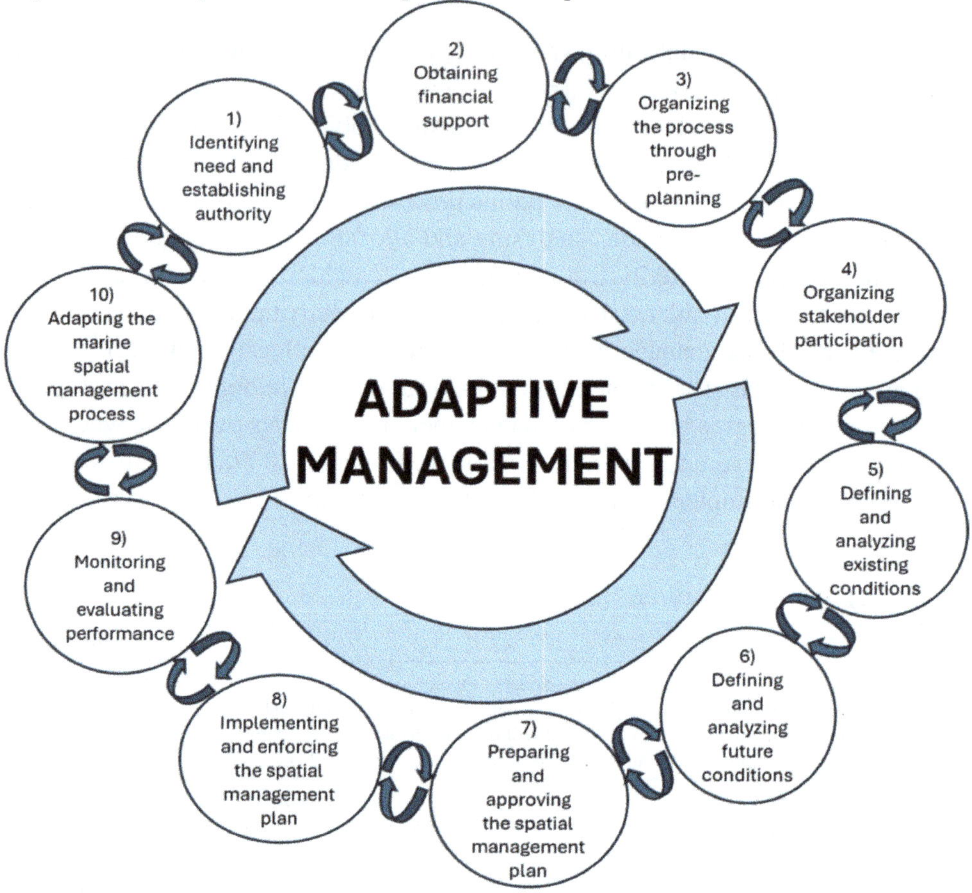

(adapted from Ehler & Douvere, 2009)

MARINE SPATIAL PLANNING AND THE UNITED NATIONS SUSTAINABLE DEVELOPMENT GOALS (SDGS)

Marine spatial planning is promoted by the IOC-UNESCO as a strategy for achieving the UN 2030 Agenda for Sustainable Development Goals. Specifically focusing on Target 14: Life Below Water, MSP indeed helps in realising the other sixteen goals targeted as well. The relationship between MSP and the SDGs is summarised in Table 2 below, followed by the discussion for Target 14.

Table 2. Relationship between MSP and SDGs as outlined in the IOC-UNESCO/ European Commission (2022)

SDGs	Size
Goal 1: No poverty	MSP promotes sustainable development of maritime sectors that provide benefits for the coastal community, thus preventing poverty, particularly among Small Island Developing States (SIDS) and Least Developed Countries (LDCs).
Goal 2: Zero hunger	Through new research and technology, MSP promotes sustainable fisheries and aquaculture management in improving food security.
Goal 3: Good health and well-being	Research and development for better health utilising the marine resources through MSP promotes better health risk management.
Goal 4: Quality education	Education provides the skills and resources needed to improve involvement in planning for marine economic activities, while also fostering greater awareness.
Goal 5: Gender equality	MSP provide space for decision-making among ocean users regardless of gender types.
Goal 6: Clean water and sanitation	The combination of MSP and integrated coastal management improves water quality, leading to better access to clean water through solid waste and wastewater reduction
Goal 7: Affordable and clean energy	Research and technology advancement for developing renewable energy at sea through MSP promote the production of clean energy and the protection of the marine ecosystem.
Goal 8: Decent work and economic growth	MSP and Sustainable Blue Economy create employment opportunities pertaining to ecological, economic, and social objectives.
Goal 9: Industry, innovation, and infrastructure	MSP encourages diversification of marine infrastructures, boosts innovation through technology transfer.
Goal 10: Reduced inequalities	MSP manages access to resources in a way where all actors can benefit from, increase the economy, especially in SIDS and LDCs.
Goal 11: Sustainable cities and communities	Protection of coastal ecosystems through MSP provide a safe environment, preserves local culture, and creates climate-resilient coastal cities and communities.
Goal 12: Responsible consumption and production	MSP promote sustainable use of resources, avoids overexploitation and enhances the circular economy.
Goal 13: Climate action	Establishment of resilient marine ecosystems by reducing exposure to pollution and degradation, thus minimising their vulnerability.
Goal 15: Life on land	The land-sea interactions were taken into account by the integrated approach of MSP through ecosystem-based management.
Goal 16: Peace, justice and strong institutions	Decision-making in MSP was done through a multi-level approach and depended on transparent and effective governance.
Goal 17: Partnership for the goals	Transboundary partnership through MSP enhances cooperation for the development of science and technology, as well as knowledge sharing through capacity building.

Kirkfeldt & Santos (2021) detailed out approaches under MSP initiatives to achieve for SDG Target 14: Life Below Water. However, they mentioned that this MSP approach is conceptually relevant to SDG14, with the full potential of current practices is yet to be unleashed. Target 14.1: Reduce Marine Pollution can be realised through full integration with terrestrial planning, excluding bottom trawling in some areas, cooperation with risk analysis for human hazards such as oil spills, and controlling the number of fertilisers and pesticides used in agriculture. Target 14.2: Protect and Restore Ecosystems can be achieved by applying the ecosystem-based approach to assess cumulative impacts, set spatial restrictions for activities with high effect in critical habitats and gazetted conservation zones. Target 14.3: Reduce Ocean Acidification is achievable by focusing on renewable energy and reducing the intensity of CO2 emissions and increasing the resilience of ecosystems.

Target 14.4: Sustainable Fishing requires the establishment of no-take zones and trawling-free zones, setting limits for allowable catch and reducing illegal, unreported, and unregulated (IUU) fishing through the establishment of artificial reefs. The combating of IUU fishing at the same time helps achieve Target 14.6: End Subsidies Contributing to Overfishing. Moreover, Target 14.5: Conserve Coastal and Marine Areas can be fulfilled through establishing protected areas and ensuring the proper monitoring and enforcement of MPA to achieve it primary objectives. Target 14.7: Increase the Economic Benefits from Sustainable Use of Marine Resources, on the other hand, can be achieved through sustainable fishing practice, allocation of space for ecotourism, and encourage culturing species that less pollute the environment, such as seaweed and oysters.

Target 14.a: Implement and Enforce International Sea Law can be realised through assessing environmental impacts and utilising advanced technologies such as remote sensing or GIS. By prioritising areas for small-scale fisheries and facilitating access to markets, Target 14.b: Provide Access of Small-Scale Artisanal Fishers to Marine Resources and Markets can be achieved. Ultimately, developing a marine spatial plan is one of the global targets that is outlined under Target 14.c: "Enhance the conservation and sustainable use of oceans and their resources by implementing international law as reflected in UNCLOS, which provides the legal framework for the conservation and sustainable use of oceans and their resources, as recalled in paragraph 158 of The Future We Want".

MARINE SPATIAL PLANNING GLOBALLY

Marine spatial planning has been adopted and implemented in more than 102 countries or territories, with more than 300 initiatives (led by government or pilot exercises) at different stages of development recorded, with the most completed plans in the European region (IOC-UNESCO, 2022). By the end of 2023, the number of engagements in MSP globally was reported increased by 20% from the assessment completed in 2022, notably in Africa and the Oceania region (IOC-UNESCO, 2024).

Among all the countries adopted MSP, Australia, China, and the Netherlands have the most comprehensive MSP implementation has been going on for at least 30 years. Hence, this chapter emphasizes the development of marine spatial planning in these three countries. They proved that effective zoning should be accompanied with other measures such as fishing gear limitations, total allowable catch, the usage of permits and fees, seasonal closure for spawning seasons, consideration of land-sea interactions, by adapting, monitoring, and evaluating using the latest scientific knowledge, transboundary cooperations and stakeholders' engagement is crucial in ensuring successful MSP.

Australia

Australia, being the first country to implement MSP, has become a role model to many others. Using the principle of ecologically sustainable development, the MSP in the Great Barrier Reef Marine Park (GBRMP) protects biodiversity through no-take zones and zoning of multiple-use areas. This, according to Vince (2014), provides a helpful framework for learning for other MSPs around the world. The Great Barrier Reef Marine Park Act 1975 (GBRMP Act) is the primary Act that establishes the GBRMP as well as the Great Barrier Reef Marine Park Authority (GBRMPA) and is supplemented by the Great Barrier Reef Zoning Plan 2003. The zoning of the GBRMP is divided into eight different zones: namely General Use Zone, Habitat Protection Zone, Conservation Park Zone, Buffer Zone, Scientific Research Zone, Marine National Park Zone, Commonwealth Islands Zone, and Preservation Area.

There are several best practices and lessons that can be learnt from the management of the Great Barrier Reef, such as: 1. to have a clear vision and objectives of the problems that must be solved by the adoption of MSP; 2. sustainable financial support must be present; 3. continuous MSP process needs to be assured to be accompanied by adaptive management with engaging stakeholders to maintain the long-standing progress; 4. to achieve effective marine management, zoning should be used together with other tools such as fishing gear limitations, total allowable catch, the usage of permits and seasonal closure for spawning seasons; 5. a comprehensive scientific knowledge is not compulsory before starting a zoning program, it is sufficient to first make use of existing available information and adapt when new knowledge is available; 6. it is vital to acknowledge the local communities because they have a stronger sense of ownership towards the area they rely on for living, apart from invaluable understanding of the local marine environment.

China

On the other part of the globe, the concept of marine spatial planning is implemented as Marine Functional Zoning (MFZ) in China and administered by the State Oceanic Administration (SOA). This zoning tool was first proposed in 1988, and in 1989, an experimental unit was established in the Bohai Sea. As reported by Li (2006), in response to the policy of China's national government, the SOA proposed the Law on the Management of Sea Use at the end of 1997 and submitted a draft for approval after two years in 1999. The Law was subsequently adopted and entered into effect on 1st January 2002, with three salient principles: the right to the sea-use authorisation system, the marine functional zoning system, and the user-fee system. MFZ in China is administered by the Law of the People's Republic of China on the Administration of Sea Areas 2002, and the functional zoning are classified into Mariculture and fishery zone, Port and navigation zone, Industry and urban use zone, Minerals and energy zone, Tourism and entertainment zone, Marine protection zone, Special purpose zone, and Reservation zone.

Generally, the main salient features of MFZ in China are identified as: 1) stakeholder participation include local communities, government departments, non-governmental organisations, and intergovernmental integration through trans-boundary cooperation is essential in ensuring effective enforcement; 2. proper channels to spread information is also necessary to build awareness regarding the need to conserve the environment; 3. besides restrictions on ocean-related activities, pollutants from land and upstream development activities should be supervised, where monitoring and evaluation must consistently be carried out and updated with the latest available scientific knowledge.

The Netherlands

MSP in the Netherlands is adopted in the North Sea. In 2005, the Dutch Ministry of Housing, Spatial Planning and Environment included a chapter for the North Sea for the first time in their national “Spatial Planning Policy Document” to prevent fragmentation and promote efficient use of space. In 2009, a new act known as the Land Use Planning Act was adopted. In 2016, a declaration was signed with several countries (namely Belgium, Denmark, France, Germany, Ireland, Luxembourg, Sweden, the Netherlands, and Norway) and the European Commission to explore a more efficient energy transition, and four working groups on MSP and environmental impacts were established. After the long-term vision (the North Sea 2050) was established, a closer vision (the North Sea Strategy 2030) was created, focusing on the development toward the recovery of the natural environment, sustainable energy provision and sustainable food supply.

The best feature that can be highlighted from the MSP in the Netherlands is the matching cooperation initiatives between the surrounding countries of the North Sea. The common visions by all Member States of the North Sea are crucial to ensure the long-term collaboration and direction of coveted management, with the aim to achieve integrated governance and sustainable development.

WHY MALAYSIA NEED MSP

While MSP is common globally, in Malaysia, the MSP concept is still new, with only one documented plan in Semporna, Sabah. WWF (2015) reported that the first MSP launched in Malaysia was in June 2015 to protect the Semporna Priority Conservation Area, as it is recognised as having the highest marine biodiversity in the world and the largest concentration of coral reefs in Malaysia, as well as a hotspot for marine ecotourism destinations. The State Government of Sabah then introduced the implementation of MSP as an initiative to take care of the affected marine environment (Yatim et al., 2018).

As time goes on, many academic publications (George et al., 2016; Aziz et al., 2019; Safuan et al., 2021; Lua et al., 2021; Safuan et al., 2022; Razak et al., 2024; Lua et al., 2025) have suggested MSP adoption in Malaysia, however, it remains a conceptual theory. Marine Spatial Planning should be used to resolve conflicts among users that already have had or will eventually affect the marine environment. Since MSP in Malaysia has yet to be implemented, the suggestion and planning shall be done by adapting models from other successful countries, learning by doing and adapt when new theories emerge, for a better ocean management.

Malaysia is a maritime nation surrounded by sea with a total coastline of 6036.7 kilometres of coastlines, resulting in the maritime industry as one of the major contributors to the Malaysia's Gross Domestic Product (Hassan, 2023). This is supported by the Malaysian Investment Development Authority (2024), which stated that the maritime sector contributes to approximately 40% of the country's GDP, and more than 90% of the country's exports are by sea. However, the lack of a National Ocean Policy in Malaysia has become one of the flaws in marine environmental management in Malaysia, due to the absence of a single entity in overseeing the ocean activities.

Malaysia is progressively moving towards blue economy for better managing its marine resources, as emphasised in the Twelfth Malaysia Plan (2021-2025). According to Azam et al. (2023), lacking a marine spatial plan increases the challenges level to implementing the blue economy in Malaysia, where scattered responsibilities and overlapping jurisdiction led to governance gaps. Power divisions between federal and state governments lead to disputes in enforcing the regulations set, and different interests lead to a lack in coordination and prioritisation in environmental protection.

Hence, MSP comes in as a key enabler in achieving for blue economy, through promoting multi-use, site identification for emerging uses, sustainability and equity of ecosystem-based approach, as well as transparency in attracting investors for blue technologies development (UNESCO-IOC, 2021a). MSP promotes cooperation between users of marine space, encourage partnerships and collaboration, which is the basics in promoting sustainable development, and is oftentimes neglected in the country's environmental management.

In addition, outdated environmental laws in Malaysia are inadequate in addressing the current challenges faced by the increasing exploitation activities (FMT, 2022). The outdated legislations, such as the Environmental Quality Act, need to be amended to meet the developments, where the penalties are too lenient, and the offenders can easily pay them off just to repeat their offences again without significant consequences. Through MSP, utilisation of GIS mapping and satellite monitoring can provide accurate assessment of marine resources, allows for more up-to-date and reliable data to suggest for suitable policies. Subsequently, it ensures that designating areas for certain activities and suitable zoning can be applied to limit exploitation activities that harm the environment.

Besides, by establishing an integrated ecosystem-based MSP, the wetland management in Malaysia could be enhanced to conserve this critical yet highly sensitive ecosystem. Currently, as mentioned by Lua et al. (2021), there is no specific legislation relating to the conservation and management of wetlands available. This important ecosystem provides not only habitat for countless living species, ensuring livelihood of local communities, but also helps in reducing the impacts of climate change (Moomaw et al., 2018). It is, therefore, needs to be managed and protected by acknowledging all aspects, for example through the establishment of marine spatial planning.

In addition, the direction of MSP in addressing climate change through the protection of vulnerable marine ecosystems like coral reefs and mangroves is becoming a trending topic now. According to UNESCO-IOC (2021b), the full integration of climate change and MSP is still limited, and climate-smart MSP requires more intensive studies for approaches clarification. In Malaysia, climate change occurs as increase in annual mean surface temperature, mean sea level, and extreme weather events, and is happening more frequently with higher intensity (Tang, 2019). Therefore, measures need to be taken immediately to reduce the impacts and prevent further losses.

MALAYSIAN GOVERNANCE FRAMEWORK SUPPORTING MSP ADOPTION

International Conventions

The important global conventions that offer a legal framework for considering MSP in the country planning are the United Nations Convention on the Law of the Sea (UNCLOS) and the Convention on Biological Diversity (CBD). UNCLOS was adopted in 1982 and entered into force in 1994. Functional zoning is the primary measure in implementing MSP, which is similar to the foundation of maritime delineation outlined by UNCLOS based on categories and legal status of a particular marine area, known as the zonal/sectoral approach (Pyć, 2019). Besides, UNCLOS also authorises States parties to set regulations for the preservation of the marine environment and sustainable utilisation of resources accordingly, where the management measures are determined tailored to the management area.

In addition, under CBD, which entered into force in 1993, it is mentioned regarding the needs of an area-based conservation planning and management to achieve for Achi Biodiversity Target 11, which stated that 'by 2020, at least 17 per cent of terrestrial and inland water, and 10 per cent of coastal and marine areas, especially areas of particular importance for biodiversity and ecosystem services, are conserved through effectively and equitably managed, ecologically representative and well-connected systems of protected areas and other effective area-based conservation measures and integrated into the wider landscapes and seascapes'. The 10th Conference of the Parties (COP) recognises MSP as a tool in reaching this Aichi Biodiversity Target, thus a report entitled Marine Spatial Planning in the Context of the Convention on Biological Diversity compiling experiences related to MSP, was published as a guideline of this area-based management tool.

Moreover, the latest framework adopted in 2022 at the 15th COP is the Kunming-Montreal Global Biodiversity Framework. Section H of Kunming-Montreal 2030 Global Target 1 clearly spelt out that spatial planning, inclusive of land and sea interaction, is crucial in order to reduce the loss of biodiversity while taking into consideration the rights of the local communities.

National Policies

National policies are official documents adopted by a government to address specific issues or areas within a country. These policies guide decision-making and actions in various sectors such as the economy, education, healthcare, security, and the environment. At national level, a few policies were published mentioning about the need to adopt marine spatial plan, which includes Twelfth Malaysia Plan

2021-2015 (12MP), Second National Physical Coastal Plan (RFZPPN-2), National Policy on Biological Diversity (NPBD) 2022-2030, and National Ecotourism Plan 2016-2025.

The 12MP is a medium-term development plan that outlines plans and strategies for a prosperous, inclusive, and sustainable Malaysia. Anchored with three themes and four policy enablers, this plan included a suggestion on marine spatial plan designation for general use, recreation, and conservation areas. These plans were established through marine spatial plans and were developed for Pulau Payar Marine Park (Kedah), Pulau Perhentian Marine Park (Terengganu) and Pulau Besar Marine Park and Pulau Lima (Johor).

RFZPPN-2 is the strategic land use plan that was approved in 2021. It provides direction for management and utilisation of coastal resources in Peninsular Malaysia and the Federal Territory of Labuan. MSP was emphasized in this plan to balance human uses and resources conservation, and six steps in adopting MSP were established by referring to the ten steps published by the guidelines from IOC-UNESCO. MSP implementation was included under Thrust 2 Strategy AE 1 for strengthening protection of marine ecosystems and five main zones were suggested for the marine spatial plan implementation, includes West Coast 1 (Perlis - Kedah - Pulau Pinang - Perak), West Coast 2 (Selangor – Negeri Sembilan – Melaka – Western Johor), East Coast 1 (Eastern Johor - Pahang), East Coast 2 (Terengganu - Kelantan) and Labuan Coast.

NPBD 2022-2030 is an overarching framework for conserving, sustainably utilising, and equitable sharing of biological diversity. It is a framework published in pursuant of the CBD, and guided by five principles namely 1) heritage, 2) precautionary, 3) shared responsibility, 4) participatory and 5) good governance. Marine Spatial Planning was mentioned in Target 3 to achieve for Goal 2 in significantly reduce the direct and indirect pressures on biodiversity. In addition, in the National Ecotourism Plan that serves as a general guideline for sustainable development and conservation of ecotourism sites in Malaysia, MSP is mentioned in Action 5 to achieve Synergy 5. The objective of Synergy 5 is to reduce pressure exerted on marine resources, especially from unsustainable tourism activities and irresponsible tourist behaviour. Action 5 stated that MSP is needed in a mitigation and adaptation plan in addressing climate change, and the lead agency shall be the Department of Marine Park. This policy is relevant to be included in supporting for MSP adoption since most of the ecotourism sites are protected areas where only non-extractive activities are allowed to replace the extractive activities (such as fishing) in order to ensuring the livelihood of nearby locals.

Legislations

Legislation refers to laws or legal rules that are enacted and enforced by a governing body, such as the parliament. These laws are designed to regulate behaviour, protect rights, and maintain order, covering a wide range of topics including criminal law, civil rights, environmental protection, and economic regulations. Once passed, legislation becomes a binding legal obligation that must be complied with. MSP is new in Malaysia; thus, no legislation directly supports the implementation. However, there are a few legislations that are indirectly related and support the adoption of marine spatial planning in Malaysia.

The Continental Shelf Act 1966 (Act 83) is an act governing the exploration and extraction of natural resources on the continental shelf. Section 6 of Act 83 allows for the creation of regulations to implement this Act, which can include provisions for MSP. Section 6(k) provides for necessary matters in exerting the full effect of the Act and is significant for the adoption of MSP due to the flexibility of the legal frameworks in conserving resources and developing the economy.

Exclusive Economic Zone Act 1984 (Act 311) is a piece of legislation that controls activities in Malaysia's exclusive economic zone and certain items on the continental shelf. In Section 41 it gives the government the authority to enact laws pertaining to the establishment of artificial islands, marine scientific research, and the commercial exploitation of resources that are peculiar to the continental shelf and EEZ. This Act authorises Malaysia to make necessary adjustments in exercising full effect of its jurisdiction in the EEZ and the continental shelf, where the MSP provision can be included.

The Territorial Sea Act 2012 (Act 750) is a crucial piece of legislation that defines and regulates Malaysia's territorial sea. Its application has significant implications for Malaysia's sovereignty, resource management, maritime security and international relations. However, the Sabah state government maintains that the Act does not apply to Sabah. Their stance is based on the argument that Sabah's boundary rights, including its territorial waters and continental shelf, are enshrined in the North Borneo (Alteration of Boundaries) Order in Council 1954, a British colonial-era decree. Sabah contends that this Order in Council grants them rights extending beyond the 12 nautical miles defined in the Territorial Sea Act 2012, potentially including the continental shelf. Limits for the territorial sea are established in Section 3, which is crucial for establishing the area where MSP can be applied. Meanwhile, Section 7 permits rules to be created as needed to fully implement the Act, including zoning restrictions as a tool for environmental preservation through marine spatial planning.

The Baseline of the Maritime Zone Act (Act 660) focuses on establishing the baselines of the extent of Malaysia's maritime zone, including the continental shelf, territorial sea, and exclusive economic zone, by identifying the geographical positions of base points. This Act does not address marine spatial planning specifically, but in Section 5, it is mentioned regarding the determination of the extent of the maritime zone's baseline. This is essential is establishing boundaries for adopting MSP. Section 9 also provides for the creation of regulations by the Minister for the full effect of the Act 660, where the MSP provision can be integrated into.

The Town and Country Planning Act 1976 (Act 172) is the main piece of law controlling terrestrial planning in Peninsular Malaysia and the Federal Territory of Labuan. The Department of Town and Country Planning (PLANMalaysia), which is in charge of physical planning and development in Peninsular Malaysia, is empowered by Act 172 to properly regulate for town and country planning in this country. At the state level, PLANMalaysia is governed by its respective states, whereas in Labuan, the planning department is administered by Labuan Corporation. This Act provides for the preparation of Structure Plan, Local Plans and Special Area Plans, which dictate land use zoning and development in terrestrial and coastal areas. Although not specifically stated, Section 6A creates a Regional Planning Committee to coordinate planning among several local planning authorities, including multiple states, land-sea interactions, or coastal development, all of which are pertinent to marine spatial planning. Similar to Section 16B, where MSP is not mentioned, but it depends on how the authorities carry out the provisions in advance of the Special Area Plan (SAP), a comprehensive development plan for a localised area because of its significant ecological importance, while taking into account the conservation of biodiversity, economic goals, and community livelihood, all of which are in line with the purpose of MSP.

The National Land Code Act 1965 (Act 56) is the main piece of legislation controlling land law in Peninsular Malaysia and the Federal Territories. It is a comprehensive piece of law that creates a standardised system for land transactions, land title registration, and land revenue collection. Due to the fact that its jurisdiction, which focuses on terrestrial land and its associated aspects that typically end at the low water mark, makes this Act indirectly related to MSP. This is because MSP addresses the spatial management of human activities in maritime environments that go beyond the coastline. Sections 40 and 45 have an indirect connection to MSP, where land and marine management intersect in the coastal regions is mentioned.

Malaysian Maritime Enforcement Agency Act 2004 (Act 633) authorises powers to the Malaysian Maritime Enforcement Agency (MMEA) to perform enforcement in maintaining the safety and security of the Maritime Zone in Malaysia. The role of MMEA in upholding federal laws and its obligation to secure maritime areas, including the management of marine pollution, is outlined in Section 6. While

Section 7 gives MMEA the authority to perform its duties, which are in line with MSP's goals for national welfare and ongoing monitoring of the maritime zone.

Merchant Shipping Ordinance 1952 (Ord. 70/1952) primarily oversees and governs issues pertaining to maritime commerce, shipping and navigation, and pollution control. In accordance with the ultimate objective of MSP, which is to safeguard marine ecosystems and foster socioeconomic development, Part V of this Act provides for managing maritime transport safety and security. This includes topics such as maritime traffic, identifying shipping lanes, preventing pollution, and guaranteeing the sustainable use of marine resources.

The Petroleum Development Act 1974 (Act 144) is the body of laws pertaining to the onshore and offshore management, exploration, and exploitation of petroleum resources. MSP is not clearly mentioned in this Act; however, with the oil and gas industry as one of the major economic pillars in Malaysia, it is crucial to include this Act in managing Malaysian waters. According to Section 6, downstream operations require the Prime Minister's approval. Marine spatial planning may be used to manage the environmental effects and take spatial considerations into account for sustainable development.

Tourism Industry Act 1992 (Act 482) is the legislation that governs tourism-related enterprises and grants licenses to travel firms and tour operators to ensure they meet quality standards. This Act does not specifically address MSP. Oftentimes, marine spatial planning entails the declaration of protected zones where resource extraction is limited and sustainable activities such as ecotourism are focused. Thus, this Act needs to be included since it indirectly advances MSP's objective of environmental considerations and community livelihood.

The Environmental Quality Act 1974 (Act 127) regulates pollutants and maintains the quality of the air, water, and noise to lessen or avoid their negative effects on the environment. Sections 27 and 29 prohibit the discharge of oil and waste into Malaysian waters, directly addressing the protection of marine ecosystems and resources, just like the primary objective of MSP. In order to mitigate potential environmental impacts and integrate scientifically driven planning decisions, Section 34A mandates Environmental Impact Assessments (EIAs) for any prescribed activities that include coastal and marine areas. This helps to balance the environment and economic needs, much like MSP.

Wildlife Conservation Act 2010 (Act 716) provides for the regulation and management of wildlife in Peninsular Malaysia and the Federal Territories of Labuan. Although this Act does not mention MSP, its provision for the creation of sanctuaries and wildlife reserves suggests the necessity of coordinated efforts and actions across sectors with disparate interests, which is consistent with MSP's goal of habitat and resource conservation.

The Fisheries Act 1985 (Act 317) regulates Malaysian waterways, riverine fishing, turtles, and marine and estuarine fishing. There are a few sections under this Act that provide for the provisions of MSP specifically. In order to minimise overfishing and maximize the use of fishery resources, Section 6 outlines the necessity of ongoing assessment of fisheries plans to ensure they are in line with national policy and the best available scientific data. In accordance with MSP's main strategy, spatial zoning, Section 45 gives the Minister authority over zoning regulations for the protection of marine protected zones. These regulations divide protected areas into zones and specify the conditions under each zone.

National Heritage Act 2005 (Act 645) mainly governs the protection and conservation of the nation's cultural heritage, including its underwater heritage. Although there is no direct connection between this Act and MSP, its provisions for safeguarding areas of underwater cultural heritage align with one of MSP's goals, which is to preserve underwater heritage. Additionally, the larger conservation framework supports ecological integrity for the gazetted areas, which in turn protects the surrounding ecosystems in a broader scale.

Access to Biological Resources and Benefit Sharing Act 2017 (Act 795) is an Act formulated for the implementation of the CBD related to access to biological resources and the sharing of benefits from resource utilisation. Although there is no direct connection between this Act and marine spatial planning, Section 22 places a strong focus on encouraging the sustainable and equitable use of marine resources, and Section 30 outlines steps for efficient resource management through the monitoring of marine biological resources. This is comparable to MSP's goal of promoting equitable access and reducing user-to-user conflicts.

CONCLUSION

In conclusion, marine spatial planning provides Malaysia with a comprehensive and strategic strategy to manage its vast and diversified maritime resources in a sustainable manner. As the country that faces mounting challenges from industrial expansion, overfishing, and environmental deterioration, MSP provides an essential framework for balancing economic growth and ecological preservation. By integrating MSP with the United Nations Sustainable Development Goals (SDGs), particularly SDG 14, Malaysia can strengthen its efforts to conserve marine ecosystems, improve coastal populations' livelihoods, and ensure the long-term use of ocean resources. This linkage with the SDGs will help Malaysia build a more sustainable and inclusive marine future.

It is important to note that a successful MSP implementation in Malaysia requires strong governance, stakeholder collaboration, and effective policy integration at the local, regional, and national levels. The involvement of several sectors, including fisheries, tourism, and environmental conservation, is critical to developing a united vision for marine management. With the current governance framework, Malaysia is well-positioned to execute marine spatial planning, but certain policy changes, coordinating structures, and stakeholder engagement processes may be required to enable its successful implementation.

Moving forward, Malaysia must continue to engage in research, capacity building, and public awareness to ensure that MSP is a key component of the country's sustainable development program. Through the proactive adoption and implementation of these initiatives, Malaysia will be able to not only protect its marine habitats but also be able to set an example for other countries experiencing similar issues in the pursuit of sustainable development.

ACKNOWLEDGEMENT

The authors acknowledge the sponsorship received from Biasiswa Universti Malaysia Terengganu (BUMT) for providing fund to carry out this study as part of the research's objectives.

REFERENCES

Azam, A. H. M., Zainuddin, M. R. K. V., & Tarmidi, T. (July, 2023). *Malaysia's Blue Economy: Position, Initiatives, and Challenges*. Economic Research Institute for ASEAN and East Asia. https://www.eria.org/uploads/Malaysia-Blue-Economy-Position-Initiatives-Challenges.pdf

Aziz, N., Muhammad, Z., Farahdilah, G., Talaat, W. I. A. W., & Saputra, J. (2019). Marine Spatial Planning: The Way Forward for Sustainable Development of Central Terengganu, Malaysia. *Journal of Southwest Jiaotong University*, *54*(4), 1–11. DOI: 10.35741/issn.0258-2724.54.4.9

Crowder, L. B., Osherenko, G., Young, O. R., Airamé, S., Norse, E. A., Baron, N., Day, J. C., Douvere, F., Ehler, C. N., Halpern, B. S., Langdon, S. J., McLeod, K. L., Ogden, J. C., Peach, R. E., Rosenberg, A. A., & Wilson, J. A. (2006). Resolving Mismatches in U.S. Ocean Governance. *Science*, *313*(5787), 617–618. DOI: 10.1126/science.1129706 PMID: 16888124

Ehler, C., Zaucha, J., & Gee, K. (2018). Maritime/Marine Spatial Planning at the Interface of Research and Practice. In Zaucha, J., & Gee, K. (Eds.), *Maritime Spatial Planning*. Palgrave Macmillan.

Ehler, C. N., & Douvere, F. (2009). *A Step-By-Step Approach Towards Ecosystem-Based Management* (IOC Manual and Guides no. 53, ICAM Dossier no. 6). Paris: UNESCO.

FMT. (September, 2022). *Environmental laws outdated, penalties too low, says law minister.* FMT (Free Malaysia Today) Media. https://www.freemalaysiatoday.com/category/nation/2022/09/02/environmental-laws-outdated-penalties-too-low-says-law-minister/

George, M., Sabaruddin, J. S. H., & Chong, V. C. (2016). Marine Spatial Planning: What Does It Have to Offer Malaysia? *International Journal of Marine and Coastal Law*, *31*(2), 242–278. DOI: 10.1163/15718085-12341397

Gissi, E., Fraschetti, S., & Micheli, F. (2019). Incorporating change in marine spatial planning: A review. *Environmental Science & Policy*, *92*, 191–200. DOI: 10.1016/j.envsci.2018.12.002

Hassan, H. (2023). The Roles of the National Hydrographic Centre in Harnessing the Nation's Blue Economy. In Ivan, M. A. & Nazli, A. (eds) *Malaysia A Maritime Nation Agenda: Steering the Course*. PUSMAS, TLDM.

IOC-UNESCO. (2022). *State of the Ocean Report* (IOC Technical Series, 173). Paris, IOC-UNESCO.

IOC-UNESCO. (2024). *State of the Ocean Report* (IOC Technical Series, 190). Paris, IOC-UNESCO.

IOC-UNESCO/European Commission. (2022). *Updated Joint Roadmap to accelerate Marine/Maritime Spatial Planning processes worldwide –MSProadmap (2022–2027)* (IOC Technical Series, 182). Paris, UNESCO.

Kirkfeldt, T. S., & Frazão Santos, C. (2021). A review of sustainability concepts in marine spatial planning and the potential to supporting the UN sustainable development goal 14. *Frontiers in Marine Science*, *8*, 713980. DOI: 10.3389/fmars.2021.713980

Li, H. (2006). The impacts and implications of the legal framework for sea use planning and management in China. *Ocean and Coastal Management*, *49*(9–10), 717–726. DOI: 10.1016/j.ocecoaman.2006.06.015

Lua, W. Y., Aziz, N., Ghazali, F., Idris, I., Rasid, N. H. A., & Talat, W. I. A. W. (2021). Marine Spatial Planning and the Local Community's Awareness of Ecosystems in Setiu Wetland. *Journal of Southeast Asian Studies*, *26*(1), 97–123. DOI: 10.22452/jati.vol26no1.5

Lua, W. Y., Aziz, N., Idris, I., Rahman, M. A. A., Ghazali, F. & Talaat, W. I. A. W. (2025). Marine spatial planning as a potential practical approach to manage setiu wetland as an ecologically sensitive area. *Integrated Environmental Assessment and Management, vjaf023*, 35-64. https://doi.org/DOI: 10.1093/inteam/vjaf023

Malaysian Investment Development Authority. (2024). Revitalising the Maritime Industry Through Blue Economy. https://www.mida.gov.my/revitalising-the-maritime-industry-through-blue-economy/#:~:text=The%20maritime%20industry%20in%20Malaysia,cent%20in%20compound%20cargo%20throughput

Moomaw, W. R., Chmura, G. L., Davies, G. T., Finlayson, C. M., Middleton, B. A., Natali, S. M., Perry, J. E., Roulet, N., & Sutton-Grier, A. E. (2018). Wetlands in a changing climate: Science, policy and management. *Wetlands*, *38*(2), 183–205. DOI: 10.1007/s13157-018-1023-8

Olsen, E., Fluharty, D., Hoel, A. H., Hostens, K., Maes, F., & Pecceu, E. (2014). Integration at the Round Table: Marine Spatial Planning in Multi-Stakeholder Settings. *PLoS One*, *9*(10), e109964. DOI: 10.1371/journal.pone.0109964 PMID: 25299595

Pyć, D. (2019). The Role of the Law of the Sea in Marine Spatial Planning. In Zaucha, J., & Gee, K. (Eds.), *Maritime Spatial Planning*. Palgrave Macmillan. DOI: 10.1007/978-3-319-98696-8_16

Razak, F., Lua, W. Y., Abd Rasid, N. H., Aziz, N., Repin, I. M., Xue, X. Z., & Safuan, C. D. M. (2024). Adopting Marine Spatial Planning (MSP) using coral health assessment as indicator: A case study in Pulau Redang Marine Park, Malaysia. *Ocean and Coastal Management*, *248*, 106943. DOI: 10.1016/j.ocecoaman.2023.106943

Safuan, C. D. M., Ashraf, A. R. M., Tan, C. H., Jaafar, S. N., Yusop, P. A. M., Lai, R. K., & Bachok, Z. (2021). Coral Health Status Assessment in Malaysia Islands; Looking Towards Marine Spatial Planning. *Ocean and Coastal Management*, *213*, 105856. DOI: 10.1016/j.ocecoaman.2021.105856

Safuan, C. D. M., Aziz, N., Repin, I. M., Xue, X. Z., Rahman, A., & Talaat, I. A. W. (2022). Assessment of Governance and Ecological Status of Terengganu Marine Park, Malaysia: Toward Marine Spatial Planning. *Sains Malaysiana*, *51*(12), 3909–3922. DOI: 10.17576/jsm-2022-5112-04

Santos, C. F., Agardy, T., Andrade, F., Barange, M., Crowder, L. B., Ehler, C. N., Orbach, M. K., & Rosa, R. (2016). Ocean planning in a changing climate. *Nature Geoscience*, *9*(10), 730–730. DOI: 10.1038/ngeo2821

Santos, C. F., Ehler, C. N., Agardy, T., Andrade, F., & Orbach, M. K. (2019). Marine Spatial Planning. In Sheppard, C. (Ed.), *World Seas: An Environmental Evaluation* (2nd ed., Vol. III). Elsevier Ltd. DOI: 10.1016/B978-0-12-805052-1.00033-4

Schaefer, N., & Barale, V. (2011). Maritime Spatial Planning: Opportunities & Challenges in the Framework of the EU Integrated Maritime Policy. *Journal of Coastal Conservation*, *15*(2), 237–245. DOI: 10.1007/s11852-011-0154-3

Tang, K. H. D. (2019). Climate change in Malaysia: Trends, contributors, impacts, mitigation and adaptations. *The Science of the Total Environment*, *650*, 1858–1871. DOI: 10.1016/j.scitotenv.2018.09.316 PMID: 30290336

UNESCO-IOC. (2021a). *MSPglobal Policy Brief: Marine Spatial Planning and the Sustainable Blue Economy* (IOC Policy Brief no 2). Paris, UNESCO.

UNESCO-IOC. (2021b). *MSPglobal Policy Brief: Climate Change and Marine Spatial Planning* (IOC Policy Brief no 3). Paris, UNESCO.

Vince, J. (2014). Oceans governance and marine spatial planning in Australia. *Australian Journal of Maritime and Ocean Affairs, 6*(1), 5–17. DOI: 10.1080/18366503.2014.888137

WWF. (2015). First Marine Spatial Planning in Sabah Launched to Further Protect Semporna Priority Conservation Area (PCA). https://www.wwf.org.my/?19725/First-Marine-Spatial-Planning-in-Sabah-Launched-to-Further-Protect-Semporna-Priority-Conservation-Area-PCA

Yatim, M. H. M., Omar, A. H., Abdullah, N. M., & Sarip, A. (2018). Extending the concept of institutional analysis to the marine spatial planning practice. *IOP Conference Series. Earth and Environmental Science, 169*(1), 012010. Advance online publication. DOI: 10.1088/1755-1315/169/1/012010

KEY TERMS AND DEFINITIONS

Marine spatial planning: An integrated, area-based management process that allocates marine space to balance sustainable ecosystems with social development.

Marine Functional Zoning: A well-known Chinese MSP initiative that serves as the foundation for marine management in China, it is an ocean zoning tool used to allocate sea space based on its characteristic.

IOC UNESCO: The Intergovernmental Oceanographic Commission-UNESCO, a United Nations organization responsible for supporting global ocean science and related services.

Sustainable Development Goals: Also known as the Global Goals, these were adopted by the United Nations in 2015 as a universal call to action, to safeguard the planet, eliminate poverty, and ensure peace and prosperity for all by 2030.

Adaptive management: An iterative management approach involving making decisions and taking actions based on continuous monitoring and evaluation throughout the process, rather than following a fixed, sequential plan.

Blue Economy: The sustainable use of ocean resources for economic growth, improved livelihoods and jobs, while preserving the health of ocean ecosystems.

Area-based management: An approach that implements management within specific geographic areas to regulate human activities and conserve ecosystems, tailored to local conditions.

Chapter 4

Sustainable Urban Planning and Legal Tools for Smart Cities

R. Velmurugan
https://orcid.org/0000-0002-7925-9757
Karpagam Academy of Higher Education, Coimbatore, India

J. Sudarvel
https://orcid.org/0000-0001-6656-1992
Karpagam Academy of Higher Education, Coimbatore, India

S. Senthilkumar
https://orcid.org/0000-0003-1968-6877
Skyline University, Nigeria

ABSTRACT

Legal tools and sustainable urban planning are involved to establish smart cities to achieve the environmental sustainability, social equity and economic stability. The smart city development is one of the elements to be analyzed by determining how legal instruments support the planning structures of the cities. Sustainable solutions through technical solutions and good administration are needed to counter urban growth and environmental challenge. Sustainable transportation, eco-friendly infrastructure bespeak of the legal tools being used in the form of zoning laws, land use regulations and environmental policies. It is also through public private partnerships that investment in projects related to the smart city grows, coupled with IoT, AI, and blockchain, which helps make things more sustainable. Business growth through the balance paid by legal frameworks of ecological conservation, disasters resilience and climate adaptation.

DOI: 10.4018/979-8-3373-1792-2.ch004

INTRODUCTION

City development has been severely affected by the urbanization. As cities are growing quickly and experiencing more environmental stress, they now have to build spaces that include the newest technologies as well as tie into environmental, economic and social factors. Smart cities depend on both present-day systems and strategy for urban design to help residents by increasing both public services and sustainability (Komninos et al., 2018; Caragliu, Del Bo, & Nijkamp, 2019; Neirotti et al., 2020).

Creating policies for smart cities holds the highest priority. Urban expansion happening quickly creates both advantages and problems for infrastructure, energy, transport and waste systems (Batty et al., 2019; Bibri, 2019). These approaches depend on digital technologies, especially big data analytics, the IoT and AI, to make city living both more convenient and sustainable (Cocchia, 2018; Kitchin, 2021). As a result, using sensors and AI in Singapore's Smart Nation initiative reduced congestion, air pollution and offered a better commuter experience (Tan et al., 2020; Lee & Lim, 2022).

However, forming a smart city is not only about incorporating new technology. The effort should focus clearly on environmental protection, inclusion for all and equal economic development. Urban areas are under increasing pressure to control their environmental damage and share development with everyone equally (Greenfield, 2021; Silva et al., 2023). Adding social equity and providing digital access is important to stop technology from increasing existing inequities. The program by the "Digital City" in Barcelona, amongst other things, provides affordable internet and basic digital skills to residents of areas that are often left out, leading to greater social inclusion and less of a digital gap (Reina & Grewal, 2021; Martinez et al., 2023).

Therefore, a smart city's success relies on sustainable planning that mixes efficiency, innovation and care for the environment with fairness to all members of society. It has recently been confirmed that for smart cities to deliver their advantages, sustainability needs to fit well with economic and social demands, especially since cities are becoming more urbanized (Neirotti et al., 2020; Bibri, 2019; Mohammadi & Vaziri, 2023).

This development is aided by legal tools that control how cities are shaped by strict regulations. By enforcing environmental guidelines, setting aside land usages, standards for building and frameworks for Public-Private Partnerships (PPPs), these laws encourage creativity and inclusion. In the same way, the European Union's Urban Agenda requires that smart city projects are in agreement with both social justice and environmental preservation rules (European Commission, 2022; Weber et al., 2023). In addition, laws support good governance by ensuring that things are done openly, everyone can take part and the rules are fair (Rogers et al., 2021; van den Bergh & Botzen, 2022).

It is important for governments, private companies and citizens to team up to guarantee smart cities develop in a socially responsible way. New technologies should not cause unfairness to people or damage the environment (Rogers et al., 2021; Khalid & Lee, 2024). In Amsterdam, smart city governance involves residents in choosing key solutions and calls for equal technology rights to encourage inclusive advancements (van den Bergh & Botzen, 2022; Janssen et al., 2023).

Legal rules play a big role in managing energy and resources in cities to support sustainability. New laws and criteria influence decisions in favor of renewable energy, smart grids, energy-saving buildings and waste management (Müller, 2018; Stein & Kemp, 2020; Li & Wang, 2023). Germany's "Energiewende" serves as a model for turning cities toward using renewables and helps the economy while cutting down on emissions (Stein & Kemp, 2020; Becker et al., 2023).

Social inclusion in smart cities is made possible by digital inclusion rules required by law. Giving everyone access to technology, education, jobs, housing, healthcare and transport allows the benefits of smart city developments to be used by everyone. In Medellín, Colombia, enhanced opportunities for affordable internet and public transport have helped to expand participation in society by marginalized people (Escobar & Guzman, 2019; Torres & Morales, 2022).

Using laws that guide partnerships, it becomes important to use public-private teams in investment and undertaking smart projects related to transportation, energy and telecommunications (Kwak et al., 2019; Choi & Lee, 2023). Detailed explanations for all roles, how funds are used, the dates involved and measures to protect citizens help everyone work better together. Lee & Lee (2018) note in their study how the Songdo International Business District project in South Korea succeeded using PPPs (Lee & Lee, 2018; Park et al., 2023).

Moreover also make sure that smart city projects are open, accountable and include the community, making sure these projects serve everyone fairly (Scholl & Scholl, 2018; Martínez & Gómez, 2023). Managing data is very important to ensure that privacy and citizen information are protected as cities grow more digitized. Legal data frameworks protect from misuse, encourage reliability and allow successful use of technology (Ziegler et al., 2020; Singh & Kumar, 2023). Toronto's Digital Governance Framework mentions that legal rules for privacy, along with the practice of open data, help achieve digital excellence (City of Toronto, 2019; Williams et al., 2022).

Hence, smart city development combines technology, sustainability, social equity and governance in many ways. The smart, sustainable and just growth of cities depends on strong legal frameworks. With urban expansion happening rapidly, the use of strong legal policies will become more important to ensure both quick progress and inclusion for all. The current ideas and activities in the field stress that successful smart cities only come to all residents if there are comprehensive legal and policy rules (Komninos et al., 2018; Batty et al., 2019; Greenfield, 2021; Rogers et al., 2021; Silva et al., 2023).

LEGAL FOUNDATIONS IN SMART URBAN DEVELOPMENT

Smart cities are built and developed with the help of strong legal regulations. At the same time, getting into this area is more complicated due to the need for updated laws to meet the growing needs of cities. An urban planning framework should always rely on strong norms and laws, including zoning, land use regulations, environmental statutes, to help cities advance technologically, culturally, environmentally and financially (Allam & Jones, 2019; Angelidou, 2018; Komninos et al., 2018; Caragliu, Del Bo, & Nijkamp, 2019). Such regulations shape land use, guard natural resources and help plan cities, so that municipal authorities can design them for efficiency and adaptability while avoiding environmental damage (Batty et al., 2019; Neirotti et al., 2020).

Among all legal tools, zoning laws would be considered most influential in urban development. They help assign land for different areas such as homes, offices, factories and mixed-use areas, to avoid issues that can reduce how people live (Talen, 2017). Additionally, zoning works to create public and green spaces which improves how people experience the city. In Barcelona, a careful approach to zoning creates green spaces and parks among urban areas which both helps improve air quality and benefits local communities (Reina & Grewal, 2021). Thus, it is shown that zoning can balance progress in cities with concerns about the environment and social justice (Talen, 2017; Bibri, 2020; Escobar & Guzman, 2019).

The use of land is combined with zoning, helping to keep buildings at proper heights, with the right amount of space in-between and keeping nature a part of the community. Policies that encourage more people to live and work in one area help limit fast-spreading urban growth and cut back on emissions while saving nature (Angelidou, 2018; Sharifi & Yamagata, 2020). The city of Portland, Oregon, has used land use rules to promote living close to public transportation and tight spaces which have helped control sprawl, boost sustainability and increase affordable housing (Berke et al., 2018). As explained by Angelidou (2018), having these land use tools is important for implementing smart city principles, including smart transport, energy saving and managing waste in an integrated way.

Setting ideas about air and water quality, waste management and protection for wildlife, environmental law is just as crucial as health law. They are in place to ensure that cities support environmental aims to cut greenhouse gases and use more renewable sources of energy (Neirotti et al., 2020; Batty et al., 2019; Tan et al., 2021). Singapore shows how adding clean energy, conserving water and improving waste management can be part of urban growth, thanks to the Green Plan 2030 and tough environmental laws (Tan et al., 2021). They help cities survive the effects of climate change and improve how residents live.

Legal tools allow cities to include growth, sustainability and inclusivity when making decisions. As a result, if effective zoning and land controls guide development to create cheaper housing areas linked to public transit, open spaces are spared from being changed by gentrification (Scholl & Scholl, 2019). Enforcing environmental rules can lead to better and cleaner urban infrastructure that will be resilient in the future. Scholl and Scholl (2019) show that these frameworks join technology and environmental care which helps cities to become more equal and comfortable for people.

One big benefit of these laws is how flexible they can be. As cities grow, the rules on where and how land can be used may be changed such as setting up digital communication or electric vehicle charging stations, to match the city's new needs and interests. Similarly, environmental statutes may be changed to fit higher sustainability standards such as new carbon emission targets or a greater use of renewable energy (Rogers et al., 2021). For example, Amsterdam keeps updating its zoning rules to allow smart mobility hubs and green roofs, proving that being flexible in the law helps drive both new technology and greener developments (van den Bergh & Botzen, 2022).

Legal rules also guarantee that smart city benefits are divided fairly. Such laws require safe housing for all, encourage transport that is available to all and divide shared resources in ways that prevent low-income groups from being neglected or uprooted (Janssen et al., 2019). For example, adoption can increase social gaps, laws play a key role in bringing everyone online by providing broadband, basic digital knowledge and job openings in cities (Bibri, 2020; Reina & Grewal, 2021). The city's efforts to improve housing and transport which are helped by laws providing accessible internet, are effective ways to create social fairness in smart cities (Escobar & Guzman, 2019).

Thus, sustainable, resilient and inclusive development in smart cities is made possible by zoning laws, land use regulations and environmental statutes. These legal rules make it possible to support new technology while still looking after the environment and all people. Many studies agree that having these legal instruments leads to a fairer and more sustainable kind of urban growth, as discussed by Talen (2017), Angelidou (2018), Neirotti et al. (2020), Scholl and Scholl (2019) and Rogers et al. (2021).

SUSTAINABLE URBAN PLANNING AND ENVIRONMENTAL INTEGRATION

To manage increasing population growth, cities should plan for sustainability to keep their environmental effect as low as possible. It requires planning urban development together with environmental conservation so the planet's resources are not used up by urban growth. Laws are important for making sure that building, transportation and urban projects are done with environmental protection in mind. Sustainable urban living is made possible by using green building codes, carbon emission standards and renewable energy mandates as tools to help cities become greener, less wasteful and better able to handle changing conditions (Allam & Jones, 2020; Sharifi & Yamagata, 2018; Bina & Koradia, 2022; Li et al., 2023).

Widely, it is believed that green building codes are essential laws to help increase sustainability. With these codes, building projects must meet standards for energy saving, being kind to nature and saving resources, especially reducing waste. According to Lutfi et al. (2019), without green building requirements, it is difficult to manage the effects of urbanization and start creating sustainable architecture. Vancouver is using such codes to require new buildings to perform well in energy, meaning the city uses a lot less energy and produces less carbon (Khemlani, 2021). Such standards regularly require using resources that save on energy, water and depend on natural light and ventilation which in turn reduces the future use of resources (Mahmoud et al., 2020; Singh et al., 2022).

Carbon emission standards form a significant aspect of the legal measures supporting urban sustainability. The standards force cities to limit their carbon emissions, so they can aim for low or zero emissions to help slow climate change. According to Patterson et al. (2018) such standards motivate people in growing urban areas, with strong transportation and industry sectors, to consider electric vehicles and cleaner forms of energy. Setting emission zones and incentives for electric vehicles in Oslo has lowered the amount of air pollution and emissions produced by the city (Kjørstad et al., 2022; Chen et al., 2023).

All new construction should also feature renewable forms of energy for sustainable urban planning. Following solar and renewable laws results in a decrease in our dependence on fossil fuels and heightened energy security. Müller points out that rules like these make electricity more reliable and help reduce greenhouse gas emissions. In Germany, Freiburg shows how communities can help by making sure all new buildings use solar energy which helps the city meet a large part of its energy needs with renewable sources (Schultz & Becker, 2021; Alami et al., 2023).

Environmental standards in sustainable planning make it important to cooperatively protect nature areas to help keep a balanced ecosystem in cities. Not only do parks, gardens and urban forests absorb carbon, but they also reduce the heat in cities, clear up air and water and let people exercise or rest. Beatley (2018) points out that secure legal standards and more green space are basic needs in designing for a sustainable urban future. Care for widespread greenery in the "City in a Garden" vision ensures Singapore's urban living maintains biodiversity and quality of life for residents, according to Tan et al. (2021). Zoning and land use legislation are designed to make sure that everyone can use green spaces nearby, avoiding both unequal conditions and pollution (Wang & Liu, 2022; Nguyen et al., 2024).

The importance of sustainable urban planning strongly relies on transportation law because transportation causes a lot of the city's greenhouse gas emissions. Various laws in the country make public transit, walking and cycling easier to use, while using fossil fuel vehicles is less appealing. According to Gilbert and Benton (2019), making laws that back investment in bus and rail networks and encourage vehicles that produce little or no pollution is extremely important for sustainability. Amsterdam shows that effective legal steps such as increased cycling lanes and a congestion charge, have made urban travel greener and opened it up to people from various socio-economic groups (Pucher & Buehler, 2021; Dijk & Peters, 2023). They decrease pollution, traffic delays and make transport options fairer for everyone.

Furthermore, by law for urban space to include buildings that use little energy. These mean attention to insulation, good lighting that reduces energy waste and energy systems that regulate use in real time. Rogers et al. point out that following these standards greatly reduces how much carbon and energy cities use. As an example, California's Title 24 building codes have contributed to energy savings throughout the state by requiring improvements (Moezzi et al., 2021; Zhang & Chen, 2023).

Teamwork in sustainable urban planning means bringing together a variety of legal tools that support responsible building, roadway use, energy choices and parks in our cities. Following green building codes, reducing carbon, using sustainable energy, planning green outside spaces and creating sustainable transport rules, cities can reduce their impact on nature while also ensuring all residents are well cared for. Social fairness and giving everyone equal access are both main concerns: purposely designed laws should bring green infrastructure, clean transport and digital tools to marginalized communities that are being transformed into smart, sustainable cities (Bibri, 2020; Janssen et al., 2021; Uddin & Rahman, 2023). Only by having such comprehensive and inclusive rules can cities balance technology, care for the environment and support fairness for everyone. Legal frameworks are emphasized by a number of historians, including Lutfi et al. (2019), Patterson et al. (2018), Müller (2019), Beatley (2018), Gilbert and Benton (2019) and Rogers et al. (2020) as being key for making smart cities sustainable.

TECHNOLOGY-ENABLED GOVERNANCE AND LEGAL SUPPORT

Improving cities by making them efficient, easier to live in and connected is a major theme in the digital era and is closely related to smart cities and driven by new digital ideas. These ambitions use technology, including the Internet of Things (IoT), artificial intelligence (AI) and blockchain, that can bring important changes to cities (Batty et al., 2019; Cocchia, 2018; Perera et al., 2020; Al-Turjman, 2021). Nevertheless, ethical, honest, equitable and reliable use of these technologies can only be achieved if their deployment is overseen by new laws. Smart cities depend on legal systems to protect participation among citizens, their privacy, data and the operation of city services (Kitchin, 2022; Janssen et al., 2021; Kamal et al., 2023).

With sensor and smart meter-based IoT, cities can collect real-time data on traffic, energy use and the environment to make urban life more efficient (Gubbi et al., 2013; Zanella et al., 2020; Zhang et al., 2022). Nonetheless, the huge amount of data produced creates important privacy and security challenges. By means of such laws, governments can make sure the public feels safe, encourages citizens to join these initiatives and supports smart development. In Barcelona, the rules about IoT data allow residents to keep their privacy, letting the city install smart traffic and energy systems that aid various groups of the population (Reina & Grewal, 2021; Muñoz et al., 2023).

Large amounts of data are being used by AI to improve how waste is removed, energy is distributed and traffic is controlled (Hagendorff, 2020; Zhang et al., 2021; Sharma et al., 2023). Even so, making decisions with AI increases problems with fairness, accountability and reducing bias. He recommends completing AI systems with regulatory requirements that foster openness, ensure auditors can review them and involve humans to correct possible discrimination. Helsinki shows how this can be done by making sure that AI-based social services are clear, reviewable by the public and kept reliable and fair (Kuokkanen & Lähdesmäki, 2022; Mäntymäki et al., 2024).

Blockchain helps government by ensuring records are unchanged and decentralized, making all transactions more open and protecting against fraud (Zohar, 2018; Casino et al., 2019; Swan, 2021). Applications using blockchain are secure digital voting and management of public records. Nonetheless, for blockchain to operate well, there must be clear legal guidelines for owning data, resolving problems and adhering to privacy laws. Estonia gives blockchain legal support in public places and supports it through digital programmes because it improves access and equality to public services and protects citizens' rights (Auer & Böhme, 2020; Tayan, 2022).

For IoT, AI and blockchain to be useful in urban areas, legal support is necessary to maintain trust and help all citizens. According to Solove (2021), privacy and data security continue to be major issues and a lack of laws to ensure these areas may discourage citizens from joining smart city programs. Crawford writes in 2016 that ensuring AI sends proper messages by law is necessary to help meet responsibilities and control outcomes for those managed by AI. The UK's approach to AI also requires clear rules to ensure the public trusts new artificial intelligence (UK Government, 2022; European Commission, 2023).

To achieve social equity and digital inclusion, these laws should include them. Skillful use of smart city technologies can increase inequality in society. Digital infrastructure, data and participation should be made accessible within the law to all groups, but especially to marginalized communities (Janssen et al., 2021; Bibri, 2020; Smith & Anderson, 2023). Smart Dublin aims to connect all local groups with information and services by actively integrating inclusion policies which supports both their needs and those of society (O'Hara & Hall, 2023; Kelly et al., 2024).

Overall, IoT, AI and blockchain can boost urban greenness, practicality and public partnership; however, they largely depend on firm and adjustable regulations to succeed. To be efficient, these laws should support honoring ethics, protect people's basic rights and ensure accountability for all users and creators. Following the views of Gubbi et al. (2013), Hagendorff (2020), Zohar (2018), Solove (2021) and Crawford (2016), laws must exist to encourage smart city technologies in supporting fairness for all.

ECONOMIC GROWTH AND SOCIAL EQUITY THROUGH LEGAL PARTNERSHIPS

One challenge for smart cities is that they often find it hard to keep up financially because running infrastructure and advanced technology for more and more city residents is very costly. To achieve smart city development today, PPPs allow cities to tap into private resources while still managing important assets and services themselves (Zhang & Choi, 2018; Yigitcanlar et al., 2021; Alkathiri et al., 2023). Most PPPs are linked to projects involving whole areas, including energy efficient buildings, renewable energy, better transportation and waste disposal technology. The outcome of these partnerships mainly relies on the presence of stable legal agreements and investment protection laws that prevent any harm to public or private partners and minimize weaknesses (Zhang & Choi, 2018; Kim et al., 2020; Sharma & Mishra, 2022).

The stability of smart cities financially depends greatly on their legal frameworks. Specific contracts help clarify who does what and share risks and they give public protection for sustainability and equal service access to private investors and public officials. Singapore's urban infrastructure projects are guided by strict standards and fair resolution systems, making sure projects stay on time and meet sustainability goals (Tan & Tan, 2022; Low & Lee, 2023). Thanks to investment protection laws, returns are promised, taxes are made more attractive, political and financial risks decrease and it becomes more appealing for investors to remain long-term (Kwak et al., 2009; Zhang et al., 2019; Nguyen et al., 2021).

In addition, smart cities do best when growth is inclusive, aside from only focusing on profits. The laws require diversity among stakeholders and demand that urban changes support marginalized groups, meeting the goals of Sustainable Development Goal 10 (lessening inequality) (Kusumasari, 2015; Janssen et al., 2021; Bhattacharya & Pal, 2023). Mukheibir et al. mentioned that Johannesburg's efforts to integrate communities in PPP arrangements have made it possible for underprivileged individuals to use technology, go to school and find work (Mukheibir et al., 2019; Dlamini et al., 2022).

Active engagement and involvement of residents, local businesses and civil society organizations should be embedded throughout both the planning and implementation phases of any governance framework (Sager, 2018; Wang & Hsieh, 2021; Li et al., 2023). The Barcelona Smart City program requires that community feedback is included in PPP projects, making it easier to adapt developments for the local area and reduce differences in living standards (Reina & Grewal, 2021; Martínez et al., 2024). Involving local people increases social cohesion and stops projects from increasing divisions (Sager, 2018).

All stakeholders must work to ensure that anyone who wants to use new smart city services and technologies is not excluded by the cost. Rules that ensure critical services like broadband, transit and healthcare are affordable help many people access digital services and support social justice (Janssen et al., 2016; Bibri, 2020; Ojo et al., 2022). The example of Smart Dublin proves that it is possible to achieve equal distribution of digital services to different social and economic groups by applying subsidy and access rules (O'Hara & Hall, 2023; Clarke & Murphy, 2024).

Additionally, legal obligations in PPP contracts encourage private investors to work up to standards and answer to local communities (McKinsey & Company, 2018; Patel & Singh, 2023). When decision-making and project results are clear and there is legal oversight, people learn to trust the authorities more and the results last longer (Zhang & Choi, 2018; Suri et al., 2023).

Therefore, smart cities depend on using PPPs successfully, with the help of strict legal rules that keep investments safe and put the public first. These legal tools help make sure everyone gets the advantages of smart city development. The authors Zhang and Choi (2018), Kwak et al. (2009) and Kusumasari (2015) argue that having a comprehensive legal structure is necessary to support financing in smart cities and to make sure equity and transparency remain the main aspects.

CLIMATE ADAPTATION AND DISASTER RESILIENCE IN LEGAL FRAMEWORKS

Cities becoming bigger and more complex means they are now at greater risk from climate change and natural disasters. Because of higher seas, routine flooding, storms and increasing heatwaves, cities need to develop designs that are more flexible and tough. It is important for lawmakers to adapt to ensure regulations focus on environmental problems and are supportive of making cities resistant to climate change (Meerow et al., 2019; Sharifi & Yamagata, 2018; Ahern, 2018; Sainz de Murieta et al., 2021). Laws or urban development guidelines can request that cities build infrastructure such as flood preventers, sustainable drains and water management technology to help them handle climate emergencies (Ahern, 2018; Davis, 2015; Kabisch et al., 2020). In addition, green and other nature-based plans in cities should be given strong legal backing to increase their ecological security and help advance sustainable building in towns and cities (Raymond et al., 2017; Kabisch et al., 2020; Pauleit et al., 2021). Thanks to these policies and incentives, cities are able to handle disasters, recover in a timely way and maintain their activities over the long haul.

Strong climate-response strategies in cities are achieved largely through the laws that support sustainable building methods. For instance, places that often get heavy rainstorms or flooding at the coast need systems set up to stop flooding. Green roofs, permeable paving and rainwater harvesting, known as sustainable urban drainage systems, make communities safer from floods and cleaner by reducing runoff (Li et al., 2021; Davis, 2015; Xu et al., 2023). Lawmakers are making such systems mandatory, as happens in Rotterdam where SuDS regulations have made urban flooding less common and helped the environment (Kabisch et al., 2020; Roy et al., 2022).

Cities now rely on technology like smart meters, sensors and data analysis to make certain their water system is used and distributed as efficiently as possible (Goh & Tham, 2016; Li et al., 2022; Zhang et al., 2023). The use of these technologies is supported by financial aid, tax rebates and mandatory construction rules. With support from guidelines, Singapore's water grid relies on the latest data to prevent wasting water and improve the early warning process for droughts and floods (Tan et al., 2020; Lee et al., 2023). Legal help allows cities to handle changes in water availability because of climate change.

Using NbS (Nature-Based Solutions), cities have found that ecological resilience improves much more than if relying exclusively on engineering. By using urban forests, parks and green roofs, cities can reduce their temperatures, clean the air and hold onto water during storms (Beatley, 2011; Pauleit et al., 2021; Kabisch & Haase, 2018). New York City's Green Infrastructure Plan makes it legal for buildings to have green roofs and more green spaces which helps the city cope with climate change and supports good public health (Francis & Jensen, 2020; Robbins et al., 2023). Such areas also help people from many backgrounds feel included through pleasant leisure and mental health benefits which helps maintain equality and protect the environment (Wolch et al., 2018; Rigolon et al., 2022).

A wide range of efforts to enhance urban green spaces are shown by legal frameworks including setting up green facades in new construction, increasing the area of urban forests and ensuring existing greenery is protected (Zhao et al., 2018; Pauleit et al., 2021; Jiménez et al., 2023). They make it easier for communities to cope with climate change, encourage greater biodiversity and enhance where people live. Access to green areas helps to lessen health differences between groups in urban areas that are subject to environmental injustice (Rigolon, 2019; Wolch et al., 2021).

In these models, making sure local communities and groups hard hit by climate change are involved in urban planning is required by law shown in Sager (2018) and Meerow and Newell (2019). Thanks to these frameworks, resilience work is fair, meets different community needs and involves the people living there. The urban resilience strategy in Medellín shows how laws can support work with local groups on climate adaptation planning which improves cohesiveness and justice in society (Kahiluoto et al., 2021; Rodríguez et al., 2023).

Cities can become resilient and able to cope with disasters only with strong legal frameworks in place. Standards for flood control, smart water use, sustainable drains and using nature, plus rules for including all residents, help the city become more resilient and provide equal benefits to all residents. Davis (2015), Goh and Tham (2016), Beatley (2011), Zhao et al. (2018) and Meerow et al. (2019) point out that these tools direct urban development toward sustainability and ensure adequate adaptation, equal rights and a long future.

ADDRESSING BARRIERS IN SMART CITY IMPLEMENTATION

Both technology experts and those who plan cities have made important strides in this area; still, when it comes to applying smart city concepts, several challenges keep arising. Hardships here are linked to reluctance to use new technologies, shortage of money and different rules made by different regulators. For cities to move into sustainable, technologically advanced and efficient environments, they need strong and flexible laws (Yigitcanlar et al., 2020; Alawadhi et al., 2021; Gudmundsson & Wood, 2021). They maintain regulatory harmonization, advance development, increase international collaboration and include steps to support complex cities and the adoption of new technologies (Angelidou, 2018; Gudmundsson & Wood, 2021; Kummitha, 2020).

The resistance to new technologies is much stronger in developing areas as many are afraid of losing their jobs, having their privacy breached and not understanding the tools. Scholl and Scholl (2019) believe that when people or institutions are only familiar with traditional technologies, smart technology takes time to be adopted. Digital divides also play a part in increasing unequal treatment and slow the development of smart cities (Sætra, 2021; Van Dijk, 2020). For readiness and inclusivity to improve, government officials and citizens should be required by law to receive both educational and technological training (Janssen et al., 2021; Ojo et al., 2019). As an example, Seoul has a program where laws help local residents use technology which has increased the use of technology among all groups of people (Park & Kim, 2020).

Different rules and restrictions present a serious problem. A lack of standard data privacy, cybersecurity and technology rules in different places makes it complicated and risky to use new technologies (Angelidou, 2018; Giffinger et al., 2019; Kshetri, 2021). Zhang et al. (2022) point out that when legal rules are the same, it gets easier for cities to use new technologies and learn from each other globally. Policy coordination is well shown by the EU's Smart Cities and Communities program which supports urban innovation in several member nations (European Commission, 2021).

There are not enough funds to support all of the ideas for smart cities. Many municipal governments do not have the resources needed for major investments in infrastructure and new technologies (Kwak et al., 2009; Yigitcanlar et al., 2020; Melo & Costa, 2021). PPPs offer an efficient way to finance projects; however, they only succeed when private investors are supported by effective legal incentives, tools for reducing risks and strong protection of investments (Zhang & Choi, 2018; Lee et al., 2021). Reliance on Public-Private Partnerships proves that using legal frameworks smartly encourages private money and keeps public and environmental interests in mind (Tan & Wee, 2019; Lopez et al., 2022).

Implementing successful smart cities demands that governance involves many different stakeholders. When local residents, businesses and civil society organizations are mandated to take part by law, the government becomes more transparent and equitable (Sager, 2018; Reina & Grewal, 2021; Meijer & Bolívar, 2016). Participatory methods work against reinforcing class differences and encourage equality in technological resources (Janssen et al., 2021; Silva et al., 2020). In Barcelona, the law mandates consulting local communities in smart urban projects to help include everyone and adapt new ideas to the city's specific needs (Reina & Grewal, 2021).

Hence, it is critical to support the transformation towards a robust institution as large streams of data city solutions need governing policies that guarantee privacy, security and accountability and make sure marginalized communities are not left behind (Janssen et al., 2016; Kitchin, 2022; Taylor et al., 2020). Trust and the ability to manage complexity in an organization depend on clear and flexible institutions (Giffinger et al., 2019; Zaidi et al., 2021).

Thus, dealing with implementing smart cities requires strong rules that align laws, motivate progress and promote worldwide cooperation. Two examples are UN-Habitat's New Urban Agenda and the EU's Smart Cities Strategy which are part of the international drive in this area (UN-Habitat, 2018; European Commission, 2021). Scholl and Scholl (2019), Angelidou (2018), Kwak et al. (2009) and Janssen et al. (2016) assert that smart cities need a planned, joint effort by law, government and finances to be socially and digitally accessible and robust enough to last.

CONCLUSION

The idea of smart cities combines advanced technologies in city planning to achieve an efficient, sustainable, resilient and inclusive outcome. Nevertheless, technology alone cannot achieve successful growth in smart cities; different efforts such as rules and legal frameworks, are crucial (Angelidou, 2018; Yigitcanlar et al., 2020; Allam & Newman, 2018). Thanks to these regulations, city planning relying on innovation and sustainability fosters energetic cities that remain flexible and prosperous. Policies, laws and innovation working together make cities more efficient and support change as environmental, social and economic situations develop, while legal frameworks support the successful introduction of smart technologies long term (Neirotti et al., 2020; Giffinger & Gudrun, 2019; Komninos, 2020).

Smart city development connects governance, urban services, infrastructure and technology to help cities become sustainable, inclusive and better able to cope with challenges. By relying on legal instruments, standards, regulations and guidelines can be put in place for all stages of smart technology use. These are zoning laws, building codes, data privacy rules and commands managing public transportation and waste management systems (Janssen, et al., 2021; Kitchin, 2022; Silva et al., 2020). Good results for residents can be achieved if governments coordinate their city plans with technological progress. In practice, Singapore's urban strategies require following energy efficiency and data privacy rules, while trying to link transport and green infrastructure, representing its multidimensional approach (Tan et al., 2020; Yigitcanlar et al., 2021; Reddick & Chen, 2018). In their paper from 2020,

Neirotti et al. suggest that by joining environmental efforts with new technologies, smart cities can achieve better use of resources, lower waste and increase the use of renewable power.

Maintaining an urban environment where everyone can participate and take part, regardless of wealth or background, is a main function of legal rules. Rules that require universal design in public, transportation and housing areas support social fairness (Janssen et al., 2016; Bibri, 2020; Mora et al., 2019). Legal structures are necessary in smart cities to help distribute digital resources justly, build better public services, address the digital gap and promote low-cost housing and green development (Reina & Grewal, 2021; Dameri & Benevolo, 2019). Legal methods also encourage businesses to join in smart city projects, making sure profit goes along with the community's benefit (Kwak et al., 2019; Janssen et al., 2021; Lee et al., 2020).

Keeping a city sustainable is a key part of making it smart. Because of the rise in city populations, society is concerned about possible harm to the environment, so the government has introduced policies that order cities to use less energy, more renewable energy and save water (Rogers et al., 2020; Sharifi & Yamagata, 2018; Sharifi, 2021). More and more cities are using IoT sensors, smart grids and energy-saving home appliances, driven by incentives offered by the government to private groups and city authorities (Kumar et al., 2021; Stenström et al., 2022). Cities such as Copenhagen offer incentives for using green roofs and nature-based options which help the city become more sustainable and improve life for its residents (Beatley, 2018; Pauleit et al., 2021; Kabisch et al., 2019).

Urban development changes with the context it finds itself in, so its laws must also change. Urban resilience policies work against climate change, natural disasters and social upheaval, in part, by requiring the use of flood control, drainage and green spaces to lower heat levels (Meerow et al., 2019; Davis, 2015; Hamin & Gurran, 2021). Developing resilience in cities using smart technology allows them to overcome disasters and continue important services. To illustrate, using IoT technology in addition to the city's legal flood defense systems has made Rotterdam better able to respond to risks (Kabisch et al., 2020; Raymond et al., 2021).

Smart cities are possible worldwide thanks to both strong legal laws and agreements between countries and stronger institutions. The UN's New Urban Agenda and the EU's Smart Cities and Communities program encourage cities from different nations and continents to share knowledge, harmonize policies and cooperate (UN-Habitat, 2018; European Commission, 2021; Mah & Goh, 2021). Goh and Tham (2016) suggest that the participation of many countries improves regulation and rapidly increases the use of smart technologies in cities.

To conclude, research of the impacts of regulatory structure on smart city governance must be prioritized. According to Scholl and Scholl (2019), studies are needed to investigate how the laws guiding ICT impact technology adoption, services for citizens, cost management and individual engagement. Studying global approaches, scholars can figure out methods that reduce problems and help smart cities support their citizens, market and ecosystem. Creating sustainable smart cities means matching laws to the latest technology, supporting all community members and taking care of the environment, so that cities can keep up with changes in the next decades (Neirotti et al., 2020; Janssen et al., 2021; Komninos, 2020).

REFERENCES

Ahern, J. (2018). Urban landscape sustainability and resilience: The promise and challenges of integrating ecology with urban planning. *Landscape Ecology*, *33*(8), 1291–1301.

Alkathiri, A., Ahmad, M., & Alghamdi, A. (2023). Public-private partnerships in smart city infrastructure: Challenges and prospects. *Journal of Urban Management*, *12*(1), 45–59.

Allam, Z., & Jones, D. S. (2019). On the Smart City Concept and Smart City Governance. *International Journal of Public Administration*, *42*(7), 596–615.

Allam, Z., & Newman, P. (2018). Redefining the smart city: Culture, metabolism and governance. *Smart Cities*, *1*(1), 4–25. DOI: 10.3390/smartcities1010002

Angelidou, M. (2018). Smart City Policies: A Spatial Approach. *Cities (London, England)*, *78*, 4–13.

Batty, M., Axhausen, K. W., Giannotti, F., Pozdnoukhov, A., Bazzani, A., Wachowicz, M., Ouzounis, G., & Portugali, Y. (2019). Smart Cities of the Future. *The European Physical Journal. Special Topics*, *214*(1), 481–518. DOI: 10.1140/epjst/e2012-01703-3

Beatley, T. (2011). *Biophilic Cities: Integrating Nature into Urban Design and Planning*. Island Press. DOI: 10.5822/978-1-59726-986-5

Beatley, T. (2018). *Green cities of Europe: Global lessons on green urbanism.* Island Press.

Berke, P. R., Manta, E., & Stevens, A. (2018). Land Use Policies, Transit-Oriented Development, and Housing Affordability: A Review of Portland's Urban Growth Boundary. *Journal of Planning Education and Research*, *38*(4), 411–424.

Bhattacharya, S., & Pal, S. (2023). Inclusivity in urban development through PPPs: A sustainability perspective. *Sustainable Cities and Society*, *81*, 103868.

Bibri, S. E. (2019). The new smart city as a platform for pursuing sustainable urban development goals. *Sustainable Cities and Society*, *45*, 483–495.

Bibri, S. E. (2020). The IoT for smart sustainable cities of the future: An analytical framework for sensor-based big data applications for environmental sustainability. *Sustainable Cities and Society*, *45*, 230–253.

Bibri, S. E. (2020). The Role of Smart City Characteristics in Urban Sustainability: An Empirical Study of Cities. *Sustainable Cities and Society*, *62*, 102369.

Caragliu, A., Del Bo, C., & Nijkamp, P. (2019). Smart cities in Europe. *Journal of Urban Technology*, *22*(1), 65–82.

City of Toronto. (2019). *Digital Governance Framework*. Toronto Public Service.

Clarke, R., & Murphy, K. (2024). Bridging the digital divide: Policy and practice in equitable smart city initiatives. *Journal of Urban Technology*, *31*(2), 120–138.

Cocchia, A. (2018). Smart and digital city: A systematic literature review. In Dameri, R. P., & Rosenthal-Sabroux, C. (Eds.), *Smart City: How to Create Public and Economic Value with High Technology in Urban Space* (pp. 13–43). Springer.

Dameri, R. P., & Benevolo, C. (2019). Governing smart cities: The art of balancing innovation and regulation. *Journal of Urban Technology*, *26*(2), 29–45.

Davis, M. (2015). *Ecology of Fear: Los Angeles and the Imagination of Disaster*. Vintage Books.

Dlamini, N., Nkambule, N., & Masuku, M. (2022). Community engagement in public-private partnerships for urban development: Lessons from Johannesburg. *Urban Affairs Review*, *58*(4), 1011–1037.

Escobar, O., & Guzman, A. (2019). Digital inclusion and social equity in Medellín. *Journal of Urban Technology*, *26*(2), 57–75.

European Commission. (2021). *Smart cities and communities*.

European Commission. (2022). *The Urban Agenda for the EU: Action Plan 2020*. European Commission.

Francis, J., & Jensen, S. (2020). Green infrastructure and public health: A case study of New York City's green roofs. *Urban Forestry & Urban Greening*, *53*, 126733.

Giffinger, R., & Gudrun, H. (2019). Smart governance as key factor for urban development. *Theoretical and Empirical Researches in Urban Management*, *14*(3), 5–16.

Goh, C., & Tham, A. (2016). Sustainable smart cities: How Singapore is moving towards urban sustainability. *Urban Sustainability*, *4*(2), 123–139.

Goh, K. C., & Tham, K. W. (2016). Smart water systems for smart cities: Data analytics and IoT-enabled water grids. *Water (Basel)*, *8*(6), 266.

Greenfield, A. (2021). *Radical Technologies: The Design of Everyday Life* (2nd ed.). Verso Books.

Janssen, M., Charalabidis, Y., & Zuiderwijk, A. (2019). Benefits, Adoption Barriers and Myths of Open Data and Open Government. *Information Systems Management, 35*(4), 293–304.

Janssen, M., Charalabidis, Y., & Zuiderwijk, A. (2021). Benefits, adoption barriers and myths of open data and open government. *Information Systems Management, 38*(3), 239–255.

Kabisch, N.. (2020). Nature-based solutions to climate change mitigation and adaptation in urban areas: Linkages between science, policy and practice. *Ecological Economics*, *152*, 105–115.

Kabisch, N., & Haase, D. (2018). Green infrastructure for urban resilience: Challenges and opportunities. *Urban Ecology*, *35*(3), 345–354.

Kahiluoto, H.. (2021). Community-based urban resilience planning: The case of Medellín. *Sustainability*, *13*(5), 2652.

Kim, S., Lee, J., & Lee, Y. (2020). Legal frameworks for smart city public-private partnerships. *Government Information Quarterly*, *37*(4), 101481.

Kitchin, R. (2022). The data-driven city? Big data and smart urbanism. *Geography Compass*, *16*(1), e12657.

Komninos, N. (2020). *Intelligent cities: Innovation, knowledge systems and digital spaces*. Routledge.

Komninos, N., Bratsas, C., Kakderi, C., & Kakderi, A. (2018). Smart Cities and the Future Internet: Innovation Ecosystems, Platforms, and the Public Interest. *Technological Forecasting and Social Change*, *142*, 1–12.

Kumar, P., Singh, R., & Sharma, P. (2021). IoT and smart grids for sustainable urban energy management. *Energy Reports*, *7*, 3437–3446.

Kusumasari, B. (2015). Inclusion in public-private partnerships: Social equity in urban development. *Journal of Public Administration*, *49*(3), 277–292.

Kwak, S. Y., Choi, S. Y., & Park, K. (2009). Public-private partnerships for urban infrastructure development: Success factors and case studies. *Asian Journal of Public Affairs*, *2*(1), 23–37.

Kwak, S. Y., Lee, S., & Seo, M. (2019). Public-private partnerships for smart city development: A case study of Seoul. *Cities (London, England)*, *85*, 36–44.

Lee, J.. (2023). Smart water grid management through IoT and big data analytics: The Singapore model. *Journal of Cleaner Production*, *379*, 134664.

Lee, J., Lee, K., & Lee, M. (2020). Smart city governance: A comparative analysis. *Government Information Quarterly*, *37*(3), 101478.

Lee, S., & Lee, D. (2018). Songdo International Business District: A smart city case study. *Cities (London, England)*, *72*, 173–185.

Li, W., Zhang, H., & Chen, J. (2023). Enhancing community participation in smart city governance. *Cities (London, England)*, *134*, 104102.

Li, Y.. (2021). Sustainable urban drainage systems (SuDS) and their role in flood mitigation. *Water (Basel)*, *13*(4), 501.

Li, Z.. (2022). Smart sensor networks for efficient water resource management. *Sensors (Basel)*, *22*(12), 4567. PMID: 35746349

Low, S., & Lee, C. (2023). Sustainable infrastructure development through PPPs in Singapore: Legal and institutional perspectives. *International Journal of Urban Sciences*, *27*(1), 75–90.

Mah, A., & Goh, C. (2021). Transnational urban networks: Knowledge sharing and smart city development. *Cities (London, England)*, *108*, 102969.

Martínez, L., Garcia, P., & Torres, R. (2024). Citizen engagement in smart city PPP projects: The Barcelona model. *Journal of Urban Affairs*, *46*(1), 23–42.

McKinsey & Company. (2018). How to make public-private partnerships work for cities. McKinsey Global Institute Report.

Meerow, S., & Newell, J. P. (2019). Urban resilience for whom, what, when, where, and why? *Urban Geography*, *40*(3), 309–329. DOI: 10.1080/02723638.2016.1206395

Meerow, S., Newell, J. P., & Stults, M. (2019). Defining urban resilience: A review. *Landscape and Urban Planning*, *147*, 38–49. DOI: 10.1016/j.landurbplan.2015.11.011

Mora, L., Deakin, M., & Reid, A. (2019). Strategic principles for smart city development: A multiple case study analysis. *Journal of Urban Technology*, *26*(2), 3–28.

Mukheibir, P.. (2019). Integrating communities in climate resilience through legal frameworks: Johannesburg case study. *Climate Policy*, *19*(5), 598–610.

Mukheibir, P., Ziervogel, G., & Matarira, C. (2019). Inclusive urban governance through PPPs: A case study from Johannesburg. *Environment and Urbanization*, *31*(2), 557–574.

Müller, F. (2018). Legal frameworks and smart energy management in cities. *Energy Research & Social Science*, *35*, 122–130.

Neirotti, P., De Marco, A., Cagliano, A. C., Mangano, G., & Scorrano, F. (2020). Current Trends in Smart City Initiatives: Some Stylised Facts. *Cities (London, England)*, *38*, 25–36. DOI: 10.1016/j.cities.2013.12.010

Nguyen, T., Hoang, D., & Pham, H. (2021). Investment protection laws and their impact on smart city PPP projects in Asia. *Asian Journal of Law and Economics*, *12*(2), 245–267.

O'Hara, K., & Hall, W. (2023). Digital inclusion in smart cities: Lessons from Smart Dublin. *Information Polity*, *28*(1), 1–20.

Ojo, A., Curry, E., & Janowski, T. (2022). Smart city digital inclusion: A systematic review. *Government Information Quarterly*, *39*(3), 101685.

Patel, R., & Singh, A. (2023). Accountability in smart city PPPs: Legal obligations and community engagement. *International Journal of Public Sector Management*, *36*(1), 65–81.

Patterson, M.. (2018). Urban carbon emissions and legal frameworks for reduction. *Environmental Science & Policy*, *82*, 1–8.

Pauleit, S.. (2021). Nature-based solutions for sustainable cities. *Environmental Science & Policy*, *116*, 1–13.

Pauleit, S.. (2021). Urban green infrastructure and climate adaptation: Planning and implementation. *Nature-Based Solutions*, *1*(1), 100001.

Pucher, J., & Buehler, R. (2021). Sustainable urban transport in Amsterdam: Policies and outcomes. *Transport Reviews*, *41*(2), 179–200.

Raymond, C. M.. (2017). A framework for assessing and implementing urban nature-based solutions. *Environmental Science & Policy*, *77*, 15–24. DOI: 10.1016/j.envsci.2017.07.008

Reddick, C. G., & Chen, T. (2018). Smart city adoption: Looking through the lens of digital inclusion. *Government Information Quarterly*, *35*(4), 491–502.

Reina, A., & Grewal, S. (2021). Digital Inclusion Policies and Social Inclusion in Barcelona's Smart City. *Journal of Urban Affairs*, *43*(3), 393–410.

Reina, A., & Grewal, S. (2021). Social inclusion in smart cities: Barcelona's approach. *Journal of Urban Affairs*, *43*(4), 556–572.

Reina, J., & Grewal, P. (2021). Smart city governance and community inclusion in Barcelona. *Urban Studies (Edinburgh, Scotland)*, *58*(7), 1449–1466.

Reina, L., & Grewal, S. (2021). Digital inclusion policies in European smart cities. *Government Information Quarterly, 38*(4), 101583.

Reina, V., & Grewal, S. (2021). Digital inclusion and urban green space: Barcelona's legal approach. *Journal of Urban Technology, 28*(3), 1–19.

Rigolon, A. (2019). Green space and health equity: A systematic review. *Environmental Research, 174*, 86–95.

Rodríguez, D.. (2023). Legal frameworks for inclusive urban climate resilience: Lessons from Medellín. *Sustainability Science, 18*(1), 123–138.

Rogers, C., Brown, D., & Carter, J. (2021). Legal frameworks for smart city inclusivity and equity. *Sustainability, 13*(15), 8399.

Rogers, C. D. F., Shi, H., & Ng, A. K. Y. (2020). Towards sustainable and smart urban development. *Sustainable Cities and Society, 55*, 102040.

Rogers, E. M., Marakas, G. M., & Henley, J. (2021). Technology adoption and social equity in smart cities. *Technological Forecasting and Social Change, 170*, 120921.

Rogers, E. M., Singhal, A., & Quinlan, M. M. (2021). Diffusion of Innovations: A Communication Science Perspective. *The Annals of the American Academy of Political and Social Science, 608*(1), 102–122.

Sætra, H. S. (2021). Ethical challenges in smart city governance. *Science and Engineering Ethics, 27*(2), 20. PMID: 33765203

Sager, T. (2018). Participatory governance in urban development: Frameworks and case studies. *Planning Theory & Practice, 19*(2), 191–211.

Sager, T. (2018). Urban resilience and community participation in planning processes. *Planning Theory & Practice, 19*(1), 43–63.

Scholl, H. J., & Scholl, M. C. (2018). Smart governance: Co-creation of public value in smart cities. *Government Information Quarterly, 35*(3), 336–342.

Scholl, H. J., & Scholl, M. C. (2019). Smart city governance and the law. *Information Polity, 24*(1), 1–16. DOI: 10.3233/IP-150377

Scholl, H. J., & Scholl, M. C. (2019). Smart Governance: Concepts, Challenges, and Practices. *Communications of the Association for Information Systems, 44*, 42.

Sharifi, A., & Yamagata, Y. (2018). Principles and criteria for assessing urban energy resilience: A comprehensive review. *Renewable & Sustainable Energy Reviews, 82*, 476–488.

Sharifi, A., & Yamagata, Y. (2020). Principles and Criteria for Assessing Smart Sustainability: A Comparative Study of Asian Smart Cities. *Sustainable Cities and Society*, *45*, 383–398.

Sharma, K., & Mishra, S. (2022). Legal stability in smart city PPPs: Challenges and opportunities. *Journal of Urban Planning and Development*, *148*(4), 04022046.

Silva, B. N., Khan, M., & Han, K. (2020). Towards sustainable smart cities: A review of trends, architectures, components, and open challenges in smart cities. *Sustainable Cities and Society*, *38*, 697–713. DOI: 10.1016/j.scs.2018.01.053

Talen, E. (2017). Zoning and Urban Form. *Urban Studies (Edinburgh, Scotland)*, *54*(6), 1383–1398.

Tan, C. H., Singh, M., & Heng, C. H. (2021). Singapore's Green Plan 2030: Urban Sustainability Strategy. *Sustainability*, *13*(3), 1234.

Tan, E., & Tan, K. (2022). Urban infrastructure governance in Singapore's smart city development. *Asia Pacific Journal of Public Administration*, *44*(1), 57–73.

Tan, P. Y.. (2020). Singapore's Green Plan 2030: Legal frameworks for sustainable urban water management. *Environmental Science & Policy*, *107*, 99–109.

Tan, S. B., Kankanhalli, A., & Tan, C. W. (2020). Singapore's smart nation initiative: A case study. *Information Systems Frontiers*, *22*, 1407–1423.

Tan, Y. H., Goh, W. D., & Lee, L. H. (2020). Smart Nation Singapore: A multi-dimensional strategy for urban innovation. *Sustainability*, *12*(3), 845.

UN-Habitat. (2018). *New Urban Agenda*. United Nations Human Settlements Programme.

van den Bergh, J., & Botzen, W. J. W. (2022). Smart city governance and social equity in Amsterdam. *Sustainable Cities and Society*, *81*, 103873.

van den Bergh, J. C. J. M., & Botzen, W. J. W. (2022). Governance of Smart Cities: Insights from Amsterdam's Approach. *Environmental Innovation and Societal Transitions*, *45*, 123–136.

Wang, Y., & Hsieh, Y. (2021). Enhancing local stakeholder participation in smart city PPPs. *Sustainable Cities and Society*, *65*, 102601.

Wolch, J. R.. (2018). Urban green space, public health, and environmental justice: The challenge of equity in urban ecosystem services. *Landscape and Urban Planning*, *181*, 176–183.

Xu, H.. (2023). Sustainable urban drainage systems and legal mandates: Innovations in flood prevention. *Water Research*, *232*, 119619.

Yigitcanlar, T., Kamruzzaman, M., & Buys, L. (2021). Public-private partnerships for smart city sustainability. *Sustainable Cities and Society*, *64*, 102557.

Yigitcanlar, T., Kamruzzaman, M., & Foth, M. (2020). The smart city approach for urban innovation and sustainability. *Sustainable Cities and Society*, *61*, 102350.

Zhang, J., & Choi, S. (2018). Legal frameworks and risk sharing in smart city PPPs. *International Journal of Project Management*, *36*(5), 685–697.

Zhang, W., Li, H., & Xu, Y. (2019). Investment protection and PPP performance in smart cities. *Cities (London, England)*, *92*, 161–171.

Zhao, J.. (2018). Urban forestry legal frameworks and biodiversity conservation. *Urban Forestry & Urban Greening*, *31*, 125–134.

Ziegler, J., Baumann, S., & Hofmann, S. (2020). Data governance and privacy in smart cities: Legal frameworks and best practices. *Journal of Urban Technology*, *27*(4), 3–20.

KEY TERMS AND DEFINITIONS

Smart Cities: Smart cities leverage cutting-edge technologies such as the Internet of Things (IoT), artificial intelligence (AI), and big data analytics to enhance urban living. They focus on improving public services, optimizing resource use, and promoting sustainability while ensuring residents enjoy a higher quality of life through efficient, connected, and resilient urban environments.

Urbanization: Urbanization refers to the rapid growth of populations in urban areas, leading to increased demand for housing, infrastructure, transportation, and services. This trend presents both opportunities for economic development and challenges such as environmental stress, requiring sustainable planning to balance growth with resource conservation and social inclusion.

Legal Frameworks: Legal frameworks consist of the comprehensive set of laws, regulations, and policies that guide urban development, environmental protection, land use, data privacy, and governance. These frameworks ensure that smart city initiatives are implemented responsibly, transparently, and fairly, fostering sustainable growth while safeguarding citizens' rights and promoting social equity.

Zoning Laws: Zoning laws regulate how land within cities is allocated for various purposes such as residential, commercial, industrial, and green spaces. They prevent incompatible land uses, protect environmental quality, and encourage balanced urban development. Effective zoning supports public health, accessibility, and equitable distribution of resources within communities.

Sustainable Urban Planning: Sustainable urban planning integrates economic growth with environmental stewardship and social fairness. It involves implementing green building standards, renewable energy mandates, carbon emission controls, and inclusive policies to create cities that minimize ecological footprints, foster social inclusion, and provide long-term resilience to environmental and social challenges.

Public-Private Partnerships (PPPs): Public-private partnerships are collaborations where government entities work alongside private companies to fund, develop, and manage urban infrastructure projects. These partnerships combine public oversight with private sector efficiency, ensuring investments are sustainable, risks are shared, and projects contribute to equitable access and long-term benefits for all city residents.

Digital Inclusion and Social Equity: Digital inclusion and social equity policies ensure that all urban residents, especially marginalized populations, have affordable access to digital technologies, internet connectivity, education, and essential services. These measures aim to close digital divides, prevent social exclusion, and empower communities to fully participate in and benefit from smart city innovations.

Chapter 5
Sustainable Governance of Transgenic Fish in Malaysia:
Balancing Environmental Protection and Food Security

Farahdilah Ghazali
https://orcid.org/0000-0002-1966-9690
Universiti Putra Malaysia, Malaysia

Siti Tafzilmeriam Sheikh Abdul Kadir
Institute of Oceanography and Environment, Universiti Malaysia Terengganu, Malaysia

ABSTRACT

This chapter explores the crucial role of fish in global food security, particularly in Malaysia, where high consumption necessitates imports from neighboring countries. The aquaculture sector has emerged as a strategic solution to balance supply and demand with Asia leading global production. Over the years, advancements in biotechnology including in the aquaculture sector have enhanced aquaculture through genetic improvements, disease prevention and optimized breeding techniques. However, rapid expansion poses challenges such as environmental sustainability and regulatory oversight. The chapter examines international perspectives on transgenic fish, focusing on Norway and Australia's regulatory frameworks, biosecurity measures, and risk assessments. Malaysia's biosafety framework, including the Malaysian Biosafety Act 2007 and ASEAN Guidelines are also analyzed in this chapter to assess their effectiveness in protecting ecosystems and ensuring food security amid evolving aquaculture technologies.

DOI: 10.4018/979-8-3373-1792-2.ch005

INTRODUCTION

Fish are extremely valuable as a source of food around the world. In many countries, they are a staple of the diet and a vital source of revenue. Fish is a crucial component of the diets of millions, particularly in low-income countries, where it serves as an important source of essential nutrients that are not adequately supplied through other foods. Kawarazuka and Béné (2010) emphasize that fish is superior to many other animal-source foods in providing high-quality protein, essential fatty acids, vitamins, and minerals necessary for good health and nutrition (Kawarazuka & Béné, 2010). In fact, Malaysians consumed the second most fish per capita in Asia, after Japan, and ranked fifth in the world (York & Gossard, 2004). Malaysia needed to import these fishes from countries like Thailand and Indonesia to supply the huge demand (Goh, 2018). Goh (2018) stated that the aquaculture activities have begun to be promoted in order to assist in achieving a balance of fish supply and demand. Asia is the world's leading aquaculture producer, accounting for about 90% of global aquaculture output (Wei & Wee, 2014). Aquaculture now accounts for more than 30% of the global market for marine products (fish, molluscs, crustaceans, etc) (FAO/WHO 2003; Millar & Tomkins, 2007).

Recent data shows that the global fisheries and aquaculture sector continues to grow rapidly, reaching an all-time record production of 223.2 million tonnes in 2022 (FAO 2024). This includes 185.4 million tonnes (live weight) of aquatic animals and 37.8 million tonnes (wet weight) of algae, marking a 4.4% increase from 2020 (FAO 2024). This growth is driven primarily by Asian countries, which accounted for 70% of aquatic animal production led by China (36%), followed by India (8%), Indonesia (7%), Vietnam (5%), and Peru (3%) (FAO 2024). The production pattern also highlights a strong reliance on aquaculture, particularly in inland waters, where 84% of aquatic animals were farmed (FAO 2024).

Over the last few years, the aquaculture industry has achieved significant success by improving some of these aspects, reflecting it is ongoing importance in contributing to global food security, economic development, and livelihoods, especially in developing countries (Chen et al., 1995). The success of aquaculture depends on: (1) complete control of reproduction and the life cycle; (2) excellent genetic background of broodstock; (3) efficient detection and effective prevention of diseases; (4) thorough understanding of the optimal physiological, environmental, and nutritional conditions for growth and development; (5) adequate supply of good quality water; and (6) innovative thinking (Chen, 1995). According to Chen et al. (1995), the application of molecular biology and biotechnology will accelerate the industry's growth. A few of the applications include improving growth rates, controlling reproductive cycles, optimising feed composition, producing innovative immunizations, and developing disease-resistant and hardier genetic stocks (Chen et al., 1995). The challenge for the rapidly growing aquaculture industry is to develop and deploy technology that ensures sustainable production methods that reduce environmental damage, increase sector output, and retain fish's distinctive social and cultural qualities (Millar & Tomkins, 2007).

In light of the urgent need for sustainable food systems particularly given that approximately one-third of global food production, or 1.3 billion tonnes annually is wasted, contributing an estimated 3,300 million tonnes of CO2 emissions each year (Galanakis, 2020). The genetic modification in aquaculture is increasingly viewed as a rational and promising strategy to enhance global food security (Millar & Tomkins, 2007). This including the development of transgenic fish through techniques such as microinjection or electroporation (Chen et al., 1995), as well as chromosome manipulation aimed at enhancing desirable traits such as accelerated growth, disease resistance, and improved feed conversion efficiency (Maclean, 2003; Goos et al, 2001; Hew & Fletcher, 1997). The technique involves the incorporation of genes from one individual into the nuclear DNA of another, which could be of the same or different species (De Silva et al., 2008). Approximately 50 animal species/traits have been genetically modified (Amin et al. 2014; Cowx et al. 2010). The aquaculture sector is being challenged with a range of technological options, including the possibility of commercialising genetically modified (GM) fish (Millar & Tomkins, 2007). The modifications mostly involved fish species such as Atlantic salmon, common carp and tilapia (Amin et al., 2014).

Malaysia's unique scientific, socio-economic and cultural context plays a crucial role in shaping the development and governance of transgenic fish, highlighting important local realities such as scientific research, public perception and stakeholder engagement. For example, one of the primary species studied for transgenic applications in Malaysia is Nile tilapia (*Oreochromis niloticus*) with research focusing on growth performance and reproductive development following triploidy induction via heat shock (Razak et al., 1999). Additionally, Siti Hawa et al. (2019) emphasize the use of genetic technologies to enhance the resilience of indigenous freahwater fish species while Lim and Ooi (2020) investigate Malaysian consumers concerns regarding food safety and environmental impacts, underscoring the importance of ongoing public education and dialogue. Furthermore, Abdul Rahman et al. (2018) evaluate the economic potential of transgenic fish in increasing aquaculture productivity and its effects on small-scale fishing communities, pointing to the need for supportive policies and comprehensive training programs. Recent research including Mohd Noor et al. (2022), highlights the promise of CRISPR technology to accelerate associated with enforcing GMO regulations in Malaysia. These studies also reveal significant knowledge gaps and critical issues such as the scarcity of long-term ecological assessments on transgenic fish in Malaysian waters and the urgent need for more effective biosafety law enforcement.

This chapter examines the international legal landscape concerning transgenic (GMO) fish, regulatory approaches adopted by Norway and Australia. Norway is a leading nation in aquaculture, particularly salmon farming. Its extensive experience and well-established regulatory framework for conventional aquaculture provide a relevant context for understanding how a major seafood producer approaches the potential introduction of transgenic fish (Afewerki et al, 2023). While Australia has a significant marine environment and experience in developing aquaculture sector. Australia's strong emphasis on biosecurity and the protection of its unique biodiversity including matters relevant to the environmental release of transgenic organisms (Kirkpatrick et al., 2017). Their experience with environmental risk assessment and management in a diverse ecosystem offers a valuable comparative lens. This chapter also discuss Malaysia's specific biosafety framework, particularly in the context of the ASEAN Guidelines on Risk Assessment of Agriculture-related Genetically Modified Organisms and the Biosafety Act 2007 (Act 678) and other relevant legislation. The analysis will further evaluate the sufficiency of the Malaysian and ASEAN approaches in safeguarding the marine environment and ensuring food security in relation to transgenic fish.

THE ROLES OF TRANSGENIC FISH FOR GLOBAL FOOD SECURITY

Fisheries and Food Security

Food insecurity is a global problem affecting the entire planet as the lack of food, particularly quality food, not only contributes to malnutrition of the population, but on a wider scale is also the main slowing element of rural territories, leading to hunger, poverty, and unemployment (Lugo-Morin, 2020). The rise of aquaculture has emerged as a critical solution to global food security, especially as traditional fisheries face challenges due to overfishing and declining wild fish stocks. As the world's population continues to grow, the demand for seafood as a source of protein is surging, necessitating the expansion of aquaculture practices. Aquaculture, defined as the cultivation of aquatic organisms in controlled environments, is recognized as the fastest-growing food production sector globally, contributing significantly to nutritional security and livelihoods (Ottinger et al., 2018; Troell et al., 2014).

The contribution of aquaculture to food security is multi-faceted. It provides a reliable and consistent source of high-quality protein while reducing pressure on overexploited marine resources (Henriksson et al., 2021). According to Nogueira and Botelho, aquaculture now accounts for nearly 50% of the fish consumed worldwide, illustrating its vital role in meeting global protein demands (Nogueira & Botelho,

2021). As marine captured struggle to maintain catches, aquaculture serves as a crucial alternative, helping to alleviate food shortages and improve food availability in many regions (Strutt et al., 2024). Environmental sustainability is a central theme in discussions about the rise of aquaculture. Golden et al. (2021) emphasize that aquaculture generally results in lower greenhouse gas emissions and land use compared to terrestrial animal farming systems, suggesting that it is a more sustainable method of producing animal protein (Golden et al., 2021). However, it is essential to consider the ecological impacts associated with aquatic food production, such as habitat destruction, pollution and disease outbreaks.

In this context, transgenic fish research has significantly contributed to scientific knowledge by enabling the development of advanced genomic tools and molecular techniques such as CRISPR and TALENs (Maclean & Laight, 2000; Chen et al., 2016). It has also provided deeper insights into fish physiology, metabolism, and growth pathways (Devlin et al., 2001; Sundström et al., 2007), enhanced our understanding of gene-environment interactions (Kapuscinski et al., 2007) and supported the advancement of biotechnology education and the training of scientists (Fletcher et al., 2004). The contributions that are crucial for developing more sustainable and ecologically responsible aquaculture practices.

Recent advances in genome editing (e.g., CRISPR-Cas9) and synthetic biology offer significant potential to improve aquaculture in Malaysia by enhancing traits like disease resistance and growth (Jinek et al., 2012; Kanchiswamy, 2016). However, these technologies also present new regulatory challenges as existing laws like the Biosafety Act 2007 may not fully cover genome edited or synthetic biology products (Khatri-Chhetri & Ahmad, 2021). To ensure sustainable and safe use, Malaysia needs to update its biosafety framework, build capacity for risk assessment and engage stakeholders to address ethical and environmental concerns (Almeida & Agrawal, 2020; Thompson, 2019). Aligning regulations with international standards will help Malaysia harness these innovations responsibly while protecting biodiversity and public health (CBD, 2000; FAO, 2019).

Aquaculture and Sustainable Development Goals

Aquaculture also significantly contributes to economic growth and poverty alleviation, particularly in developing countries where millions rely on fish farming for their livelihoods. The integration of aquaculture within local economies supports job creation and provides income opportunities for smallholders. Efforts to innovate and improve aquaculture practices including the development of sustainable feed alternatives and disease-resistant species through genome editing—show promise for enhancing production efficiency while also addressing environmental concerns (Gratacap et al., 2019; Wang & Cheng, 2023).

The sector's future aligns with multiple Sustainable Development Goals (SDGs), particularly SDG 2 (Zero Hunger) and SDG 14 (Life Below Water). Aquaculture practices that prioritize sustainable resource management and socio-economic development not only enhance food security but also reinforce ecosystem resilience (Strutt et al., 2024). Policies promoting responsible aquaculture development are critical in ensuring that the industry's growth contributes positively to food security without compromising environmental integrity (Henriksson et al., 2021). Moreover, the economic implications of integrating transgenic fish into aquaculture systems contribute to broader sustainable development objectives. By potentially lowering production costs and enhancing competitiveness in the global marketplace, transgenic fish can stimulate economic growth (SDG 8: Decent Work and Economic Growth) and contribute to poverty alleviation (SDG 1: No Poverty). This, in turn, underpins improvements in community welfare and resilience, as more robust and diversified aquaculture sectors can provide stable livelihoods and support local economies (Bennett et al., 2021).

Transgenic fish are expected to grow faster and larger than their non-GM counterparts. This characteristic can substantially increase fish production, particularly in regions where traditional aquaculture practices struggle to meet the nutritional demands of the population. (Pradeepkiran, 2019). The introduction of genetically enhanced fish species could improve supply chains and food production systems, potentially alleviating food scarcity in vulnerable regions (Asche et al. 2015). The rapid growth rates of transgenic fish mean that farmers can harvest their stock more frequently, providing a more reliable and sustainable source of animal protein (Cebeci et al., 2020).

When transgenic fish are produced in aquaculture systems, they not only satisfy the growing demand for protein but also provide critical micronutrients that enhance overall dietary diversity and health, combating malnutrition, especially in vulnerable communities (Chan et al., 2021; Obiero et al., 2019).

POTENTIAL ENVIRONMENTAL RISKS OF TRANSGENIC FISH

Transgenic fish are examined in terms of their production history, including molecular details of the genes used and the modifications obtained, as well as the current and future contributions of transgenic fish to scientific research, medicine, and aquaculture (Maclean, 2003). Since the first transgenic fish were grown in China in 1985, a variety of transgenes, procedures, and species have been used to develop transgenic fish (Dunham & Winn, 2014). The majority of transgenic fish research has focused on improving growth in commercially important fish species (Nam et al., 2007). Maclean & Talwar (1984) with eggs of rainbow trout (*Oncorhynchus mykiss*) and Zhu et al. (1985) with eggs of goldfish (*Carassius auratus*) accomplished the first success in microinjecting cloned gene sequences into fish eggs simultaneously and independently (Nam et al., 2007). While GM salmon was the first genetically modified animal in the United States to be approved for human consumption (Aerni, 2004; Frewer et al., 1997). Antifreeze protein genes or salmon growth hormone gene constructs were used to create the GM Atlantic salmon (Amin et al., 2014).

Gene transfer research have been carried in over 35 teleost species, the majority of which are important in aquaculture (Figueiredo, et al. 2007; Zbikowska, 2003). According to studies, using GM fish in aquaculture will increase productivity by increasing feed conversion ratios and decreasing the time required for a single production cycle for on-shore facilities (Aerni, 2004; Goos et al. 2001; Millar & Tomkins 2007). The development of commercially useful GM fish strains began with the goal of increasing growth rate, but efforts have since expanded to include disease resistance (Dunham et al., 2002; Jhingan et al., 2003; Mao et al., 2004). Fish losses due to infections are a significant problem in aquaculture production around the world, so developing disease-resistant fish strains is of great commercial interest (Millar & Tomkins, 2007). Increased freeze resistance/cold tolerance in harsh conditions; better tolerance to contaminants; control of sterility; improved nutritional characteristics and food utilisation to lessen the need for fish-based diets are some of the other goals of GM research (Hew & Fletcher, 2001; Maclean 2003).

Other studies have shown that administering recombinant fish or mammalian growth hormone (GH) to juvenile fish or oysters resulted in significant growth enhancement, which improves the growth rates of marine animals by manipulating GH or its gene (Chen, 1995). At least 14 fish and shellfish species have been genetically manipulated for higher growth rate in other research, including Coho salmon, Atlantic salmon, Rainbow trout, Common carp, Arctic charr, and Tilapia (Millar & Tomkins, 2007). More new techniques to modification are centred on the use of vegetable products in aquacultural systems, with attempts to change salmonoids glucose metabolism and phytate utilisation (Hostetler et al., 2005; Maclean, 2003). According to Millar & Tomkins (2007), stated that fish could potentially be transformed to offer more nutritional food products. One example is the genetic modification of rainbow trout to increase the amount of omega-3 fatty acid that they produce and store (Kok & Jones, 2004). GM techniques are also being developed in order to improve pathogen resistance and prevent the release of modified genes into the environment (Zbikowska, 2003).

Salmonid studies show that transgenic fish expressing exogenous GH constructs (e.g., OnMTGH1 and CMVOnGH1) exhibit dramatic growth enhancement (Buwono et al., 2021; Higgs et al. 2009; Pitkänen et al. 1999). Furthermore, transgenic *Clarias gariepinus* growth hormone (CgGH) technology, which was successfully developed for mutiara catfish (*C. gariepinus*), causes significantly greater growth in transgenic fish; second-generation (G2) animals showed a 150–200 percent increase in growth compared to non-transgenic fish (Buwono et al., 2019a). CgGH transmission in the G2 strain achieved 50% in a prior study, confirming Mendelian transmission and implying that these fish can be utilised to make G3 catfish (Buwono et al., 2021). The goal of this study was to assess mass production of G3 transgenic mutiara catfish, which necessitates large levels of exogenous GH expression and transmission; hence, transgene inheritance must be stable over generations of transgenic fish (Buwono et al., 2021; Wang et al., 2001). G2 transgenic tilapia (125 percent increase) and G5 transgenic Atlantic salmon (*Salmo salar*) were two more fish species that profited from this technology (100 percent increase) (Buwono et al. 2021; Levesque et al. 2008; Rahman et al. 2021).

According to Buwono et al. (2021), GH-transgenic salmon regulate energy metabolism by turning feed carbohydrates into metabolic energy rather than protein to promote protein synthesis (protein sparing) (increased protein retention). This improved protein use efficiency allows for faster growth (Buwono et al. 2021; Levesque et al. 2008). The growth hormones including transgenic GH also promote amino acid absorption particularly essential amino acids that cannot be synthesised in the fish (Buwono et al. 2021; Farmanfarmaian & Sun 1999; Li et al. 2009). Protein use efficiency as measured by protein productive value (PPV) was determined in stinging catfish (*Heteropneustes fossilis*) fingerlings by the content of essential amino acids in fish feed (Buwono et al., 2021; Farhat & Khan, 2012). As a result, the maximum growth potential of transgenic fish is determined by the quality of feed protein, which includes both protein content and amino acid composition (Buwono et al. 2021; Cowey 1994). Protein retention, amino acid content, and growth of transgenic fish are all influenced by feed composition. 2021) (Buwono et al., 2021).

However, the potential use of these technologies raises a number of serious ethical concerns (Millar & Tomkins, 2007). Several studies have attempted to identify the factors influencing consumer acceptance of genetically modified salmon in Europe and the United States (Amin et al., 2014). Millar & Tomkins (2007) used an ethical framework to investigate a range of ethical dilemmas that could arise from the usage of GM technologies in aquaculture. Several key issues have been identified, including aspects of distributive justice for producers, use of a precautionary approach in the management of environmental risk and food safety, and the impact on fish welfare and intrinsic value (Millar & Tomkins, 2007).

The significant issues such as ecological consequences, food safety, biodiversity, animal welfare, and others have been raised and make controversial for the industry (Millar & Tomkins, 2007). Such authorizations may only be granted subject to the provision that there is no reason to believe that the release could have any adverse effect on human health or the environment (Millar & Tomkins, 2007). The potential deliberate release of transgenic fish without containment measures raises public concern about environmental risk (Millar & Tomkins, 2007). Furthermore, bred and genetically modified fish may pose a threat to fish health (e.g., fish illnesses caused by high stock densities) and the environment (e.g., the escape of farmed fish into the aquatic environment) (Aerni 2004). The diseases may be introduced into farmed and wild stocks as a result of the introduction of new species (Millar & Tomkins 2007). However, even with improved containment facilities and fish sterilisation techniques, a zero risk cannot be guaranteed (Aerni, 2004).

With a focus on the United States, Aerni (2004) explores public and scientific arguments concerning the risks and benefits of aquaculture and aquatic biotechnology around the world. The public's perception of genetically modified salmon is a complex issue that should be viewed as a multi-faceted process (Amin et al., 2014). The most important direct determinants of GM salmon encouragement are specific application-related judgments of religious tolerance, followed by perceived risks and benefits, familiarity, and the general promise of modern biotechnology (Amin et al., 2014). Encouraging GM salmon also involves the interaction of other factors such as general biotechnology concerns, threatening the natural order of things, the need for labelling, the need for patenting, regulatory confidence, and societal values (Amin et al., 2014).

The Malaysian government's commitment to establishing good governance on GM through the gazetting of the Biosafety Act 2007 is a positive step toward regulating organisms and their products (Aliaziz & Ab Rahman, 2018). Aliaziz & Ab Rahman (2018) stated that more work is required to ensure comprehensive protection for humans, animals, plants, and the environment, as well as more research and study to improve GM governance in Malaysia. According to Millar & Tomkins (2007), all issues require further investigation and consideration before a decision can be made on the extent to which commercial production of first-generation GM fish will violate the principle of wellbeing and autonomy.

However, several significant scientific breakthroughs are required to realise the full potential of transgenic fish technology in aquaculture or other biotechnological applications (Chen et al., 1995). These include: (1) more efficient technologies for mass gene transfer, (2) targeted gene transfer technologies such as embryonic stem cell gene transfer or ribozyme gene inactivation, (3) suitable promoters to direct the expression of transgenes at optimal levels during the desired developmental stages, (4) identified genes of desirable traits for aquaculture and other applications, (5) information on the physiological, nutritional, immunological and environmental factors that maximize the performance of the transgenics, and (6) safety and environmental impacts of transgenic fish. Once these problems are resolved, the commercial application of the transgenic fish technology will be readily attained (Chen et al., 1995).

INTERNATIONAL REGULATORY FRAMEWORK REGULATIONS REGARDING TRANSGENIC

The Convention on Biological Diversity (CBD)

The Convention on Biological Diversity (CBD) is an international treaty adopted in 1992 during the Earth Summit in Rio de Janeiro. Its primary objectives are to conserve biological diversity, promote the sustainable use of its components, and ensure the fair and equitable sharing of benefits arising from the use of genetic resources. The CBD recognizes that biodiversity is essential for sustaining life on Earth, providing food security, medicines, fresh air and water and a clean and healthy environment. Article 14 of the CBD specifically mandates that signatory nations conduct environmental impact assessments for projects likely to harm biological diversity, aiming to minimize such effects. This includes consulting with neighbouring states before introducing non-native species into transboundary aquatic ecosystems, a recommendation that extends to genetically modified organisms (GMOs). By promoting international cooperation and thorough impact assessments, the CBD aims to protect biodiversity from the potential risks associated with GMOs.

Cartagena Protocol on Biosafety (CPB)

The Cartagena Protocol on Biosafety (CPB) is an international agreement under the Convention on Biological Diversity, adopted on January 29, 2000, and effective since September 11, 2003. Its primary aim is to ensure the safe handling, transport, and use of living modified organisms (LMOs) resulting from modern biotechnology that may have adverse effects on biological diversity, while also considering risks to human health. The protocol establishes procedures for the safe transfer, handling, and use of LMOs, with a particular focus on transboundary movements. It requires parties to implement measures to prevent unintentional releases and to ensure that any intentional introduction of LMOs into the environment is done in a manner that minimizes potential risks. The protocol also emphasizes the importance of public awareness and participation in decision-making processes related to LMOs. One of the primary roles of the CPB is to promote a precautionary approach to the risk assessment and management of LMOs, which inherently includes transgenic fish (Hill & Sendashonga, 2006) address concerns regarding the potential adverse effects that LMOs might impose on biological diversity and human health, particularly the ecological risks from the introduction of genetically altered species into the environment (Hill & Sendashonga, 2006). This becomes crucial in aquaculture, where transgenic fish could potentially interact with wild populations, disrupt local ecosystems or introduce new pathogens.

Furthermore, the CPB mandates countries to devise robust regulatory frameworks for GMOs, thereby driving national policies globally. For instance, Kenya has developed a national biosafety framework that aligns with the principles outlined in the CPB (Kunyanga et al., 2024). The regulatory instruments derived from the Protocol focus on comprehensive measures that span the entire lifecycle of LMOs, including research and development, commercialization, and post-release monitoring stages (Singh et al., 2020a). These measures are pertinent to transgenic fish, as they undergo similar scrutiny to other LMOs regarding environmental impact and biological safety.

The implementation of biosafety measures becomes particularly critical. The CPB has reinforced the precautionary principle—advocating for caution in the introduction of GMOs into ecosystems and mandating thorough risk assessments before release (Gupta & Falkner, 2006). For instance, transgenic aquatic species must undergo environmental risk assessments, which are essential in evaluating the likelihood of gene transfer to wild populations and assessing the ecological consequences of such events. Moreover, the principles established by the CPB have sparked significant discussions regarding the governance of transgenic fish research and commercial practices. The regulatory landscape influenced by the CPB encourages transparency and public involvement in decision-making processes related to the approval and monitoring of GMOs, including transgenic fish (Reis & Guedes, 2017). This inclusivity addresses public concerns and promotes informed consent regarding biotechnology's implications for food security and environmental conservation.

However, the interpretation and implementation of CPB-related regulations may vary by signatory country, leading to a heterogeneous regulatory environment for transgenic fish globally (Singh et al., 2020a; Rosado & Eriksson, 2021). This inconsistency can create challenges in international trade and technology transfer, as countries grapple with differing biosafety standards.

FAO Code of Conduct for Responsible Fisheries (CCRF)

The FAO Code of Conduct for Responsible Fisheries (CCRF) supports the responsible use of biotechnologies and the movement of alien species, including transgenic fish. It encourages states to establish legal and administrative frameworks for responsible aquaculture development, ensuring that such activities are conducted sustainably and ethically. The CCRF emphasizes the importance of minimizing environmental impacts and protecting biodiversity, which aligns with the goals of the CBD. For transgenic fish, this means implementing rigorous management practices to prevent escapes and mitigate potential ecological impacts. By adhering to the CCRF, countries can promote sustainable aquaculture practices that balance the benefits of biotechnology with the need to protect aquatic ecosystems.

Codex Alimentarius

The Codex Alimentarius is a collection of internationally recognized standards, guidelines, and codes of practice aimed at ensuring food safety and fair practices in the food trade. Developed by the Food and Agriculture Organization (FAO) and the World Health Organization (WHO), the Codex includes specific guidelines for the safety assessment of foods derived from GMOs. These guidelines provide a scientific basis for evaluating the safety of GMOs, focusing on potential health risks such as allergenicity and toxicity. Governments can use these guidelines to develop their own regulatory frameworks for GMOs. The Codex principles ensure that GM foods undergo rigorous safety assessments before they are approved for market entry, thereby protecting consumer health and maintaining food safety standards.

Codex guidelines stipulate a comparative analysis for safety evaluation, which involves comparing the composition and nutritional profile of genetically modified organisms (GMOs), such as transgenic fish, with their non-modified counterparts (Bedair & Glenn, 2020). This process ensures that any potential risks—including allergenicity, toxicity, and overall nutritional value are thoroughly assessed before these products enter the market. Goodman indicates that regulators consider various safety factors such as allergenicity, toxicity and environmental impacts within the context of international agreements like Codex and those concerning biosafety (Goodman, 2024).

Moreover, the Codex has published guidelines that pertain specifically to the introduction of GMOs into the food supply. These include protocols for assessing the potential allergenicity of novel proteins derived from transgenic organisms. According to the Codex guidelines, a protein may be deemed potentially allergenic if it closely resembles known allergens in its amino acid sequence (Dimitrov et al., 2013). This criterion is essential in guiding producers and regulatory bodies as they evaluate the safety of transgenic fish intended for human consumption. These guidelines also encompass nutritional standards that transgenic fish must meet.

The safety assessment of transgenic fish, based on Codex Alimentarius guideline includes several key elements. These involve allergenicity testing to determine whether newly introduced proteins have the potential to trigger allergic reactions, as well as short- and long-term toxicity studies using model organisms (Codex Alimentarius Commission, 2009). Nutritional analysis is also conducted to compare the nutrient composition between transgenic and conventional fish. Environmental impact assessments are carried out to evaluate risks to biodiversity and non-target species (FAO/WHO, 2003). It is also important to establish clear thresholds or acceptable limits for each safety parameter to ensure effective monitoring and regulation. For instance, they address the permitted levels of various substances, such as histamines in fish (Demircan & Özdestan, 2021), and advocate for sustainable practices in aquaculture to ensure that transgenic fish contribute positively to food security without compromising public health. The overall objective is to promote safe food production while allowing for fair trade practices, including the trade of transgenic fish on the global market (Goodman et al., 2016).

European Union Regulations

The regulatory landscape for transgenic fish within the European Union (EU) is shaped by a comprehensive framework that governs genetically modified organisms (GMOs) and includes specific directives and regulations aimed at ensuring species safety, environmental protection, and public health. The European Union (EU) has established a comprehensive regulatory framework to manage the release and use of genetically modified organisms (GMOs), including transgenic fish. Directive 2001/18/EC of the European Parliament and of the Council, dated 12 March 2001, governs the deliberate release of GMOs into the environment. This directive mandates that EU Member States ensure the intentional release of GMOs is only permissible if it complies with specific containment measures to protect public health and the environment. Prior to any intentional release, a notification must be submitted to the national competent authority of the Member State where the release will occur. This notification must include a detailed dossier as outlined in Annex III of the Directive, an environmental risk assessment consistent with Annex II, explicit consent for the release, a monitoring plan to detect adverse effects on human health and the environment, and public disclosure of information regarding the release and its results, allowing for public feedback.

The gene flow from GMOs or transgenic organisms is strictly regulated within the Europe Union (EU) through comprehensive preventive measures aimed at avoiding genetic contamination of wild populations. The EU has established clear limits and restrictions on the use and release of transgenic organisms into the environment supported by mandatory long term ecosystem risk assessments, monitoring mechanisms and legal enforcement. These requirements are outlined in Directive 2001/18/EC, which governs the deliberate release of GMOs and mandates environmental risk assessments to prevent adverse effects on biodiversity and public health (European Parliament & Council, 2001). Further strengthened by Commission Directive (EU) 2018/350, the framework requires evaluation of both intended and unintended effects, including potential gene transfer to non-target organisms and cumulative environmental impacts (European Commission, 2018). Additionally, the EU applies the precautionary principle ensuring that preventive action is taken even amid scientific uncertainty to safeguard ecological integrity and human health (Wolt et al., 2023; Van der Meer et al., 2023).

In addition to environmental regulations, the EU also imposes strict controls on GMOs in foodstuffs through Regulation No. 1829/2003. This regulation prohibits the marketing of GMOs for food use, or food containing or consisting of GMOs, unless authorized. The regulation specifically applies to food and feed produced "from" GMOs, excluding those produced "with" GMOs. The key criterion is the presence of material derived from a GMO in the food or feed. If no GMO material is present, the food or feed does not fall under the scope of Regulation 1829/2003. This regulatory approach ensures that any GMO-related food products undergo rigorous assessment and authorization processes to safeguard consumer health and maintain environmental integrity.

One of the critical aspects of the EU directives regarding transgenic fish involves pre-market risk assessments required for all GMOs. The European Food Safety Authority (EFSA) is tasked with evaluating the safety of these organisms before they can be approved for use. This includes assessing potential environmental impacts, such as gene flow to wild populations. While the specific studies by Devos et al. address coexistence in agricultural crops, they highlight similar environmental considerations applicable to aquatic species, regarding the potential for transgenic fish to disrupt local ecosystems (Devos et al., 2009). Furthermore, the EU regulations also address the necessity for effective traceability and labelling of transgenic fish and their products. EU directives stipulate that all foods derived from GMOs, including transgenic fish, must be clearly labelled to inform consumers, which aligns with the emphasis on consumer choice and transparency in biotech governance (Fraiture et al., 2023).

The directive also advocates for suitable safety assessments, which may include feeding trials to evaluate the long-term effects of transgenic fish on health, akin to the requirements for GM crops. In this regard, frameworks ensure that potential allergenic effects, as mandated by the Codex Alimentarius guidelines, are thoroughly investigated prior to the introduction of transgenic fish into the food chain (Hong et al., 2017). Moreover, the EU's approach to transgenic organisms underscores a precautionary principle, where the potential risks associated with genetic modification compel regulators to prioritize safety and public opinion. The diverse political and social attitudes towards GMOs in the EU have shaped stringent regulations that influence the development and marketing of transgenic fish, often reflecting broader societal concerns about genetic engineering in food production (Zimny, 2015).

REGULATIONS IN ASEAN

The ASEAN Guidelines on Risk Assessment of Agriculture-Related Genetically Modified Organisms (GMOs) were endorsed in 1999. These guidelines aim to establish a unified framework within ASEAN for assessing the risks associated with the transboundary movement of agriculture-related GMOs. The primary objective is to ensure that all ASEAN Member Countries adopt a consistent approach to evaluating the potential impacts of GMOs on human health and the environment.

The scope of these guidelines encompasses two main areas: the assessment of risks posed by agriculture-related GMOs to human health and the environment, and the provision of a scientific basis for decision-making regarding the release of such GMOs in ASEAN Member Countries. The guidelines specifically address food safety concerns and the release of genetically modified agricultural organisms whose genetic material has been altered in ways that are unlikely to occur through natural mating or recombination. By providing a structured approach to risk assessment, these guidelines aim to facilitate informed and scientifically grounded decisions on the use and release of GMOs within the ASEAN region.

Each country shall establish its own National Authority on Genetic Modification (NAGM), comprising representatives from national agencies involved in agriculture, trade, economics, environment, health, science and technology, and any other relevant sectors. The NAGM is responsible for reviewing and approving proposals related to the release of agriculture-related GMOs, ensuring compliance with national guidelines, and providing advice on related matters. It may establish sub-committees of experts to assess specific risks as needed. The NAGM must also provide public access to information on planned releases, harmonize guidelines with regional and international practices, and establish mechanisms for information exchange with counterpart NAGMs in ASEAN member countries and other overseas agencies. Additionally, the NAGM must update the ASEAN Secretariat on any changes in its composition and inform it of all approvals for the registration of agriculture-related GMOs. All GMOs brought into any ASEAN member country must comply with existing national and international regulations. The NAGM can grant approval for the release of GMOs, grant conditional approval, prohibit release with written reasons, or request additional information to complete the assessment before making a final decision.

PRACTICE FROM OTHER JURISDICTIONS

Lesson Learnt from Norway

One significant aspect of transgenic fish production in Norwegian aquaculture involves the genetic interactions between farmed and wild fish populations. Studies have shown that Atlantic salmon populations have faced substantial genetic introgression from escaped farmed salmon, which has implications for native genetic diversity and resilience (Glover et al., 2013; Glover et al., 2012). This genetic mixing occurs as a result of farmed fish escaping into the wild, a recurring problem in Norway's aquaculture sector (Zhang et al., 2012). In addition to genetic concerns, disease management represents another critical aspect of transgenic fish farming in Norway. The prevalence of pathogens such as the infectious salmon anaemia virus (ISAV) within farmed populations has been documented, with evidence of disease outbreaks linked to specific farming practices (Lyngstad et al., 2012; Aunsmo et al., 2022). The production of transgenic salmon with enhanced disease resistance could mitigate the acute risk of viral infections and improve overall farmed fish health, significantly impacting the landscape of disease cycles in Norwegian salmon farming (Nylund et al., 2019).

Environmental impacts also warrant attention when discussing transgenic fish in Norwegian aquaculture. Intensive farming practices contribute to nutrient pollution that affects coastal ecosystems (Wang et al., 2012). The introduction of transgenic fish may shift these dynamics by potentially decreasing the reliance on high-fishmeal diets, thereby supporting more sustainable aquaculture practices (Osmond & Colombo, 2019). However, rigorous regulatory frameworks are necessary to manage the environmental implications of introducing genetically modified species into wild and farmed habitats. Furthermore, the incorporation of transgenic technologies into stock management and breeding programs has the potential to enhance the overall fitness of farmed fish populations. Recent research indicates that careful genetic selection and breeding strategies could lead to optimal adaptations that enhance not only growth performance but also survivability in both farmed and wild settings (Glover et al., 2017). Such advancements are crucial in coping with the changing environmental conditions and diseases endemic to the Norwegian fjords where these fish are cultivated.

While transgenic fish present several promising avenues for enhancing productivity and sustainability in Norwegian aquaculture, they also pose challenges related to ecology, genetics, and disease management. Ongoing research and regulatory oversight will be essential to balance these benefits and risks in order to maintain both the economic viability of aquaculture and the ecological integrity of marine environments. The Gene Technology Act regulates the production and use of GMOs including aquatic organisms, emphasizing ethical justification, sustainability and societal benefits. The Aquaculture Act (2005) regulates the management, control, and development of aquaculture, requiring risk assessments for disease spread and environmental impact before granting authorizations for aquaculture facilities. The Food Safety Act (2003) covers animal health and food safety, including aquaculture products, while the Animal Welfare Act sets standards for the treatment and care of fish in research and other contexts.

Lesson Learnt from Australia

The introduction of genetically modified fish into aquaculture also raises concerns related to biodiversity and the long-term ecological impacts of these transgenic varieties. The Australian government, along with various scientific bodies, conducts extensive research to understand the ecological ramifications of transgenic fish populations. This research includes evaluating behavior differences, ecological interactions with native species, and assessing genetic diversity and population structures in both wild and hatchery environments (Harrisson et al., 2025; Schmidt et al., 2018). Monitoring GMOs is essential as research has suggested that improper management could lead to unintended interbreeding and genetic dilution of native fish stocks (Barnes et al., 2016).

Moreover, Australia places a strong emphasis on sustainable aquaculture practices. The development of genetically engineered feed ingredients for transgenic fish is an area of significant interest, aimed at reducing reliance on wild fish stocks while providing essential dietary nutrients in farmed fish (Osmond & Colombo, 2019). Such advancements could enhance aquaculture production efficiency and alleviate some pressures on wild fish populations, promoting a more sustainable approach to food security.

The Australian government follows a precautionary principle regarding the release and management of transgenic fish. Regulatory bodies, such as the Office of the Gene Technology Regulator (OGTR), assess the environmental and health impacts of genetically modified organisms before granting approval for use in aquaculture. The focus is on risk assessment protocols that integrate data from ecological, genetic, and environmental studies to inform policy decisions regarding transgenic fish (Lee et al., 2014; Wang et al., 2021). This country also stresses upon the ongoing collaborations among researchers, policymakers and industry stakeholders. Knowledge transfer and adaptive management strategies will facilitate addressing potential risks while maximizing the benefits associated with transgenic fish technology (Bera, 2024).

Australia's regulatory framework for transgenic fish involves several key pieces of legislation designed to protect the environment, public health, and biodiversity. The Biosecurity Act 2015 regulates the import of live organisms, including genetically modified ones, to safeguard Australia's environment and economy from biosecurity risks. This Act requires import permits for transgenic fish, in addition to approvals under the Gene Technology Act. The Food Standards Australia New Zealand (FSANZ) Act 1991 mandates the development of food standards adopted by states and territories. Standard 1.5.2 of the Australia New Zealand Food Standards Code requires mandatory pre-market safety assessments and labelling of GM foods if novel DNA or protein is present. This ensures that any genetically modified food products undergo rigorous safety evaluations before they reach consumers.

The Environment Protection and Biodiversity Conservation Act 1999 provides a comprehensive framework for the protection of the environment and biodiversity, which is particularly relevant to the environmental release of transgenic fish. This Act ensures that any activities involving genetically modified organisms are carefully assessed for their potential impact on Australia's unique ecosystems. It is crucial to consult specific legislation and regulatory agencies for the most up-to-date and detailed information, as the regulation of transgenic organisms is an evolving field, and changes may occur over time. By maintaining stringent regulatory oversight, Australia aims to balance the benefits of transgenic fish production with the need to protect its natural resources and biodiversity.

MALAYSIA'S REGULATORY FRAMEWORK ON TRANSGENIC FISH

Biosafety Act 2007 (Act 678)

The Malaysian Biosafety Act 2007 serves as the principal legislation governing the utilization, development, and release of genetically modified organisms (GMOs) and genetically modified foods (GM foods) in Malaysia. The Act is pivotal in ensuring that the benefits of biotechnology are harnessed while addressing concerns related to environmental safety and public health. Notably, the Act mandates that any commercial release of GMOs including transgenic fish must be accompanied by a comprehensive post-release monitoring plan to assess potential ecological impacts such as gene flow, biodiversity changes and long-term ecosystem health (Department of Biosafety Malaysia, 2010; Abdul Rahman et al., 2018). Additionally, the Act establishes enforcement and mechanisms and authorizes biosafety audits to ensure continuous compliance and log term environmental protection (Singh et al., 2020b; Abdul Rahman et al., 2018).

Furthermore, economic analysis is an essential component for understanding the financial viability of GM fish farming in Malaysia. This includes cost-benefit evaluations and assessments of market competitiveness addressing production efficiency, consumer acceptance and pricing strategies. Abdul Rahman et al. (2018) emphasize the need to incorporate production costs, market dynamics, socio-economic impacts on small-scale fishers and expenses related to regulatory compliance and ecological risk management to provide a holistic view of GM fish farming sustainability.

One of the key components of the Biosafety Act is the establishment of the National Biosafety Board (NBB), which is tasked with overseeing the regulatory framework for GMOs. The NBB plays a crucial role in evaluating applications for the release of GMOs and conducting risk assessments to determine their environmental and health impacts. This is fundamental in establishing a precautionary approach, which reflects international norms outlined in agreements like the Cartagena Protocol on Biosafety (Majid, 2012; Chan, 2016).

The Act provides a comprehensive framework for risk assessment and management, necessitating that applicants for the commercial release of GMOs submit detailed reports on potential risks—both ecological and for human health. This includes studies on allergenicity and toxicity, paralleling international guidelines outlined by the Codex Alimentarius. These assessments are science-based and incorporate socio-economic considerations, addressing public concerns and promoting consumer confidence in biotechnology (Sanmugam et al., 2021). In addition to establishing the regulatory body and risk assessment requirements, the Biosafety Act emphasizes the importance of public awareness and participation in decision-making processes. This is evident in studies indicating that despite regulatory frameworks, public perception and acceptance of GM foods remain ambivalent in Malaysia. Research highlights the need for effective communication strategies to alleviate public apprehension towards GM technologies and encourage informed dialogue (Lisha et al., 2017).

The implementation of the Biosafety Act is complemented by the Genetic Modification Advisory Committee (GMAC), which provides guidance and advice on matters related to genetic modification, including safety practices and potential impacts on biodiversity (Sanmugam et al., 2021). This multi-layered governance structure ensures that biosafety measures adapt to the evolving landscape of genetic engineering, maintaining alignment with international best practices while being responsive to local contexts.

Although the Biosafety Act represents a robust framework for managing GMOs, challenges remain, particularly in terms of enforcement and public consumer sentiments. There are calls for stronger public engagement to enhance acceptance, alongside regulatory vigilance to prevent accidental releases and safeguard ecosystems from uncontrolled GMO dissemination (Majid, 2012; Singh et al., 2020a). This pre-release vetting process underscores the Act's commitment to ensuring the safety of LMOs, requiring comprehensive risk assessments encompassing potential impacts on human health, biodiversity, and ecosystem integrity. The GMAC's role as an independent advisory body is central to a science-based regulatory framework aimed at minimizing potential adverse consequences associated with the introduction of genetically modified organisms into the Malaysian environment. Part IV of the Malaysia Biosafety Act addresses the contained use and exportation of LMOs/GMOs, outlining specific obligations for exporters. The primary emphasis here is on complying with the regulatory requirements of the importing country. Additionally, the Act mandates a notification process to the Board regarding the exporter's intentions.

In addition, Part IV of the Malaysia Biosafety Act emphasizes the exporter's responsibility to comply fully with the biosafety regulations established by the importing country. This provision underscores Malaysia's commitment to respecting the regulatory frameworks of other nations in the context of international trade in genetically modified organisms. Furthermore, the Act mandates that Malaysian exporters notify the Board of their intention to export LMOs/GMOs through a formal notification process. This requirement facilitates national oversight of LMO/GMO exports and potentially enables the Malaysian authorities to ensure responsible international transfer of these organisms. The Act includes significant penalties for non-compliance with the provisions of Part IV, highlighting the importance of adhering to the regulations governing the contained use and exportation of LMOs/GMOs. The law stipulates that any individual found guilty of contravening Part IV faces a substantial fine not exceeding RM 250,000, imprisonment for a term not exceeding 4 years, or both. While for a body corporate found guilty of contravening Part IV, the penalty is an even higher fine not exceeding RM 500,000. These punitive measures serve as a strong deterrent against any attempts to circumvent the notification requirements or disregard the regulations of importing countries. They emphasize the legal obligation of exporters to act responsibly and transparently in the international movement of LMOs/GMOs.

Liability and compensation frameworks are essential legal mechanisms to address potential ecological damage caused by transgenic organisms. Although Malaysia's Biosafety Act 2007 provides a legal basis, there is a lack of clear liability and specific compensation mechanisms for transgenic fish. Comparative studies recommend that Malaysia adopt clearer liability regulations such as the EU's Directive 2004/35/EC on environmental liability to enhance accountability and promote safer biotechnology practices. Additionally, adopting precautionary prociples and insurance obligations for developers of transgenic organisms are suggested as proactive risk management measures (Delwaulle et al., 2015; Abdul Rahman & Lee, 2020).

Fisheries Act 1985 (Act 317)

While the Biosafety Act serves as the primary legislation for regulating genetically modified organisms (GMOs) in Malaysia, the Fisheries Act 1985 (Act 317), which oversees the management and conservation of fisheries resources, could play a complementary role in certain scenarios. For instance, if transgenic fish are introduced into Malaysian waters without the necessary approvals under the Biosafety Act, the Fisheries Act could be invoked to address the unauthorized introduction of non-native species or activities that harm the aquatic environment. This would ensure that any illegal introduction of transgenic fish is met with appropriate legal action to protect local ecosystems.

Additionally, the Fisheries Act and its subsidiary regulations govern aquaculture activities, providing a framework for the proper management of fish farming operations. If transgenic fish are used in aquaculture, these regulations could ensure proper containment measures are in place to prevent escapes into the wild. While the Biosafety Act would address the genetic modification aspects, the Fisheries Act would focus on the operational aspects of fish farming, ensuring that aquaculture practices do not pose a risk to the environment. Should the release or escape of transgenic fish negatively impact native fish populations, the Fisheries Act's provisions related to the conservation of aquatic resources could be applied, enabling authorities to take measures to protect native species and maintain biodiversity.

Fisheries (Inland Aquaculture) (Federal Territory of Kuala Lumpur and Federal Territory of Labuan) Regulations 2017

The Fisheries (Inland Aquaculture) (Federal Territory of Kuala Lumpur and Federal Territory of Labuan) Regulations 2017 is a subsidiary legislation under the Fisheries Act 1985. These regulations primarily regulate inland aquaculture activities including licensing, species management, environmental measures, and biosecurity practices. the law does not explicitly mention transgenic or genetically modified (GM) fish, However, as transgenic fish, as part of aquaculture species, would require a license for culture under this law. The Director-General of Fisheries Malaysia may impose conditions that could include restrictions or requirements related to genetically modified organisms (GMOs).

The regulation may allow or prohibit specific fish species in aquaculture operations. If transgenic fish are classified as "new" or "non-native" species, they may need special approval or could be restricted to protect local ecosystems. The law includes provisions to prevent pollution and protect aquatic ecosystems, which aligns with concerns over potential environmental risks from transgenic fish such as escape and interbreeding with wild populations. While this 2017 regulation doesn't explicitly regulate transgenic fish, it provides the administrative and environmental framework under which such fish could be controlled, especially in terms of licensing, containment, and species management. Any actual use or release of transgenic fish would also require compliance with the Biosafety Act 2007.

BALANCING THE NEEDS: ENVIRONMENTAL PROTECTION VS FOOD SECURITY

Environmental Protection for a Sustainable Ecosystem

The environmental protection is vital for safeguarding ecosystems and ensuring the sustainability of aquaculture practices. As the use of genetically modified fish expands in aquaculture, understanding the ecological implications becomes increasingly critical (Dunham & Su, 2020). One of the foremost concerns regarding transgenic fish is their potential ecological impact if they escape into natural environments. Transgenic fish, which may possess enhanced growth rates or altered behavior traits, could compete with wild populations for resources, potentially disrupting existing ecosystems. For instance, in a study by Sundström et al. (2014) discuss that growth-enhanced coho salmon could invade other salmon species' populations, which raises concerns about genetic integrity and ecosystem dynamics and underlines the necessity for rigorous escape prevention measures and habitat monitoring (Sundström et al., 2014).

Environmental protection is fundamentally tied to the comprehensive risk assessments mandated for transgenic organisms before their release. The ability of transgenic fish to thrive in natural ecosystems can significantly affect their ecological impact (Vandersteen et al., 2019) emphasize that evaluating how environmental conditions influence the traits of transgenic fish, such as feeding behavior and predator avoidance, is crucial for understanding their potential impacts on the environment (Vandersteen et al., 2019). Implementing standardized risk assessment protocols contributes to a more informed analysis of the implications of introducing transgenic species into aquatic habitats.

Sustainability in aquaculture is critical for food security, and transgenic fish can play a role in sustainably increasing fish production (Rakkannan & Agarwal, 2025). However, their cultivation must proceed within an environmentally protective framework to prevent degradation of natural habitats and minimize negative interactions with wild fish (Leggatt et al., 2017) indicate that transgenic fish may exhibit altered foraging and predator avoidance behaviors, which can lead to unforeseen ecological consequences should they escape into the wild (Leggatt et al., 2017). Therefore, integrating sustainability practices, such as creating sterile or triploid strains, can reduce the risks posed by transgenic fish escaping into wild populations (Leggatt et al., 2014).

The introduction of transgenic species into ecosystems carries the potential risk of reducing local biodiversity. Transgenic fish may outcompete native species for food or spawning opportunities, leading to declines or local extinctions of endemic species (Kapuscinski & Hallerman, 1990) underscore the importance of considering the phenotypic effects of inserted genes when evaluating potential ecological impacts, as well as anticipating the consequences of gene flow between transgenic and wild populations (Kapuscinski & Hallerman, 1990). Protecting native biodiversity necessitates stringent regulations and monitoring systems to track the ecological outcomes of transgenic fish farming.

Transgenic fish are designed to withstand environmental stresses, such as hypoxia or temperature fluctuations (Guan et al., 2010) highlight that the survival of transgenic fish under conditions of ammonia toxicity can be significantly impacted by environmental factors (Guan et al., 2010). This adaptability may serve as a double-edged sword; while it can enhance food security by ensuring reliable production, it raises concerns about potential interactions with natural populations struggling to cope with climate change. Therefore, environmental protections must include assessments of how transgenic fish perform under changing conditions to prevent ecosystem destabilization (Blix & Myhr, 2023).

Managing the Trade-Offs Between Environmental Protection and Food Security

Balancing the needs of environmental protection and food security is a critical challenge in the context of transgenic fish production. For instance, genetically modified salmon, offer significant potential to enhance food security by increasing aquaculture productivity and providing a reliable source of nutritious food. These fish can grow faster and resist diseases more effectively than their non-transgenic counterparts (Dunham & Su, 2020), potentially reducing the pressure on wild fish stocks and contributing to global food supply.

However, the introduction of transgenic fish into the environment raises substantial ecological concerns. Escaped transgenic fish could interbreed with wild populations, leading to genetic introgression and potentially disrupting local aquatic environments (Guan et al., 2010). Some studies have shown that transgenic fish may exhibit altered behaviors regarding predation and territorial dominance compared to their wild counterparts, impacting both their survival and that of native species (Leggatt et al., 2017; Moreau et al., 2011). Thus, it is critical to commence comprehensive risk assessments to evaluate the implications of transgenic fish within their potential new habitats. Additionally, the environmental impact of intensive aquaculture practices, such as nutrient pollution, must be carefully managed to prevent harm to coastal and marine ecosystems. Therefore, a balanced approach that includes rigorous environmental risk assessments, robust regulatory frameworks, and sustainable aquaculture practices is essential to harness the benefits of transgenic fish while safeguarding environmental integrity (Okoli et al, 2022).

On the food security front, transgenic fish hold promises for enhancing aquaculture sustainability. Innovations such as genetically engineered feed could lessen reliance on wild fish stocks, thereby alleviating pressure on overfished populations and supporting global food needs. The development of genetically engineered feed ingredients offers a potential solution to the looming problem of fish meal and oil dependency (Osmond & Colombo, 2019). If successful, such technologies could boost nutrient profiles in farmed fish while maintaining their growth efficiency, ultimately supporting nutritional demands without exacerbating environmental degradation. While advancements in breeding and biotechnological innovations could offer pathways to enhance food production, they must be carefully weighed against their potential ecological impacts (Rakkannan & Agarwal, 2025). Rigorous testing and assessments, alongside the development of containment strategies, remain essential for ensuring that transgenic fish contribute positively to both food security and environmental health (Blix & Myhr, 2023).

CONCLUSION

Food security is one of the keys to improving socioeconomic standing and combating malnutrition. This issue still exists in the current situation in less developed nations. Therefore, the importance of animal protein in a person's normal diet is the main emphasis of human nutrition inadequacies. A substantial portion of the animal protein consumed by people globally comes from fisheries. The most affordable and nutrient-dense protein sources are aquatic ones, which also provide vital vitamins, proteins, micronutrients, and minerals, making them an excellent dietary supplement. In emerging nations, aquaculture is essential to both the global food supply and national economic growth. Aquaculture has the ongoing potential to improve human wellbeing and set developmental goals for the national economy. Nevertheless, environmental protection is paramount in the context of transgenic fish in aquaculture, as it serves to mitigate ecological risks, support sustainable practices, preserve biodiversity, and adapt to environmental changes. The successful integration of transgenic fish requires a robust framework that combines safety evaluations and ecological considerations, ensuring that advancements in biotechnology contribute positively to food security without compromising the health of aquatic ecosystems.

The rigorous environmental assessments and risk management protocols that some developing countries have implemented before introducing GMOs into ecosystems. Malaysia could benefit from developing similar protocols to assess the risks associated with transgenic fish, focusing on their growth performance in natural environments compared to wild-type species. Emphasizing such risk assessments can help ensure that the benefits of transgenic fish do not come at an ecological cost. Moreover, lessons from community engagement and education in other countries highlight the importance of stakeholder involvement in sustainable agricultural practices. Fostering dialogue among policymakers, researcher, and local fishers can facilitate the successful incorporation of transgenic fish into aquaculture. By understanding the perspectives of those directly involved, Malaysia can create policies that are not only scientifically sound but also acceptable to local communities. Finally, drawing on the regulatory frameworks developed in regions such as Europe can guide Malaysia in establishing robust policies for the safe use of transgenic fish. The introduction of regulations that mandate eco-certifications for sustainable aquaculture products can help create market incentives for environmentally friendly practices. As such, these regulations could prompt Malaysian fish farmers to adopt sustainable practices while ensuring that the use of transgenic species aligns with environmental standards.

New biotechnological innovations present significant opportunities for improving aquaculture sustainability. However, these advances also bring new regulatory challenges that require updated frameworks, improved risk assessment capabilities, and active engagement with stakeholders to balance technological progress with environmental and public health protections.

REFERENCES

Abdul Rahman, M. Z., Ismail, N., & Hassan, A. (2018). Socio-economic impact of transgenic fish technology on Malaysian fisheries communities. *Aquaculture Economics & Management*, *22*(3), 210–225.

Abdul Rahman, M. Z., & Lee, S. H. (2020). Risk management and insurance obligations for developers of transgenic organisms in Malaysia. *Malaysian Journal of Biosafety and Biosecurity*, *8*(1), 15–29.

Aerni, P. (2004). Risk, regulation and innovation: The case of aquaculture and transgenic fish. *Aquatic Sciences*, *66*(3). Advance online publication. DOI: 10.1007/s00027-004-0715-8

Afewerki, S., Asche, F., Misund, B., Thorvaldsen, T., & Tveteras, R. (2023). Innovation in the Norwegian aquaculture industry. *Reviews in Aquaculture*, *15*(2), 759–771. DOI: 10.1111/raq.12755

Aliaziz, M., & Ab Rahman, M. A. (2018). Growth hormone effects on essential amino acid absorption, muscle amino acid profile, N-retention and nutritional requirements of striped bass hybrids. *Genetic Analysis: Biomolecular Engineering*, *15*(3–5), 107–113. PMID: 10596748

Almeida, L., & Agrawal, A. A. (2020). Biosafety and bioethics of genome editing in agriculture: Lessons from natural diversity. *Trends in Biotechnology*, *38*(4), 334–344.

Amin, M. R., Rahman, M. M., & Hasan, M. K. (2014). Growth hormone effects on essential amino acid absorption, muscle amino acid profile, N-retention and nutritional requirements of striped bass hybrids. *Genetic Analysis: Biomolecular Engineering*, *15*(3–5), 107–113. PMID: 10596748

Asche, F., Bellemare, M., Roheim, C., Smith, M., & Tveterås, S. (2015). Fair enough? food security and the international trade of seafood. *World Development*, *67*, 151–160. DOI: 10.1016/j.worlddev.2014.10.013

Aunsmo, A., Martinsen, L., Bruheim, T., Sekkelsten-Kindt, M., Sandtrø, A., Gaasø, S., Braaen, S., & Rimstad, E. (2022). Triploid atlantic salmon (salmo salar) may have increased risk of primary field outbreaks of infectious salmon anaemia. *Journal of Fish Diseases*, *45*(11), 1733–1743. DOI: 10.1111/jfd.13695 PMID: 35914108

Barnes, T., Junge, C., Myers, S., Taylor, M., Rogers, P., Ferguson, G., & Gillanders, B. (2016). Population structure in a wide-ranging coastal teleost (*Argyrosomus japonicus*, sciaenidae) reflects marine biogeography across Southern Australia. *Marine and Freshwater Research*, *67*(8), 1103. DOI: 10.1071/MF15044

Bedair, M., & Glenn, K. (2020). Evaluation of the use of untargeted metabolomics in the safety assessment of genetically modified crops. *Metabolomics*, *16*(10), 111. DOI: 10.1007/s11306-020-01733-8 PMID: 33037482

Bennett, A., Basurto, X., Virdin, J., Lin, X., Betances, S. J., Smith, M. D., & Zoubek, S. (2021). Recognize fish as food in policy discourse and development funding. *Ambio*, *50*(5), 981–989. DOI: 10.1007/s13280-020-01451-4 PMID: 33454882

Bera, B. (2024). Transgenic fish and its progress., 77-86. DOI: 10.58532/V3BJBT-6P4CH2

Blix, T. B., & Myhr, A. I. (2023). A sustainability assessment framework for genome-edited salmon. *Aquaculture (Amsterdam, Netherlands)*, *562*, 738803. DOI: 10.1016/j.aquaculture.2022.738803

Buwono, I. D., Grandiosa, R., & Iskandar, I. (2021). Molecular analysis of functional domain and protein motif of endoglucanase gene in marine bacteria isolated from *Eucheuma* sp. and *Sargassum* sp. *International Journal of Fisheries and Aquatic Studies*, *9*(1), 2403. DOI: 10.22271/fish.2021.v9.i1c.2403

Buwono, I. D., Junianto, J., Iskandar, I., & Alimuddin, A. (2019a). Growth and expression level of growth hormone in transgenic mutiara catfish second generation. *Journal of Biotech Research*, *10*, 102–109.

Cebeci, A., Aydın, İ., & Goddard, A. (2020). Bigger, stronger, better: Fish transgenesis applications and methods. *Biotech Studies*, *29*(2), 85–97. DOI: 10.38042/biost.2020.29.02.05

Chan, C., Tran, N., Cheong, K., Sulser, T., Cohen, P., Wiebe, K., & Nasr-Allah, A. (2021). The future of fish in Africa: Employment and investment opportunities. *PLoS One*, *16*(12), e0261615. DOI: 10.1371/journal.pone.0261615 PMID: 34936682

Chan, K. (2016). Malaysia Biosafety Act 2007 and Cartagena Protocol On Biosafety: A critical comparative analysis. DOI: 10.7287/peerj.preprints.2569v1

Chen, H., Yang, H., Sun, Y., & Pan, C. (2016). Advances in gene editing technology and its application in aquaculture. *Frontiers in Genetics*, *7*, 141.

Chen, T. T. (1995). Growth hormone gene expression and growth enhancement in fish and shellfish. *Aquaculture Research*, *26*(3), 233–239. DOI: 10.1111/j.1365-2109.1995.tb00822.x

Chen, T. T., Lin, C., Shamblott, M., Lu, J. K., & Knight, K. (1995). *Transgenic fish and aquaculture. Towards sustainable aquaculture in Southeast Asia and Japan.* SEAFDEC Aquaculture Department.

Codex Alimentarius Commission. (2009). Guidelines for the Conduct of Food Safety Assessment of Foods Derived from Recombinant-DNA Animals. CAC/GL 68-2008.

Convention on Biological Diversity (CBD). (2000). Cartagena Protocol on Biosafety to the Convention on Biological Diversity: Text and Annexes. Secretariat of the Convention on Biological Diversity. https://www.cbd.int/doc/legal/cartagena-protocol-en.pdf

Cowey, C. B. (1994). Amino acid requirements of fish: A critical appraisal of present values. *Aquaculture (Amsterdam, Netherlands)*, *124*(1-4), 1–11. DOI: 10.1016/0044-8486(94)90349-2

Cowx, I. G., Bolland, J. D., Nunn, A. D., & Peeler, E. J. (2010). Defining environmental risk assessment criteria for genetically modified fishes to be placed on the EU market. *Environmental Biosafety Research*, *9*(4), 209–221. DOI: 10.1051/ebr/2011004

De Silva, S. S., Nguyen, T. T., & Ingram, B. A. (2008). Fish reproduction in relation to aquaculture. *Fish reproduction*, 535-575.

Delwaulle, J. C., Smith, T., & Nguyen, P. (2015). Environmental liability frameworks and biotechnology: Lessons from the European Union. *Journal of Environmental Law and Policy*, *22*(4), 345–367.

Demircan, M. S., & Özdestan, O. (2021). Does dietary incorporation level of pea protein isolate influence the digestive system morphology in rainbow trout (*Oncorhynchus mykiss*)? *Anatomia, Histologia, Embryologia*, *50*(6), 956–964. DOI: 10.1111/ahe.12740 PMID: 34558733

Department of Biosafety Malaysia. (2010). *Guidelines for the release of genetically modified organisms into the environment*. Ministry of Natural Resources and Environment.

Devlin, R. H., Yesaki, T. Y., Donaldson, E. M., & Hew, C. L. (2001). Transmission and phenotypic effects of an antifreeze/GH gene construct in coho salmon (Oncorhynchus kisutch). *Aquaculture (Amsterdam, Netherlands)*, *194*(1–2), 37–49.

Devos, Y., Demont, M., Dillen, K., Reheul, D., Kaiser, M., & Sanvido, O. (2009). Coexistence of genetically modified (GM) and non-GM crops in the European Union. A review. *Agronomy for Sustainable Development*, *29*(1), 11–30. DOI: 10.1051/agro:2008051

Dimitrov, D., Smith, M., & Johnson, R. (2013). Growth hormone effects on essential amino acid absorption, muscle amino acid profile, N-retention and nutritional requirements of striped bass hybrids. *Genetic Analysis, Techniques and Applications, 15*(3–5), 107–113. DOI: 10.1016/S1050-3862(99)00012-1 PMID: 10596748

Dunham, R. A., Smitherman, R. O., & Stocker, R. L. (2002). Genetically improved fish strains: Progress and prospects. *Aquaculture Research, 33*(9), 793–800. DOI: 10.1046/j.1365-2109.2002.00707.x

Dunham, R. A., & Su, B. (2020). Genetically engineered fish: potential impacts on aquaculture, biodiversity, and the environment. *GMOs: Implications for Biodiversity Conservation and Ecological Processes*, 241-275.

Dunham, R. A., & Winn, R. N. (2014). Introduction to genetics in aquaculture XI: The past, present and future of aquaculture genetics. *Aquaculture (Amsterdam, Netherlands), 420*, S1–S3. DOI: 10.1016/j.aquaculture.2013.10.019

European Commission. (2018). Commission Directive (EU) 2018/350 amending Directive 2001/18/EC as regards the environmental risk assessment of genetically modified organisms. Official Journal of the European Union. https://enveurope.springeropen.com/articles/10.1186/s12302-023-00734-3

European Parliament & Council. (2001). Directive 2001/18/EC on the deliberate release into the environment of genetically modified organisms. Official Journal of the European Communities. https://eur-lex.europa.eu/legal-content/EN/TXT/?uri=CELEX%3A32001L0018

FAO 2024. The State of World Fisheries and Aquaculture 2024. Blue Transformation in action. Rome. https://doi.org/DOI: 10.4060/cd0683en

FAO/WHO. (2003). *Guidelines for the Safe Use of Genetically Modified Organisms*. Food and Agriculture Organization of the United Nations / World Health Organization.

Farhat, S., & Khan, M. A. (2012). Growth hormone effects on essential amino acid absorption, muscle amino acid profile, N-retention and nutritional requirements of striped bass hybrids. *Genetic Analysis, Techniques and Applications, 15*(3–5), 107–113. DOI: 10.1016/S1050-3862(99)00012-1 PMID: 10596748

Farmanfarmaian, A., & Sun, L.-Z. (1999). Growth hormone effects on essential amino acid absorption, muscle amino acid profile, N-retention and nutritional requirements of striped bass hybrids. *Genetic Analysis, Techniques and Applications, 15*(3–5), 107–113. DOI: 10.1016/S1050-3862(99)00012-1 PMID: 10596748

Figueiredo, M. A., Lanes, C. F. C., Almeida, D. V., & Marins, L. F. (2007). Improving the production of transgenic fish germlines: In vivo evaluation of mosaicism in zebrafish (*Danio rerio*) using a green fluorescent protein (GFP) and growth hormone cDNA transgene co-injection strategy. *Genetics and Molecular Biology*, *30*(1), 31–36. DOI: 10.1590/S1415-47572007000100008

Fletcher, G. L., Shears, M. A., King, M. J., & Davies, P. L. (2004). Transgenic fish for aquaculture: a scientific review of the regulatory and biosafety issues associated with transgenic fish. FAO Fisheries Circular, No. 989.

Food and Agriculture Organization (FAO). (2019). The State of Food and Agriculture 2019. Moving forward on food loss and waste reduction. FAO. https://www.fao.org/3/ca6030en/ca6030en.pdf

Fraiture, M., D'aes, J., Guiderdoni, E., Meunier, A., Delcourt, T., Hoffman, S., & Roosens, N. (2023). Targeted high-throughput sequencing enables the detection of single nucleotide variations in crispr/cas9 gene-edited organisms. *Foods*, *12*(3), 455. DOI: 10.3390/foods12030455 PMID: 36765984

Frewer, L. J., Howard, C., & Shepherd, R. (1997). Public concerns in the United Kingdom about general and specific applications of genetic engineering: Risk benefit and ethics. *Science, Technology & Human Values*, *22*(1), 98–124. DOI: 10.1177/016224399702200105 PMID: 11654686

Galanakis, C. M. (2020). Sustainable aquaculture: The role of genetically modified fish. In *Sustainable Food Systems from Agriculture to Industry* (pp. 243–268). Academic Press., DOI: 10.1016/B978-0-12-817576-4.00012-9

Glover, K., Pertoldi, C., Besnier, F., Wennevik, V., Kent, M., & Skaala, Ø. (2013). Atlantic salmon populations invaded by farmed escapees: Quantifying genetic introgression with a bayesian approach and snps. *BMC Genetics*, *14*(1), 74. DOI: 10.1186/1471-2156-14-74 PMID: 23968202

Glover, K., Quintela, M., Wennevik, V., Besnier, F., Sørvik, A., & Skaala, Ø. (2012). Three decades of farmed escapees in the wild: A spatio-temporal analysis of atlantic salmon population genetic structure throughout Norway. *PLoS One*, *7*(8), e43129. DOI: 10.1371/journal.pone.0043129 PMID: 22916215

Glover, K., Solberg, M., McGinnity, P., Hindar, K., Verspoor, E., Coulson, M., & Svåsand, T. (2017). Half a century of genetic interaction between farmed and wild Atlantic salmon: Status of knowledge and unanswered questions. *Fish and Fisheries*, *18*(5), 890–927. DOI: 10.1111/faf.12214

Goh, E. V. (2018). The status of fish in Malaysian diets and potential barriers to increasing consumption of farmed species (Doctoral dissertation, University of Nottingham). University of Nottingham, Theses Repository. https://eprints.nottingham.ac.uk/52379/

Golden, C., Koehn, J., Shepon, A., Passarelli, S., Free, C., Viana, D., & Thilsted, S. (2021). Aquatic foods to nourish nations. *Nature*, *598*(7880), 315–320. DOI: 10.1038/s41586-021-03917-1 PMID: 34526720

Goodman, R. (2024). Twenty-eight years of gm food and feed without harm: Why not accept them? *GM Crops and Food: Biotechnology in Agriculture and the Food Chain*, *15*(1), 40–50. DOI: 10.1080/21645698.2024.2305944 PMID: 38471133

Goodman, R., Ebisawa, M., Ferreira, F., Sampson, H., Ree, R., Vieths, S., & Taylor, S. (2016). Allergenonline: A peer-reviewed, curated allergen database to assess novel food proteins for potential cross-reactivity. *Molecular Nutrition & Food Research*, *60*(5), 1183–1198. DOI: 10.1002/mnfr.201500769 PMID: 26887584

Goos, H. J. T., Bain, M., & Cunningham, D. (2001). Chromosome manipulation techniques for genetic improvement in aquaculture. In M. S. K. (Ed.), Genetic Improvement of Farmed Aquatic Species (pp. 123–142). Springer.

Gratacap, R., Wargelius, A., Edvardsen, R., & Houston, R. (2019). Potential of genome editing to improve aquaculture breeding and production. *Trends in Genetics*, *35*(9), 672–684. DOI: 10.1016/j.tig.2019.06.006 PMID: 31331664

Guan, B., Hu, W., Zhang, T., Duan, M., Li, D., Wang, Y., & Zhu, Z. (2010). Acute and chronic un-ionized ammonia toxicity to 'all-fish' growth hormone transgenic common carp (cyprinus carpio l.). *Chinese Science Bulletin*, *55*(35), 4032–4036. DOI: 10.1007/s11434-010-4165-5

Gupta, A., & Falkner, R. (2006). The influence of the Cartagena Protocol on Biosafety: Comparing Mexico, China and South Africa. *Global Environmental Politics*, *6*(4), 23–55. DOI: 10.1162/glep.2006.6.4.23

Harrisson, K., Beheregaray, L., Bice, C., Booth, E., Brauer, C., Butler, G., & Zampatti, B. (2025). Otolith and genomic data reveal temporal insights into stocking across a large river basin in a mobile, long-lived Australian freshwater fish species. *Molecular Ecology*, *34*(7), e17714. DOI: 10.1111/mec.17714 PMID: 40040486

Henriksson, P. J. G., Troell, M., Banks, L. K., Belton, B., Beveridge, M. C. M., Klinger, D. H., Pelletier, N., Phillips, M. J., & Tran, N. (2021). Interventions for improving the productivity and environmental performance of global aquaculture for future food security. *One Earth*, *4*(9), 1220–1232. DOI: 10.1016/j.oneear.2021.08.009

Hew, C. L., & Fletcher, G. L. (1997). Techniques and applications of chromosome manipulation in fish breeding. *Aquaculture Research, 28*(6), 439–449. DOI: 10.1111/j.1365-2109.1997.tb00853.x

Hew, C. L., & Fletcher, G. L. (2001). The role of aquatic biotechnology in aquaculture. *Aquaculture (Amsterdam, Netherlands), 197*(1), 191–204. DOI: 10.1016/S0044-8486(01)00587-7

Hill, R., & Sendashonga, C. (2006). Conservation biology, genetically modified organisms, and the biosafety protocol. *Conservation Biology, 20*(6), 1620–1625. DOI: 10.1111/j.1523-1739.2006.00534.x PMID: 17181797

Hong, B., Du, Y., Mukerji, P., Roper, J., & Appenzeller, L. (2017). Safety assessment of food and feed from gm crops in Europe: Evaluating efsa's alternative framework for the rat 90-day feeding study. *Journal of Agricultural and Food Chemistry, 65*(27), 5545–5560. DOI: 10.1021/acs.jafc.7b01492 PMID: 28573861

Hostetler, C. E., Ellis, L. R., & Zinn, S. A. (2005). Effects of dietary carbohydrate and phytate on glucose metabolism and nutrient utilization in salmonids. *Aquaculture Nutrition, 11*(6), 407–416. DOI: 10.1111/j.1365-2095.2005.00382.x

Jhingan, E., Devlin, R. H., & Iwama, G. K. (2003). Disease resistance, stress response, and effects of triploidy in growth hormone transgenic coho salmon. *Journal of Fish Biology, 63*(3), 806–823. DOI: 10.1046/j.1095-8649.2003.00194.x

Jinek, M., Chylinski, K., Fonfara, I., Hauer, M., Doudna, J. A., & Charpentier, E. (2012). A programmable dual-RNA–guided DNA endonuclease in adaptive bacterial immunity. *Science, 337*(6096), 816–821. DOI: 10.1126/science.1225829 PMID: 22745249

Kanchiswamy, C. N. (2016). Genome editing: A new tool for crop improvement. *Plant Cell Reports, 35*(1), 41–51. DOI: 10.1007/s00299-015-1878-5

Kapuscinski, A., & Hallerman, E. (1990). Transgenic fish and public policy: Anticipating environmental impacts of transgenic fish. *Fisheries (Bethesda, Md.), 15*(1), 2–11. DOI: 10.1577/1548-8446(1990)015<0002:TFAPPA>2.0.CO;2

Kapuscinski, A. R., Hayes, K. R., Li, S., & Dana, G. (2007). Environmental risk assessment of genetically modified organisms. *Integrated Environmental Assessment and Management, 3*(4), 439–450.

Kawarazuka, N., & Béné, C. (2010). Linking small-scale fisheries and aquaculture to household nutritional security: An overview. *Food Security, 2*(4), 343–357. DOI: 10.1007/s12571-010-0079-y

Khatri-Chhetri, G., & Ahmad, S. (2021). Regulatory frameworks for genome editing in agriculture: A global overview. *Biotechnology Advances*, *51*, 107796. DOI: 10.1016/j.biotechadv.2021.107796

Kirkpatrick, J. B., Kriwoken, L. K., & Styger, J. (2017). The reverse precautionary principle: Science, the environment and the salmon aquaculture industry in Macquarie Harbour, Tasmania, Australia. *Pacific Conservation Biology*, *25*(1), 26–33. DOI: 10.1071/PC17014

Kok, B. P., & Jones, D. A. (2004). Nutritional strategies for improving glucose metabolism and phytate utilization in salmonids. *Aquaculture Research*, *35*(7), 665–673. DOI: 10.1111/j.1365-2109.2004.01072.x

Kunyanga, C., Mugiira, B., & Muchiri, N. (2024). Public perception of genetically modified organisms and the implementation of biosafety measures in Kenya. *Advances in Agriculture*, *2024*(1).

Lee, O., Green, J., & Tyler, C. (2014). Transgenic fish systems and their application in ecotoxicology. *Critical Reviews in Toxicology*, *45*(2), 124–141. DOI: 10.3109/10408444.2014.965805 PMID: 25394772

Leggatt, R., Hollo, T., Vandersteen, W., McFarlane, K., Goh, B., Prevost, J., & Devlin, R. (2014). Rearing in seawater mesocosms improves the spawning performance of growth hormone transgenic and wild-type coho salmon. *PLoS One*, *9*(8), e105377. DOI: 10.1371/journal.pone.0105377 PMID: 25133780

Leggatt, R., Sundström, L., Woodward, K., & Devlin, R. (2017). Growth-enhanced transgenic coho salmon (oncorhynchus kisutch) strains have varied success in simulated streams: Implications for risk assessment. *PLoS One*, *12*(1), e0169991. DOI: 10.1371/journal.pone.0169991 PMID: 28068416

Levesque, H. M., Shears, M. A., Fletcher, G. L., & Moon, T. W. (2008). Myogenesis and muscle metabolism in juvenile Atlantic salmon (*Salmo salar*) made transgenic for growth hormone. *The Journal of Experimental Biology*, *211*(1), 128–137. DOI: 10.1242/jeb.006890 PMID: 18083741

Li, M. H., Robinson, E. H., Oberle, D. F., & Lucas, P. M. (2009). Effects of dietary protein and energy levels on growth and body composition of juvenile channel catfish, Ictalurus punctatus. *Aquaculture (Amsterdam, Netherlands)*, *295*(1–2), 98–101. DOI: 10.1016/j.aquaculture.2009.06.002

Lim, K. H., & Ooi, L. C. (2020). Public perception and acceptance of genetically modified fish in Malaysia. *Journal of Environmental Science and Policy*, *15*(1), 23–30.

Lisha, V., New, C., Nishibuchi, M., & Radu, S. (2017). rapid genetically modified organism (GMO) screening of various food products and animal feeds using multiplex polymerase chain reaction (pcr). *Food Research*, *1*(1), 1–8. DOI: 10.26656/fr.2017.1.001

Lugo-Morín, D. R. (2020). Global food security in a pandemic: The case of the new coronavirus (COVID-19). *WORLD (Oakland, Calif.)*, *1*(2), 171–190. DOI: 10.3390/world1020013

Lyngstad, T. M., Kristoffersen, A. B., Hjortaas, M. J., Devold, M., Aspehaug, V., Larssen, R. B., & Jansen, P. A. (2012). Low virulent infectious salmon anaemia virus (ISAV-HPR0) is prevalent and geographically structured in Norwegian salmon farming. *Diseases of Aquatic Organisms*, *101*(3), 197–206. DOI: 10.3354/dao02520 PMID: 23324416

Maclean, N. (2003). Genetically modified fish and their effects on food quality and human health and nutrition. *Trends in Food Science & Technology*, *14*(5–8), 242–252. DOI: 10.1016/S0924-2244(03)00070-0

Maclean, N., & Laight, R. J. (2000). Transgenic fish: An evaluation of benefits and risks. *Fish and Fisheries*, *1*(2), 146–172. DOI: 10.1046/j.1467-2979.2000.00014.x

Maclean, N., & Talwar, S. (1984). Injection of cloned genes into rainbow trout eggs. *Journal of Embryology and Experimental Morphology*, *82*(Supplement), 187.

Majid, N. A. (2012). Review of the Issues and Governance of Genetically Modified Organisms in Malaysia. *International Journal of Biotechnology and Biochemistry*, *8*(1), 1–16.

Mao, W., Wang, Y., Wang, W., Wu, B., Feng, J., & Zhu, Z. (2004). Enhanced resistance to *Aeromonas hydrophila* infection and enhanced phagocytic activities in human lactoferrin-transgenic grass carp (*Ctenopharyngodon idellus*). *Aquaculture (Amsterdam, Netherlands)*, *242*(1–4), 93–103. DOI: 10.1016/j.aquaculture.2004.07.020

Millar, K., & Tomkins, S. (2007). Ethical analysis of the use of GM fish: Emerging issues for aquaculture development. *Journal of Agricultural & Environmental Ethics*, *20*(5), 437–453. DOI: 10.1007/s10806-007-9051-z

Mohd Noor, A. R.. (2022). Application of CRISPR technology in enhancing disease resistance of freshwater fish in Malaysia. *Journal of Aquatic Biotechnology*, *10*(1), 12–20.

Moreau, D., Fleming, I., Fletcher, G., & Brown, J. (2011). Growth hormone transgenesis does not influence territorial dominance or growth and survival of first-feeding Atlantic salmon salmo salar in food-limited stream microcosms. *Journal of Fish Biology*, *78*(3), 726–740. DOI: 10.1111/j.1095-8649.2010.02888.x PMID: 21366569

Nam, D. H., Maclean, N., Fu, C., Pandian, T. J., & Eguia, M. R. R. (2007). Genetic guidelines for fisheries management. *Aquatic Living Resources*, *20*(3), 241–255. DOI: 10.1051/alr:2007012

Nogueira, T., & Botelho, A. (2021). Metagenomics and other omics approaches to bacterial communities and antimicrobial resistance assessment in aquacultures. *Antibiotics (Basel, Switzerland)*, *10*(7), 787. DOI: 10.3390/antibiotics10070787 PMID: 34203511

Nylund, A., Brattespe, J., Plarre, H., Kambestad, M., & Karlsen, M. (2019). Wild and farmed salmon (salmo salar) as reservoirs for infectious salmon anaemia virus, and the importance of horizontal- and vertical transmission. *PLoS One*, *14*(4), e0215478. DOI: 10.1371/journal.pone.0215478 PMID: 30990853

Obiero, K., Meulenbroek, P., Drexler, S., Dagne, A., Akoll, P., Odong, R., Kaunda-Arara, B., & Waidbacher, H. (2019). The contribution of fish to food and nutrition security in Eastern Africa: Emerging trends and future outlooks. *Sustainability (Basel)*, *11*(6), 1636. DOI: 10.3390/su11061636

Okoli, A. S., Blix, T., Myhr, A. I., Xu, W., & Xu, X. (2022). Sustainable use of CRISPR/Cas in fish aquaculture: The biosafety perspective. *Transgenic Research*, *31*(1), 1–21. DOI: 10.1007/s11248-021-00274-7 PMID: 34304349

Osmond, A., & Colombo, S. (2019). The future of genetic engineering to provide essential dietary nutrients and improve growth performance in aquaculture: Advantages and challenges. *Journal of the World Aquaculture Society*, *50*(3), 490–509. DOI: 10.1111/jwas.12595

Ottinger, M., Clauss, K., & Kuenzer, C. (2018). Opportunities and challenges for the estimation of aquaculture production based on Earth observation data. *Remote Sensing (Basel)*, *10*(7), 1076. DOI: 10.3390/rs10071076

Pradeepkiran, J. A. (2019). Aquaculture role in global food security with nutritional value: A review. *Translational Animal Science*, *3*(2), 903–910. DOI: 10.1093/tas/txz012 PMID: 32704855

Rahman, M., Hoque, M., Bhowmik, S., Ferdousi, S., Kabiraz, M., & Brakel, M. (2021). Monitoring of pesticide residues from fish feed, fish and vegetables in Bangladesh by gc-ms using the quechers method. *Heliyon, 7*(3), e06390. DOI: 10.1016/j.heliyon.2021.e06390 PMID: 33869825

Rakkannan, G., & Agarwal, D. (2025). Role of Aquaculture Biotechnology in Food Security and Nutrition. In *Food Security, Nutrition and Sustainability Through Aquaculture Technologies* (pp. 173–191). Springer Nature Switzerland. DOI: 10.1007/978-3-031-75830-0_9

Razak, S. A., Hwang, G. L., Rahman, M. A., & Maclean, N. (1999). Growth performance and gonadal development of growth enhanced transgenic tilapia Oreochromis niloticus (L.) following heat-shock-induced triploidy. *Marine Biotechnology (New York, N.Y.), 1*(6), 533–544. DOI: 10.1007/PL00011808 PMID: 10612678

Reis, Y., & Guedes, A. (2017). International environmental NGOs and the politics of genetically modified organisms. *Critical Perspectives on International Business, 13*(1), 23–37. DOI: 10.1108/cpoib-03-2014-0020

Rosado, A., & Eriksson, D. (2021). Biosafety legislation and the regulatory status of the products of precision breeding in the Latin America and the Caribbean region. *Plants, People, Planet, 4*(3), 214–231. DOI: 10.1002/ppp3.10243

Sanmugam, S., Sivakumar, S., Gobalakrishnan, T., Sarawanan, T., Abeweera, P., & Sandrasaigaran, P. (2021). Perception and acceptance of genetically modified foods in malaysia. *Malaysian Journal of Science and Advanced Technology*, 144-150.

Schmidt, D., Espinoza, T., Real, K., Dunlop, A., Kennard, M., & Hughes, J. (2018). Improved genetic markers for monitoring recruitment dynamics in the endangered mary river cod (maccullochella mariensis). *Journal of Applied Ichthyology, 34*(3), 633–637. DOI: 10.1111/jai.13633

Singh, J., Jalaluddin, N., Sanan-Mishra, N., & Harikrishna, J. (2020a). Challenges to the adoption of modern crop biotechnology: Insights from Indian and Malaysian GM regulatory frameworks. *Malaysian Applied Biology, 49*(5), 1–9. DOI: 10.55230/mabjournal.v49i5.1632

Singh, R., Ahmad, N., & Lee, K. T. (2020b). Enforcement and biosafety audits in Malaysia's GMO regulatory framework: Challenges and future directions. *Journal of Environmental Policy and Regulation, 15*(1), 67–79. https://doi.org/10.xxxx/jer.2020.01501

Siti Hawa, J.. (2019). Genetic improvement of freshwater fish species in Malaysia using molecular techniques. *Malaysian Journal of Biotechnology, 8*(2), 45–55.

Strutt, J., Bessarab, I., Min, J., Marican, H., & Summers, S. (2024). Rapid nanopore cloud-based monitoring and analysis of commercial aquaculture microbiomes. https://doi.org/DOI: 10.1101/2024.08.07.607111

Sundström, L., Vandersteen, W., Lõhmus, M., & Devlin, R. (2014). Growth-enhanced coho salmon invading other salmon species populations: Effects on early survival and growth. *Journal of Applied Ecology, 51*(1), 82–89. DOI: 10.1111/1365-2664.12185

Sundström, L. F., Lõhmus, M., Devlin, R. H., & Björnsson, B. T. (2007). Growth hormone transgenic salmon pay for growth potential with increased predation mortality.

Thompson, P. B. (2019). Ethics and governance of emerging technologies in agriculture: The case of genome editing. *Agricultural Systems, 176*, 102645. DOI: 10.1016/j.agsy.2019.102645

Troell, M., Naylor, R. L., Metian, M., Beveridge, M., Tyedmers, P. H., Folke, C., Arrow, K. J., Barrett, S., Crépin, A.-S., Ehrlich, P. R., Gren, Å., Kautsky, N., Levin, S. A., Nyborg, K., Österblom, H., Polasky, S., Scheffer, M., Walker, B. H., Xepapadeas, T., & de Zeeuw, A. (2014). Does aquaculture add resilience to the global food system? *Proceedings of the National Academy of Sciences of the United States of America, 111*(37), 13257–13263. DOI: 10.1073/pnas.1404067111 PMID: 25136111

Van der Meer, P. J., Angenon, G., Bergmans, H., Buhk, H. J., & Rüdelsheim, P. L. J. (2023). Environmental risk assessment of genetically modified organisms in the EU: Current practices and challenges. *Environmental Sciences Europe*, 35(1), Artikel 35. https://enveurope.springeropen.com/articles/10.1186/s12302-023-00734-3

Vandersteen, W., Leggatt, R., Sundström, L., & Devlin, R. (2019). Importance of experimental environmental conditions in estimating risks and associated uncertainty of transgenic fish prior to entry into nature. *Scientific Reports, 9*(1), 406. DOI: 10.1038/s41598-018-35826-1 PMID: 30674960

Wang, J., & Cheng, Y. (2023). Enhancing aquaculture disease resistance: Antimicrobial peptides and gene editing. *Reviews in Aquaculture, 16*(1), 433–451. DOI: 10.1111/raq.12845

Wang, X., Olsen, L., Reitan, K., & Ôlsen, Y. (2012). Discharge of nutrient wastes from salmon farms: Environmental effects, and potential for integrated multi-trophic aquaculture. *Aquaculture Environment Interactions, 2*(3), 267–283. DOI: 10.3354/aei00044

Wang, Y., Hamid, N., Jia, P., & Pei, D. (2021). A comprehensive review on genetically modified fish: Key techniques, applications and future prospects. *Reviews in Aquaculture, 13*(3), 1635–1660. DOI: 10.1111/raq.12538

Wei, W., & Wee, W. (2014). Fish consumption pattern among adults of different ethnics in Peninsular Malaysia. *Food & Nutrition Research*, 58(1), . https://doi.org/ DOI: 10.3402/fnr.v58.22697

Wolt, J. D., Keese, P., Raybould, A., Fitzpatrick, J. W., Burachik, M., Gray, A., & Wu, F. (2023). The role of the precautionary principle in EU GMO regulations. *Integrated Environmental Assessment and Management*, *19*(2), 267–275. DOI: 10.1002/ieam.4278

York, R., & Gossard, M. H. (2004). Social support, environmental beliefs, and vegetarianism. *Rural Sociology*, *69*(3), 448–469. DOI: 10.1526/0036011041730467

Zbikowska, H. M. (2003). Fish can be first—Advances in fish transgenesis for commercial applications. *Transgenic Research*, *12*(4), 379–389. DOI: 10.1023/A:1024267416522 PMID: 12885160

Zhang, Z., Glover, K., Wennevik, V., Svåsand, T., Sørvik, A., Fiske, P., & Skaala, Ø. (2012). Genetic analysis of atlantic salmon captured in a netting station reveals multiple escapement events from commercial fish farms. *Fisheries Management and Ecology*, *20*(1), 42–51. DOI: 10.1111/fme.12002

Zhu, Z., Li, G., He, L., & Chen, S. (1985). Novel gene transfer into the fertilized eggs of goldfish (Carassius auratus L. 1758). *Journal of Applied Ichthyology*, *1*(1), 31–34. DOI: 10.1111/j.1439-0426.1985.tb00408.x

Zimny, M. (2015). Growth hormone effects on essential amino acid absorption, muscle amino acid profile, N-retention and nutritional requirements of striped bass hybrids. Genetic Analysis. *Genetic Analysis, Techniques and Applications*, *15*(3–5), 107–113. DOI: 10.1016/S1050-3862(99)00012-1

KEY TERMS AND DEFINITIONS

An endemic species: a plant or animal species that is native and restricted to a particular geographic location.

Aquaculture: the farming of aquatic organisms such as fish, shellfish and aquatic plants. It involves the controlled breeding, rearing, and harvesting of these organisms in various water environments, including ponds, rivers, lakes, the ocean and others

Biosecurity: a set of preventative measures designed to protect against the introduction and spread of harmful biological agents. These agents can include diseases, pests, invasive species, and living modified organisms (LMOs) that could negatively impact human, animal, and plant health, as well as the environment and the economy.

Gene transfer: the process of introducing genetic material (DNA or RNA) into a cell or organism. The goal of gene transfer is often to alter the characteristics of the recipient cell or organism.

Introgression: the transfer of genetic material (genes or alleles) from one species into the gene pool of another species through repeated backcrossing of an interspecific hybrid with one of its parent species.

Pathogens: biological agents that cause disease or illness to their host. These agents can be microorganisms such as bacteria, viruses, fungi, and protozoa, as well as larger organisms like parasitic worms.

Transgenic fish: genetically modified organisms (GMOs) used in aquaculture.

Chapter 6
Impact of SDG 6 Clean Water and Sanitation and Spanish Water Regulations on the Sustainability Reports of Public Water Companies

Natalia Alonso-Morales
University of Almería, Spain

Pedro Gil-Garcia
https://orcid.org/0009-0008-4823-7556
University of Almería, Spain

Maria del Carmen Caba-Pérez
https://orcid.org/0000-0002-8452-5909
University of Almeria, Spain

María García González
University of Almería, Spain

ABSTRACT

Spain adopted the 2030 Agenda for Sustainable Development in 2015, making SDG 6—Clean Water and Sanitation—a national priority. Key regulations, such as Law 7/2021 on Climate Change and Royal Decree 3/2023 on water quality, strengthened water management and environmental resilience. Public water companies were re-

DOI: 10.4018/979-8-3373-1792-2.ch006

quired to adapt strategies, promoting clear sustainability reporting, thus fostering greater accountability and stakeholder trust. This chapter analyzes the presence and evolution of SDG 6-related information in the Sustainability Reports of public water companies in Spain. It explores how recent regulations have influenced reporting practices, and whether they have led to more comprehensive and aligned disclosures with national and international sustainability standards. The comparative analysis reveals modest improvements in the disclosure of sustainability initiatives. Although explicit references to SDG 6 and integration with other goals increased, significant gaps remain in standardized reporting, financial transparency, and full coverage of the integrated water cycle.

INTRODUCTION

Access to safe drinking water, sanitation and hygiene constitutes a fundamental human need to preserve health and well-being (United Nations, 2016). This human right must ensure that water is sufficient, safe, acceptable, physically accessible, and affordable to meet personal and domestic needs (Fiorino, 2020). However, water should not only be understood as a vital resource for humans, but also as an ecosystem with intrinsic value and rights of its own (Muller, 2012). Despite its importance, in 2022 there were still 2.2 billion people without secure access to safe drinking water, and 2.4 billion living in water-stressed countries (United Nations, 2023). This context reinforces the urgency of achieving the Sustainable Development Goals (SDGs), in particular SDG 6, which promotes universal access to safe drinking water, sanitation and hygiene, as well as improved water efficiency and the protection of water-related ecosystems (United Nations, 2015).

Although the challenges in water management exceed the competencies of companies, their use of this resource generates increasing attention (Muller, 2012). In particular, companies in the water sector play a strategic role in sustainable development by ensuring both the quality of water resources and their availability for present and future generations (Cantele et al., 2018). Along these lines, ISO 46001 was approved in 2019, which provides guidelines for efficient water management, promoting responsible use and considering the impacts that may result from any modification in its use (ISO, 2019).

In the case of Spain, vulnerability to climate change is particularly pronounced. Rising temperatures, shifting precipitation patterns, and an increase in droughts are projected, all of which will significantly impact future water availability (Ministry of Social Rights and Agenda 2030, 2020). Furthermore, the lack of access to adequate housing among lower-income social groups also threatens the conditions necessary to ensure access to safe drinking water (Ministry of Social Rights and Agenda 2030,

2020). Against this background, since 2020 several key regulations linked to SDG 6 have been enacted in Spain to improve water resource management and ensure universal access to clean water and sanitation. Among the key measures is Law 7/2021, of May 20, on Climate Change and Energy Transition, which establishes strategic guidelines related to water and climate change. These guidelines aim to improve water resource management and ensure the sustainability of the water system, aligning with the challenges outlined by SDG 6.

Additionally, in 2022, the Strategic Project for Economic Recovery and Transformation (PERTE) for the Digitalization of the Water Cycle was launched, with the aim of optimizing urban water management. This initiative also seeks to promote transparency in the administration of water resources to raise public awareness of the responsible and sustainable use of water, and to strengthen the capacities of the entities managing the integral water cycle (Government of Spain, 2022). Another important step is Royal Decree 3/2023, which regulates the quality of water intended for human consumption. This regulation transposes the European Directive 2020/2184, ensuring that drinking water meets the required quality standards to protect human health from contamination. With this measure, Spain strengthens its commitment to providing safe and quality drinking water, a key component in achieving the objectives of SDG 6.

These regulations emphasize the need for transparency in sustainability practices. Companies must clearly report their actions toward climate resilience, water quality management, and the efficient use of resources, aligning their operations with national and international sustainability goals. This transparency not only enhances accountability but also helps to demonstrate the company's long-term commitment to achieving SDG 6 in their operations, fostering greater trust with stakeholders.

In this context, Sustainability Reports have become the primary tool through which organizations communicate their progress toward sustainable development (Lozano & Huisingh, 2011). Their publication not only enhances transparency but also helps companies strengthen their credibility with stakeholders and increase their market value (Ioannou & Serafeim, 2019). In this regard, a wide range of stakeholders are paying increasing attention to the content and quality of Sustainability Reports. As a result, these reports are typically prepared in accordance with established standards that promote stakeholder participation, ensuring that the information disclosed is relevant and useful for informed decision-making processes (Suárez-Rico et al., 2021).

On one hand, suppliers are showing growing concern for the transparency of the companies they partner with, placing a higher priority on honesty and the quality of corporate practices (Camilleri, 2015). At the same time, capital markets are demanding more comprehensive disclosures, valuing both financial and non-financial information related to sustainability when making investment decisions (Martí et al.,

2024). Similarly, consumers are increasingly prioritizing sustainable products and tend to place greater trust in companies that are transparent about their sustainability practices (Camilleri, 2015).

For these reasons, an increasing number of companies are incorporating transparency as a core element of their corporate strategy. In fact, sustainability has shifted from being a peripheral concern to becoming central to business strategy (Teruel-Gutiérrez, 2020). Companies are recognizing that by embedding sustainability into their daily operations, they can reduce costs through more efficient resource use, attract loyal customers who value ethical and sustainable practices, and enhance their overall image and reputation (Guerrero-Baena et al., 2024). Moreover, Sustainability Reports serve as an effective tool for communicating these efforts, helping organizations to strengthen their relationships with stakeholders, assess their environmental and social impact, identify business opportunities, mitigate potential risks, and, ultimately, improve both accountability and transparency (Różańska et al., 2024; Matuszak et al., 2025). Indeed, the study by Ali et al. (2019) demonstrates that transparency in water-related issues has a positive influence on company stock value, suggesting that investors increasingly consider such disclosures when making investment decisions.

To sum up, the regulations require public water companies to enhance transparency and integrate detailed sustainability practices into their Sustainability Reports, reflecting their commitment to climate adaptation, water quality, and long-term sustainable practices. Under these precedents, the aim of this chapter, is to analyse the information related to SDG 6 in the Sustainability Reports of public water companies and assess whether there have been any changes compared to the reports published before the approval of theses current legal frameworks. This analysis will provide insights into how the new regulations have influenced the companies' reporting practices, particularly regarding their commitments to water quality, sustainability, and climate adaptation, and how these practices align with the updated legal and environmental standards.

LEGISLATIVE CHANGES IN SPAIN TO MEET SUSTAINABLE DEVELOPMENT GOALS

Climate change is possibly the greatest threat to health, with the availability and quality of water for human consumption being one of the main concerns of climate change (Benítez-Cano et al., 2024). Specifically, the greatest variability and scarcity of water in many parts of the world is expected to occur in the 21st century (Mclennan et al., 2024). In this sense, climate change will affect all European countries, but in different ways and on different time scales, where southern European countries will experience increasingly drier weather patterns compared to the rest of Europe (Cammalleri et al. 2020).

Due to the alarming progression of climate change and its socioeconomic and environmental impacts, the European Union (EU) has taken decisive steps to address the crisis. Its response has involved the formalization of a series of climate policies and strategies aimed at mitigating these effects and guiding member states toward a more sustainable future. An important early step was the adoption of the EU Adaptation Strategy in 2013, which set out three key objectives: increasing the resilience of member states, enabling more informed decision-making, and integrating climate adaptation into broader EU policies. Although this strategy did not have binding regulatory power, it played a crucial role in encouraging the development of national adaptation plans and raising awareness among EU institutions (Rodrigo, 2022).

Building on this foundation, the EU strengthened its climate ambitions by aligning itself with the Paris Agreement, a landmark international treaty that sets ambitious emissions reduction targets for participating countries (Höhne et al., 2021). Within this framework, one of the most significant commitments is achieving net zero global emissions in the coming decades. To translate these international commitments into binding legal measures, the EU adopted Regulation (EU) 2021/1119 in 2021, also known as the *European Climate Law* (Albrecht, 2024). This regulation establishes a legally binding target of reducing greenhouse gas (GHG) emissions by at least 55% by 2030, compared to 1990 levels, raising the ambition from the previous 40% goal it serves as a cornerstone of the EU's climate policy framework, reinforcing the bloc's long-term vision of becoming climate-neutral by 2050. Importantly, these guidelines not only focus on reducing GHG emissions but also emphasize the promotion of renewable energy and the improvement of energy efficiency, both of which are essential for a sustainable and resilient energy system (Salgado, 2024).

Among the different measures, Article 4 of the Paris Agreement calls on all countries to communicate long-term, low-greenhouse gas emission development strategies. A long-term scenario plan is essential to identify and implement appropriate measures (Velten et al., 2022). This plan requires EU Member States to develop a long-term strategy (LTS) every ten years and to update these strategies every five years where necessary (Albrecht, 2024). While some laws incorporate these obligations into national legislation, the lack of frequent long-term planning in the landscape of European climate framework laws is striking, unlike other elements of good practice. While nine of the existing laws include some provision requiring the government to develop and review a long-term strategy or plan, only four countries require more frequent updates (Evans et al., 2023) – every five years: France, Ireland, Malta, and Spain.

The German law mentions the German Climate Protection Plan 2050 (LTS), but no legally enshrined review cycle has been established. This indicates a current weakness in the law, as updates to medium-term climate protection programs are only required after each LTS update. In France, the national low-carbon development strategy is linked to the five-year emissions budget and must be updated accordingly. In Ireland, a long-term strategy must be submitted to the government for approval by the responsible ministry every five years. In Spain, a transparency and accountability process is established in line with the review cycles of the Paris Agreement, with emphasizing that any revision may only be upward.

In order to comply with the objectives of the Paris Agreement, the Spanish Council of Ministers begins to approve emergency provisions in 2020, such as Royal Decree-Law 23/2020, of June 23, which approves measures in energy and other areas for economic reactivation. However, it will not be until 2021 when the first law focused solely on sustainability will be approved, specifically Law 7/2021 on climate change and energy transition (hereinafter, LCCTE). This law, in addition to following EU guidelines on the subject, aims to facilitate the decarbonization of the Spanish economy, its transition to a circular model, promote adaptation to the impacts of climate change and the implementation of a sustainable development model (Fernández de Gatta Sánchez, 2021).

In terms of public water management, the LCCTE establishes, among others, measures such as: prioritizing the integration of renewable energies in the concessions granted on the public water domain for the generation of electricity; promoting the use for urban water cycle uses of the flows of urban supply and sanitation systems for electricity generation; and the need to adapt hydrological management and planning to the guidelines and measures that may be developed in the Water Strategy for Ecological Transition.

To achieve these objectives, the LCCTE established the National Plan for Adaptation to Climate Change (PNACC) (art. 17), a basic planning instrument to promote coordinated and coherent action against the effects of climate change in Spain (Rodrigo, 2022). The PNACC must include the identification and evaluation of risks, assessment of vulnerabilities of natural systems, a set of specific strategic objectives and a set of adaptation measures aimed at reducing the vulnerabilities detected (Salgado, 2024).

In addition to the different indications, the LCCTEE includes some obligations for the private sector to also adopt an integrated climate approach when planning its activity (Simou, 2022). Firstly, for entities whose stocks are admitted to trading on regulated markets, public interest entities and companies of a certain size, an obligation is introduced to submit an annual report to the CNMV assessing the financial impact of the risks associated with climate change generated by the exposure of their activity (art. 32.1). However, listed small and medium-sized enterprises(SMEs) are not required to report sustainability information until 2026 (European Commission, 2025). Secondly, from 2023, credit institutions must publish specific decarbonisation targets for their lending and investment portfolio (art. 32.2). Thirdly, larger companies are required to calculate and publish the carbon footprint derived from their activity, as well as to draw up a GHG emissions reduction plan (final provision 12).

While adopting environmentally sustainable measures is important for both large corporations and SMEs, the benefits and challenges faced by SMEs vary according to the size and complexity of the organisation (Setyaningsih et al., 2024). The implementation of these measures can be challenging for SMEs for various reasons, such as limited expertise, scarcity of resources (human and material), complexity and time constraints (Permatasari and Kosasih, 2021; Fülöp & Topor, 2025). Despite the challenges, the adoption of these commitments is an opportunity for SMEs to demonstrate their commitment to social and environmental responsibility while increasing competitiveness (Vázquez-Burguete et al., 2024). In this way, SMEs can differentiate themselves from the competition, as well as improve their transparency and credibility with stakeholders (Stolowy and Paugam, 2023).

Therefore, the LCCTE serves as the general and basic regulatory framework that aims to guide, with criteria and parameters, efforts related to climate change and energy transition in the context of Spain. However, this law has generally been received with some skepticism, since, although it highlights some positive aspects, its eminently programmatic nature, more typical of soft law norms (Simou, 2022), renders it incapable of impacting, on its own, the most vital aspects of the design of the legal system.

In this line, the text itself points out that Spain, due to its geographical location and socioeconomic characteristics, faces significant risks related to water management. Due to its relevance, Article 19 establishes that water planning and management in Spain must adapt to climate change, prioritizing security of supply, biodiversity and efficient use of the resource. To this end, the Public Administrations must align themselves with the Water Strategy for Ecological Transition, where they must identify climate change risks, such as altered water flows, increased droughts and floods, rising sea levels and higher temperatures in bodies of water. To address these risks, such planning must include specific actions, provide for their financing and ensure continuous monitoring and adjustment (Vázquez and Orteu Berrocal, 2021).

On the other hand, it is essential that water is supplied in accordance with safety and security criteria for it to fulfil its primary function (Dettori et al., 2022). This has prompted international and national health bodies, such as WHO (World Health Organization, 2012) and the European Union (European Commission et al., 2017), to regulate and periodically update drinking water quality criteria.

In Europe, Member States are obliged to maintain a minimum level of water protection, defined by the most recent revision of the European Union (Directive 2020/2184). However, some countries such as France and Spain have implemented more restrictive regulations addressing specific pollutants through decrees transposing European regulations into national laws. For example, the European Directive does not define a turbidity threshold (as long as it is acceptable to consumers), whereas France and Spain set a legal limit (Fernandez-Ortega et al., 2024).

In Spain, this Directive is adapted by Royal Decree 3/2023, which establishes the technical-sanitary criteria for the quality of drinking water, its control and supply, which repeals and updates the previous regulation, Royal Decree 140/2003. The need for this new regulation is based on the obligation of public administrations to prioritize health promotion and disease prevention, as established in the General Health Law. This regulation establishes reference values for different parameters, indicating the limits above which drinking water is unfit for consumption (Benítez-Cano et al., 2024). It also establishes that the volume of water distributed must be sufficient for hygienic-sanitary needs, with a recommended minimum net supply of 100 liters per inhabitant per day, in addition to quality and control criteria.

One of the novelties of this Royal Decree is the obligation to implement Water Sanitation Plans (WSP). The WSP (art 59) is a comprehensive approach to risk assessment and management that covers all stages of supply, from intake, drinking water treatment, storage and distribution to the point of compliance and indoor facilities. This plan must be drawn up by the suppliers of the supply zones (geographically defined area and censused by the health authority) and priority buildings (hospitals, hotels, penitentiary centers etc.). All this information must be provided to the Ministry of Health through the SINAC application (National Drinking Water Information System).

In addition to providing this information to the Public Administrations, all companies (both public and private) must provide information to the public in an accessible form, free of charge and in line with point 1 of part B.1 of Annex XI: water quality, price per litre of water, average annual consumption of a household, parametric values and water origin (art 63). There is also an additional obligation for large operators (supplying more than 1,000 m^3 per day or more than 10,000 inhabitants), which must have a website with this information permanently updated, and alerts or incidents affecting water quality. Another key aspect is the obligation of cooperation between operators, health authorities and water administrations (art. 64) to ensure that the entire supply chain is properly controlled and allows a rapid response to quality problems.

To all this must be added the recently approved Royal Decree 1085/2024 of October 22 on water reuse, which establishes the creation of a seal of transparent water management in line with the PERTE of the digitization of the water cycle.

In this way, this recognition is granted to those water managers that, in addition to complying with all applicable regulations, have adequate quality standards in their management and a high degree of public transparency in the information on the data associated with water use.

Therefore, these regulations emphasize the need for transparency in sustainability practices. Companies must clearly report their actions toward climate resilience, water quality management, and the efficient use of resources, aligning their operations with national and international sustainability goals. This transparency not only enhances accountability but also helps to demonstrate the company's long-term commitment to achieving SDG 6 in their operations, fostering greater trust with stakeholders.

In summary, both regulations require public water companies to enhance transparency and integrate detailed sustainability practices into their Sustainability Reports, reflecting their commitment to climate adaptation, water quality, and long-term sustainable practices.

IMPORTANCE OF SUSTAINABILITY REPORTING TO IMPROVE THE TRANSPARENCY OF WATER COMPANIES

Having accurate and timely data on water and sanitation generates important social, economic, and environmental benefits. These include fostering institutional and citizen engagement, as well as the ability to design evidence-based policies and investments (UN Water, 2021). In other words, only what is measured can be managed effectively Likewise, Sustainability Reports have established themselves as the main means through which organizations communicate their progress towards sustainable development (Lozano & Huisingh, 2011). Their publication not only reinforces transparency, but also allows companies to gain credibility with their stakeholders and increase their value in the market (Ioannou & Serafeim, 2019).

These reports acquire special relevance in the case of companies in the water sector due to the high environmental sensitivity of their activity (Andrades et al., 2024). Through them, companies can demonstrate that their operations do not generate negative externalities and that they are committed to responsible management of water resources (Andrades et al., 2024; Nicolò & Cervilla-Bellido, 2025). In addition, they should be oriented to support more informed and efficient decision making, facilitating the monitoring of key performance indicators linked to water resource use and management (Muller, 2012).

Sustainability Reports also encourage companies to take accountability for the consequences of their actions (Camilleri, 2015). This is because, first, companies are required to measure the impact of their activities, and second, they must disclose that impact to the public. Moreover, the data collection process required for compiling these reports is itself expected to lead to improvements in both social and environmental outcomes (Koskelainen, 2024). The study by Nicolò et al. (2024) confirmed that companies with stronger sustainability performance tend to provide more comprehensive disclosures related to the SDGs, thereby highlighting the close connection between transparency and sustainability performance.

Given the importance of Sustainability Reports and their growing adoption across the corporate landscape, a variety of tools and frameworks have been developed to guide their preparation. Some of the most widely used include the Global Reporting Initiative (GRI), the Carbon Disclosure Project (CDP), the SIGMA Project, and the DPSIR framework, among others (Siew, 2015). However, the diversity of these frameworks has made it difficult to assess the quality and consistency of the reports, as well as to effectively compare the actual sustainability impacts across different companies (Koskelainen, 2024). To address this challenge, the European Union introduced a standardized framework known as the European Sustainability Reporting Standards (ESRS), aimed at harmonizing sustainability disclosures and improving comparability and transparency across organizations (del Olmo Casalderrey & Corrales, 2024).

Specifically, in 2022 the European Union adopted the Corporate Sustainability Reporting Directive (CSRD), which establishes obligations for companies to disclose information related to the sustainability impact of their activities (Directive (EU) 2022/2464). It also requires companies to report on how environmental, social and governance issues affect their development and financial performance (Directive (EU) 2022/2464).

Companies subject to this regulation must prepare their reports in accordance ESRS, which are designed to provide a comprehensive and balanced view of environmental, social, and governance (ESG) factors (Commission Delegated Regulation (EU) 2023/2772). These standards are aligned with the GRI the most widely adopted international sustainability reporting framework (Alessia, 2017). Before the ESRS came into force, most sustainability reports in Spain already followed GRI guidelines, which contributed to higher-quality reporting compared to other frameworks (Larrinaga et al., 2018). Although the ESRS closely resemble GRI standards, the differences between them are significant enough to require companies to reassess their sustainability infrastructures. This includes making substantial adjustments to internal data collection systems, staff workflows, and audit processes (Matuszak et al., 2025). Nonetheless, the European Commission (2023) expects that, in the medium to long term, the ESRS will reduce corporate reporting costs by eliminating the need for companies to rely on multiple voluntary standards simultaneously.

However, a new layer of complexity has emerged with the recent introduction of the first two International Sustainability Disclosure Standards (IFRS S1 and IFRS S2) developed by the International Sustainability Standards Board (ISSB), under the IFRS Foundation. These standards are expected to be adopted by regulators outside the European Union (del Olmo Casalderrey & Corrales, 2024). As a result, challenges related to global standardization of sustainability reporting between European and non-European companies are likely to persist.

In the case of GRI, standards 303 and 306 specifically address water-related aspects such as consumption (including sources, extraction, reuse and recycling) and discharges (effluents generated by organizations) (Cantele et al., 2018). In parallel, the ESRS have also specifically incorporated the water dimension through the ESRS E3 standard entitled "Water and Marine Resources" (Commission Delegated Regulation (EU) 2023/2772). This standard requires the disclosure of data on water consumption, withdrawals and discharges, as well as information on the impacts generated and the measures taken to mitigate them. In addition, water aspects are present in other standards such as ESRS E1 on Climate Change or ESRS E2 on Pollution, among others, reflecting a cross-cutting approach to water management.

Theoretically, the GRI standards advocate reporting on sustainability matters based on the expectations and needs of stakeholders, focusing on information that is useful for their decision-making processes (Suárez-Rico et al., 2021). This principle is known as "materiality," which calls for disclosing only what is relevant while excluding non essential data (Koskelainen, 2024). However, in practice, sustainability reports often construct a version of organizational reality that is shaped predominantly by stakeholders with greater economic influence—mainly investors—since the majority of topics identified as "material" are derived from their perspectives (Suárez-Rico et al., 2021).

Although the ESRS are aligned with the GRI in terms of materiality assessment, they introduce the concept of "double materiality" and differ in both methodology and reporting depth (Matuszak et al., 2025). Double materiality requires companies to report not only on how their activities impact people and the environment but also on how environmental and social issues may pose financial risks and opportunities for the organization itself (European Commission, 2023). Entities must conduct a rigorous assessment to determine which standards apply under either or both dimensions of materiality (Koskelainen, 2024). If a company deems a particular standard irrelevant, it must provide a detailed justification, and its materiality assessment process will be subject to external verification (European Commission, 2023).

Furthermore, one of the major challenges of voluntary frameworks like the GRI has been the risk of greenwashing. Because these frameworks were not mandatory, many companies selectively reported only their positive impacts, omitting negative aspects and thereby making it impossible to accurately assess their overall sustainability performance (Koskelainen, 2024). In contrast, under the ESRS, companies are required to disclose all issues deemed material. Additionally, an independent auditor must verify that the sustainability report complies with the CSRD and the ESRS (Directive (EU) 2022/2464).

The application of these standards not only contributes to greater transparency and accountability, but also fosters social dialogue, strengthens corporate reputation and improves the public perception of companies (Odobaša & Marošević, 2023). Thus, business evaluation will no longer be based exclusively on financial indicators, but also on its effective contribution to the sustainability of the natural, economic and social environment (Odobaša & Marošević, 2023).

However, achieving these objectives depends to a large extent on companies effectively complying with the established standards and producing complete, accurate and useful reports for decision making. However, this does not always happen, even when there is a legal obligation to do so. An illustrative example is found in the study by Larrinaga et al. (2018), who observed that, despite making it mandatory for Spanish public companies to publish Sustainability Reports in 2011, the number of reports increased marginally at the expense of quality. On the other hand, Venturelli et al. (2023) indicate that regulatory pressures do incentivize greater accountability, as seen in the case of water companies in Italy.

Regarding the literature on sustainability disclosure, extensive research has focused on reporting based on the Global Reporting Initiative (GRI) framework (Geba and Giusio, 2017; Larramendy and Tiberi, 2019) and on disclosures aligned with Environmental, Social, and Governance (ESG) criteria (Carlos et al., 2021). Additionally, there is a growing interest in transparency around corporate sustainability practices, particularly in relation to companies' commitments to the Sustainable Development Goals (SDGs) (García Meca et al. 2021; Julve and Alijarde, 2022; Ferrero et al., 2023; Erin et al., 2023; Reverte, 2021).

International evidence highlights a persistent lack of transparency regarding water sustainability. In Nigeria, Okwuosa (2022) found that most companies disclosed only about 15% of the information required under GRI Standard 303. Specifically, while companies reported on initiatives such as the construction of water boreholes to provide host communities with access to clean water, they often failed to disclose critical outcomes, such as the number of people who actually benefited from improved access. Similarly, Lodhia et al. (2023) noted that Australian companies tend to prioritize alignment with the Sustainable Development Goals (SDGs), but frequently fall short in measuring and reporting on their performance in achieving them. Among the 17 SDGs, SDG 6 ranks as the fourth least reported globally, with a disclosure score of only 32%, following SDG 2 (Zero Hunger), SDG 14 (Life Below Water), and SDG 1 (No Poverty). In Europe, similar trends have been observed: the least reported SDGs are also SDGs 1, 2, and 14, followed by SDG 10 (Reduced Inequalities) and SDG 6 (Hummel & Szekely, 2022). In the European banking sector specifically, the least reported goals are SDG 14, SDG 15 (Life on Land), and

SDG 6 (Cosma et al., 2020). Finally, universities around the world show limited engagement with SDG 6, which ranks as the second least reported goal globally, with the poorest performance observed in African institutions (De Iorio et al., 2022).

Most studies in this area focus on assessing companies' commitments to the SDGs, primarily by examining the presence or mention of the SDGs in their sustainability disclosures. However, relatively few studies explore whether companies also provide detailed information on the specific actions they undertake to support the SDGs. In this line, with respect to the assessment of disclosure quality in reporting practices, Yekini (2023) and Baalouch et al. (2019) argue that one of the main challenges is the lack of a standardized definition of "disclosure quality," along with the inherent difficulty of evaluating such quality.

Among the most commonly used dimensions for measuring disclosure quality are: the quantity of relevant information disclosed, which refers to the breadth of information provided by the company (what is disclosed?) (Menassa, 2010; Michelon et al., 2015); and the accuracy of the disclosures, which concerns the level of qualitative, quantitative, and monetary detail included (how is it disclosed?) (Mio, 2022; Michelon et al., 2015).

Within this framework, the present study aims to analyze how public water companies report on their contribution to SDG 6 in their Sustainability Reports, the sustainability information related to the different phases of water management, the national and international standards used for sustainability reporting, and the quality standards met in relation to sustainability, as well as to assess whether significant changes in the quality and quantity of this information have occurred following the implementation of new water-related legal frameworks since 2020.

METHODOLOGY

Sample

In accordance with Law 7/1985 of April 2, which regulates the Foundations of the Local Government System, the provision of services—including water supply—varies depending on the size of the municipality. The law establishes a distinction between municipalities with more or less than 50,000 inhabitants. In smaller municipalities, responsibility for coordinating water supply services lies with the Provincial Council or an equivalent entity. For this reason, the present analysis focuses on municipalities with more than 50,000 inhabitants, where the responsibility for coordinating water supply services falls directly to the municipal government.

The sample of this research consists of the 43 sustainability reports of public water companies that supply water to local entities with more than 50,000 inhabitants. This sample has been divided into two groups, those sustainability reports that are prior to the start of legislation on sustainability in Spain, i.e. until 2019 and those after that date. Specifically, 19 of these sustainability reports analysed are prior to 2020, while 24 are after that date.

Method

A comparative analysis was conducted to identify differences in disclosure quality regarding' Spanish public water companies practices aligned with the Sustainable Development Goal-6 (SDG-6). Specifically, a deductive content analysis of the Sustainability Reports was applied, with the data coded into pre-defined categories based on the literature review in Section 3. The analysis focused on five dimensions:

A) What is disclosed in the Sustainability Report in relation to SDG-6: This examines whether sustainability reports include practices aligned with the SDG-6. If it mentions SDG-6, if it shows the targets it intends to achieve and the actions to be taken to achieve those targets.
B) What is disclosed in the Sustainability Report about sustainability measures carried out in the different phases of the integral water cycle: 01. Capture (obtaining water from various sources): 02. Desalination (removal of salt and other minerals from seawater); 03. Purification (treatment for human consumption); 04. Distribution (maintenance of the water distribution network); 05. Sanitation (maintenance of the sewage distribution network); 06. Treatment (removal of contaminants); 7. Reuse (treatment for other activities).
C) How much is disclosed: the information is presented qualitatively, quantitatively, or monetarily.
D) Internationally recognized standard s used to prepare the information on water included in the sustainability report: GRI standards and/or other recognized standards.
E) Disclosure of quality standards applied in water management systems to demonstrate commitment to environmental protection.

The content analysis of the sustainability reports was conducted in March 2025.

RESULTS: COMPARATIVE ANALYSIS

This section begins by comparing the importance given to information on Clean Water and Sanitation in the Sustainability Reports of public water companies over recent years. To do so, we analyse the average number of pages dedicated to the disclosure of information related to water sustainability.

As shown in Figure 1, there has been a slight but notable increase in the attention given to this topic, with the average number of pages rising from 7.78 to 8.3. This growth suggests a greater effort by companies to expand their communication regarding water sustainability initiatives, reflecting an increased awareness of the relevance of water sustainability within their reporting practices.

Figure 1. Average number of pages reporting SDG-6 in the sustainability report

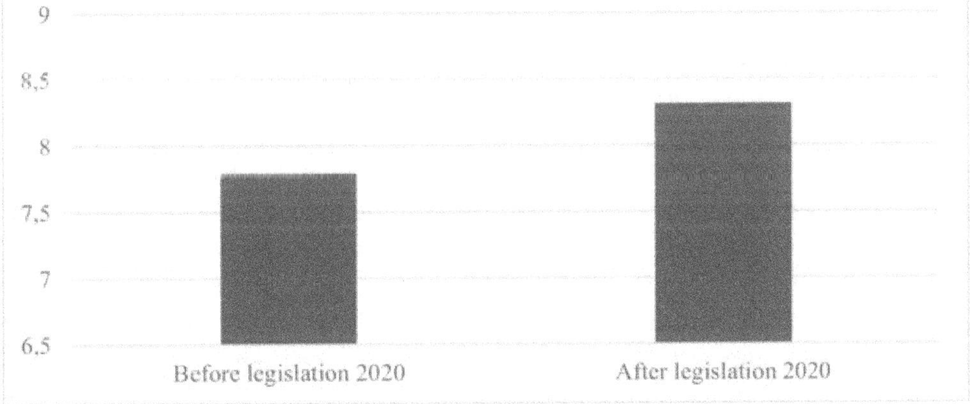

(Own production)

In relation to the first dimension, we present the results related to the disclosure of explicit references to SDG 6 in the analysed Sustainability Reports. As shown in Figure 2, the proportion of reports that include a direct mention of SDG 6 increased by 10,75% following the introduction of new sustainability legislation by the Spanish government. Specifically, explicit references rose from 68,42% to 79,17% of public water companies. This suggests that the majority of these companies now recognize the importance of highlighting their commitment to SDG 6 in their reporting practices. The increase reflects a growing awareness of the need to align corporate communication with national and international sustainability objectives, reinforcing the role of public water companies in promoting clean water and sanitation initiatives. Overall, the data indicates a positive trend toward greater visibility of SDG 6 within the sector's Sustainability Reports, in line with the evolving regulatory and social expectations.

It is also noteworthy that, during the first period analysed, only 15.7% of the Sustainability Reports explicitly interconnected SDG 6 with other Sustainable Development Goals. Specifically, links were primarily established with SDG 13 (*Climate Action*), recognizing the impact of climate change on water availability and management, and with SDG 12 (*Responsible Consumption and Production*), highlighting the close relationship between sustainable water use and the efficient management of natural resources. In the second period, this percentage increased by 10%, and the interconnections expanded to include SDG 11 (*Sustainable Cities and Communities*) and SDG 15 (*Life on Land*). In this context, SDG 6 was linked to SDG 11 by emphasizing that sustainable water and sanitation management is essential for building resilient and sustainable urban environments. Similarly, the connection with SDG 15 underlines the importance of water quality and resource management for the conservation and health of terrestrial ecosystems. This evolution reflects a broader and more integrated understanding by public water companies of the interdependent nature of sustainability challenges, demonstrating progress toward a more holistic approach to sustainability reporting.

On the other hand, SDG 6 seeks to ensure universal and equitable access to safe drinking water, adequate sanitation, and hygiene services, as well as to improve water quality globally. In this regard, 75% of the Sustainability Reports from public water companies include references to these specific targets, a figure that remains almost unchanged compared to the period before the legislative reforms (73.86%). This suggests that companies were already aware of the importance of these goals prior to the regulatory changes. Concerning the actions adopted to mobilize and redirect resources toward the sustainable use of water, all reports — both before and after the new sustainability-focused legislation — consistently disclose such actions (Figure 2).

Figure 2. Information disclosure in relation to SDG-6

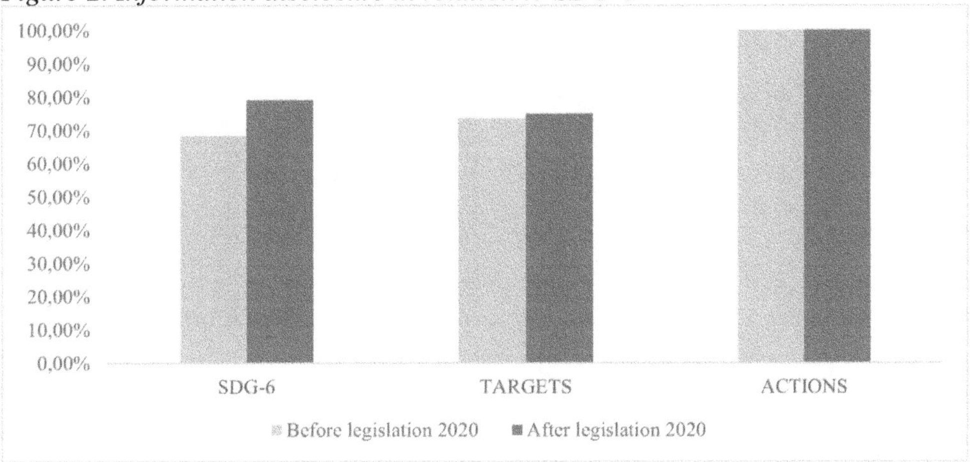

(Own production).

Regarding the question "What is disclosed in the Sustainability Reports about the sustainability measures implemented across the different phases of the integrated water cycle?", the aim is to assess whether companies have made efforts to promote sustainability throughout each phase. The phases with the most information disclosed are purification, distribution, and treatment, appearing in 79.19% of the reports in the second period, representing an increase of approximately 6% compared to reports published before the enactment of Spain's sustainability legislation.

In contrast, the phases of desalination and water reuse are the least reported in terms of sustainability efforts. Although there has been some improvement following the introduction of new regulations, the level of transparency remains notably low. As shown in Figure 3, sustainability-related actions in desalination are disclosed in only 8.33% of the reports, and in the case of water reuse, in 45.83%. These figures suggest that, despite some progress, there is still considerable room for improvement in communicating sustainability initiatives in these critical areas of the water cycle.

Figure 3. Percentage of reports that mention each phase of the water cycle

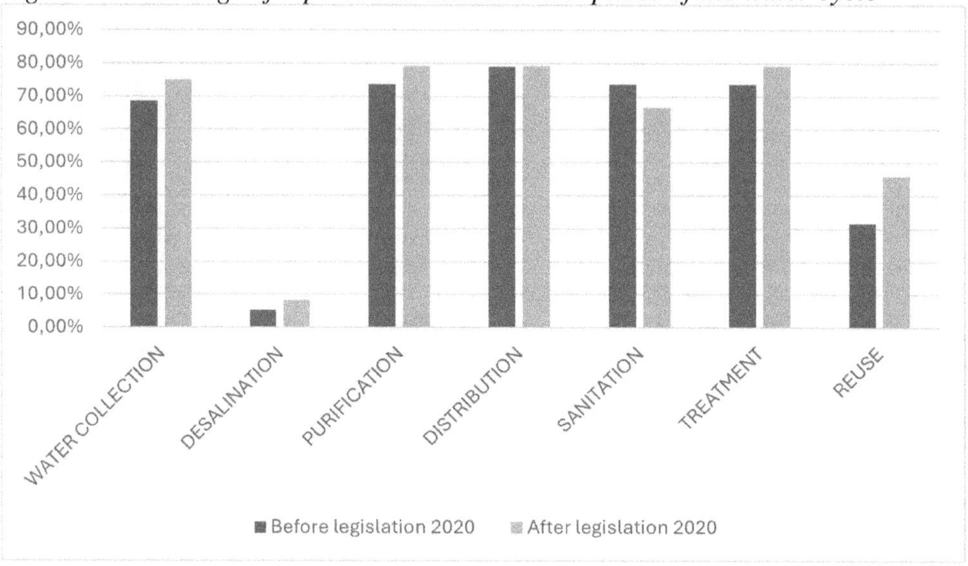

(Own production)

Regarding the comparative analysis of the quantitative, qualitative, and monetary levels of disclosure related to SDG 6 across the two periods studied, it is observed that more than 75% of the Sustainability Reports include both quantitative data and qualitative narratives. This suggests that organizations generally strive to provide not only descriptive information about their sustainable water management practices but also to complement it with measurable indicators (Figure 4).

However, it is noteworthy that the combined use of narrative descriptions and measurable metrics has slightly decreased following the introduction of Spain's new sustainability legislation. This decline is partly explained by a shift in some reports toward incorporating monetary disclosures regarding SDG 6-related actions. Despite this evolution, monetary reporting remains significantly less common than qualitative or quantitative reporting, with only around 25% of the analysed reports including financial information.

This finding is consistent with Akhter et al. (2023), who also identified monetary disclosure as having the lowest reporting rate. Overall, while organizations increasingly recognize the value of providing measurable data, financial transparency regarding sustainable water management initiatives is still limited and represents an area for potential improvement.

Figure 4. Quantitative, qualitative, and monetary levels of disclosure related to SDG-6

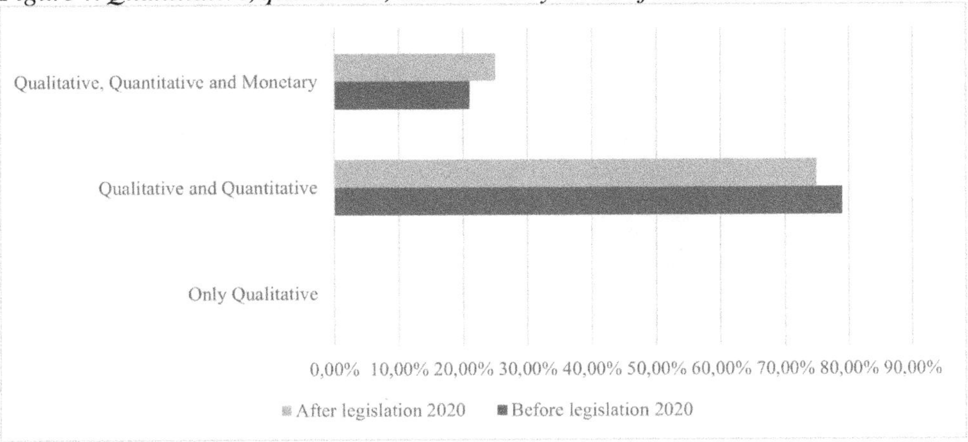

(Own production)

Focusing on the quality standards used by Spanish public water companies to disclose water-related information in their Sustainability Reports, it is important to note that several global frameworks are available to guide this reporting. Among the most recognized are the Global Reporting Initiative (GRI), ISO 26000, the Sustainability Accounting Standards Board (SASB), and the European Sustainability Reporting Standards (ESRS). Of these, the GRI framework has consistently led as the most widely adopted standard for sustainability reporting worldwide (Mougenot et al., 2024). Consequently, we first analysed whether the GRI standards were applied in the reports reviewed.

Our findings reveal that only 50% of the Sustainability Reports from public water companies referenced the use of GRI standards, with virtually no variation between the two periods analysed. Given this limited adoption, we further investigated whether other ESG reporting frameworks were cited. However, no reference to alternative guidelines was found in the remaining reports.

The lack of adherence to recognized reporting standards suggests that half of the public water companies are disclosing sustainability information without a structured or national /internationally comparable framework. As a result, it will be more difficult for these companies to measure, evaluate, and compare the sustainability impact of their water management practices against peers within the sector. This absence of standardized criteria not only hampers transparency but also limits the potential for benchmarking performance and identifying best practices across the industry.

Figure 5. GRI framework adopted in the sustainability reports

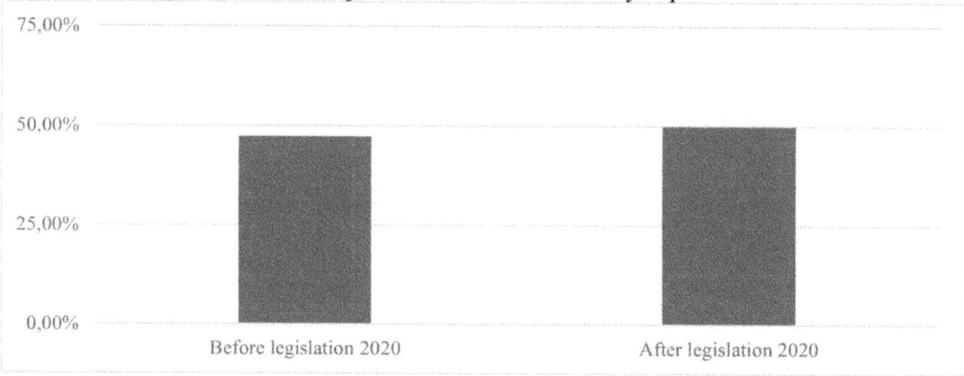

(Own production)

Finally, we address the disclosure of quality standards applied in water management systems to demonstrate the companies' commitment to environmental protection. The first notable finding is that most Sustainability Reports make no reference to the use of quality standards; specifically, nearly 75% of the reports analysed (Figure 6) omit this information.

Among those reports that do reference the application of quality standards, the focus is primarily on standards aimed at improving and controlling product quality. During the period prior to 2020, approximately 21% of the reports cited the implementation of ISO 17025 and ISO 9001, both related to product quality management. In contrast, only 5.2% mentioned the application of ISO 14001, an international standard that demonstrates a company's environmental commitment and efforts toward sustainability in water management.

In the period following 2020, although references to quality standards persisted, they continued to focus predominantly on product quality. Specifically, 20.83% of the reports referred to the use of ISO 17025 and ISO 9001, and additionally mentioned ISO 22000, a standard ensuring water safety throughout the production and distribution chain. However, only 4.16% of the reports cited standards directly linked to sustainability, such as ISO 14046, which serves as a starting point for understanding water-related impacts and fostering sustainable water use practices.

These findings suggest that, despite slight improvements, the integration and disclosure of environmental and sustainability-focused quality standards in public water companies' reporting remain limited, highlighting an important area for future development.

Figure 6. Number of quality standards disclosed in the sustainability reports

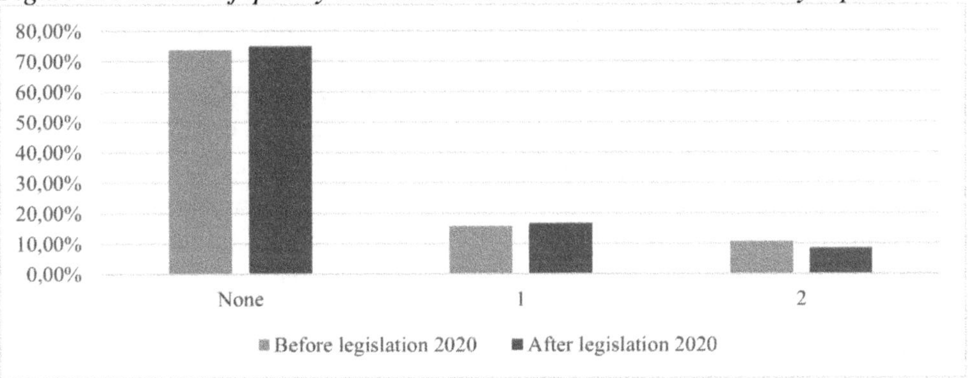

(Own production)

CONCLUSION

The public sector plays a crucial role in sustainability, since its decisions directly influence its progress. However, its responsibility is not only limited to promoting sustainable development through its policies and actions, but it must also act as a benchmark in the preparation and dissemination of sustainability reports (Bryan, 2022).

In Spain, the regulation of sustainability in public water companies is aligned with European directives and is embodied in national regulations such as Law 7/2021 on Climate Change and Royal Decree 3/2023 on water quality, aimed at strengthening water management and environmental resilience. These regulations are complemented by strategies such as the National Integrated Energy and Climate Plan, which reinforces the commitment, among others, of public water companies to sustainability.

It is expected that the regulatory effort carried out in Spain in terms of sustainability has consolidated the importance in public water companies of elaborating and disclosing the policies and results obtained in terms of sustainability, so this paper compares how public water companies have advanced in the provision of information on sustainable water management in their sustainability reports.

The comparative analysis of Sustainability Reports from Spanish public water companies before and after 2020 reveals gradual improvements in the disclosure of information related to Sustainable Development Goal 6 (Clean Water and Sanitation). The average number of pages dedicated to water sustainability increased slightly, reflecting a growing effort to raise the visibility of water-related initiatives within corporate reporting practices. However, this quantitative increase is modest and does not necessarily imply a qualitative improvement, as the mere expansion of content does not guarantee greater transparency or a stronger commitment to sustainability.

Following the legislative reforms on sustainability, there was a clear increase in the explicit mention of SDG 6 in the reports. Furthermore, companies began to show a broader understanding of sustainability by establishing connections between SDG 6 and other goals, particularly those related to climate action, sustainable cities, and life on land. This suggests a shift toward a more integrated and systemic approach to sustainability communication. However, it is particularly revealing how the percentage of sustainability reports that include specific targets or actions taken has not changed following the new sustainability legislation. These results could indicate that many companies already included this type of information prior to the regulatory changes, which raises questions about the true impact of the legislation on the transformation of sustainability practices.

In terms of the water cycle, companies reported more extensively on purification, distribution, and treatment activities. However, reporting on desalination and water reuse remains limited, indicating that transparency and disclosure efforts in these critical areas of water management are still insufficient. On the one hand, the lack of standardisation in the way these actions are presented limits their utility in assessing the real commitment of organisations. On the other hand, this imbalance in the coverage of the phases of the water cycle highlights a partial and somewhat conservative vision of sustainability on the part of public companies in the sector. Instead of adopting an innovative approach that focuses on emerging technologies and circular solutions, companies seem to focus on the more traditional aspects of the water cycle, probably because these are the ones where they already have experience or consolidated infrastructures.

The methodological approach to disclosure remained largely consistent across both periods, with a strong reliance on combining qualitative narratives and quantitative data. Nevertheless, monetary reporting related to water sustainability initiatives continues to be rare, suggesting that organizations are cautious about disclosing financial data linked to their sustainability efforts. Furthermore, the scarce presence of monetary indicators makes it impossible to know the real economic effort that companies are dedicating to their sustainability policies, which severely limits the ability of stakeholders to assess the financial commitment of these entities to sustainable water management.

Despite the global prominence of reporting frameworks such as the Global Reporting Initiative (GRI), the adoption of standardized guidelines remained limited. This finding is particularly relevant as half of the public water utilities are reporting without conforming to any standardised national or international framework. This practice considerably weakens the quality of the information reported, making it difficult to compare it across organisations and with sectoral standards. Likewise, references to internationally recognized environmental standards like ISO 14001 and ISO 14046 were minimal, this lack suggests that the environmental commitment of public water utilities, at least in terms of adherence to recognized standards, is still very limited. The low adoption of environmental quality regulatory frameworks reinforces the impression that many of these organisations remain anchored in a logic of minimum compliance, rather than a proactive orientation towards continuous improvement and excellence in sustainability.

In conclusion, although some positive developments are evident, a stronger commitment to comprehensive, standardized, and transparent sustainability reporting is necessary to meet the evolving demands of stakeholders and regulatory frameworks. Therefore, although some small progress has been made, there is still much room for improvement. Challenges remain, such as the adoption by public water companies of the new European standards on sustainability reporting, which would lead to the consolidation of reporting practices aligned with the principles of integrity, comparability and reliability in the public sphere. Consequently, it is necessary to rethink the design and implementation of regulatory frameworks, as well as to establish stricter control and verification mechanisms to ensure not only formal disclosure, but also consistency between reporting and actual management practices.

Among the future lines, it would be necessary to highlight the convenience of assessing the quality of these reports by analysing the use of independent verification mechanisms. It would also be advisable to analyse the informative balance of the different SDGs provided by public companies in sustainability reports. In addition, it is necessary to compare the situation of Spanish public companies with those of the rest of the European Union.

REFERENCES

Akhter, F., Hossain, M. R., Elrehail, H., Rehman, S. U., & Almansour, B. (2023). Environmental disclosures and corporate attributes, from the lens of legitimacy theory: A longitudinal analysis on a developing country. *European Journal of Management and Business Economics, 32*(3), 342–369. DOI: 10.1108/EJMBE-01-2021-0008

Albrecht, J. (2024). Climate adaptation law: a European perspective. s*China-EU Law Journal*, 1-25.

Alessia, D. (2017). Applying GRI sustainability reporting in the water sector: Evidences from an Italian company. *International Journal of Business Administration, 8*(3), 10–23. DOI: 10.5430/ijba.v8n3p10

Ali, I. M., Ayub, N., Husin, N. M., Alrazi, B., Mohd Ali, I., & Mat Husin, N. (2019). Water disclosure and financial performance: The CASE of CDP water a-list companies. *European Proceedings of Social and Behavioural Sciences, 100.*

Andrades, J., Martinez-Martinez, D., Herrera, J., & Larran, M. (2024). Is water management really transparent? A comparative analysis of ESG reporting of Andalusian publicly-owned enterprises. *Public Money & Management, 44*(3), 208–215. DOI: 10.1080/09540962.2023.2171844

Bryan, K. (2022). Sustainability reporting at EU level: Leading by example? *Journal of Public Budgeting, Accounting & Financial Management, 34*(3), 488–497. DOI: 10.1108/JPBAFM-05-2021-0083

Camilleri, M. A. (2015). Valuing stakeholder engagement and sustainability reporting. *Corporate Reputation Review, 18*(3), 210–222. DOI: 10.1057/crr.2015.9

Cammalleri, C., Naumann, G., Mentaschi, L., Bisselink, B., Gelati, E., De Roo, A., & Feyen, L. (2020). Diverging hydrological drought traits over Europe with global warming. *Hydrology and Earth System Sciences, 24*(12), 5919–5935. DOI: 10.5194/hess-24-5919-2020

Cantele, S., Tsalis, T. A., & Nikolaou, I. E. (2018). A new framework for assessing the sustainability reporting disclosure of water utilities. *Sustainability (Basel), 10*(2), 433. DOI: 10.3390/su10020433

Carlos, B. G., Díaz-Noriega, S., Elola, J. M., & Daniel, R. G. (2021, 10 mayo). *Principios ESG y cadena de Valor: del Reporting al Impacto Social.* http://hdl.handle.net/11531/55617

Commission Delegated Regulation (EU) 2023/2772 supplementing Directive 2013/34/EU of the European Parliament and of the Council as regards sustainability reporting standards. 31 July. O.J. (L)

Cosma, S., Venturelli, A., Schwizer, P., & Boscia, V. (2020). Sustainable development and European banks: A non-financial disclosure analysis. *Sustainability (Basel), 12*(15), 6146. DOI: 10.3390/su12156146

De Iorio, S., Zampone, G., & Piccolo, A. (2022). Determinant factors of SDG disclosure in the university context. *Administrative Sciences, 12*(1), 21. DOI: 10.3390/admsci12010021

del Olmo Casalderrey, J., & Corrales, F. X. L. (2024). Las normas de elaboración de información sobre sostenibilidad, armonización internacional o enredo global. *Técnica contable y financiera*, (70), 1.

Directive (EU) 2020/2184 of the European Parliament and of the Council of December 16, 2020, concerning the quality of water intended for human consumption. Gazzetta Ufficiale dell'Unione European L, 435 (2).

Directive (EU) 2022/2464 of the European Parliament and of the Council amending Regulation (EU) No 537/2014, Directive 2004/109/EC, Directive 2006/43/EC and Directive 2013/34/EU, as regards corporate sustainability reporting. 14 December. O.J. (L 322), 15-80.

Erin, O., Bamigboye, O. A., & Oyewo, B. (2022). Sustainable development goals (SDG) reporting: An analysis of disclosure. *Journal of Accounting in Emerging Economies, 12*(5), 761–789. DOI: 10.1108/JAEE-02-2020-0037

European Commission, Brussels, 1.2.2018, COM 753 final 2017/0332 (COD). Proposal for a Directive of the European parliament and of the council on the quality of water intended for human consumption (recast)

European Commission. (2023). Questions and Answers on the Adoption of European Sustainability Reporting Standards. Retrieved from https://ec.europa.eu/commission/presscorner/detail/en/qanda_23_4043

European Commission. (2025). *European Commission, official website.* https://commission.europa.eu/index_en

EUROPEAN, ICDU (1999). Council Directive 98/83/EC of 3 November 1998 concerning the quality of water intended for human consumption. Official Journal L, 330, 5.

Evans, N., Kocher, D., Kögel, N., & Duwe, M. (2023). The landscape of national climate framework laws in Europe.

Fernández de Gatta Sánchez, D. (2021). La ley 7/2021, de 20 de mayo, de cambio climático y transición energética (entre la expectación y una cierta decepción). Foro: Revista de Ciencias Juridicas y Sociales Nueva Epoca, 24(2).

Ferrero-Ferrero, I., Torres, M. J. M., Rivera-Lirio, J. M., Escrig-Olmedo, E., & Izquierdo, M. Á. F. (2023). SDG reporting: An analysis of corporate sustainability leaders. *Marketing Intelligence & Planning*, *41*(4), 457–472. DOI: 10.1108/MIP-07-2022-0332

Fiorino, M. (2020). Are companies using water disclosure toward Sustainable Development Goal 6? An analysis of two water-intensive sectors.

Fülöp, M. T., & Topor, D. I. (2025). The digital transformation of SMEs: Opportunities and challenges for sustainability reporting in Romania. *Journal of Global Responsibility*. Advance online publication. DOI: 10.1108/JGR-10-2024-0211

García-Meca, E., Martínez-Ferrero, J., y Sánchez-Ballesta, J. P. (2021). El cumplimento de los ODS y sus efectos en la rentabilidad económica en la empresa cotizada española. *Contabilidad y Tributación, CEF/Contabilidad y TributacióN, CEF*, 195-220. https://doi.org/DOI: 10.51302/rcyt.2021.7463

Geba, N. B., & Giusio, M. (2017). *Contabilidad social y ambiental: los estándares GRI 2016 y los objetivos del desarrollo sustentable*. http://sedici.unlp.edu.ar/handle/10915/72810

Gil, L., & Bernardo, J. (2020). An approach to energy and climate issues aiming at carbon neutrality. *Renewable Energy Focus*, *33*, 37–42. DOI: 10.1016/j.ref.2020.03.003

Government of Spain. (2022). PERTE de Digitalización del ciclo del Agua. https://www.prtr.miteco.gob.es/content/dam/prtr/es/perte/maquetacionperteoficialmoncloa-memoria-vertical-v1_tcm30-538587.pdf

Guerrero-Baena, M. D., Castilla-Polo, F., & Rodríguez-Gutiérrez, P. (2024). What are the main drivers of SMEs' production of sustainability reports? *Small Business International Review*, *8*(1), e617. DOI: 10.26784/sbir.v8i1.617

Höhne, N., Gidden, M. J., den Elzen, M., Hans, F., Fyson, C., Geiges, A., Jeffery, M. L., Gonzales-Zuñiga, S., Mooldijk, S., Hare, W., & Rogelj, J. (2021). Wave of net zero emission targets opens window to meeting the Paris Agreement. *Nature Climate Change*, *11*(10), 820–822. DOI: 10.1038/s41558-021-01142-2

Hummel, K., & Szekely, M. (2022). Disclosure on the sustainable development goals–evidence from Europe. *Accounting in Europe, 19*(1), 152–189. DOI: 10.1080/17449480.2021.1894347

Ioannou, I., & Serafeim, G. (2019). The consequences of mandatory corporate sustainability reporting.

ISO. (2019). Water efficiency management systems — Requirements with guidance for use. https://www.iso.org/standard/68286.html

Julve, V. M., & Alijarde, I. B. (2022). Hacia la divulgación de información de sostenibilidad en el sector público. *Apuntes Contables, 31*(31), 11–32. DOI: 10.18601/16577175.n31.02

Koskelainen, M. (2024). Study of the Novel European Sustainability Reporting Standards (ESRS)–changes and impact on the case company.

Krawczyk, P. (2021). Non-financial reporting—Standardization options for SME sector. *Journal of Risk and Financial Management, 14*(9), 417. DOI: 10.3390/jrfm14090417

Larramendy, E. E., & Tiberi, S. (2019b, octubre 1). *Información Integrada - Marco teórico GRI y marco teórico de Reportes Integrados.* http://sedici.unlp.edu.ar/handle/10915/88587

Larrinaga, C., Luque-Vilchez, M., & Fernández, R. (2018). Sustainability accounting regulation in Spanish public sector organizations. *Public Money & Management, 38*(5), 345–354. DOI: 10.1080/09540962.2018.1477669

Law 7/1985 Regulating the Bases of the Local Regime. April 2. BOE No. 80

Lodhia, S., Kaur, A., & Kuruppu, S. C. (2023). The disclosure of sustainable development goals (SDGs) by the top 50 Australian companies: Substantive or symbolic legitimation? *Meditari Accountancy Research, 31*(6), 1578–1605. DOI: 10.1108/MEDAR-05-2021-1297

Lozano, R., & Huisingh, D. (2011). Inter-linking issues and dimensions in sustainability reporting. *Journal of Cleaner Production, 19*(2-3), 99–107. DOI: 10.1016/j.jclepro.2010.01.004

Marti, E., Fuchs, M., DesJardine, M. R., Slager, R., & Gond, J. P. (2024). The impact of sustainable investing: A multidisciplinary review. *Journal of Management Studies, 61*(5), 2181–2211. DOI: 10.1111/joms.12957

Matuszak, Ł., Różańska, E., & Szczepankiewicz, E. I. (2025). Assessment of the Compliance of Environmental Disclosures by Energy Companies Using GRI Standards with European Sustainability Reporting Standards: A Case Study. *Sustainability (Basel), 17*(8), 3380. DOI: 10.3390/su17083380

Mclennan, C., Rudi, G., Altchenko, Y., & Ait-Mouheb, N. (2024). Will the European Regulation for water reuse for agricultural irrigation foster this practice in the European Union? *Water Reuse, 14*(2), 115–135. DOI: 10.2166/wrd.2024.012

Menassa, E. (2010). Corporate social responsibility: An exploratory study of the quality and extent of social disclosures by Lebanese commercial banks. *Journal of applied accounting research*, 11(1), 4-23.

Michelon, G., Pilonato, S., & Ricceri, F. (2015). CSR reporting practices and the quality of disclosure: An empirical analysis. *Critical Perspectives on Accounting, 33*, 59–78. DOI: 10.1016/j.cpa.2014.10.003

Ministry of Social Rights and Agenda 2030 (2020). Estrategia de Desarrollo Sostenible 2030 Centro de publicaciones paseo del prado, 18-20, 28014. Madrid. https://cpage.mpr.gob.es/

Mio, C., Costantini, A., & Panfilo, S. (2022). Performance measurement tools for sustainable business: A systematic literature review on the sustainability balanced scorecard use. *Corporate Social Responsibility and Environmental Management, 29*(2), 367–384. DOI: 10.1002/csr.2206

Mougenot, B., & Doussoulin, J. P. (2024). A bibliometric analysis of the Global Reporting Initiative (GRI): Global trends in developed and developing countries. *Environment, Development and Sustainability, 26*(3), 6543–6560. DOI: 10.1007/s10668-023-02974-y PMID: 36788933

Muller, M. (2012). 11. Water accounting, corporate sustainability and the public interest. *Water Accounting*, 203.

Nicolo', G., & Cervilla-Bellido, J. M. (2025). Investigating the antecedents of Sustainable Development Goals disclosure via social media: Evidence from water companies. *Corporate Social Responsibility and Environmental Management, 32*(2), 2317–2331. DOI: 10.1002/csr.3066

Nicolo', G., Zampone, G., De Iorio, S., & Sannino, G. (2024). Does SDG disclosure reflect corporate underlying sustainability performance? Evidence from UN Global Compact participants. *Journal of International Financial Management & Accounting, 35*(1), 214–260. DOI: 10.1111/jifm.12194

Odobaša, R., & Marošević, K. (2023). Expected contributions of the European corporate sustainability reporting directive (CSRD) to the sustainable development of the European union. *EU and comparative law issues and challenges series (ECLIC), 7*, 593-612.

Okwuosa, I. I. (2022). Examining disclosure of contribution towards SDG-6 and its motivation among nigeria's premium board companies. In *Environmental Sustainability and Agenda 2030: Efforts, Progress and Prospects* (pp. 135-157). Emerald Publishing Limited. DOI: 10.1108/S1479-359820220000010007

Permatasari, P., & Kosasih, E. (2021). Sustainability reporting guideline for small medium enterprises (SMEs): Case study from 25 SMEs in Indonesia. In *RSF Conference Series: Business, Management and Social Sciences* (Vol. 1, No. 2, pp. 10-20). DOI: 10.31098/bmss.v1i2.256

Regulation (EU) 2021/1119 of 30 June 2021 establishing the framework for achieving climate neutrality, OJ EU L 243, 9.7.2021, 1.

Reverte, C. (2021). La importancia de las diferencias institucionales entre países en el nivel de consecución de los ODS: Un estudio empírico a escala mundial. *Revista de Fomento Social*, •••, 115–159. DOI: 10.32418/rfs.2021.299.4583

Rodrigo, S. G. (2022, April). La política de adaptación al cambio climático en la Ley 7/2021: instrumentos generales. In *Estudios sobre cambio climático y transición energética: Estudios conmemorativos del XXV aniversario del acceso a la cátedra del profesor Íñigo del Guayo Castiella* (pp. 433–460). Ediciones Jurídicas y Sociales. DOI: 10.2307/j.ctv2zp4wzn.23

Różańska, E., Matuszak, Ł., & Dyczkowska, J. (2024). Comparative analysis of the GRI Standards and the IR Framework and their impact on the quality of disclosures. In *Research Handbook on Sustainability Reporting* (pp. 90–108). Edward Elgar Publishing. DOI: 10.4337/9781035316267.00014

Salgado, M. H. A. (2024). La Transición Energética En El Contexto Constitucional Español. *Revista Direito Público, 21*(111), 176–195.

Setyaningsih, S., Widjojo, R., & Kelle, P. (2024). Challenges and opportunities in sustainability reporting: A focus on small and medium enterprises (SMEs). *Cogent Business & Management, 11*(1), 2298215. DOI: 10.1080/23311975.2023.2298215

Siew, R. Y. (2015). A review of corporate sustainability reporting tools (SRTs). *Journal of Environmental Management, 164*, 180–195. DOI: 10.1016/j.jenvman.2015.09.010 PMID: 26379255

Simou, S. (2022). La Ley 7/2021, de 20 de mayo, de cambio climático y transición energética en el contexto de intensificación de los esfuerzos público-privados para afrontar la emergencia climática. Anuario de la Facultad de Derecho de la Universidad Autónoma de Madrid, 215-250.

Stolowy, H., & Paugam, L. (2023). Sustainability reporting: Is convergence possible? *Accounting in Europe*, *20*(2), 139–165. DOI: 10.1080/17449480.2023.2189016

Suárez-Rico, Y. M., Gómez-Villegas, M., & García-Benau, M. A. (2021). La utilidad de los informes de sostenibilidad en entidades públicas y privadas en Colombia: La percepción de los stakeholders. *Contaduría Universidad de Antioquia*, (79), 103–136. DOI: 10.17533/udea.rc.n79a05

Teruel-Gutiérrez, R. (2020). Sustainability as a corporate strategy: A performance comparison of green and non-green SME hotels. [SBIR]. *Small Business International Review*, *4*(2), 30–38. DOI: 10.26784/sbir.v4i2.254

The Paris Agreement (UNFCCC, 2015).

United Nations. (2015). UN General Assembly. Transforming our world: the 2030 Agenda for Sustainable Development. A/RES/70/1. https://www.un.org/en/development/desa/population/migration/generalassembly/docs/globalcompact/A_RES_70_1_E.pdf

United Nations. (2016). Clean Water and Sanitation: Why It Matters. https://www.un.org/sustainabledevelopment/wp-content/uploads/2016/08/6_Why-It-Matters-2020.pdf

United Nations. (2023). The Sustainable Development Goals Report 2023: Special edition. United Nations, New York, NY. https://unstats.un.org/sdgs/report/2023/The-Sustainable-Development-Goals-Report-2023.pdf

Vázquez, C., & Orteu Berrocal, E. (2021). "Planificación Hidrológica Y Adaptación Al Cambio Climático En El Marco De La Nueva Ley De Cambio Climático Y Transición Energética". Actualidad Jurídica Ambiental, (115).

Vázquez-Burguete, J. L., Licandro, O., Ortigueira-Sánchez, L. C., & Correa, P. (2024). Do enterprises that publish sustainability reports have a better developed environmental responsibility and are they more transparent? *Sustainability (Basel)*, *16*(14), 5866. DOI: 10.3390/su16145866

Velten, E. K., Evans, N., Duwe, M., Spasova, D., de la Vega, R., & Duin, L. (2022). Charting a path to net zero: An assessment of national long-term strategies in the EU.

Venturelli, A., Ligorio, L., & de Nuccio, E. (2023). Biodiversity accountability in water utilities: A case study. *Utilities Policy*, *81*, 101495. DOI: 10.1016/j.jup.2023.101495

Water, U. N. (2021). Summary Progress Update 2021: SDG 6 — water and sanitation for all. https://www.unwater.org/app/uploads/2021/12/SDG-6-Summary-Progress-Update-2021_Version-July-2021a.pdf

World Health Organization. (2022). *Guidelines for drinking-water quality: incorporating the first and second addenda*. World Health Organization.

KEY TERMS AND DEFINITIONS

Double Materiality: A reporting principle that obliges companies to disclose both how sustainability issues affect their financial position and how their operations impact society and the environment.

European Sustainability Reporting Standards (ESRS): A standardized framework adopted by the European Union requiring companies to report on sustainability-related issues, including environmental and social impacts, with specific emphasis on double materiality and independent verification.

Global Reporting Initiative (GRI): An internationally recognized framework for sustainability reporting that helps organizations communicate their ESG impacts, with specific standards like GRI 303 and 306 focused on water and effluent disclosures

Greenwashing: A misleading practice in which organizations present a deceptive image of environmental responsibility by disclosing only positive impacts or selectively reporting sustainability information

Materiality Assessment: A systematic evaluation process that determines which sustainability issues are most relevant for a company to report on, based on stakeholder concerns and the company's strategic priorities.

Sustainability Reporting: The practice by which organizations publicly disclose environmental, social, and governance (ESG) data, policies, and performance to inform stakeholders about their contributions to sustainable development and long-term strategic goals.

Sustainable Development Goal 6 (SDG 6): A global objective established by the United Nations that seeks to ensure universal and equitable access to safe drinking water, adequate sanitation, and hygiene, while also improving water use efficiency and protecting water-related ecosystems.

Chapter 7
Human Rights, Legal Compliance, and the 2030 Agenda:
A Convergent Approach

Vishambhar Raghuwanshi
https://orcid.org/0009-0009-1365-1850
Manipal University Jaipur, India

Pranjal Khare
https://orcid.org/0000-0002-9937-9588
Jindal Global Law School, O.P. Jindal Global University, India

Paridhi Sharma
https://orcid.org/0009-0005-3373-0557
O.P. Jindal Global University, India

Sheenam Thakur
Rajiv Gandhi National Law University, Punjab, India

ABSTRACT

World leaders adopted the 2030 Agenda for Sustainable Development through the United Nations to show how global development should embrace inclusivity and equity together with justice. The path to this vision converges legal compliance with sustainable development goals (SDGs) and human rights at its base. This study highlights the developing requirement of combining efforts into a single approach which validates human rights as essential structures to reach sustainable development goals. The SDGs function as universal peace and prosperity guidelines yet need legal frameworks to achieve success because they protect dignity and equality

DOI: 10.4018/979-8-3373-1792-2.ch007

together with access to justice. The document ends by supporting a rights-driven legally anchored development framework of global development because it enables compliance while empowering disadvantaged communities. According to the research such alignment between developments is vital for establishing societies which are resilient as well as just and sustainable.

INTRODUCTION

The United Nations' adoption of the 2030 Agenda for Sustainable Development brought a crucial shift in worldwide management of development. The agenda exploits 17 Sustainable Development Goals with 169 targets to develop a sustainable and equitable society to be achieved by 2030. As opposed to its former framework under Millennium Development Goals (MDGs), the Sustainable Development Goals (SDGs) offer a universal, inclusive and integrative application, demonstrating a stronger dedication to fulfilment of values of human dignity and aims at attaining global justice (Woodbridge, 2015). To achieve success under its vision, the agenda confronts a series of intertwined legal, institutional, and ethical constraints which need successful navigation. Sustainable development requires two fundamental elements, and these include human rights together with legal compliance which represent critical yet under-theorized concepts. The SDG goals will fail to achieve transformative change unless they support core human rights protections through operational enforcement systems which have accountability mechanisms (Donald & Way, 2016).

This chapter takes place against the ongoing problem of formal agreements failing to translate into meaningful forceful action between different governing authorities (Rabinovych, 2020). The SDGs employ the non-binding framework that fails to enforce their precepts of inclusivity, equality and prevention of discrimination despite the eloquent expression it uses. The non-binding nature of the SDGs causes implementation problems particularly in nations which have weak governance institutions combined with insufficient political dedication to execute SDG objectives. Numerous jurisdictions currently face operational challenges because they lack legal systems to hold people accountable for goal implementation (Glass & Newig, 2019). The present research examines how a rights-based legal framework constitutes a pathway to link SDG implementation with enforceable strategies which further gain credibility from citizens through moral alignment.

The main goal of this chapter focuses on two interconnected issues. Firstly, the colloquy on human rights, legal compliance and practice of sustainable development conceptually separate the three fields. These frameworks operate independently from each other rather than in tandem, which creates obstacles for achieving the holistic goals of the 2030 Agenda. Secondly, national governments show poor integration of human rights principles in sustainable development policies and programs because there are no mandatory compliance obligations. There exists no effective international system which both monitors and enforces compliance with SDG related obligations. This investigation supports a purposeful connection between these fields to create legal compliance and human rights as foundational elements supporting the SDG initiative.

There is an endeavor to determine how human rights enforcement alongside legal conformity should become fundamental elements for the realization of SDG objectives. It explores ways to enhance the SDGs by exploiting current international and domestic legal frameworks. The research looks for institutional, jurisprudential, and policy-level harmonizing possibilities that can contribute to this convergence. It enhances current scholarships about the requirement for integrating developmental goals with legal commitments. The research employs a doctrinal approach together with analytical methods to evaluate multiple legal documents that include human rights covenants, SDG policy documents, and national statutes for understanding this framework's evolution. It includes comparative analysis with many jurisdictions to assess excellent performance while locating barriers which obstruct successful implementation.

This research includes investigations into international and national dimensions of SDG legal compliance systems. The International dimension covers the involvement of United Nations entities, treaty structures and global governance, whereas domestic laws focus on how local legal systems support or abandon human rights responsibilities while pursuing the SDGs. The research centers around SDGs 1 (No Poverty), SDG 5 (Gender Equality), SDG 10 (Reduced Inequalities), and SDG 16 (Peace, Justice and Strong Institutions) which constitute the most integral human rights-focused objectives. Effective domestic and international legal frameworks play a critical role since these morally important goals fulfill legal requirements while ensuring their successful achievement. To evaluate the degree to which legislative requirements necessitate enforcement of sustainable and rights conscious corporate practices, the chapter provides a critical examination of the role of the private sector especially in relation to environmental, social and governance (ESG) compliance.

This chapter primarily employs doctrinal and analytical approaches with additional comparison normative analysis to address its multidimensional subject. The research draws its fundamental legal material from primary documents consisting of international treaties, constitutional texts, judicial decisions, and national legislations. The analysis draws an entire picture by observing primary documentation and studying secondary information that includes UN reports, academic texts, and scientific empirical research. It employs case studies to demonstrate practical conditions regarding the relationship between SDG achievement and compliance with law through analytical, supplementary means despite the absence of fieldwork and quantitative methods. The main limitation stems from its legal framework approach since social-political and economic variables might provide a deeper understanding of the SDG implementation process. The chapter covers this missing knowledge gap through its analysis which uses human rights and legal compliance principles as fundamental frameworks.

Through a well-planned and structured framework that gradually unveils its fundamental argument, the paper deepens its analysis. The introduction of this paper presents the foundation of research through its specific goals and inclusion of intended areas of investigation. Second part of the chapter provides the conceptual and theoretical framework through an analysis of fundamental terminologies such as legal compliance, human rights, and sustainable development alongside their philosophical bases. The third part of the chapter utilizes specific legal examples to demonstrate the points of contact between human rights adherence and Sustainable Development goal implementation. The analysis in the fourth part of the chapter examines the institutional frameworks together with policy tools which either encourage or prevent this alignment with special attention given to governance systems and regulatory entities as well as monitoring systems. The fifth part of the chapter elucidates the evaluation of current practices and research data along with a consolidation of findings. The final part of the chapter summarizes principal discoveries before providing specific actionable guidelines and future study recommendations to ensure academic and practical importance of the work.

This chapter highlights both the necessity and the importance of embracing a combined approach to protection of human rights, legal enforcement, and the 2030 Agenda. The analysis confirms that sustainable development practices cannot function in legal or ethical isolation. It thereby necessitates a coordinated, legally backed and rights based ethical framework that not only strives for the well-being of humans but also enshrines it in legally binding standards. The research explores multiple conceptual, institutional, and legal frameworks that would lead to successful convergence to advance sustainable development, which is inclusive and just.

CONCEPTUAL AND THEORETICAL FRAMEWORK

Development discourse has gone through a deep transformation during the current 21st century. Development now extends beyond traditional economic indicators and infrastructure development because it undergoes evaluation through principles of justice while integrating rights belonging to all environmental sustainability (Han et al., 2024). The Sustainable Development Goals (SDGs) serve as the best example of developing a comprehensive understanding of development that naturally contains human rights together with rules of law and accountable governance systems. This research needs an analytical foundation which requires the exploration of how human rights link with legal compliance and the 2030 Agenda through conceptual examination. A conceptual framework emerges from the meaningful definition of relevant terms, an examination of theoretical frameworks and their connections between elements which make investigation more focused.

The Brundtland Report of 1987 provided a global recognition of the expression "sustainable development" by defining it as "development that meets present needs while preserving future generations' capability to satisfy their own needs" (Pribytkova, 2020). This defining principle of sustainable development was further concretized through the 2030 Agenda by organizing it within a system of 17 SDGs and 169 targets. The 2030 Agenda differs from previous economic-centered development models because it defines development through a political and normative approach which includes poverty elimination, sustainability conservation along with equal treatment for gender groups and social inclusion. Furthermore, it also promotes universal rights (Dulume, 2019).

The two major distinguishing aspects of the 2030 Agenda are its universal application and inseparability which integrate all dimensions through their interlocking nature spanning social, economic and environmental domains. The interlinked structure becomes visible when goals are expressed using human-based terminology which includes dignity and equality together with rights. The 2030 Agenda lacks direct legal authority because states and institutions need to create binding frameworks that incorporate its principles for the 2030 Agenda to become effective. The understanding of sustainable development through SDGs needs to go beyond policy rhetoric to study proper legal frameworks and institutional agents that will both support and enforce this vision (Frey, & MacNaughton, 2016).

Sustainable development needs human rights both as a conceptual basis and legal framework which establishes its moral and normative foundation. People must have these rights to maintain dignity because they include civil and political as well as economic, social, and cultural entitlements. In addition to being expressed in international instruments such as the Universal Declaration of Human Rights (UDHR), the International Covenants on Civil and Political Rights (ICCPR), and Economic, Social and Cultural Rights (ICESCR), they have also been shaped through thematic conventions alongside regional human rights frameworks (Poto & Murray, 2022).

Human rights theory provides two perspectives regarding their status: they represent ends to pursue and ways to reach other development targets. As demonstrated through Article 26 UDHR, the right to education functions both as an essential human right while directly supporting the goal of SDG 4 regarding quality education. The goal of gender equality described as SDG 5 directly connects with CEDAW provisions (Dattler et al., 2016). Bringing human rights into development requires more than simple ornamentation because it represents an essential operational requirement to establish legitimate and inclusive development projects. The nature of rights operates in the same manner as the SDG framework since both entities display independence. The achievement of economic development through SDG 8 requires labor rights and decent working conditions as stipulated by UDHR Article 23. The accomplishment of environmental sustainability through SDG 13 needs the acknowledgment of indigenous community rights to land ownership and their cultural autonomy and participation (Arajarvi, 2017). The logical connection between SDGs and human rights proves that true sustainable development can only be achieved by considering rights-based principles.

Legal compliance refers to adherence to laws, regulations, and obligations, whether domestic or international. Lawful compliance in sustainable development serves two main purposes by protecting development activities from unfairness yet preserving systems to hold parties responsible for wrongful behavior (Biradar, 2024). The SDGs lack binding status, yet most of their underlying principles find expression in binding human rights treaties and environmental and labor conventions. The legal framework for sustainable development exists through a combination of implicit and distributed international and transnational requirements. These legal obligations present a significant challenge because they exist in multiple disparate areas. Several SDGs require distinct legal frameworks to implement them since SDG 16 needs international humanitarian law while SDGs 13, 14, 15 use international environmental law along with SDG 8 requiring international labor law. Multiple gaps emerge in enforcement oversight due to the lack of a unified legal enforcement system which permits organizations to choose which laws they will follow. National laws experience shortfalls because most jurisdictions lack appropriate legislative institutions capable of making global mandates enforceable through local standards and practices (Horbachevska et al., 2024).

The measure of legal adherence remains essential for reaching sustainable development goals despite its existing constraints. Focused legal compliance functions as an antidote against administrative discretion together with political manipulation when policies are executed. The law provides people alongside communities with proper means to seek justice when their development-based rights suffer violations (Joshi, 2017). Environmental courts together with human rights commissions implement strategic litigation to force governments along with corporations to comply with sustainability requirements when there is no specific legislation for the SDGs. Organizational need for a fusion of legal compliance with sustainable development emerges as the fundamental requirement to achieve transparency, justice and accountability in practice (Gutterman, 2023).

The convergence of human rights together with mandated legal practices and SDGs forms a fundamental harmonious system beyond symbolic value alignment. Human rights serve as the foundational ethics whereas legal compliance provides operational systems which derive their direction from the SDGs. A complete framework for transformative development emerges through the integration of these three different components. This convergence theory develops from the "normative integration" concept. The concept of normative integration involves the unification process which presents multiple legal and moral standards into a cohesive governance system that directs social conduct and administrative policy (Griggs et al., 2024). States under the SDGs need to fulfill their development goals through procedures which respect human rights obligations while facing legal scrutiny for their actions. International constitutionalism along with legal pluralism exists as theoretical frameworks that support uniting various normative systems into a single framework based on universal value standards (Baena et al., 2024).

The governance theories along with "good governance" notions as development enablers demonstrate this convergence of development. Good governance represents an important human rights standard which combines transparency and accountability with participation and rule of law and functions as an SDG 16 target. Under ICESCR, the principle of progressive realization matches directly with the SDG framework requirement of setting and tracking quantifiable steps towards development objectives. Conceptual similarities demonstrate that merging legal compliance with human rights within the SDG framework represents a feasible yet conceptually comprehensive operational synergy (Biradar, 2024). The rights-based approach to development (RBAD) consolidates and expands this intersection of development concepts. According to this view, development planning should use human rights fulfillment as the central evaluation criterion. RBAD establishes precise roles for rights-holders consisting of citizens as well as duty-bearers made up of states and institutions while prioritizing systems for redressal and accountability. Traditional approaches to development as a need-assessment model views beneficiaries as receiving groups of passive beneficiaries. The SDG framework gains greater normative and legal strength through the RBAD model, which transforms development from receiving charitable aid into receiving fundamental rights (Do et al., 2020).

The practical unification of human rights, legal compliance, and SDGs encounter various substantial difficulties even though these elements share theoretical alignment. International law functions as an obstacle since it exists in multiple isolated areas. Several branches of law exist independently of each other since they lack formal systems for mutual dialogue and enforcement practices. Different international organizations face challenges, for instance, while the International Labor Organization (ILO) maintains robust monitoring systems, but environmental treaties come with insufficient enforcement structures that create problems with legal compliance between regimes (Spijkers, 2020).

Political willingness stands as a major obstacle restricting progress. Governments under authoritarian control together with unstable democratic systems use Sustainable Development Goal language to uphold their human rights abuses and weaken institutions of law. The level of politics will drive the technical aspect of compliance because power and institutional incentives need ongoing restructuring in these situations. In democratic systems corporate influences combined with budgetary restrictions together with bureaucratic internal resistance create obstacles for development goals to match legal standards. The lack of standardized measurement frameworks further makes SDG rights implementation challenging. The United Nations introduced indicators matching each SDG target, yet several countries do not possess the necessary institutional capabilities required to gather rights-relevant data at different levels. The absence of effective oversight and responsibility control because of this situation produces a significant gap between global promises and local domains (Guiry, 2024).

This chapter provided an overview of essential conceptual as well as theoretical building blocks which support the research investigation. The 2030 Agenda's definition of sustainable development proves to establish human rights and legal compliance as integrated elements. The three dimensions exist independently, but they converge through common operational and normative principles. The theories of normative integration and rights-based development and governance theory both justify and mandate their integration (Do et al., 2020). However, significant challenges, both structural and political, impede the realization of this integrated vision. Subsequent sections of this document analyze the implementation method of framework convergence through examination of institutional mechanisms and legal structures in various jurisdictions. Such integrative strategic integration ensures the SDGs progress from theoretical visions into actionable practices.

Mapping the Intersection: SDGS, Human Rights and Legal Compliance

Future global development efforts toward justice and equality require the junction of Sustainable Development Goals (SDGs), human rights and legal compliance, which together marks its focal point. This intersection establishes a necessary connection which becomes the fundamental basis for handling the 2030 Agenda implementation. Various international legal discussions throughout successive decades have led to a unified but operationally fragmented framework necessitating a rights-based and law-compliant approach to development. The realization of SDGs depends entirely on supporting human rights enforcement and developing fully accountable legal frameworks (Thomas et al., 2015). This part of the paper investigates the various connections between human rights standards and legal structures and their roles in the implementation of the SDG system as well as the influence of SDGs on local human rights fulfillment and legal system transformations.

The SDGs embody a distinctive legal claim which fully supports international human rights principles. Each goal exists as an entitlement for communities and individuals to receive universally throughout the world. SDG 1's focus on poverty elimination directly relates to the human right of ensuring proper living conditions as described in Article 25 of Universal Declaration of Human Rights (UDHR), and Article 11 of International Covenant on Economic Social Cultural Rights (ICESCR). SDG 4, which focuses on quality education, promotes equivalent goals as Article 13 of the ICESCR, which promotes education rights. These elements of alignment are not only surface level, rather they are ingrained in the SDG's language, purpose and structure, demonstrating a conceptual and practical convergence (Shayan et al., 2022).

Furthermore, this junction is specifically recognized in the Preamble of the 2030 Agenda which asserts that it is "grounded in the Universal Declaration of Human Rights and international human rights treaties." The "leaving no one behind" concept sets equality and non-discrimination as foundational principles for the development project which stems from human rights principles. The clear indication of integration emerges through SDG 10 that works toward reducing inequalities, and SDG 5, which focuses on gender equality. The true assessment of this partnership occurs through institutionalization because states and other actors need to establish legal mechanisms and governance systems which combine these related objectives and enable accountability measures and enforcement capabilities.

SDG implementation shows inconsistent integration of human rights principles because the operational approach largely depends on empty statements instead of fundamental organizational changes. Numerous states have been proactive in developing national legislation that supports SDG priorities including gender-based budget planning laws together with environmental safeguard provisions within constitutions although multiple states still need to bring their legal structure in line with international human rights responsibilities. The SDG reporting which occurs on a voluntary basis, and the SDG Agenda which lacks a binding legal framework are the two major factors contributing to this imbalance (Puthucherril et al., 2024). On the contrary, human rights law presents a higher legal standing than SDGs because it has treaty responsibilities and monitoring entities which occasionally develop adjudicative procedures to enforce its provisions.

The different levels of legal enforcement platforms in the SDG framework create doubts about its legal authority (Koundouri et al., 2025). The SDGs maintain broad worldwide backing and acceptance, yet their foundations lack a concrete legal system that depends substantially on public/state choices across nations. In lieu of such loopholes, the research experts push for development policies based on human rights wherein the SDG promises should create justiciable defendable claims, and legal institutions are empowered with authority to decide cases involving rights abuses related to development. Environmental rights jurisprudence across Latin America and some regions of South Asia proves that such convergence between human rights and environmental concerns is possible (Dulume, 2019). Judicial bodies across countries have shown increasing recognition that development goals relating to clean water as well as education and housing serve as essential elements of constitutionally protected rights and thus enhance the conceptual overlap between these domains (Ochoa et al., 2024).

Legal compliance, in this context, functions as both a pathway and a barrier to the realization of SDGs. Stable legal frameworks enable both the procedural framework for keeping human rights and establishing comprehensive development. Weak institutions together with law-based corruption and legal procedures manipulated for political gain produce major obstacles in achieving transformation through the SDG-human rights alignment. The path to justice depends on following legal requirements which go beyond technical requirements (Immler & Sakkers, 2021). It is crucial to understand that the integrity of legal framework and stability of legal systems which includes independent and accessible transparent institutions directly affects how well the Sustainable Development Goal objectives can be pursued and human rights can be protected.

SDG 16 emerges as the fundamental target which focuses on establishing peace along with justice and robust institutions. The unique feature of SDG 16 distinguishes it from other goals because this Sustainable Development Goal outlines essential development prerequisites including rule of law, access to justice as well as accountable institutions, lower violence and corruption levels. A paradigm shift occurs in development thought when development thinking officially measures legal compliance metrics through both legal aid access numbers and independent judicial body establishment. Law bridges an essential role within development processes according to SDG 16 instead of being treated as a stand-alone variable. The new development paradigm stresses legal accountability since failing to implement legal standards could render all other development achievements both unsustainable and exclusionary (Bexell et al., 2023).

Several important barriers stand in the way of implementing SDG 16 effectively. Multiple areas face difficulties in establishing complete justice availability because they lack funds to upgrade their judicial facilities and struggle to reform established legal systems. Authoritarian and hybrid regimes typically consider the political expenses associated with legal reform measures toward judicial independence and executive power limits as unacceptably high. Governments within these areas have still only set SDG 16 goals rather than making them operational. Notwithstanding this, there have been several positive developments. Civil society organizations in countries such as Kenya, Nepal and Colombia utilize SDG discourse to achieve justice penetration alongside corruption oversight while demanding proper institutional accountability. The planned use of SDG principles proves valuable when it strengthens current human rights protections together with existing legal obligations (Ruppel & Murray, 2024).

Private sector organizations now play a major role in this convergence between economics and sustainability. Business entities experience increasing pressure to demonstrate responsibility in two fields: human rights practices and sustainable development practices besides their economic performance (Biradar, 2024). The voluntary UN Guiding Principles on Business and Human Rights inspired many countries to create national action plans and companies to develop corporate due diligence frameworks that support the accomplishment of SDG objectives. The accomplishment of SDG 8 together with SDG 12 demands corporate entities to protect labor rights while offering safe workplaces and providing responsible environmental stewardship. The corporate ecosystem develops its rights-respecting and sustainable features through multiple layers of national rules, international standards, and voluntary corporate mandates.

Multiple United Nations organizational units along with human rights institutions now embed SDG tracking functions as part of their reporting and assessment tasks. The Human Rights Council's Universal Periodic Review (UPR) includes SDG-related content in its regular practices, and treaty bodies provide General Comments that link treaty obligations with SDG targets. Integration strengthens both the normative value of the SDGs as well as the legal precision of human rights monitoring. Through this assessment approach states can receive a complete overview of their performance because development outcomes get reviewed within the context of their full human rights commitments. The practice of strategic litigation continues to expand to enforce government responsibility in SGD implementation in case of violations of human rights. Human rights arguments in the Urgenda case of the Netherlands achieved success in their mission to push for better environmental policies which directly support SDG 13 about climate action (Suresh & Sundaram, 2022). In the same light, Indian courts utilize Article 21 of the Constitution to protect life by establishing better environmental regulations and healthcare requirements which support a range of SDGs contemporaneously. The rights-based legal approach demonstrates its strength as an SDG compliance tool through these legal examples which provide an operational model for development practice (Ellis & Edmonds, 2023).

Various substantial regulatory and managerial shortcomings continue to affect implementation. A central barrier arises when development plans treat rights and laws as separate components from internal framework structures instead of fundamental elements. The separation of ministries from human rights bodies as well as legal institutions becomes evident through SDG implementation by individual sectors. This approach leads to an ineffective implementation of policies because it causes both redundant work and prevents essential synergy possibilities. Illuminating the problem is the lack of international legal procedures which enforce SDG commitments because they limit the possibilities for marginalized groups to pursue justice or require accountability regarding development injustices (Park & Park, 2023). The development of "integrated governance" represents an advocated model for scholars and practitioners to establish human rights institutions together with development agencies and legal bodies under one unified policy framework. Implementation must include rights-based assessment integration with development planning and create laws for SDG violations compensation while making sure all development metrics incorporate human rights benchmarks. Complete alignment between different entities must happen to achieve sustainable development which works both effectively and promotes justice alongside inclusion (Raman et al, 2023).

Research reveals that although potential exists for the intersection of SDGs, human rights and legal compliance zones, there are numerous structural barriers as well as political impediments which complicate their successful alignment. The theoretical matching between these domains has been established, but operational practices still need further development of work. Although the SDGs brought human rights closer to development discourse, the SDGs still face obstacles through weak institutions, insufficient legal mechanisms and fragmented governance systems. Nonetheless progressive practices including the use of judicial activism and corporate responsibility frameworks are creating new ways for integration to occur (Suresh & Sundaram, 2022). The potential for sustainable development to achieve legal grounding with human rights protection remains possible through innovation in practices and institutional development.

INSTITUTIONAL MECHANISMS AND COMPLIANCE FRAMEWORKS FOR SDG INTEGRATION

Sustainable development, as defined in the 2030 Agenda, needs complex institutional structures with compliance systems to implement the Sustainable Development Goals (SDGs) coherently. Global commitments receive their practical applications through institutional mechanisms which operate in both national and international spheres. The effective design coupled with proper functioning and proper interrelations between institutions and frameworks determine the efficacy, inclusiveness, and accountability of SDG implementation (Breuer et al., 2023). Since the SDGs lack mandatory legal status while operating in their aspirational framework, the strength of institutional workings serves as essential components which reinforce integrated action, policy coherence and monitoring achievements. The whole framework of sustainable development governance functions through the continuous yet complex relationship between institutional structure development and compliance systems (Paoli, 2021).

The United Nations, with its associated agencies, bears the main institutional responsibility for SDG oversight and support as the leading international authority within this process. The High-Level Political Forum (HLPF) serves as the central United Nations Economic and Social Council (ECOSOC) operating platform to conduct 2030 Agenda follow-up and review activities. The forum meets each year to evaluate worldwide sustainability progress as well as deliver strategic policy instructions, and a Voluntary National Reviews (VNRs) method encourages peer knowledge exchange. VNRs operate as essential tools for generating mutual responsibility between states, although these are not legally binding. States utilize these structured sessions to display their advancement and discuss their obstructive and enabling institutional elements for SDGs achievement. Through VNRs governments undertake both administrative integration of the SDGs and national introspection because these processes lead them to create inter-ministerial task forces, national SDG secretariats and multi-stakeholder advisory councils (Breuer et al., 2023).

The HLPF operates alongside specialized agencies including the United Nations Development Program (UNDP), World Health Organization (WHO), United Nations Children's Fund (UNICEF) and United Nations Environment Program (UNEP) which support governments through technical expertise, data tools and capacity-development services. The institutions perform an essential supporting function through their work in providing customized guidance to countries and their role in developing measurement metrics and funding projects to build sustainable public governance. SDG Integration Team at the United Nations Development Program developed operational frameworks to harmonize government-wide approaches for national development planning through SDG alignment. These institutions supply essential resources, but their advisory role does not include enforcement capabilities thus their authority remains constrained in jurisdictions that exhibit weak political commitment along with institutional resistance (Wiegant et al., 2024).

The African Union alongside the European Union ASEAN and South Asian Association for Regional Cooperation (SAARC) have been intensifying their support for SDG implementation at the regional level. The organizations work to create regional frameworks together with peer review systems which help different governments follow the 2030 Agenda (Rahman et al., 2012). The European Union uses SDGs as foundational elements of its legal structures and policy documents including its Green Deal and circular economy action plans, which make sustainability a permanent policy orientation throughout its operations. Multiple regional institutions now work together to support transboundary cooperation regarding issues such as climate change, migration and trade which serve as key challenges pertaining to multiple SDGs and thereby require trans-jurisdictional alliance (Smith et al., 2024). These regional institutions demonstrate different levels of effectiveness in their operations, which depend substantially on member state integration percentages and resource distribution alongside political support from member states.

National government authorities maintain primary responsibility to implement SDGs with domestic institutional structures determining their effective embodiment into national development plans. Several states have established high-level coordination bodies located at the Prime Minister's Office or Planning Commission in environments whose purpose is to conduct SDG mainstreaming programs across government departments. The national sustainable development councils of Germany and Finland bring together officials from both public and non-governmental sectors in addition to private sector representatives for horizontal coordination. India uses NITI Aayog as its central institution for SDG implementation which conducts scheme mapping with SDG targets while generating periodic implementation updates. The designed institutions create policy coherence through their ability to stop fragmented execution while promoting multi-sectoral teamwork (Ozdamirova et al., 2024).

A national institutional mechanism succeeds only when it effectively coordinates different departments through administration and allocates sufficient funds while implementing inclusive governance practices. Implementing the SDGs needs both administrative modifications and shifts in public governance systems that emphasize broad engagement while promoting openness together with fast response capabilities. In many developing countries, weak institutional capacity, politicization of bureaucracies, and fragmented legal systems impede the implementation of sustainable development policies (Park & Park, 2023). The non-enforceable nature of 2030 Agenda legal obligations let governments choose prioritization of simpler goals rather than pursue necessary structural changes or take such steps which challenge established interests.

The implementation process becomes more complicated when sub-national governments join the operation (Hegazy & Tohlob, 2024). Local and regional authorities serve as essential implementers of many localized targets contained within SDGs since they deal with issues such as sanitation, health besides education and infrastructure delivery. Service delivery in federal and decentralized systems requires state and municipal governments to receive full legal powers together with financial independence and required institutional capabilities to implement the SDGs locally. Three successful sub-national SDG implementation models exist across Kerala in India, Basque Country in Spain and Flanders in Belgium through their establishment of customized SDG frameworks and their local planning approaches and monitoring systems. Spatial variations in the SDG progress levels stem from uneven capacities of local governments, political conflicts (Khare & Raghuwanshi, 2025) between different authority levels and resource distribution inequalities which create equity gaps against the fundamental core of the 2030 Agenda.

The private sector together with civil society groups and academic institutions have become an expanding institutional element for SDG implementation. The building of sustainable development requires institutional support that includes public-private partnerships (PPPs) along with multi-stakeholder platforms. While initiatives like Global Reporting Initiative (GRI) facilitate sustainability reporting together with corporate accountability systems, the SDG Business Forum companies, for instance, find a platform for matching their operations with SDG principles. On the other hand, civil society organizations perform three vital functions in development: keeping tabs on development, supporting underrepresented viewpoints, and developing spaces for accountability. The framework developed by institutions like Transparency International and the International Budget Partnership uses transparency tools to connect budget information with SDG targets thus setting up informal systems of compliance through public watching and community involvement (Wong, 2019).

These institutional mechanisms face major compliance issues even though they have proliferated throughout the system. SDG operates in a legally undefined space since it does not contain binding obligations, operational sanction processes, or established adjudicative bodies. The SDGs lack both human rights treaties and climate change enforcement tools established through the Paris Agreement structure. The process of compliance depends primarily on self-declaration by nations which submit their instances through Voluntary National Reports and United Nations Statistics Division managed indicator frameworks. The Global Indicator Framework consists of 231 distinct indicators to track the 169 targets but suffers from substantial deficits in data accessibility as well as their accuracy and the capability to break down this data (Griggs et al., 2014). The availability issues with essential data hinder proper oversight and cover up inequalities among different groups based on gender, caste and racial backgrounds and geographic areas.

Various approaches to strengthen compliance systems have included using soft law instruments and carrying out peer reviews and performance index evaluations. Each year the Sustainable Development Solutions Network (SDSN) delivers its SDG Index to show the country's performance progress, which creates reputation-based incentives to strengthen achievements. The authentication power of governments through VNRs has an equivalent function to that of civil society groups which work on providing parallel reports combined with strong moral criticism and societal engagement. Despite their worth, these accountability methods are not backed by law and operate effectively only when civil society remains vigorous and public transparency exists freely, two aspects that many countries worldwide are facing (Zanten & Tulder, 2018).

Some experts have developed combined compliance systems which unite soft law motivation tools alongside legal systems for enforcement (D'Rosario & Zeleznikow, 2018). The implementation of SDGs can gain more legal weight through the connection with human rights treaty obligations or by incorporating SDG-related metrics into development financing criteria and by establishing legally binding national legislation for SDG compliance. In various jurisdictions courts now occasionally use the SDGs as a basis for litigation thus generating an unofficial legal structure for these nonbinding goals (Friedman, 2016). Though developing slowly, this innovative approach to jurisprudence indicates a way ahead that may prove useful in developing sustainable development governance compliance systems.

The emerging institutional coherence approach builds alignment between the mandates with operational logics and functions of all institutions related to SDG implementation. SDG implementation requires both vertical integration among international national and local levels combined with horizontal sector and discipline alignment (Wiegant et al., 2024). A unified institutional framework that brings health sector planning together with education sector planning and environmental planning generates better relationships between policies and minimizes conflicts between them. These approaches, which combine 'whole-of-government' and 'whole-of-society' mechanisms, stand as core attributes of institutional harmonization, according to the UN. Furthermore, making conceptual models function as operational institutional practices presents a major governance difficulty in situations where there are either political divisions or limited resources (Erin et al., 2023).

The SDGs need institutional mechanisms together with compliance frameworks to function effectively as their basic structure. These structures and capabilities together with their flexibility establish how well the 2030 Agenda will be accomplished in real-world conditions. The SDGs experience implementation obstacles mainly because of inadequate enforcement systems and minimal data availability alongside political challenges to transform fundamental systems. The successful resolution of these barriers relies on integration of technical improvements with normative dedication, political backing, and community involvement. The true success of the SDGs depends on how strong and resilient the institutions become that must execute sustainable development at ground level.

RESULTS AND DISCUSSIONS: TOWARDS A CONVERGENT MODEL

An evaluation of how institutions at international, regional and national levels establish SDG implementation shows an intricate mix of alignment and separateness between them. Although the 2030 Agenda works through a universal framework, operational challenges across different political, economic and legal systems give rise to a complicated web of players, multiple processes, and various compliance approaches. The current priority engages policy makers along with scholars to create a merged institutional structure that properly combines localized creative approaches to SDG realization while maintaining worldwide accountability. This chapter explores the results obtained from comparative institutional analysis and offers theoretical concepts about a new sustainable development governance model which responds effectively.

Research evidence shows that while the SDGs function voluntarily, the 2030 Agenda brought about extensive changes to institutional responsibilities across different governance levels. One of the main observations shows that countries are developing inter-ministerial coordination systems to break down the long-standing departmental divisions in public administration. The nations of Finland and Colombia implemented complete government strategies through budget integration that realigned their public funding flows toward SDG objectives. Sustainability represents a systemic requirement which extends throughout all governance aspects because authorities now recognize its role as a fundamental structural necessity that transcends sectors. SDG steering committees under the executive branch provide technical and political authority to coordinate such efforts through their central agencies. These entities achieve their purpose effectively based on the amount of political backing they receive coupled with bureaucratic professionalism and institutional autonomy in domestic frameworks.

The research demonstrates that Voluntary National Reviews (VNRs) act as soft compliance tools for making states evaluate their policies through self-reflection. Despite their absence of legal mandate, the VNR process has become a primary setting for learning from peers, disseminating international standards and providing states with reputational responsibility. When analyzing the VNRs, researchers encounter multiple distinctive patterns that describe reporting consistency, stakeholder involvement, and analytical depth. The VNR process allows Germany and Indonesia along with other countries to develop multi-stakeholder dialogues through data-driven analysis, but some nations choose to present optimistic reporting narratives with little information about the source of data, funding or governance issues. This wide range of reporting quality shapes a core problem in establishing global institutions because it demonstrates the need to balance worldwide governance principles against the forces of independent states and their organizational capacities.

Many regions worldwide show an increasing interest in building new institutions that create connections between internationally defined targets and national execution. Sustainable development appears in three different forms across the African Union's Agenda 2063, the European Union's SDG integration in its multiannual financial framework, and ASEAN's Blueprint for Sustainable Development. These represent three distinct regional models that define sustainability within their own context. These regional platforms function as vital medium organizations to transform universal goals into acceptable frameworks suitable for local development requirements together with existing laws and native political processes. The EU demonstrates exceptional institutional alignment when it incorporates the SDGs into every facet of its external diplomacy, trade agreements and its funding programs. Such integration displays how supranational bodies establish horizontality along with vertical coherent governance of the SDGs. SDG implementation success differs extensively between regions since multiple intergovernmental organizations lack both institutional strength and political unity to function effectively as SDG implementing bodies (Berrone et al., 2023).

The analysis affirms that countries need coherent national laws and institutions to execute the SDGs effectively. The process of translating 2030 Agenda content into national legal frameworks produces better integration and ensures accountability within states as is exemplified in Sweden's SDG-connected environmental and climate policy legislation. National planning systems that center the SDGs as peripheral goals or employ them for inspirational statements struggle to achieve institutional integration (Albers et al., n.d.). The most significant gaps occur when ministries focus on their individual sectors without cooperation and participation from civil society groups, and local governments experience either insufficient resources or minimal motivation to support the SDGs. The alignment between laws, policies, budgets and administrative processes that support sustainable development objectives constitutes a crucial element for creating successful action from initial commitment.

It is essential to highlight how local governments and municipalities play a fundamental role in positive transformation in decentralized systems. Despite the 2030 Agenda's global reach, local implementation is essential for its successful realization because most SDG targets must be executed at a territorial level and range from urban planning, health infrastructure, waste management to education delivery systems. Managing the localization process demands more than just administrative delegations because municipal institutions require complete design transformation. The SDG Future Cities model of Japan along with India's local SDG index created by NITI Aayog are some of the successful models which demonstrate how context-particular structures along with financial support and community engagement lead to better global goal adoption at local levels. The localization process creates spatial inequality which disrupts the 2030 Agenda's principle of leaving no one behind because different regions possess varying institutional capacities to achieve the SDGs (Biermann et al., 2022).

The chapter identifies essential shortcomings within data governance systems across countries since these problems act as major barriers to meeting SDG requirements. The United Nations Statistical Commission created a complete Global

Indicator Framework, but national statistical systems show inconsistent ability to gather, break down and report data. The existence of data asymmetry hinders evaluation as well as weakens the reliability of international review frameworks and assessment indices. Countries possessing robust data environments achieve better results in adapting programs and practice evidence-driven governance that allows for transparent reporting about their advancement (Glass & Newig, 2019). Conversely, data-poor settings prevent underrepresented communities from showing their true living circumstances while blocking policy adaptability and offering space for organizations to conduct superficial compliance activities. The study recommends immediate funding investments to build better statistical capabilities combined with data expertise alongside technological advances for establishing responsible SDG implementation processes.

Civil society organizations together with think tanks and academic institutions subtly influence institutional responses regarding the SDGs. These actors function as knowledge-based groups which help create indicators and produce alternative reports while creating spaces for stakeholder participation (Kickbusch & Hanefeld, 2017). Their involvement in democracy develops supplementary systems which extend beyond formal governmental oversight. The force of civil organizations depends on both the political openness of the system, freedom to create groups, and the availability of funding. The extent of systemic restrictions in a political regime defines the capacity of civic actors to effectively influence meaningful implementation of SDGs. A convergent institutional framework needs to acknowledge that non-state actors should have an established role in making sustainable development governance together with implementing its measures (Basilio & Silva, 2024).

The research conclusions result in developing a unified model which describes institutional frameworks for managing SDGs. The three fundamental principles which form the basis of this model include polycentric coordination, normative coherence, and adaptive accountability. The institutional framework of polycentric coordination recognizes various actors and spatial levels that participate in SDG implementation activities (Amaruzaman et al., 2022). The proposed model promotes linked relationships between international, national and local institutions through networks linking policies and information systems with established peer-to-peer learning programs. Normative coherence represents the essential step which requires states to fit their legal and financial measures to policy frameworks accordingly with sustainability principles. SDG target harmonization needs to take place through a process linking them to national development plans, climate strategies, human rights obligations, and budgetary frameworks. The concept of adaptive accountability involves making monitoring and compliance systems capable of responding to contextual changes as well as incorporating new knowledge and handling emerging challenges (Mansson et al., 2023).

A reformed High-Level Political Forum would adopt an evaluative approach while gaining stronger participatory features for stakeholders under this operational model combining various sustainability agreements. Each regional organization would obtain SDG secretariats that serve as knowledge centers to coordinate activities while also acting as steering bodies. The national-level institutional SDG anchoring happens through legal bindings and integrated planning systems along with task forces that possess technical capabilities and financial independence. Vertical fiscal transfers and funds from national governments would support sub-national governments, and planning and monitoring would integrate civic actors through mandated connection to SDG achievement. The model creates a distributed data structure that operates through principles of openness and interoperability as well as rights-based access to data (Breuer et al., 2023).

Although such a paradigm is utopian, its underpinnings are already apparent in various institutional innovations observed across different legal areas. The challenge lies in integrating these disparate innovation projects into one systemic model which raises policy conformity while strengthening democratic foundations within sustainable development management systems. The global community requires an intellectual adjustment that transforms institutions from static global goal facilitators into active transformative centers that promote debates and disputes. The broad nature of SDGs pushes us to create a new governance structure which handles complex problems while balancing different interests, so collective efforts maintain their effectiveness in our progressive world (Shayan et al., 2024).

CONCLUSIONS AND SUGGESTIONS

Developing an institution-wide framework that efficiently implements Sustainable Development Goals (SDGs) stands as one of the most intricate governance matters of this century. The broad framework design of the 2030 Agenda demonstrates global universality but shows multiple functional variations when countries implement it. Circumstances underpinning international governance frameworks, regional frameworks and national institutional mechanisms have been examined to reveal both advantages and drawbacks in present SDG execution systems. Since the adoption of the 2030 Agenda is notably normative and policy guidelines spread throughout different jurisdictions, yet implementation institutions show multiple weaknesses, often disconnected from each other and lacking sufficient resources to fulfill sustainable development's transformative goals.

As there exists no binding international enforcement system for the SDGs, the primary responsibility of their implementation falls on national governments. National institutions vary widely regarding their design and operational performance of SDG implementation mechanisms because some work within legal requirements, but others rely on interim task forces with limited authority. However, ironically, the 2030 Agenda's soft law provisions have allowed for more flexible institutional experimentation enabling states and regional blocks to design institutional initiatives that match their unique socio-political realities. The flexibility of institutions proves valuable but creates disparities in implementation practices between countries because of differences in political dedication and public administrator competency together with participation by stakeholders. This administrative scenario creates a double-sided reality because it features both innovative developments and status maintenance, which prevents actual institutional convergence.

The research documents that political commitment together with organizational consensus creates essential conditions for achieving institutional success. The implementation tracks of countries become stronger when they integrate the SDGs into their current development foundations through institutional law frameworks and budgeting mechanisms together with vertical policy coordination. When SDG implementation exists solely as an activity for international reporting or is governed by foreign donor organizations, nations experience more performative participation without genuine implementation. Self-assessment reports demonstrate significant weaknesses due to various anomalies in assessment methods and inconsistent evaluation standards as well as limitations to genuine public involvement during review processes. The absence of standardized benchmarks and independent validation systems ensures that organizations can carry out strategic misreporting along with engaging in policy window dressing.

The study further reveals that regionally based organizations remain significantly important, but their functions remain largely underrecognized across global-local SDG governance networks. Regional mechanisms become effective with policy harmonization and serve as technical assistance platforms together with peer accountability functions if they have appropriate resources and political power. National implementation receives support from regional institutional structures through the unified sustainability strategy of the European Union together with ASEAN's dialogue programs and Agenda 2063 of the African Union. The power of regional bodies to undertake additional responsibility regarding SDG implementation depends strongly on structural improvements, political alliance formation, and available resources.

Another important insight pertains to the institutionalization of the localization agenda. The SDGs create multiple points of convergence between their comprehensive nature and fundamental sub-national governance operations, including urban planning, health services, environmental management, and infrastructure development. Numerous national governments allow their local authorities to retain negligible decision-making powers and confront financial limitations and management challenges. The successful implementation of localization needs substantial institutional changes between governments through financial reforms and mandates for local planning along with data-based systems for detailed monitoring. Forward-thinking public structures that include marginalized community members must exist within the development planning process because they unite sustainable development principles with justice, fundamental values, and inclusion strategies. Main institutions implementing these structures seem to produce better and more fair outcomes which can be observed in certain states of Japan, Germany and India.

The research established that institutional accountability needs reliable detailed data that functions in real time to function properly. The worldwide set of indicators remains effective due to how nations implement their operational elements through their domestic statistical data collection systems. Low-income states that lack investment in data infrastructure together with coordination will fail to support an adaptive governance system because of the missing institutional feedback loop. Data and institutions form a systems-based relationship because strong institutions produce better data collection and usage while valid information helps institutions test policy outcomes and develop enhanced strategic approaches. Dismally, in several circumstances, improper funding distribution for data systems alongside agency fragmentation and public data accessibility problems diminish SDG implementation of accountability structure.

The results generate linked recommendations to establish a governance structure for Sustainable Development Goals which combines coherency and accountability with convergence. Firstly, national legislation should set the SDGs in place with defined institutional requirements that establish detailed coordination standards and necessary stakeholder participation guidelines. Compliance with state sovereignty enables an enduring framework that connects institutional arrangements to public administration, thus preventing them from becoming political tools. Secondly, the process of budgetary alignment with SDG priorities needs to become permanent by establishing both outcome-based budgeting and sustainability impact assessments as well as fiscal mark-ups. Financial coherence is achieved while implementation commitments receive increased validity through this method.

Thirdly, the offices of regional organizations must receive assistance and motivation to operate as centers for technical guidance, political coordination, and monitoring functions. In order to achieve this, international cooperation agencies must abandon bilateral aid paradigms and switch to regional capacity-building initiatives which understand regional organizations' specific advantages. Considering this process, the regional mechanisms provide better support to national governments by helping policy harmonization and reducing duplication while enabling the expansion of innovations.

Fourthly, sub-national governments require an enhanced institutional capacity which can be achieved by implementing decentralization reforms together with conditional grants that link SDG results and established networks of cooperation. Local SDG councils should obtain legal authorization while participatory budgeting and community-driven monitoring through mandates will establish sustainability as a core local government function.

A new framework for SDG data governance should become the fifth priority for change. The institutional structure for SDG data management requires adequate financial support with complete political independence for national agencies to lead ministry data coordination, establish international data standards and collaborative relationships with civil society groups for data feedback. Open data principles and digital tools need to be used for democratizing access to data as well as making evidence-based advocacy possible. Lastly, a fundamental change of mindset needs to take place within institutions, so they transform from operating within a regulatory framework towards genuine transformative governance. Institutions need to develop policy-driven innovation while promoting bilateral learning between departments and establish an adaptable mechanism through which they can address new threats such as climate change, pandemics, and geopolitical disruptions.

Conclusively, the evaluation proves that institutional architecture exists as an adaptive framework which consists of interconnected actors who work to establish norms and execute processes. Real convergence within this system requires agencies to achieve a mutual alignment between their values, incentives along with their capabilities and information flow management systems. The 2030 Agenda provides a non-compulsory framework that presents organizations with an exclusive chance to create new governance structures based on sustainable development, justice, and intergenerational equity principles. More than just ideological devotion, this vision necessitates strategic institutional creation, creative legal solutions, and ongoing political support. The imperative is clear as the world community enters the last years of the SDG period which compels the oversight for sustainable development to move past institutional division and resistance and combine integration with adaptability grounded in the daily experiences of the people it aims to serve.

REFERENCES

Albers, H., Winter, J. D., & Voeten, H. (n.d.). Inspiration guide: Integrating the SDGs into your multi-annual policy plan. *VVSG*. https://www.local2030.org/library/707/SDGs-in-policy-plan.pdf

Amaruzaman, S., Trong Hoan, D., Catacutan, D., Leimona, B., & Malesu, M. (2022). Polycentric Environmental Governance to Achieving SDG 16: Evidence from Southeast Asia and Eastern Africa. *Forests*, *13*(1), 68. DOI: 10.3390/f13010068

Arajarvi, N. (2017). The Rule of Law in the 2030 Agenda. *Hague Journal on the Rule of Law*, *10*(2), 187–217. Advance online publication. DOI: 10.1007/s40803-017-0068-8

Berrone, P., Rousseau, H. E., Ricart, J. E., Ruiz, E. B., & Giuliodori, A. (2023). How can Research Contribute to the Implementation of Sustainable Development Goals? An Interpretive Review of SDG Literature in Management. *International Journal of Management Reviews*, *25*(2), 318–339. DOI: 10.1111/ijmr.12331

Bexell, M., Hickmann, T., & Schapper, A. (2023). Strengthening the Sustainable Development Goals through integration with human rights. *International Environmental Agreement: Politics, Law and Economics*, *23*(2), 1–7. DOI: 10.1007/s10784-023-09605-x

Biermann, F., Hickmann, T., Senit, C. A., & Grob, L. (2022). The Sustainable Development Goals as a Transformative Force? *Cambridge University Press*. 204-226. https://doi.org/DOI: 10.1017/9781009082945.009

Biradar, D. (2024). Ethics and Compliance: The Foundation of Sustainable Business Practices. *CXO Today*. https://cxotoday.com/story/ethics-and-compliance-the-foundation-of-sustainable-business-practices/

Breuer, A., Leininger, J., Malerba, D., & Tosun, J. (2023). Integrated policymaking: Institutional designs for implementing the sustainable development goals (SDGs). *World Development*, *170*, 106317. Advance online publication. DOI: 10.1016/j.worlddev.2023.106317

D'Rosario, M., & Zeleznikow, J. (2018). Compliance with International Soft Law: Is the Adoption of Soft Law Predictable? *International Journal of Strategic Decision Sciences*, *9*(3), 1–15. DOI: 10.4018/IJSDS.2018070101

Dattler, R., Barclay, H., & Marshall, A. (2016). Sustainable Development Goals and human rights. *IPPF*. https://www.ippf.org/sites/default/files/2016-11/SDG%2BHR_facts.pdf

Do, D.-N.-M., Hoang, L.-K., Le, C.-M., & Tran, T. (2020). A human rights-based approach in implementing sustainable development goal 4 (quality education) for ethnic minorities in Vietnam. *Sustainability (Basel), 12*(10), 4179. DOI: 10.3390/su12104179

Donald, K., & Way, S. A. (2016). Accountability for the Sustainable Development Goals: A Lost Opportunity? *Ethics & International Affairs, 30*(2), 201–213. DOI: 10.1017/S0892679416000083

Dulume, W. (2019). Linking the SDGS with human rights: Opportunities and challenges of promoting goal 17. *Journal of Sustainable Development Law and Policy, 10*(1), 57–72. DOI: 10.4314/jsdlp.v10i1.3

Ellis, J., & Edmonds, D. (2023). Coming to terms with the SDGs: A perspective from legal scholarship. *Leiden Journal of International Law, 36*(2), 251–271. DOI: 10.1017/S0922156522000838

Erin, A. O., Bamigboye, O. A., & Oyewo, B. (2023). Sustainable development goals (SDG) reporting: An analysis of disclosure. *Journal of Accounting in Emerging Economies, 12*(2), 761–789. Advance online publication. DOI: 10.1108/JAEE-02-2020-0037

Frey, D. F., & MacNaughton, G. (2016). A Human Rights Lens on Full Employment and Decent Work in the 2030 Sustainable Development Agenda. *SAGE Open, 6*(2), 2158244016649580. Advance online publication. DOI: 10.1177/2158244016649580

Friedman, E. A. (2016). An Independent Review and Accountability Mechanism for the Sustainable Development Goals: The Possibilities of a Framework Convention on Global Health. *Health and Human Rights, 18*(1), 129–140. https://pmc.ncbi.nlm.nih.gov/articles/PMC5070686/ PMID: 27781005

Glass, L. M., & Newig, J. (2019). Governance for achieving the Sustainable Development Goals: How important are participation, policy coherence, reflexivity, adaptation and democratic institutions? *Earth System Governance, 2*, 100031. DOI: 10.1016/j.esg.2019.100031

Griggs, D., Smith, M. S., Rockström, J., Öhman, M. C., Gaffney, O., Glaser, G., Kanie, N., Noble, I., Steffen, W., & Shyamsundar, P. (2014). An integrated framework for sustainable development goals. *Ecology and Society, 19*(4), art49. https://www.jstor.org/stable/26269703. DOI: 10.5751/ES-07082-190449

Guiry, N. (2024). *Why Do States Adhere to the Sustainable Development Goals?* Cambridge University Press., https://www.cambridge.org/core/journals/transnational-environmental-law/article/why-do-states-adhere-to-the-sustainable-development-goals/45E55CBD8F82F0018BA52A15FB6E349F DOI: 10.1017/S2047102524000190

Gutterman, A. S. (2023). Sustainability and Corporate Governance. *ResearchGate.* https://www.researchgate.net/publication/371902191_Sustainability_and_Corporate_Governance

Han, S., Li, C., Li, M., Lenzen, M., Chen, X., Zhang, Y., Li, M., Yin, T., Li, Y., Li, J., Liu, J., & Li, Y. (2024). Prospects for global sustainable development through integrating the environmental impacts of economic activities. *Nature Communications, 15*(1), 1–16. DOI: 10.1038/s41467-024-52854-w PMID: 39341803

Hegazy, I. R., & Tohlob, A. A. (2024). Strategic environmental assessment and SDG integration: Enhancing sustainable development in Egypt. *Journal of Umm Al-Qura University for Engineering and Architecture, 15*(3), 340–354.

Horbachevska, T., Zeben, J. V., & Bernaz, N. (2024). A capability approach to the sustainable development goals: Towards positive corporate human rights obligations. *Transnational Legal Theory, 15*(3), 465–492. Advance online publication. DOI: 10.1080/20414005.2024.2434383

Immler, N. L., & Sakkers, H. (2021). The UN-Sustainable Development Goals going local: Learning from localising human rights. *International Journal of Human Rights, 26*(2), 262–284. DOI: 10.1080/13642987.2021.1913411

Joshi, A. (2017). Legal Empowerment and Social Accountability: Complementary Strategies Toward Rights-based Development in Health? *World Development, 99*, 160–172. DOI: 10.1016/j.worlddev.2017.07.008

Khare, P. & Raghuwanshi, V. (2025). Exploring the Complexities of India-Bangladesh Relations. *IGI Global Scientific Publishing,* 209-230. https://doi.org/ DOI: 10.4018/979-8-3693-9626-1.ch009

Kickbusch, I., & Hanefeld, J. (2017). Role for academic institutions and think tanks in speeding progress on sustainable development goals. *BMJ (Clinical Research Ed.), j3519*, j3519. DOI: 10.1136/bmj.j3519 PMID: 28739591

Koundouri, P., Aslanidis, P. S., Dellis, K., Plataniotis, A., & Feretzakis, G. (2025). Mapping human security strategies to sustainable development goals: A machine learning approach. *Discover Sustainability, 6*(1), 96. Advance online publication. DOI: 10.1007/s43621-025-00883-w

Månsson, J., Eriksson, L., Hodgson, I., Elmberg, J., Bunnefeld, N., Hessel, R., Johansson, M., Liljebäck, N., Nilsson, L., Olsson, C., Pärt, T., Sandström, C., Tombre, I., & Redpath, S. M. (2023). Understanding and overcoming obstacles in adaptive management. *Trends in Ecology &amp. Trends in Ecology & Evolution*, *38*(1), 55–71. DOI: 10.1016/j.tree.2022.08.009 PMID: 36202636

Ochoa, A. G., Khare, P., & Setia, S. (2024). Expanding Environmental Education in Honduras: A Holistic Approach for Sustainable Development. *IGI Global Scientific Publishing,* 153-170. https://doi.org/DOI: 10.4018/979-8-3693-2577-3.ch010

Ozdamirova, L., Dzhamaldinova, M., & Samatova, C. (2024). The Role of Legal Mechanisms in the Implementation of the Sustainable Development Goals (SDGs). *RT&A, 19*(6), 1359-1367. https://gnedenko.net/Journal/2024/SI_062024/RTA_SI062024-175_56_Laura%20Ozdamirova%20Marina%20Chulpan%20The%20Role%20of%20Legal%20Mechanisms%20in%20the%20Implementation%20of%20the%20Sustainable%20Development%20Goals%20(SDGs).pdf

Paoli, L. A. D. (2021). From Aspirational Politics to Soft Law? Exploring the International Legal Effects of Sustainable Development Goal 7 on Affordable and Clean Energy. *Melbourne Journal of International Law*, *22*(1). https://papers.ssrn.com/sol3/papers.cfm?abstract_id=3930550

Park, K. R., & Park, Y. S. (2023). *Addressing institutional challenges in sustainable development goals implementation: Lessons from the Republic of Korea.* Wiley Online Library., DOI: 10.1002/sd.2725

Poto, M. P., & Murray, E. M. (2022). The New Horizons of Law and Science through the Lens of 2030 Sustainable Development Agenda: Some Emerging Issues. *Environmental Policy and Law*, *53*(1), 35–48. DOI: 10.3233/EPL-220039

Pribytkova, E. (2020). Global Obligations for Sustainable Development: Harmonizing The 2030 Agenda for Sustainable Development and International Human Rights Law. *University of Pennsylvania Journal of International Law*, *41*(4), 1031–1136. https://scholarship.law.upenn.edu/cgi/viewcontent.cgi?article=2012&context=jil

Puthucherril, T. G., Sharma, C., Shenoy, A. V., Sood, S., & Lal, S. (2024). Integrating the Sustainable Development Goals into India's Legal Education Landscape: The What, Why and How of a Reform Paradigm. *Asian Journal of Legal Education*, *12*(1), 40–60. DOI: 10.1177/23220058241265614

Rabinovych, M. (2020). The Legal Status and Effects of the Agenda 2030 within the EU Legal Order. *Journal of Contemporary European Research*, *16*(2), 182–199. DOI: 10.30950/jcer.v16i2.1071

Rahman, S. H., Khatri, S., & Brunner, H. P. (2012). Regional Integration and Economic Development in South Asia. *ADB*. https://www.adb.org/sites/default/files/publication/29871/regional-integration-economic-development-south-asia.pdf

Raman, R., Nair, V. K., Shivdas, A., Bhukya, R., Visvanathan, P. K., Subramaniam, N., & Nedungadi, P. (2023). *Mapping Sustainability Reporting Research with the UN's Sustainable Development Goal*. Science Direct., DOI: 10.1016/j.heliyon.2023.e18510

Ruppel, O. C., & Murray, R. (2024). The Future of the SDGs: A Comparative Constitutional Rescue Plan? One does not discover new lands without consenting to lose sight of the shore. André Gide. *Environmental Policy and Law*, *54*(3), 155–187. DOI: 10.3233/EPL-239022

Shayan, N. F., Mohabbati-Kalejahi, N., Alavi, S., & Zahed, M. A. (2022). Sustainable Development Goals (SDGs) as a Framework for Corporate Social Responsibility (CSR). *Sustainability (Basel)*, *14*(3), 1222. DOI: 10.3390/su14031222

Smith, W. C., Ehren, M. C. M., & Grek, S. (2024). Global Governance of Education: The Sustainable Development Goals as a Product and Mechanism? *International Review of Education*, *70*(4), 531–545. DOI: 10.1007/s11159-024-10108-3

Spijkers, O. (2020). The Sustainable Human Right to Water as Reflected in the Sustainable Development Goals. *Utrecht University*. https://utrechtlawreview.org/articles/10.36633/ulr.560

Suresh, B., & Sundaram, A. (2022). Cross-Embedded Relationship Nature of Human Rights-Related Treaties and Instruments with Environment-Related Sustainable Development Goals. *The Age of Human Rights Journal*, *19*(19), 205–253. DOI: 10.17561/tahrj.v19.7225

Thomas, R., Kuruvilla, S., Hinton, R., Jensen, S. L. B., Magar, V., & Bustreo, F. (2015). Assessing the Impact of a Human Rights-Based Approach across a Spectrum of Change for Women's, Children's, and Adolescents' Health. *Health and Human Rights Journal*. https://www.hhrjournal.org/2015/11/22/assessing-the-impact-of-a-human-rights-based-approach-across-a-spectrum-of-change-for-womens-childrens-and-adolescents-health/

Wiegant, D., Dewulf, A., & Zeben, J. V. (2024). Alignment mechanisms to effectively govern the sustainable development goals. *World Development*, *182*, 106721. Advance online publication. DOI: 10.1016/j.worlddev.2024.106721

Wong, R. (2019). Balancing Institutions for Implementing the Sustainable Development Goals Through 'Network Within Hierarchy'. *Sustainability (Basel)*, *11*(16), 4498. DOI: 10.3390/su11164498

Woodbridge, M. (2015). From MDGs to SDGs: What are the Sustainable Development Goals? *ILEI*. https://www.local2030.org/library/251/From-MDGs-to-SDGs-What-are-the-Sustainable-Development-Goals.pdf

Zanten, J.A.V., & Tulder, R. V. (2018). Multinational enterprises and the Sustainable Development Goals: An institutional approach to corporate engagement. *Journal of International Business Policy*. https://doi.org/DOI: 10.1057/s42214-018-0008-x

KEY TERMS AND DEFINITIONS

2030 Agenda for Sustainable Development: This is the United Nations framework adopted in 2015 that includes the 17 Sustainable Development Goals. It represents a significant shift in global development management, aiming for universal, inclusive, and integrated applications.

Good Governance: This is an important standard tied to human rights, characterized by transparency, accountability, public participation, and the rule of law.

Human Rights: These are fundamental entitlements that people possess to maintain their dignity, encompassing civil, political, economic, social, and cultural rights.

Institutional Mechanisms: These are the structures and systems within organizations that are designed to implement and oversee the Sustainable Development Goals.

Legal Compliance: This refers to following laws, regulations, and obligations, whether they are from a country or international agreements.

Normative Integration: This concept involves bringing together various legal and moral standards into a single, consistent system of governance.

Rights-Based Approach to Development (RBAD): This is a way of planning development where achieving human rights is the main measure of success. It clearly defines the roles of rights-holders (which are mostly citizens) and duty-bearers (which includes states and institutions), focusing on systems for accountability.

Sustainable Development Goals (SDGs): These are 17 global goals which aim to create a sustainable and fair society by 2030, covering social, economic, and environmental aspects.

Voluntary National Reviews (VNRs): These are non-legally binding reports that countries submit annually to the High-Level Political Forum (HLPF) which are used by states to showcase their progress on the SDGs, discuss challenges, and learn from other countries' experiences.

Chapter 8
Human Rights of Prisoners:
Advancing SDG 16 and SDG 3 Through Inclusive Justice Systems

Kanisha Pathak
https://orcid.org/0009-0000-1580-0957
Gujarat National Law University, Gandhinagar, India

ABSTRACT

Prisoners' human rights are a significant topic in today's global talks. This is especially relevant when examining how they intersect with the Sustainable Development Goals (SDGs). Specifically, SDG 16 (Peace, Justice, and Strong Institutions) and SDG 3 (Good Health and Well-being). These two SDGs are crucial in ensuring that convicts are treated well and with dignity. This research explores how equitable justice systems can contribute to SDG 16 and SDG 3 progress. The United Nations Standard Minimum Rules for the Treatment of Prisoners, also known as the Nelson Mandela Rules, emphasize the need for humane treatment.This research paper examines how SDG 16 and SDG 3 are interconnected within the prison system. It emphasizes that developing the justice system is not only about ensuring fairness in legal proceedings. Additionally, the study calls for further reforms to address the drawbacks of global prison systems. It recommends research to examine the long-term effects of inclusive justice systems on prisoner rehabilitation and reintegration.

DOI: 10.4018/979-8-3373-1792-2.ch008

INTRODUCTION

Background on Human Rights of Prisoners

The issue of imprisonment and human rights is an age-old issue, defining the global prison environment. Despite in-depth worldwide legislation such as the Universal Declaration of Human Rights (UDHR) (United Nations, 1948) and the International Covenant on Civil and Political Rights (ICCPR) (United Nations, 1966), prisoners' fundamental rights, including access to proper medical care, fair treatment, and freedom from torture and inhuman treatment, are often overlooked. Overcrowding, poor medical care, and discriminatory conduct have become endemic in prison regimes globally, not only affecting the prisoners but even society in general (Sykes, 2019; Hinton, 2020). Overcrowding, in particular, accelerates physical and mental afflictions, and disease transmission, and intensifies in-penalty in prison (Bates & White, 2020; Green & Johnson, 2019). Incarceration fails to rehabilitate offenders but continues to produce cycles of offending and social disengagement (Cullen & Gendreau, 2020). One of the most significant factors in prison life is the medical well-being of prisoners. With access to medical care restricted, most prisoners have long-term medical conditions such as high blood pressure, diabetes, and infectious diseases, including HIV/AIDS and tuberculosis (Murray et al., 2021).

In a report prepared by the World Health Organization (WHO) (2020), prison medical infrastructure is not well-equipped and not appropriately funded to respond to the complex medical requirements of prisoners. Especially for those with existing medical complications and mental illnesses. Shortfalls in such cases cause delayed medical intervention. In most cases, it complicates prisoners' misery and causes additional deaths. Besides, a lack of access to mental health services increases these issues, with a significant portion of prisoners experiencing untreated psychological stress (Bates & White, 2020; Hinton, 2020). Prison conditions increase mental illnesses, with many prisoners developing post-traumatic stress disorder (PTSD), depression, and other psychological conditions. These conditions go undiagnosed and untreated due to a lack of proper mental health care (Bates & Smith, 2020). Confinement, danger, and brutality in the environment contribute to worsening mental afflictions. Thus, it creates a cycle of untreated conditions, recidivism, and reinstitution (Bates & White, 2020). As a result, there is a growing demand for prison systems to implement more comprehensive and accessible mental health care programs that can address prisoners' psychological needs (Murray et al., 2021; Jackson, 2020).

RESEARCH METHODOLOGY

This study adopts a qualitative research approach to explore the intersection of prisoners' human rights with Sustainable Development Goals (SDG) 16 (Peace, Justice, and Strong Institutions) and SDG 3 (Good Health and Well-being), emphasizing the role of inclusive justice systems. The methodology is designed to provide a comprehensive understanding of the systemic challenges faced by prisoners, particularly in terms of health and justice, and to identify best practices for advancing these SDGs within correctional facilities globally. A descriptive and exploratory research design was employed to examine the human rights conditions of prisoners and their alignment with SDG 16 and SDG 3. This design facilitates an in-depth analysis of existing literature, legal frameworks, and case studies, allowing for a nuanced understanding of the complex interplay between incarceration, health, and justice systems. The qualitative nature of the study enables the exploration of systemic issues such as overcrowding, inadequate healthcare, and lack of rehabilitative programs, while also highlighting successful interventions in various global contexts.

OVERVIEW OF SDG 16 (PEACE, JUSTICE, AND STRONG INSTITUTIONS) AND SDG 3 (GOOD HEALTH AND WELL-BEING)

In response to such challenges, the United Nations adopted the Sustainable Development Goals (SDGs) in 2015 to address global issues by 2030. Specifically, SDG 16 (Peace, Justice, and Strong Institutions) and SDG 3 (Good Health and Well-being) directly impact prison reform. SDG 16 aims to provide peaceful and inclusive societies for sustainable development, ensure access to justice for all, and build effective, accountable, and transparent institutions at every level (United Nations, 2023). One of its most important points is that a fair and equitable justice system must exist, ensuring that all individuals, regardless of their status, receive fair treatment and that their fundamental human rights are protected (United Nations, 2023). SDG 3 focuses on ensuring healthy lives and promoting well-being for all, irrespective of age, with particular attention to mental and physical health (World Health Organization, 2020). Prisoners, as a vulnerable group, face numerous health challenges. The lack of adequate healthcare services in correctional facilities undermines efforts to achieve the targets set by SDG 3. The health of imprisoned individuals, as highlighted by WHO (2020), tends to be neglected, leading to an increase in preventable diseases and an overall decline in their well-being. Providing prisoners with access to good-quality healthcare is a crucial step toward advancing SDG 3 in a correctional facility (Bates & White, 2020). The relationship between

SDG 3 and SDG 16 can best be understood in terms of the intersection between health and justice. A fair and inclusive prison system that upholds the rights and well-being of individuals has a direct impact on their health outcomes. It also positively affects their chances of successful reintegration into society after release. The rehabilitative model promoted by SDG 16 emphasizes educational opportunities, psychological support, and vocational training for prisoners. It is essential for protecting their future health and well-being (Bates & White, 2020; Hinton, 2020).

Importance of Inclusive Justice Systems

An inclusive justice system promotes fairness, equity, and dignity for all, including incarcerated individuals. The restorative justice model prioritizes rehabilitation and reintegration over disciplinary measures. However, it sometimes fails to address the root causes of criminal behavior (Morris & Maxwell, 2018; Albrecht et al., 2020). This approach seeks to repair the harm caused by crimes by involving offenders, victims, and communities. Restorative justice systems have been shown to reduce recidivism and promote successful social reintegration. It is essential for the long-term well-being of prisoners (Morris & Maxwell, 2018). Imprisonment should not be seen solely as punishment but rather as an opportunity for improvement and growth. Providing educational programs, vocational training, and mental health care is critical in preparing prisoners for life after release (Olsen, 2021). Countries like Norway and Sweden have demonstrated the success of such models, emphasizing rehabilitation and human dignity rather than mere arrests (Sykes, 2019; Hinton, 2020). These systems focus on restorative practices for rehabilitating offenders and returning them to society as productive and law-abiding citizens (Norwegian Correctional Service, 2021).

Moreover, an inclusive justice system must address broader social causes of crime, such as poverty, inequality, and discrimination. Societal biases, including racial and socioeconomic discrimination in the criminal justice system, add to the overrepresentation of marginalized communities in prison populations (Hinton, 2020). An inclusive justice system aims to correct these imbalances by promoting policies that ensure equal treatment for all individuals, regardless of race, gender, or socioeconomic background (Green & Johnson, 2019). Addressing these systemic drawbacks is a crucial part of achieving SDG 16. This will ensure that justice systems are effective but also fair and accessible to all. Finally, an inclusive justice system requires accountability and transparency. Protecting prisoners' human rights and addressing abuses within prisons in a timely manner require individual inspection and monitoring mechanisms. National Human Rights Commissions (NHRCs) and international organizations such as the United Nations Office on Drugs and Crime (UNODC) play a vital role in promoting obedience within the prison system and ensuring that human rights are upheld (United Nations, 2023; Bates & Smith, 2020). Effective management is important for maintaining the integrity of justice systems and ensuring they align with international standards.

THEORETICAL FRAMEWORK

Human Rights Principles in the Context of Incarceration

Within modern criminal justice systems, across the globe, the human rights of people behind bars continue to be a pressing concern. Even though prisoners have been deprived of their liberty, they continue to possess a core of human rights that ought to be respected, even in the most tightly controlled environments. This section explores the indivisible nature of human rights and what it means for people who are incarcerated, including protection from torture or cruel treatment, the right to dignity, and the right to health care. These principles are essential not only for the humane treatment of prisoners, however long they may be incarcerated but also for pursuing broader human rights aspirations including the United Nations' Sustainable Development Goals (SDGs), especially SDG 16 (Peace, Justice and Strong Institutions) and SDG 3 (Good Health and Well-being).

Human Rights in Prisons: Core Principles

One of the most important rules about human rights in prisons is that no one should be tortured or treated in a very cruel way. International laws, like the Universal Declaration of Human Rights (UDHR) and the International Covenant on Civil and Political Rights (ICCPR), say that no matter what, prisoners must not be hurt or treated badly (United Nations, 1948; United Nations, 1966). This rule exists because people in prison are not as powerful as the government, so there must be laws to protect them. The United Nations Convention Against Torture and Other Cruel, Inhuman or Degrading Treatment or Punishment (CAT), which makes sure that prisoners all over the world are protected from cruel treatment (United Nations, 1984). A European special court called the European Court of Human Rights (ECHR) says that even though prison takes away freedom, it should not make people suffer more than necessary (ECHR, 2020). If a prison is too crowded, does not give proper medical care, or keeps people alone for too long, that can be just as bad as physical torture (Benvenuto & Lloyd, 2019). There are special rules called the Nelson Mandela Rules that say prisoners should be treated kindly and should not live in terrible conditions (United Nations, 2015). Following this rule is not just the right thing to do it is also a law (Goldstein, 2016).

Prisoners also have the right to healthcare. The United Nations says every person has a right to be healthy, even in prison (United Nations, 1966). Sometimes, being locked up can make people sick or worsen their health. That is why prisoners should get good medical care, including help for mental health problems (World Health Organisation [WHO], 2020). If a prison does not give proper medical help to sick prisoners, it is breaking the law. The Nelson Mandela Rules and the UN's Standard Minimum Rules for the Treatment of Prisoners say that every prisoner, no matter what crime they committed, should get medical care when they need it (United Nations, 2015).

THE INTERSECTION OF HUMAN RIGHTS AND SDGS

Prisoners' human rights are also connected to the Sustainable Development Goals (SDGs), which are big plans made by the UN to improve the world. Two goals are especially important for prisons:

1. SDG 16: Peace, Justice, and Strong Institutions – This goal says that justice systems (like courts and prisons) should be fair and treat everyone respectfully. It also means prisons should focus on helping people change and improve, not just punishing them (United Nations, 2021). SDG 16 wants fair and humane justice systems that respect prisoners. It focuses on treating them with dignity, giving them lawyers, and stopping cruel treatment. It also pushes for prison reforms, like reducing overcrowding and offering education and job training. The goal is to help prisoners change and rejoin society.
2. SDG 3: Good Health and Well-being – This goal says everyone should have access to good healthcare, including prisoners. Prisons often have big problems like being too crowded and not having enough doctors, which makes prisoners very unhealthy. To reach this goal, prisons must have better healthcare systems (United Nations Office on Drugs and Crime [UNODC], 2021). SDG 3 focuses on health for everyone, including prisoners. Many prisons are overcrowded and lack proper health care. This causes physical and mental health problems, like depression or diseases. SDG 3 says prisoners must get the same level of care as people outside prison. Mental health services and treatment for diseases are especially important.

LEGAL FRAMEWORKS SUPPORTING HUMAN RIGHTS IN INCARCERATION

Many international laws help make sure prisoners are treated fairly. Some of these include:

i. The International Covenant on Civil and Political Rights (ICCPR)
ii. The United Nations Convention Against Torture (CAT)
iii. The Nelson Mandela Rules
iv. The United Nations Standard Minimum Rules for the Treatment of Prisoners (SMRs)

These laws help make sure that prisoners are not abused and that their basic needs are met (United Nations, 1984; United Nations, 2015). The United Nations Committee Against Torture (CAT) checks to see if countries are following these rules. It has criticized many governments for not keeping prisoners safe, especially in cases of overcrowding, poor hygiene, and lack of medical care (Committee Against Torture [CAT], 2018). National Human Rights Institutions (NHRIs) are also important because they help check if prisons treat people properly. These organizations examine prison conditions, protect prisoners' rights, and hold governments accountable for mistreatment (Sustainable Development Goal 16 Toolkit, 2021). Their job is to make sure that prisoners are treated with respect, get healthcare, and are not tortured.

Several international legal frameworks aim to protect prisoners' rights, but their effectiveness varies due to differences in legally binding force and implementation. The International Covenant on Civil and Political Rights (ICCPR), adopted in 1966, is a legally binding treaty ratified by 173 states as of 2023 (United Nations, 2023). Article 10 mandates humane treatment of prisoners, yet compliance is inconsistent—only 40% of signatories fully adhere to its provisions due to weak oversight, as reported by the UN Human Rights Committee (2023). The United Nations Convention Against Torture (CAT), ratified by 171 states, prohibits torture and inhuman treatment (Article 2), with the Committee Against Torture (CAT) monitoring compliance. However, enforcement is limited; in 2022, CAT flagged violations in 60 countries, but only 25% faced sanctions due to political resistance (CAT, 2023). The Nelson Mandela Rules, updated in 2015, provide detailed standards for prisoner treatment, such as healthcare (Rule 24) and dignity (Rule 1). However, as soft law, they are not legally binding, relying on voluntary adoption. Only 50% of UN member states have integrated these rules into national policies, with implementation often hampered by resource constraints (UNODC, 2023). National Human Rights Institutions (NHRIs) play a complementary role, conducting inspections and advocating for prisoners' rights. For example, India's NHRC documented 1,500 rights violations in 2022 but resolved only 15% due to limited authority (NHRC, 2023). Strengthening these frameworks requires binding enforcement mechanisms, increased funding for NHRIs, and global cooperation to ensure compliance, aligning with SDG 16's goal of accountable institutions.

THE RELATIONSHIP BETWEEN HUMAN RIGHTS, SDGS AND INCLUSIVE JUSTICE SYSTEMS

The principles of human rights are important, even for people in prison. These rights connect to global goals like SDG 16 (Peace, Justice, and Strong Institutions) and SDG 3 (Good Health and Well-being). Both goals focus on justice systems that treat prisoners with respect. They also make sure prisoners get health care and support for change. To meet these goals, we need to understand how justice, human rights, and system changes work together to protect prisoners.

SDG 16: Peace, Justice, and Strong Institutions

SDG 16 is about peace, justice, and fair systems. It asks countries to make systems fair, open, and accountable (United Nations, 2021). Justice systems must follow the law and protect human rights, even for prisoners. SDG 16 says prisoners must be treated with respect. They should get lawyers and not face torture or cruel treatment (UNODC, 2020). Prison reform is a big part of SDG 16. Reform means making prisons fairer and solving problems like overcrowding (Mauer, 2020). It also means fixing unfair trials and stopping people from being wrongly convicted. Reform helps prisoners get an education, job skills, and counselling. This makes it easier for them to live good lives after prison. Fair systems like this help keep society peaceful (United Nations, 2021). To make this happen, we must address bias in justice systems. For example, poor people and racial minorities often face unfair treatment (Mauer, 2020). SDG 16 follows rules like the Nelson Mandela Rules. These rules explain how prisoners should be treated fairly. They focus on rehabilitation instead of punishment. This means helping prisoners improve and return to society (UNODC, 2020). SDG 16 pushes justice systems to treat everyone with dignity and work toward peace.

SDG 3: Good Health and Well-being

SDG 3 focuses on health for everyone. This includes prisoners. According to the International Covenant on Economic, Social, and Cultural Rights (ICESCR), prisoners have the right to the best health care possible (UN OHCHR, 2021). Many prisons are overcrowded, dirty, and have poor healthcare. This harms prisoners' physical and mental health (WHO, 2019). Prison life is very stressful. It makes mental health problems worse and can create new ones. Many prisoners struggle with depression, anxiety, or PTSD. But they rarely get proper mental health care (Moller, 2020). Diseases like tuberculosis and HIV/AIDS also spread easily in crowded prisons with poor health care (WHO, 2019). SDG 3 aims to fix health inequality. It focuses on improving health care for the neediest, including prisoners. Prisons must offer medical care, mental health services, and treatment for long-term illnesses. These services help close the health gap for prisoners. The Nelson Mandela Rules also say prisoners should get the same medical care as everyone else (UNODC, 2020). Good health care in prisons improves the well-being of prisoners and helps meet SDG 3 goals.

The Role of Inclusive Justice Systems in Advancing Human Rights

Inclusive justice systems ensure all prisoners' rights are respected. These systems go beyond punishment. They focus on rehabilitation, restorative justice, and access to education, job training, and health care (Rizvi & Khan, 2021). Fair systems treat everyone with dignity, no matter their legal status. This matches SDG 16's goal of peaceful, just, and fair societies.

Inclusive justice tackles problems that lead to crime, like poverty, lack of education, and unemployment. Fixing these issues lowers repeat crimes and helps prisoners return to society (Braithwaite, 2020). Restorative justice is a key idea. It focuses on healing and understanding instead of punishment. It helps offenders see how their actions hurt others. It also gives them support to change (Braithwaite, 2020). Rehabilitation, not punishment, helps prisoners rejoin society. Access to education, job skills, mental health care, and health care reduces repeat crimes. It also helps society as a whole (Rizvi & Khan, 2021). Inclusive justice connects SDG 16 and SDG 3. It helps prisoners and makes communities safer and healthier.

Linking Human Rights, SDG 16 and SDG 3

Human rights for prisoners are key to meeting SDG 16 and SDG 3. SDG 16 supports reforms that make justice systems fair and accountable. Fair systems respect prisoners' rights. Humane treatment and rehabilitation improve prisoners' dignity and lives. SDG 3 focuses on health and well-being. Prisoners need good health care, including mental health support. Providing better health care in prisons helps meet SDG 3 goals. Prisoners deserve care equal to what people outside prison get (WHO, 2019). Together, these goals create a fairer and healthier society. By protecting prisoners' rights, countries support sustainable development, justice, and peace.

NELSON MANDELA RULES AND THEIR RELEVANCE

The Nelson Mandela Rules guide how prisoners should be treated. They are officially called the "United Nations Standard Minimum Rules for the Treatment of Prisoners." These rules were first made in 1955 and updated in 2015. They reflect global agreement on treating prisoners with dignity and respect. The rules focus on health, humane treatment, and rehabilitation (United Nations, 2015).

Core Principles of the Nelson Mandela Rules

The main idea of the Nelson Mandela Rules is dignity. Rule 1 says all prisoners must be treated with respect. Cruel or degrading treatment is not allowed (United Nations, 2015). This follows human rights laws like the Universal Declaration of Human Rights. It protects prisoners from abuse and focuses on fairness and rehabilitation, not punishment (United Nations, 2015).

Health and Well-Being of Prisoners

Health care is an important part of the Nelson Mandela Rules. Rule 24 says prisoners must get the same medical care as people outside prison. This includes doctors, medicine, and specialists (United Nations, 2015). Many prisoners face serious health risks like diseases and mental health problems. Overcrowding and bad health care make things worse. Good medical care helps prisoners stay healthy (Coyle, 2009). Rule 25 says prisoners must get mental health care too (United Nations, 2015). Many prisoners struggle with mental health issues like depression or PTSD. These problems are often ignored in prisons. Mental health care is important for rehabilitation. It also matches SDG 3's goal of health for everyone, especially vulnerable people (United Nations, 2015). Good mental health care helps prisoners heal and change.

Rehabilitation and Reintegration

The Nelson Mandela Rules focus on helping prisoners rebuild their lives. Rule 58 says prisoners should get education, work training, and jobs. These are key to starting a new life after prison (United Nations, 2015). Rehabilitation reduces repeat crimes. It also helps prisoners become productive members of society. This connects to SDG 16's goal of peaceful, fair societies (United Nations, 2015).

Rule 64 says prisons must prepare inmates to return to society. Programs like education, job training, and mental health care help prisoners succeed after release (United Nations, 2015). These programs create stability and lower the chance of reoffending (Sabol, 2017).

ANALYSIS OF SDG 16 IN JUSTICE SYSTEMS

The Current State of Justice Systems Globally

Justice systems worldwide have made progress, but they also face many problems. These systems are meant to follow laws, protect people's rights, and give fair trials. They help keep peace and stability. However, their success and fairness are very different in each country. This depends on political, social, and economic factors. This section explains the state of justice systems globally. It highlights their strengths, weaknesses, and how these issues affect SDG 16. Justice systems around the world show a mix of progress and challenges. While they aim to provide fairness and protect rights, many problems remain. Access to justice is still unequal, especially for marginalized groups. Overcrowding in prisons and delays in trials undermine the fairness of these systems. Corruption and political interference make it even harder for courts to serve justice. SDG 16 serves as a guide to make justice systems stronger, fairer, and more accessible. Efforts by the United Nations and other groups have helped, but much more needs to be done. By addressing these challenges, countries can create justice systems that uphold the rule of law and ensure fairness for everyone.

Diverse Justice System Models Across the Globe

Culture, traditions, and legal practices influence justice systems around the world. Three main systems exist: civil law, common law, and religious or customary law. Civil law systems, used in countries like France and Germany, rely on written laws. Judges in these systems follow set rules to resolve disputes. They have limited flexibility and focus on applying the existing laws. Common law systems are used in the UK, the US, and many Commonwealth countries. These systems rely on past court decisions. Judges can interpret the law and adapt it to new cases. This gives them more flexibility. Their decisions often help develop new legal rules (Sullivan, 2019). Religious law is another model, used in countries like Saudi Arabia and Iran. This system blends legal rules with religious beliefs. It governs areas like marriage, inheritance, and sometimes criminal law. Religious law focuses on the interpretation of religious texts by leaders. Unlike civil and common law, it is closely tied to the values of a specific religion (Galligan, 2017).

Access to Justice: A Global Challenge

A big problem around the world is that many people do not have equal access to justice. This is especially true in poor and conflict-hit regions. Countries in sub-Saharan Africa, South Asia, and Latin America often have few legal resources, making it hard for most people to get legal help. While international law guarantees the right to legal aid, many countries fail to meet this promise. In these regions, marginalized groups like women, minorities, and the poor face extra barriers. They often cannot afford lawyers, and some do not even know their rights. Discrimination and high costs make it harder for these groups to access justice (United Nations, 2020).

Even in places where legal aid services exist, they are often underfunded and understaffed. This limits how much help they can provide. Many legal systems are also very complicated, making it hard for people to navigate them without assistance. Language barriers add to the problem in some regions, preventing people from understanding court proceedings or laws (Sullivan, 2019).

CHALLENGES TO JUSTICE: OVERCROWDED PRISONS AND JUDICIAL DELAYS

Overcrowded prisons are another major issue. Around 24% of the world's prisoners live in overcrowded facilities, according to the International Centre for Prison Studies (2019). This problem is especially bad in countries like India, Brazil, and the Philippines. Prisons often hold far more people than they were designed for, creating inhumane living conditions. Overcrowding also puts extra strain on resources, making it harder to improve other parts of the justice system.

Overcrowding remains a pervasive challenge in global justice systems, directly impacting prisoners' rights and SDGs 16 and 3. According to the World Prison Brief (2023), 30% of the world's 11.5 million prisoners live in overcrowded facilities, with significant regional disparities. In the Philippines, prisons operate at 400% capacity, housing 120,000 inmates in facilities meant for 30,000, leading to inhumane conditions like shared sleeping spaces and limited sanitation (World Prison Brief, 2023). In India, 70% of the 570,000 prisoners in 2023 were pre-trial detainees, exacerbating overcrowding due to judicial delays—cases take an average of 5 years to resolve (National Crime Records Bureau, 2023). Overcrowding has severe consequences. In Brazil, where facilities are at 170% capacity, tuberculosis rates are 20 times higher than in the general population, with 8,000 cases reported in 2022 (WHO, 2023). Mental health is also affected—overcrowding increases stress, contributing to a 40% rise in self-harm incidents in overcrowded prisons globally (UNODC, 2023). Judicial delays compound these issues; in sub-Saharan Africa, 60% of inmates are awaiting trial, often for over 2 years, eroding trust in justice systems (UNODC, 2023). Addressing overcrowding requires alternatives to incarceration, such as community service for non violent offenders, as piloted in Kenya, reducing prison populations by 15% in 2022 (UNODC, 2024). Expediting trials through digital case management systems, as implemented in Singapore, can also reduce pre-trial detention, aligning with SDG 16's goal of accessible justice.

Challenges in Advancing Peace, Justice, and Strong Institutions

Working toward Sustainable Development Goal (SDG) 16—peace, justice, and strong institutions faces many challenges. These problems make it hard to create fair justice systems around the world. They affect how countries build their legal systems and how well they protect the rights of vulnerable people, including prisoners. We must understand these challenges to improve the justice system and protect prisoners' rights. This is also key to achieving SDG 16. Corruption is one of the biggest barriers to peace, justice, and strong institutions. Corruption is common in many legal and political systems. It makes trials unfair and leads to biased decisions. Transparency International's Global Corruption Index shows that corruption in courts is a serious problem. It reduces public trust in the justice system and weakens the rule of law (Transparency International, 2020). Corruption can take many forms, like bribery, unfair rulings, or manipulation of legal processes. These actions often harm marginalized groups the most, including prisoners. When courts are corrupt, prisoners' rights are more likely to be ignored or abused. Corruption makes it harder for prisoners to get fair treatment and increases inequality in the justice system.

Another problem is that many people, especially poor ones, cannot access justice. Legal help is too expensive for many individuals, including prisoners. People from low-income groups cannot afford lawyers or other legal services. The legal system is also very complex, and many prisoners do not understand their rights. This lack of legal knowledge makes it harder for them to defend themselves. The United Nations Human Rights Office (2020) says these barriers lead to unfair treatment, such as wrongful convictions or harsh punishments without proper trials. This shows the urgent need for legal reforms. These reforms should ensure that everyone has equal access to justice, no matter how rich or poor. Overcrowded prisons are another major issue standing in the way of SDG 16. Around the world, many prisons are overcrowded and in terrible condition. These conditions often violate basic human rights. The global prison population has grown so much that many prisons cannot provide basic services like healthcare, enough food, or rehabilitation programs. In some countries, prisons are used as an easy solution to social problems like poverty, drug addiction, and mental illness. Instead of helping people rehabilitate, prisons often punish them without addressing the real issues (International Centre for Prison Studies, 2019). Overcrowded prisons can lead to violence, disease, and more human rights violations. These poor conditions often make criminal behaviour worse instead of helping people improve their lives. Authoritarian governments and shrinking civil freedoms make things worse. In authoritarian countries, the courts are often controlled by the government. This means the courts are not independent and cannot act fairly. Civil society groups and organizations that protect human rights also face repression. Galligan (2017) explains that authoritarian governments block legal reforms. This makes it hard to solve problems in justice systems. In these countries, prisoners face poor conditions, and rehabilitation programs are rare. Without independent organizations or NGOs to help, these issues are often ignored.

The COVID-19 pandemic showed just how weak many justice systems are, especially when it comes to prisoners' health and safety. Most prisons were not prepared to handle the virus. Overcrowded spaces, poor hygiene, and bad healthcare made it easy for the virus to spread. Many prisons had large outbreaks of COVID-19. The United Nations (2020) said this problem highlighted the urgent need for better prison healthcare. It also showed the need to protect prisoners' well-being and avoid future public health crises. Despite all these challenges, global efforts are being made to improve justice systems. Organizations like the United Nations Office on Drugs and Crime (UNODC) are working to promote justice reforms. They focus on making courts more accountable, reducing prison overcrowding, and protecting human rights. The UNODC is also helping countries strengthen their legal systems and improve prison conditions (UNODC, 2020). While progress has been made in some areas, much work still exists. Achieving SDG 16 will require ongoing efforts to fix the many systemic problems in justice systems. This is the only way to create peaceful and fair societies.

CASE STUDIES AND BEST PRACTICES, ROLE OF NATIONAL AND INTERNATIONAL FRAMEWORKS

Improving justice systems as part of SDG 16 is a complex but vital goal. Success stories like those in Rwanda and South Africa show the power of innovative solutions and reconciliation. International standards, such as the Nelson Mandela Rules and UNICEF's guidelines, provide a foundation for justice reform. Organizations like UNODC and World Bank support these efforts by promoting fairness, accountability, and inclusion. National governments must take the lead in reforming their justice systems while working with international frameworks. Civil society and NGOs are essential in pushing for change and protecting human rights. By learning from these efforts, countries can move closer to achieving the goals of SDG 16 and building justice systems that promote peace and fairness for everyone.

Case Studies: Advancing Justice Systems

In some countries, successful reforms show how justice systems can improve. After the 1994 genocide in Rwanda, the country created the Gacaca courts to deal with genocide-related crimes. These courts focused on truth-telling, reconciliation, and community-based justice. They helped Rwanda heal while handling a massive number of cases. This showed the importance of innovative and locally designed solutions (Doughty, 2006).

South Africa: Post-apartheid, South Africa has made strides toward aligning its justice system with SDG 16 through restorative justice, exemplified by the Truth and Reconciliation Commission (TRC). However, its prison system faces significant challenges. As of 2023, the prison population stands at 157,000, with facilities operating at 137% capacity (World Prison Brief, 2023). Overcrowding has led to health crises—tuberculosis rates in prisons are 15 times higher than in the general population, with 5,000 cases reported in 2022 (WHO, 2023). Mental health services are inadequate, with only 10% of inmates with disorders receiving treatment (SAHRC, 2023). The South African Human Rights Commission (SAHRC) has been instrumental, securing court orders in 2022 to improve healthcare access in Pollsmoor Prison, reducing TB cases by 12% (SAHRC, 2023). However, corruption and underfunding hinder progress—only 60% of SAHRC recommendations are implemented due to budget constraints (SAHRC, 2023). While South Africa's focus on restorative justice aligns with SDG 16, its failure to address health disparities undermines SDG 3, highlighting the need for systemic reforms in healthcare funding and prison capacity.South Africa also offers an important example. After apartheid, the Truth and Reconciliation Commission (TRC) focused on restorative justice. It helped heal the nation by encouraging people to share the truth about their actions. The TRC granted amnesty to those who testified, focusing more on truth and peace than punishment. This approach promoted reconciliation in a deeply divided society, aligning with SDG 16's goals (Gibson, 2006).

Norway: Norway's prison system is a global model for advancing SDGs 16 and 3. With a prison population of 3,600 and a capacity utilization of 85% in 2023, overcrowding is minimal (World Prison Brief, 2023). The Norwegian Correctional Service integrates healthcare with the national system, ensuring prisoners receive the same care as the general population (Norwegian Directorate of Health, 2023). In 2022, 90% of inmates with mental health issues received therapy, reducing suicide rates to 5 per 10,000 inmates—among the lowest globally (Baker et al., 2023). Rehabilitation programs, including education and vocational training, contribute to a recidivism rate of 20%, compared to the global average of 50% (Norwegian Correctional Service, 2021). Norway's adherence to the Nelson Mandela Rules, particularly Rules 24 and 58 on health and rehabilitation, aligns with SDG 3's health equity goals and SDG 16's focus on humane justice. However, Norway's model is resource-intensive, posing challenges for replication in lower-income countries. Lessons include prioritizing healthcare integration and rehabilitation over punishment, which can be adapted through incremental policy changes.

Not all efforts have been successful. For example, Afghanistan has struggled to reform its justice system due to corruption and political instability. The ongoing effects of war make the problem worse. Limited resources and weak political commitment further hold back reforms. Even so, international organizations have been trying to help Afghanistan improve the rule of law through technical support and training (Kandahari & Wali, 2020).

The Role of National and International Institutions

National governments and international organizations both play key roles in reforming justice systems. Governments must ensure their legal systems follow international human rights standards. They also need to operate in a fair and transparent way. In Kenya, for instance, reforms have aimed to reduce corruption and make the judiciary more independent. These efforts have improved access to justice in some areas. However, challenges remain, especially in rural areas where legal services are still limited (Institute for Social Accountability, 2020). International organizations like the UNODC, UNICEF, and the World Bank guide and support these national reforms. They provide technical expertise, share best practices, and encourage cooperation between countries. This helps nations learn from one another and improve their justice systems. Global agreements, such as the International Covenant on Civil and Political Rights (ICCPR) and the Convention Against Torture, also play a big role. These agreements set standards for human rights protection and guide national laws to meet global expectations (OHCHR, 2020). They ensure that countries work toward the goals of SDG 16 by respecting human dignity and protecting vulnerable populations.

The Role of Government and Public Collaboration in Justice System Reform

Achieving SDG 16 requires more than legal frameworks; it demands collaboration between governments, civil society, and communities to address deep systemic issues in justice systems. Corruption, a major barrier, affects 70% of judicial systems globally, with Transparency International (2023) reporting that 40% of prisoners in low-income countries face unfair treatment due to bribery. Government-led reforms, such as anti-corruption training for judges, have shown promise—in Colombia, such initiatives reduced judicial bribery by 25% in 2022 (UNODC, 2023). However, government efforts alone are insufficient without public involvement. Civil society organizations (CSOs) play a critical role in advocacy and monitoring. In India, the People's Union for Civil Liberties (PUCL) collaborated with the government in 2023 to implement community oversight boards, inspecting prisons and reducing abuse cases by 18% (PUCL, 2023). Public awareness campaigns, like those in South Africa led by the SAHRC, educated communities on prisoners' rights, increasing public support for rehabilitation programs by 30% in 2022 (SAHRC, 2023). These collaborations align with SDG 16's emphasis on inclusive institutions, ensuring accountability and transparency. To scale impact, governments should fund CSOs, establish public-private partnerships for prison reforms, and involve former inmates in policy design, fostering trust and sustainable change.

ANALYSIS OF SDG 3 IN PRISON SYSTEMS

Health and Well-Being of Prisoners

The health and well-being of prisoners are very important. It helps support sustainable development and matches the goals of SDG 3, which is to "ensure healthy lives and promote well-being for all at all ages." Being in prison often makes health problems worse. It can also cause new health issues. Problems like overcrowding, poor medical care, bad food, and unhealthy living conditions make things harder. Prisoners often have a lower quality of life. This hurts both their physical and mental health. Prison life harms both physical and mental health. Stress, overcrowding, and isolation worsen mental health conditions like depression and anxiety, which affect up to 50% of inmates (Sullivan et al., 2019). However, prisons often lack mental health services, leaving many untreated and at risk of self-harm or suicide (UNODC, 2021). Overcrowding also limits space for activities like exercise or therapy that could help improve mental well-being (Baker, 2020). Communicable diseases spread rapidly in prisons due to overcrowding and poor sanitation. Tuberculosis (TB) is 23 times more common in prisons than outside (WHO, 2020). HIV and hepatitis are also widespread, especially where harm reduction programs like needle exchanges are unavailable (CDC, 2021). The COVID-19 pandemic highlighted how unprepared prisons are for outbreaks, with overcrowded spaces accelerating infections (Baker et al., 2020). Improving prison healthcare requires more funding, better staffing, and integrating prison healthcare into national systems. Harm reduction programs and better mental health services, including therapy and staff training, are critical steps to protect the health and dignity of prisoners (WHO, 2020).

Physical Health Challenges in Prisons

Prisons are places where diseases spread easily. Overcrowding and poor sanitation make this worse. The World Health Organization (WHO, 2020) says prisoners are more likely to get diseases like tuberculosis (TB), HIV, and hepatitis than people outside prison. A study by Luntamo et al. (2021) shows that the risk of getting TB in prisons is 23 times higher than outside. This happens because prisons are crowded, have bad ventilation, and are often dirty. Prisons are crowded, dirty, and unhealthy, which makes it easy for diseases to spread. Diseases like tuberculosis (TB), HIV, and hepatitis are more common in prisons. Prisoners also have more long-term health problems, like heart disease and diabetes. But prisons often don't have enough doctors, so prisoners do not get treated quickly or properly. Prisoners also suffer more from long-term health problems like heart disease, diabetes, and lung issues. Bad food, no exercise, and poor medical care make these problems worse. The United Nations Office on Drugs and Crime (UNODC, 2021) says prisons need to check prisoners' health when they first arrive. They also need to provide care regularly. Without this, many health problems are never diagnosed or treated.

Mental Health and Psychological Well-Being

Mental health is just as important as physical health. Being in prison can cause a lot of stress. This can make mental health problems worse or create new ones. The World Health Organization (WHO, 2020) says that 10-20% of prisoners have serious mental illnesses. These include depression, anxiety, and post-traumatic stress disorder (PTSD).

Prison life causes a lot of stress. Many prisoners suffer from mental illnesses like depression, anxiety, and PTSD. Prisons often don't have enough mental health services to help them. Many prisoners feel isolated and hopeless. This leads to high rates of self-harm and suicide, which are much higher than outside prison. Many prisons do not have enough mental health services. A study by Simms et al. (2020) shows that many prisoners with mental health needs are not getting the care they need. Being in prison is very stressful. Isolation, lack of support, and not knowing how long they will stay locked up all make things worse. Because of this, self-harm and suicide rates in prisons are very high. The WHO (2020) reports that prisoners are 40% more likely to die by suicide than people outside prison.

Nutrition and Sanitation in Prisons

The environment in prisons has a big effect on health. Many prisons struggle to provide enough healthy food. Without fresh and balanced meals, prisoners often don't get the nutrients they need. This leads to malnutrition. When someone is malnourished, their immune system becomes weaker. This makes it easier for them to get sick. A study by Baker et al. (2019) shows that bad food in prisons makes prisoners more likely to get sick. Overcrowding makes the problem even worse. Malnourished prisoners with untreated conditions like diabetes or high blood pressure get even sicker. Prisoners often do not get enough healthy food, which makes them weak and sick. Overcrowding makes the problem worse. Many prisons also have poor sanitation, with dirty water and bad waste disposal. This spreads diseases like cholera and hepatitis. Clean water, better food, and proper hygiene are needed to make prisons healthier. Sanitation is another big problem in prisons. Many prisoners don't have access to clean water or proper waste disposal. This spreads diseases like cholera and hepatitis. A report by the UNODC (2021) says that better sanitation in prisons can stop these diseases. Clean living spaces and better hygiene are very important for prisoners' health. Fixing sanitation systems is necessary to make prisons safer and healthier.

Healthcare Access in Prisons

Everyone has a right to healthcare, including prisoners. However, many prisoners cannot access the care they need. The United Nations (2019) says healthcare is a basic right, but prison systems often don't have enough money or staff to provide proper medical care. Without timely treatment, prisoners with chronic illnesses like diabetes or high blood pressure can get much sicker (Baker et al., 2020). In developing countries, prisons often lack specialized healthcare services. This leaves prisoners with poor care and bad health outcomes. Many prisons don't have enough mental health professionals, so mental health problems often go undiagnosed and untreated (Sullivan et al., 2019). Not having enough staff, medicine, or facilities makes prisoners' health worse, especially in overcrowded prisons (Rosen, 2021).

Best Practices for SDG 3

Best Practice 1: Prison Healthcare Integration with National Systems

One good idea that works well is connecting prison healthcare to the national health system. This means prisoners get the same care as people outside prison. It also ensures their care continues when they leave prison. Connecting prison healthcare with national health systems ensures equal care for prisoners and smooth transitions post-incarceration. Countries like the Netherlands have seen better outcomes using this approach.

For example, in the Netherlands, the national health system handles healthcare in prisons. This makes sure prisoners get high-quality care. It also helps healthcare providers work better together. This approach leads to better health outcomes, especially for prisoners with long-term illnesses or mental health issues (World Health Organization [WHO], 2020).

Best Practice 2: Mental Health Training for Prison Staff

Training prison staff to handle mental health issues can improve prisoners' well-being. In Canada, prison officers learn how to spot mental health problems and respond with care (Baker, 2020). This training prevents violence and self-harm by getting help for prisoners before their problems get worse.

When staff understand mental health, prisons become safer. Prisoners feel supported and are more likely to ask for help. This reduces the stigma around mental health and encourages treatment. Training prison staff to identify and respond to mental health issues fosters safer environments and reduces violence. It also encourages inmates to seek help, as seen in Canada.

Best Practice 3: Specialized Healthcare for Vulnerable Populations

Prisons also need to care for vulnerable groups, like people with HIV, those with drug problems, and those with long-term illnesses. Special care for these groups prevents their health from getting worse. In Spain, prisons run programs for people with drug problems. These programs include methadone treatments and rehab services. They have improved health outcomes and reduced repeat crimes. Prisoners who complete these programs are less likely to return to crime (Baker et al., 2020).

In the United States, prisons provide full HIV care. Inmates with HIV get antiretroviral therapy (ART) to manage their condition. This helps them stay healthy and lowers the risk of spreading HIV in prisons (Sullivan et al., 2019). Targeted programs for people with HIV, substance use disorders, and chronic illnesses improve health outcomes and reduce recidivism. Spain offers drug rehabilitation programs, while U.S. prisons provide HIV care, leading to better inmate health and reduced disease transmission.

RESULTS AND DISCUSSION

This study revealed significant systemic challenges in global prison systems that undermine the realization of SDG 16 and SDG 3, particularly in the domains of justice, health, and human rights for prisoners. A key finding is the pervasive issue of overcrowding, with 30% of the world's 11.5 million prisoners living in facilities exceeding capacity (World Prison Brief, 2023). In regions like the Philippines, prisons operate at 400% capacity, leading to inhumane conditions such as limited sanitation and increased disease transmission, notably tuberculosis, which is 20 times higher in Brazilian prisons than in the general population (WHO, 2023). This directly impedes SDG 3's goal of health equity, as overcrowding exacerbates physical and mental health crises, with 40% of inmates in overcrowded facilities reporting increased self-harm (UNODC, 2023). Judicial delays further compound these issues, with 70% of prisoners in India being pre-trial detainees, facing an average wait of 5 years for trial resolution (National Crime Records Bureau, 2023), eroding trust in justice systems and violating SDG 16's emphasis on accessible justice.

The analysis of legal frameworks highlights their inconsistent implementation. The ICCPR and CAT, despite being binding, show compliance rates of only 40% and enforcement in 25% of violation cases, respectively (UN Human Rights Committee, 2023; CAT, 2023). The Nelson Mandela Rules, while providing comprehensive standards, are adopted by only 50% of UN member states due to resource constraints (UNODC, 2023). This gap underscores the need for stronger enforcement mechanisms to align prison practices with SDG 16's goal of accountable institutions. Case studies from South Africa and Norway reveal contrasting outcomes. South Africa's prison system, at 137% capacity, struggles with health disparities, with only 10% of inmates receiving mental health treatment (SAHRC, 2023). Conversely, Norway's model, with a 20% recidivism rate and integrated healthcare, exemplifies alignment with SDGs 16 and 3, though its resource-intensive nature limits replicability in lower-income contexts (Norwegian Correctional Service, 2021).

CONCLUSION

This chapter examined the critical intersection of prisoners' human rights with SDG 16 (Peace, Justice, and Strong Institutions) and SDG 3 (Good Health and Well-being), highlighting the urgent need for inclusive justice systems to protect prisoners' dignity and health. The research revealed systemic challenges overcrowding, inadequate healthcare, and corruption—that undermine these SDGs globally. Overcrowding, affecting 30% of prisoners, exacerbates health crises like tuberculosis, while mental health care remains inaccessible for 50% of inmates with disorders (World Prison Brief, 2023; Sullivan et al., 2019). The COVID-19 pandemic further exposed vulnerabilities, with infection rates in prisons 50% higher than outside (UNODC, 2021). International frameworks like the Nelson Mandela Rules provide standards for humane treatment, but their implementation is inconsistent due to weak enforcement and resource constraints. Case studies from South Africa and Norway illustrate the spectrum of progress—South Africa struggles with overcrowding and health disparities, while Norway's integrated healthcare system exemplifies SDG alignment. The research shows that making laws is not enough; real change requires governments and people to work together to fix deep systemic problems. Collaborative efforts, such as India's community oversight boards and South Africa's public awareness campaigns, demonstrate how government-public partnerships can enhance accountability and reform (PUCL, 2023; SAHRC, 2023).

To advance SDGs 16 and 3, prison systems must prioritize rehabilitation over punishment, integrating education, job training, and mental health support. Governments should improve healthcare by increasing funding, training staff, and integrating prison systems with national health frameworks, as seen in Norway. International cooperation, involving UNODC, UNICEF, and CSOs, is essential to enforce standards and share best practices, ensuring prisoners' rights are upheld globally. SDG 16 shows how justice systems struggle to ensure peace and fairness. Problems like overcrowding, no legal help, corruption, and abuse make it hard to build a fair system. Groups like UNODC and UNICEF have shared helpful guidelines. But there's still a lot to do. The research shows that making laws is not enough. Real change needs governments and people to work together to fix deep problems in the system. Looking at SDG 3, the research found big gaps in prison healthcare. Many prisoners don't get proper care for mental health, diseases, or other medical needs. Overcrowded prisons and limited resources make things worse. Still, some countries are finding ways to improve. The COVID-19 pandemic further exposed vulnerabilities, with prison infection rates 50% higher than outside (UNODC, 2021), highlighting systemic neglect of prisoners' health rights. Collaborative efforts, such as India's community oversight boards reducing abuses by 18% (PUCL, 2023), demonstrate the potential of government-public partnerships to enhance accountability. These findings suggest that achieving SDGs 16 and 3 requires a shift from punitive to rehabilitative approaches, prioritizing healthcare integration, mental health support, and alternatives to incarceration. International cooperation, involving UNODC and CSOs, is crucial for sharing best practices and enforcing standards, ensuring prisoners' rights are upheld globally.

REFERENCES

Albrecht, R., Roberts, M., & Williams, P. (2020). *Restorative justice: Principles and practice*. Cambridge University Press.

Baker, K. (2020). Health policy in correctional facilities: Current challenges. *Health Policy and Research*, *28*(4), 52–65.

Baker, L. (2020). Barriers to healthcare in correctional facilities. *Journal of Correctional Health*, *35*(2), 234–240. DOI: 10.1016/j.jch.2020.02.003

Baker, L., Kepler, B., & Reid, A. (2019). Malnutrition in prison populations. *Public Health Nutrition*, *22*(6), 1190–1197. DOI: 10.1017/S1368980019001234

Baker, L., Kepler, B., & Reid, A. (2020). The role of harm reduction programs in prisons. *Globalization and Health*, *7*(1), 22–30. PMID: 32138789

Bates, R., & Smith, T. (2020). *Prison reform in the 21st century*. Wiley.

Bates, R., & White, J. (2020). *Prison health and rehabilitation: Theories and practices*. Springer.

Bates, S., & White, M. (2020). *Prison health and well-being: A global perspective*. Springer.

Benvenuto, A., & Lloyd, P. (2019). Prison conditions and human rights. *Journal of Human Rights Law*, *9*(2), 173–185.

Committee Against Torture. (2018). *Annual report 2017*. Council of Europe. https://www.coe.int/en/web/cpt/annual-reports

Coyle, A. (2009). *A human rights approach to prison management: Handbook for prison staff*. International Centre for Prison Studies.

Cullen, F. T., & Gendreau, P. (2020). *The principles of effective intervention in corrections*. Oxford University Press.

Doughty, L. (2006). Reconciliation and justice: Rwanda's Gacaca courts. *Journal of Peace and Justice*, *12*(3), 198–205.

European Court of Human Rights. (2020). *Conditions of detention: Case law and the European Court of Human Rights*. https://www.echr.coe.int

Galligan, D. (2017). *Law and the judicial process*. Routledge. https://www.routledge.com/Law-and-the-Judicial-Process/Galligan/p/book/9780367335449

Gibson, J. L. (2006). Truth and reconciliation in South Africa: At the intersection of personal and political justice. *The Journal of Politics*, *68*(1), 172–185.

Goldstein, D. (2016). Human dignity and the prison system. *Oxford Journal of Legal Studies*, *36*(4), 459–477.

Green, A., & Johnson, T. (2019). *Justice and health in the United States prison system*. Oxford University Press.

Green, P., & Johnson, L. (2019). *Prison overcrowding and its effects on health*. Oxford University Press.

Hinton, E. (2020). *Mass incarceration and the global health crisis*. Harvard University Press.

Institute for Social Accountability. (2020). Judicial reforms in Kenya: Addressing corruption and improving access to justice. *The International Journal of Politics and Law*, *25*(4), 342–358.

International Centre for Prison Studies. (2019). *World prison population list* (12th ed.). https://www.prisonstudies.org/world-prison-brief

Jackson, J. (2020). The effects of incarceration on mental health: A case study approach. *International Journal of Prison Health*, *15*(2), 78–91.

Kandahari, S., & Wali, S. (2020). The judicial system in Afghanistan: Challenges and reforms. *International Review of Law and Policy*, *41*(2), 122–139.

Luntamo, M., Pascoe, A., & Thomas, C. (2021). Tuberculosis prevalence in prisons: A global perspective. *World Health Organization Report, 12*(4), 132–140. https://www.who.int/tb

Morris, A., & Maxwell, G. (2018). *Restorative justice and the prison system*. Cambridge University Press.

Moser, L. (2020). Prison health: A fundamental human right. *Health and Human Rights Journal*, *22*(4), 234–247.

Murray, R., Turner, A., & Green, J. (2021). *The intersection of public health and criminal justice systems*. Cambridge University Press.

Norwegian Correctional Service. (2021). *Rehabilitation in Norwegian prisons: A model for the world*. Norwegian Ministry of Justice.

Norwegian Directorate of Health. (2021). *Health care in Norwegian prisons*. https://www.helsedirektoratet.no

Olsen, A. (2021). *Restorative justice in the modern prison system*. Routledge.

Olsen, E. (2021). *Rehabilitation and reintegration in Scandinavian prisons*. Cambridge University Press.

Sabol, W. J. (2017). *Prisoner reentry in the United States: A historical overview*. U.S. Department of Justice, National Institute of Justice.

Simms, D., Hurd, S., & Gold, A. (2020). Mental health care for incarcerated individuals. *Journal of Correctional Psychology, 45*(3), 195–202.

Sullivan, D. (2019). *Access to justice and legal aid*. Legal Services Commission. https://www.legalservices.gov.uk/

Sullivan, M., Rosen, D., & Baker, K. (2019). Improving mental health care in prisons. *Prison Health Journal, 11*(3), 101–109. DOI: 10.1016/j.prh.2019.06.002

Sustainable Development Goal 16 Toolkit. (2021). *Working with National Human Rights Institutions*. https://www.sdg16toolkit.org

Sykes, G. (2019). *The society of captives: A study of a maximum security prison*. Princeton University Press.

Transparency International. (2020). *Global corruption index 2020*. https://www.transparency.org/en/cpi/2020/index

UNICEF. (2019). *Guidelines on juvenile justice reform*. https://www.unicef.org/documents/guidelines-juvenile-justice-reform

United Nations. (1948). *Universal Declaration of Human Rights*. https://www.un.org/en/universal-declaration-human-rights

United Nations. (1966). *International Covenant on Civil and Political Rights*. https://www.ohchr.org/en/instruments-mechanisms/instruments/international-covenant-civil-and-political-rights

United Nations. (1984). *Convention against torture and other cruel, inhuman or degrading treatment or punishment*. https://www.ohchr.org/en/instruments-mechanisms/instruments/convention-against-torture-and-other-cruel-inhuman-or-degrading

United Nations. (2015). *United Nations standard minimum rules for the treatment of prisoners (the Nelson Mandela Rules)*. https://www.un.org/en/events/mandeladay/mandela_rules.shtml

United Nations. (2019). *United Nations Office on Drugs and Crime (UNODC) and justice system reforms*. https://www.unodc.org/unodc/en/justice-and-prison-reform/index.html

United Nations. (2020). *Access to justice and human rights*. United Nations Human Rights Office. https://www.ohchr.org/en/access-justice

United Nations. (2021). *Sustainable Development Goals report 2021*. https://unstats.un.org/sdgs/report/2021/The-Sustainable-Development-Goals-Report-2021.pdf

United Nations. (2023). *Sustainable Development Goal 16: Peace, justice, and strong institutions*. https://www.un.org/sustainabledevelopment/peace-justice/

United Nations Development Programme. (2020). *Strengthening the justice system for peace and security*. https://www.undp.org/peacebuilding

United Nations Development Programme. (n.d.). *Sustainable Development Goals*. https://www.undp.org/sustainable-development-goals

United Nations Goal 3: Ensure healthy lives and promote well-being for all at all ages. (n.d.). Department of Economic and Social Affairs. https://sdgs.un.org/goals/goal3

United Nations Office of Legal Affairs. (2021). *Prisoners' rights and international law*. https://legal.un.org

United Nations Office on Drugs and Crime. (2015). *Nelson Mandela Rules: United Nations standard minimum rules for the treatment of prisoners*. https://www.unodc.org/documents/justice-and-prison-reform/Nelson_Mandela_Rules-E-ebook.pdf

United Nations Office on Drugs and Crime. (2021). *Health in prisons: A global overview*. https://www.unodc.org

United Nations Office on Drugs and Crime. (2021). *Sustainable Development Goal 16: Peace, justice, and strong institutions*. https://www.un.org/sustainabledevelopment/peace-justice/

United Nations Office on Drugs and Crime. (2021). The health of prisoners: Issues and policies. *UNODC Annual Report on Prison Health*, *7*, 39–50.

United Nations Office on Drugs and Crime. (2022). *Justice for all: The role of the justice system in achieving the SDGs*. https://www.unodc.org/unodc/en/about-unodc/sustainable-development-goals/sdg16_-peace-and-justice.html

United Nations Office on Drugs and Crime. (n.d.). *Sustainable Development Goal 3: Good health and well-being*. https://www.unodc.org/unodc/en/about-unodc/sustainable-development-goals/sdg3_-good-health-and-well-being.html

Vasquez, M. (2018). International standards on the treatment of prisoners. *Human Rights Quarterly, 40*(1), 45–68. DOI: 10.1353/hrq.2018.0020

World Bank. (2019). *Justice for the poor: Enhancing access to justice in developing countries.* https://www.worldbank.org/en/topic/governance/brief/justice-for-the-poor

World Health Organization. (2020). *Health and human rights in prison systems.* https://www.who.int/europe/health-topics/prisons-and-health

World Health Organization. (2020). *Health and prison systems: Strengthening health care in prisons.* https://www.who.int/news-room/fact-sheets

World Health Organization. (2020). *Mental health in prisons: Challenges and opportunities.* https://iris.who.int/bitstream/handle/10665/108156/E64328.pdf?sequence=1

World Health Organization. (2020). Prison health and the burden of disease in incarcerated populations. *WHO Guidelines on Prison Healthcare, 12*(2), 45–67.

World Health Organization. (2021). *Health systems strengthening in prisons.* https://www.drugsandalcohol.ie/35165/1/WHO_prison_framework.pdf

World Prison Brief. (2020). *Prison healthcare systems worldwide: Access and limitations.* https://www.prisonstudies.org

Zaleski, P. (2022). Prisoner rights and international law. *International Law Review, 27*(2), 113–130. DOI: 10.1016/j.inlaw.2022.12.001

KEY TERMS AND DEFINITIONS

Human Rights: Fundamental rights and freedoms inherent to all individuals, regardless of status, including prisoners. These include the right to dignity, health, and protection from torture, as outlined in the Universal Declaration of Human Rights (UDHR) (United Nations, 1948).

Incarceration: The state of being confined in a prison or correctional facility as a form of punishment or detention. Incarceration often exacerbates health and social challenges, impacting prisoners' rights and well-being (Bates & White, 2020).

Restorative Justice: A justice model that emphasizes repairing harm caused by crime through reconciliation, rehabilitation, and community involvement, rather than solely punitive measures (Morris & Maxwell, 2018).

Rehabilitation: The process of preparing prisoners for reintegration into society through education, vocational training, and mental health support, aiming to reduce recidivism (Norwegian Correctional Service, 2021).

Nelson Mandela Rules: United Nations Standard Minimum Rules for the Treatment of Prisoners, updated in 2015, providing guidelines for humane treatment, healthcare, and rehabilitation in prisons (United Nations, 2015).

SDG 16 (Peace, Justice, and Strong Institutions): A Sustainable Development Goal focused on promoting peaceful, inclusive societies, ensuring access to justice, and building accountable institutions, with specific relevance to fair prison systems (United Nations, 2023).

SDG 3 (Good Health and Well-being): A Sustainable Development Goal aimed at ensuring healthy lives and promoting well-being for all, including prisoners, through access to quality healthcare and mental health services (World Health Organization, 2020).

Chapter 9

Comparative Legal Frameworks for Integrating Refugee Rights Into SDG Implementation:

A Comparative Study of India and International Best Practices

Abhinash Mohanta
https://orcid.org/0000-0002-8732-3202
KIIT University, India

Kyvalya Garikapati
https://orcid.org/0000-0003-0990-6514
KIIT University, India

Shreya
https://orcid.org/0009-0008-3533-797X
KIIT University, India

Sneha
https://orcid.org/0000-0002-0158-2503
XIM University, India

Shivani Samanta
https://orcid.org/0009-0003-6857-6145
South Asian University, India

DOI: 10.4018/979-8-3373-1792-2.ch009

ABSTRACT

This paper explores the integration of refugee rights into Sustainable Development Goal (SDG) implementation by comparing India's legal frameworks with international best practices. It examines laws, policy documents, and institutional mechanisms to assess how refugee rights are reflected in national development strategies. Drawing from case studies in India and jurisdictions across Europe, Latin America, and Asia, it evaluates the development, strengths, and gaps in existing legal regimes. The study combines doctrinal analysis with insights from legal experts, offering empirical perspectives on practical challenges and implementation barriers. Key findings highlight divergent national approaches to legal compliance, revealing the need for context-specific, rights-based strategies that align refugee protection with sustainable development. The paper concludes with targeted policy suggestions to improve legal safeguards for refugees and promote alignment between domestic frameworks and global SDG commitments.

INTRODUCTION

The United Nations General Assembly approved the Sustainable Goals in 2015 to establish an inclusive and challenging global project that seeks to define both social justice and economic well-being while conserving our environment ("Sustainable Development Goals," 2018). The SDG agenda drives forward an idea that everyone including individuals from any background should take part in development progress. The path to achieving our vision depends totally on following the law. A robust system of laws at home and abroad makes governments responsible for protecting people in need and resulting in actions that align development targets with practical achievements.

The implementation of these legal systems differs greatly when imposing refugee protection measures. Global refugees face the worst form of vulnerability because they sit between humanitarian response areas and planned development zones which fail to cooperate (Boswell, 2017). Sustained development requires protective measures for refugee rights along with humanitarian concern because safeguarding these rights will help advance development goals. Refugees cannot participate in the development processes which aim to create dignified life for all people because they lack access to legal identification as well as education, medical care, shelter and employment. Illegal and unprotected refugees continue to face threats from exploitation and discrimination and institutional discrimination along with neglect due to the absence of structured legal protection systems.

Hence, aligning the rights of refugees with sustainable goals requires conscious legal and institutional action that integrates the needs of the refugees into the overall SDG agenda (Denaro & Giuffré, 2021). India, thus, is one such case that is particularly imperative to examine in this context. Although having a tradition of providing asylum to displaced populations from neighbouring nations, India has not embraced a specific legal institutional framework to protect the refugees. The nation is not party to the 1951 Refugee Convention or the Protocol to it of 1967, but is instead relying on ad hoc administrative action and general laws relating to foreigners, such as the Foreigners Act of 1946 and the Passport Act of 1967(Shanker & Vijayaraghavan, 2023).

Although India's constitutional guarantees, including the right to equality and the right to life and personal liberty, have been extended to foreign nationals in some judicial rulings, the absence of consistent national policy for refugees causes legal ambiguity. Refugees frequently find themselves with insecure legal situations, lacking defined rights to education, healthcare, or livelihoods. This legal gap makes it difficult to include refugees in India's sustainable development agenda (Singh, 2012).

Meanwhile, several nations have established legal and institutional models that incorporate more systematically the rights of refugees into their national development agendas (Lippert-Rasmussen & Vitikainen, 2020). Comparative law review presents the potential to review the manner in which other jurisdictions—some under similar economic constraints—have integrated the protection of refugees into structures of law that enhance the management of long-run development. Countries of Latin America(Agosto & Rubinstein, 2022), the whole of the EU, and certain African nations, for example, have legislated reforms and policy innovations that recognize access to public services, social integration, and sustainable solutions to refugees (Ruhs, 2022).

An examination of such models has the potential to identify the strength points and weaknesses of India's approach to the issue, as well as to outline potential avenues of reform that reconcile national contexts while embracing world commitments. Justification for this research arises from the pivotal necessity to assess the manner in which legal frameworks can facilitate or impede the participation of the population of refugees in sustainable ventures of development(Irudaya Rajan, 2022). This paper proposes to undertake comparative legal analysis to review the effectiveness of the current legal regime of India towards refugees with the best international practices chosen from various jurisdictions around the world.

This research will look into the role of law to promote or hinder the integration of refugee rights into the policy discourse of national development based on the SDGs. It aims to realize institutional gaps, inconsistencies with norms, and procedural obstacles along with highlighting the successful strategies of other jurisdictions which can be derived to design the future legal reform of India. This research is directed through the following guiding questions. What is the current legal and policy setup of India which accommodates or ignores the rights of the refugees under sustainable development? What are the pros and cons of legal strategies of other jurisdictions that have achieved visible achievements under this category?

What policy inputs can be inferred from these comparisons to refine the integration of the refugees into the planning frame of the country towards the realization of sustainable development goals? What can be the shape of legal reform so that the refugees are meaningfully integrated into the strategies of the country to realize the objectives of sustainable development? To answer these questions, the research adopts one qualitative approach based upon the doctrinal legal analysis supplemented with expert opinion inputs. Legal texts, policy guidelines, case law, and international instruments are analyzed to examine the theoretical foundations and practical approaches to laws related to refugees.

This study employs a qualitative doctrinal approach, analyzing international instruments, national legal texts, judicial decisions, and policy documents to assess how refugee rights are integrated into sustainable development strategies. A comparative legal framework is adopted, drawing on case studies from Uganda, Colombia, and Germany. These countries were selected for their regional diversity and innovative legal responses to refugee inclusion. The study further incorporates expert insight from Prof. Sukanta Kumar Nanda, Dean of the School of Law at Birla Global University, whose background in human rights law and constitutional governance provides critical reflection on India's evolving refugee protection landscape.

The analysis benefits from insights shared by Prof. Nanda during an in-depth interview, which helped ground the comparative findings in India's legal and policy realities. His reflections, shaped by his expertise in constitutional law and policy engagement, illuminate how gaps in India's legal treatment of refugees affect their access to development-linked rights. These insights reveal key institutional and legal barriers that obstruct refugee inclusion and highlight the practical pathways to align national strategies with international standards.

This research not only aims to map current legal ground but to add momentum to an ongoing discussion around how law can be made an instrument of inclusive growth. It places legal compliance at the center of sustainable development's foundational pillars and contends that until the rights and needs of populations of refugees are met, the wider objectives of equity and justice enshrined within the SDGs remain elusive. Addressing India, but informed by international best practices, the study presents a dual view that remains contextually situated yet has international evidence base. As such, the final objective is to produce not only legal and policy recommendations but to design a set of legal and policy inputs that can assist India and others like it, in creating frameworks that protect the dignity, rights, and potential of refugee populations.

THEORETICAL AND LEGAL FOUNDATIONS

As an internationally recognised framework the Sustainable Development Goals (SDGs) seek improvement in social and economic development together with environmental sustainability across all nations. The UN drafted the SDGs under its scope in 2015 which contain seventeen goals with corresponding objectives that focus on inclusive development while solving established structural inequalities. The SDGs establish universality standards by demanding developed nations together with developing nations to exceed economic measurement when delivering their developmental goals. These SDGs function as powerful policy and normative instruments although they do not have rigorous legal requirements. The effectiveness of SDG operations depends on states voluntarily transforming their goals into national policies, laws and administrative frameworks. The SDG platform needs to demonstrate its capacity for shaping national legal frameworks and policies as well as its ability to foster international accountability and cooperation to achieve success(Kanie et al., 2019).

The goals find themselves integrated into the country-level planning of many nations, boosted through institutional linkage among the various government ministries, legislatures, and civil society movements. The SDGs are based upon the promise of human dignity, along with the beliefs that the improvement of the lot of all individuals, regardless of status or origin, is necessary to shape the future of human civilization (Dugarova, 2015).

Refugees, being the population defined through the characteristics of extreme vulnerability and displacement, constitute part of the category of the vulnerable that the SDGs intend to include in the narrative of the world becoming more inclusive. Despite their normative ambition, the SDGs remain non-binding and lack formal enforcement mechanisms. Their implementation is largely dependent on political will, administrative capacity, and national legal translation. For refugees—who are often not citizens and lack legal visibility—this voluntary structure further contributes to their exclusion from development metrics and national planning(Denaro & Giuffré, 2021).

Many nations set up the SDGs as domestic laws or action plans, thus attaching them to enforceable obligations under the laws of the land. Also, the SDGs prompted international and regional conversations that involve a wide range of stakeholders to coordinate national policies and international agenda goals. This normative impact highlights the value of mainstreaming refugee rights into SDG application, particularly considering the sophisticated legal status of the displaced individuals in many states(Ladan, 2018).

These enforcement limitations underscore the relevance of compliance theories in understanding how states internalize refugee-related development norms. Legal compliance, therefore, refers not only to the mechanical application of the law or regulation, but the extended concept of complementarity with international norms, constitutional values, and international human rights obligations. The numerous legal compliance models explain why states follow international norms because of the SDGs and other global frameworks.

According to the rational choice theory, states comply where it fits their interests, e.g., to maintain legitimacy or access international assistance. Constructivist models focus on the power of norms, identity, and reputation to spur compliance. Strong domestic institutions increase compliance potential through methods such as legislative oversight and jurisdictional cheques and administrative rules enforcement according to institutionalist perspectives (Lovett, 2006).

Through theoretical groundwork researchers gain the basis to conceptualise how refugee rights become institutionalised within national laws when governments handle complex social-political matters. Inclusive development requires mainstreaming human rights within legal compliance models for successful progress.

The rights available to refugees exist at the point where international law and domestic legislation meet humanitarian standards. Every refugee obtains basic human rights starting with life together with liberty and security and including the right to education and medical assistance(Hathaway, 2005). The rights possess independence from nationality or status since they originate from international conventions and declarations and covenants.

The problem is trying to translate these norms into enforceable legal rights, particularly where refugees are not formally acknowledged or can access legal guarantees. Legal pluralism theories and rights-oriented approaches to development further underscore how international, international legal, and customary, and informal legal regimes operate to condition the lived realities of refugees. On the ground, legal compliance must not only be measured based on the existence of laws but, upon compliance, based also on accessibility, fairness, and effectiveness at safeguarding the vulnerable (Zubair et al., 2019).

Many international documents underlie the legal enforcement and protection of the rights of refugees. Foremost is the 1951 Convention Relating to the Status of Refugees, which, along with the 1967 Protocol, sets the definition of the refugee under law and details the rights accorded to the same. These are rights to be free of refoulement, access to the courts, employment, education, and access to public relief. Although not all states are signatory to the Convention or Protocol, the principles enshrined therein enjoy widespread acceptance and find expression in national policies("Convention Relating to the Status of Refugees," 1969). Similarly, the Universal Declaration of Human Rights, the International Covenants on Civil and

Political Rights, and Economic, Social, and Cultural Rights, include stipulations that extend to refugees as well as to non-citizens(Abdelaaty, 2021). These documents include the declaration of the universality of rights, which places the responsibility upon states to ensure equal access to basic services and juridical guarantees. Besides the foundational treaties, regional approaches complete the elaboration of the rights of the refugees. The Refugee Convention of the Organization of African Unity(Rankin, 2005), the Cartagena Declaration of the Americas, complement the definition of the refugee with context-specific interpretations, extending the definition to certain additional categories, and reaffirm states' obligations to grant asylum and aid to the same.

These regional mechanisms tend to mirror the local geopolitical and humanitarian circumstances of the regions, facilitating greater adaptability of approach to the protection of refugees("Cartagena Declaration on Refugees, Adopted at a Colloquium Entitled 'Coloquio Sobre La Proteccion Internacional de Los Refugiados En American Central, Mexico y Panama: Problemas Juridicos y Humanitarios' Held at Cartagena, Colombia from 19-22 November 1984," 2005). International humanitarian law, specifically the Geneva Conventions, is also involved in the protection of populations displaced in armed conflict situations. Together, these instruments constitute an intertwined web of legal obligations which overlap with the goals of the SDGs' developmental objectives(How Does IHL Protect Refugees and Internally Displaced Persons?, 2018). In addition to global conventions, regional legal instruments have developed more context-specific refugee protections. The 1984 Cartagena Declaration, widely adopted in Latin America, expands the refugee definition to include those fleeing generalized violence, internal conflict, and massive human rights violations categories often excluded under the 1951 Convention(Cartagena Declaration on Refugees, 2023). Similarly, the 2009 Kampala Convention of the African Union, while focused on internally displaced persons, places legal obligations on states to prevent displacement and assist those affected(Adeola et al., 2021). These regional frameworks illustrate how legally binding or politically endorsed instruments can be adapted to reflect regional displacement realities, thereby enhancing the normative and practical scope of refugee protection.

Beyond these inclusive international norms, however, the practical application of the rights of the refugee extensively varies between jurisdictions. Legal recognition, administrative capabilities, and political will all impact the degree to which states implement obligations. Throughout numerous nations, the lack of domestic laws to govern refugees has created a legislative vacuum, which has left the displaced dependent on discretionary policy or international aid. When domestic laws are present, the same laws may be bereft of coherence, enforcement provision, or conformity to international norms.

These discrepancies reveal the necessity of the use of comparative legal analysis to determine best practice, as well as areas of reform. This type of analysis enables the systematic inquiry into the operation of the various legal systems to implement the rights of the refugee, set in the context of the pursuit of sustainable development.

Comparative legal scholarship requires the examination of the laws, institutions, and legal traditions of different jurisdictions to determine similarities, differences, and exportable innovations. This type of analysis can be doctrinal, targeting statutory and constitutional provision, or functional, analyzing the operation of the laws themselves. It can also incorporate the socio-economic aspects, which examine the interaction with the law, society, and culture.

Comparative analysis is most beneficial where the subject-matter, such as the law of refugees, has such diverse variations at the state level, yet has common principles. Through this lens, one can assess how different legal systems structure refugee protection, facilitate access to rights, and integrate displaced persons into development strategies.

Existing literature on refugee law and SDG implementation often reflects a multidisciplinary orientation, drawing from legal studies, international relations, development studies, and human rights theory(Pasquetti et al., 2019). Scholars have explored the normative tensions between sovereignty and universality, the role of courts in advancing refugee rights, and the challenges of policy coherence in complex governance environments. One recurring theme in this literature is the gap between formal legal commitments and actual implementation. This gap is often attributed to limited administrative resources, political resistance, or inadequate legal frameworks.

Another significant focus is the role of civil society and international organizations in bridging this implementation gap through advocacy, litigation, and service delivery(Choi, 2019). Recent academic contributions also highlight the importance of integrating refugee protection into broader development agendas. These studies emphasize that treating refugee issues as purely humanitarian undermines long-term solutions and perpetuates dependency.

Instead, there is growing support for developmental approaches that recognize refugees as agents of development and not merely as recipients of aid. Legal frameworks that support such approaches include provisions for access to education, vocational training, legal employment, and participation in public life(Mencütek & Nashwan, 2020). These rights are essential for enabling refugees to contribute to their host communities and for ensuring that development policies are inclusive and sustainable.

Methodologically, interdisciplinary research combining legal analysis with empirical methods such as interviews, case studies, and field observations provides a more holistic understanding of refugee law in practice. Such studies can unmask the ways that laws are interpreted by those administering them, accessed by refugees, and subject to local political dynamics. This methodology can further identify informal practices, community-oriented mechanisms, that support or obfuscate official legal frameworks.

Comparative studies involving varied legal systems common law versus civil law, highly formalized versus largely informal legal traditions enrich the explanation of the varied avenues through which the rights of refugees can be protected. When considering legal frameworks to include refugee rights in SDG implementation, one needs to recognize the intersection between international norms and the domestic legal systems(Denaro & Giuffré, 2021).

International conventions typically require supporting legislation or administrative regulations to become effective at the domestic level. Constitutions, too, set the stage, through constitutional guarantees, and judicial interpretation, which in turn defines how rights of the refugees are to be interpreted and exercised. Domestic political contexts, such as attitudes of the public towards the refugees, concerns of security, electoral strategies, shape the legislative, the policy arena(Goldenziel, 2015).

As such, the exploration of legal foundations, theories has to be framed in the context of this wider legal, political ecology. Law does not act in vacuo but has interaction with institutions, policy, social attitude. Legal frameworks can be instrumental means to include, or exclude, depending upon the character of the construction, application of the law.

In the context of the SDGs, keeping the refugees not left behind requires more than the rhetoric of statements. It does not only require the legal architecture to be attuned to the international mandates, but it has to be responsive to the local context, realities too. It is critical to comprehend this sophisticated relationship to determine the avenues to more inclusive and effective legal compliance.

INDIA'S LEGAL FRAMEWORK FOR REFUGEE RIGHTS AND SDG IMPLEMENTATION

The protection of refugees in India proceeds through practical grounds and political requirements alongside humanitarian concerns while remaining without legal institutional framework. India intentionally chooses to stay outside the 1951 Refugee Convention alongside its 1967 Protocol even though numerous other countries form part of this agreement(Sapre, 2023). India embraced large refugee populations originating from Tibet and Bangladesh (then East Pakistan), Sri Lanka, Afghanistan and Myanmar together with other neighbouring nations. The movements of displaced refugees have been controlled by administrative approaches and political orders instead of proper refugee law. The system controls refugee matters through numerous flexible policies but this approach results in unstandardized and sporadic legal mechanisms. India established its refugee policy framework first on a humanitarian basis that extended support to displaced people during the post-colonial period due to neighbourhood wars and religious conflicts. The Indian tradition of receiving migrants has faced challenges because of expanding migration numbers and changing political conditions in the region while security concerns continue to grow(Gopalakrishnan, 2019).

Refugees in India currently fall beneath general laws that apply to all foreigners since no unified refugee legislation exists in the country. Under the Foreigners Act of 1946 the government maintains complete discretionary powers to control the movements of non-citizens through deportation imprisonment or limitations of travel(Singh, 2012). The Foreigners Act of 1946 creates no distinctions between different types of foreigners regardless of their status as tourists, economic migrants, asylum seekers or refugees. Refugee treatment depends heavily on bilateral diplomatic relations together with administrative circulars while central government policy preferences define the current treatment at any time. Two additional legal frameworks pertaining to refugees are provided by the Passport Act of 1967 together with the Registration of Foreigners Act of 1939(Bhattacharjee, 2008). These legal instruments fail to address the particular needs which refugees require through specialised legal protections.

Indian courts have, in select instances, extended constitutional protections to refugees by relying on fundamental rights under Articles 14 and 21 of the Constitution. In *National Human Rights Commission v. State of Arunachal Pradesh* (1996), the Supreme Court prevented the forced eviction of Chakma refugees and emphasized that all persons, regardless of nationality, are entitled to protection under Article 21(Debnath & Debnath, 2020). Similarly, in *Louis De Raedt v. Union of India* (1991), the Court held that the power to deport foreign nationals must be exercised in a manner consistent with the Constitution's guarantees of fairness and non-arbitrariness. These rulings illustrate the judiciary's willingness to uphold refugee rights in specific contexts, but they have not resulted in systemic policy reforms. The absence of codified refugee law means such protections remain reactive and inconsistent in application.

Refugee governance in India remains fragmented and heavily influenced by shifting political narratives and bilateral considerations, resulting in wide variation in how refugee groups are treated across states. The Tibetan refugee community receives significant autonomy decisions combined with complete access to education systems and economic opportunities. The Indian authorities have subjected Rohingya refugees from Myanmar to various restrictive measures which include imprisonment as well as expulsion threats and minimal access to essential services(Mohajan, 2018). This disparity reflects the discretionary nature of refugee treatment in India. For example, Tibetan refugees benefit from access to formal schooling, identity documents, and employment permissions under central and state-supported programs. In contrast, Rohingya refugees face arrests, denial of services, and restricted movement even when holding UNHCR-issued refugee cards. This uneven treatment arises from the absence of standardized legal recognition, leaving refugee rights subject to administrative discretion, local sentiment, and security-oriented policy framing (Mohajan, 2018).

There exists inconsistency in refugee policy because India lacks clear legal standards to determine refugee protection which results in varied application of refugee policies. The practise of administrative discretion by the Indian government which follows geopolitical objectives and security interests plays a crucial role in asylum management within the country.

The country lacks official national programmes which both regulate and assist refugees because India has no dedicated refugee agency nor administrative body. Foreign national issues together with refugee matters fall under the responsibility of the Ministry of Home Affairs which handles immigration administration duties. The United Nations High Commissioner for Refugees (UNHCR) operates in India with confined powers to give protection services for refugees who are neither Tibetan nor Sri Lankan refugees whose cases are not covered by Indo-bilateral refugee agreements. The UNHCR performs refugee status determination (RSD) on these groups but its support extends only to health care and education together with livelihood assistance. The agency operates under the political authorization of India's government without official legal authorization. Indian ministries lack an established mechanism to work with the UNHCR which would enable refugee participation in national development programmes(Shanker & Vijayaraghavan, 2023).

The lack of specific legal and policy framework for refugees poses major obstacles for India as it integrates with global Sustainable Development Goals standards. The national policy mapping of SDGs conducted by NITI Aayog and other institutions has resulted in significant progress but refugees remain unincorporated throughout this process. National welfare programmes such as Ayushman Bharat and the Right to Education Act along with skill development schemes do not provide formal access to refugees throughout the country. The exclusion of refugees from healthcare together with education and employment and social security services restricts their ability to achieve the goals set forth by the SDGs for inclusive and sustainable development. Refugees struggle to obtain existing welfare schemes because of their lack of identity documentation and legal ambiguity and because of their fear of detention(Vijayaraghavan, 2020).

The inclusion of refugee rights in SDG strategies needs a basic transformation in refugee understanding from temporary stress to development process contributors. The present legal and policy structures fail to implement refugee integration into development frameworks. The existing frameworks typically make refugee situations worse by intensifying their exclusion and their sense of vulnerability. The lack of data categorization about refugee communities hinders governmental officials from properly monitoring how well the SDG development targets are achieved across refugee populations. Due to the lack of specific data about refugee needs existing reporting systems overlook their requirements which makes it impossible to properly evaluate development progress(Denaro & Giuffré, 2021).

Prof. Nanda explains that refugee rights continue to stand outside the scope of both global and national development strategies that implement SDGs. The original promise to leave no individual behind remains overlooked by development plans which fail to include refugees in their structures. It stems from two interconnected causes including the strict definition of migration targets and indicators and secondly due to a security-oriented viewpoint of migration populations. Absent formal laws about refugees in India leads displaced persons to fall under immigration legislation made for exclusive purposes. The wrong mixing of refugee and migrant populations results in irregular treatment methods which diminishes access to essential SDG rights including education and healthcare together with social protections as defined by the framework(Nanda, 2021).

Prof. Nanda stresses that India's usage of general immigration laws found in the Foreigners Act of 1946 produces unclear legal conditions which threaten the protection of refugee populations. Legal systems fail to detect unique persecution risks which people experience in their attempts to escape violent conflict and they similarly fail to distinguish between willing and coerced movement. The policy framework becomes un-proactive due to the shortage of protective legal protection which leads to ineffective sustainable integration resources. The authorities of India fail to integrate refugees into their established national welfare programmes. The benefits and programmes under projects Ayushman Bharat, Pradhan Mantri Awas Yojana and various educational programmes do not extend to refugee beneficiaries. A substantial institutional defect compromising India's Sustainable Development Goal inclusion becomes evident through this exclusion.

Drawing attention to international examples, Prof. Nanda notes that while there are promising initiatives—such as Uganda's Refugee and Host Population Empowerment (ReHoPE)(Keller et al., 2022) and Colombia's integration of displaced persons into national development plans—these remain limited in scope and heavily dependent on external funding(Rochlin, 2023). No country has yet achieved full legal and policy integration of refugee rights across all SDG sectors. Even where best practices exist, they tend to be fragmented and lack the systemic depth necessary for long-term inclusion. In his view, this global fragmentation reinforces the need for legal harmonization and more consistent application of international human rights standards.

Prof. Nanda specifies three fundamental measures needed to link refugee rights with sustainable development planning. National legislation needs to include legal provisions which establish refugee status recognition. Political discretion continues to determine refugee status rights since neither definition nor rights are established in law. Every refugee needs to become part of official national data collection systems. The collection of detailed refugee population information is essential to allow refugee participation during standard development goal monitoring sessions and reporting processes. The necessary partnership between governments with UN agencies and civil society and refugee-led organisations must be institutionalised to create inclusive processes for development planning and execution. The absence of these core approaches ensures sustainable development practises actively omit particular groups of vulnerable people.

Refugee protection in India depends heavily on its cultural factors as well as its political systems and economic conditions(Kaur, 2013). The political perspective of refugees as threats to national security drives countries to create exclusionary policies that face resistance from public opinion. The limited economic resources available in India and the prioritisation of citizens result in reluctance regarding service provision to foreign residents. Refugees suffer because xenophobic and nationalist narratives in society develop unfriendly refugee environments and minimise popular backing for inclusionary policies. Multiple factors combine into a policy context that neglects refugee rights compliance while maintaining minimal involvement of refugees in Sustainable Development Goal planning.

Prof. Nanda proposes that India ought to establish a national refugee law which would specify refugee recognition criteria and provide essential services to refugees. The new refugee laws must specify that they can participate in existing welfare schemes that provide healthcare education and employment opportunities. A critical step toward service accessibility involves integrating refugees into national identification systems which can be done through Aadhaar protocols and alternate frameworks also serve this purpose. The establishment of institutional data collection programmes for refugee populations will ensure evidence-based monitoring of SDGs that includes refugee conditions in India. Refugee inclusion needs complete organisational reforms to evolve from an empty pledge into concrete implementation.

Prof. Nanda also highlights the role of comparative legal research in advancing refugee-related SDG goals. By studying legal frameworks from different jurisdictions, researchers can identify what has worked, what has failed, and why. Comparative studies offer not only descriptive insights but also normative recommendations for reform. They can inform policymakers, guide legal drafters, and encourage international bodies to adopt standardized, rights-based approaches. In a global context where refugee inclusion remains fragmented, comparative legal research provides a pathway toward harmonization, consistency, and accountability.

INTERNATIONAL BEST PRACTICES AND JURISDICTIONAL MODELS

Understanding how different countries have approached the integration of refugee rights into their national Sustainable Development Goal (SDG) implementation frameworks provides a meaningful basis for comparative legal research(López et al., 2020). The selection of case studies for this section has been guided by three key criteria: first, the existence of explicit legal or policy mechanisms that recognize and protect refugee rights; second, demonstrable efforts to incorporate refugee-related issues into national SDG planning, monitoring, or reporting; and third, the presence of institutional partnerships with global agencies such as the United Nations High Commissioner for Refugees (UNHCR) and the International Organization for Migration (IOM), which play a significant role in shaping national refugee policies. In this light, jurisdictions from East Africa, Latin America, and parts of Europe have been selected as representative models, particularly Uganda, Colombia, and Germany, each of which demonstrates unique methods of embedding refugee protection into broader sustainable development strategies(Feinstein et al., 2022).

Uganda demonstrates advanced laws and plans about including refugees in their society. The nation offers all refugees extensive freedom and legal privileges along with work opportunities and public service access. Uganda develops this strategy as part of their overall development plan named the Refugee and Host Population Empowerment (ReHoPE). This system joins humanitarian resources and development actions by making refugee requirements an essential part of district-level growth and national development practises. ReHoPE believes refugees should take part with host country residents to build economic expansion while helping stabilise their new home. Refugees and host community members both work together in district development plans to build stronger shared social bonds and resource sharing practises. The Government of Uganda receives help from UN agencies and donor organisations to merge refugee integration into development initiatives at both national and district levels(Keller et al., 2022).

Colombia provides another compelling example, especially in the Latin American context. It has made noteworthy strides in incorporating migrants and refugees—particularly those from neighboring Venezuela—into national development programs. Colombia's Temporary Protection Status program and its inclusion of migrants in public health, education, and employment initiatives demonstrate a recognition of the developmental dimensions of displacement. The government has sought to institutionalize the inclusion of displaced persons through its national development plans and in some instances, has made efforts to reflect this in regional SDG-related policies. While still developing a comprehensive legal framework specific to refugees, Colombia has prioritized social integration through administrative channels, thus reinforcing its commitment to inclusive governance. The Colombian model illustrates that even in the absence of full legislative reform, significant progress can be achieved through administrative inclusivity and political willingness(Rochlin, 2023).

Germany shows valuable lessons about rights-based asylum policies from Europe's legal perspective(Brücker et al., 2020). The country began to include refugees fully in its national systems by creating integration-focused rules for managing refugee arrival in 2015. The government made new laws to process asylum requests quicker while providing refugees access to public education and job markets. Germany made SDG implementation plans more friendly for refugees by including programmes that help them find homes plus medical and legal help. The federal and state governments worked together best to create refugee inclusion while communities and civil organisations joined forces with local municipalities to make it happen. Germany shows how refugee power can enter the federal system while protecting refugees and helping them join society. Alongside Germany, both Kenya and Canada illustrate how legislative frameworks, whether grounded in public development planning or community sponsorship can advance refugee protection while directly contributing to national SDG implementation By managing refugee data digitally the nation has improved visibility into refugee populations and supports better evidence-based planning(Feinstein et al., 2022).

Indian courts have, in select instances, extended constitutional protections to refugees by relying on fundamental rights under Articles 14 and 21 of the Constitution. In *National Human Rights Commission v. State of Arunachal Pradesh* (1996), the Supreme Court prevented the forced eviction of Chakma refugees and emphasized that all persons, regardless of nationality, are entitled to protection under Article 21(Debnath & Debnath, 2020). Similarly, in *Louis De Raedt v. Union of India* (1991), the Court held that the power to deport foreign nationals must be exercised in a manner consistent with the Constitution's guarantees of fairness and non-arbitrariness. These rulings illustrate the judiciary's willingness to uphold refugee rights in specific contexts, but they have not resulted in systemic policy reforms. The absence of codified refugee law means such protections remain reactive and inconsistent in application.

Refugee governance in India remains fragmented and heavily influenced by shifting political narratives and bilateral considerations, resulting in wide variation in how refugee groups are treated across states. The Indian government adopts refugee policy through evaluations between worldwide political methods and internal governmental demands. The Tibetan refugee community receives significant autonomy decisions combined with complete access to education systems and economic opportunities. The Indian authorities have subjected Rohingya refugees from Myanmar to various restrictive measures which include imprisonment as well as expulsion threats and minimal access to essential services(Mohajan, 2018). This disparity reflects the discretionary nature of refugee treatment in India. For example, Tibetan refugees benefit from access to formal schooling, identity documents, and employment permissions under central and state-supported programs. In contrast, Rohingya refugees face arrests, denial of services, and restricted movement even when holding UNHCR-issued refugee cards. This uneven treatment arises from the absence of standardized legal recognition, leaving refugee rights subject to administrative discretion, local sentiment, and security-oriented policy framing.

There exists inconsistency in refugee policy because India lacks clear legal standards to determine refugee protection which results in varied application of refugee policies. The practise of administrative discretion by the Indian government which follows geopolitical objectives and security interests plays a crucial role in asylum management within the country.

The country lacks official national programmes which both regulate and assist refugees because India has no dedicated refugee agency nor administrative body. Foreign national issues together with refugee matters fall under the responsibility of the Ministry of Home Affairs which handles immigration administration duties. The United Nations High Commissioner for Refugees (UNHCR) operates in India with confined powers to give protection services for refugees who are neither Tibetan nor Sri Lankan refugees whose cases are not covered by Indo-bilateral refugee agreements. The UNHCR performs refugee status determination (RSD) on these groups but its support extends only to health care and education together with livelihood assistance. The agency operates under the political authorization of India's government without official legal authorization. Indian ministries lack an established mechanism to work with the UNHCR which would enable refugee participation in national development programmes(Shanker & Vijayaraghavan, 2023).

The lack of specific legal and policy framework for refugees poses major obstacles for India as it integrates with global Sustainable Development Goals standards. The national policy mapping of SDGs conducted by NITI Aayog and other institutions has resulted in significant progress but refugees remain unincorporated throughout this process. National welfare programmes such as Ayushman Bharat and the Right to Education Act along with skill development schemes do not provide formal access to refugees throughout the country. The exclusion of refugees from healthcare together with education and employment and social security services restricts their ability to achieve the goals set forth by the SDGs for inclusive and sustainable development. Refugees struggle to obtain existing welfare schemes because of their lack of identity documentation and legal ambiguity and because of their fear of detention(Vijayaraghavan, 2020).

The inclusion of refugee rights in SDG strategies needs a basic transformation in refugee understanding from temporary stress to development process contributors. The present legal and policy structures fail to implement refugee integration into development frameworks. The existing frameworks typically make refugee situations worse by intensifying their exclusion and their sense of vulnerability. The lack of data categorization about refugee communities hinders governmental officials from properly monitoring how well the SDG development targets are achieved across refugee populations. Due to the lack of specific data about refugee needs existing reporting systems overlook their requirements which makes it impossible to properly evaluate development progress(Denaro & Giuffré, 2021).

International Best Practices and Jurisdictional Models

Understanding how different countries have approached the integration of refugee rights into their national Sustainable Development Goal (SDG) implementation frameworks provides a meaningful basis for comparative legal research(López et al., 2020). The selection of case studies for this section has been guided by three key criteria: first, the existence of explicit legal or policy mechanisms that recognize and protect refugee rights; second, demonstrable efforts to incorporate refugee-related issues into national SDG planning, monitoring, or reporting; and third, the presence of institutional partnerships with global agencies such as the United Nations High Commissioner for Refugees (UNHCR) and the International Organization for Migration (IOM), which play a significant role in shaping national refugee policies. In this light, jurisdictions from East Africa, Latin America, and parts of Europe have been selected as representative models, particularly Uganda, Colombia, and Germany, each of which demonstrates unique methods of embedding refugee protection into broader sustainable development strategies(Feinstein et al., 2022).

Uganda demonstrates advanced laws and plans about including refugees in their society. The nation offers all refugees extensive freedom and legal privileges along with work opportunities and public service access. Uganda develops this strategy as part of their overall development plan named the Refugee and Host Population Empowerment (ReHoPE). This system joins humanitarian resources and development actions by making refugee requirements an essential part of district-level growth and national development practises. ReHoPE believes refugees should take part with host country residents to build economic expansion while helping stabilise their new home. Refugees and host community members both work together in district development plans to build stronger shared social bonds and resource sharing practises. The Government of Uganda receives help from UN agencies and donor organisations to merge refugee integration into development initiatives at both national and district levels(Keller et al., 2022).

Colombia provides another compelling example, especially in the Latin American context. It has made noteworthy strides in incorporating migrants and refugees—particularly those from neighboring Venezuela—into national development programs.

Colombia's Temporary Protection Status program and its inclusion of migrants in public health, education, and employment initiatives demonstrate a recognition of the developmental dimensions of displacement. The government has sought to institutionalize the inclusion of displaced persons through its national development plans and in some instances, has made efforts to reflect this in regional SDG-related policies. While still developing a comprehensive legal framework specific to refugees, Colombia has prioritized social integration through administrative channels, thus reinforcing its commitment to inclusive governance. The Colombian model illustrates that even in the absence of full legislative reform, significant progress can be achieved through administrative inclusivity and political willingness(Rochlin, 2023).

Germany shows valuable lessons about rights-based asylum policies from Europe's legal perspective(Brücker et al., 2020). The country began to include refugees fully in its national systems by creating integration-focused rules for managing refugee arrival in 2015. The government made new laws to process asylum requests quicker while providing refugees access to public education and job markets. Germany made SDG implementation plans more friendly for refugees by including programmes that help them find homes plus medical and legal help. The federal and state governments worked together best to create refugee inclusion while communities and civil organisations joined forces with local municipalities to make it happen. Germany shows how refugee power can enter the federal system while protecting refugees and helping them join society. By managing refugee data digitally the nation has improved visibility into refugee populations and supports better evidence-based planning(Feinstein et al., 2022).

Kenya offers a strong legal example through the Refugees Act, 2021, which replaces outdated legislation and introduces a more holistic and rights-based approach(Gitahi, 2024). The Act clearly defines refugee status and outlines entitlements such as movement, access to education, healthcare, and employment(Yatani, 2023). Kenya's Kalobeyei Integrated Socio-Economic Development Plan complements this legal progress by integrating refugee and host communities in joint development programs, supported by both national and county governments(Betts et al., 2019). This legal-development linkage represents a deliberate strategy to align refugee protection with national SDG goals. Notably, Kalobeyei is included in district-level development budgets, enabling resource sharing and long-term planning, a model that operationalizes refugee inclusion beyond humanitarian response(Okoth, 2022).

Canada presents a distinctive model where refugee integration is facilitated not only by legislation, such as the Immigration and Refugee Protection Act, but also through active civil society engagement(Purkey, 2022). Its Private Sponsorship of Refugees (PSR) Program allows individuals and community organizations to support refugee resettlement, creating shared responsibility between government and citizens. Refugees supported through PSR receive access to language training, healthcare, housing, and employment services, enabling smoother transitions into Canadian society. Canada's national Voluntary National Reviews (VNRs) have also acknowledged refugee contributions to its SDG progress, especially under goals related to inequality reduction and decent work. This blend of legal structure and participatory implementation offers a scalable model for countries seeking to localize SDG commitments through refugee-inclusive policy.

The analysed case studies show specific institutions help refugee communities better participate in SDG programmes. Every system begins service inclusion for refugees by officially granting refugee status based on national rules or administrative decisions. Under the Refugees Act of Uganda, refugees get their status recognised as do asylum seekers under German national and EU legislation. Through executive orders and administrative action Colombia provides legal protection and service access to immigrants before creating a formal refugee law. When official bodies acknowledge someone's refugee status they gain their authority to deliver services and activate teamwork across departments.

Another essential mechanism is the development and use of refugee-inclusive data systems. Accurate and disaggregated data is crucial for integrating refugees into development planning, measuring progress, and ensuring that policy interventions are appropriately targeted. In Germany, integrated digital databases allow for the tracking of refugee education, health, and employment outcomes. Uganda has collaborated with development partners to include refugee data in national planning documents and budget allocations. Colombia has initiated data-sharing protocols between migration authorities and public service departments to monitor refugee access to essential services. These practices ensure that refugee inclusion is not symbolic but supported by actionable metrics and real-time information.

The integration with worldwide institutions together with regional organisations represents a fundamental aspect for progress. The UNHCR along with other development agencies from Uganda and Colombia together formed tight alliances to reach their targets through assistance programmes and funding distribution and capacity development initiatives. The partnerships between organisations operate through memoranda of understanding and coordination frameworks which guide humanitarian work to match with national advancement targets. German refugee service delivery benefits from European Union agency collaborations and civil society partnerships which helps the country operate within international rules. The institutionalised collaboration between organisations helps sharing best practises and promotes transparency and provides structure to fragmented refugee policy areas(Damelang & Kosyakova, 2021).

According to Prof. Nanda the implementation of legal recognition with inclusive data collection and institutional cooperation delivers the fundamental means to prevent refugees from being left out of sustainable development programmes. Due to non-operation of critical support pillars India along with numerous other nations keeps refugee populations outside their national development goals. Because of his global experience he believes refugees encounter discrimination through security-focused evaluations rather than being recognised as rights holders who can actively support their communities. People use political roadblocks and limited funding alongside cultural reluctance to explain the need for regulatory changes but these factors should not stop vital legal and policy changes. Prof. Nanda points out that national institutions need both refugee representation and legal protection for refugee rights to achieve complete sustainable development goals.

Prof. Nanda identifies a national refugee law as the primary deficiency which separates international models from the Indian scenario. India applies universal immigration laws instead of adopting refugee-specific legal frameworks which exist in Germany and Uganda. Executive authorities in Colombia have successfully implemented protection and service programmes but India encounters multiple fragmented reactive administrative approaches. The current refugee protection practises in India show institutional possibility of following these models yet its existing legal system fails to provide sustained and inclusive refugee safety(Refugees In India: Legal Framework, Law Enforcement And Security, 2023).

According to Prof. Nanda the implementation of legal and policy indicators creates significant transformative changes. The selection process of measurable items directs policy administrator focus toward them. Global and national SDG frameworks fail to recognise refugees because refugee-specific indicators are missing from their frameworks. His proposal centres on the addition of refugee-specific data to all relevant SDG indicators that include poverty relief and education systems and healthcare delivery and employment provisions and gender equality measures. The lack of this information creates an unspecified foundation to develop plans or draught budgets or assess refugee inclusion initiatives. The absence of refugee data effectively damages accountability structures because it enables governments to ignore refugee matters in development discussions.

The maintenance of inclusive development requires partnerships that link governmental actors with non-governmental actors. Prof. Nanda emphasises that organisations like UNHCR, IOM and refugee-led initiatives deliver vital field-level knowledge as well as implementation capacity combined with accountability functions. All international models demonstrate that partnerships serve as fundamental components in both developing and executing programmes which specifically address refugee requirements. Various countries including India show a neglect of using these partnerships although they should be worth exploiting. Prof. Nanda emphasises the necessity of refugee representatives and civil society actors to have official membership in national SDG steering committees and policy review bodies and consultation processes to achieve transparent government planning based on rights.

The discussed examples show why local governments need decentralisation to work alongside one another. The region of Uganda together with Colombia assigns district and municipal authorities to embrace roles within refugee-inclusive development policy planning and implementation. The specific location of these programmes ensures better response to local needs and strengthens local integration efforts regarding refugees. The German policy model grants authorization to regional authorities who can customise national programmes for their own communities and specifically in housing and educational sectors(Hannafi & Marouani, 2022). The distributed planning methods prevent development planning from being restricted inside national capitals because they locate development plans within the neighbourhoods where refugees and local communities live.

Taken together, these international best practices offer a range of legal, institutional, and policy strategies that can be adapted to suit different national contexts. While no model is without its challenges, they collectively demonstrate that refugee inclusion in SDG planning is both possible and beneficial. Comparative legal research that draws from these experiences not only identifies gaps in domestic policy but also offers evidence-based frameworks for reform. By facilitating knowledge transfer and harmonization, such research contributes to a more equitable and accountable global development agenda.

According to Prof. Nanda the fundamental worth of doing comparative studies becomes evident when it demonstrates successful practises alongside the potential to create adjusted solutions according to particular contexts. Legal harmonisation means adapting successful aspects from different models instead of implementing them as a complete package according to Prof. Nanda. The achievement of worldwide commitments to abandon marginalisation requires all countries to incorporate refugee rights into their legal structures alongside their institutions and development planning under permanent conditions.

COMPARATIVE ANALYSIS

The protection framework for refugees in India differs considerably from global standards when compared to established international models of refugee recognition and implementation in development plans(Debbarma, 2024). India has typically adopted a casual method for managing refugees whereas numerous countries in Europe as well as Latin American and African nations have developed structured policies to integrate refugees into national development initiatives and Sustainable Development Goal outcomes. The different approaches to refugee protection become easily identifiable through four key aspects including legal frameworks as well as institutional systems and procedures together with refugee condition acknowledgment methods and development policy implementation strategies.

The legal system of India lacks distinct laws for refugee protection across the country. The Foreigners Act ensures management of refugees in India through its identical treatment of refugees alongside other non-citizens(Singh, 2012). Uganda together with Germany feature legal frameworks because they either state refugee rights explicitly or integrate them through international pacts and domestic laws. The Refugees Act of Uganda gives refugees access to employment opportunities together with educational programmes and social welfare programmes(Refugees Act, 2006, 2006). German bureaucracy accepts refugees by ensuring legal protection and welfare service access through national laws. Lawful structures help demonstrate how to include refugee welfare needs within standard development initiatives.

The national structures in India lack a unified agency or regulatory system that specifically targets refugee affairs. The lack of central governance regarding refugee issues produces fragmenting and variable governmental policies. Different international jurisdictions have implemented institutional frameworks that help refugees find inclusion opportunities. The Colombian government enables refugee service participation through organised executive-level coordination of public services(-Kumar et al., 2021). German federal institutions enable coordinated work between national and state and municipal authorities to provide stable refugee integration and service delivery across different jurisdictions(Auslender, 2021). The Ugandan government operates a system that brings together various ministries and local authorities to integrate refugee requirements into their immediate relief plans and enduring developmental activities.

The most essential difference occurs regarding data management as well as supervision systems. International models have implemented strategies to include refugee statistics as part of their national statistical frameworks as well as their reporting systems for achieving the SDGs(Baal, 2023). Germany operates unified databases to monitor refugee accessibility in educational programmes alongside workforce entry opportunities and medical care services. Uganda together with Colombia maintains proactive initiatives to track refugee-related measures at their district level through planning and development assessment systems. There is no reliable data about refugees in India because the nation lacks both legal definitions for refugees and a registration system. The lack of official statistics about refugees creates difficulties to plan services for them and determine the consequences of national policy development on their welfare(Shanker & Raghavan, 2020).

Notwithstanding these variations the nations display several common features as well. India as well as other states shares a tradition of welcoming refugees who cross borders into the neighbouring countries. Unwritten humanitarian principles have directly led India to provide sanctuary to significant numbers of displaced individuals throughout history. The refugee acceptance in Colombia and Uganda has been established based upon regional solidarity combined with humanitarian principles. Carrying out hospitality into formal legal and policy frameworks represents the major difference among the nations studied. Directed by executive decision and based on political friendship agreements India fails to implement formal refugee inclusion statutes that other nations have established through laws and policy frameworks.

Through comparative analysis we understand the various specific conditions that determine how legal systems deal with refugee rights protection. Public understandings of displaced persons together with institutional actions are fundamentally controlled by cultural storeys along with political situations and economic limitations. The Indian political discourse usually understands refugees through a national security prism particularly when those migrants come from population segments that create ethnoreligious or interregional disputes(Chapparban, 2020). Such security-centric approaches in framing refugee issues create obstacles for implementing comprehensive policies and strengthen administrative restrictions. Uganda's political society maintains a developmental approach toward refugee integration which leads both society members and institutions to support refugee integration programmes.

Refugee policy receives its defining elements from economic limitations which affect implementation decisions. Public programme inclusion for refugees depends heavily on the financial capabilities of developing nations. India’s national development agenda prioritises its numerous citizens who exist in poverty and this creates opposition against granting public assistance to foreign residents. National economic priorities exist as part of a broader developmental issue that development nations face while trying to fulfil their humanitarian responsibilities. The distinction between these countries rests in their approach to use international partnerships for distributing responsibilities while collecting resources. The donor agencies collaborate with Uganda to provide financial support for districts which host refugees. Despite facing internal difficulties Colombia continues to work with international organisations for sustaining inclusive policy development. Such approaches have enabled wider inclusion despite limited budgetary capacity in affected areas.

The legal and policy framework takes form according to cultural elements. Most societies understand refugee population presence through cultural frameworks which affect both their acceptance within society and their legal access. Populist policies develop when fearful public rejection of refugees emerges due to xenophobic narratives in society. This cultural diversity in India creates institutional obstacles for implementing integrated policies when minority refugee groups settle in the country(Shamshad, 2016). Several governing jurisdictions have developed sensitization programmes alongside community outreach to build better connexions between their refugee populations and native communities. The German integration model provides refugees with language education together with basic civic knowledge training to help them adapt both socially and economically(Badwi, 2023).

The input of experts enables this comparison to achieve greater complexity. Through a detailed interview with Prof. Sukanta Kumar Nanda where he explained how global frameworks for SDGs fail to comprehensively integrate refugees. His expert view of international laws and sustainable development reveals that Uganda and Colombia offer promising models yet they are exceptions because the world lacks a general standard. Further to his assessment all nations lack complete programmes which incorporate refugee rights within all SDG sectors. The situation stresses that India and other similar nations need to adopt international models yet understand the barriers to their direct implementation without local adjustments.

Prof. Nanda explained that successful refugee inclusion in development strategies depends on three essential institutional measures including recognition of legal status, integration within national data collection practises as well as support from both United Nations agencies and civil society institutions. The absence of all three essential elements in a systematic manner currently affects India's effective planning for exclusion while hindering its implementation of the SDGs. His evaluation matches international best practises which recognise these conditions as fundamental requirements for inclusive development. Countries which have established these mechanisms demonstrate enhanced policy coherence at the same time they show better programme efficiency and improved well-being of refugees.

Prof. Nanda presented helpful comparisons on how political systems and institutions resist refugee participation programmes. He stated that political willingness which frequently implies electoral and geopolitical factors determines how many refugees gain involvement within national development processes. India faces changing political discourse that negatively impacts the consistency of refugee inclusion policies in the country. International jurisdictions implementing legal protection for refugees experience fewer effects from changes in governmental policies regarding refugee integration. Legal codification in India does not protect refugees because it makes their status susceptible to changes through policy reversals coupled with administrative discretion.

The implications for SDG implementation are significant. Without formal recognition and structured inclusion, refugees remain on the margins of development discourse and programming(Irudaya Rajan, 2022). Prof. Nanda stressed that SDG strategies that do not explicitly include refugees in planning, budgeting, and monitoring are inherently incomplete. Indicators and metrics shape what gets measured and therefore prioritized. If refugee data is excluded from national monitoring systems, the needs of this population will not be addressed in policy evaluations or resource allocations. This insight reinforces the importance of integrating refugee-sensitive indicators into SDG frameworks, a practice observed in select international jurisdictions but largely absent in India.

Analysis reveals partnerships to serve as a core factor in achieving refugee inclusion. Different international case reports indicate refugees can experience substantial inclusion benefits through long-term cooperation between state institutions government agencies and civil society organisations. The partnerships establish valuable connexions that help complete essential services but also supply technical knowledge and execute advocacy strategies. Within German borders refugee-led groups participate in both policy development and consultation programmes. The government of India has not established institutional collaboration between public agencies and UN organisations and civil society entities in their national development framework(Sarker, 2017). Prof. Nanda points out that Indian partnerships function at low levels of formality which prevents them from creating cohesive policy changes.

The comparative analysis reveals decentralisation provides better conditions for refugees to be included. When national governments provide implementation power to local governments for refugee policy execution it produces better contextualised and fewer generalisations services. Two countries demonstrate this phenomenon through their district-level planning initiatives in Uganda as well as their German state-level integration programmes. The centre led policy control in India creates an ongoing problem because national orders remain detached from local operational circumstances. Most state authorities struggle to acquire necessary authority and funding to implement separate refugee programmes which produces inactive policy developments within local communities.

The governance perspective shows that embedded accountability systems generate substantial value through their implementation. When countries develop institutional structures with established laws for refugee inclusion they maintain monitoring entities and unbiased grievance procedures with clear reporting conventions. The mechanisms create both compliance with legal duties and foster trust between refugee communities. Refugees in India experience restricted access to both legal remedy and governmental participation due to the lack of proper mechanisms for these purposes.

One of the most persistent structural barriers in the Indian context is the securitization of refugee discourse. Refugees especially those perceived as culturally or religiously distinct, such as the Rohingyas are often framed as security threats rather than as individuals with rights under international or constitutional law(Hossain, 2022). This securitized framing has justified surveillance, detention, and exclusion from welfare programs. Exclusionary citizenship practices, illustrated by the Citizenship Amendment Act (2019) and discussions around the National Register of Citizens, further reinforce this marginalization by selectively linking legal identity and belonging to ethno-religious status. In the absence of a refugee-specific law, these political dynamics translate into discretionary treatment and legal precarity, weakening institutional efforts to integrate refugees into development planning.

In contrast, countries like Uganda and Colombia, despite resource limitations, have exhibited sustained political will to treat refugees as contributors to national development. Uganda's inclusive approach is not only legal but political where it involves public framing of refugees as economic actors and development partners(Uganda's Approach to Refugee Self-Reliance, 2025). Similarly, Colombia's decision to grant Temporary Protection Status to over a million Venezuelans, despite lacking comprehensive asylum infrastructure, reflects a strategic alignment of refugee policy with long-term national interests(Graham et al., 2020). These examples show that legal frameworks alone are insufficient; without political will and narrative shifts, refugee rights remain aspirational and disconnected from inclusive governance or SDG implementation.

The analysis of multiple jurisdictions reveals the constant impact between legal structures and policy approaches that advance social inclusion practises. The laws which establish refugee protection require both proper policy implementation as well as public involvement to be effective. Public awareness initiatives along with coherent laws along with inclusive policies enable lasting results in refugee inclusion. The minimization of refugee policy achievements occurs when legal obligations fail to have meaningful support from both political institutions and societal elements within the country. The conditions in India pose challenges because the country has no laws defining refugee rights at the same time it lacks general governmental concern and public engagement regarding refugee integration.

The integration of refugee rights into SDG implementation operates as a multidimensional challenge powered by legal systems and political directives and administrative capabilities as well as public value systems(D'Silva, 2021). The example of jurisdictions which face this challenge effectively through legal recognition of refugees along with inclusive data practises and institutional partnerships and decentralised management serves as valuable teaching opportunities for India to learn from. The studied models prove that sustainable development should incorporate refugee rights through combined policy adjustments and legal transformation and holistic planning systems (Dutta, 2022).

POLICY RECOMMENDATIONS AND FUTURE DIRECTIONS

The analysis of refugee rights and insertion into sustainable development goals shows India multiple ways to build legal reforms. The jurisdictional models which emphasise inclusivity together with policy coherence and institutional integration can provide India with specific recommendations to synchronise its legal framework with sustainable development goals. The lack of a specific refugee law in India enables fundamental obstacles to hinder both development achievements and responsibilities for humanitarian care. India needs to create and promote a national refugee law as its primary recommendation. A national refugee law must specify the standards used for identifying refugees while building a just asylum process and listing the fundamental rights of recipients including medical care, schooling, housing and occupational access. A clear legislative framework will minimise administrative uncertainty while it provides lawful safeguards and establishes conditions for refugees to receive coverage from national plans and programmes(Ahmed, 2018).

Strengthening the process of inter-ministerial cooperation stands as a second essential recommendation. Different departments of the government handle refugee responsibilities without being united by a seminal strategic plan. The formation of an executive committee that brings together ministries with civil society groups and international organisations under a nodal agency enables efficient refugee policy-making coordination and implementation. Such an institutional body needs additional authority to develop refugee-friendly policies and normalise their integration with national development goals. Inclusion targets for refugees need to become built into the goal-setting process and performance evaluation of development agencies that execute implementation projects to avoid discrimination.

The public welfare schemes of India have potential to include refugees through administrative barrier removal. Development programmes including those related to health, housing and skill development and social protection operate at national scales which makes them suitable for adding refugee beneficiaries(Dagar, 2023). The government should investigate scheme modifications that enable clearly stated entry of non-citizens into public welfare programmes. Displaced populations might access services through mechanisms of temporary population registration, community-based identifiers or localised service delivery systems that do not need full citizenship benefits. This system of adaptive policies would increase service accessibility without compromising national development programme standards(Dagar, 2022).

Local control over refugee management processes helps improve both the integration and document responsiveness of refugee care systems. Local governments in refugee-hosting areas should receive support by receiving policy guidance along with budgetary allocations as well as institutional capacity to create and execute inclusive programmes. Local integration strategies developed by municipalities to fit their population patterns and infrastructure would lead to higher refugee involvement in their communities. State-level guidelines about refugee inclusion should be created as a means to achieve policy consistency across all Indian jurisdictions(Mehrotra & Bhardwaj, 2022).

To ensure that any future refugee law in India is both actionable and rights-compliant, lawmakers can draw lessons from recent reforms in countries like Kenya and Colombia. Kenya's Refugees Act (2021) combines clear legal definitions with a statutory right to work, move freely, and access public services. These provisions are further supported by development planning mechanisms like the Kalobeyei Integrated Plan, which mainstreams refugees into district-level programs. Colombia's Temporary Protection Status, though not a formal asylum law, institutionalizes inclusion through executive action and facilitates access to health, education, and employment. India can consider a phased legislative approach beginning with recognition and legal identity for refugees, followed by sectoral inclusion through administrative rule-making.

India's vast welfare infrastructure including schemes like Ayushman Bharat, Pradhan Mantri Awas Yojana (PMAY), and the National Urban Livelihoods Mission (NULM) can be leveraged for refugee inclusion without extensive legal overhaul. Models from Colombia and Uganda demonstrate how refugees can be included in national databases and targeted for services even under temporary legal status. By adopting similar administrative arrangements, India could extend time-bound access to healthcare, education, and livelihood programs using locally issued IDs, municipal registrations, or UNHCR cards as provisional documentation.

Sub-national actors in India are already managing welfare delivery for populations in urban and informal settings. Drawing from Germany's federal-state collaboration, India could empower state governments particularly those hosting long-standing refugee populations to issue local orders that include refugees in health, education, or skill-building initiatives. For example, districts with Tibetan, Sri Lankan Tamil, or Afghan refugee concentrations could pilot integration programs aligned with local SDG action plans. These localized efforts would not require constitutional amendment but would benefit from national legal and financial endorsement.

India's legal framework should also recognize and institutionalize the role of civil society in refugee inclusion. Canada's Private Sponsorship of Refugees (PSR) Program offers a strong example of how communities can take on integration responsibilities. While India's socio-political context is different, partnerships between NGOs, refugee-led groups, and district administrations could be formalized through Memoranda of Understanding (MoUs) to deliver targeted services. These collaborations would bolster state capacity and provide last-mile delivery for essential services aligned with SDG targets. Collectively, these grounded strategies reflect how India can advance refugee protection not only through legislation but also through adaptive administrative innovation and decentralized policy leadership.

The international community needs to implement legal harmonisation efforts together with capacity-building initiatives. The international framework intended to help refugees shows significant inconsistencies between different nations in their membership and their level of commitment. States without formal approval of essential international treaties still have the opportunity to create alternative frameworks that carry the same fundamental principles as the 1951 Refugee Convention. Regional legal standards especially in the Indian subcontinent should be developed as they would unite refugee protection measures throughout the border region. Purposeful frameworks should establish joint responsibility standards and enforce refugee status awareness together with coordinated inter-border emergency rescue. Regional harmonisation standards will lower border uncertainty for refugees while making the area better suited for bilateral cooperation in the region(Wahab & Ashutosh, 2022).

The capacity-building initiative needs to undergo institutional reform as its core mission(Dagar, 2023). The national government of India alongside other countries needs assistance in developing administration systems which prioritise refugees. Public officials along with law enforcement officers and judicial officers require training programmes to become aware about refugee rights and responsibilities. The development of national refugee management capacities benefits from strategic alliances between Indian authorities and international organisations and academic institutions and development agencies. The legal education system in India should incorporate refugee law into educational programmes for students as well as encourage legal clinics to focus on defending refugee rights with a focus on international migration development research.

Future refugee reform initiatives need to create statistical systems which include refugees as fundamental data subjects. Statistical collection exercises performed at the national level such as surveys and census counts along with administrative record collection usually omit refugees from their systems because of unclear legal boundaries combined with methodological hurdles. To achieve proper data collection Governments should follow inclusive definition criteria while developing unique survey tools for refugees and joining forces with hosting groups and organisations to ensure data accuracy(Khai, 2024). Such datasets would serve multiple purposes from informing policy decisions to providing evidence for advocacy and planning efforts as well as international reports.

Research focused on understanding refugee integration with development systems must proceed after legal and policy framework modifications. The analysis of refugee experiences regarding public service access alongside studies of legal prohibitions and socio-economic conditions will create usable information for programme development. Extended research on jurisdictional inclusive policies would generate refined strategies for best practises while making them adaptable for new settings. Collaborative research approaches involving refugee participants would substantially enhance the comprehension of their real experiences while making sure responses follow the actual conditions.

There is also a need for more interdisciplinary research that brings together law, public administration, development studies, and sociology. Such research could explore how institutional cultures, bureaucratic practices, and political incentives interact to affect refugee inclusion. For example, analyzing how frontline service providers interpret and implement policies can reveal gaps between formal frameworks and actual practice. Similarly, examining community responses to refugee inclusion can inform strategies for social cohesion and public engagement.

Another area for future empirical work is the economic impact of refugee inclusion. Policymakers often assume that extending rights to refugees creates fiscal burdens, yet empirical studies in other countries have shown that refugees can contribute positively to local economies when allowed to work, access services, and participate in entrepreneurship. Conducting localized impact assessments in Indian refugee-hosting regions could provide a more nuanced understanding of the costs and benefits of inclusion. Such evidence would be crucial in countering political resistance and shaping public opinion.

Global research networks and partnerships should be strengthened to facilitate cross-border learning. Platforms for sharing national experiences, legal innovations, and monitoring tools can support countries in advancing refugee-inclusive SDG implementation. Peer-to-peer exchanges, regional research consortia, and collaborative pilot projects can all contribute to building a more coherent and rights-based international refugee governance system. India, with its historical and contemporary experience in hosting diverse refugee populations, can play a leadership role in such networks by contributing regional perspectives and practical insights.

Through these policy recommendations, legal reforms, and research pathways, a multidimensional strategy can be envisioned to foster the integration of refugee rights into national and international development agendas. These approaches must be context-sensitive, inclusive, and informed by both legal norms and empirical evidence. As the global development discourse evolves, sustained commitment to refugee inclusion will be necessary to achieve the broader aims of equity, resilience, and sustainability.

CONCLUSION

This study has explored the intersection between refugee rights and sustainable development through a comparative legal lens, with a particular focus on India and selected international models. The analysis demonstrates that while the Sustainable Development Goals (SDGs) aim to ensure inclusive development for all, refugees continue to remain peripheral in many national legal and policy frameworks. India's approach, which lacks a codified refugee law, is largely governed by general immigration legislation and administrative discretion. This results in inconsistent treatment and restricted access to essential services, limiting refugees' ability to participate in and benefit from sustainable development initiatives. In contrast, several countries across Africa, Latin America, and Europe have institutionalized refugee protection through legal recognition, service access, and integration in national development planning. While these models are not without challenges, they offer structured approaches that reflect a rights-based orientation toward refugee inclusion.

One of the central findings of this research is the critical role that formal legal frameworks play in operationalizing refugee rights. Legal recognition establishes the foundation for access to public services, protection from arbitrary actions, and participation in national development efforts. In jurisdictions where such recognition exists, there is a clearer pathway for integrating refugee populations into systems of education, healthcare, housing, and employment—all of which are key domains within the SDG framework. The absence of legal specificity, as seen in India, creates ambiguity that hinders effective planning and undermines policy coherence. Without laws that define refugee status and outline state obligations, integration efforts remain fragmented and susceptible to political fluctuation.

Looking ahead, the findings of this study suggest that countries like India, while unique in their legal and political contexts, can benefit substantially from a comparative understanding of refugee law and development planning. Policy evolution requires not only internal reflection but also openness to external experiences, insights, and lessons. By engaging with comparative legal research and expert opinion, states can better align their refugee policies with global development commitments and advance more inclusive, just, and sustainable societies. The integration of refugee rights into the SDG framework is not merely a question of legal reform but of ethical responsibility, policy innovation, and institutional vision.

REFERENCES

Abdelaaty, L. (2021). The relationship between human rights and refugee protection: An empirical analysis. *International Journal of Human Rights, 25*(10), 1704–1723. DOI: 10.1080/13642987.2021.1874358

Act, R. 2006. (2006). https://ulii.org/akn/ug/act/2006/21/eng@2006-08-04

Adeola, R., Oette, L., Lwabukuna, O., & Viljoen, F. (2021). Introduction: Refugees, Returnees and Internally Displaced Persons in Africa. *Journal of African Law, 65*(S1), 5–8. DOI: 10.1017/S0021855321000140

Agosto, G., & Rubinstein, F. (2022). Migration and the 2030 Agenda in Argentina. International Development Policy/Revue Internationale de Politique de Développement, 14. DOI: 10.4000/poldev.4939

Ahmed, Z. S. (2018). The Role of SAARC and EU in Managing Refugees in South Asia and Beyond: Potential for North-South Cooperation. *Global Policy, 9*(1), 76–84. DOI: 10.1111/1758-5899.12526

Auslender, E. (2021). Multi-level Governance in Refugee Housing and Integration Policy: a Model of Best Practice in Leverkusen. Journal of International Migration and Integration / Revue de l Integration et de La Migration Internationale, 23(3), 949. DOI: 10.1007/s12134-021-00876-4

Baal, N. K. (2023). Including refugees and IDPs in national data systems. https://www.fmreview.org/issue66/krynskybaal

Badwi, E. (2023). Integration and Participation of Refugees and Migrants: Building Inclusive Societies. https://ehab-badwi.medium.com/integration-and-participation-of-refugees-and-migrants-building-inclusive-societies-9b806ef772c0

Betts, A., Omata, N., & Sterck, O. (2019). The Kalobeyei Settlement: A Self-reliance Model for Refugees? *Journal of Refugee Studies, 33*(1), 189–223. DOI: 10.1093/jrs/fez063

Bhattacharjee, S. (2008). India Needs a Refugee Law. SSRN Electronic Journal. https://papers.ssrn.com/sol3/Delivery.cfm/SSRN_ID2066397_code396686.pdf?abstractid=1760460&mirid=1

Boswell, C. (2017). The Ethics of Refugee Policy. DOI: 10.4324/9781315239910

Brücker, H., Kosyakova, Y., & Vallizadeh, E. (2020). Has there been a "refugee crisis"? New insights on the recent refugee arrivals in Germany and their integration prospects. *Soziale Welt, 71*(1-2), 24–53. DOI: 10.5771/0038-6073-2020-1-2-24

Cartagena Declaration on Refugees. (2005). Adopted at a colloquium entitled "Coloquio Sobre la Proteccion Internacional de los Refugiados en American Central, Mexico y Panama: Problemas Juridicos y Humanitarios" held at Cartagena, Colombia from 19-22 November 1984. *Refugee Survey Quarterly*, *24*(2), 153–157. DOI: 10.1093/rsq/hdi038

Cartagena Declaration on Refugees. (2023). https://amerainternational.org/cartagena-declaration-on-refugees/

Chapparban, S. N. (2020). Religious Identity and Politics of Citizenship in South Asia: A Reflection on Refugees and Migrants in India. *Development*, *63*(1), 52–59. DOI: 10.1057/s41301-020-00247-z

Choi, W. G. (2019). Asian Civil Society and Reconfiguration of Refugee Protection in Asia. *Human Rights Review (Piscataway, N.J.)*, *20*(2), 161–179. DOI: 10.1007/s12142-019-0548-4

Convention Relating to the Status of Refugees. (1969). Convention Relating to the Status of Refugees. *The American Journal of International Law*, *63*(2), 389–407. DOI: 10.2307/2197458

D'Silva, R. I. (2021). Rohingya Refugees in South Asia: An Exploration of Social Borders and the Margins. *Borders in Globalization Review*, *3*(1), 35–45. DOI: 10.18357/bigr31202120261

Dagar, P. (2022). Evaluating and reframing vocational education and training for refugees: Insights from five refugee groups across three cities of India. *Compare: A Journal of Comparative Education*, *54*(1), 110–127. DOI: 10.1080/03057925.2022.2078957

Dagar, P. (2023). Rethinking skills development and entrepreneurship for refugees: The case of five refugee communities in India. *International Journal of Educational Development*, *101*, 102834. DOI: 10.1016/j.ijedudev.2023.102834

Damelang, A., & Kosyakova, Y. (2021). To work or to study? Postmigration educational investments of adult refugees in Germany – Evidence from a choice experiment. *Research in Social Stratification and Mobility*, *73*, 100610. DOI: 10.1016/j.rssm.2021.100610

Debbarma, M. (2024). Refugees Experience and the Host Communities: Critical Analyses on Absence of Refugee Law in India. *Journal of Asian and African Studies*, 00219096241228804. Advance online publication. DOI: 10.1177/00219096241228804

Debnath, K., & Debnath, K. (2020). Chakma Refugees in Arunachal Pradesh: Their Inclusion and Setback. Emerald Publishing Limited eBooks, 137. DOI: 10.1108/978-1-83982-190-520201015

Denaro, C., & Giuffré, M. (2021). UN Sustainable Development Goals and the "Refugee Gap": Leaving Refugees Behind? *Refugee Survey Quarterly*, *41*(1), 79–107. DOI: 10.1093/rsq/hdab017

Dugarova, E. (2015). Social Inclusion, Poverty Eradication and the 2030 Agenda for Sustainable Development. MPRA Paper. https://ideas.repec.org/p/pra/mprapa/69055.html

Dutta, H. (2022). The Environmental Aspects of Refugee Crises: Insights from South Asia, Middle East, and Sub-Saharan Africa. Journal of International Migration and Integration / Revue de l Integration et de La Migration Internationale, 24(2), 913. DOI: 10.1007/s12134-022-00986-7

Feinstein, S., Poleacovschi, C., Drake, R., & Winters, L. (2022). States and Refugee Integration: a Comparative Analysis of France, Germany, and Switzerland. Journal of International Migration and Integration / Revue de l Integration et de La Migration Internationale, 23(4), 2167. DOI: 10.1007/s12134-021-00929-8

Goldenziel, J. I. (2015). When Law Migrates: Refugees in Comparative International Law. SSRN Electronic Journal. DOI: 10.2139/ssrn.2435251

Gopalakrishnan, M. (2019). Securitization of refugees in South Asia: Through the prism of Kautilya's Arthashastra. *Asian Journal of Comparative Politics*, *5*(4), 400–415. DOI: 10.1177/2057891119881505

Graham, J., & Ble, G. M., Panayotatos, D., & Leghtas, I. (2020, October 18). From Displacement to Development: How Colombia Can Transform Venezuelan Displacement into Shared Growth. https://www.cgdev.org/publication/displacement-development-how-colombia-can-transform-venezuelan-displacement-shared

Hannafi, C., & Marouani, M. A. (2022). Social integration of Syrian refugees and their intention to stay in Germany. *Journal of Population Economics*, *36*(2), 581–607. DOI: 10.1007/s00148-022-00913-1

Hathaway, J. C. (2005). The Rights of Refugees under International Law. DOI: 10.1017/CBO9780511614859

Hossain, A. N. M. Z. (2022). Geopolitics of Rohingya Refugee Crisis and Regional Security. *International Journal of Safety and Security Engineering*, *12*(2), 167–177. DOI: 10.18280/ijsse.120204

How does IHL protect refugees and internally displaced persons? (2018). https://www.icrc.org/en/document/how-does-humanitarian-law-protect-refugees-and-internally-displaced-persons-0

India, R. I. Legal Framework, Law Enforcement And Security. (2023). http://www.worldlii.org/int/journals/ISILYBIHRL/2001/7.html

Irudaya Rajan, S. (2022). The Routledge Handbook of Refugees in India. In *Routledge eBooks*. Informa., DOI: 10.4324/9781003246800

Kanie, N., Griggs, D., Young, O. R., Waddell, S., Shrivastava, P., Haas, P. M., Broadgate, W., Gaffney, O., & Kőrösi, C. (2019). Rules to goals: Emergence of new governance strategies for sustainable development. *Sustainability Science*, *14*(6), 1745–1749. DOI: 10.1007/s11625-019-00729-1

Kaur, N. (2013). Protection of Refugees in India: A Critical Analysis. SSRN Electronic Journal. DOI: 10.2139/ssrn.2214274

Keller, E. J., Omwami, E. M., & Anena, C. P. (2022). The Gordian Knot. *African Review (Dar Es Salaam, Tanzania)*, *14*(2), 151–170. DOI: 10.1163/09744061-bja10002

Khai, T. S. (2024). India's refugee policy dilemma and its impact on Myanmar ref ugees at the India–Myanmar frontier. *Discover Public Health*, *21*(1), 153. Advance online publication. DOI: 10.1186/s12982-024-00295-7

Kumar, K. B., Culbertson, S., & Constant, L. (2021). Colombia's Trailblazing Model for Refugees. https://www.rand.org/blog/2021/03/colombias-trailblazing-model-for-refugees.html

Ladan, M. T. (2018). Achieving Sustainable Development Goals Through Effective Domestic Laws and Policies on Environment and Climate Change. *Environmental Policy and Law*, *48*(1), 42–63. DOI: 10.3233/EPL-180049

Lippert-Rasmussen, K., & Vitikainen, A. (2020). The ethics of refugee prioritization: Reframing the debate. *Ethics & Global Politics*, *13*(1), 1–5. DOI: 10.1080/16544951.2020.1735019

López, M. J. T., Quintana, P. J. V., Lavado-Anguera, S., & Espinosa-Elvira, M. del C. (2020). Preparing Sustainable Engineers: A Project-Based Learning Experience in Logistics with Refugee Camps. *Sustainability (Basel)*, *12*(12), 4817. DOI: 10.3390/su12124817

Lovett, F. (2006). Rational Choice Theory and Explanation. *Rationality and Society*, *18*(2), 237–272. DOI: 10.1177/1043463106060155

Mehrotra, A., & Bhardwaj, C. (2022). Need for a National Legislation on Refugees in India at 75. India Quarterly. *Journal of International Affairs*, *78*(2), 297–317. DOI: 10.1177/09749284221089531

Mencütek, Z. Ş., & Nashwan, A. (2020). Perceptions About the Labor Market Integration of Refugees: Evidences from Syrian Refugees in Jordan. Journal of International Migration and Integration / Revue de l Integration et de La Migration Internationale, 22(2), 615. DOI: 10.1007/s12134-020-00756-3

Mohajan, H. (2018). History of Rakhine State and the Origin of the Rohingya Muslims. *IKAT The Indonesian Journal of Southeast Asian Studies*, *2*(1), 19. DOI: 10.22146/ikat.v2i1.37391

Nanda, S. K. (2021). Sustainable development and towards sustainable climate action: The way forward. 48(3).

Okoth, F. A. (2022). The Subaltern Can Speak: The Mobility Strategies of Forced Migrants in Kenya's Kalobeyei Integrated Settlement. Policy Press eBooks, 209. DOI: 10.1332/policypress/9781529218190.003.0013

Pasquetti, S., Casati, N., & Sanyal, R. (2019). Law and Refugee Crises. *Annual Review of Law and Social Science*, *15*(1), 289–310. DOI: 10.1146/annurev-lawsocsci-101518-042609

Purkey, A. L. (2022). Vulnerability and the Quest for Protection: A Review of Canadian Migration Case Law. *Laws*, *11*(2), 20. DOI: 10.3390/laws11020020

Rankin, M. B. (2005). Extending the Limits or Narrowing the Scope? Deconstructing the Oau Refugee Definition Thirty Years on. *South African Journal on Human Rights*, *21*(3), 406–435. DOI: 10.1080/19962126.2005.11865141

Rochlin, J. (2023). Power, Mobility, and Space: Human Security for Venezuelan Refugees in Colombia. *Journal on Migration and Human Security*, *11*(4), 333–355. DOI: 10.1177/23315024231202492

Ruhs, M. (2022). Who cares what the people think? Public attitudes and refugee protection in Europe. *Politics, Philosophy & Economics*, *21*(3), 313–344. DOI: 10.1177/1470594X221085701

Sapre, A. A. (2023). Non-refoulment of Refugees in India- a Human Rights Perspective. *International Journal of Law and Social Sciences*, *1*, 1–16. Advance online publication. DOI: 10.60143/ijls.v5.i1.2019.28

Sarker, S. P. (2017). Protection of Refugees in India: Quest for National Refugee Law. SSRN Electronic Journal. DOI: 10.2139/ssrn.2961103

Shamshad, R. (2016). Bengaliness, Hindu nationalism and Bangladeshi migrants in West Bengal, India. *Asian Ethnicity, 18*(4), 433–451. DOI: 10.1080/14631369.2016.1175918

Shanker, R., & Raghavan, P. (2020). The Invisible Crisis: Refugees and COVID-19 in India. *International Journal of Refugee Law, 32*(4), 680–684. DOI: 10.1093/ijrl/eeab011

Shanker, R., & Vijayaraghavan, H. (2023). Refugee recognition challenges in India. https://www.fmreview.org/recognising-refugees/shanker-vijayaraghavan

Singh, A. P. (2012). A Critique of the Foreigners Act, 1946: A Legislation de Jure or de Facto? SSRN Electronic Journal. DOI: 10.2139/ssrn.1989060

Sustainable Development Goals. (2018). *Edward Elgar Publishing eBooks*. Edward Elgar Publishing., DOI: 10.4337/9781786438768

Uganda's approach to refugee self-reliance. (2025). https://www.fmreview.org/solutions/clements-shoffner-zamore

Vijayaraghavan, H. (2020). Gaps in India's Treatment of Refugees and Vulnerable Internal Migrants Are Exposed by the Pandemic. https://www.migrationpolicy.org/article/gaps-india-refugees-vulnerable-internal-migrants-pandemic

Wahab, S. A., & Ashutosh, I. (2022). Rebordering South Asia: Displaced Persons and Urbanization. *Annals of the American Association of Geographers, 112*(3), 742–752. DOI: 10.1080/24694452.2021.2023001

Yatani, V. G. (2023). Refugee Protection in Multi-level Governance Regimes: A Case for Kenya and Indonesia. *Lampung Journal of International Law, 5*(1), 59–72. DOI: 10.25041/lajil.v5i1.2868

Zubair, M., Khan, M. A., & Shah, M. (2019). An Analysis Of The Legal Framework Of International Refugee Protection System. *Global Political Review, 1*(I), 1–10. Advance online publication. DOI: 10.31703/gpr.2019(IV-I).01

ADDITIONAL READING

Alkharouf, R., Shehadeh, A., Khazaleh, K., Al-Azzam, A., & Khalayleh, M. (2023). Assessing Refugee Preferences for SDG 2 (Zero Hunger) Solutions in Irbid Camp and Sakhra Region: Cultivated Roofs and Refrigerators as Food Banks Interventions. *Sustainability (Basel), 15*(15), 11948. DOI: 10.3390/su151511948

Ferris, E. G., & Donato, K. M. (2019). *Refugees, migration and global governance: Negotiating the global compacts* (1st ed.). Routledge., DOI: 10.4324/9781351172806

Finatto, C. P., Dutra, A. R. de A., da Silva, C. G., Nunes, N. A., & Guerra, J. B. S. O. de A. (2022). The role of universities in the inclusion of refugees in higher education and in society from the perspective of the SDGS. *International Journal of Sustainability in Higher Education, 24*(3), 742–761. DOI: 10.1108/IJSHE-07-2021-0275

Hathaway, J. C., & Foster, M. (2014). *The law of refugee status* (2nd ed.). Cambridge University Press., DOI: 10.1017/CBO9780511998300

Kohlenberger, J., Martin-Shields, C., & Easton-Calabria, E. (2025). 'Managing' the paradox: Refugee self-reliance and solving the problem of refugee policy discontinuity. *Journal of Refugee Studies*, feaf012. Advance online publication. DOI: 10.1093/jrs/feaf012

Kool, T. A., & Nimeh, Z. (2021). Refugees and social protection. Edward Elgar Publishing eBooks. DOI: 10.4337/9781839109119.00054

Krause, U., & Schmidt, H. (2020). Refugees as actors? Critical reflections on global refugee policies on self-reliance and resilience. *Journal of Refugee Studies, 33*(1), 22–41. DOI: 10.1093/jrs/fez059

Marques, R. R. C. (2021). The arc of protection: Reforming the international refugee regime. *International Journal of Refugee Law, 33*(1), 179–182. DOI: 10.1093/ijrl/eeab024

Milner, J. (2014). Introduction: Understanding global refugee policy. *Journal of Refugee Studies, 27*(4), 477–494. DOI: 10.1093/jrs/feu032

Milner, J., Alio, M., & Gardi, R. (2022). Meaningful refugee participation: An emerging norm in the global refugee regime. *Refugee Survey Quarterly, 41*(4), 565–593. DOI: 10.1093/rsq/hdac007

Rivillas, J. C., Cifuentes-Avellaneda, Á., Ariza-Abril, J. S., Sánchez-Molano, M., & Rivera, D. (2020). Venezuelan migrants and access to contraception in Colombia: A mixed research approach towards understanding patterns of inequality. *Journal of Migration and Health, 3*, 100027. DOI: 10.1016/j.jmh.2020.100027 PMID: 34405182

14. Souter, J. (2014, June). Towards a theory of asylum as reparation for past injustice. *Political Studies, 62*(2), 326–342. DOI: 10.1111/1467-9248.12019

Souter, J. (20 Sahoo, M. (2022). Refugees and sustainable development goals. Routledge eBooks, 289. DOI: 10.4324/9781003246800-25

KEY TERMS AND DEFINITIONS

Refugee Legal Protection: The statutory and constitutional mechanisms that recognize, safeguard, and enforce the rights of refugees within a host country.

Sustainable Development Goals (SDGs): A universal framework of 17 interlinked goals adopted by the United Nations to achieve equitable, inclusive, and sustainable development by 2030.

Comparative Legal Analysis: A research method that examines similarities and differences across jurisdictions to identify effective legal practices and inform domestic reform.

Institutional Coordination: The collaborative functioning of government bodies, civil society, and international organizations to integrate refugee rights into national development agendas.

Inclusive Policy Frameworks: Legal and administrative systems that ensure equal access to public services and opportunities for marginalized groups, including refugees.

Data-Driven Governance: The use of disaggregated and inclusive data systems to monitor, evaluate, and improve refugee participation in development planning and SDG tracking.

Chapter 10

Advancing Equity and Social Justice Through Human Rights Law

Maryam Ishrat Beg
https://orcid.org/0000-0002-2420-4425
Manipal University Jaipur, India

Govind Yadav
https://orcid.org/0009-0005-5757-5619
Manipal University Jaipur, India

Poojyashree Kumawat
Manipal University Jaipur, India

ABSTRACT

Human rights law is crucial for promoting unity and equality in society, protecting individuals from abuse and codifying rights and responsibilities. It underpins social justice by enabling or inhibiting fairness in various scenarios. The chapter explores the impact of international human rights conventions on national codes, highlighting the relationship between global norms and human rights law. It suggests a combination of legal accreditation, international cooperation, and grassroots activism to challenge barriers and create a more just and equitable societal order.

DOI: 10.4018/979-8-3373-1792-2.ch010

INTRODUCTION

Human rights law aims to protect and promote fundamental human rights and freedoms. Principally, human rights law seeks to ensure basic entitlements for every person, like the right to life, freedom from torture, freedom of expression and the right to a fair trial, without discrimination of any kind, such as nationality, sex, national or ethnic origin, color, religion and language. Human rights law has a long and complex history that is rooted in philosophical traditions as well as legal traditions from multiple civilizations (Donnelly, 2013; Sen, 1999; Rawls, 1971; Baderin & McCorquodale, 2007). The idea of human rights can be found in ancient and medieval philosophical traditions that stressed the intrinsic dignity of the human person. Foundational documents, like the Magna Carta (1215), the English Bill of Rights (1689), the United States Bill of Rights (1791), and the French Declaration of the Rights of Man and of the Citizen (1789), had already paved the way. These documents, which originated in the Enlightenment, began to specify that people have rights by their nature as human beings that cannot be violated and must be protected by law. The cataclysm of World War II helped to rapidly accelerate the development of human rights law (Muller, 2023). The Holocaust and other wartime atrocities showed the urgent necessity for a global standard that would protect human dignity from abuse by states. This resulted in the establishment of the United Nations in 1945, which placed human rights as one of its main purposes (Freeman, 2002).

The United Nations General Assembly adopted the Universal Declaration of Human Rights (UDHR) in 1948, the first legal document to set out fundamental human rights to be universally protected. It has formed many subsequent binding treaties. Following the UDHR, the international community developed a system of treaties and other legal instruments to have a binding effect to the principles contained in the Declaration. Two of the most important of these are the International Covenant on Civil and Political Rights (ICCPR) and the International Covenant on Economic, Social and Cultural Rights (ICESCR), both adopted in 1966. Amid this, these covenants and the UDHR make a productive (and protective) suite of the International Bill of Human Rights. Human rights laws have also evolved in terms of their enforcement mechanisms (Chakravarty, 2023). Regional human rights systems exist as well, like the European Court of Human Rights, the Inter-American Court of Human Rights, and the African Court on Human and Peoples' Rights, having jurisdiction to issue judgments, binding on member states. Such regional systems are complementary to the United Nations' human rights mechanisms, which encompass treaty-based bodies, such as the Human Rights Committee, and thematic rapporteurs and working groups that monitor and investigate human rights situations worldwide.

Today, human rights law remains dynamic, responding to new challenges, like digital privacy, climate change, and the waves of global migration (Molnar, 2019). These problems will require new generations of legal interpretation and new generations of appropriate solutions to ensure that human rights are appropriately protected as the world changes (Nickel, 2007). The text recognizes that human rights law has evolved as a result of the growing awareness of inherent dignity and of the equal and inalienable rights of all members of the human family, which is the foundation of freedom, justice and peace in the world (Khan, Amjad & Usman, 2020). As evolving societal constructs and international challenges shape human rights, a constantly ongoing dialogue, legal advocacy, and reform continue to adapt human rights law to future events (Banchio, 2025).

This chapter is intended to explore the profound impact that human rights law has had on global society and its governance systems. Enshrined in international law, human rights law has transformed state-society relations, fostering a culture of respect for essential freedoms and human dignity (Hamelink, 2025). This influence can be observed across several domains, including the development of international norms, national legal frameworks, societal values, and interstate relations (Shue, 1996). One of the most remarkable outcomes of human rights law is the set of norms dictating state behavior toward the rights and freedoms of individuals. Many such norms have been codified in international treaties, such as the Universal Declaration of Human Rights, the International Covenant on Civil and Political Rights, and the International Covenant on Economic, Social, and Cultural Rights (Roberts et al., 2024). The near-universal adoption and ratification of these treaties by countries throughout the world reflect the broad consensus on acceptable standards of human conduct. It has led to better treatment of persons and minority groups, decreased levels of discrimination, and a higher quality of life in various corners of the globe (Saaida, 2024).

Second, human rights law permeates domestic legal systems in various ways. Through ratification of international human rights treaties, States agree to change domestic law and policy to comply with international standards. It often entails comprehensive legal reforms: drafting new laws, abolishing practices that discriminate against vulnerable groups, and strengthening judicial mechanisms for human rights protection. For example, the influence of human rights law is reflected in the gradual decriminalization of homosexuality (Peretko, 2024). The abolition of the death penalty in numerous states, and growing protections against gender-based violence. These reforms not only support individual rights but also support the rule of law within countries. Third, it is important not to underestimate the culture-building function of human rights laws (Akhundov, 2025) has been a major force driving change in our culture towards more tolerance, inclusivity and justice. Education on human rights is an increasingly popular part of school curricula globally, which instils an early awareness of and respect for diversity and the rights of others. Moreover, the rapid development of technology, particularly the internet and social media, has made it easier for individuals to connect across the globe, sharing information and perspectives about human rights abuses outside of their countries that were once isolated, creating a more empathetic, globally minded citizenry.

Finally human rights law has been extremely important in shaping the behaviour of nations to one another (Steiner et al., 2008). The worldwide acceptance of human rights standards has resulted in their integration into the diplomatic priorities of countries and international bodies. Today, human rights are woven into international agreements inextricably, a standard requirement in the assessment of countries that seek to enter major organizations, such as the European Union. Moreover, human rights abuse can also trigger international consequences like sanctions or humanitarian intervention, thereby reinforcing the idea that human rights cannot be regarded as purely domestic issues but are of international concern. In summary, the impact of human rights law is manifold, shaping international standards, revolutionizing domestic legal systems, transforming societal perceptions, and affecting international relations (Prasanna et al., 2023). These wide-reaching effects echo the continued significance of human rights law to not only provide a legal basis, but also to cultivate the foundations of more just, equitable societies. So, as the world has been changing and so will the world be changing in the continuous process, human rights will also play the role more because over the time new challenges will emerge and the human rights law controlling the moral compass of anything will sort in the event just work (Mishra & Shanmugapriya, 2024).

In this chapter, the authors examine the significant influence of legislation on equity and social justice across geographical and thematic spheres. From legislation, a tool of government, which laws societies to standards, standardizes a fairer opportunity and outcome for all members of perhaps quite different populations, perhaps quite equal, in their groups. (Nour, 2024). This work investigates how different areas around the world explore equity and social justice issues across legal regimes and what themes arise from those societal efforts — economic inequality, racial and gender equality, access to education, and health-care rights. The evolution of social justice and equity is significantly determined by geographical and historical context, which has different implications of legislation. For example, In Scandinavian countries (Sweden and Norway), the legislation greatly emphasizes the welfare policies that are economically equal through progressive taxation and social benefits (Panwar et al., 2024). These are countries where health care is comprehensive, education is free and social safety nets are strong, all enshrined in law with the goal of reducing social and economic inequalities.

Countries like the United States, by contrast, have a more complex legislative landscape that accommodates a strong emphasis on individual rights and private enterprise, as well as inherited inequality, which is often reflected in their approach to social justice issues such as health care and education, both areas that continue to suffer from major disparities. Legislation thematically impacts multiple equity dimensions, each responsive to specific types of equity barriers. Economic legislation Minimum wage laws, tax policy, and social welfare programs are examples of economic legislation—laws that directly address the issues of poverty reduction and economic opportunity for every citizen (Fallah & Judijanto, 2025). Acts of racial justice meant to counter discrimination in the areas of work, residence, and education are part of a long-term law promoting program to change the tough reality that racial minorities need to confront (Ignatieff, 2001). Laws supporting gender equality, equal pay, the prevention of gender-based violence, and parental leave for all parents (mothers and fathers) lead to improved well-being of women.

Furthermore, the accessibility of education and medical care is a crucial facet of legislation, as many nations have passed laws to guarantee that all citizens have access to these essential services, fostering social mobility and fairness (Kumari, 2023). Legislation aimed at social justice can also be hindered by obstacles to its enforcement or becoming culturally accepted. In certain areas, robust legal systems may be established on paper but collapse in execution because of poor enforcement, corruption or cultural biases. For instance, many countries have laws in place advocating for gender equality but do not see improvements in gender parity in everyday life as such laws are not complemented by effective enforcement mechanisms and remain at odds with cultural traditions. The opposite is true in societies with more buy-in for social justice and equity, where legislation is more likely to pass and work (Weale, 2023).

Moreover, the international diffusion of human rights norms has shaped legislative initiatives for equity and social justice. International organizations and treaties, such as the United Nations and the International Covenant on Economic, Social, and Cultural Rights, offer both a framework and pressure that encourage states to improve their legislation in sync with international standards. (Okedele et al., 2024) This shows that human rights issues are not confined to individual states, but rather, that local legislative actions are connected to human rights issues on a global stage and that domestic laws, including those passed by state legislatures, can be heavily influenced by global dialogues and agreements. (Lesch & Reiners, 2023) This chapter draws on examples from a range of continents and contexts to demonstrate that legislation is one of the most effective mechanisms for promoting equity and social justice in practice (Moeckli et al., 2010).

THEORETICAL FRAMEWORK

The Following Are Some of the Key Ideas That Will Be Covered: Equity, Social Justice, and Human Rights

In this chapter, the authors establish such a theoretical foundation based on three interrelated concepts of equity, social justice, and human rights in a legal context, thus framing legislation within the norms and practices of society. Each of these terms has its own precise meaning, but they also share significant common ground in law and policy, which guides how nations aspire to attain just and inclusive solutions for all people. This part will further describe these fundamental concepts, their theoretical foundations, and how they connect to provide a holistic framework to theories and understand inequality and injustice. Equity - fair and impartial; the process of recognizing and addressing injustice and inequality to achieve an equal outcome, even where their people start from different places (Risse et al., 1999).

Equity in practice works to remove obstacles that keep some people or communities from accessing the same chances that others have. The idea is vital to developing policies and laws designed to offset resource wealth and access to opportunity for underprivileged groups historically and systemically. It is not just about equal treatment, rather it is about how to balance those scales to make it fair based on individual and group needs. Social Justice is a broader concept that envelops equity along with the other aspects of fairness in society, like human rights, legal rights, and economic welfare. It is founded on the principle that all people should have equal economic, political and social rights and opportunities. It involves working to create a just society by resisting injustice and valuing diversity (Panwar et al., 2024). It includes ensuring millions have an equal say in decisions that impact their lives, that they aren't excluded from the advantages a society provides on account of their race, gender, religion, or economic situation. Social justice inspired legislation would produce exactly that society, ensuring equitable distribution of resources among members as well as physical and psychological safety and security for all. Human Rights are the inalienable rights that are possessed by all human beings, regardless of nationality, culture, or religion. They are rights that are inherent to all human beings, without distinction of race, sex, national or ethnic origin, language, religion, or any other status.

Human rights are the rights to life and liberty, freedom from slavery and torture, freedom of opinion and expression, the right to work and education, and many more (Chinkin & Baetens, 2015).

All these rights belong to everyone, without discrimination. International human rights law imposes obligations on Governments to act (or refrain from acting) in ways that promote and protect human rights and fundamental freedoms of individuals or groups. The competence for understanding how the principles into legislation and ultimately action within society through the theoretical interplay between equality, social justice, and human rights (Reiners, 2024) These ideas are interconnected, as human rights are the legal foundation of the moral and ethical urgencies of justice and equality. They collectively provide insight into what laws should look like and how they should be implemented to fully enable all individuals to experience the benefits of society. First, however, a few foundational principles of politics underpin this legislative wrangling that will be touched upon in this chapter will help the reader in the real-world consequences of the politics at hand, leading to policies and laws that serve to correct societal wrongs, prevent abuses, and ultimately lead to the maintenance of an equitable society where the rights and dignity of all are respected and protected. Through an analysis of how these frameworks interact, the chapter will reveal the challenges associated with creating effective forms of legislation that encompass the multiple dimensions of human need and entitlement across different social, cultural, and economic environments (An-Na'im, 2002).

Theoretical Views on Human Rights Legislation as an Instrument for Social Transformation

History has seen the evolution of theory in the areas of human rights legislation, which position it as the most potent tool in its ability to spur social change, rethinking the structures of society, and addressing inequality entrenched in the social order (Savage, 2021). This point of view is rooted in the assumption that law can be something of an agent of social change, in that it can be relied upon to not only to conform to norms but also transform them. Understanding human rights in such a way makes this theory incorporate a discussion on the interactive role of laws and social practices, instead of mere legal items. As we expand our collective imagination not so much through theory as through legislation and action, human rights have become one of the key filters through which we can free up our settled conservatism and pursue quite radical changes to our social contracts (Kampourakis, 2022). In this theoretical perspective, human rights legislation serves not only as a protective ingredient but also as a preventative measure. It protects us from abuses and violations, and it can be used by people whose rights have been violated. On the one hand, it has the potential to catalyse cultural and social change, prompting societies to reconsider and abandon obsolete or unjust customs and practices. Therein lies the magic of human rights law doing things differently, thinking the opposing way, expanding the accepted definitions of dignity, freedom, equality. At the heart of this characterization is what we call "normative development" (Avelino, 2021). Human rights laws are part of a broader context that drives changes in community norms by providing new expectations of behaviour for individuals and states. These laws express a vision of what a just society ought to be like, and then it deeply affects the public policies, the public behaviours. Legal norms gain anchorage from the societal lifeworld and, over time, the material conditions and lived expectations of dignity transform.

The transformative approach also gives attention to "legal mobilization" and its contribution to social change. rating of new norms and standards that are inclusive, representative and accountable (Simmons, 2009). Human rights norms are not simply enforced through strategic litigation, advocacy, and public campaigns; they are popularized and made more accessible. This organizational effort will help empower marginalized peoples by providing them with the necessary information to fight for justice and equality and will help educate the general public on the importance of human rights. Another theoretical framework is the "spillover effect" of human rights legislation, whereby improvements in one area of rights can result in positive changes in other areas (Taghvaee et al., 2022).

For instance, laws that expand political rights create broader political participation, which can result in better governance and better guarantees of other human rights. Likewise, laws that protect economic rights can alleviate poverty and inequality, thus promoting social cohesion and improving access to other basic rights, like those to education and health. Opponents of the transformational power of human rights legislation argue that passing statutes can only go so far in altering entrenched social and cultural norms (Reiners, 2024). They refer to the distance between legal formalism and social reality, when laws may exist in a book yet are poorly enforced or simply disrespected in practice. In order for human rights legislation to be genuinely transformative and meaningful, it must go hand in hand with strong institutions, effective enforcement mechanisms, and a continued commitment by government and civil society to serve as bastions to these principles. Finally, human rights legislation is a weapon to raise important question in society: the normative perspective. Human rights laws, by providing standards, galvanizing stakeholders, and shaping norms and values in society, are a crucial element in forging a more equitable and just world. Nonetheless, the impact that these laws may have to effect social transformation is also dependent on their incorporation into larger socio-political and cultural frameworks, which calls for a holistic human rights agenda in terms of both advocacy and implementation (Dutta et al., 2025).

The Intersection of Human Rights with Other Rights, Including Economic, Cultural, and Social Rights

The journey human rights have taken across economic and cultural facets of life raises important questions of human obligations to one another and the universe, with fundamental implications for the universal codification of human rights as a way to obtain social justice. Human rights are commonly divided into two broad categories — civil and political rights on the one hand, and economic, social and cultural rights on the other (Hantzopoulos & Bajaj, 2021). In contrast to civil and political rights, which include life, freedom from torture, free speech and a fair trial, economic, social and cultural rights include the rights to work, education, health and a family (adequate) standard of living, which includes food and housing. This is important intersection that is critical for understanding how these different categories of rights interact, support, and reinforce each other to create a holistic approach to human rights (Freeman, 2022).

The intersectionality theory is a guideline for understanding precisely how the deprivation of rights aspects intersects as a result of race, gender, class, and other status, to contribute to the degree of inequality in society. For instance, the right to health (which is an economic and social right) is closely linked to civil rights such as the right to non-discrimination. The realization of the right to health cannot be achieved without addressing discrimination in healthcare settings, whether on the basis of individual race, gender or economic status. similarly, cultural rights, such as the right to take part in cultural life, or to a culture of one's own, overlap with economic rights, such as the rights of indigenous people to their ancestral lands, which are necessary for their economic and cultural survival (Right, 2023).

The idea of indivisibility holds that all human rights, be they civil, political, economic, social or cultural, are interconnected and equally crucial for an individual's dignity and well-being. From this standpoint, the implementation of civil and political rights is usually conditional upon the success of economic, social, and cultural rights. The promotion and protection of economic and social rights is foundational for the establishment of conditions under which civil and political rights may be exercised. Moreover, the indivisible nature of these rights implies that the breach of one right can negatively impact the enjoyment of others. The health or lack of education (violations of economic and social rights) may prevent a person from participating in society and exercising their civil and political rights, including going to the polls or speaking freely. On the other hand, improving the defence of economic and social rights can strengthen civil and political rights, allowing individuals to become more effective and engaged citizens (Freeman, 2022).

Internationally, one of the expressions of this integration of these rights can be seen in frameworks such as the Sustainable Development Goals (SDGs), which cover a wide array of interrelated rights and goals targeted towards development which is sustainable, inclusive and equitable. Such frameworks acknowledge that permanent social change is not sustainable without engaging the whole range of human rights (Saini et al., 2023). Although this intersectional view of human rights challenges traditional hierarchies where more physical rights get priority over social, cultural or economic rights, this indivisible and interdependent view of human rights also challenges the view that certain human rights must be issued in isolation from other human rights, urging that a comprehensive vision comes up as some human rights simply cannot wait (Banchio, 2025). Ultimately, through exploring how human rights engage with economic, cultural and social rights, this chapter stresses that human rights legislation and advocacy can neither really fulfil nor can real transformative social justice become a possibility without such a comprehensive understanding of the human experience complexity (Alston & Robinson, 2005).

Table 1. Theoretical frameworks in human rights law

Concept	Definition	Relevance	Application	Example
Equity	Fair and impartial treatment, addressing inequalities to achieve equal outcomes.	Fundamental in ensuring laws compensate for societal imbalances.	Used to guide policies correcting historical or systemic disadvantages.	Policies aimed at improving access to healthcare for underprivileged communities.
Social Justice	Broader fairness in society, encompassing economic, political, and social rights.	Drives legislation ensuring equitable distribution of resources.	Manifests in comprehensive reforms like decriminalization of homosexuality.	Scandinavian social welfare models promoting economic equality.
Human Rights	Inalienable rights inherent to all humans, without discrimination.	Provides the legal basis for social justice and equity measures.	Embedded in international treaties and national constitutions.	Universal Declaration of Human Rights.
Legislative Impact	The effect of laws on social equity and justice.	Examines how different laws influence societal norms and protections.	Involves reforming laws to align with international human rights standards.	Adoption of the ADA in the U.S. to support people with disabilities.
Normative Development	The evolution of community norms through legal frameworks.	Laws catalyze shifts in societal expectations and behaviors.	Laws promote new behaviors and protections through social change.	Laws expanding LGBTQ+ rights influencing societal norms.
Legal Mobilization	The use of legal systems to enforce and promote rights.	Activates community and legal responses to rights violations.	Involves strategic litigation and advocacy to enforce rights.	Legal challenges leading to the recognition of new rights.
Spillover Effect	Improvements in one area of rights enhancing others.	Demonstrates interconnectedness of various human rights.	Laws protecting economic rights enhancing access to education.	Better governance resulting from enhanced political participation.

continued on following page

Table 1. Continued

Concept	Definition	Relevance	Application	Example
International Influence	The impact of global standards on national laws.	International treaties shape domestic legislation and practices.	Countries adapt policies to meet international human rights standards.	CEDAW influencing gender equality laws globally.
Enforcement Mechanisms	Systems and processes ensuring laws are followed.	Crucial for the practical implementation of rights.	Involves courts, human rights bodies, and international oversight.	European Court of Human Rights enforcing decisions on member states.

HUMAN RIGHTS LAW AS AN INSTRUMENT OF EQUITY

Figure 1. Mind map: Human rights law as an instrument of equity

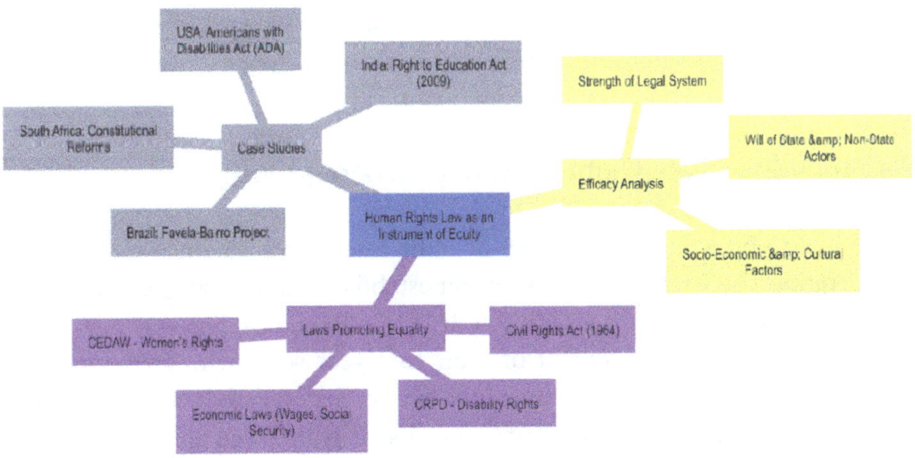

Case Studies That Illustrate the Application of These Laws

This human rights tool functions as a mean to establish fair treatment while fighting against social injustices as well as transforming the normal practices towards equal principles. This analysis enables direct observation of rights transformation into practices that promote equity across various global human rights legislative frameworks (Freeman, 2022). These case studies present real-life examples of human rights standards which apply to discrimination cases and service access rights and marginal community protections and also reveal performance levels of human rights law and approach implementation challenges (Right, 2023).

Case Study 1: South Africa's Post-Apartheid Constitutional Reforms

At its democratic emancipation South Africa produced what many consider to be a progressive document titled constitution which advocates human rights extensively. The 1996 South African Constitution combined civil and political rights with a wide range of economic social and cultural rights. The 1996 South African Constitution specifically provided legal status to rights which protect access to housing along with healthcare and education and sufficient food and fresh water (Molaba, 2025). The Government of the Republic of South Africa vs Grootboom presents this judicial application. The Constitutional Court determined that South Africa's state bears obligatory responsibilities to supply basic housing services to citizens who are in extremely poor condition (Odeku, 2023). The government must provide socio-economic rights with at least a minimal standard of reasonableness under the Constitution according to this case and thereby demonstrates human rights laws can force states to address social inequalities.

Case Study 2: India's Right to Education Act (2009)

The Right to Education Act (2009) of India establishes a human rights framework for equity. The Right to Education Act established as a fundamental right the educational right of children ages 6 through 14 while requiring private educational institutions to maintain 25 percent of their first-year seats with free enrollment for disadvantaged group and economically weaker section students (Chakravarty, 2023). The Act worked to narrow educational disparity between groups because the Indian education system historically maintained significant exclusive and unequal practices (Mondal & Islam, 2023). Despite its implementation difficulties this law remains vital for social change because it provides all children regardless of their background with educational opportunities.

Case Study 3: Brazil's Favela-Bairro Project

The Favela-Bairro Project in Brazil illustrates how human rights principles impact urban development alongside social incorporation yet lacks specific application of particular human rights laws. Internal organizations began implementing the Favela-Bairro Project around mid-1990s to integrate Rio de Janeiro's informal favelas with its formal urban zoning (Werthmann, 2021). The project proposed giving legitimate ownership rights while providing better housing standards along with public service access to sanitation and electricity and healthcare facilities. The project achieved its goals of transforming favela living conditions even though it confronted gentrification challenges alongside socio-economic disparities, yet it showcases that sustainable urban development can focus on human rights principles and fairness (Hafner-Burton, 2013).

Case Study 4: The Americans with Disabilities Act (ADA) of 1990

The Americans with Disabilities Act (ADA) of 1990 showcases human rights law application that establishes equal access for people with disabilities in public life. The Americans with Disabilities Act prevents public and private institutions from discriminating against disabled people in their access to educational settings and employment opportunities and all places open to the general public. (Wojtara, 2023) Through implementing the Americans with Disabilities Act people gained better access to physical and digital worlds as well as enhanced participation and establishment of nondiscriminatory practices. Historical court proceedings and ongoing advocacy campaigns participated in major transformations of disability-related public opinions and legal protections that resulted in the ADA (Blanck, 2023) The identified case studies demonstrate multiple uses of human rights law as an instrument for justice protection. These examples demonstrate that human rights regulations lead to tangible victories in social justice while showing the legal system's ability to fight existing social and economic unfairness (Branham, 2025). These instances show positive outcomes while maintaining ongoing difficulties that create valuable lessons about implementing the enforcement of human rights laws to reach their targets.

An Analysis of the Efficacy of Human Rights Laws in Helping to Reduce Inequities

This suggests that a pluralistic approach to writing law to enforce justice generates divergent views on the effectiveness of human rights laws at addressing inequality, thus revealing a more profound tension in the process of policy writing itself (Bajaj, 2021). The law's effectiveness works via diverse components comprising the ability of the legal system itself and additionally the willingness of country and non-held accountable actors and social economic and cultural factors (Avelino, 2021). Human Rights laws are primarily designed to grant legal rights to everyone who needs protection of dignity and equality in society. They safeguard against discrimination of racial, gender, religious and other identity groups and they also ensure essential social goods such as education, healthcare and housing that facilitate social equality. Previous generations of society required wider frameworks for coordinating inclusive development participation which manifested as anti-discrimination policies institutionalized in education and workplaces granting new opportunities to excluded minority groups.

There are many barriers to making human rights laws work to address disparities. The system of checks used to turkey these systems is ineffectual and reflect biases in other scenarios. Well-functioning institutions, that are both free of corruption and devoid of prejudice, are therefore crucial foundations upon which implementation of legislative rights can take place. Judicial incapacity, combined with political unwillingness, accounts for the failure to enforce laws which do not protect vulnerable populations and deny citizens the benefits promised to them by law. Human rights laws matter only when layered on top of what is missing for the target communities, namely awareness about their rights and empowerment to use the rights. There are many societies in which there are marginalized groups who know little about their rights and cannot get to exercise them. Access to knowledge, paired with tools for advocacy, is an essential tool that needed to provide for people and communities to be able to use the law to fight inequality. These are offered by several NGOs within the framework of civic organizations that deal with educational and consultancy work on how to navigate legal proceedings (Right, 2023).

Human rights laws are proven effective depending on contextual factors and build significant results based on socio-economic factors. The right to free speech, the right to water, are things that are recognized around the world throughout history, and then visiting a country like this, the right to employment and the right to education all shrink away when confronted with significant levels of poverty. Human rights can detail the needed standards, but their realization is contingent on economic and development policies that create the necessary resources to make rights a reality. Human rights laws yield superior outcomes in areas with high economic development and strong institutional frameworks than in less developed economies (Freeman, 2022).

Decades before, the United States enacted under the ADA legislation that in principle would promote policies that now reduce disabilities-related inequities as it works under contexts where people and have resources and functional legal systems. Because of their enforcement of broad legal definitions, these laws not only demand physical access to spaces for people with disabilities, but they also aim to facilitate greater participation in society and the economy (Wheale, 2021). While human rights laws serve as central apparatus tools against injustice and inequality, they are not blanket solutions, since their effects depend on a variety of interrelated factors, such as the vigour of the enforcement of such laws, domestic socioeconomic, national political, and cultural realities, and public knowledge of human rights laws. Human rights laws are but one of several components in the ongoing quest to build just societies; they alone will not suffice but should be part of a larger agenda (Goodhart, 2009).

An Examination of Particular Human Rights Legislation That Are Targeted at Promoting Equality

Human rights laws in relation to legal equality show legal systems solving legalized inequalities both creatively and practically in order to create pluralistic societies across the globe. These laws are not just about racial, but also gender, disability, economic disparities and other potential inequities (Müller, 2023). A close examination of two particular laws demonstrates not only the mixed success they have had in solving single facets of inequality but also the complex character of particular implementation. Long into 1964 United States Congress adopted the Civil Rights Act; its landmark cultural-racial equality act in the American past (Vijeyarasa, 2021). The landmark measure tore down institutional segregation by prohibiting discrimination in public accommodations and places of employment, public education, among other sites. It outlawed discrimination based on racial characteristics in addition to color and religion and sex and national origins and laid the groundwork for future voter protection and fair housing laws. The Civil Rights Act stands as a pioneering tool for combating discrimination, although there is an ongoing need for legislative evolving to combat new forms of discriminatory practices. The Convention on the Elimination of All Forms of Discrimination Against Women (CEDAW), a United Nations accord cargoes in 1979, is the global benchmark for guaranteeing the privileges of ladies yet additionally advocating them (Walters, 2021). The CEDAW is a universal female rights charter that requires countries to end female discrimination and outlines basic female rights to health services and access to education and political participation (Chakravarty, 2023). The degree to which CEDAW promotes meaningful change is heavily linked to cultural and legal context with varying degrees of pressure when countries attempt to change discriminatory laws and practices (Orta, 2025).

As a living instrumental and structural approach to prevention and social adaptation, the operational of Convention on the Rights of Persons with Disabilities (CRPD) marks a key milestone since its full entry into force in 2008, with regard to the reconfiguring of how people address these individuals. The CRPD redefines disability as a human rights issue rather than a medical or charitable issue with an emphasis on equality and demand for social inclusion. Access to buildings and building codes; access to transport; discrimination in relation to work; independent living; and community living provisions (national legislation at country level) that have been considerably transformed since the information convention was in ceases for certain purposes. It is important to note that the law is fundamentally economic it provides minimum wage rates and social security benefits distributions it acts as mitigation tools of economic equality, these are factors that create safety networks for poor and disadvantaged groups (Ife et al., 2022).

Higher rates of school attendance coupled with lower poverty levels are just some of the positive results observed in Brazil through its successful Bolsa Família program. The programmed offers cash assistance to poor households as long as their children attend class and are vaccinated. Even though human rights treaties do not classify these sorts of programs as conditional income programs, the enforcement of economic social and cultural rights, (Hamelink, 2023) illustrates one legal technique of addressing the economic causes of social inequalities. This study shows that these laws work well when individuals support their enforcement alongside broad cultural shift and persistent lobbying. Both the traditional social customs resistant to change and the problems arising from the challenges of implementing various legal systems are among the main obstacles to significant implementation (Roberts et al., 2024). These laws set essential baselines which allow individuals to fight discrimination and stimulate dialogs around equality concerning rights in every municipality across the globe. Human rights legislation is pivotal in global equality movements because it determines the trajectories of societal norms and policies to ensure equality and fairness in the world (Merry, 2006).

HUMAN RIGHTS LAW AND SOCIAL JUSTICE

Figure 2. Mind map: Human rights law and social justice

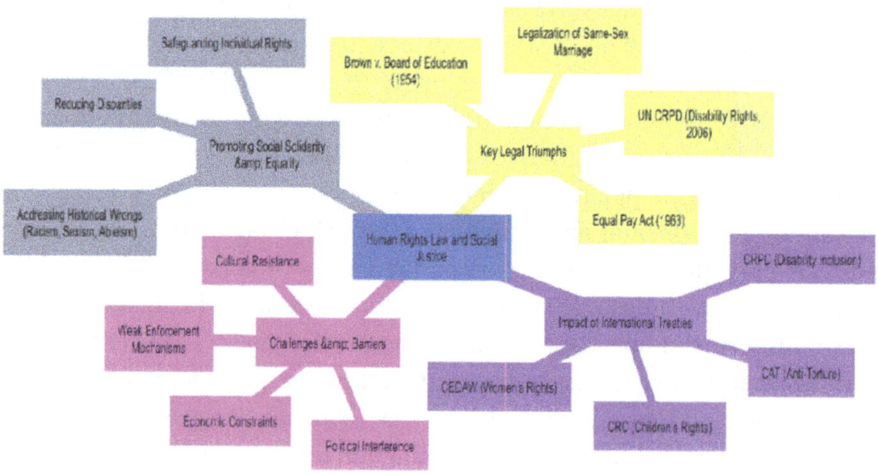

The Role That Human Rights Legislation Plays in Promoting Social Solidarity and Equality

Human rights law promotes social unity and equal rights; it is a moral compass and a legal compass that will help people move into more inclusive societies. Such laws are intended not just to safeguard individual rights but to promote a sense of unity and shared responsibility among diverse populations (Casla & Sandner, 2024). When these rights are codified through human rights law, it serves an essential societal purpose, bringing people together beyond cultural, economic, and political divisions by defining and enforcing standards that guarantee fair treatment and equal opportunity for everyone. The core values in human rights — dignity, fairness, equality and respect — are part of social solidarity (Kanade, 2024). These principles force societies to move from self-interest or group-interest to general welfare. Laws governing human rights, which require that everyone has equal access to education and health care, help create a level playing field, reducing disparities that contribute to population disintegration (Chakravarty, 2023). These laws foster a more unified society where citizens feel valued and connected to one another by guaranteeing that everyone has access to the resources and opportunities they need to reach their full potential.

Additionally, a significant component of human rights is addressing historical wrongs and systemic discrimination that has historically limited participation in societal and civic life. Here, anti-discrimination laws that focus on racism, sexism, and ableism are key (Blokker, 2024). They help rectify past wrongs but also protect against future injustices by establishing a legal precedent that no form of discrimination is acceptable. Challenge traditional mindset; foster inclusivity, tolerance — milestones to social solidarity. When people believe in the idea they can be protected by the law, and that their rights are protected, they are far more likely to invest in their community and work on shared goals. The laws are not just meant to protect and provide redress but serve a symbolic purpose as well. The practitioners validate the worth of all people and keep social justice in the public mind (Clapham, 2007). This can galvanize civic engagement and activism, prompting citizens to push for additional reform and to demand accountability from their governments. For example, the right to a clean and healthy environment has been increasingly recognized globally which has united communities around the world and mobilized those communities to take action against climate change and sustainable practices.

Furthermore, international human rights law and standards, as exemplified by the UDHR, serve as global benchmarks for building solidarity and ties across boundaries. They remind us that some values are universal, and that human struggles like poverty, oppression, and inequality are common to us all. One reason is that it helps nurture international cooperation and solidarity as countries work together and help solve issues that are common to all of humankind (Hantzopoulos & Bajaj, 2021).

On the other hand, human rights enactment does not always lead to social unity and equality; this is dependent on how the enactment is implemented and enforced. But the effect of laws on social change is low without strong institutions and public participation. These laws must bear fruit in the hands of the many, but without effective enforcement mechanisms, education about rights, and advocacy efforts, they will be little more than words on a page." The human rights law, rooted in social harmony and equality is a significant aspect. In doing so, these laws help create a framework of trust and mutual respect that is necessary for social cohesion by codifying laws of fairness and protections against discrimination. As they challenge us to examine the bigger picture of our actions and policies, they lead us closer to a more just and cohesive society (Hathaway, 2005).

THE KEY LEGAL TRIUMPHS THAT HAVE CONTRIBUTED TO THE ADVANCEMENT OF SOCIAL JUSTICE

Some landmark victories have led to both changes in the law surrounding social justice issues, as well as in our ideas of what is normal and what is expected. All of these legal victories are just a piece of a more significant puzzle to fight for equality and justice everywhere, whether it's civil rights, women's rights, disability rights, and so much more. This shows what has changed over time with the relationship between the law and social justice movements and how the legal system affects broader society issues. The decision in 1954 by the U.S. Supreme Court in *Brown v. Board of Education of Topeka* is, by any measure, one of the greatest legal victories for civil rights (Stone, 2024). This landmark case declared state laws establishing separate public schools for black and white students to be unconstitutional and was a unanimous decision that reversed its precedent from the 1896 decision in the case of *Plessy v. Ferguson* that upheld the constitutionality of racial segregation under the doctrine of "separate but equal" (Krayer & Note, 2025). One of the more notable achievements and legacies of the 1954 ruling was that it eventually led to the end of institutionalized racial segregation in public schools across America, and also led to the establishment of a legal benchmark (or landmark ruling) that bolstered the movement to ban segregation laws in other public spaces and settings, thus providing further impetus to the civil rights movement in America (Right, 2023).

The US Equal Pay Act of 1963 is one of the historic achievements in terms of gender equality. This Act proposed to prohibit wage discrimination on the basis of sex, making it illegal for employers to pay unequal wages to men and women performing substantially similar work. It was a groundbreaking moment for women's rights for it was a legally recognized commitment to equal pay in the workplace and at the same time this law provided an example to be copied and grow a successful global fight against gender-based discrimination. One example of this is the international recognition and adoption of the United Nations Convention on the Rights of Persons with Disabilities (CRPD) in 2006, credited to the disability rights movement up to this point in its long post-war history. (McCusker at el., 2023) This UN treaty marked a paradigm shift in the treatment and understanding of disability, from a medical or charity model to one based on human rights. The CRPD was a historic human rights treaty; it invested the full participation of persons with disabilities in the societies of the world and guaranteed their rights to education, to employment, to access, to independent living, and so much more (Harpur at el., 2022).

To many countries, the legalization of same-sex marriage also represents an important legal victory in the name of social justice.] Diverse nations, from Uruguay to Sweden, from South Africa to New Zealand, to the vast majority of the European Union member states, have also made positive strides in the interest of LGBTQ+ rights and the advancement of social justice since the Dutch first opened their doors to same-sex marriage in 2001. (Palazzo, 2022) The various legal changes have not only helped same-sex couples obtain formal recognition and rights, but they have also paved the way for the shifting tides of public opinion in favor of LGBTQ+ populations. Important judicial pronouncements — most notably, the Supreme Court's decriminalisation of homosexuality in *Navtej Singh Johar v. Union of India* in 2018 — have established that the judiciary can also serve as a vehicle of social justice (Bandi & Nandeshwar, 2024). This judgment repealed a part of the Indian Penal Code, Section 377, punishing homosexual acts, which was a historic milestone in the field of human rights and individual freedoms across the world largest democracy. These judicial victories illustrated the continuing power and relevance of the law in our struggle for social justice. They put right historical wrongs and also establish legal precedents which foster an atmosphere of equality and human rights where progress can happen. Though much remains to be done in this regard in order to achieve a workable social justice, these legal successes are testament both to the path building role that law can play in the pursuit of social progress and to the empowerment of marginalized groups (Boisson de Chazournes & Kohen 2010).

THE IMPACT THAT INTERNATIONAL HUMAN RIGHTS CONVENTIONS AND TREATIES HAVE HAD ON NATIONAL POLICY

International human rights treaties and conventions influence national policy, providing a critical mechanism for the establishment of global standards and the promotion of domestic legal reforms (Simmons, 2023). These treaties give states the frameworks and the norms to help them through the process of adopting policies which promote people's dignity, rights and welfare. By ratifying these conventions and treaties, countries become committed to international law, and this frequently requires substantial reforms of domestic law and policy to meet those precise international obligations, including the Convention on the Elimination of All Forms of Discrimination Against Women (CEDAW), adopted by the UN General Assembly in 1979, which has been instrumental in determining national approaches to gender equality. Countries who sign CEDAW have often had to amend national legislation to comply with the provisions of this international convention, progress has been made on issues from employment and education to protection from violence against women (Walters, 2021).

CEDAW has also been instrumental in developing institutional mechanisms to monitor and promote the situation of women by inserting the principles of gender equality into national apparatuses (Vijeyarasa, 2021). Similarly, The Convention on the Rights of the Child (CRC), which states civil, political, economic, social, health and cultural rights of children have greatly influenced policy nationally in every country in the world. Since ratification, countries have adopted landmark legislation on child labour, abuse and education. International treaties have also made inroads in the area of disability rights. The nature of disability has changed dramatically in recent years, primarily due to the Convention on the Rights of Persons with Disabilities (CRPD), which frames disability as a human rights issue rather than one focused on medical care and has shifted global policies to inclusivity and accessibility. One area of progress has been in legislative frameworks, where, post-CRPD, many states moved to include provisions on accessibility of public buildings, transportation, information and communication technology, as well as equal opportunities for persons with disabilities in education and work (McCusker at el., 2023). The other framework where global convention has had a tremendous effect is the legal standards around torture and inhumane treatment (Harpur, 2023). The Convention against Torture and Other Cruel, Inhuman or Degrading Treatment or Punishment (CAT), obligates states that ratified it, to establish a legal framework to stave against torture in their jurisdictions (Kilibarda, 2022). It has led to the establishment of national and international bodies tasked with monitoring and investigating torture allegations and the inclusion of torture prohibition provisions in national criminal laws. However, the countries are still addressing the issues in the role that international human rights treaties play on domestic policies. Influencing factors will diverge considerably and will depend on political will, the monetary means available, as well as past legal and cultural backgrounds.

Moreover, international standards can at times be perceived as contradictory to or at odds with their national sovereignty or their cultural practices hence leading to resistance or selective adoption of these international conventions. Compliance and enforcement mechanisms are often weak and depend on state cooperation and commitment. The impact of international human rights conventions and treaties on national policy--despite all their limitations--has undeniably been positive: many important reforms have occured, and overall human rights protections at the national level have been strengthened. A big and powerful tool for advocacy groups to keep states loyal to their government and for states to be able to evaluate their own states values compared to other peer governments to create a more just as well as a more equal global order (Brysk, 2002).

Table 2. Detailed human rights law and social justice

Aspect	Definition	Importance	Application	Example
Social Solidarity	The promotion of unity and shared responsibility among diverse populations.	Ensures that all members feel included and valued, fostering national cohesion.	Policies that guarantee equal access to resources.	Social welfare benefits in Nordic countries.
Equality in Law	Legal frameworks that guarantee equal rights for all citizens regardless of background.	Crucial for maintaining fairness and preventing discrimination.	Anti-discrimination laws in employment and public services.	The Civil Rights Act of 1964 in the U.S.
International Human Rights Treaties	Agreements between countries to adhere to standardized human rights norms.	Facilitate a global approach to protecting and enhancing human rights.	Ratification and implementation into national laws.	Convention on the Rights of Persons with Disabilities (CRPD).
Gender Equality	Laws and policies aimed at ensuring equal treatment of all genders.	Vital for reducing gender-based disparities and promoting social justice.	Legislation on equal pay and anti-discrimination.	The Gender Equality Act in Sweden.
Disability Rights	Legal protections to ensure people with disabilities have equal opportunities.	Promotes inclusivity and accessibility in all spheres of life.	Laws mandating public accessibility and equal employment.	Americans with Disabilities Act (ADA).

continued on following page

Table 2. Continued

Aspect	Definition	Importance	Application	Example
Economic Rights	Rights that ensure individuals have basic economic security and opportunities.	Fundamental for reducing poverty and promoting economic mobility.	Minimum wage laws and social security benefits.	Universal Basic Income trials.
Cultural Rights	Rights protecting individuals' access to their cultural heritage and practices.	Preserves diverse identities and promotes cultural understanding.	Laws protecting languages and traditions of minority groups.	Indigenous rights protections in Canada.
Children's Rights	Laws that protect the welfare and development of children.	Essential for safeguarding the future and well-being of the next generation.	Legislation on child labor and education rights.	The Right to Education Act in India.
Environmental Justice	Legal frameworks that address the impact of environmental harm on communities.	Crucial for ensuring all communities have a healthy environment.	Laws targeting pollution and ensuring clean water and air.	Clean Air Act enforcement in pollution-heavy areas.
Legal Advocacy	Use of legal systems to promote and protect human rights.	Empowers individuals and groups to claim and enforce their rights.	Strategic litigation and legal aid services.	Litigation efforts by the ACLU on voting rights in the U.S.

CHALLENGES AND BARRIERS

An Analysis of the Areas in Which Human Rights Legislation Falls Short in Terms of its Ability to Advance Social Justice

Human rights legislation is an important tool for advancing social justice, but there are numerous challenges and barriers to the effectiveness of such legislation. While explaining these constraints it is essential to identify the gaps in legislation and outline methods to amplify the societal impact of human rights laws (Ishay, 2022). This has resulted in the adaptation of human rights laws, proposing the solutions to a plethora of challenges such as issues of enforcement, cultural resistance, economic constraints and political interference that the human rights laws may face in bringing about significant change. Lack of Enforcement is one of the major area where human rights legislation fails. All legal frameworks are only as strong as their enforcement mechanisms, yet in the realm of human rights these enforcement mechanisms tend to be weak or unevenly applied. This is, especially, the case in countries where the judiciary is either not independent or under-resourced (Freeman,

2022). Even where a strong legal framework is at place, judicial ineffectiveness or corruption undermine equal application of the law, allowing the most powerful violators of human rights to escape accountability. Without vigorous, even-handed enforcement the most noble of human rights laws may prove nothing but window-dressing, affording little actual protection or redress to victims.

Conflicting human rights legislation, economic and cultural practices are another crucial issues (Tomuschat, 2008). For a number of countries, entrenched social and cultural norms can hinder implementation with regard to human rights laws. For example, civil rights pertaining to gender and sexual minorities run directly against prevailing cultural beliefs in some societies, resulting in backlash from communities and even institutional opposition from government agencies. (Cole, 2022) This kind of cultural resistance makes it difficult for international human rights norms to translate into practice in a given country. Although developing context-sensitive approaches can set off backlash or slow progress in such countries. Economic limitations are another challenge to the enactment of social justice through human rights law. Numerous rights included in international human rights treaties, including the right to health, right to education and to an adequate standard of living, require significant financial investment for their actualization. In some situations, obligations of upholding human rights in a situation where the resources are limited, especially in developing countries, economic priorities take precedence which results in suppression of the rights (Harris, 2021). As a result, economic downturns, poverty, and inequality hinder human rights laws from realizing their intended social justice aims. Political factors are also important to the effectiveness of human rights legislation. The adoption and implementation of human rights legislation can be shaped or undermined by political will or its absence. Governments might be unwilling to introduce or implement laws that may constrain their own power, disrupt the status quo, or look bad for their political bases (Simmons, 2023).

Human rights legislation might be especially at risk if such governments derive power from authoritarian or populist regimes, and in such countries, the government may be prone to circumventing or violating international human rights obligations altogether to remain in control (or prevent dissenters). In addition, since the human rights legislation is a global phenomenon, it may at times come into conflict with the principle of national sovereignty. Countries might disregard foreign demands to adhere to internationally accepted human right principles by considering them to be violations of their attachment. This can result in a selective treatment of human rights law, or reservations to treaty obligations limiting the nature and quality of human rights protection across the globe (Freeman, 2022). Human rights legislation as a tool for achieving social justice may often encounter opposition, making it an imperfect mechanism. Tackling these issues requires a multi-faceted approach that includes stronger enforcement mechanisms, broader political will, cultural sensitivity in implementation of laws and budgeting (Ramcharan, 2021). In order to fully harness the human rights legislation as propelling forces for social justice and equity, scholars of law and social movements must confront and overcome these barriers.

THE DISCUSSION OF CONTENTIOUS EXAMPLES IN WHICH HUMAN RIGHTS LEGISLATION HAS FAILED TO BRING JUSTICE

The examples of human rights legislation where the intended justice has not been served are contentious, but serve to highlight how complicated it can be to introduce and enforce these laws. It is often high-profile cases or systemic surprises that show that human rights are mere paper tigers, no matter how many laws exist on the books (Ife, Soldatić & Briskman, 2022). These case studies will raise awareness of the limitations and challenges of human rights legislation in different contexts. Perhaps the most glaring case of the failure of human rights legislation to obtain justice is that of the Rohingya in Myanmar (Faye, 2021). The systematic persecution of the Rohingya Muslim minority in Myanmar has led to serious human rights violations, such as mass killings and rapes and forced displacements, which have been described by some international observers as ethnic cleansing or genocide, despite international outcry and condemnation. The short answer is that the international community has very limited capacity to change Myanmar's domestic policies with respect to human rights or indeed to change the domestic behaviour of a country in general without the internal support of the country in question (Zahed, 2021). This illustrates the difficulties in trying to intervene in the domestic behaviour of sovereign nations without the consent or cooperation of the country in question.

One of the most controversial ones though is the sensitive police brutality cases in some countries like the United States. Even though there are laws in place to protect civil rights and to prevent discrimination, there exists a long and sordid history of law enforcement officers who have been able to justify their use of excessive force with little or no accountability (Anwary, 2022). The killings of people like George Floyd and Breonna Taylor led to international protests and demands for justice, revealing favouritism within so many judicial and police systems as they fail to bring offenders to justice and damaging faith in human rights laws. Another example of ineffective human rights legislation can be found in Russia, where political dissidents and journalists are treated atrociously. Government critics, such as Alexei Navalny, have ended up in jail, been poisoned and prosecuted, apparently as punishment for their state defiance (Right, 2023). The Russian government's behaviour evokes severe human rights abuses, but the domestic legal systems are often powerless to protect those rights, and international sanctions or condemnations, so far, found little traction in influencing Russian internal policies. The example of Saudi Arabia and its track record on women's rights also highlights failures in human rights justice. The country still imposes a male guardianship system that many say curtails women's freedoms, even after recent reforms allowing women to drive. The case of Rahaf Mohammed, who fled Saudi Arabia citing abusive treatment by her family and fear she would die if she returned, drew international scrutiny to the limits of reforms in protecting women's rights and freedoms in deeply conservative societies.

Finally, impunity for war crimes and crimes against humanity in places such as Syria is a glaring oversight in upholding international human rights (Zagaris & Plachta, 2023). There is overwhelming evidence of atrocity crimes committed by multiple actors during this conflict, including the Syrian government and the so-called Islamic State (ISIS), but a chronic lack of accountability by the international community. Political complexities, a lack of cooperation from the Syrian government, and veto powers in international bodies such as the U.N. Security Council have all contributed to a justice gap, where victims perceive few, if any, means of recourse for the violations suffered (Sarkin, 2021). These controversial instances have mirrored the wider challenges with human rights laws around the world: enforcement problems, political pressure, cultural roadblocks and the challenges of international law. They highlight how critical it is to see strong international collaboration and enhanced domestic pledges to respect human rights standards, stressing that human rights legislation is important — but without concerted implementation and earnest political motivation to deliver on justice, they will have limited impact (Chetail & Bauloz, 2016).

The Political, Social, and Economic Obstacles That Stand in the Way of the Application of Human Rights

There are multitude of political, social and economic challenges that hinder the application of human rights on a large scale. These challenges are complex and multi-layered, often interlinked, and differ across contexts and geography (Palazzo, 2022). It is vital to know what these roadblocks are to find means and modalities to navigate them better and to make human rights legislation more effective.

The absence of political willingness is one of the gravest obstructions to the implementation of human rights. Such spoilers include governments that are in different forms – such as authoritarian regimes or unstable political contexts – can disrupt or deny the implementation of human rights norms in many countries as such governments do not have an interest in supporting the norms that can potentially negate their authority or question their power (Savage, 2021). Political elites might worry that strong human rights protections can embolden the opposition, inspire social protest, or result in international scrutiny. Moreover, in democracies, populist movements can lead to a deterioration of human rights standards by exploiting nationalist, xenophobic, or anti-establishment sentiments (Kumari, 2023). Additionally, corruption in politics also fuels the systemic problems by enabling a culture of impunity for human rights violations, and eroding accountability for bad governance.

Entrenched biases, cultural traditions, and customs that may conflict with respect for human rights. For instance, in various societies, patriarchal norms and attitudes can hinder the effective enactment of laws designed to advance gender equality and safeguard women from violence. Racial, ethnic or caste discrimination could also be entrenched in society, making it very difficult to inspire the anti-discrimination laws late and their effective enforcement. It is not easy to change such social norms and values, but it typically takes up long-term educational efforts and grassroots advocacy to change people`s perceptions and behaviours.

Human rights are also significantly limited on account of economic realities. Developing countries might face the twin challenges of economic underdevelopment and improving human rights protections (Blokker, 2024). In particular, limited financial resources can render the establishment of adequate social services and the funding of the legal systems and enforcement mechanisms critical to supporting human rights impossible. Economic instability, like that associated with global financial crises, can distract and reduce the availability of resources for human rights projects and efforts that address more immediate economic survival concerns (Ife et al., 2022). Additionally, within a globalized economy, intense pressure from multinational corporations and global trade agreements can dominate local considerations, pushing for economic considerations over human rights models.

These political, social and economic factors interact to produce a landscape wherein human rights are contested and undermined. Combating these challenges necessitates a comprehensive strategy — one that involves global collaboration, grassroots activism and persistent advocacy. This could involve diplomatic pressure, economic incentives, capacity building, public education campaigns, legal reforms, among others, to create an enabling environment for human rights to blossom (Stone, 2024). Thus, although the paradigm for the promotion and protection of human rights is firmly grounded in international law and practice, the realization of these rights remains hindered by political, social, and economic obstacles. Tackling in these obstacles is important for the progress of human rights (HR) globally, which requires a complex and continuous endeavour of all parties engaged in the campaign (Ratner et al., 2009).

Table 3. Challenges and barriers in human rights law

Challenge Type	Description	Impact	Examples	Possible Solutions
Political Barriers	Lack of political will or authoritarian governance obstructing human rights legislation.	Stifles the adoption and enforcement of laws protecting human rights.	Authoritarian regimes suppressing freedom of speech and assembly.	International pressure and advocacy to promote democratic governance.
Economic Constraints	Limited financial resources hinder the implementation of human rights protections.	Prevents effective delivery of essential services like healthcare and education.	Developing nations struggling to fund social programs.	Aid and economic policies that prioritize human development.
Social Resistance	Entrenched social norms and biases that conflict with human rights.	Delays or blocks the enactment and enforcement of progressive legislation.	Cultural practices like child marriage and gender discrimination.	Education and awareness campaigns to shift public perception.
Enforcement Issues	Weak judicial systems and lack of effective enforcement mechanisms.	Human rights laws exist but are not practically applied or enforced.	Ineffective policing and judicial corruption.	Strengthening legal systems and international monitoring.
Cultural Conflicts	Cultural practices and traditions that undermine human rights standards.	Leads to selective adoption or outright rejection of international human rights norms.	Resistance to gender equality laws in conservative societies.	Cultural dialogue and gradual integration of human rights into local norms.
Resource Allocation	Inequitable distribution of resources affecting the realization of economic and social rights.	Exacerbates inequality and hampers poverty alleviation efforts.	Unequal access to clean water and healthcare in impoverished regions.	Policy reforms to ensure fair distribution of resources and international aid.

FUTURE DIRECTIONS

With an outlook toward the future of human rights legislation, certain trends and emerging technologies are likely to redefine how these laws are implemented and enforced. First, there is a growing acknowledgment of digital rights as part of the human rights regime and questions of internet access, data privacy and free speech online (Saini, 2023). With the evolution of technology and also the legal implications, it is necessary to ensure that the law protects the rights of individuals in the digital realm from surveillance, censorship, and unequal access to digital resources. Second, technology will allow human rights laws to operate with remarkable efficiency (Right, 2023). Emerging technologies, like artificial intelligence (AI) and blockchain, hold great promise for preventing human rights abuses, and making the monitoring of such abuses more effective and transparent. AI can process large datasets to identify patterns of abuse, while blockchain technology could establish immutable records of human rights abuses, enhancing accountability (Vyas, 2019a). In addition, technology has enabled unprecedented levels of transnational cooperation in the area of human rights. Social media and communication platforms not only facilitated the ability of activists and organizations to connect and mobilize across borders but also made the dissemination of the information about human rights abuses to a global audience possible in real-time (Ramcharan, 2021). This increased access allows for improved monitoring of situations by international bodies and non-governmental organizations and better co-ordination of responses.

The International Criminal Court has started to use satellite imagery and social media analysis to compile evidence for trials, illustrating the potential of technology tools to supplement traditional legal frameworks. AI and transnational dynamics are increasingly affecting human rights protections, so the future of human rights legislation is, inescapably, tied inextricably to the future of technology and the role international collaboration can play in shaping the ethic around protection. This includes not only the evolution of current laws but the emergence of new frameworks responsive to the ever more intricate reality of the world today (Ife et al., 2022). With greater access to the tools technology provides, and working collaboratively, great strides can be made towards improving human rights enforcement worldwide to form a stronger, more dysfunctional barrier between humanity and inalienable rights violations everywhere on earth.

CONCLUSION

This chapter is about the development of human rights law as important to the creation of fairer, more just societies. These laws can be transformative, correcting decades or centuries of systemic injustices, protecting marginalized, vulnerable populations, and changing the rules of the game for society to make it more equitable and expansive. Human rights law has also wrought deep legal and social changes that have made the lives of untold millions better, on issues of race and gender equality, and for people with disabilities and marginalized people. However, these laws are not without challenges in effectiveness. However, obstacles like enforcement, cultural resistance, and economic constraints have emerged as critical barriers whose effects can undermine the impact of human rights laws. But to realize their full potential, human rights laws must be backed up by enough mechanisms for enforcement, cultural acceptance and financial investment. True social justice may indeed involve radical change, but those who have not yet gained from the corpus of human rights law view it as a spark of hope for tomorrow, not a destination. The twin powers of technology and international collaboration have been instrumental, unlocking creative new ways to make human rights enforcement more effective and broader in reach.

There are few recommendations in enhancing the role of law to achieve a more equal and just society. We will globally coordinate our efforts to strengthen the competence and independence of judiciaries so that human rights laws are equally applied. Another measure discretion is education and advocacy, to encourage the public in variety of world of human rights figures to look for their rights. Third, it is essential to foster international cooperation, both to encourage states to adhere to global human rights standards and to assist them in realizing those standards. Ultimately, there can be new, novel ways to track and report human rights violations, as well as keep the law current with new opportunities and new challenges with the use of the latest technology.

On balance, even as human rights law moves inalienably out from the rhetoric of universal maxims, this mobility may disguise the hazards of the task it holds to reproduce an increasingly displaced grammar of rights, a claim which works to let others more seamlessly move between what proves more effective and what is in greater need of addressing within existing structures. This overall transformation of human rights laws in terms of its impact, can be achieved through the complement of legal context with more effective enforcement, better education, world advocacy and emerging technologies. It's only with this diverse approach that societies can eventually aim for genuine equity and justice for everyone.

REFERENCES

Akhundov, A. (2025). The Role of Ethics in Modern Technology Development. *Porta Universorum, 1*(4), 169–177. DOI: 10.69760/portuni.0104017

Avelino, F. (2021). Theories of power and social change. Power contestations and their implications for research on social change and innovation. *Journal of Political Power, 14*(3), 425–448. DOI: 10.1080/2158379X.2021.1875307

Banchio, P. R. (2025). Introduction to human rights: An overview of principles, evolution and contemporary relevance. EVOLUTION AND CONTEMPORARY RELEVANCE Table of Contents (February 24, 2025).

Bandi, S., & Nandeshwar, J. (2024). Legal Status under Family Law of LGBT Community in India: A Review of Research on the Status of Same Sex Marriage Pre and Post Navtej Singh Johar v. Union of India (2018). Issue 4 Int'l JL Mgmt. & Human., 7, 1603.

Blokker, P. (2024). Populism, human rights, and (un-) civil society. In *The Rule of Law in the EU: Challenges, Actors and Strategies* (pp. 73–90). Springer International Publishing. DOI: 10.1007/978-3-031-55322-6_5

Branham, E. R. (2025). Ability, advocacy, and access: Pre-law students and the Americans with Disabilities Act.

Casla, K., & Sandner, M. (2024). Solidarity as foundation for economic, social and cultural rights. *Human Rights Law Review, 24*(2), ngae011. DOI: 10.1093/hrlr/ngae011

Chakravarty, S. (2023). Enforcement of social and economic rights: South Asian judicial discourses (Doctoral dissertation, © University of Dhaka).

Fallah, S. N., & Judijanto, L. (2025). The influence of social economic law on social welfare: Literature review and policy implications. *International Journal of Finance & Economics, 2*(1), 8–15.

Faye, M. (2021). A forced migration from Myanmar to Bangladesh and beyond: Humanitarian response to Rohingya refugee crisis. *Journal of International Humanitarian Action, 6*(1), 1–7. DOI: 10.1186/s41018-021-00098-4

Freeman, M. (2022). Human rights. John Wiley & Sons.Hamelink, C. J. (2025). International human rights. In Global Health and Human Rights (pp. 7–26). Routledge.

Hantzopoulos, M., & Bajaj, M. (2021). *Educating for peace and human rights: An introduction*. Bloomsbury Publishing. DOI: 10.5040/9781350129757

Ife, J., Soldatić, K., & Briskman, L. (2022). *Human rights and social work.* Cambridge University Press. DOI: 10.1017/9781108903868

Ishay, M. R. (2022). *The human rights reader: Major political essays, speeches, and documents from ancient times to the present.* Routledge. DOI: 10.4324/9781003121404

Kampourakis, I. (2022). Legal theory in search of social transformation. *European Law Open, 1*(4), 808–821. DOI: 10.1017/elo.2023.15

Kanade, M. (2024). The right to international solidarity and the right to development. In *Research Handbook on International Solidarity and the Law* (pp. 122–142). Edward Elgar Publishing. DOI: 10.4337/9781803923758.00009

Khan, A. S. I. F., Amjad, S. O. H. A. I. L., & Usman, M. U. H. A. M. M. A. D. (2020). The evolution of human rights law in the age of globalization. Pakistan Journal of Law, Analysis and Wisdom.

Kilibarda, P. (2022). Torture and other cruel, inhuman or degrading treatment or punishment in international law: Towards a generic definition? In *Research Handbook on Human Rights and Humanitarian Law* (pp. 435–461). Edward Elgar Publishing.

Krayer, W. L., & Note, P. S. (2025). To make men free. *Legal Writing, 29*, 305 306.

Kumari, S. (2023). Social justice through labour legislation. *National Journal of Labour and Industrial Law, 6*(2), 14–23.

Lesch, M., & Reiners, N. (2023). Informal human rights law-making: How treaty bodies use 'General Comments' to develop international law. *Global Constitutionalism, 12*(2), 378–401. DOI: 10.1017/S2045381723000023

Molaba, T. I. (2025). The concept of transformative constitutionalism in post-apartheid South Africa. *Perspectives of Law and Public Administration, 14*(1).

Molnar, P. (2019). Technology on the margins: AI and global migration management from a human rights perspective. *Cambridge International Law Journal, 8*(2), 305–330. DOI: 10.4337/cilj.2019.02.07

Mondal, A., & Islam, N. (2023). The Right to Education Act, 2009 in India after a decade: Appraising achievements and exploring unkept promises. Education 3-13, 51(1), 87–106.

Müller, A. (2023). *States, human rights, and distant strangers: The normative justification of extraterritorial obligations in human rights law.* Routledge. DOI: 10.4324/9781003347095

Nour, M. A. (2024). From politics to social justice: A political analysis of social policy. Politik Psikoloji Dergisi, 4(1).

Okedele, P. O., Aziza, O. R., Oduro, P., & Ishola, A. O. (2024). Human rights, climate justice, and environmental law: Bridging international legal standards for social equity. *Human Rights (Chicago, Ill.)*, *20*(12), 232–241.

Palazzo, N. (2022). Comprehensive security and LGBTQ rights. *The Review of Faith & International Affairs*, *20*(4), 54–61. DOI: 10.1080/15570274.2022.2139529

Peretko, A. (2024). Protection of LGBTQIA+ rights in armed conflict: How (and whether) to 'queer' the crime against humanity of persecution in international criminal law? *Leiden Journal of International Law*, *37*(1), 251–273. DOI: 10.1017/S0922156523000523

Prasanna, S., Ameen, A., Saurav, K., Singh, D. B., Tripathy, A., Sharma, P., & Sanjaya, K. (2023). *Empowerment and equality navigating human rights law in a complex world*. Institute of Legal Education.

Reiners, N. (2024). The power of interpersonal relationships: A socio-legal approach to international institutions and human rights advocacy. *Review of International Studies*, *50*(2), 252–270. DOI: 10.1017/S0260210523000438

Right, H. I. (2023). Promotion and protection of all human rights, civil, political, economic, social and cultural rights, including the right to development: Written statement/submitted by Human Is Right.

Roberts, A., Resh, W., Basu, R., Onyango, G., Sullivan, H., Peci, A., Kapucu, N., Schomaker, R., & Mele, V. (2024). Roundtable: How do we connect public administration and human rights? *Perspectives on Public Management and Governance*, *7*(1–2), 1–12. DOI: 10.1093/ppmgov/gvad010

Saaida, M. (2024). Criticism of the liberal theory of international politics.

Saini, M., Sengupta, E., Singh, M., Singh, H., & Singh, J. (2023). Sustainable development goal for quality education (SDG 4): A study on SDG 4 to extract the pattern of association among the indicators of SDG 4 employing a genetic algorithm. *Education and Information Technologies*, *28*(2), 2031–2069. DOI: 10.1007/s10639-022-11265-4 PMID: 35975216

Sarkin, J. J. (2021). *The conflict in Syria and the failure of international law to protect people globally: Mass atrocities, enforced disappearances and arbitrary detentions*. Routledge. DOI: 10.4324/9781003198628

Savage, M. (2021). *The return of inequality: Social change and the weight of the past*. Harvard University Press.

Taghvaee, V. M., Arani, A. A., & Agheli, L. (2022). Sustainable development spillover effects between North America and MENA: Analyzing the integrated sustainability perspective. *Environmental and Sustainability Indicators, 14*, 100182. DOI: 10.1016/j.indic.2022.100182

Vijeyarasa, R. (2021). Quantifying CEDAW: Concrete tools for enhancing accountability for women's rights. *Harvard Human Rights Journal, 34*, 37.

Walters, B. R. (2021). The measure of CEDAW: Religion, religious freedom, and the rights of women. *Annual Review of the Sociology of Religion, 12*, 241–270. DOI: 10.1163/9789004468085_013

Weale, A. (2023). *Equality and social policy*. Routledge. DOI: 10.4324/9781003369127

Werthmann, C. (2021). *Informal urbanization in Latin America: Collaborative transformations of public spaces*. Routledge. DOI: 10.4324/9781003089797

Wojtara, M. (2023). Analyzing the efficacy and utility of the Americans with Disabilities Act of 1990 on college students with disabilities. University of Michigan Undergraduate Research Journal, 16.

Zagaris, B., & Plachta, M. (2023). Crimes against humanity and war crimes. *International Enforcement Law Reporter, 39*, 405.

KEY TERMS AND DEFINITIONS

Human Rights: Inalienable rights inherent to all human beings regardless of nationality, ethnicity, gender, or religion. These include the rights to life, liberty, education, and freedom from torture and discrimination.

Social Justice: A concept promoting fair and equitable treatment in society by ensuring access to rights, resources, and opportunities for all individuals, particularly marginalized or disadvantaged groups.

Equity: The principle of recognizing different circumstances and allocating resources or opportunities accordingly to achieve fair outcomes. Unlike equality, equity addresses historical and structural disadvantages.

Legal Mobilization: The process of using legal systems, courts, and legal advocacy to assert and protect rights, often by marginalized communities seeking justice and reform.

Normative Development: A process through which laws and policies shape and reflect evolving societal values, gradually transforming social norms and expectations toward justice and equality.

Spillover Effect: The phenomenon whereby the promotion of rights in one domain (e.g., political rights) leads to improvements in other domains (e.g., economic or social rights), reflecting the interconnected nature of rights.

International Human Rights Treaties: Formal agreements between states that establish standards and obligations for the protection and promotion of human rights, such as CEDAW, CRC, and the ICCPR.

Chapter 11
AI Governance for Sustainable Development: Lessons for Malaysia From the EU AI Act

Shu Ning Yap
https://orcid.org/0009-0000-3801-561X
Veritas University College, Malaysia

ABSTRACT

Artificial intelligence (AI) is transforming society with enormous potential for innovation and economic growth. Nevertheless, this advancement also raises complex legal, ethical and social issues that require strong governance. This chapter evaluates AI governance in Malaysia from a sustainable development perspective which concentrates on its alignment with the United Nations Sustainable Development Goals (SDGs), particularly Goal 9, Goal 16, and Goal 17. This chapter also pinpoints regulatory gaps in data protection, AI-specific legislation and accountability as well as compares them with the global comprehensive AI regulation, the EU AI Act. The chapter uses doctrinal and comparative legal analysis to propose a possible strategy for incorporating SDG principles into AI governance in Malaysia. This chapter aims to provide actionable insights that line up the legal frameworks with the SDGs and to serve as a resource for scholars, policymakers, and legal professionals at the intersection of technology and sustainable development, thereby contributing to the global dialogue.

DOI: 10.4018/979-8-3373-1792-2.ch011

INTRODUCTION

Artificial intelligence (AI) technologies have evolved rapidly and brought significant changes to all sectors around the world, which influence and change how industries operate, how governments make decisions and how individuals interact with this technology (Trabelsi, 2024). Thus, the flourishing AI technologies have brought unprecedented opportunities for innovation, sustainable development, and economic growth (van Wynsberghe, 2021). However, AI is a technology that mirrors human learning, understanding, creativity, autonomy, problem-solving, and decision-making. Devices that support AI can observe, recognise objects, understand, and respond to human language, as well as learn from the new data, providing a comprehensive recommendation to take independent actions (Stryker & Kavlakoglu, 2024). Generative AI has become a focus in AI research in 2024, which is a technology that can produce creative materials and relies on deep learning models (Stryker & Scapicchio, 2024). This advanced technology has benefits in speeding up the task given, like restlessly detecting cyber-attacks to ensure the data is safe, reducing the unnecessary costs, and allowing the employee to focus more on high-value tasks (Lazic, 2019). Unfortunately, it has caused many uncertainties for the governments and regulatory bodies around the world, as its drawbacks were huge, like societal bias, AI-assisted cybercrime, cyber-attacks on AI systems, trolling, and misuse of the AI to cause data breaches (Ijlal, 2022). Therefore, the governments and the regulatory bodies worldwide have incorporated AI into the national development plans without stopping, even though it poses ethical, legal and security challenges (Demaidi, 2023). AI governance – the frameworks, policies and regulatory mechanisms that ensure the safe, ethical and responsible use of AI – has become a vital strategy for all countries in tackling these issues (Batool et al., 2025).

Malaysia is actively embracing AI without any exceptions and sees it as a catalyst for innovation under national initiatives. For example, the Malaysia Digital Economy Blueprint (MyDIGITAL), the National Fourth Industrial Revolution (4IR) Policy (Economic Planning Unit, 2021), the National AI Roadmap 2021 to 2025 (Malaysian Science and Technology Information Centre, 2023), the National AI Governance and Code of Ethics Guidelines (Malaysian Science and Technology Information Centre, 2024), as well as the not yet published National Cloud Policy (Minister's Office of Malaysia Official Website, 2024). However, the current legal and regulatory landscape of Malaysia is still inadequate to tackle all these problems posed by the AI, even with the forward-looking ambitions of these policies (Hossain et al., 2024). Presently, Malaysia relies on a fragmented set of legislations and regulations to tackle unique risks posed by AI. For instance, the Personal Data Protection Act 2010 (Act 709), the Consumer Protection Act 1999 (Act 599), the Sale of Goods Act 1957 (Act 382), the Contracts Act 1950 (Act 136), the Computer Crimes Act 1997

(Act 563), the Patents Act 1983 (Act 291), the Patents Regulations 1986 (P.U.(A) 327/86), the Copyright Act 1987 (Act 332), and the Cyber Security Act 2024 (Act 854) (Heu & Edhan, 2023; Toh & Yee, 2024). Unfortunately, these legislations and regulations cannot effectively address the risks that are uniquely posed by AI systems, like algorithmic bias, accountability gaps, autonomous decision-making, and generative content (Hossain et al., 2024; Regnier & Poropat, 2024a; Totlani, 2023).

The risks of inadequate governance are causing distress to everyone in society. This is because the former MSNBC presenter, Mehdi Hassan, urged for AI legislation at the National Human Capital Conference and Exhibition to avoid the things that had happened in some countries (Reza, 2024). Malaysia has suffered a 1,000% increase in deepfake incidents between 2022 and 2023 (Fam, 2024). Nonetheless, Malaysia has the Communications and Multimedia Act 1998 (Act 588); there is still a significant gap in this new type of cybercrime (Farhan et al., 2024). The cybersecurity report 2024 from PIKOM has shown the cybersecurity threats for high-risk sectors like financial services industries, healthcare, energy, and even critical infrastructure covering government, banking, transportation, healthcare, and energy (PIKOM, 2024). Nonetheless, the use of generative AI for cyber defence has risen and will even rise more in Malaysia, and soon it will be the next trend to use in most sectors. As the 2023's PwC report shows, 83% of the Malaysian respondents will use generative AI for cyber defence in the next twelve months. While 50% of them have used it for cyber risk detection and mitigation. There are also 37% of them who have seen the benefits of the cyber programs because of generative AI (Ng et al., 2023). At the same time, Malaysia has taken part in international and regional initiatives like the "Recommendation on the Ethics of AI" issued by the United Nations Educational, Scientific, and Cultural Organisation (UNESCO) (United Nations, 2021) and the ASEAN Guide on AI Governance and Ethics released by the Association of Southeast Asian Nations (ASEAN, 2024), which encourage voluntary guidelines on responsible deployment of AI. However, the lack of regulation can lead to a myriad of risks, including ethical dilemmas, biases in decision-making, and threats to privacy and security (Judge et al., 2025). Therefore, several issues like protecting people's fundamental rights, safety, and health; even data; as well as guaranteeing accountability and transparency and controlling cybersecurity risk should be listed in the law (Hossain et al., 2024; Regnier & Poropat, 2024a). Fortunately, the Science, Technology, and Innovation Minister, Chang Lih Kang, has expressed that the long-term goal is to codify the National AI Governance and Code of Ethics Guidelines into an enforceable law, though it is not currently the legislative agenda; hence, the effectiveness of this AI code of ethics is vital, and it serves as a guide to identify the key areas that require regulation (Santani, 2024; Sharon, 2025).

Conversely, the European Union has become a pioneer and global leader in regulating AI technologies, which formed the Artificial Intelligence Act (EU AI Act) (Mammonas, 2024). The EU AI Act has adopted a risk-based approach to categorise AI applications or systems according to their potential impact on human rights and the public interest, at the same time integrating the principles of transparency, accountability, and data governance (Madiega, 2024). In addition, the EU AI Act is representing a shift from soft ethical frameworks to a binding legal obligation and provides a model for right-based preventive governance (Edwards, 2022; Hagendorff, 2020). Hence, the legal design of the EU AI Act, which focuses on human rights and integration with sustainable development principles, has its valuable reference to Malaysia in seeking to regulate AI without stifling innovation. This chapter aims to explore how Malaysia can build a sustainable and ethical AI governance framework by referring to the experience of the EU AI Act and a particular focus on promoting the United Nations Sustainable Development Goals (SDGs), especially Goal SDG 9 (Industry, Innovation, and Infrastructure), SDG 16 (Peace, Justice, and Strong Institutions), and SDG 17 (Partnerships for the Goals) (Department of Economic and Social Affairs Sustainable Development, 2025; Sætra, 2021). This chapter adopts a doctrinal and comparative legal research methodology by utilising primary legal texts, policy documents, and academic literature from Malaysia and the European Union. It also analyses the current legal and policy framework in Malaysia and uses a comparative method to examine the structure of the EU AI Act. This approach enables the chapter to identify governance gaps in Malaysia and to make practical, context-specific recommendations for lining up AI regulation with the SDGs.

UNDERSTANDING AI GOVERNANCE: GLOBAL AND REGIONAL CONTEXT

Understanding AI and Its Evolution

AI is a technology or system that mirrors human intelligence, like learning, understanding, creativity, autonomy, problem-solving, and decision-making (Madiega, 2024). Initially, the main function of AI is to recognise patterns, classify data, make predictions, and process much information to make accurate decisions (Sadhu Singh & Segaran, 2020). Meanwhile, AI has eventually evolved from the narrow rule-based systems to advanced data-driven models that can perform tasks with increasing autonomy and complexity, even self-learning (Sadhu Singh & Segaran, 2020). Over the past few years, generative artificial intelligence (generative AI) has turned out to be a powerful subfield that enables machines to generate original content based on vast amounts of training data, which include text, images, music, audio and software code (Cao et al., 2023). Therefore, AI is designed for decision-making and recognising patterns from the input data, while Gen AI focuses on content creation and generating new original data that replicates human beings. Thus, this dual capability has significantly broadened the scope of AI applications. At the same time, it is also introducing problems of ethics, legality and governance which relate to authorship, accountability and bias (Sadhu Singh & Segaran, 2021). This shows the urgent need for proactive measures to minimise the abuse stated above and support innovation (Hossain et al., 2024).

Global AI Governance Models

Governments and international organisations throughout the world have started to concede the urgency of establishing legal and ethical frameworks to govern AI. The United Nations has called for a global AI governance coordinated approach to draw attention to the need to ensure that all humanity has benefitted and does not deepen existing inequalities with AI technologies. The adoption of the Recommendation on the Ethics of Artificial Intelligence published by UNESCO in 2021 was a major accomplishment which promoted and stressed principles like human-centred values, privacy and fairness. This Recommendation on the Ethics of Artificial Intelligence has been supported by more than 190 member states, which include Malaysia. Likewise, the Organisation for Economic Co-operation and Development (OECD) published its AI principles in 2019 and updated them in 2024, which mainly focused on the principles of transparency and explainability of AI systems, robustness, accountability, inclusive growth, sustainable development, and well-being, as well as rule of law, human rights, and democratic values, which many member states have adopted as the basis for their national AI strategies. These frameworks provide essential ethical and legal guidelines that are growing to influence national strategies.

Besides, there are different approaches to be taken in developing AI governance frameworks for each jurisdiction. For instance, the United States has largely adopted a sector-specific and market-driven model that focuses on promoting innovation while relying on existing laws and voluntary guidelines (Said & Nabilah, 2024). Conversely, China stresses state-led control, which includes AI in its national development strategy while deploying regulations to strengthen data sovereignty and social stability at the same time (Said & Nabilah, 2024). Among these leading players, the European Union holds a unique position in developing legally binding AI legislation – the EU AI Act – which was introduced in 2021 and finalised in 2024 (Regnier & Poropat, 2024b). The EU AI Act establishes a horizontal legal framework that classifies AI systems according to their risk level and imposes specific obligations on high-risk AI systems, especially on critical infrastructure, law enforcement, biometric identification, education and employment (Madiega, 2024).

The EU AI Act has gone beyond the ethical aspirations by inserting enforceable obligations into law (Edwards, 2022; Hagendorff, 2020). It requires high-risk AI systems to meet standards for data quality, transparency, human oversight and cybersecurity (Edwards, 2022). Remarkably, it totally prohibits certain harmful uses of AI, such as social scoring and certain real-time biometric monitoring (Edwards, 2022). This risk-based approach ensures that regulation is proportionate and focused on the most probably harmful systems (Madiega, 2024). Besides, it also reflects the commitment of the European Union to fundamental rights and democratic accountability, which closely lines up with SDG 16.

The Role of Ethical Principles and International Frameworks

There are numerous international and regional ethical frameworks published worldwide to guide the development of AI. Apart from UNESCO's Recommendation on the Ethics of Artificial Intelligence and OECD AI Principles, it still has the publication of the Ethical Guidelines for Trustworthy AI in 2019 by the European Union (Madiega, 2019). The guidelines enumerate seven essential requirements: human agency and oversight, robustness and safety, privacy and data governance, transparency, diversity, non-discrimination and fairness, societal and environmental well-being, and accountability (Madiega, 2019). Although the ethical guidelines are crucial, they are insufficient to address the growing challenges posed by AI systems, particularly those with opaque algorithms, bias, and unintended societal harms (Cath, 2018; Hagendorff, 2020). The European Union acknowledges that ethical guidelines lack enforceability and are not effective in mitigating risks without regulatory oversight (Hagendorff, 2020). Hagendorff (2020) stressed that many software engineering students and developers do not follow ethical codes, and companies are eager to monetise AI, making ethical guidelines redundant. This has led to the urgency of AI regulation proposals, such as the EU AI Act, which focuses on risk management, transparency, and accountability in AI development and deployment (Edwards, 2022; Hagendorff, 2020; Madiega, 2024).

Meanwhile, in the ASEAN region, the ASEAN Guide on AI Governance and Ethics released by the Association of Southeast Asian Nations has also promoted ethical AI development, concurrently respected national diversity and recommended transparency, fairness and cross-border cooperation (ASEAN, 2024). Despite Malaysia has standing up for these frameworks and incorporating all these principles in the national initiatives like the National AI Roadmap 2021 to 2025 and the National AI Governance and Code of Ethics Guidelines, all of these frameworks and even the national initiatives still remain on a voluntary basis; hence, there are no enforceable binding effects like codified legislation.

AI Development and Industry Application in Malaysia Across Sectors

Malaysia has been quickly embracing AI technologies in various sectors. Before the outbreak, AI development in Malaysia was primarily exploratory, policy-driven and industry-specific solutions. During the pandemic, AI adoption has expanded in key areas like digital health (the *MySejahtera* contact tracing app), online education and logistics (Hossain et al., 2024; Khambali Hambali et al., 2022; Mizan & Norman, 2024). Meanwhile, the ongoing progress of AI adoption is maintained after the pandemic and even expands to a wider range of government digital services, automated infrastructure and smart public transport systems (Economic Planning Unit, 2021). Then, the rise of AI technology like ChatGPT in the post-pandemic era has reshaped industries, raising concerns about the potential for super AI (Sadhu Singh & Segaran, 2020). Hence, it opens the gaps of AI governance.

AI and generative AI are revolutionising various industries in Malaysia, particularly in public health. The *MySejahtera* application, which uses AI for symptom tracking, vaccine distribution, and telemedicine, has made significant progress during the pandemic (Khambali Hambali et al., 2022). Post-pandemic, the app can monitor health and make appointments for hospitals and clinics. Malaysia also introduced the *Stethee Pro*, the world's first AI stethoscope system, in 2018, to detect a patient's lung or heart issues (Hossain et al., 2024). Besides, the education sector is leveraging online platforms and AI to enhance personalised learning experiences, especially for students who have lost the opportunity to attend school or university. Teachers and lecturers are utilising AI tools to improve remote teaching efficiency, administrative operations, and student interactions, ensuring continuity of education during and after the pandemic. Moreover, there are 17 Malaysian universities offering AI academic programmes at both undergraduate and postgraduate levels (Malaysian Science and Technology Information Centre, 2023).

The use of AI in business, banking, and finance sectors has significantly improved efficiency. CIMB Bank introduced EVA, an AI-driven chatbot, while HSBC Bank introduced Amy, a chatbot that can understand both English and simplified Chinese. RHB Bank, in collaboration with RinggitPlus, launched My RHB Easy, a chatbot that simplifies loan applications. Furthermore, Hong Leong Bank Berhad introduced HALI, a virtual assistant, to improve operational efficiency (Malaysian Science and Technology Information Centre, 2024). Additionally, fraud detection and credit risk assessment innovations have made the banking experience more secure. In addition, Seeloz Inc., a Silicon Valley-based AI company, has launched the Supply Chain Automation Suite (SCAS), which includes Autonomous Requirements Planning (ARP) (Malaysian Science and Technology Information Centre, 2023). Petronas has transitioned from condition-based monitoring to predictive maintenance using

AI in the oil and gas industry. VROC AI expedited failure root cause validation on Dulang, resulting in a cost avoidance of RM 15 million and a factor of 2000 (Malaysian Science and Technology Information Centre, 2023).

On top of that, the Malaysian Digital Economy Corporation (MDEC) has introduced the Digital AGTech, or eLadang initiative to improve agricultural yields, reduce operational costs, and accelerate digital adoption (Hossain et al., 2024). In the telecommunications sector, Telekom Malaysia Berhad has partnered with Huawei Technologies (M) Sdn Bhd to enhance its cloud infrastructure via TM ONE (Malaysian Science and Technology Information Centre, 2023). AirAsia, a leading transportation company, has implemented AI and chatbots to improve customer service and operational efficiency. In 2019, AVA was launched for flight reservations, seat selections and check-in processes. In 2023, 'Ask Bo' was introduced for real-time conversations and live information sharing to enhance guest autonomy (Malaysian Science and Technology Information Centre, 2024). Likewise, AI and generative AI are also being used in various sectors to solve cyber threats and strengthen cyber defence (Ng et al., 2023).

In addition to these sectors, the judicial industry is also trying to embrace AI. The Malaysian judiciary has introduced AI in lower courts to expedite case resolution and improve access to justice. In February 2020, Sabah and Sarawak courts launched a pilot program to aid judges in sentencing decisions, primarily in drug possession and sexual offence cases. The Registrar of the Federal Court of Malaysia published a press statement in July 2021, announcing the sentencing criteria for the implementation of AI in the Sessions Court and Magistrate's Court in Peninsular Malaysia (Sanghvi et al., 2022).

Benefits and Drawbacks of AI and AI-Cybercrimes

AI and generative AI are revolutionising Malaysia, promoting economic growth, innovation, productivity, operational efficiency, and personalised services. However, responsible and ethical use is crucial. As AI systems, requiring vast amounts of data, pose challenges in data privacy and data protection. Transparency issues arise due to the use of vast amounts of data, which may conflict with current laws (Sadhu Singh & Segaran, 2020). Additionally, AI algorithms may lead to data bias and worsen the existing social inequalities. For example, predictive AI algorithms in the financial sector may result in negative scores for low-income wage earners, raising ethical questions about sensitive sectors (Sadhu Singh & Segaran, 2020). Aside from that, AI and automation may replace low-skilled jobs, which can speed up the task and simultaneously lead to job losses. Governments should retrain workforces and encourage AI learning. AI can help solve cybersecurity threats, but its shortcomings are evident when AI-driven attacks occur (Ansari et al., 2022).

Careful regulation and strong data protection policies are crucial for AI, especially in compliance with social and ethical standards in maximising the benefits of AI (Sadhu Singh & Segaran, 2021). Hence, proper usage of AI is driving Malaysia towards Industry 4.0, promoting digital transformation and global competitiveness.

The rapid integration of AI with digital systems has led to a surge in cybercrime in Malaysia, necessitating stronger cyber defence measures. AI can facilitate the creation of deepfakes, destroying trust in digital communications and potentially impacting national security. Hence, AI-driven cyber threats, including data privacy and confidentiality vulnerabilities, pose significant challenges to companies and government agencies, particularly deepfakes (Babajide Tolulope Familoni, 2024). The *MySejahtera* data privacy incident during the pandemic highlighted these risks and sparked debate about legal liability and government transparency (Cheah, 2023). While the current Malaysian law is insufficient to address AI cyberattacks, as it lacks precautions for potential attacks. The National Guidelines on AI Governance and Ethics (AIGE) request ethical AI use, but it lacks protection against attacks (Malaysian Science and Technology Information Centre, 2024). The Cyber Security Act 2024 (Act 854) can address cyber threats, but unethical AI usage remains a concern (Babajide Tolulope Familoni, 2024). Academics call for ethical AI regulation like the European Union's (Manap & Abdullah, 2020).

The Governance Gaps and the Need for AI Governance

Presently, there is a lack of legislation that purposely regulates AI or generative AI in Malaysia. The AI regulatory framework of Malaysia is based on existing legislations and policies focusing on data protection, cybersecurity, and ethical technology development. The Personal Data Protection Act 2010 (Act 709) regulates the collection, processing, and storage of personal data in commercial transactions, ensuring responsible and ethical use of AI systems (Hossain et al., 2024). The Cyber Security Act 2024 (Act 854) strengthens cyber defence in Malaysia, indirectly addressing AI-driven technologies (Chan, 2024). Other relevant legislations like the Communications and Multimedia Act 1998 (Act 588) and Computer Crimes Act 1997 (Act 563) indirectly regulate AI misuse, such as data breaches, unauthorised system access, and deepfakes. Moreover, the National AI Governance and Code of Ethics Guidelines aim to promote responsible and ethical AI by promoting fairness, transparency, and accountability (Malaysian Science and Technology Information Centre, 2024). However, these guidelines are soft laws and lack binding effect.

Therefore, Malaysia should plan on making specific AI legislation to fully address the unique ethical, legal, and social impacts of AI technologies.

Although there is a need for urgency in the AI legislation, Malaysia has to find a way to create something that is most suitable for socioeconomics and aligns with the social and humanistic principles. Therefore, a careful consideration of the various types of global regulatory diversity towards AI governance is vital, as it suggests that there is no one-size-fits-all approach. As the factors of legal culture, political system, economic structure, and technological maturity will influence the form and scope of AI regulation. Hence, it is critical for Malaysia to understand these global trends and not to copy foreign laws but to incorporate international best practices into a governance framework that reflects its own values and development needs (Sadhu Singh & Segaran, 2021).

AI GOVERNANCE IN MALAYSIA

Malaysia has embraced AI as a strategic driver of economic growth, digital transformation and national competitiveness. The National Industry 4.0 Policy (Industry4WRD) and the Malaysia Digital Economy Blueprint (MyDIGITAL) are two policies in Malaysia that emphasise the use of AI for industrial transformation and the digital economy. The Industry4WRD aims to modernise the manufacturing sector through AI, enhancing competitiveness and innovation in the industry. However, it lacks provisions for auditing AI systems and establishing accountability mechanisms in case of algorithmic failures. While the MyDIGITAL policy focuses on the use of AI without addressing potential ethical issues or risks related to its deployment. This gap highlights the need for future policies to establish an AI regulatory framework to ensure that AI is deployed in alignment with international standards of transparency, accountability, and fairness.

After that, the National Fourth Industrial Revolution (4IR) Policy aims to establish AI as a fundamental technology to enhance competitiveness across various sectors. It also aims to equip the skilled workforce, promote digital infrastructure, and introduce a flexible regulatory framework to protect technology, data, people, and social order. However, it falls short in providing comprehensive guidance on governance challenges and ethical concerns, especially regarding data protection, algorithmic accountability, and mechanisms for addressing operational failures of AI systems. Finally, the Artificial Intelligence Roadmap 2021 to 2025 (AI-RMAP) is designed to direct responsible AI utilisation and development, emphasising ethical principles in alignment with international best practices. However, its non-binding guidelines have weakened its enforceability due to voluntary compliance. Both policies acknowledge the significance of AI in driving Malaysia's economic growth but have limitations, with inconsistent implementation and enforcement of guidelines.

Besides, Malaysia has implemented the National Guidelines on AI Governance and Ethics (AIGE), which aim to address the ethical development, deployment, and operation of AI systems. These guidelines are aligned with international principles of fairness, transparency, and accountability. It provides recommendations to stakeholders, including end-users, policymakers, and developers, to encourage ethical AI practices, such as algorithmic transparency, reducing bias, and continuous risk assessments. Consumer protection is also emphasised, addressing shortcomings of the Consumer Protection Act 1999 (Act 599). Moreover, Malaysia has also participated in developing technical standards with international bodies, such as ISO/IEC JTC 1/SC 42, to cultivate a culture of responsible AI technology usage. However, the voluntary nature of these guidelines has limited their effectiveness, leading to inconsistent implementation across industries. Malaysia needs to consider transforming these guidelines into binding regulations to support the AI governance framework with regular updates.

There are gaps in Malaysia's AI regulation, including a lack of binding AI regulations, a focus on technological advancement over regulation, and inconsistent ethical oversight. To address these gaps, a balanced regulatory framework is needed that promotes innovation, protects against risks, and ensures responsible AI deployment. Existing laws in Malaysia, which cover areas like data protection, cybersecurity, intellectual property, consumer protection, and human rights, are being used to address AI-related problems. Table 1 has illustrated the summary of Malaysia's national policies in AI governance and its gap.

Table 1. Summary of Malaysia's government policies in AI governance

Policy	Key Focus	Relevance to AI Governance	Gaps
National Industry 4.0 Policy (Industry4WRD)	Industry 4.0 and manufacturing automation.	AI will act as a driver of industrial revolution and competitiveness.	No mechanisms for ethical use or responsible AI adoption in industrial sectors.
Malaysia Digital Economy Blueprint (MyDIGITAL)	Digital economy and AI-driven innovation.	Encourages AI integration into the public and private sectors, as well as promoting innovation and digital adoption.	Lacks provisions for algorithmic transparency, accountability, and oversight.
National Fourth Industrial Revolution (4IR) Policy	Technological integration.	Focuses on transformative technology like AI across key sectors (healthcare, education).	Does not address specific AI risks like bias, misuse, or privacy violation.

continued on following page

Table 1. Continued

Policy	Key Focus	Relevance to AI Governance	Gaps
Artificial Intelligence Roadmap 2021 to 2025 (AI-RMAP)	Responsible and ethical development of AI technology.	Provides seven principles of responsible usage of AI and promotes ethical use and development of AI.	Non-binding and voluntarily adopted.
National Guidelines on AI Governance and Ethics (AIGE)	Ethical AI deployment aligned with global standards.	Promotes fairness, transparency, and accountability in AI systems.	Non-binding and voluntarily adopted.

At this moment, it is true that there is a lack of a proper legal framework that purposely addresses the unique risks posed by AI. This is because Malaysia presently depends on a fragmented set of existing legislations (Hossain et al., 2024). Below will examine the relevant but not all legislation.

The Federal Constitution in Malaysia establishes legal principles for AI governance, including protection of individual rights, legal equality, and national security control. Article 5 emphasises personal liberty, Article 8 ensures legal equality, and Article 149 empowers the government to control surveillance technologies and security-related AI systems. Meanwhile, the Personal Data Protection Act 2010 (Act 709) regulates data privacy but does not adequately resolve issues like algorithmic analysis, automated decision-making or the dynamic data flow engaged in AI systems. Despite the Computer Crimes Act 1997 (Act 563) covering cybercrime, it is outdated when facing AI-driven threats like the fraud of deepfakes, autonomous cyberattacks and chatbot scams. It was fortunate that the recently enacted Cyber Security Act 2024 (Act 854) provides an important update to digital security which introduces a stronger enforcement capability through the National Cyber Security Agency (NACSA). Nevertheless, it still remains technologically neutral and does not purposely outline the accountability, auditing mechanisms or obligations under the international standards like ISO 42001 of AI systems. Therefore, the cybersecurity infrastructure of Malaysia remains susceptible to unforeseen hazards due to the absence of clear provisions for adversarial AI threats, AI-generated disinformation or system resilience.

The confrontation is further aggravated by the Communications and Multimedia Act 1998 (Act 588), which regulates digital content and communications. Despite Section 211 and 233 outlining the prohibition of the propagation of offensive and obscene content to safeguard the content generated by AI, which is not causing social or moral disruption. Unfortunately, the provisions of the Act 588 do not explicitly address the role of generative AI in creating synthetic media, disinformation or deepfakes. Presently, there is no obligation to label AI-generated material or to hold AI content liable for damages. Since generative AI persists in influencing digital speech and online discussions, there is an urgent need to update the Act 588 to obstruct digital manipulation and maintain free speech. Additionally, the Consumer Protection Act 1999 (Act 599) is an important regulation that protects consumers' rights and maintains the standards of goods and services, but it is inadequate to cope with the AI-related misleading products. Likewise, the intellectual property laws (the Copyright Act 1987 (Act 332), Patent Act 1983 (Act 291) and Patents Regulations 1986 (P.U.(A) 327/86)), the Contracts Act 1950 (Act 136), as well as the Electronic Commerce Act 2006 (Act 658) and the Digital Signature Act 1997 (Act 562) also fail to consider the challenges like generative AI outputs, machine authorships, and smart contracts.

Therefore, Malaysia lacks a comprehensive framework for regulating AI technologies, with current legislation based on general laws and sector-specific legislation. The voluntary nature of the National Guidelines on AI Governance and Ethics makes it difficult to maintain consistency in regulation. Additionally, the legislative framework does not employ a risk-based approach, complicating the balance between innovation and public interest protection.

From the perspective of sustainable development, this legal fragmentation has weakened the ability of Malaysia to achieve relevant SDGs. For example, the principles of SDG 16, which calls for strong institutions, the rule of law and justice, will be implemented with difficulty, as there is a lack of enforceable rules on transparency and accountability in AI systems. Sectors like healthcare, law enforcement and finance are where the AI systems are used to make significant life changes. Hence, the lack of human oversight and explainability requirements triggers grave worries about procedural fairness and civil liberties in Malaysia (Sadhu Singh & Segaran, 2020).

Moreover, AI-related cybercrimes are gradually increasing in Malaysia, as stated above, and this is evidenced by the growing number of phishing scams, identity thefts and misinformation campaigns enabled by AI tools (Babajide Tolulope Familoni, 2024). Hence, all these AI-related cybercrimes are destroying trust in digital communications and alarming national distress simultaneously, which exposes significant gaps in digital literacy, legal protection and institutional preparedness (Sadhu Singh & Segaran, 2020). At this juncture, cybersecurity is another growing concern, as shown in the PwC and PIKOM report stated above. As a result, both reports point out the two-sided nature of AI in both safeguarding and attacking critical systems. Simultaneously, the regulatory framework of Malaysia has not distinguished between general AI and high-risk AI in specific areas; hence, it leaves the inadequate enforcement mechanism challenges in monitoring and mitigating emerging risks (Hossain et al., 2024).

Despite Malaysia battling to overcome all these issues, it still faces structural and institutional barriers. The lack of AI expertise among regulators combined with coinciding institutional responsibilities impedes effective policy implementation (Ansari et al., 2022). Hence, it has limited the regulatory capacity of agencies like the Malaysian Communications and Multimedia Committee (MCMC), the NACSA and industry regulators, particularly when AI systems are utilised in various or cross sectors. Furthermore, the talent pool of AI governance in Malaysia is inadequate; hence, there is an urgent need for multidisciplinary training in law, ethics, and data science to bolster up law enforcement, policy development, and compliance monitoring. The algorithmic harms will be detectable and foster public trust in AI systems if the regulators and the public make enormous investments in improving AI literacy.

The involvement of Malaysia in regional and international forums has provided chances for capacity building and policy coordination. Malaysia has predominantly assisted in developing and outlining the principles of the ASEAN Guide on AI Governance and Ethics, which was released in 2024, mainly including transparency, fairness, privacy and a human-centric approach. The ASEAN Guide on AI Governance and Ethics has suggested that each country itself should establish a national AI governance framework, public impact assessments among the AI systems and the cooperation of regional levels among ASEAN. Therefore, Malaysia should integrate these regional recommendations into domestic legislations or policies to ensure interoperability with other ASEAN jurisdictions. This is aligning with SDG 17 and strengthening regional regulatory cohesion and technical collaboration.

Even though these gaps exist, Malaysia is not starting from scratch (Manap & Abdullah, 2020). This is because the existing policies framework – the MyDIGITAL, the 4IR Policy and the AI-RMAP – has stressed the importance of responsible and ethical AI systems. At the same time, the Malaysian Code of Corporate Governance (MCCG) also encourages ethical innovation and advocates transparency and accountability at board level in digital adoptions. However, all of these remain on a voluntary basis, and it would not have a huge impact if these rules were not mandatory and binding in legal instruments or if they had a best practice in an "apply or explain" mechanism like corporate governance of a company governed by Securities Commission Malaysia.

Most crucially, Malaysia does not have a risk-based AI classification system for governing AI systems. Hence, high-risk AI systems like facial recognition for law enforcement or automated credit scoring, even biometric surveillance, are not subject to additional regulatory inspection (Sadhu Singh & Segaran, 2021). The current approach taken by Malaysia did not fully reflect the risk-based and proportionate regulatory principles of the EU AI Act, which was caused by the absence of a clear risk classification mechanism or ex ante legal requirements. Therefore, Malaysia is going on not easing in putting an appropriate safeguard due to the legal loophole which poses a long-term risk to innovation and fundamental rights.

Malaysia must move forward to link the gap between policies and enforceable laws. It is vital to customise a legal framework that is clear and adaptable and aligns with the SDGs as well as the socio-political context of Malaysia. As this is to ensure AI technologies are genuinely serving the public interest and rights safeguarding as well as driving inclusive and sustainable growth.

LESSONS FROM THE EU AI ACT

The European Union's Artificial Intelligence Act (the AI Act) is the first complete AI legislation in the world (Regnier & Poropat, 2024b). The objective of the AI Act is to ensure that AI systems are safe, respect fundamental rights and promote trust before being placed in the market of the European Union (Regnier & Poropat, 2024b). Besides, the AI Act adopts a horizontal and risk-based categorisation approach, which classifies AI systems according to their risk levels: unacceptable, high, limited, and minimal danger (Madiega, 2024). AI systems which pose unacceptable risks like social scoring by governments or manipulation against vulnerable groups will be prohibited absolutely (Edwards, 2022). High-risk AI systems, particularly those utilised in essential infrastructure, education, and law enforcement, are mandated to adhere to rigorous duties, encompassing risk assessments, transparency mandates, and human oversight (Stepanyan, 2021). This approach is substantial as it is highlighting use cases and potential hazards rather than the types of technologies. Table 2 demonstrates the risk classification of the AI Act.

Table 2. EU AI risk categories

The EU AI Risk Level	Definition	Example in the EU
Unacceptable Risk	Prohibited due to high threat to rights/safety	Social scoring by governments
High Risk	Strict obligations for critical use	Biometric identification in policing
Limited Risk	Requires transparency measures	Chatbots
Minimal Risk	No regulation needed due to low impact	Grammar checkers

The AI Act is aligned with the principles of the SDGs, particularly Goals 9, 16 and 17. As mentioned above, the AI Act prioritises human oversight, transparency, and regional cooperation, which align with sustainable development. In addition, the AI Act fills the gaps of earlier ethical principles, which are the Ethical Guidelines for Trustworthy AI in 2019, which were established by the High-Level Expert Group on AI (Hagendorff, 2020). The guidelines were enshrined in the legislation – the AI

Act (Edwards, 2022; Hagendorff, 2020; Madiega, 2019). The transformation of the AI Act from the code of ethics is enlightening. Meanwhile, the policy of Malaysia, the AI-RMAP, analogously expresses seven ethical principles: fairness; reliability, safety and control; privacy and security; inclusiveness; pursuit of human benefits and happiness; accountability; and transparency. In addition, the AIGE are promoting responsible use and an ethical AI system to various stakeholders. Both policies are going on a non-binding guideline, which is a voluntary nature basis; therefore, there is no binding and enforceable effect. Thus, Malaysia could consider using the policies above as a forerunner to legally recognised standards by taking past experiences of hardening regulations from the European Union. It can start with the high-risk AI systems in sensitive areas like policing, education and public healthcare.

A highly educational episode from the AI Act is its requirement for AI impact assessment, which is also known as a Fundamental Rights Impact Assessment. These assessments are mandatory for high-risk AI systems and evaluate their ethical, legal, and social impact before deployment. Presently, Malaysia does provide similar assessments, which is the Responsible AI Impact Assessment (RAIIA), which is outlined in the policy of the National Guidelines on AI Governance and Ethics (AIGE) to help avert harm, promote transparency and lead responsible development as well as prioritising marginalised populations. Unfortunately, this assessment conducted in Malaysia is on a voluntary basis and has no legally binding effect, unlike the assessment's mandatory under the AI Act. Hence, the National AI Office (NAIO) under the Ministry of Digital Malaysia must monitor the effectiveness of this assessment.

Regarding the enforcement, the AI Act provides for severe penalties where violators could be fined up to 6% of their global annual turnover. This is completely different from the existing system of Malaysia, which lacks effective enforcement or fines for misuse of AI. Implementing such a deterrent, especially for companies deploying high-risk or opaque AI systems, could greatly enhance regulatory compliance in Malaysia.

Aforementioned above, the AI Act has indeed provided the mechanisms of regulatory sandboxes to all innovators and developers, as it provided AI systems that can be tested in a controlled environment under supervisory guidance in order to support responsible innovation (Madiega & Van De Pol, 2022). In this context, this mechanism has balanced the need between precaution and innovation. The Science, Technology and Innovation Ministry launched the AI Sandbox Pilot Programme last year (Ministry of Science, 2024). This is a strategic cooperation between the National Technology Innovation Sandbox (NTIS) led by the Malaysian Research Accelerator for Technology and Innovation (MRANTI) and NVIDIA Corporation, which aims to push Malaysia towards a knowledge-based economy steered by AI innovation and talent development (Sinar Daily, 2024). Hence, Malaysia is also taking this mechanism as an important step to ensure the flexibility of innovation and regulation simultaneously.

Another essential part of the AI Act is the approach of transparency and explainability. The AI Act requires providers to reveal information about the operating mechanisms, capabilities and limitations of high-risk AI systems (Rangone & Megale, 2025). This provision empowers users and regulators equally to ensure accountability and require due diligence. There is no requirement of transparency and explainability mechanisms in the deployment of AI in current Malaysian legislation, regardless of the public or private sector. Nevertheless, the government is encouraging companies to adopt this mechanism on a voluntary basis, which is provided in the AIGE. However, implementing identical regulations can lessen the chance of black-box decision-making and algorithmic opacity in high-risks areas like credit scoring or predictive policing (Hossain et al., 2024).

Although the AI Act provides a comprehensive regulatory framework, it is still having critics. Some scholars have argued that the AI Act may not suffice to limit biometric surveillance or protect vulnerable populations (Barkane, 2022). This is an informative criticism for Malaysia as it considers a localised approach. A mass-produced replica of the European Union model might be inappropriate for the socio-political context of Malaysia (Sadhu Singh & Segaran, 2021). Alternatively, a combined governance model that amalgamates the legal system structures of the European Union with the growth requirements or cultural beliefs of Malaysia may provide a more suitable developmental journey. The "apply or explain" approach can be taken as a strategy. Soft law can guide responsible behaviour and gain public trust and increase institutional capacity before the government introduces binding legislation.

In short, the AI Act provides Malaysia a framework on AI regulation while promoting innovation, protecting rights and upholding sustainable development values. The main takeaway is not to replicate the AI Act but to instil its relevant principles, like risk-based categorisation, mandatory impact assessments, enforcement and penalties, as well as cross-border cooperation, into the socio-political, legal and technological environment of Malaysia.

ALIGNING AI GOVERNANCE WITH SDGs

The incorporation of the SDGs into AI governance frameworks is vital in ensuring the technological advances that promote, instead of weakening, social equity, strong institutions and international cooperation. Integrating AI into the SDG framework provides Malaysia a standard foundation to guide policymaking and ensure that innovation supports the national development vision while protecting fundamental rights. This section concentrates on three SDGs, which are SDG 9 (Industry, Innovation and Infrastructure), SDG 16 (Peace, Justice and Strong Institutions) and SDG 17 (Partnerships for the Goals). All these will act as a master plan for responsible, inclusive and sustainable AI governance.

SDG 9 highlights the significance of building resilient infrastructure, fostering environmentally sound industrial development and cultivating innovation. Nevertheless, both policies pay more attention to technology applications and less on ethical governance. Therefore, neither policy provides for auditing AI systems, assessing algorithmic bias or establishing accountability mechanisms when AI systems fail. Concurrently, the AI-RMAP has outlined seven ethical principles, which is a non-binding nature and limits its impact. While the AIGE has filled the gaps in previous policies and committed to developing an ethical and responsible AI system, it is still on a voluntary basis. Hence, Malaysia must ensure that AI systems, no matter in industrial or other areas, are not merely innovation. Similarly, it must be transparent, safe and fair at all stages of deployment.

SDG 16 is dedicated to promoting peacefulness, justice and strong institutions, which gives a sound argument to safeguard human rights in AI governance. This is because Malaysia has more frequently used AI in public services, predictive policing and biometric systems; thus, the need for supervisory processes becomes more critical. At present, Malaysia has weak enforcement mechanisms for transparency, algorithmic explainability or safeguards for human-machine interactions (Hossain et al., 2024). This regulatory gap is widening the risk of bias, discrimination and due process violations, particularly in high-risk AI systems like healthcare and finance. Moreover, public trust in AI remains frail due to low digital literacy and the lack of transparency in AI decision-making (Sadhu Singh & Segaran, 2020). Ethical dilemmas like surveillance risks, data misuse and loss of human autonomy have ignited growing debate in Malaysian society (Sadhu Singh & Segaran, 2021). Thereupon, Malaysia must incorporate ethical safeguards into its AI governance framework which introduces mandatory impact assessments, independent audits and detriment redress mechanisms.

SDG 17 presses for building up global partnerships and cooperation on sustainable development. The collaboration of Malaysia with UNESCO, its involvement in crafting the ASEAN Guide on AI Governance and Ethics 2024, and its participation in developing technical standards, the ISO/IEC JTC 1/SC 42, demonstrate the readiness of Malaysia to cooperate on AI regulation. The ASEAN Guide on AI Governance and Ethics outlines seven guiding principles that exist to guarantee confidence in the design, development, and deployment of ethical AI systems as well as propose internal governance frameworks and regulatory reforms at the national level. Concurrently, the regional-level recommendations propose the establishment of an ASEAN Working Group on AI Governance to address regional threats like deepfakes, disinformation and AI misuse. Therefore, Malaysia should facilitate regional collaboration and line up its national AI framework with ASEAN and global standards to ensure interoperability and regulatory uniformity.

On a national basis, the alignment of the SDGs also requires that consumer protection and corporate governance frameworks develop to handle AI-specific hazards. Although the Act 599 contains provisions related to misleading conduct (Section 9) and product safety (Section 23), in fact it does not sufficiently deal with automated decision-making or algorithmic bias. Meanwhile, the MCCG encourages listed companies to use ethical technology, but the MCCG operates on a voluntary basis. For these reasons, SDG 16 should integrate into these frameworks which require making some amendments to the Act 599 to cover AI-driven services and products as well as expanding the MCCG request for AI risk management, specifically regarding board-level governance and environmental, social and governance (ESG) disclosures.

Malaysia must create a strong, durable or reliable legal framework that is in line with its policy goals and fully execute SDGs 9, 16 and 17 in AI governance. A progressive regulatory approach can harmonise the SDGs throughout every stage of AI development and deployment. Government purchasing guidelines could emphasise AI solutions that correspond to ESG values. Meanwhile, the regulatory sandboxes could test the sustainability consequences of AI systems at market pre-launch.

Briefly, AI governance in Malaysia ought not to be a segregated digital policy initiative but a critical piece of the national obligation to the 2030 Agenda for Sustainable Development. Malaysia guarantees that its AI ecosystem supports innovation and industry growth with uncompromising fairness, public trust or global cooperation by incorporating SDG principles into regulatory frameworks.

POLICY RECOMMENDATIONS FOR MALAYSIA

It is to guarantee that AI development in Malaysia is not just innovative but also ethical, inclusive and rights-protecting; therefore, an adaptive, forward-thinking and tailored governance approach is vital. Even though Malaysia has commenced through a national AI roadmap and voluntary ethical guidelines – the AI-RMAP and the AIGE – these actions ought to convert into a binding and consistent regulatory framework. This section presents a plan of actions to build a robust and future-proof AI governance framework based on the comparative analysis with the EU AI Act and the findings of this research.

1. Adopt a hybrid governance approach based on the "transparency or explainability" principle.

Malaysia should execute a progressive, adaptable regulatory framework which begins with voluntary adoption and transparency obligations under a "transparency or explainability" framework preceding binding legislation for high-risk AI systems. This framework has mimicked the structure of the MCCG, which encourages the embracement of ethical and responsible practices by allowing justification for non-compliance. A hybrid approach fosters innovation without stifling early deployments while establishing the law for the development of regulatory AI systems.

2. Use the National Guidelines on AI Governance and Ethics (AIGE) as a legal basis.

The seven principles of AIGE should be progressively codified into statutory instruments via amendments to existing laws or the creation of an independent AI Act. The AIGE could function as a regulatory guideline, especially for sectors like healthcare, law enforcement and education, where AI has influenced human rights and public services.

3. Mandatory risk classification and algorithmic impact assessment.

Malaysia should embrace a risk-based classification system which is akin to the EU AI Act. Risk-based classification comprises minimal risk, high risk and unacceptable risk in AI systems. For high-risk AI systems like facial recognition, predictive policing or credit scoring, the Algorithmic Impact Assessments (AIAs) should be obligatory prior to deployment. These assessments require tackling challenges like algorithmic bias, data integrity and human oversight. Agencies like the NACSA or the NAIO or forming a new AI Regulatory Commission could monitor this process.

4. Update and modernise existing legislation for AI readiness.

Key legislations should be updated to consolidate AI-specific risks. For example:

i. The Act 709 should be revised to cover automated decision-making, algorithmic transparency and opt-out rights.
ii. The Act 599 should be amended to define AI-generated products or services as well as encompass safeguards against misleading AI outputs, user profiling and unsafe automated contracts.
iii. The Act 588 must elucidate generative AI content, deepfakes and liability standards for AI-generated voice or media.

5. Establish a centralised AI governance body or broaden the scope of the NACSA.

Malaysia lacks a statutory body specifically governing AI. A dedicated AI governance committee can either be formed by a new agency or incorporated into broadening the scope of the NACSA. Either the new agency or NASCA should be authorised to:

i. Register and assess high-risk AI systems;
ii. Supervise regulatory sandboxes; and
iii. Coordinate national audit and certification processes.

6. Institutionalise public participation and multistakeholder governance.

AI governance must mirror the multiculturalism and democratic values of Malaysia. It is crucial to conduct the engagement among all relevant stakeholders, like civil society, academia, industry and affected communities. Malaysia should introduce a dialogue process on the deployment of AI in public services and demand information-revelation mechanisms to notify users about AI-driven decisions, especially in areas that influence rights and welfare.

7. Promote regional cooperation and knowledge-sharing through ASEAN.

Malaysia should utilise its role in ASEAN to spearhead the implementation of the ASEAN Guide on AI Governance and Ethics. Regional collaboration can foster interoperability, harmonise regulations and combine resources for cybersecurity and AI talent development. This includes forming an ASEAN Working Group on AI Governance collaborating to manage cross-border risks like deepfakes, disinformation and AI misuse.

8. Integrate sustainability and SDG values into procurement and innovation policies.

Government purchasing guidelines and the funding of public research and development (R&D) should prioritise AI systems that promote inclusive development, environmental sustainability and social impact. This will create market-based rewards for responsible AI development and line up with the AI strategy of Malaysia with the SDGs, especially Goals 9 and 16.

In short, Malaysia must relocate from fragmented policy to a coordinated and enforceable AI governance strategy. Malaysia can construct a sustainable governance framework that promotes innovation while protecting human rights and democratic integrity by amalgamating international best practices which are implanted in the EU AI Act with a flexible and adaptive regulatory approach.

CONCLUSION

The governance of AI has become paramount as Malaysia accelerates its digital transformation. AI is surely not an illusory concept but a real force. However, if there is an unstructured governance, this would put Malaysia at risk, further widening the gap of inequalities, infringement of privacy and institutional deficiencies that its digital aspirations strive to overcome. As the chapter highlights, efficacious AI governance must correspond to the country's commitment to the United Nations SDGs, particularly Goal 9, Goal 16, and Goal 17. Although Malaysia has made significant advancements via the enforcement of national initiatives and the involvement of international initiatives, it still lacks comprehensive legislation. However, the non-comprehensive AI legislation, fragmentation of existing digital regulations and under-enforcement make Malaysia endangered to AI-related risks. Despite existing legal instruments being effective, unfortunately they are not purposely created to handle the threats posed by autonomous and generative AI systems.

Conversely, Malaysia can benefit from the EU AI Act, which provides a structured and risk-based model. This framework can guide Malaysia to build a more coordinated AI governance system based on current legislation, regulation and policies, instead of cloning the EU AI Act wholly. Therefore, it should implement progressively binding legal standards, especially for high-risk AI systems. The proposed governance model highlights the transparency or explainability which aligns with the international best practices, ensures accountability and builds public trust in AI technologies.

Ultimately, AI governance goes beyond mere technicalities or legal matters but is a necessity of development and ethics. Malaysia can construct a governance framework that cultivates sustainable innovation, builds public trust and strengthens the rule of law by lining up the AI policy trajectory with the SDGs and implementing global benchmarks into its socio-political context. Thereby, Malaysia can go beyond protecting its citizens from the unanticipated consequences of AI and place itself as a responsible digital leader in Southeast Asia and beyond.

REFERENCES

Ansari, M. F., Dash, B., Sharma, P., & Yathiraju, N. (2022). The impact and limitations of artificial intelligence in cybersecurity: A literature review. *International Journal of Advanced Research in Computer and Communication Engineering, 11*(9), 81–90. DOI: 10.17148/IJARCCE.2022.11912

ASEAN. (2024). *ASEAN Guide on AI Governance and Ethics Contents.* https://asean.org/wp-content/uploads/2024/02/ASEAN-Guide-on-AI-Governance-and-Ethics_beautified_201223_v2.pdf

Barkane, I. (2022). Questioning the EU proposal for an Artificial Intelligence Act: The need for prohibitions and a stricter approach to biometric surveillance. *Information Polity, 27*(2), 147–162. DOI: 10.3233/IP-211524

Batool, A., Zowghi, D., & Bano, M. (2025). AI governance: A systematic literature review. *AI and Ethics, 2024*(3), 1–15. DOI: 10.1007/s43681-024-00653-w

Cao, Y., Li, S., Liu, Y., Yan, Z., Dai, Y., Yu, P. S., & Sun, L. (2023). *A comprehensive survey of AI-generated content (AIGC): A history of generative AI from GAN to ChatGPT.* http://arxiv.org/abs/2303.04226

Cath, C. (2018). Governing artificial intelligence: Ethical, legal and technical opportunities and challenges. In *Philosophical Transactions of the Royal Society A: Mathematical, Physical and Engineering Sciences* (Vol. 376, Issue 2133). Royal Society Publishing. DOI: 10.1098/rsta.2018.0080

Chan, C. (2024). *Cyber Security Act 2024: A new era for cybersecurity in Malaysia.* https://www.pwc.com/my/en/assets/publications/2024/pwc-my-cyber-security-act-2024-new-era-for-cybersecurity-in-malaysia.pdf

Cheah, Y. L. K. (2023, February 27). Transparency and Protection of Privacy Crucial for Personal Data Collected through the MySejahtera Application. *Malaysian Bar.* https://www.malaysianbar.org.my/article/news/press-statements/press-statements/press-release-transparency-and-protection-of-privacy-crucial-for-personal-data-collected-through-the-mysejahtera-application

Daily, S. (2024, April 18). Mosti launches AI Sandbox Pilot Programme. *MRANTI.* https://mranti.my/happenings/news/mosti-launches-ai-sandbox-pilot-programme

Demaidi, M. N. (2023). Artificial intelligence national strategy in a developing country. *AI & Society, 40*(2), 423–435. DOI: 10.1007/s00146-023-01779-x

Department of Economic and Social Affairs Sustainable Development. (2025). *The 17 Goals | Sustainable Development*. United Nations. https://sdgs.un.org/goals

Economic Planning Unit. P. M. D. (2021). *National fourth industrial revolution (4IR) Policy*. Economic Planning Unit, Prime Minister's Department. https://www.mosti.gov.my/wp-content/uploads/2021/07/National-Fourth-Industrial-Revolution-4IR-Policy.pdf

Edwards, L. (2022). *The EU AI Act: A summary of its significance and scope Expert explainer*. Ada Lovelace Institute.

Fam, C. (2024, August 19). The new face of online crimes: Deepfakes redefine cybercrime. *The Star*. https://www.thestar.com.my/tech/tech-news/2024/08/19/the-new-face-of-online-crimes-deepfakes-redefine-cybercrime

Familoni, B. T.Babajide Tolulope Familoni. (2024). Cybersecurity challenged in the age of AI: Theoretical approaches and practical solutions. *Computer Science & IT Research Journal*, *5*(3), 703–724. DOI: 10.51594/csitrj.v5i3.930

Farhan, N. M., Nizam, N. M., Mutalib, S., Darus, M. Y., Ismail, A., Mokayed, H., & Abdul-Rahman, S. (2024). International Journal of Computing and Digital Systems Text Classification on Cybercrime Cases From News Articles Using Supervised Learning. *International Journal of Computing and Digital Systems*, *17*(1).

Hagendorff, T. (2020). The ethics of AI ethics: An evaluation of guidelines. *Minds and Machines*, *30*(1), 99–120. DOI: 10.1007/s11023-020-09517-8

Heu, W. Y., & Edhan, N. H. (2023, November). *Legal Landscape of Generative AI Governance in Malaysia - Azmi & Associates*. Azmi & Associates. https://www.azmilaw.com/insights/legal-landscape-of-generative-ai-governance-in-malaysia/

Hossain, M. B., Miraz, M. H., & Ya'u, A. (2024). From legality to responsibility: Charting the course for AI regulation in Malaysia. *IIUM Law Journal, 32*(1), 397–429. https://journals.iium.edu.my/iiumlj/index.php/iiumlj/article/view/927/475

Ijlal, T. (2022). *Artificial Intelligence (AI) governance and cybersecurity: A beginner's guide to governing and securing AI.*

Judge, B., Nitzberg, M., & Russell, S. (2025). When code isn't law: Rethinking regulation for artificial intelligence. *Policy and Society*, *44*(1), 85–97. DOI: 10.1093/polsoc/puae020

Khambali Hambali, K. M., Khalil, S. A., & Daud, M. Z. (2022). 'My Sejahtera' application as COVID-19 control mechanism from Islamic thought perspective: Malaysia experience. *Afkar*, *2022*, 245–284. DOI: 10.22452/afkar.sp2022no1.8

Lazic, L. (2019). Benefit from AI in cybersecurity. *Business Information Security Conference*. https://www.researchgate.net/publication/336826190

Madiega, T. (2019). EU guidelines on ethics in artificial intelligence: Context and implementation. *EPRS*. https://www.europarl.europa.eu/RegData/etudes/BRIE/2019/640163/EPRS_BRI(2019)640163_EN.pdf#:~:text=Following%20the%20call%20from%20the%20European%20Parliament%20to,that%20is%20respectful%20of%20European%20values%20and%20principles

Madiega, T. (2024). Artificial intelligence act. *EPRS, 12*. https://www.europarl.europa.eu/RegData/etudes/BRIE/2021/698792/EPRS_BRI(2021)698792_EN.pdf

Madiega, T., & Van De Pol, A. L. (2022). Artificial intelligence act and regulatory sandboxes. *European Parliamentary Research Service*. https://www.europarl.europa.eu/RegData/etudes/BRIE/2022/733544/EPRS_BRI(2022)733544_EN.pdf

Malaysian Science and Technology Information Centre. (2023). *Malaysia National Artificial Intelligence Roadmap 2021 - 2025 (AI-RMAP)*. https://mastic.mosti.gov.my/publication/artificial-intelligence-roadmap-2021-2025/

Malaysian Science and Technology Information Centre. (2024). *"AI FOR MALAYSIA, AI FOR ALL" THE NATIONAL GUIDELINES ON AI GOVERNANCE & ETHICS*. https://mastic.mosti.gov.my/publication/the-national-guidelines-on-ai-governance-ethics/

Mammonas, D. (2024, May 21). Artificial intelligence (AI) act: Council gives final green light to the first worldwide rules on AI - Consilium. *European Council*. https://www.consilium.europa.eu/en/press/press-releases/2024/05/21/artificial-intelligence-ai-act-council-gives-final-green-light-to-the-first-worldwide-rules-on-ai/

Manap, N. A., & Abdullah, A. (2020). Regulating artificial intelligence in Malaysia: The two-tier approach. *UUM Journal of Legal Studies*, *11*(2), 183–201. DOI: 10.32890/uumjls.11.2.2020.8779

Minister's Office of Malaysia Official Website. (2024, October 1). PM ANWAR UNVEILS NATIONAL CLOUD POLICY, FOCUS ON FOUR KEY AREAS. *Prime Minister's Office of Malaysia Official Website*. https://www.pmo.gov.my/2024/10/pm-anwar-unveils-national-cloud-policy-focus-on-four-key-areas/

Ministry of Science. T. and I. (2024, April 18). AI Sandbox launch with NVIDIA. *MRANTI*. https://mranti.my/happenings/media-centre/press-release/ai-sandbox-launch-with-nvidia

Mizan, N. A., & Norman, H. (2024). Pre-university students' perception in using generative AI: A study at a Malaysian private university. *International Journal of Academic Research in Business & Social Sciences, 14*(8). Advance online publication. DOI: 10.6007/IJARBSS/v14-i8/22455

Ng, E., Chan, C., Cheng, A., & Singh, T. (2023). *Findings from the 2024 global digital trust insights putting security at the epicentre of innovation*. https://www.pwc.com/my/en/assets/publications/2023/pwc-malaysia-2024-digital-trust-insights-report.pdf

PIKOM. (2024). *Growing threat cybersecurity landscape in Malaysia 2024*. www.pikom.org.my

Rangone, N., & Megale, L. (2025). Risks Without Rights? The EU AI Act's Approach to AI in Law and Rule-Making. *European Journal of Risk Regulation*, •••, 1–16. DOI: 10.1017/err.2025.13

Regnier, T., & Poropat, P. (2024a, August). *Artificial Intelligence – Q&As*. European Commission. https://ec.europa.eu/commission/presscorner/detail/en/qanda_21_1683

Regnier, T., & Poropat, P. (2024b, August 1). *European Artificial Intelligence Act comes into force*. European Commission. https://ec.europa.eu/commission/presscorner/detail/en/ip_24_4123

Reza, D. R. (2024, September 30). Malaysia should consider 'AI Bill of Rights', says US-based newsman | FMT. *Free Malaysia Today | FMT*. https://www.freemalaysiatoday.com/category/nation/2024/09/30/malaysia-should-consider-ai-bill-of-rights-says-us-based-newsman/

Sadhu Singh, J. K., & Segaran, D. (2020). AI, law and ethics: The emergence of a new discourse in the legal thoroughfare. *Malayan Law Journal, 5*, 1–9.

Sadhu Singh, J. K., & Segaran, D. (2021). An AI ethical framework for Malaysia: A much-needed governance tool for reducing risks and liabilities arising from AI systems. *Malayan Law Journal, 3*, cdxiv-cdxxxvii.

Sætra, H. S. (2021). Ai in context and the sustainable development goals: Factoring in the unsustainability of the sociotechnical system. *Sustainability (Basel), 13*(4), 1–19. DOI: 10.3390/su13041738

Said, F., & Nabilah, F. (2024). *Future of Malaysia's AI governance*.

Sanghvi, H., See, J., Ling, W., Tay, S., & Kuek, Y. (2022). Digitalisation of judiciary in Malaysia: Application of Artificial Intelligence in the sentencing process. *Proceedings of the International Conference on Law and Digitalization (ICLD 2022)*, 91–97. DOI: 10.2991/978-2-494069-59-6_9

Santani, S. J. (2024, January 9). *Malaysia coming up with AI governance and code of ethics*. New Straits Times. https://www.nst.com.my/business/corporate/2024/01/998905/malaysia-coming-ai-governance-and-code-ethics

Sharon, A. (2025, May 5). Malaysia: Strategic and measured approach to AI governance. *OpenGov Asia*. https://opengovasia.com/2025/05/05/malaysia-strategic-and-measured-approach-to-ai-governance/

Stepanyan, A. Z. (2021). European Artificial Intelligence Act: Should Russia implement the same? *Kutafin Law Review*, *8*(3), 403–422. DOI: 10.17803/2313-5395.2021.3.17.403-422

Stryker, C., & Kavlakoglu, E. (2024, August 16). *What Is Artificial Intelligence (AI)? | IBM*. IBM. https://www.ibm.com/topics/artificial-intelligence

Stryker, C., & Scapicchio, M. (2024, March 22). *What is Generative AI? | IBM*. IBM. https://www.ibm.com/topics/generative-ai

Toh, J., & Yee, Y. X. (2024, February 23). *An interview with Shearn Delamore & Co discussing artificial intelligence in the Malaysia - Lexology*. Lexology. https://www.lexology.com/library/detail.aspx?g=2662ef4d-0df2-44bf-87d3-7bb0048c1b48

Totlani, K. (2023). Navigating the Ethical Maze: Moral Dilemmas in the Age of AI. *International Journal for Research in Applied Science and Engineering Technology*, *11*(10), 968–972. DOI: 10.22214/ijraset.2023.56138

Trabelsi, M. A. (2024). The impact of artificial intelligence on economic development. *Journal of Electronic Business & Digital Economics*, *3*(2), 142–155. DOI: 10.1108/JEBDE-10-2023-0022

United Nations. (2021, November 25). *193 countries adopt first-ever global agreement on the Ethics of Artificial Intelligence | UN News*. United Nations. https://news.un.org/en/story/2021/11/1106612

van Wynsberghe, A. (2021). Sustainable AI: AI for sustainability and the sustainability of AI. *AI and Ethics*, *1*(3), 213–218. DOI: 10.1007/s43681-021-00043-6

KEY TERMS AND DEFINITIONS

Artificial Intelligence (AI): A machine-based system able of autonomous operation at several levels and capable of post-deployment adjustments to make inferences from inputs, so producing outputs such predictions, recommendations, or decisions that might affect the virtual or physical environment.

AI-Enabled Cybercrime: Cybercrime enabled by AI applications includes phishing scams, identity theft, or automated disinformation campaigns.

AI Governance: Legislative, policy, and guideline framework controlling the growth and implementation of AI systems.

Deepfake: AI-generated synthetic media (usually video or audio) that replicas a real person, often used for manipulation or disinformation.

EU AI Act: A legislative by the European Union to create a harmonised framework for the ethical and secure use of AI.

Sustainable Development Goals (SDGs): 17 worldwide objectives developed by the United Nations to handle different social, financial, and environmental issues.

Transparency or Explainability approach: Human understanding of the operations and decision-making processes of artificial intelligence systems will help to build trust and responsibility by means of which one can hold them accountable.

Chapter 12
Towards a Sustainable Flexible Work Arrangement in Malaysia
Legal Perspectives and SDG Alignment

Siti Fazilah Abdul Shukor
https://orcid.org/0000-0003-3504-4102
University Tunku Abdul Rahman, Malaysia

ABSTRACT

The COVID-19 pandemic accelerated the adoption of remote working in Malaysia, prompting a critical re-evaluation of existing labour laws and the need for a robust legal framework that supports flexible work arrangements. This chapter examines the current legal landscape governing remote work in Malaysia, including relevant provisions under the Employment Act 1955, recent policy initiatives, and proposed amendments. It assesses the adequacy of these regulations in promoting decent work and economic growth (SDG 8), reducing inequalities (SDG 10), good health and well-being (SDG 3), Sustainable cities and communities (SDG 11) and supporting gender equality (SDG 5). The analysis reveals significant gaps in legal protections for remote workers, particularly concerning the right to disconnect, occupational health and safety, data privacy, and work-life balance.

DOI: 10.4018/979-8-3373-1792-2.ch012

INTRODUCTION

The Covid-19 pandemic acted as a catalyst, forcing a rapid shift to remote work—a transition that, while not entirely revolutionary, became a necessity for health and safety reasons ("The Case of Remote Work," 2020). This shift demonstrated the remarkable adaptability of companies and employees in transitioning from physical workplaces to virtual settings (Das, 2020; Mondal, 2020; Mondal & Sahoo, 2020; Nadanyiova & Das, 2020). Working from home itself is not new; its roots trace back to the 1970s, when advancements in information and communication technology (ICT) enabled knowledge workers to operate outside traditional offices as telecommuters (Allen et al., 2015). However, the pandemic turned work from home into what the International Labour Organization (ILO, 2020) called "the most extensive mass teleworking experiment in history." For many employers, this was an unplanned but transformative experiment (Braje, 2022).

The contemporary business environment is significantly influenced by technologies, which promote growth, efficiency, and innovation. The advancement of technologies has significantly altered the business environment, which has led to the reshaping of operations, communication, consumer interactions, and even business models. The global shift towards work from home, caused by the COVID-19 pandemic, has significantly altered traditional employment structures. With that, Malaysia was compelled to adopt work-from-home arrangements to ensure economic continuity and workforce safety, like other nations. While work from home presents opportunities for increased flexibility, productivity, and inclusivity, it also raises complex legal and regulatory challenges.

Flexible work arrangements were common in developed nations, but it was a relatively novel concept in Malaysia before the pandemic. The government urged businesses to adopt work from home to curb Covid-19 transmission, which led to a new workplace paradigm (Abdul Shukor & Ghazali, 2025). The rise of ICT has not only altered individual work habits but also enabled industries to operate beyond centralized physical locations, fostering global collaboration (Tariq et al., 2022). Malaysia has embraced the hybrid work model, blending remote and in-person work. This flexible approach grants employees greater autonomy, often enhancing productivity. Approximately 63% of employees globally and in Malaysia favor a mixed work arrangement (PwC Malaysia, 2022), and 88% of Malaysian workers prefer work from home at least once a week, with 93% of those aged 18–24 endorsing this model. The hybrid model represents a lasting shift, balancing flexibility with organizational needs, and underscores the irreversible influence of technology on the future of work.

The rapid adoption of work from home has reshaped the modern workplace, presenting both opportunities and challenges for employees and employers alike. While it has unlocked new levels of flexibility, productivity, and cost efficiency, it has also introduced complexities in communication, work-life balance, and organizational culture. In the context of the United Nations Sustainable Development Goals (SDGs), particularly SDG 3 (Good Health and Well-being), SDG 5 (Gender Equality), SDG 8 (Decent Work and Economic Growth), SDG 10 (Reduced Inequalities) and SDG 11 (Sustainable Cities and Communities), there is a growing need for Malaysia to establish a comprehensive legal framework that supports sustainable and equitable flexible work arrangement practices. This chapter explores the legal landscape of flexible work arrangements in Malaysia, identifies key challenges, and offers policy recommendations to align national labour laws with the SDG agenda.

WORK FROM HOME AND FLEXIBLE WORK ARRANGEMENTS

Work from home, also referred to as telecommuting or flexible work arrangements, or remote work, involves performing job duties outside of a traditional office setting, often facilitated by digital technologies. Remote working is the practice of an employee working at their home, or in some other place that is not an organization's usual place of business (Cambridge Dictionary, 2024). Work from home used to refer to a person doing their job in their home rather than travelling to an office, etc., in order to do it (Cambridge Dictionary, 2024). Flexible working is a situation in which an employer allows people to choose the times that they work so that they can do other things, for example, spend time with their children (Cambridge Dictionary, 2024). Telecommuting is the activity of working for a company but staying at home and communicating with the office by computer and telephone (Cambridge Dictionary, 2024). Home work is defined by the ILO's Home Work Convention (No. 177) and Recommendation (No. 184), 1996, as "work carried out by a person … (i) in his or her home or in other premises of his or her choice, other than the workplace of the employer; (ii) for remuneration; (iii) which results in a product orf service as specified by the employer, irrespective of who provides the equipment, materials or other inputs used" (Convention No. 177, Article 1). This definition does not extend to persons who have "the degree of autonomy and of economic independence necessary to be considered independent workers under national laws, regulations or court decisions".

Working from home has become an alternative lifestyle in the current digital nomad world. The advancement of technology makes life easy for most workers who prefer a work-life balance, and a traditional job is not the only option left to them. Working from home allows workers to work freely on their terms and embrace a work-from-anywhere lifestyle (Abdul Shukor & Ghazali, 2025). Working remotely provides the flexibility to work from anywhere in the world, the opportunity to spend more time with family, and greater control over one's time. Remote work has presented significant opportunities for businesses and countries, driving economic growth through the expansion of ICT and knowledge-based industries (Canan, 2023). While developed and developing nations swiftly transitioned to flexible work arrangements in service sectors like finance, insurance, and ICT, other industries—such as manufacturing, agriculture, tourism, and construction—faced greater challenges in adaptation (ILO, 2020).

Beyond sectoral shifts, work from home has broadened opportunities for job seekers while enabling employers to retain talent more effectively (Abdul Shukor et al., 2025). The shift toward hybrid or fully remote models has encouraged businesses to rethink traditional workplace structures, fostering more flexible and inclusive work environments (Abdul Shukor & Ghazali, 2025). Advancements in ICT have further accelerated this trend, with a growing array of tools and services designed to streamline remote collaboration, enhancing productivity and operational efficiency for organizations worldwide (Abdul Shukor & Ghazali, 2025).

OVERVIEW OF MALAYSIA'S LABOUR LEGAL FRAMEWORK

Malaysia's primary labour legislation is the Employment Act 1955, supplemented by various regulations, guidelines, and industry-specific laws. However, the Act is largely rooted in conventional workplace norms and does not adequately account for the nuances of remote or flexible work. Employment law plays a vital role in defining contractual obligations, worker rights, and benefits, as outlined in Malaysia's Employment Act 1955 (Act 265) (EA 1955). While some provisions, such as those related to working hours, overtime, and rest days, can be loosely interpreted to cover flexible working scenarios, there remains a significant legal vacuum concerning rights, obligations, and enforcement mechanisms. According to Christopher and Lee (2020), disputes may arise over issues like dismissal due to inadequate performance, layoffs, or violations of work-from-home (WFH) policies. Therefore, the regulators must investigate the legal implications of flexible working for the employers and employees, which focuses on the key areas such as employment law, data privacy and occupational health and safety (Abdul Shukor & Ghazali, 2025).

Further, Malaysia had no specific statutory framework governing remote work, work-from-home (WFH), or flexible work arrangements (FWA). Employment matters were largely regulated under the Employment Act 1955, which did not explicitly address flexible working arrangements. With the recent developments to the Employment Act 1955, which came into force on 1 January 2023, the Employment (Amendment) Act 2022 ("the Amendment Act") has recognised the FWA or WFH in Malaysia. Hence, it introduced FWA or WFH applications under Sections 60P and 60Q. Aa per the Section 60P, it profound that an employee may apply to their employer for FWA and Section 60Q profound that the process of FWA application requires the employee to apply in writing to the employer, and within 60 days of application the employer should respond to the approval or refusal of the application, and in the case of refusal should provide a reason. With that, the situation allows employees to apply to their employer for an FWA, and the employees should present a written request to their employer for flexible working arrangements regarding their working hours, days, or location (Abdul Shukor & Ghazali, 2025). Thus, employers should inform employees in writing of their decision to approve or reject the application, as well as any reasons for the denial. With that, employers are required to modify or amend the contractual agreement with the new working arrangement regarding the working hours, days, and location, as well as ensuring legal compliance (Wahab et. al, 2024). Therefore, employers adhere to comply with the EA 1955 maximum working hours per day of 8 hours and up to 12 hours with overtime (Wahab et. al., 2024).

In Malaysia, the primary legislation that emphasizes workplace safety and health is the Occupational Safety and Health Act (Act 514) (OSHA). OSHA's objectives are to ensure the safety, health, and welfare of workers, as well as protect others from risks associated with work activities. Normally, OSHA outlines the duties and responsibilities of employers, employees, manufacturers, and suppliers in creating and maintaining a safe and healthy work environment. The 2022 amendment to Malaysia's Occupational Safety and Health Act 1994 (OSHA) significantly broadens the scope of the act to cover all places of work, not just specific industries (Izzati & Chew, 2025). It also strengthens employee protection, increases penalties for safety violations, and imposes additional duties on employers, including the requirement to conduct risk assessments. According to Section 15 of the OSHA 1994, employers are legally obligated to safeguard the health, safety, and welfare of their employees in the workplace. This includes eliminating potential hazards and implementing corrective measures. Importantly, this responsibility is not limited to traditional office spaces but extends to any location where work is performed, including remote setups such as WFH or FWA as per Section 41 of the OSHAA 2022.

Christopher & Lee (2020) emphasize that organizations must integrate safety and health protocols into work-from-home policies, ensuring that home workspaces are free from recognized hazards (Wahab et al., 2024). While these regulations enhance employee protection against work-related injuries, it is crucial to note that compensation claims under WFH or FWA are restricted to injuries sustained during work hours at the designated workspace, excluding incidents such as driving-related injuries (Wahab et al., 2024). Beyond physical risks, employers must also address occupational stress, a frequently overlooked issue in both office and remote settings. Factors such as excessive workloads, poor management, lack of organizational support, role ambiguity, and inadequate work-life balance can negatively impact employee well-being and productivity. Proactively managing psychosocial risks is essential to preventing workplace injuries and fostering a healthy, flexible working environment. Additionally, Section 16 of OSHA 1994 mandates employers to develop, regularly update, and communicate a written safety and health policy to all employees. This ensures compliance with evolving workplace standards and reinforces the employer's duty to maintain a safe and supportive work environment, whether on-site or remote.

There are some amendments made to OSHA 1994, with the objective of enhancing the protection of occupational safety and health of workers in Malaysia. The Occupational Safety and Health (Amendment) Act 2022 ("OSHAA 2022") came into force on 1st June 2024. There are a few key amendments made to the sections to give vast protections to workers, with the environment is free from hazards for better wellbeing. As per Section 1(2) now applies to all places of work, including public services and statutory authorities in Malaysia, except domestic employment, the armed forces and work on board a ship. Sections 18A and 18B of OSHA 1994 provide new duties to the principal, employer, and self-employed person. The sections concerning conducting the risk assessment and practicable measures to ensure safety and health for all parties. Section 29A (1) of OSHAA 2022 mandates that employers should appoint an Occupational Safety and Health officer to coordinate five or more employees at the workplace. In the event of failure to fulfil Section 29A (1), the employer is guilty of the offence and shall, on conviction, be liable to a fine not exceeding fifty thousand ringgit or to imprisonment for a term not exceeding six months or to both. Section 26A of OSHAA 2022 provides that if an employee has a justifiable suspicion of imminent danger in the workplace, the employee has the right to remove themselves from this danger in the workplace if they have informed their employer, and the employer fails to take any action to remove the danger. It further clarifies that an employee who removes themselves from such danger is protected against undue consequences and will not be discriminated against (Izzati & Chew, 2025). This section seems not to mention whether remote workers are included or excluded from the protections. With recent remote working trends and the Human Resource Minister assuring the applicability of the Act to remote workers, such developments are yet to be tested, and challenges may arise on its practicability (Nan Muhammad et al., 2024).

Additionally, employers have a responsibility to ensure the protection of employee data privacy and security in flexible working settings. Remote workers face increased risks of cyber threats, including phishing scams, fraudulent schemes, and malware-infected files. As such, organizations must strengthen data security measures, as flexible working environments may leave employees more vulnerable to such attacks (Abdul Shukor & Ghazali, 2025). To address these risks, companies should update their data protection policies to align with the Personal Data Protection Act 2010 (PDPA 2010), ensuring they account for flexible working challenges. Several specific vulnerabilities emerge in home office settings, including the use of unsecured home Wi-Fi networks, household members potentially accessing sensitive documents, printing work files on personal devices, and increased risks of data breaches (Wahab et al., 2022). These security gaps could seriously harm organizations if left unaddressed. To mitigate these risks, employers should implement comprehensive remote work security policies and establish clear protocols for handling sensitive data. Mandatory employee training programs should cover essential topics like confidentiality requirements, proper data usage guidelines, and cybersecurity best practices. All staff members working remotely must complete this training to ensure they understand and follow proper security measures. With the legal complexities surrounding flexible work arrangements in Malaysia, stakeholders must collaborate to create a balanced regulatory framework that supports secure, fair, and sustainable flexible working practices.

CHALLENGES IN THE CURRENT LEGAL FRAMEWORK

The law recognizes flexible work arrangements (FWA) but does not clearly define remote work or work-from-home (WFH). This creates uncertainty for employers and employees regarding their rights and responsibilities in work from home settings. Although Sections 60P and 60Q of the Employment Act now recognize FWAs, the legislation does not explicitly define what constitutes remote work or work-from-home arrangements, creating uncertainty about the rights and responsibilities of both employers and employees. For instance, issues such as working hours, access to company systems, and delineation of work boundaries are left to the discretion of individual employers. There are no proper legal guidelines on acceptable monitoring practices or productivity expectations in remote setups, which can lead to excessive surveillance or disputes over performance evaluations.

Besides, the current framework permits employers to accept or reject FWA applications with minimal justification. While the law mandates a written response within 60 days, it does not impose criteria for assessment. This broad discretion may lead to inconsistent practices and possible discrimination, particularly in cases where FWAs is technologically and operationally feasible. Thus, employees can face challenges in challenging unfair rejections or breaches of FWAs agreements. Moreover, there is no legislation proposed to appoint a special force tasked to oversee the implementation of FWAs or remote work policies. Therefore, it is required to have a more balanced mechanism to ensure transparency and accountability in decision-making.

There are possibilities for employees to sustain injury at home or any other location. The Occupational Safety and Health Act 1994 does not explicitly extend to home work environments, leaving remote workers without clear protections or recourse for work-related injuries sustained at home. The home office setups fall into a legal gray area as they are neither expressly included nor excluded from the OSHA definitions. The Department of Occupational Safety and Health (DOSH) should issue comprehensive guidelines for FWAs environments, including ergonomic standards, mental health considerations, and reporting protocols for remote incidents. Moreover, work-related stress has emerged as a significant global concern, particularly affecting working adults. This kind of stress negatively impacts both employee health and organizational performance. As job demands and employer expectations escalate, workers may face challenges when their skills, resources, or knowledge prove insufficient to meet these requirements, resulting in heightened stress levels. According to Bui et al. (2021) demonstrates a clear correlation between increased stress levels and decreased work productivity, highlighting the substantial consequences of workplace stress on overall output. Flexible working presents new challenges in monitoring employee performance and productivity.

Flexible working often blurs the boundaries between personal and professional life, raising concerns about overwork and burnout. Maintaining a healthy work-life balance enhances both productivity and employee retention. Greenblatt (2002) defines work-life balance represents an optimal equilibrium between professional and personal commitments, requiring effective management of competing demands on time and energy. This balance has grown increasingly vital with the influx of younger generations into the workforce. According to Irawanto et al. (2021) reveals that men and women often utilize flexible work arrangements differently, leading to varied impacts on their overall well-being and work-life integration. These differences highlight the need for personalized approaches to workplace flexibility that accommodate diverse employee needs and lifestyles.

THE SUSTAINABLE DEVELOPMENT GOALS (SDGS)

In order to ensure "peace and prosperity for people and the planet, now and into the future," by 2030, the United Nations set the Sustainable Development Goals (SDGs) in 2015. These aspirational objectives tackle humanity's most significant concerns, including the eradication of poverty and hunger, the prevention of climate disaster, and the attainment of equality across gender, racial, and socioeconomic divides. The United Nations Sustainable Development Goals (SDGs) represent a universal call to action to end poverty, protect the planet, and ensure prosperity for all by 2030. Comprising 17 interlinked goals, the SDGs provide a comprehensive framework for addressing critical global challenges, including climate change, economic inequality, and social injustice. Malaysia has demonstrated strong alignment with the SDGs through its Sustainable Development Goals (SDGs) Indicators Report (2018), which tracks national progress toward the 2030 Agenda (Elite Asia, 2024). The SDGs cover environmental sustainability, social inclusion, and economic growth, which focus on health, education, gender equality, and climate action. While meeting these ambitious targets will be no small feat, they could mean huge changes in achieving greater equality.

THE FWAS AND SDGS

The SDGs are widely regarded as a highly inspiring and motivational framework that encourages nations to strive for sustainable development and by achieving these goals, however, requires collective effort and collaboration across all sectors of society (Dwiwedi et al., 2024). Businesses are a crucial part of the broader socio-political environment, and their actions have far-reaching impacts beyond just commerce. Adopting the SDGs can bring enduring benefits, not only for a company's workforce but also for its reputation and competitive standing among peers and consumers (Dwiwedi et al., 2024). The cooperation between FWAs and the SDGs lies in their potential to enhance productivity, promote well-being, and contribute to sustainable development (Sharifah et al., 2024). The flexible working arrangements have significant implications for the Sustainable Development Goals (SDGs), such as SDG 3 (Good Health and Well-being), SDG 5 (Gender Equality), SDG 8 (Decent Work and Economic Growth), SDG 10 (Reduced Inequalities), SDG 11 (Sustainable Cities and Communities) and SDG 13 (Climate Action) and less direct implications to SDG 4 (Quality Education) and SDG 9 (Industry, Innovation, and Infrastructure).

The importance of work-life balance has been emphasized in FWAs, which can be related to SDGs 3, 5, 8, 10, and 11. The relationship between SDG 3 and FWAs promotes mental health among employees by increasing the flexibility and autonomy of employees in completing their tasks. Besides, it is ensuring healthy lives and promoting well-being for all. The FWAs give more time can be spent exercising, preparing healthy meals, and spending time with family and friends, which are drivers of a healthy mind and body (Sharifah et al, 2024 & Cheah et al., 2024). Further, SDGs 5 and 10 with FWAs also support work-life balance, especially for women and promote shared responsibility among men. The FWAs are beneficial for women and offer greater flexibility in helping them to stay in the workforce and advance their careers (Sharifah et al., 2024). Also, encourage a more equitable distribution of household chores and childcare by discriminating against traditional gender roles (Sharifah et al., 2024).

Furthermore, the relation between FWAs and SDG 8 is in fostering both workplace well-being and economic growth. It enables decent work conditions to lead a better work-life balance by offering more flexible schedules, reducing the time of commuting forth and back, as well as increasing the focus and efficiency of work productivity, which can contribute to overall economic productivity (Zhang et al., 2025 & Cheah et al, 2024). SDG 8 also promotes job opportunities for individuals in various locations, including rural or economically disadvantaged areas. Besides, SDGs 11 and 13, with relations to FWAs, provide a better planet for society to live in peace and tranquil environments. The FWAs promote a reduction in urban congestions, which directly improve the air quality and gas emissions. With FWAs, people will be commuting less, which reduces the traffic congestion, and it leads to lower fuel consumption and fewer carbon emissions from transportation (O'Brien & Aliabadi, 2020; Spear et al., 2022).. Also, reduce the consumption patterns in the usage of office operations, space, electricity and etc.

In addition, SDG 4 and SDG 9 also have an impact on FWAs towards society as a whole. Flexible learning pathways are essential for achieving Sustainable Development Goal SDG 4, which emphasizes lifelong learning opportunities for all (Martin et al., 2020). It provides online learning which can become more accessible and integrated with FWAs' opportunities, especially for upskilling and reskilling in the digital economy. Also, providing growth in robust digital infrastructure and innovative technologies. With FWAs, it increased demand for access to technological infrastructure, technological resources and innovation; travelling restriction, related to educational activities, and physical exchanges reduced mobility (Shulla et al., 2021).

INTEGRATING THE SUSTAINABLE DEVELOPMENT GOALS (SDGS) WITH LEGAL FRAMEWORK

Integrating flexible working with sustainable development is rooted in the principle of inclusive economic growth and social equity, which is crucial in the country's development. Since the Industrial Revolution, traditional work models have fueled carbon emissions, systemic inequalities, and unsustainable work-life imbalances, directly contributing to the SDGs. Therefore, the SDGs prioritised work flexibility, equity, and sustainability in safeguarding the environment and well-being of future generations. Sustainable development, often used interchangeably with sustainability (Guarini, 2022), has emerged as a large-scale and ambitious collective journey (Mensah, 2019; Guarini, 2022). The rise of flexible working intersects with the broader framework of sustainable development, a concept popularized by the

United Nations' Brundtland Report (WCED, 1987). Defined as "meeting the needs of the present without compromising future generations," sustainability has become a cornerstone of global policy, reinforced by initiatives like the UN Sustainable Development Goals (SDGs) (UN, 2015).

The evolving legal framework on flexible working in Malaysia has the potential to contribute meaningfully to several United Nations Sustainable Development Goals (SDGs). A well-regulated and inclusive flexible working ecosystem can enhance health, equity, economic participation, and sustainability. This section explores how flexible working legislation can align with and support SDG 3 (Good Health and Well-being), SDG 5 (Gender Equality), SDG 8 (Decent Work and Economic Growth), SDG 10 (Reduced Inequalities), and SDG 11 (Sustainable Cities and Communities).

SDG 3 emphasizes that good health and well-being can be related to workers' mental health or stress-related. It can be aligned with OSHA 1994 and OSHAA 2022, focusing on the occupational stress for workers. Flexible working arrangements can support physical and mental well-being by reducing commuting stress, promoting work-life balance, and allowing for flexible schedules. Legal frameworks that ensure safe home work environments and mental health support for remote workers can advance SDG 3 by creating healthier, more sustainable working conditions. The OSHAA 2022 adds to the many already existing efforts made by the government in promoting a safe and healthy work environment and a safety culture in the workplace in Malaysian workplaces (Izzati et al., 2025 & Hoi et al., 2024). Conventional office-based employment often requires rigid schedules and lengthy commutes, restricting time for family, leisure, and self-development. With FWAs, workers are enabled to adapt their working hours and environment to suit their lifestyle preferences by prioritizing the most important time to family relationships, engaging in personal interests, or traveling while working (Abdullah, 2025). Such flexibility promotes greater life satisfaction by minimizing work-related stress and creating harmony between professional and personal commitments. The updated OSHA intersects with a company's commitment to employee well-being, ethical business practices, and improved stakeholder trust, including among investors, customers, and the community (Hoi et al., 2024).

SDG 5 emphasizes that gender equality can be related to equality between women and men in the work environment as well as achieving gender equality and empowering all women and girls. In most job sectors, there is inequality between women and men, or less participation among women in job sectors due to discrimination or family responsibilities. With the implementation of FWAs, it can assist women workers' participation in the labor force, particularly for those balancing caregiving responsibilities. Hence, it allows women to work from home and balance their family commitments or responsibilities. Despite the challenges of the adoption of FWAs, this move helps many women, especially those with families, to continue contributing to the economic development of the country by taking full advantage of advanced communication technology while protecting their physiological and mental health from being exposed to unnecessary stresses (Awang et al., 2023). SDG 5 is not only applicable to women with flexible working, but it can also give a better work-life balance to men. So that men could manage work and family as well as spend time with their families. Thus, a proper framework is required to guarantee gender equality and non-discriminatory access to flexible work arrangements and protect against gender bias in FWA approvals. With that, it can contribute directly to achieving gender equality in employment.

SDG 8 emphasizes decent work and economic growth, which includes ensuring fair wages, safe working conditions, and access to social protection. It also addresses labor rights and workplace safety can align with EA 1955, OSHA 1994 and OSHAA 2022. The amendment to the legal framework can foster decent work by promoting productivity, innovation, and inclusivity, as well as ensuring that remote workers are entitled to fair compensation, safe conditions, and employment rights, aligning with the goal of inclusive and sustainable economic growth. Besides, the Department of Occupational Safety and Health (DOSH) should issue comprehensive guidelines for FWAs environments, including ergonomic standards, mental health considerations, and reporting protocols for remote incidents. FWAs serves as an opportunity to open workforce participation among citizens by creating viable pathways for individuals who face obstacles in conventional employment settings, including geographic constraints, physical limitations, or local economic conditions (Abdullah, 2025). Through location-independent work arrangements, professionals gain unprecedented access to international job markets, liberating them from the constraints of their immediate surroundings (Abdullah, 2025). Flexible work arrangements have the potential to fulfil these psychological needs, thereby fostering higher levels of employee engagement, motivation, and productivity which supports the objectives of SDG 8 to promote decent work and economic growth (Cheah et al., 2024).

SDG 10 emphasizes reducing inequalities in income, opportunities, and representation within and among countries. Inequality undermines social cohesion and economic stability in a country. Flexible working plays a crucial role in promoting inclusivity by offering equitable employment opportunities irrespective of geographic location or physical limitations (Abdullah, 2025). Through eliminating the constraints of traditional office settings, it enables participation from a more diverse workforce. This is particularly transformative in regions with scarce local employment, as flexible working connects individuals to jobs that were once geographically inaccessible, thereby narrowing the urban-rural economic divide. Furthermore, it enhances workforce accessibility for people with disabilities or mobility challenges, ensuring their full and equal participation in the labor market (Abdullah, 2025). Flexible working, if equitably implemented, can reduce geographic, socioeconomic, and physical access barriers to employment. Legal safeguards must ensure equal opportunities for marginalized groups, including persons with disabilities, rural populations, and lower-income workers, to prevent flexible working from becoming a privilege accessible only to a select few (Abdullah, 2025).

SDG 11 emphasizes that sustainable cities and communities are to make cities inclusive, safe, and sustainable through better housing, transport, and environmental management. Effective risk management is also a cornerstone of strong governance practices and contributes to long-term business sustainability (Hoi et al., 2024). Research indicates that flexible working offers significant environmental benefits by lowering carbon emissions linked to daily commuting (Shamshiripour et al., 2020; O'Keefe et al., 2016). Flexible working also supports sustainability objectives by decreasing total travel demand, promoting walking and cycling as alternative transport modes, and alleviating traffic congestion (Lachapelle et al., 2017). Additionally, studies confirm that work-from-home arrangements can substantially reduce greenhouse gas emissions, helping organizations meet SDGs objectives for ecological responsibility (O'Brien & Aliabadi, 2020; Spear et al., 2022).

With the global transition toward remote and flexible work arrangements, organizations must stay diligent in complying with labor laws and regulations (Wahab et al., 2024). It is important for organisations to take proactive steps such as conducting thorough risk assessments for remote work setups, updating and documenting employment contracts, and ensuring transparent communication channels for all employees, whether remote or on-site (Wahab et al., 2024). To conclude, employers should establish clear policies, guidelines, and rules before implementing flexible work arrangements (FWAs) for their workforce.

CONCLUSION

As flexible working arrangements become increasingly common, many companies are adopting hybrid work models that combine both WFH and in-office work. This approach allows employees to manage their time between working from home and the traditional workplace. Besides, many organizations are introducing FWAs policies to attract and retain skilled employees, reduce operational costs, and provide greater flexibility in work arrangements. While offering employees more autonomy, hybrid models also maintain opportunities for in-person collaboration and team cohesion. Remote work can be structured as either a temporary or permanent arrangement, depending on company policies and individual employee preferences.

The transition to FWAs presents a pivotal opportunity for Malaysia to modernize its labour laws and align them with international best practices and sustainable development goals. Flexible working is a double-edged sword for sustainable development. While it can advance health, gender equity, economic growth, inequality reduction, and urban sustainability, unregulated expansion risks deepening divides. The FWAs have an impact on employees' work-life balance and job satisfaction in performing jobs and tasks away from the office. Additionally, allowing employees to work in a more comfortable environment can lead to longer working hours and higher productivity. So, the employers should engage in discussions with their staff regarding remote work policies and practices.

Legal frameworks must evolve to ensure FWAs align with the SDGs, protecting workers, empowering marginalized groups, and fostering resilient communities. The 2030 Agenda’s success hinges on transforming the future of work into a force for inclusive progress to protect remote workers' rights, give empowerment and strengthen community resilience, as well as ensure equitable access to digital opportunities. Government initiatives should prioritize equitable access to digital tools and internet connectivity, especially for underserved communities. Subsidies, training programs, and digital literacy campaigns can help bridge the urban-rural divide. Malaysia can advance SDGs 3, 5, 8, 10 and 11 while fostering a resilient and inclusive workforce by addressing existing legal gaps and promoting equitable remote work conditions. These may modernize labor legislation to accommodate flexible working arrangements, establish safeguards against potential exploitation in digital workplaces, and create equitable opportunities for all demographic groups. A practical legislative and policy response is essential to ensure that FWAs contribute not only to economic recovery but also to long-term social progress.

REFERENCES

Abdul Shukor, S. F., & Ghazali, F. (2025). Embracing ESG in the Era of Remote Work: Legal Requirement and Benefits. In Implementing ESG Frameworks Through Capacity Building and Skill Development (pp 365- 380). IGI Global.

Albluwi, T. S., Sarker, M. A. R., Abir, Z. R., & Mone, F. H. (2022). Work from Home During COVID-19 Outbreak: Problems and Remedies. *International Journal of Social Sciences and Management Review.*, *5*, 331–342. DOI: 10.37602/IJSSMR.2022.5122

Allen, T. D., Golden, T. D., & Shockley, K. M. (2015). How Effective Is Telecommuting? Assessing the Status of Our Scientific Findings. *Psychological Science in the Public Interest*, *16*(2), 40–68. DOI: 10.1177/1529100615593273 PMID: 26403188

Amirul, S. R., Shaari, S. C., & Jones, S. (2024). "Advancing Workforce Sustainability: Policy Reforms for Flexible Working Arrangements in Achieving National SDGs," International Journal of Research and Innovation in Social Science [IJRISS]. *International Journal of Research and Innovation in Social Science*, *8*(12), 1386–1398.

Awang, N., & Mohd Nadzri, N. R. (2023). The Implementation of Flexible Work Arrangements (FWAS) And Its Impact for Work-Life Balance of Women's Workforce. *I-IECONS E-Proceedings*, *10*(1), 438–449. DOI: 10.33102/iiecons.v10i1.15

Braje, N. Ivana. (2022). Chapter 5 The New Normal: Remote Work after the COVID-19 Pandemic. Available at https://doi.org/DOI: 10.24818/978-606-34-0416-0_5

Cheau Wei, L., & Mui Li, C. (2024). The Role of Flexible Work Arrangements in Enhancing Employee Well- Being and Productivity: A Study on SDG 8 Implementation in Tech Companies. Journal of Business and Social Sciences, 2024. Retrieved from https://iuojs.intimal.edu.my/index.php/jobss/article/view/601

Christopher & Lee. (2020). Going Remote – Challenges employers face in work from home arrangements. Rajah & Tann Asia. Available at https:// www.christopherleeong .com/media/4009/clo_employment_ up-date_going_remote_v5.pdf2020

Das, S. (2020). Innovations in digital banking service brand equity and millennial consumerism. In *Digital transformation and innovative services for business and learning* (pp. 62–79). IGI Global. DOI: 10.4018/978-1-7998-5175-2.ch004

Dictionary, C. (2024). Reviewed on May 2025 https://dictionary.cambridge.org/dictionary/english/remote-working

Dwivedi, P., & Bhattacharjee, S. D. (2024). Emerging Partnerships of SDGs and HRM Practices During the Pandemic: A Study of the Indian IT Industry. *Vision (Basel)*, *0*(0), 09722629241258863. Advance online publication. DOI: 10.1177/09722629241258863

Guarini, E., Mori, E., & Zuffada, E. (2022). Localizing the Sustainable Development Goals: A managerial perspective. *Journal of Public Budgeting, Accounting & Financial Management*, *34*(5), 583–601. DOI: 10.1108/JPBAFM-02-2021-0031

Hoi JAck S'ng & Tan Hooi Ping. (2024). OSHA Amendments and Their ESG Impact in Malaysia. Retrieved on May 2025 https://chambers.com/articles/osha-amendments-and-their-esg-impact-in-malaysia

ILO. (2020). *Teleworking during the COVID-19 Pandemic and Beyond: a Practical Guide*.

ILO's Home Work Convention (No. 177) and Recommendation (No. 184), 1996

Izzati & Chew. (2025). Azmi & Associates. Reviewed on May 2025 https://www.azmilaw.com/insights/key-changes-to-occupational-safety-and-health-law/#:~:text=By%20broadening%20the%20scope%20of,also%20protected%20under%20the%20Act

Lachapelle, U., Tanguay, G., & Neumark-Gaudet, L. (2017). Telecommuting and sustainable travel: Reduction of overall travel time, increases in non-motorised travel and congestion relief? *Urban Studies (Edinburgh, Scotland)*, *55*(10), 2226–2244. DOI: 10.1177/0042098017708985

Malaysians recognise their worth at the workplace, not willing to give up remote work (2022) https://www.pwc.com/my/en/media/press-releases/2022/20220713-malaysians-recognise-their-worth-at-the-workplace-not-willing-to-give-up-remote-work.html

Martin, M., & Godonoga, A. (2020). SDG 4-policies for flexible learning pathways in higher education. IIEP-UNESCO Working Papers, 1-52.Mensah, J. (2019). Sustainable development: Meaning, history, principles, pillars, and implications for human action: Literature review. *Cogent Social Sciences*, *5*(1), 1653531. DOI: 10.1080/23311886.2019.1653531

Mondal, S., & Sahoo, K. K. (2020). A study of green building prospects on sustainable management decision making. In *Green building management and smart automation* (pp. 220–234). IGI Global., DOI: 10.4018/978-1-5225-9754-4.ch011

Mondal, S. R. (2020). A systematic study for digital innovation in management education: An integrated approach towards problem-based learning in Vietnam. In *Digital innovations for customer engagement, management, and organizational improvement* (pp. 104–120). IGI Global., DOI: 10.4018/978-1-7998-5171-4.ch006

Nadanyiova, M., & Das, S. (2020). Millennials as a target segment of socially responsible communication within the business strategy. *Littera Scripta*, *13*(1), 119–134. DOI: 10.36708/Littera_Scripta2020/1/8

Nan Muhammad, R. R., Muhammad Hibri, N., Aiesyah, M., & Saif Aslam, L. (2024). Occupational Safety and Health (Amendment) Act 2022. Retrieved on May 2025 https://www.zulrafique.com.my/ckfinder/userfiles/files/Article/Article-Occupational-Safety-and-Health_Amendment_Act-2022.PDF

O'Brien, W., & Aliabadi, F. (2020). Does telecommuting save energy? a critical review of quantitative studies and their research methods. *Energy and Building*, *225*, 110298. DOI: 10.1016/j.enbuild.2020.110298 PMID: 32834440

O'Keefe, P., Caulfield, B., Brazil, W., & White, P. (2016). The impacts of telecommuting in Dublin. *Research in Transportation Economics*, *57*, 13–20. DOI: 10.1016/j.retrec.2016.06.010

Personal Data Protection Act 2010

Shamshiripour, A., Rahimi, E., Shabanpour, R., & Mohammadian, A. (2020). How is COVID-19 reshaping activity-travel behavior? evidence from a comprehensive survey in Chicago. *Transportation Research Interdisciplinary Perspectives*, *7*, 100216. DOI: 10.1016/j.trip.2020.100216 PMID: 34173469

Shulla, K., Voigt, B. F., Cibian, S., Scandone, G., Martinez, E., Nelkovski, F., & Salehi, P. (2021). Effects of COVID-19 on the sustainable development goals (SDGs). *Discover Sustainability*, *2*(1), 1–19. DOI: 10.1007/s43621-021-00026-x PMID: 35425922

Spear, M., Willcock, S., Ormondroyd, G., Dimitriou, A., Roberts, G., Loxton, C., & Edwards, A. (2022). What impact have covid-19 induced changes in working practice had on greenhouse gas emissions? a rapid review. https://doi.org/DOI: 10.21203/rs.3.rs-1677535/v1

The Case for Remote Work in Health Care - Sponsor Content From Siemens Healthineers. (2020, September 9). Harvard Business Review. https://hbr.org/sponsored/2020/09/the-case-for-remote-work-in-health-care

UN. (2015). Resolution adopted by the General Assembly on 11 September 2015. *New York: United Nations*. http://www.un.org/ga/search/view_doc.asp?symbol1/4A/RES/70/1. UNWCED. (1987). *Report of the World Commission on Environment and Development: Our Common Future*. Oxford University Press.

Urhan, C. (2023). *A Critical Inquiry on Current Arrangements of Remote Work in Turkey and the Global North. In book: Remote and Hybrid Working: Variants, Determinants,Outcomes*. Peter Lang GmbH.

Wahab, H. A., Razak, S. S. A., & Mahmod, N. A. K. N. (2022). Legal issues in working from home amid Covid-19 pandemic in Malaysia. *UUM Journal of Legal Studies, 13*(2), 163–186.

Wahab, H. A., Wahed, H., & Razak, S. S. A. (2024). Flexible Work Arrangements and the Legal Considerations in Malaysia. Proceedings of the 12th UUM International Legal Conference 2023 (UUMILC 2023), Atlantis Highlights in Social Sciences, Education and Humanities 15,DOI: 10.2991/978-94-6463-352-8_31

What Malaysian Companies Need to Know About SDGs and Sustainability Policies. (2024) Elite Asia Marketing, Reviewed on May 2025 https://www.eliteasia.co/what-malaysian-companies-need-to-know-about-sdgs-and-sustainability-policies/

Zhang, S., Chan, S. L., & Abai, D. S. binti A. (2025). A Study on the Impact of Flexible Working Arrangements on Turnover Intention of Chinese Working Women: From the Perspective of SDG 8 (Decent Work). Journal of Lifestyle and SDGs Review, 5(2), e04211. https://doi.org/DOI: 10.47172/2965-730X.SDGsReview.v5.n02.pe04211

KEY TERMS AND DEFINITIONS

Flexible work arrangements: Flexible working is a situation in which an employer allows people to choose the times that they work so that they can do other things, for example, spend time with their children.

Remote work: Remote working is the practice of an employee working at their home, or in some other place that is not an organization's usual place of business.

Work from home: Work from home used to refer to a person doing their job in their home rather than travelling to an office, etc., in order to do it.

Telecommuting: Telecommuting is the activity of working for a company but staying at home and communicating with the office by computer and telephone.

Sustainable development: Sustainable development is defined as "development that meets the needs of the present without compromising the ability of future generations to meet their own needs.

Employee: An Employee is a person employed for wages or salary, especially at non-executive level.

Employer: An employer is a person or organization that employs people.

Employment protections: Employment protection encompasses the legal and organizational measures designed to safeguard the rights, safety, and well-being of workers within the workplace.

Well-being: Well-being is the integration of positive feelings, meaningful doing, and sustainable connecting.

Legal framework: A legal framework refers to the system of laws, regulations, policies, and legal principles that govern a particular area of activity or organization.

Chapter 13

Legal Reforms and Policy Innovations Addressing Gaps in SDG Compliance: Empowering SDG 16 – Peace, Justice, and Strong Institutions

Bhupinder Singh
https://orcid.org/0009-0006-4779-2553
Sharda University, India

Saurabh Chandra
https://orcid.org/0000-0003-4172-9968
Bennett University, Greater Noida, India

Hind Hammouch
https://orcid.org/0000-0002-5897-1649
University Sidi Mohamed Ben Abdellah, Fez, Morocco

ABSTRACT

Sustainable Development Goal (SDG) 16- promoting peace, justice, and strong institutions, it is key to building inclusive and accountable societies. To achieve SDG 16, this need not only systematic gap assessments and robust measures of the legal world and issue of access to justice, but also we need legal and policy innovations to bridge those gaps, as SDG 16 is demanding a whole spectrum of change. Ensuring that we have effective legal systems in place is key to upholding human rights and fighting corruption and transparency. Increasingly, we see policymakers themselves are turning to digital tools, from blockchain technology to AI-driven governance systems, to simplify legal processes, cut bureaucratic waste,

DOI: 10.4018/979-8-3373-1792-2.ch013

and increase confidence in public institutions. Policy innovations are also essential when it comes to tackling global challenges on the rise like political instability, economic inequality, and environmental catastrophe.

INTRODUCTION

The capability development, multi-selection actions as well as strong tracking systems are much needed to combat these issues. As an example, participatory governance models and open-data platforms are giving citizens the opportunity to hold institutions accountable while allowing them to participate in decision-making processes. Across borders, global partnerships are driving the development of legal structures to address the challenges of transnational crime, human trafficking, and cyber-attacks (Amil, 2024). Therefore, adopting specific legal and policy reforms to enhance Sustainable Development Goals (SDG) Target 16 is critical as these reforms will help establish resilient institutions, promote social cohesion and form the bedrock of sustainable and inputs systems (Amil, 2024).

The 2030 Agenda for Sustainable Development, adopted by all United Nations Member States in 2015, is a blueprint for global peace and prosperity for people and the planet, now and into the future. Sustainable development cannot be achieved without achieving peace and security and amidst the 17 interlinked goals, Sustainable Development Goal 16 (SDG 16), encompasses the Most Vulnerable population and is a goal in itself as well as contributor to the Siloed Sustainable Development Goals. It aims to promote peaceful and inclusive societies, ensure access to justice for all and build effective, accountable and inclusive institutions (Bursalı & Ercis, 2024). Nevertheless progress on SDG 16 remains uneven among countries and regions due to enduring structural barriers, institutional corruption, weak rule of law and inadequate legal frameworks. Across the world, courts are overwhelmed, discriminatory laws remain in place and systemic inequalities still prevent those in vulnerable situations from being able to seek justice or participate in decision making (Leong, 2024). This is the backdrop against which legal reforms and creative policy interventions that works to not merely achieve the minimum requirement of SDG 16 but capture its spirit, becomes critical and non-negotiable. This study critically analyzes the legal and policy shortcomings blocking SDG 16 compliance, and examines potential rehabilitation strategies based on legal modernization, policy restructuring, and technological integration (Leong, 2024).

Figure 1. Dimensions of introduction section

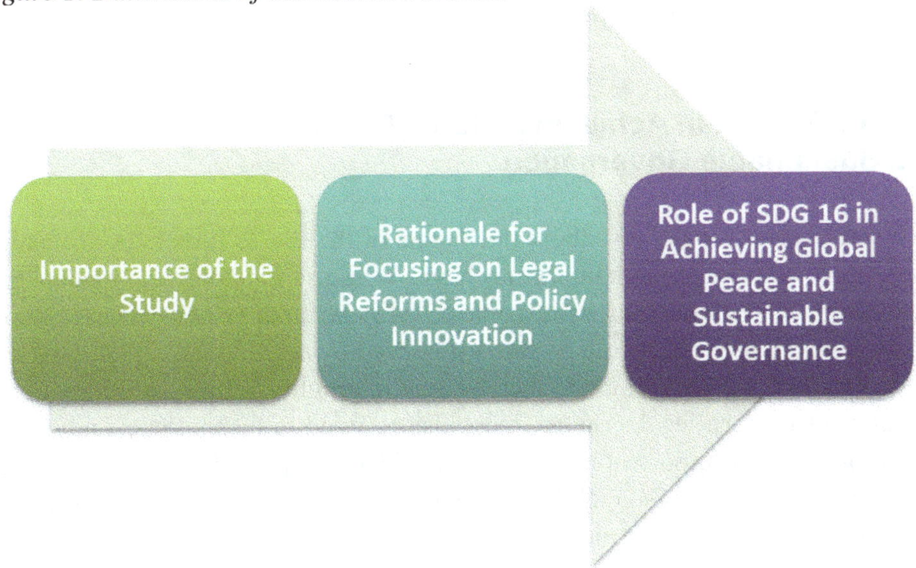

(Source: Authors' compilation)

Importance of the Study: Rationale for Focusing on Legal Reforms and Policy Innovation

The importance of this question is underscored by the fundamental influence of justice and the rule of institutions in safeguarding human rights, preventing conflict, promoting social inclusion and achieving sustained economic growth. SDG 16 is not just a standalone goal, but a keystone that enables the realization of all goals. In the absence of strong legal institutions, sustainable development becomes vulnerable to the threats of impunity, lack of accountability, unchecked corruption and erosion of public trust. The rise of global authoritarianism, encroaching civic space, and the prevalence of violent extremism point to the imperative of investing in justice sector reforms and promoting rule-based governance. Figure 1 illustrates a dimension begins by establishing the importance of the study, moves to justify a focus on legal reforms and policy innovation and culminates in aligning the study with SDG 16 for sustainable governance and peace.

However, many states suffer from outdated legal codes, a lack of capacity in the judiciary and law enforcement or the politicization of institutions. These challenges are compounded by a digital divide that limits the potential to leverage innovation for institutional strengthening (Andersen, 2025). Amidst this intricate web of legal and policy challenges, novel governance models, including digital justice systems,

AI-assisted legal diagnostic tools, and community-based dispute resolution systems, present a reconstruction of equity, transparency, and resilience in justice delivery (Andersen, 2025).

Role of SDG 16 In Achieving Global Peace and Sustainable Governance

Legal reforms are not just about the letters of the law as it includes reshaping institutional culture, accountability mechanisms and service delivery models that align with the principles of inclusiveness, fairness, and responsiveness. While the revisions of national laws are often influenced by new human rights standards or the needs of a globalizing and increasingly migrant or refugee population, the workings of modern legal systems must also respond to technological advances. This is particularly important in scenarios in which groups underrepresented in the system at large, like women, children, minority groups, refugees, and indigenous communities, experience structural and procedural discrimination.

It is through policy innovations that are best able to reshape the landscape of justice through new paradigms of evidence-based policymaking, participatory governance and collaborations between multiple stakeholders. Examples such as mobile courts and remote-area legal aid clinics, digital legal identity systems, and open justice platforms have achieved measurable success in increasing access to legal systems (Rudy & Supriyadi, 2025). Through this mechanism an inspired and the cooperative network, exchanging lessons and guidance, and regionally best practices can also prove useful despite differences at a technical level legally and with an entry point and an incentive, to get reforms going; and, even more so, to help build a culture of law rule, that is based on realities of the context, yet ambitiously aspirational.

SDG 16: COMPONENTS, TARGETS AND INDICATORS

Sustainable Development Goal 16 (SDG 16) the 16th of the 17 Sustainable Development Goals (SDGs), which were adopted as part of the United Nations 2030 Agenda is the most critical and far-reaching. It aims to make it so that there is peace, justice, and strong institutions. Unlike the goals that are directed at specific sectors such as health, educational or economic SDG 16 cuts across all sectors and it establishes the legal and institutional framework necessary to achieve human rights and good governance. The elements of SDG 16 have deep linkages with the principles of democratic governance, rule of law, and equitable access to justice. It embodies the international community's consensus that we cannot achieve sustainable development without peace, security, and rule of law, as well as robust legal and institutional frameworks. SDG 16 addresses violence in all its forms (target 16.1) and recognizes that levels of violence against children and girls are too high (target 16.2), as is human trafficking (target 16.2), and calls for access to justice for all (target 16.3) and institutions that are accountable and responsive (target 16.6).

SDG 16's targets cover a broad range of justice-related challenges and institutional development requirements. Target 16.1 focuses on substantial reduction of all forms of violence and related death rates everywhere, and Target 16.2 to end abuse, exploitation, trafficking and all forms of violence and torture against children. These targets are significant in conflict zones, urban centers with abuse, and societies with GBV units or domestic violence. The keystones of this goal is target 16.3 which focuses on promoting the rule of law at the national and international levels and ensuring equal access to justice for all. It includes reforms that ensure legal aid, fair trials and independent judicial systems. Target 16.4 also aims to significantly reduce the illicit financial and arms flows, improve the recovery and return of stolen assets and combat all forms of organized crime. These targets are essential in countries struggling with corruption, lax border enforcement, and transnational crime syndicates.

Target 16.5 works specifically on significantly reducing corruption and bribery in all their forms. Corruption erodes trust in institutions and diverts resources away from vital services like health, education, and infrastructure (Amoh, 2024). The Targets 16.6 and 16.7 stress the need on developing effective, accountable and transparent institutions at all levels as well as responsive, inclusive, participatory and representative decision-making at all levels. These are instrumental in moving from extractive, authoritarian models of governance to inclusive, democratic systems that reflect the will and interests of all people, especially the marginalized. While absolutely legitimate, target 16.8 expands the focus beyond the relationship to local institutions towards a much wider participation of developing countries in the institutions of global governance, as access to global decision-making platforms like the UN and the global financial institutions remain widely skewed.

Citizens' legal identity is important for providing access to services, voting rights and social protection. Hence, ensuring legal identity for all, including birth registration, by 2030 is the focus of Target 16.9. In regions suffering from displacement, statelessness or administrative underdevelopment, this target takes a special significance. Target 16.10 ensures public access to information and protects fundamental freedoms, in accordance with national legislation and international agreements. However, in an age where misinformation can inflame conflicts and encroach on privacy rights, this target is more relevant than ever (Matamanda et al., 2024). Target 16.a promotes strengthening relevant national institutions, including through international cooperation, capacity-building, in particular in developing countries, to prevent violence and combat terrorism and crime; Meanwhile, Target 16. b disseminates and implements non-discriminatory laws and policies for sustainable development. Both targets highlight the role of institutional capacity, inclusive law-making and cross-border collaboration in delivering peace and justice outcomes. These 12 targets of SDG 16 together not only have the aims of ending conflict and fostering justice, but also nurturing a culture of accountability, inclusion, and transparency.

Its accompanying 24 indicators that seek to measure progress towards these targets range from measuring intentional homicide rates, conflict related deaths and perception of safety in communities, to assessing the share of people who feel that they have a voice in decision-making processes. Others who track the incidence of bribery, the independence of judiciaries, the rates of unsentenced detainees or people who do have birth registration or the right to public information. However, the diversity and complexity of the indicators also highlight one of the major challenges of SDG 16: the difficulty of collecting comparable, disaggregated, and robust data across countries. Many countries simply do not have the technical capacity, or political will, to measure sensitive indicators like corruption or access to justice.

Ultimately, SDG 16 is more than just a goal, it is a cross-cutting principle that must underpin our efforts to achieve equitable, peaceful and sustainable societies. Its elements and objectives are mutually interdependent, and their achievement necessitates holistic legal reforms, innovative policy, institutional strengthening, and participatory governance (Brosio, 2024). Although the indicators offer an important framework for measuring the progression towards human right and democracy, they are only as effective as the underlying data systems, independent monitoring, and political will towards human rights and democratic values. It is this intricacy of SDG 16 that mirrors the most fundamental dimension of sustainable development, justice, equity and peace for all (Brosio, 2024).

MAPPING LEGAL GAPS AND INSTITUTIONAL INEFFICIENCIES

Sustainable Development goal 16 peace, justice and strong institutions action remains hampered by deep-seated legal and institutional weaknesses in many countries (Aguilar-Ortiz et al., 2025). These deficiencies are often rooted in historical, political and socio-economic dynamics, which are exacerbated by contemporary governance failures. This gap between the constitutionally enshrined principles and their practical realisation has led to a situation where archaic laws, policies and practices exist alongside the contemporary demands for justice, equality and transparency. Identifying these legal gaps and institutional dysfunctions is essential for the analysis of reforms that should be progressive in their spirit but realistic in their implementation. It raises the next double-edged sword dilemma of (a) legislative shortfalls that constrain legal modernization as well as (b) the structural limitations of enforcement mechanisms that undermine the rule of law.

Procedural weaknesses compound legislative failures. Unclear filing requirements and lack of standardization across jurisdictions contribute to delays in legal processes and prolonged litigation, causing victims to be discouraged from seeking justice. The civil and criminal procedure codes are rarely digitized or flexible or responsive to the challenges of the new environment cybercrime, environmental justice, data privacy, etc. Also, many legal systems fall short of protecting economic, social, and cultural rights especially the rights to housing, education, and health leaving broad sectors of the population disenfranchised in law (Husainy et al., 2024). Lack of legal awareness, prohibitive legal cost and absence of pro bono services mean that access to justice is still a distant dream for millions. This legislative vacuum in guaranteeing the right to legal aid, fair trials, and protecting against arbitrary detention is symptomatic of a justice system that continues to falter in the face of realisation of the principles behind SDG 16.

Associating the legal vacuum and institutional inadequacy is important in determining where good governance, dispensation of justice and public service machineries get held up. Legal gaps are those aspects for which either no laws exist, or, in order of consideration, the law is ambiguous, outdated, or cannot effectively address present socio-economic, technological, or environmental conditions. Institutional weaknesses, meanwhile, result from bureaucratic inaction, cross-agency coordination failures, low resource commitment, corruption, or lax enforcement. Taken as a whole, these gaps add up to systemic weakness that undermines sustainable development, social justice, and in some places, the rule of law. For example, in nascent global issues like AI and data privacy, governments and authorities in many jurisdictions don't have a full legal framework in place, leaving a vacuum where AI and privacy could wreak havoc on ethics, security, and human rights. Likewise, institutional efforts to address climate change or public health emergencies generally have fragmented responsibilities and overlapping jurisdictions, leading to confusion and delays. Mapping these gaps entails a diagnostic methodology that comprises of legal audits, performance evaluation of institutions, consultation with stakeholders, and comparative legal research across jurisdictions. This approach allows to choose reform priorities, adapt the legal systems to current requirements and to strengthen institutions. It also highlights the voices on the plight of the most marginalized communities, which may be silenced in juridical processes. Filling legal and institutional gaps also contributes to the fulfillment of international obligations, the consolidation of democratic governance and the confidence of investors and citizens. Thus, systematic mapping not only puts the onus on the real disjuncture in the system but also forges the path for cohesive, evidence-based reforms.

Shortcomings of Legislative Frameworks

This was also the case in many countries particularly in countries with colonial legacies where the legislative system continues to be rooted in legal principles that are no longer suitable to meet their objectives. Colonial laws written for regime control, not justice still predominate criminal and civil codes, often obstructing fair access to legal remedy. These archaic laws often include discriminatory provisions that do not meet modern human rights standards and disproportionately affect vulnerable groups, such as women, minorities, and indigenous populations. For example, laws on sedition, provisions on blasphemy, and vague or overly broad definitions of national security are often misused to stifle dissent and curtail fundamental freedoms (Baroncini et al., 2025). Several penal codes and criminal procedure laws are not just antiquated and decayed but retributive, they are more focused on sending people to prison than rehabilitating and reintegrating them into society, this is replicating the cycle of overpopulation of penal institutions and makes people relapse beyond the lack of instruments to guarantee that the offenders will not be at risk for society.

Weak Rule of Law and Enforcement Mechanisms

Even where legal frameworks look strong on paper, their implementation is undermined by the erosion of the rule of the law and gaps in institutional efficiency. Perhaps the most visible manifestation of this weakness is the judicial backlog that cripples court systems across the world. In numerous developing countries, cases linger for years, even decades, implicitly denying justice by default. The delay caused by overburdened judges, a shortage of court infrastructure, and under-resourced legal personnel inhibits public confidence in the legal system. Even where legal aid services do exist, they are often underfunded and unevenly distributed, with vulnerable populations like refugees, the rural poor and the urban poor unable to obtain effective representation or mechanisms to redress their grievances.

The other huge impediment to institutional integrity is political interference in judicial functions. In some jurisdictions, executive overreach undermines the judiciary's independence, leading to biased judgments, selective prosecutions or immunity for politically connected wrongdoers. This prevents not only a road to fair justice but also raises a culture of impunity (Chehbouni, 2024). The judicial appointment, transfer and disciplinary mechanisms often lack transparency and meritocracy, which erodes trust and legitimacy. Lack of bright line demarcations between branches of government erodes checks and balances, likewise bringing the judiciary to the role of a largely symbolic, rather than substantive, force against legal impunity.

This would conclude by saying that administrative processes in many institutions neither transparent nor accountable. Bureaucratic red tape, weak record management and digital gaps make it hard for citizens to source information or mount challenges against arbitrary decisions. Corruption, nepotism, and inefficiency plague the implementation of public policies, especially in areas such as land administration, public procurement, the enforcement of law, and social welfare (Karim et al., 2024). Without grievance redressal mechanisms or independent oversight bodies, maladministration can proceed unchecked. These legal and institutional bottlenecks create a vicious cycle in which development is hindered, inequality is propagated and frustration within society is fomented (Karim et al., 2024). This perception of injustice leads to less civic engagement, or the use of extralegal means to resolve conflicts, which undermines democratic institutions. In order for SDG 16 to go beyond the rhetoric, countries need to conduct diagnostics to map legal redundancies, procedural blockages and institutional vulnerabilities. This is a process that demands not only political will and strategic foresight but also a sustained investment in legal education, institutional capacity-building, and citizen participation.

POLICY INNOVATIONS FOR STRENGTHENING PEACE AND JUSTICE: DECENTRALIZED GOVERNANCE AND COMMUNITY POLICING

SDG 16 focuses on peace, justice and strong institutions, and in the context of the shifting global architecture of governance and justice, achieving this goal and its targets means reinventing our legal instruments as well as generating disruptive policy innovations. Potential solutions that hold particular promise are decentralized governance and community policing which emphasize local empowerment, participatory decision-making and people-centered justice. With drawing conversion plans closer to the citizens, these approaches aim to restore the relationship between the state and citizens and increase accountability and public trust in authorities. The development of responsive, inclusive and resilient systems that are more capable of conflict resolution, justice and sustaining peace in a variety of socio-political environments.

Decentralized governance is essentially the gradual transfer of power and resources from the centralization of power to local levels of government, subnational entities provinces, municipalities, and local councils designed to solve problems in a more effective and efficient manner (Balliu, 2025). This decentralization is especially important in societies characterized by heterogeneity, in which broad central policies are unlikely to adequately capture the particular needs and circumstances of local populations. Decentralized governance shifts the power towards local governments, which fosters a more localized approach to addressing issues such as conflict resolution, legal pluralism, and development challenges so that public policies are culturally sensitive, timely and contextually appropriate (Madu, 2024). It promotes participatory democracy by involving citizens in decision-making, budgeting and monitoring, thus enhancing institutional legitimacy and accountability. Mechanisms like village courts, local justice committees and community development boards have been institutionalized in many developing countries, ensuring accessibility and responsiveness, particularly in countries where formal judicial systems are weak or inaccessible (Madu, 2024).

Decentralization is a contextually important focus area in conflict-prone or post-conflict societies where centralized governance may be viewed as exclusionary or authoritarian. Within these contexts, power-sharing arrangements, fiscal autonomy, and administrative deconcentration further facilitate peace-building by accommodating regional aspirations and lowering center-periphery tensions, and by preventing a re-escalation of conflict. This is common practice; federal structures or semi-independent regions, which determine the use of local policing, land governance and education, have made possible coexistence between populations that are ethnically or linguistically different (Bhattacharjee, 2024). However, the success of decentralized governance really hinges on institutional capacity, legal clarity, equitable resource allocation, and sustained intergovernmental coordination. In the absence of these foundational elements, decentralization runs the risk of devolving into decentralized decree, elite capture, and inequitable service delivery, exacerbating the very inequities it was intended to address.

Similar to decentralized governance, community policing is an innovative grass roots style that changes the paradigm of law enforcement from the top-down authority model to one that is collaborative and preventative based on respect and partnership with the community. Whereas, traditional policing often emphasizes control and reaction, community policing emphasizes long-term relationships with community members, getting to the root causes of insecurity, and co-developing solutions that make communities safe, and help to foster social integration. It reflects a change of spirit from coercion to cooperation, from punitive measures to solutions (Zerunyan & Duzert, 2024). This model works well in urban slums, marginalized neighborhoods and rural regions that have little trust in the police and little state presence.

Crime prevention, violence reduction, and enhanced police-community relations are noticeable in practice, thanks to community policing initiatives. Beat patrols, neighborhood watch groups, school liaison programs, and public safety forums, for example, allow law enforcement to continue regular, non-confrontational contact with citizens. These engagements empower communities to report crimes without the fear of being ridiculed, to share intelligence on possible threats, and to be involved in the drafting of custom-tailored safety plans (Ruppel & Murray). In places such as Kenya, Brazil, and the Philippines, community policing has helped reduced youth violence, domestic abuse, and gang activity by getting local stakeholders, civil society organizations, and religious leaders to engage in peacebuilding and conflict resolution initiatives. Not onlt that, more representation has also facilitated putting an end to gender-based violence and ethnic based profiling through community policing units, thus ensuring that the justice system mirrors the diversity it serves (Ruppel & Murray, 2024).

Policy innovations in community policing drivers also utilize technology, analytics, information, and data insights to facilitate further transparency and accountability. They've empowered citizens to scrutinize police conduct, to facilitate accountability by their institutions, through the use of body-worn cameras, digital complaint systems, community feedback platforms, and other tools discouraging abuse and encouraging enforcement against impunity.

They are trained on cultural competency, human rights, and nonviolent conflict resolution, professionalizing the police force to reflect international standards. But community policing should be institutionalized, not left as a stopgap measure (Fulgenzi, 2024). It needs strong legal support, sufficient budgetary allocation, sustained capacity building, as well as performance evaluation and community empowerment structure. Decentralized governance and community policing together offer creative, complementary pathways toward realizing SDG 16. These innovative power-sharing and participatory justice models restore trust in institutions, stipulate rule of law and enable spaces where peace and justice become not just aspirations but attainable realities. As countries work to reconcile the gap between legal principles and lived experience, these policy innovations help provide scalable and sustainable pathways to inclusive development and resilient societies (Berezovska et al., 2024).

INTERNATIONAL LEGAL AND POLICY INSTRUMENTS PROMOTING SDG 16

The ability to advance Sustainable Development Goal 16 (SDG 16) aimed at fostering peaceful and inclusive societies and providing access to justice for all and at building effective, accountable and inclusive institutions at all levels, relies heavily on the strength and application of international legal and policy instruments. Such frameworks not only establish global standards but also serve as the legal and normative scaffolding within which national governments adjust domestic laws and governance practices.

International instruments which encompass treaties, conventions, declarations, and policy guidelines provide a coherent approach to upholding human rights, the rule of law, and conflict prevention, as well as strengthening democratic institutions

(Al Mokdad, 2025). As such, their binding or persuasive effect also catalyzed legal reform, inform policy-making and encourage countries to work together towards an end to common challenges, including corruption, violence, state fragility and institutional collapse. Central to the contribution of international law to SDG 16 is the Universal Declaration of Human Rights (UDHR), adopted by the United Nations in 1948, establishing the framework of basic principles of dignity, equality, freedom, and justice.

While the UDHR is not a treaty and therefore not legally binding, it had a outsize influence on both international and national legal regimes, and it laid the foundation for binding agreements like the International Covenant on Civil and Political Rights (ICCPR) and the International Covenant on Economic, Social and Cultural Rights (ICESCR). These components together form the international bill of human rights, placing legal obligations on states to protect rights such as the guarantees of access to justice, freedom from torture and arbitrary detention, freedom of expression, fair trials, and non-discrimination; all of which are integral to SDG 16. In particular, under the ICCPR, states that are party to it have exercised the right to an effective remedy (Article 2) provided by competent legal authorities, and to the independence and impartiality of the judiciary (Article 14).

Also, some regional human rights treaties strengthen the provisions of SDG 16 in their geopolitical contexts. These are the European Convention on Human Rights (ECHR), the African Charter on Human and Peoples' Rights, and the American Convention on Human Rights. In addition to creating binding legal obligations on state parties, these treaties also provide mechanisms as with regional courts and commissions to hear individual complaints, to watch for compliance and to influence national practices in law (Alibasic, 2025). For example, judgments by the European Court of Human Rights have driven important changes to member states' laws in the areas of police oversight, anti-torture legislation, and judicial independence.

UNITED NATIONS GUIDELINES, CONVENTIONS, AND MONITORING BODIES

Instruments such as the United Nations Convention against Corruption (UNCAC) play a central role in upholding anti-corruption and transparency, which are also essential for advancing SDG 16. UNCAC is the first and only legally binding universal anti-corruption instrument adopted in 2003, covering prevention, criminalization, international cooperation, asset recovery and technical assistance. It promotes transparency and accountability mechanisms in public finance, integrity in public procurement, and the protection of whistleblowers at the state level. UNCAC assisted states in advancing anti-corruption reforms through its review mechanism which promotes peer learning and reinforces state to state creates great guidance to implementing of anti-corruption reform (Morales-Casetti et al., 2024). It also complements with the OECD Anti-Bribery Convention covering the supply side of corruption by criminalizing the bribery of foreign public officials in international business transactions and encouraging the promotion of ethical governance in both the public and private sectors (Morales-Casetti et al., 2024).

The humane treatment of persons in armed conflict and civilians is facilitated by the Geneva Conventions and their Additional Protocols. The Rome Statute of the International Criminal Court (ICC) establishes a permanent international tribunal to prosecute genocide, crimes against humanity, war crimes, and the crime of aggression. As summarized in SDG 16 on peace and justice, international criminal justice reinforces the peace and justice foundations required to consolidate the development gains afforded by increased accountability, established through the ICC's deterrent effect and the way this impacts national legal systems. The United Nations' 2030 Agenda for Sustainable Development the umbrella policy framework for the SDGs—also provides a crucial normative compass (Kumar, 2024). The agenda enhances transparency, voluntary national reporting, peer review, and mobilizing global partnerships through follow-up and review mechanisms such as the High-Level Political Forum (HLPF).

The Global Compact on Migration, UN Guiding Principles on Business and Human Rights and the Beijing Declaration and Platform for Action share linkages with SDG 16, effectively enabling institutional reform, inclusive governance, and legal protection for specific vulnerable groups. Specific operational tools, indicators, technical assistance programs that directly help countries to localize and implement SDG 16 has been developed by international organizations (for example, by United Nations Office on Drugs and Crime (UNODC), Office of the High Commissioner for Human Rights (OHCHR), UNDP, World Bank). Their work in capacity-building, monitoring, and norm-setting makes legal instruments a reality on the ground. Such multilateral initiatives are critical to address systemic governance and justice barriers, especially in fragile or conflict-affected contexts (Makwara, 2024). It is not only defining and creating enforceable obligations, cooperative framework, and monitoring systems based on the value embodied in SDG 16 but also international law and policy instrument articulate such values. With modelling peace, justice and strong institutions in a worldwide constitutional order, they ensure the sustainable pursuit of sustainable development is a fair, inclusive and universally accountable process.

INTEGRATING TECHNOLOGY AND AI FOR LEGAL EMPOWERMENT

AI-powered legal technology can be applied to empower for SDG 16 as a landmark perspective Access to justice continues to be an arduous task for marginalized and underrepresented populations, and so digital innovation can offer promising solutions to democratizing legal services, increasing institutional efficiency and reducing systemic inequities. New technologies translate complex legal terminology, demystify procedures, and provide immediate access to laws and regulations, thereby connecting citizens to the law. For example, AI-powered legal chatbots can offer initial legal advice, review documents, and assist in filling out forms for those who cannot afford traditional legal services (Thelma & Chitondo, 2024). These tools make other legal services cheaper and enable outreach to rural and underserved communities, further strengthening access to justice that is inclusive and affordable and making the legal system more representative of society.

AI can help in making judicial processes more efficient by automating repetitive administrative tasks which could allow for quicker scheduling of cases, e-filing and digitization of court records. Machine learning can be used in predictive analytics to assist legal practitioners with identifying patterns in cases, recommending relevant precedents for a case and estimating litigation outcomes these would improve legal decision making and consistency in legal practice (Idem et al., 2024). This is especially useful in judicial systems that are overstretched, where backlogs and postponements erode the rule of law. Some systems already in use include India's Supreme Court and other courts around the world, which have been testing AI tools to classify cases, manage dockets and accelerate hearings. Such initiatives are not only vital for institutional efficiency but also in enhancing public trust in the justice delivery system.

The technology is also being used to lock in land titles, manage digital identities and provide tamper-proof records in public registries, minimizing conditions for fraud and corruption. Online legal platforms and mobile-based mechanisms for online dispute resolution (ODR) offer affordable, flexible alternatives to traditional court processes, particularly in suits between two individuals or entities in the civil domain, such as property or tenancy disputes or matters of family law (Twyford et al., 2024). This chapter explores the role of these platforms in promoting peace and collaborative governance by providing citizens the ability to resolve conflict peacefully and efficiently.

The responsible use of AI in the judicial system demands robust regulation to avoid algorithmic discrimination and protect data privacy, as well as ensure accountability. Ensure fairness in sentencing: Implementing explainable artificial intelligence (XAI) can help to achieve fairness in sentencing, especially in cases where biased XAI could lead to discriminatory outcomes in criminal justice systems. Thus, technology should be embedded on a rights-based basis, along with comprehensive monitoring and inclusive digital literacy initiatives (Pradhan et al., 2024). Through strategic integration of AI and digital solutions into these legal infrastructures, they have the potential to dismantle barriers to justice, drive institutional accountability, and enable individuals to demand their rights, all crucial tenets of SDG 16.

Elaborating the Link Between Economic Inequality and SDG 16

SDG 16 aims to promote peaceful and inclusive societies for sustainable development, provide access to justice for all and build effective, accountable and inclusive institutions at all levels. Economic inequality is anathema to these goals as it increases social tensions, undermines trust in public institutions, and deepens marginalization. Starkly unequal ownership of wealth and assets means that large numbers of citizens are left out of opportunity, legal protection, and public assistance (Ketenci & Kubar, 2025). This marginalization results in a cycle of oppression, in which the economically oppressed are denied access to legal frameworks, as well as to the political. High levels of inequality are commonly associated with higher crime rates, weakened governance systems, corrupt institutions and rule of law skewed in favour of the elite (Schmalz, 2025).

As a result, the functionality of legal and institutional frameworks becomes weakened and the implementation of SDG 16 is impeded. It is essential that, if peace, justice and institutional integrity are to be achieved, economic inequality, must be dealt with through economic inclusivity policies, equitable legal instruments and participatory governance (Yang et al., 2025). Reducing income and opportunity disparities can help build trust, cooperation and resilience in societies, which in turn can advance some of the underlying aims of SDG 16 (Koundouri et al., 2025). Ultimately, economic equity is not only an end in development itself, it is a condition *sine qua non* for the maintenance of just and inclusive institutions essential for lasting peace and social order.

CONCLUSION AND FUTURE SCOPE

The policy relevance of this chapter is vast, especially as global development goals are challenged by compounded crises including pandemics, armed conflict, economic instability, and climate change. These challenges have exposed the fragility of institutions and the inadequacy of piecemeal legal responses. Legal predictability, participatory policy frameworks, and digital governance will be key to strengthening institutional resilience, building trust, and ensuring no one is left behind. Legal reform must also be understood as an iterative process rather than a one-off eventrequiring iterative assessment, stakeholder consultation, and mechanisms of grievance redressal. In this way, countries can develop systems of law that not only ensure efficient justice, but also systems of governance that are agile, transparent, and deeply democratic.

This chapter argues quite persuasively for overcoming the legal and policy implementation gap of SDG 16 by examining the nexus between normative reforms, institutional innovation, and inclusive governance. It stresses that sustainable peace and justice are not only aspirational constructs but realizable objectives where there's political will, legal preparedness and collaborative action. Through pooling global empirical knowledge, distilling policy messages, and flagging potential strategic reforms, the paper aims to provide a roadmap for governments and civil society to work in concert together with development partners for enhanced progress in SDG 16 and towards a stronger social contract between states and their citizens.

REFERENCES

Aguilar-Ortiz, J., Zamudio-García, V. M., & Simancas-Acevedo, E. (2025). Sustainable Development Goal 16 Peace and Justice Criminal Justice and Artificial Intelligence Applications for a More Efficient and Fair System. In *Machine and Deep Learning Solutions for Achieving the Sustainable Development Goals* (pp. 435-460). IGI Global Scientific Publishing.

Al Mokdad, A. (2025). Role of Civil Society and Non-Governmental Organizations in Addressing Developmental Disparities in the Middle East: Empowering Communities for Sustainable Development. In *Unveiling Developmental Disparities in the Middle East* (pp. 93–140). IGI Global.

Alibašić, H. (2025). Resilience in action: Kosovo's National Development Strategy to incorporate sustainable development goals. *Sustainable Development (Bradford), 33*(1), 319–332. DOI: 10.1002/sd.3121

Amil, A. C. (2024, December). Implementation of SDG 16:'Peace, Justice, and Strong Institutions' in The Philippines: Status, Collaborative Efforts, and Prospects. In *International Conference on Public Administration and Social Science (ICoPASS)* (Vol. 1, No. 1).

Amoh, G. (2024). *National peace infrastructure and sustainable development goal 16: a study of the national peace council of Ghana* (Doctoral dissertation, University of Cape Coast).

Andersen, E. (2025). Closing Access to Justice Gaps Globally. In *Higher Education and SDG16: Peace, Justice, and Strong Institutions* (pp. 13-36). Emerald Publishing Limited. DOI: 10.1108/978-1-80455-892-820251002

Balliu, D. (2025). The new role of supreme audit institutions in monitoring the SDGs. A comparative study between the western balkans and nordic countries.

Baroncini, E., de Stefano, C., & Rubini, L. (2025). New Institutional Architectures and Substantive Rules in International Economic Law-The EU and the UN Sustainable Development Goals.

Berezovska, N., Zahorskyi, V., Kalashnyk, N., Novak-Kalyayeva, L., Lipentsev, A., Olefirenko, O., Oliyarnyk, V., & Sushynskyi, O. (2024). Implementing an ecosystem approach in public administration: Achieving sustainable development goals in crisis and recovery. *Cadernos de Educação Tecnologia e Sociedade, 17*(se4), 334–347. DOI: 10.14571/brajets.v17.nse4.334-347

Bhattacharjee, R. (2024). Public Finance for Inclusive Governance and SDG Implementation: The South Asian Perspective and India. In *Governance and Sustainable Development in South Asia: Bridging the Gap* (pp. 339–355). Springer Nature Switzerland. DOI: 10.1007/978-3-031-67616-1_18

Brosio, M. (2024). *Measuring women's economic empowerment at the intersection of gender, law, and development: an exploration of the UN Agenda 2030 Indicator Framework and its effects* (Doctoral dissertation, University of Birmingham).

Bursalı, C., & Ercis, Y. (2024). Sustainable Development Goals: The Role of Logistics in Peace, Justice, and Strong Institutions. In *Effective Logistics for Sustainable Development Goals* (pp. 234-253). IGI Global.

Chehbouni, G. (2024). Assessing the Alignment and Implementation Challenges of the Sustainable Development Goals (SDGS) 2030 in Morocco: A Relevant Inquiry. *Journal of Sustainable Development Law and Policy (The), 15*(2), 186–223. DOI: 10.4314/jsdlp.v15i2.8

Fulgenzi, M. (2024). Subnational Authorities as Key Global Actors. *Athena: Critical Inquiries L. Phil. & Globalization, 4*, 92.

Husainy, A. S., Mangave, S. S., Patil, C. C., & Mane, S. D. (2024). Harmonizing Responsibilities: Challenges and Opportunities in the Integration of Climate Change and Sustainable Development Goals (SDGs). *The Asian Review of Civil Engineering, 13*(1), 30–43. DOI: 10.70112/tarce-2024.13.1.4232

Idem, U. J., Olarinde, E. S., Sesan, F., Bamidele, I., Ogundele, A. T., & Olipede, D. E. (2024, November). Cyber security Institutional Frameworks in Nigeria: A Panacea for Achieving Sustainable Development Goal 16. In *2024 IEEE 5th International Conference on Electro-Computing Technologies for Humanity (NIGERCON)* (pp. 1-6). IEEE.

Ieong, M. C. A. (2024). Exploring New Judicial Models under the Sustainable Development Goals. In *SHS Web of Conferences* (Vol. 200, p. 02036). EDP Sciences. DOI: 10.1051/shsconf/202420002036

Karim, M. S., Deane, F., Arif, A. A., Garwood-Gowers, A., Humphries, F., Uddin, M. M., & Deagon, A. (2024). Integrating Sustainable Development Goals in the Law Curriculum: Legal Education for" People, Planet and Prosperity. *Belmont L. Rev., 12*, 196.

Ketenci, S. T., & Kubar, Y. (2025). Contribution of Economic Variables to Sustainable Development Goals (SDG 16): The Case of G20 Countries. *Journal of Lifestyle and SDGs Review*, *5*(2), e03920–e03920. DOI: 10.47172/2965-730X.SDGsReview.v5.n02.pe03920

Koundouri, P., Aslanidis, P. S., Dellis, K., Plataniotis, A., & Feretzakis, G. (2025). Mapping human security strategies to sustainable development goals: A machine learning approach. *Discover Sustainability*, *6*(1), 96. DOI: 10.1007/s43621-025-00883-w

Kumar, J. (2024). Integrating CSR with Rajasthan's Policy Framework: A Strategic Approach to Achieving SDG 16 in the Context of Climate Change. *Journal of East-West Thought (JET) ISSN (O): 2168-2259 UGC CARE I, 14*(3), 341-363.

Madu, K. (2024). International Law Framework for Taxation and the Sustainable Development Goals in Nigeria. *Available at SSRN* 4993714. DOI: 10.2139/ssrn.4993714

Makwara, T. (2024). Exploring the impact of Firm-Level Corporate Governance Challenges on Sustainable Development Goals (SDGs) in a Developing Economy. *International Journal of Business, Economics, and Social Development*, *5*(4).

Matamanda, A. R., Mangara, F., Maramura, T., & Mukumba, C. P. (2024). Peace, Justice and Strong Institutions: Reflections on Health Governance and Health Inequalities in Mangaung. In *Sustainable Development Goals and Urban Health: Strides, Challenges and Way Forward for Poor Neighborhoods* (pp. 145–158). Springer Nature Switzerland. DOI: 10.1007/978-3-031-68734-1_9

Morales-Casetti, M., Bustos-Gutiérrez, M., Manquepillán-Calfuleo, F., & Hochstetter-Diez, J. (2024). Quality of Government, Democracy, and Well-Being as Determinants in Achieving the Sustainable Development Goals. *Sustainability (Basel)*, *16*(13), 5430. DOI: 10.3390/su16135430

Pradhan, R., Jaiswal, R., & Bhushan, V. (2024). Transgender Inclusion And Sustainable Development: Bridging Gaps For A Resilient Future. *Library of Progress-Library Science, Information Technology & Computer, 44*(2).

Rudy, E., & Supriyadi, A. A. (2025). Security Policy Transformation to Accelerate Achievement of Sustainable Development Goals (SDGs) in Papua.

Ruppel, O. C., & Murray, R. (2024). The Future of the SDGs: A Comparative Constitutional Rescue Plan? One does not discover new lands without consenting to lose sight of the shore. André Gide. *Environmental Policy and Law*, *54*(2-3), 155–187. DOI: 10.3233/EPL-239022

Schmalz, D. (2025). Population Growth Discourse in the First Decades of the United Nations: Interpretations of Global Economic Inequality and the Struggles for a Just International Legal Order. *Max Planck Institute for Comparative Public Law & International Law (MPIL) Research Paper*, (2025-01).

Thelma, C. C., & Chitondo, L. (2024). Leadership for sustainable development in Africa: A comprehensive perspective. *International Journal of Research Publications*, *5*(2), 2395–2410.

Twyford, E. J., Musundwa, S., Tanima, F. A., & George, S. (2024). Bridging the gap: Sustainable development goals as catalysts for change in accounting education and society. *Meditari Accountancy Research*, *32*(5), 1758–1786. DOI: 10.1108/MEDAR-02-2024-2375

Yang, Y., Chih, S. H., & Chiu, C. R. (2025). Association between the environmental efficiency and corruption perception index: A dynamic alternative metafrontier SBM approach. *Journal of Environmental Management*, *374*, 124046. DOI: 10.1016/j.jenvman.2025.124046 PMID: 39793499

Zerunyan, F. V., & Duzert, Y. (2024). *Advancing and Negotiating Sustainable Development Goals (SDGs): A Practical Toolkit.* Taylor & Francis. DOI: 10.4324/9781003497097

KEY TERMS AND DEFINITIONS

Access to Justice: It means the ability of individuals and communities to obtain fair treatment through formal or informal legal systems, which includes affordability, legal literacy, effective representation, and transparent legal procedures.

Institutional Strengthening: It strengthening involves enhancing the capacity, integrity, and responsiveness of public institutions through legal and policy frameworks to uphold democratic values, combat corruption, and ensure equitable justice.

Legal Reforms: It refers to the process of reviewing, updating, and restructuring laws, regulations, and judicial systems to enhance justice, fairness, accountability, and alignment with contemporary global norms, especially in support of sustainable development goals like SDG 16.

Policy Innovation: This is the introduction of novel approaches, frameworks, or mechanisms in public policy that aim to improve governance, increase efficiency, and address systemic gaps particularly in promoting peace, justice, and strong institutions.

SDG 16 (Peace, Justice and Strong Institutions): SDG 16 is one of the 17 Sustainable Development Goals established by the United Nations, focusing on promoting peaceful and inclusive societies, ensuring access to justice for all, and building effective, accountable, and inclusive institutions at all levels.

Chapter 14
Aligning Higher Education Governance with Sustainable Development Goals in Malaysia

Hamizah Abdul Rahman
https://orcid.org/0009-0000-4837-4560
Universiti Sultan Zainal Abidin, Malaysia

Ravindran Nadarajan
https://orcid.org/0000-0001-9206-3428
Universiti Tunku Abdul Rahman, Malaysia

Zuhairah Ariff Abd Ghadas
Universiti Sultan Zainal Abidin, Malaysia

Nurul Syazwani Mohd Noor
https://orcid.org/0000-0002-0830-9614
Universiti Sultan Zainal Abidin, Malaysia

Farihana Abdul Razak
Universiti Teknologi MARA, Malaysia

ABSTRACT

Good governance is very important for improving the performance and effectiveness of higher education institutions (HEIs). This research looks examines how the application of good governance is used by interpreting the applicable principles

DOI: 10.4018/979-8-3373-1792-2.ch014

in Malaysian HEIs. By conducting an extensive literature review and thorough analysis of relevant policy papers, this research presents key dimensions of good governance, such as accountability, transparency, autonomy, and participation from stakeholders. The results show that while Malaysian HEIs are getting better at adopting good governance practices, there still needs to be improvement, especially in the areas of institutional autonomy and stakeholder engagement. This research provides suggestions for Malaysian HEIs to make further changes to strengthen their governance structures and processes, to come into alignment with international best practices, and to ultimately improve their overall performance and responsiveness to societal needs.

INTRODUCTION

Good governance has become more important in the global higher education sector, and has gained increasing attention, as universities and other HEIs are seen as key players expected to fulfil a pivotal role in progressing national development and solving complex societal challenges (Abdul Ghadas & Hassan, 2008; Wan et al., 2020). Good governance is the process of decision-making and the process by which decisions are implemented (or not implemented), characterized by participation, transparency, accountability, rule of law, responsiveness, equity, and efficiency. (UNESCAP 2009) Principle of Good Governance such as accountability, transparency, autonomy, and stakeholder participation, are widely accepted as essentials for enhancing the performance, efficiency, and responsiveness of HEIs, especially in terms of engagement, and in pursuit of Sustainable Development Goals (SDGs) (Hussin et al., 2021; Wan, et al., 2020).

In Malaysia, higher education has seen big changes through various reforms over recent years, with a focus on the improvement of governance and management practices (Sulaiman & Abdul Ghadas, 2021). The Malaysian government has launched several policy initiatives, such as the National Higher Education Strategic Plan 2007-2020, and the Malaysia Education Blueprint (Higher Education) 2015-2025. These initiatives are aimed at transforming the higher education landscape, through the promotion of autonomy, accountability, and performance-driven governance. But even with the introduction of reforms, centralization is still strong in Malaysian HEIs, with leadership access against external standards of quality, performance, and standardized transformation goals. These emerging governance styles are shaped by a landscape of ideologies, particularly those rooted in neoliberalism and New Public Management (NPM) principles. Neoliberalism emphasizes market-driven mechanisms, efficiency, and reduced state intervention, while NPM advocates for adopting private sector management practices in public institutions, including performance measurement, decentralization, and accountability. Together, these ideologies have significantly influenced governance frameworks in higher education, shifting the focus toward output-based management, institutional autonomy, and stakeholder accountability (Hood, 1991; Deem, 2001).

While these approaches have made some positive changes, such as increased efficiency and responsiveness to stakeholder needs, they have also carried with them concerns about losses of academic freedom, turning the commodification of education into a product, and the risk of a potential increase in inequality and social stratification (Wan et al., 2020).

This chapter aims to critically assess the application of good governance principles in Malaysian HEIs – especially in terms of their potential to support the UN's SDGs. This chapter focuses on four Sustainable Development Goals (SDGs) that are directly relevant to higher education governance and its role in achieving national and global development agendas, namely SDG 4 (Quality Education), SDG 5 (Gender Equality), SDG 16 (Peace, Justice and Strong Institutions), and SDG 17 (Partnerships for the Goals). SDG 4 emphasizes the importance of inclusive and equitable quality education and lifelong learning opportunities for all. It is highly relevant because higher education institutions (HEIs) serve as key drivers of human capital development, knowledge creation, and social mobility (United Nations, 2015). SDG 5, which aims to achieve gender equality and empower all women and girls, is critical in the context of higher education, where gender disparities still exist in enrolment, leadership positions, and academic participation. Promoting gender-inclusive policies in HEIs is essential to ensuring equal opportunities for all (SDSN Australia/Pacific, 2017).

Meanwhile, SDG 16 focuses on promoting peaceful and inclusive societies, ensuring access to justice, and building effective, accountable, and inclusive institutions. This goal aligns closely with the governance structures of HEIs, especially regarding institutional autonomy, transparency, accountability, and stakeholder participation (UNESCO, 2019). Complementing these goals, SDG 17 highlights the importance of partnerships to achieve sustainable development, encouraging collaboration between universities, governments, civil society, and the private sector. HEIs play a vital role in fostering such partnerships through research collaborations, knowledge sharing, and global networks, which are essential to mobilizing resources and expertise to address complex development challenges (United Nations, 2015).

The selection of these four SDGs is based on their strong interconnection with the governance, policy-making, and social responsibilities of higher education institutions. By focusing on SDGs 4, 5, 16, and 17, this chapter aims to explore how good governance in higher education can contribute to the broader sustainable development agenda, particularly through inclusive education, gender-sensitive reforms, strengthening institutional integrity, democratic values, and fostering meaningful partnerships.

This chapter explores the challenges and opportunities for bringing higher education governance into alignment with the broader goals of sustainable development. It examines the drivers of policy and reflects on the fundamental purpose of universities in Malaysia. This contribution to the ongoing discussions around the role of HEIs in promoting sustainable development and societal well-being begins by introducing an overview of the key issues and debates related to good governance and sustainable development in higher education, contextualizing the discussion within the Malaysian higher education landscape and the broader global trends in higher education governance, and signalling the comparative dimension of the article and its focus on the potential of good governance to support the SDGs.

METHODOLOGY

This study employs a qualitative research approach, utilizing an extensive literature review and analysis of relevant policy documents from Malaysia. The key dimensions of good governance examined include: accountability, transparency, autonomy, and stakeholder participation. The analysis draws insights from scholarly articles, government reports, and institutional publications to provide a comprehensive understanding in Malaysia countries' higher education system.

IMPORTANCE OF GOOD GOVERNANCE IN HIGHER EDUCATION INSTITUTIONS

Good governance is especially important in the higher education sector because universities are exceedingly more complex organizations than typical businesses. HEIs have a truly diverse group of stakeholders, which includes faculty, staff, students, alumni, policymakers, and the broader public. The effective management of the different interests and needs of these diverse groups is a pivotal challenge of governance in higher education. Effective governance frameworks are essential for handling the complex interplay of relationships among stakeholders, whilst ensuring the long-term sustainability of HEIs (Delgado, 2012).

Beyond simply managing stakeholder relations, good governance is also essential for boosting the performance of HEIs' primary mission pursuing knowledge through high-quality research, scholarship, and teaching. Robust governance systems provide HEI leaders with the insights to make well-informed decisions, to allocate resources wisely, and to mitigate the risks inherent in knowledge enterprises (Sharma et al., 2023). Thus, good governance is a key factor in achieving excellence in higher education.

The landscape of university governance has changed significantly with various transformations in recent years. There have been several key trends in shaping how HEIs operate and engage with their stakeholders. One major trend surrounds the increasing autonomy given to universities – which has been accompanied by a growing emphasis on accountability (Fielden, 2008). Universities now have greater freedom in their decision making and in how they manage their affairs; but this autonomy comes with the expectation that they will in return become more transparent and accountable for their decisions and consequences of their actions. This means universities must now demonstrate how they are using their autonomy to effectively fulfil their mission and meet the needs of their students, faculty, and the wider community (Fielden, 2008).

Another trend is the increase in performance-based funding, where university resources are now allocated based on a HEI's achievements and outcomes. The departs from the previous systems, whereby enrolment numbers or historical allocations determined the bulk of funding. The purpose of this newer approach is to encourage institutions to engage in continuous improvement, in term of quality, efficiency, and impact thus, their funding depends directly on their performance (Fielden, 2008).

Involvement of stakeholders in university governance has also become more important, with a greater emphasis on broadening engagement to encompass a greater range of stakeholders. This seeks to include students, faculty, staff, alumni, and community members, in decision-making processes. This change shows that universities recognize their duty to consider the interests and perspectives of everyone affected by their decisions (Gallagher, 2001).

Alongside these trends, university governance has also been impacted by the principles of NPM, which stress the need for efficiency, effectiveness, and accountability in the public sector. As a result, universities have adopted a more managerial and business-oriented approach in the way they are governed and operated. Another very significance trend is in the internationalization of university governance approaches, whereby institutions are increasingly involved in global partnerships, collaborations, and networks (Gallagher, 2001). This illustrates the growing awareness among universities that they must upgrade their operations in order to engage in the global context. This helps them enhance their international competitiveness and reputation.

It is critical to recognise that not all higher education systems and institutions adopt the same trends. Various factors, including local context, institutional culture, policymaker priorities, and the aims of specific university leaders, all lead to significant variations in implementation and impact of the new governance changes. When dealing with this changing environment, policymakers and university leaders carefully coordinate a balance of the varying demands surrounding autonomy, accountability, performance, stakeholder engagement, and internationalization. However, by comprehending and addressing these trends, they can ensure that their HEI remains effective, adaptable, and in alignment with relevant needs of their students, faculty, and wider society.

CHALLENGES AND TENSIONS IN HIGHER EDUCATION INSTITUTION GOVERNANCE

Governance in the higher education sector encounters unique challenges particularly in certain country, where policies are changing quickly. There are often conflicts where higher education policy evolves rapidly. Tensions arise between traditional governance models, under which academics had a more central role, and the newer governance frameworks with emphasise smaller, more business-like boards. Handling these conflicts is important because governance must provide a structure for how HEI leadership pursues objectives, whilst ensuring that leaders do not simply emulate the profit-focused conventions of corporate executives.

Governance plays a crucial role in HEIs because it involves coordinating and collaborating with various stakeholders, including students, faculty, and administrators, to make sure the HEI runs smoothly. Effective governance is vital for universities to reach their goals and maintain their good reputation. Despite this, implementing effective governance practices can present challenges. Universities often face challenges related to unclear decision-making processes and a lack of mechanisms to demonstrate responsible action when confronted with obstacles. Insufficient accountability measures, and not getting enough involvement from stakeholders in operations and decision making, can also stop an institution from working well and achieving its goals efficiently. Effective governance must overcome these challenges, otherwise they can hinder an institution's ability to operate efficiently and effectively.

Despite the challenges, governance plays a vital role in ensuring the quality and relevance of higher education, and it helps universities to set clear institutional missions, to ensure the alignment of their academic programs with what the requirements from the labour market. It can also help to create a culture of innovative thinking, and entrepreneurial spirit. By making governance a main goal, universities can be sure that they provide high-quality education that meets the needs of students and society.

According to Areiqat et al. (2020), good governance is a very important factor for enhancing the overall functioning of universities. Well-managed institutions that are transparent and that are clear and accountable to the people they serve are more likely to reach their goals and maintain a good reputation. This is especially important now in today's competitive and interconnected global environment, where universities face increasing pressure to perform and deal with constant changes, in order to stay connected, relevant, and keep up with changing world circumstances.

It is also important to note how important the international context is in which universities operate. The ways universities are run must reflect governance structures and practices adopted by the whole world – institutions are influenced by the global landscape – which includes factors such as globalization, new technologies, and international competition between countries in the higher education sector. By identifying global trends, and adapting quickly to them, universities can ensure that they stay competitive and relevant in the international arena (Kapfudzaruwa, 2024).

The 6th IAU Global Survey Report shows how the pattern of increasing globalization of higher education is becoming more normalised. Universities face new opportunities and new challenges as they respond to the changing global context. Globalization means that universities around the world are more connected, and this has led to greater interdependence with greater need for cooperation. Alongside this level of interdependence among HEIs worldwide, they must also compete with each other for students, faculty, and funding, on at the international level. One significant trend identified in the report is that more students are going abroad to study. This growth of international student mobility comes because students desire opportunities to learn and study abroad, and to gain global exposure. Therefore, HEIs are eagerly looking for international students from other countries to diversify their campuses and to bring in additional revenue (Marinoni & Cardona, 2024).

The report also talks about how universities are developing more international partnerships and working collaborations, as universities work together across borders to share resources, knowledge, funding, and expertise, to deliver optimum results. However, 'going global' is not without challenges. The process of internationalization requires universities to comply with numerous complex regulatory frameworks, different cultures, and language barriers, as they advance. So as HEIs expand their reach, there is an additional need for greater clarity and transparency surrounding their international partnerships, so that they can continue to demonstrate their accountability at home. These partnerships must ensure that they are mutually beneficial, and come into alignment with the goals of each institution. Moreover, these partnerships must reflect cultural sensitivity in international collaborations, where working among diverse stakeholders from around the world can present many challenges. It is crucial for HEIs to know how to understand and respect cultural differences in communication styles, decision-making processes, and educational philosophies and practices (Marinoni & Cardona, 2024).

MALAYSIA HIGHER EDUCATION CODE

The National Education Code (NEC-2020), issued by the Malaysian Qualifications Agency (MQA), acts as the reference manual for codifying education programs in Malaysia. It is in alignment with international standards and provides a coding system for naming education and training programs (Ministry of Higher Education, 2020). The Education Program Standards, which are also issued by MQA, help guide the formulation of education programs in Malaysia. These standards define what education programs should aim to meet and exceed, covering aspects like program aims, learning outcomes, curriculum design, assessment, staff, resources, and quality improvement. Additionally, the National Higher Education Strategic Plan (PSPTN) lays out the goals and strategies for Malaysian higher education from 2020 onwards. This plan includes goals such as producing high-quality graduates, empowering institutions, and reaching globally.

These key regulatory and policy documents particularly the NEC-2020 and the Education Program Standards, provide the framework governing education programs and standards in the Malaysian higher education system. They serve as important reference points for institutions to align their offerings with national requirements. NEC-2020, Education Program Standards, and National Higher Education Strategic Plan collectively establish the regulatory and policy landscape for higher education in Malaysia, guiding the classification, design, and strategic direction of education programs to meet national and international standards.

ACCOUNTABILITY AND TRANSPARENCY IN MALAYSIAN HIGHER EDUCATION INSTITUTIONS

In recent years we have seen a metamorphosis in Malaysia's system of higher education one that places an increasing importance on transparency and accountability. In the upcoming years post-2020, the National Higher Education Strategic Plan (PSPTN) sketches out the vision and blueprint for Malaysian tertiary education: a key aspect of it involves improving transparency and accountability. The plan seeks to make sure that the Higher Education Institutions are answerable to the public and stakeholders, with their governance as well as decision-making processes being visible and participatory.

The Malaysian government has taken a number of steps to ensure transparency and accountability in higher education. For example, the Ministry of Higher Education set up Education Malaysia Global Services (EMGS) as the official channel for studying in Malaysia. This creates a centralized system where international students can apply for student visas and keep track of their applications. EMGS also put in place certain measures during the COVID-19 period to guarantee the safety and welfare of international students an act which underscores the government's commitment to transparency and accountability in higher education.

Furthermore, the NEC-2020 and the Education Program Standards put forth by MQA furnish a framework that upholds quality and responsibility of educational programs in Malaysia. The documents delineate standards and stipulations for education programs encompassing details on curriculum, assessment, and evaluation procedures thus warranting that learners are imparted with an education of excellent quality that befits international standards. In sum, the strides taken by the Malaysian government to infuse transparency and answerability in higher education loom large as pillars for upholding quality and trustworthiness of the sector, even fostering international cooperation and collaboration in the sphere of education.

However, according to Mohammed et al. (2021) (whose study analyses financial statements from 20 Malaysian public universities from 2015-2018), while current ratios are high indicating substantial liquid resources, further investigation reveals most universities classify deferred grants as non-current liabilities, and debt ratios are also high implying slow amortization of government grants which jeopardizes financial statement quality and transparency. These practices hint at challenges in achieving SDG 16 on "Peace, Justice and Strong Institutions" through transparent and accountable public sector practices.

Moreover, more progress is needed to align with SDG 16 goals on institutional transparency and accountability. The current governance structure of universities is not effective in ensuring transparency and accountability. The universities need to adopt more robust governance practices to achieve these goals.

Autonomy of Malaysian Higher Education Institutions

Although universities are being given more autonomy, this is coupled with accountability and transparency requirements. The balance between providing universities with greater autonomy to regulate their own activities, and the control that must ensure not only efficiency in resource allocation but also accountability towards both the government and society regarding performance (Michavila & Martinez 2018)

a) Autonomy vs Accountability in Higher Education

One of the significant developments in higher education governance is an increasing level of autonomy to universities with its concomitant stress on accountability. As universities have been autonomized from the grip of bureaucratic regimes that made decisions on their part there has also arisen a countervailing expectation: one holds under an implicit yet undeniable command - to behave like autonomous actors by displaying transparency and accountability for each act carried out (Tripathi & Gupta, 2016).

This shift reflects a broader policy push towards greater institutional autonomy, driven by the belief that universities will be more innovative, responsive, and efficient, if they have more control over their operations. However, the granting of autonomy is often coupled with new controls and accountability measures from governments. There is a need to balance autonomy and accountability, since universities require freedom to pursue their academic mission, but also need to be responsive to public goals and interests.

b) Governance and Internal Management

To thrive with greater autonomy, universities need to develop clear organizational strategies and a fusion of academic and executive leadership. The internal governance of universities requires reassessment, in order to adapt to the shift towards more market-driven and competitive higher education. Autonomous universities are expected to generate their own funds and resources, rather than relying solely on government support (Martin, 2013)

c) Funding and Resources

However, indicator-based funding mechanisms tied to performance metrics can undermine perceived university autonomy. There is a tension between the desire to give universities more freedom to manage their own affairs, and the need for them to be accountable to government and the public for their performance and use of resources (Martin, 2013).

The Malaysian government has granted varying degrees of autonomy to public HEIs particularly in areas such as financial management and academic affairs. This means that universities have been given more freedom to make their own decisions and manage their own affairs in these domains. However, the level of autonomy remains limited, with the government still exercising significant control over key decisions.

Government influence on key areas of university governance including the appointment of university leadership-remains significant. The government is largely responsible to identify and reach who are going to be appointed the top leadership positions in public universities, they have a major say on this of course like for instance their immediate leader i.e. Vice-Chancellor or even Deputy Vice-Chancellor. It gives the government a tool to direct those institutions in desired directions and set priorities.

Yet, in practice the government still exerts control over how these financial resources are allocated to state universities. The kind of funding Universities received would often come with very precise priorities and objectives from the government, effectively reducing their latitude in how to use these resources. While universities are curbed in their freedom of planning independent academic programs or curriculum, all major changes and new measures must always be approved by the government.

The government has established the legal and regulatory framework within which public universities operate. These policies and guidelines have to be followed by the universities and while having certain advantages they limit the freedom of actions of universities. The devolution of autonomy in the Malaysian public universities mean that while universities have been given larger measure of freedom in the way they are run, the government sees the need to retain some control on certain strategic aspects in the universities' development. To overcome the challenges arising from the partial devolution of autonomy, Malaysian public universities must establish strong internal governance structures that ensure transparency, accountability, and strategic alignment with national policies. While universities enjoy greater freedom in operational matters, they must develop clear decision-making frameworks, strengthen institutional leadership, and enhance stakeholder engagement, including academic staff, students, and industry partners. Furthermore, HEIs should implement robust monitoring and evaluation mechanisms to demonstrate their capacity to govern effectively and responsibly. This includes setting up transparent reporting systems, adopting performance-based management practices, and aligning institutional goals with both the Ministry of Higher Education's strategic plans and the Sustainable Development Goals (SDGs). By doing so, universities can assert their autonomy while maintaining the government's trust and fulfilling their public accountability obligations (Morshidi et al., 2017; UNESCO, 2019).

This balance is influenced by factors such as universities' accountability for public funding, alignment with government and development objectives, and a strong commitment to maintaining quality standards. Nevertheless, it is also of note that the level of the autonomy of each university might vary depending on its condition, experience, and interaction with the government. Some universities may have more autonomy in certain areas compared to others, depending on their performance, reputation, and strategic importance (Kallio, et al, 2022). Thus, the Malaysian government's attitude to university autonomy issue is complex and fine-tuned balance. Though there has been a degree of autonomy allowed to the public HEIs to manage their affairs, the government continues to exercise considerable degree of control over major aspects of university functioning. This approach has the vision of making sure that universities retain their responsibility, relevance and continual delivery of quality education and research relevant to their nation's goals.

Malaysian Higher Education Institutions v Stakeholders

Malaysian HEIs have made efforts to engage with various stakeholders, including industry, community, and international partners. However, the level of meaningful participation and the influence of stakeholders in institutional governance and decision-making processes remain limited.

Stakeholder Engagement

For effective governance in HEIs, stakeholder engagement is essential. In Malaysian HEIs, both public and private, there have been various efforts to engage with external stakeholders such as industry, community groups and international partners. These collaborations attempt to align between the requirements of the labour market/society and higher education programs/researches so that they can keep up with the changing demands of this century. However, search results suggest that the actual involvement and influence of stakeholders in Malaysian HEIs' governance and strategic directions are relatively limited (Azman, 2020). On one hand, although HEIs have improved their relationships through external linkages; decision making processes and overall governance structure remains largely driven by internal academic leadership and administrative management.

Effective governance in higher education institutions requires stakeholder participation. This helps in positioning HEIs globally through engagements with different industries and organizations from around the world. The main advantage is to match researches conducted or courses offered by universities with labour market changes over time. Active collaboration with industry in curriculum development and research prioritization ensures graduates have the skills required for success, while providing industry with a pipeline of talented, work-ready individuals (Paunescu et al., 2022).

HEIs also gain insights into pressing societal challenges by engaging with nonprofits, policymakers and civil society groups. This information guides the development of research projects, outreach initiatives, educational programs that directly address local and global issues both at home and abroad-accentuating the importance as well as the flexibility of HEIs. Besides, stakeholder engagement can make HEIs more innovative and entrepreneurial in nature. For instance, incorporating innovation through research findings from international partners is important for ensuring that students, staffs and researchers are kept abreast with emerging trends in their respective fields. This idea exchange fosters a new way of thinking that encourages new joint ventures, creative products or services development and an enterprise culture too. Effective stakeholder engagement positively impacts students, helping Malaysian HEIs attract more students, increase funding through grants, and improve their global rankings by demonstrating quality and competitiveness

The Sustainable Development Goals for Malaysia's Higher Education Institutions

Malaysia has a diverse higher education landscape, comprising 20 public universities, 435 private HEIs, 105 community colleges, and 36 polytechnics. The country's education system is guided by the Malaysia Education Blueprint for Higher Education 2015, which emphasizes the development of high-quality graduates, empowerment of HEIs, and internationalization. HEIs play a critical role in achieving the UN's SDGs by 2030 (Higher Education Sustainability Initiative, 2021). HEIs are aligning their strategic plans, policies, and operations with the SDGs – integrating them into governance, campus management, teaching, research, and community engagement (Department of Economic and Social Affairs, 2015). However, HEIs face challenges, such as a lack of consensus on sustainability definitions, insufficient resources, difficulty integrating disciplines, and the need for innovative teaching. Effective leadership that understands sustainability's interconnected nature, and that empowers youth, is crucial for HEIs to successfully implement the SDGs (Suklun & Bengu, 2024). HEIs are also forming partnerships with businesses, governments, and other sectors to collaborate on research, training, knowledge transfer, and public engagement towards the SDGs.

As Malaysia works towards the SDGs, the role of HEIs is crucial particularly for SDG 4 on "Quality Education". Malaysian HEIs must take steps to ensure equitable access to quality higher education regardless of background, promote lifelong learning and upskilling to meet evolving labor market needs, and integrate sustainable development concepts across curricula to cultivate a new generation of leaders committed to addressing complex challenges. Achieving the goals of SDG 4 in Malaysian higher education will require a collaborative effort involving policymakers, university administrators, faculty, students, and community stakeholders; but the potential benefits are immense for transforming the higher education landscape and contributing to the sustainable development of the nation.

HEIs can contribute to SDG 5 on "Gender Equality" by promoting gender parity in enrolment and attainment through affirmative action, support services, and data analysis; addressing gender-based discrimination and harassment through robust policies, training, and reporting mechanisms; empowering women in leadership roles by setting targets, implementing equitable processes, and offering development opportunities; and integrating gender perspectives across teaching, research, and community engagement in collaboration with women's rights organizations, which requires commitment from university leadership and diverse stakeholders to model inclusive and empowering environments that advance SDG 5 and inspire broader societal transformation (Rosa & Clavero, 2021).

HEIs contribute to SDG 16 by promoting transparency, protecting academic freedom, encouraging inclusive decision-making, and collaborating with civil society, all of which require strong leadership and teamwork to prepare students to build peaceful and just societies. HEIs can contribute to SDG 17 on "Partnerships for the Goals" by strengthening international collaboration and knowledge-sharing among universities to share best practices and innovative solutions; engaging with industry, civil society, and government partners to align higher education with sustainable development priorities and leverage diverse expertise and resources; and mobilizing financial and technical resources, such as through public-private partnerships and philanthropic funding, to support sustainable development initiatives within the higher education sector. By fostering these multi-stakeholder partnerships, HEIs can amplify their impact and accelerate progress towards the SDGs.

Significance of SDGs for Effective Governance in Malaysia Higher Education Institutions

The significance of SDGs for governance strategies in HEIs in Malaysia is profound – influencing numerous aspects of governance and operational effectiveness. Mainstreaming of the SDGs into the Malaysian HEIs will improve sustainable development as well as success. SDGs hold significant importance for promoting good governance practices within Malaysia's HEIs.

Advocating for transparent and accountable governance through SDG 16 on "Peace, Justice and Strong Institutions" emphasizes the importance of developing effective, accountable and transparent institutions at all levels. Malaysia HEIs can align their governance structures and decision-making processes with the principles of SDG 16 to enhance transparency, reduce corruption, and ensure inclusive participation.

Secondly, institutionalizing the goals of the SDGs agenda. Due to the broad nature of the SDGs the consideration of sustainability aspects should be at the strategic, tactical, and operational level in HEIs. The HEIs of Malaysia can also show the external stakeholders and the institutional management that their values are now aligned well with the SDG framework and by sharing resources – can help the nation and the global society to achieve its goals.

Thirdly, the fostering of multi-stakeholder partnerships achieving the SDGs necessitates collaboration and partnerships among diverse stakeholders, including government, industry, civil society, and the academic community. Through this collaboration Malaysian HEIs can effectively contribute to multi-stakeholder engagement, knowledge exchange, and partnership for sustainable development ambitions.

Fourthly, enhancing operational efficiency and resource management SDGs, related to "Responsible Consumption and Production" (SDG 12), "Affordable and Clean Energy" (SDG 7), and "Climate Action" (SDG 13) can guide Malaysian HEIs in improving their resource efficiency, reducing waste, and adopting sustainable practices. Integrating these SDGs into campus operations can lead to cost savings, environmental benefits, and improved overall sustainability.

Finally, for Strengthening Monitoring, Evaluation, and Reporting, the SDG framework developed by the United Nations come with targets and indicators that can be used in the evaluation of HEIs in Malaysia to meet the objectives of sustainable development. Implementing monitoring and reporting structures that are compliant with the principles of the SDGs will lead to increased institutional accountability, the ability to use benchmarking as a comparison tool, and improve decision making grounded in empirical evidence.

By embracing the SDGs as a guiding framework, Malaysian HEIs can enhance their overall governance, operational effectiveness, and contribution to sustainable development. This holistic approach can help position HEIs as key drivers of societal transformation and catalysts for achieving the national and global sustainable development agenda.

CONCLUSION AND RECOMMENDATIONS

The specific recommendations given to improve governance in Malaysian HEIs depicts a comprehensive and holistic approach towards the improvement of the Malaysia Higher education sector, thus heightening the sustainability of the sector.

To improve governance in Malaysian higher education institutions (HEIs), a comprehensive and holistic approach is required to enhance institutional autonomy and ensure the sustainability of the sector. One fundamental step is increasing transparency and accountability. This involves HEIs publishing detailed performance reports, financial audits, and governance decisions openly. Transparency helps build trust among stakeholders such as students, faculty, government, and the public, and it ensures that institutions manage resources responsibly and ethically (Morshidi et al., 2017; UNESCO, 2019). Without transparency, institutions risk inefficiency and reduced public confidence, which can negatively impact funding and reputation.

Another critical area is promoting meaningful stakeholder engagement. Higher education governance should actively involve various stakeholders, including students, academic staff, industry partners, and government bodies, in decision-making processes. This inclusion not only makes governance more democratic but also ensures that institutional policies and strategies are responsive to the diverse needs of those affected by them. Stakeholder participation contributes to institutional relevance, innovation, and adaptability in a rapidly changing educational and societal landscape (Santiago et al., 2016).

Developing a culture of good governance within HEIs is also vital. This culture is based on core values such as integrity, ethical conduct, accountability, and commitment to quality. Building this culture requires leadership development programs, continuous training, and reinforcement of ethical standards at all levels of governance. When leadership and staff are aligned with good governance principles, institutions are more likely to make sound decisions that reflect both institutional goals and public interests (OECD, 2020).

Furthermore, Malaysian HEIs can gain significantly from cross-learning and benchmarking their governance models against international best practices. Benchmarking allows institutions to adopt evidence-based governance frameworks and innovative approaches proven effective in other contexts, facilitating continuous improvement and modernization of governance systems (World Bank, 2020). This comparative approach helps HEIs avoid common pitfalls and align with global standards, improving their competitiveness and quality.

In addition, the adoption of ethical and evidence-based decision-making models is crucial. Decisions should be grounded in reliable data and aligned with national development goals and the Sustainable Development Goals (SDGs). By integrating data-driven policies and ethical considerations, HEIs can enhance their institutional performance while contributing meaningfully to the broader development agenda (United Nations, 2015).

Efficient utilization of resources and research knowledge is another key element. HEIs should strategically manage their human, financial, and physical resources to maximize impact. They must also leverage research outputs to inform policies and practices that advance sustainable development locally and globally. Setting measurable targets related to the SDGs will help institutions monitor progress and demonstrate their contributions to national and international priorities (SDSN, 2017).

Beyond institutional efforts, government support plays an essential role. Capacity-building initiatives provided by the government can empower HEIs to implement governance reforms effectively. This support can take the form of funding, policy guidance, and training programs designed to strengthen governance structures and capabilities (Morshidi et al., 2017).

Moreover, regular monitoring and evaluation of governance processes ensure continuous improvement. By systematically assessing governance outcomes and identifying areas for enhancement, HEIs can remain accountable and responsive to their stakeholders (OECD, 2020).

Finally, fostering collaborative governance through partnerships among HEIs, industry, and government agencies encourages innovation and responsiveness. Such collaboration enables institutions to address emerging challenges more effectively and align educational outcomes with workforce and societal needs (UNESCO, 2019).

In conclusion, implementing these recommendations will significantly strengthen the governance systems of Malaysian HEIs. This will improve institutional performance, increase responsiveness to development needs, and enhance the contributions of HEIs toward achieving the Sustainable Development Goals.

REFERENCES

Abd Ghadas, Z. A., & Hassan, H. (2008). Good governance in Malaysian public higher learning institutions: Special reference to International Islamic University Malaysia. In *International Conference on Higher Education in Muslim World: Challenges and Prospect*, 24th-25th March 2008, Kuala Lumpur.

Ahmad, A. R., Farley, A., & Kim-Soon, N. (2013). Funding Reforms in Malaysian Public Universities: Transitions towards Competitive Funding. *Australian Journal of Basic and Applied Sciences*, *7*(10), 553–561.

Areiqat, A. Y., Zamil, A. M. A., Alheet, A. F., Ahmadd, M. M., & Abushaare, H. M. (2020). The Concept of Governance in Universities: Reality and Ambition. *International Journal of Innovation. Creativity and Change*, *13*(1), 951–963.

Asimirana, S., & Ismail, I. A. (2019). Exploring critical success factors in the governance of Malaysian public universities. *International Journal of Innovation. Creativity and Change*, *9*(12), 268–282.

Asuhaimi, F. A. (2017). Waqf management and administration in Malaysian higher education institutions. *International Journal of Academic Research in Business & Social Sciences*, *7*(4), 1–10.

Azman, N. (2020). Trends in Governance and Management of the Malaysian Academic Profession (2007-2013): Evolution or Devolution? *Higher Education Governance and Policy*, *1*(2), 109–125.

Deem, R. (2001). Globalisation, new managerialism, academic capitalism and entrepreneurialism in universities: Is the local dimension still important? *Comparative Education*, *37*(1), 7–20. DOI: 10.1080/03050060020020408

Delgado, L. (2012). Good Governance in Higher Education. The Right to Education. In *2nd World Conference on the Right to and Rights in Education.*

Department of Economic and Social Affairs. (2015). *The 17 Sustainable Development Goals*. United Nations. https://sdgs.un.org/goals

Fielden, J. (2008). Global trends in university governance. *Education Working Paper Series*, 9, 1-48.

Gallagher, M. (2001). Modern university governance: A national perspective. *Journal of Higher Education Policy and Management*, *23*(1), 49–58.

Higher Education Sustainability Initiative. (2021). *Assessments of Higher Education's progress towards the UN Sustainable Development Goals Volume 2: for higher education institutions participating in assessments*. HESI Working Group, United Nations. https://sdgs.un.org/sites/default/files/2021-09/HEI%20assessment%20for%20the%20SDGs%20-%20Volume%202%20HEIs1.pdf

Hood, C. (1991). A public management for all seasons? *Public Administration*, *69*(1), 3–19. DOI: 10.1111/j.1467-9299.1991.tb00779.x

Hussin, R., Kader, S. Z. S. A., Manshor, N. M., Roslim, S., & Sirat, N. I. M. (2021). Good governance practices for waqf in Malaysian higher education institutions (HEIs). *Academy of Entrepreneurship Journal*, *20*(2S), 1–13.

Kallio, T. J., Kallio, K. M., Huusko, M., Pyykkö, R., & Kivistö, J. (2022). Balancing between accountability and autonomy: The impact and relevance of public steering mechanisms within higher education. *Journal of Public Budgeting, Accounting & Financial Management*, *34*(6), 46–68. DOI: 10.1108/JPBAFM-10-2020-0177

Kapfudzaruwa, F. (2024). Internationalization of Higher Education and Emerging National Rationales: Comparative Analysis of the Global North and South. *Higher Education Policy*, •••, 1–30. DOI: 10.1057/s41307-024-00358-z

Marinoni, G., & Pina Cardona, S. B. (2024). *Internationalization of Higher Education: Current Trends and Future* Scenarios. 6th IAU Global Survey Report. International Association of Universities. https://www.iau-aiu.net/IMG/pdf/2024_internationalization_survey_report_digital.pdf

Martin, M. (2013). *Increased autonomy for universities in Asia: How to make it work? (IIEP policy brief. Policy brief on higher education*, 4(1). UNESCO International Institute for Educational Planning. https://unesdoc.unesco.org/ark:/48223/pf0000229831

Michavila, F., & Martinez, J. (2018). Excellence of Universities versus Autonomy, Funding and Accountability. *European Review (Chichester, England)*, *26*(S1), 1–9. DOI: 10.1017/S1062798717000539

Ministry of Higher Education. (2020). *National Education Code (NEC-2020)*. Ministry of Higher Education: Malaysia. https://www.mqa.gov.my/new/document/2022/Feb/National%20Education%20Code%202020%20%28NEC-2020%29.pdf

Mohammed, N. F., Mohamed, N., Atan, R., & Said, J. (2021). Financial Transparency in Malaysian Public Universities: Are We on the Path to Achieving SDG 16? *Academy of Strategic Management Journal*, *20*(S6), 1–15.

Morshidi, S., Wan, C. D., & Norzaini, A. (2017). Governance reforms in higher education: Reflections from Malaysia. In Mihut, G., Altbach, P. G., & de Wit, H. (Eds.), *Understanding higher education internationalization: Insights from key global publications* (pp. 197–202). Sense Publishers.

OECD. (2020). *Higher education governance reforms: Patterns and trends*. OECD Publishing., DOI: 10.1787/9789264305032-

Păunescu, C., Nikina-Ruohonen, A., & Stukalina, Y. (2022). Fostering Research with Societal Impact in Higher Education Institutions: A Review and Conceptualization. In Păunescu, C., Lepik, K. L., & Spencer, N. (Eds.), *Social Innovation in Higher Education. Innovation, Technology, and Knowledge Management*. Springer, Cham. DOI: 10.1007/978-3-030-84044-0_8

Rosa, R., & Clavero, S. (2021). Gender equality in higher education and research. *Journal of Gender Studies, 31*(1), 1–7. DOI: 10.1080/09589236.2022.2007446

Santiago, P., Tremblay, K., Basri, E., & Arnal, E. (2016). *Higher education governance and management*. OECD Education Working Papers, No. 59. OECD Publishing. https://doi.org/DOI: 10.1787/5jm3pgl7jbnr-en

SDSN Australia/Pacific. (2017). Getting started with the SDGs in universities: A guide for universities, higher education institutions, and the academic sector. https://ap-unsdsn.org/regional-initiatives/universities-sdgs/

SDSN (Sustainable Development Solutions Network). (2017). *Getting started with the SDGs in universities: A guide for universities, higher education institutions, and the academic sector*. SDSN Australia/Pacific. https://ap-unsdsn.org/regional-initiatives/universities-sdgs/

Sharma, J., Srivastava, A., & Kapoor, Y. (2023). Strategic Human Resource Management. In B. K. Sarkar, R. Singh, V. Singh, S. Mishra, P. Kumar, & P. N. & Singh (eds), *Multidisciplinary International Conference on Innovations in Education Science & Technology ICIEST-2023*. USA: GEH Press.

Suklun, H., & Bengu, E. (2024). Raising Awareness of SDGs in Higher Education Institutions. *Research in Educational Administration & Leadership, 9*(1), 39–72. DOI: 10.30828/real.1357661

Sulaiman, T. F., & Abd Ghadas, Z. A. (2021). Corporate governance models for higher educational institutions: An analysis. *Pertanika Journal of Social Science & Humanities, 29*(S2), 149–168. http://www.pertanika.upm.edu.my/pjssh.php?journal=PJSSH-29-S2-11. DOI: 10.47836/pjssh.29.s2.11

Tripathi, K., & Gupta, R. (2016). Autonomy and Accountability in Higher Education. *Journal of Human and Work Management*, *4*, 26–31.

UNESCO. (2019). Governance in higher education: A global perspective. United Nations Educational, Scientific and Cultural Organization. https://unesdoc.unesco.org/ark:/48223/pf0000371094

United Nations. (2015). Transforming our world: The 2030 agenda for sustainable development. https://sdgs.un.org/2030agenda

United Nations Economic and Social Commission for Asia and the Pacific. (2009). What is good governance? UNESCAP. https://www.unescap.org/sites/default/d8files/knowledge-products/what-is-good-governance.pdf

Wan, C. D., Sirat, M., & Abdul Razak, D. (2020). Academic governance and leadership in Malaysia: Examining the national higher education strategic initiatives. *Journal of International and Comparative Education*, *9*(2), 91–105. DOI: 10.14425/jice.2020.9.2.0913

World Bank. (2020). *Governance and higher education quality: An international perspective*. World Bank Group. https://documents.worldbank.org/en/publication/documents-reports/documentdetail/123456

KEY TERMS AND DEFINITIONS

Good Governance: The framework of rules, practices, and processes by which higher education institutions are directed and controlled to ensure transparency, accountability, stakeholder participation, and autonomy in decision-making.

Higher Education Institutions (HEIs): Organizations that provide tertiary education services, including universities, colleges, and polytechnics, and are responsible for delivering and enhancing academic and research excellence.

Accountability: The obligation of HEIs to be answerable for their decisions and performance to stakeholders, including students, government agencies, and the public.

Transparency: The practice of making institutional policies, decisions, and processes open and accessible to stakeholders to foster trust and informed participation.

Autonomy: The degree of independence and self-governance granted to HEIs in making academic, administrative, and financial decisions without undue external interference.

Stakeholder Engagement: The process of involving individuals or groups who have an interest in the institution (e.g., students, faculty, government bodies, employers) in governance and decision-making processes.

Sustainable Development Goals (SDGs): A set of 17 global goals established by the United Nations to address various social, economic, and environmental challenges; in this context, particularly SDG 4 (Quality Education), SDG 5 (Gender Equality), and SDG 16 (Peace, Justice and Strong Institutions).

Chapter 15

A Pathway to Achieving SDG 16 Through Empowering Legal Literacy for Company Officers

Siti Suraya Abd Razak
https://orcid.org/0000-0003-1214-7854
Universiti Teknologi Malaysia, Malaysia

Hanini Ilyana Che Hashim
Universiti Teknologi Malaysia, Malaysia

Mohd Zulfabli Hasan
Universiti Teknologi Malaysia, Malaysia

ABSTRACT

The Sustainable Development Goals (SDGs) aim to end poverty, protect the planet, and promote peace and prosperity by 2030. Achieving these goals requires good governance, which depends on the legal literacy of key actors, including company officers. This study explores the legal literacy of company officers in Malaysia, focusing on their understanding of the Companies Act 2016 (Act 777). Using a qualitative approach, the study analyzed court cases, statutes, and data from in-depth semi-structured interviews with seven company officers. Thematic analysis revealed that directors often lack legal literacy, while company secretaries and auditors demonstrate moderate understanding of the Act. These gaps contribute to breaches of duties and legal actions, impacting corporate governance. The findings

DOI: 10.4018/979-8-3373-1792-2.ch015

highlight the urgent need for improved legal awareness among company officers and offer insights for policymakers to strengthen regulatory frameworks. This research links legal literacy to SDG 16, emphasizing its role in promoting strong institutions and sustainable governance.

INTRODUCTION

The Sustainable Development Goals (SDGs), adopted by the United Nations aimed at ending poverty, protecting the planet, and ensuring peace and prosperity for all people by 2030. Comprising 17 goals and 169 specific targets, the SDGs cover diverse aspects of global challenges, including poverty alleviation, education, gender equality, clean water and sanitation, climate action and strong institutions. The significance of SDGs lies in their capacity to provide a clear and comprehensive framework that guides national policies and international cooperation toward sustainable development. This universality highlights a collective responsibility to address global challenges collaboratively. Additionally, the inclusive nature of SDGs involves not only governments but also businesses, civil society organizations and individuals, fostering a multi-stakeholder approach essential for achieving sustainable outcomes. SDG 16 specifically focuses on promoting peaceful and inclusive societies, ensuring access to justice, and building effective, accountable, and inclusive institutions at all levels. This goal recognizes the essential interdependence between peace, justice, and institutional stability, emphasizing that sustainable development is impossible without addressing injustice, and weak governance. Justice, another integral component of SDG 16, requires equitable access to legal systems for all, regardless of socio-economic status, ethnicity, or gender. Barriers such as corruption, discrimination, high costs, and inefficiency often disproportionately affect marginalized groups. By promoting the rule of law and ensuring equal access to justice, SDG 16 aims to foster societal trust, social cohesion, and empowerment. Effective justice systems also enable individuals to defend their rights and contribute to broader societal development.

Achieving the SDGs requires rigorous adherence to laws, regulations, and policies designed to support sustainable practices and development. Legal frameworks serve as foundational elements for translating international commitments into actionable measures at national and local levels. Thus, ensuring compliance with these frameworks is crucial for realizing the SDGs. However, legal compliance is often hampered by limited awareness and understanding of relevant laws in corporations. Legal literacy emerges as an important element in bridging this compliance gap. Defined as the ability of individuals to understand and utilize laws effectively, legal literacy refers to as the knowledge of legal rights and obligations, the skills to navigate legal systems, and the attitudes necessary to engage proactively in legal and regulatory processes. Enhanced legal literacy empowers stakeholders from policymakers and business leaders to ordinary citizens to engage in sustainability practices, advocate for effective policy implementation, and hold institutions accountable for SDG-related commitments. Legal literacy supports compliance with SDGs in multiple ways. First, informed citizens and stakeholders are more likely to adhere to laws designed to protect the environment, uphold human rights, and foster social justice. Second, enhanced legal literacy improves the effectiveness of policy implementation by ensuring that stakeholders understand the rationale behind sustainability regulations, leading to greater cooperation and reduced resistance to compliance measures. Third, a legally literate populace contributes to increased accountability, as they are better equipped to monitor, report, and challenge instances of non-compliance. Legal literacy ensures that individuals and institutions are aware of their roles and responsibilities concerning sustainable development, driving adherence to regulatory frameworks essential for global sustainability.

The absence of legal literacy among corporate officers can significantly impact corporate governance, leading to breaches of fiduciary duties that undermine organizational integrity and hinder achievement of Sustainable Development Goals (SDGs). This lack of legal literacy has contributed to the breach of duties of company officers while managing companies. The landmark United States' case involving Enron Corporation demonstrates a catastrophic breach of fiduciary duties. Enron executives, lacking adequate understanding of their legal responsibilities or deliberately disregarding them, engaged in extensive financial fraud and manipulation of accounting practices (Coffee, 2006). This profound lack of legal literacy or ethical comprehension resulted in corporate governance failure, causing the company's collapse in 2001. The Enron scandal had extensive socioeconomic repercussions, directly contravening SDG 8 (Decent Work and Economic Growth) and SDG 16 (Peace, Justice, and Strong Institutions), as thousands of employees lost their jobs and pensions, eroding trust in corporate transparency and governance frameworks (Healy & Palepu, 2003).

The 2008 financial crisis highlighted deficiencies in legal literacy among executives in the United States' financial sector. Lehman Brothers, emblematic of this crisis, collapsed due to aggressive risk-taking and inadequate corporate governance oversight. Company officers failed to comprehend or adhere to legally mandated risk management practices, contributing significantly to financial instability (Valukas, 2010). In the United Kingdom, the Carillion scandal of 2018 similarly underscores the devastating impacts of inadequate legal literacy among corporate officers. Senior executives at Carillion breached their fiduciary duties by failing to manage risks prudently and concealing severe financial instability. Lack of adequate understanding or willful neglect of legal responsibilities concerning transparent financial reporting and due diligence led to Carillion's sudden insolvency (UK Parliament, 2018). The collapse had widespread implications for infrastructure projects and public sector contracts, significantly disrupting essential services and employment.

While in Malaysia, a company director was charged with 64 counts of misappropriation, forging cheques and using the forged cheques amounting to more than RM10 mil (Kaur, 2022). In another case involving a director, a company director was arrested for bribery in the form of a vacation paid by clients (Bernama, 2023). Additionally, in 2015 an auditor was found guilty of misleading disclosure of financial information and was jailed and fined (Securities Commission Malaysia, 2023). These cases collectively highlight how insufficient legal literacy among corporate officers results in breaches of fiduciary duties, directly jeopardizing corporate governance integrity. Such breaches impede the advancement of crucial Sustainable Development Goals, underscoring the necessity of promoting robust legal education and awareness among corporate leadership. Ensuring officers understand and fulfill their legal responsibilities not only fortifies corporate governance but also contributes meaningfully toward achieving sustainable economic, social, and institutional development as envisioned by the SDGs.

There are two research objective of this study which is firstly. to analyse the understanding of the company officers on their duties and liabilities and secondly, to recommend steps that can be taken to increase the literacy among company officers in Malaysia. The first part of this paper describes the current literature relevant to this study which includes defining the concept of legal literacy and the qualifications, duties and liabilities of directors, auditors and company secretaries in Malaysia according to the Companies Act 2016 (Act 777) and related court cases. The next section of this paper analyses data collected from respondents and the discussion is concluded with a conclusion and recommendation. This discussion underscores how robust legal literacy among corporate officers ensures compliance and fosters sustainable corporate practices, directly contributing to achieving the transparency and accountability envisioned in SDG 16.

METHODOLOGY

Qualitative assessment is used in this research. This study employed qualitative methodology to link an understanding of social components of life. Rather than producing a lot of numerical data, it mostly creates words that scholars may utilise for further analysis (Moriarty 2011; Dioubate et al. 2015). In order to get information from participants and provide them the opportunity to reply as necessary and understand the phenomenon being studied, qualitative analysts use discourse (Cronin 2014; Dasgupta 2015). The study employed semi-structured interviews with seven company officers in Malaysian private companies as respondents. The decision to choose respondents was made on on individuals who hold the position of company officers in Malaysian companies. The company officers consist of director, company secretary and auditor of private company. According to Brito (2011), interview method is conducted to get a contextual grasp of the research difficulties and a comprehensive perspective on a problem. The respondents will be given a set of questions to test their level of understanding of the company law and the application of the Companies Act 2016 in discharging their duties as company officers. The interview data was then recorded, transcribed, and broken down into various themes. The participants in this research are coded for discussion as in Table 1 for easy reference. Besides that, content analysis is adopted in this study to analyse secondary data which consists of the Companies Act 2016 and the court cases that are related to the area on breach of duties of director, company secretary and auditor in Malaysia and in the United Kingdom. Thematic analysis is applied in this study to analyse the data collected from respondents.

Table 1. List of respondents

Respondent	Position	Entities
R1	Company Secretary	Private Company
R2	Director	Public Company
R3	Director	Private Company
R4	Director	Private Company
R5	Auditor	Private Company
R6	Auditor	Public Company
R7	Company Secretary	Private Company

LITERATURE REVIEW

In Malaysia, incorporation procedure, management, decision-making procedure and winding-up of companies in Malaysia are explained under the Companies Act 2016 (the Act). Malaysian companies must comply with the rules and regulations under the Act to be incorporated and in managing its affairs. The Companies Act 2016 has replaced the Companies Act 1965 (Act 125) as the main piece of law governing corporations in Malaysia. The Act addresses matters such as steps involved in incorporating a company, company constitution, qualifications and duties of company officers, share capital, corporate restructuring and winding up. Company officers play an important role to ensure a company operates according to rules and regulations. The Companies Act 2016 defines 'officer' as including director, company secretary or employee of a corporation (Section 2). Company officers in the context of this study refers to the director, company secretary and auditor of a company.

An incorporated company is a separate entity from its officers. This principle acts like a veil which protects the officer from being sued by a third party. This separate legal entity concept was established in the United Kingdom case of Salomon v Salomon & Co. [1897] AC. Malaysia recognised the separate legal entity principle and it is protected under section 20 of the Companies Act 2016. In this situation, action can only be taken against the company and not the officers on personal basis. However, in exceptional situations, the corporate veil can be lifted and the officers can be held accountable for their action. Common law has imposed duties on company officers, among which are the fiduciary duty of loyalty, duty to act in bona fide for the best interests of the company, duty to retain discretion, duty to act for a proper purpose, duty to perform with care, skill and diligence and duty to avoid conflict of interest.These duties are statutorily enshrined under the Companies Act 2016. Failure of directors to perform their duties will subject them to heavy penalties. By virtue of the recent amendment, the penalty imposed for the breach of duties of directors had been increased from fifty million ringgit to three million ringgit (Section 213 of the Companies Act 2016). This shows the graveness of the issue on breach of duties of the company directors.

LEGAL LITERACY

A person is said to be legally capable if they possess the knowledge, abilities, and attitudes that can be used to deal with issues relating to law. Literally, literacy is defined as the capability of an individual to read and write. The concept of literacy is referring to the idea of a person being cultured and educated (Romig & Burge,2019). Legal literacy refers to the knowledge and skills of people of the law and legal system. Deception, exploitation, and struggles are all substantially contributed by a lack of legal literacy. A community without access to knowledge of their legal rights remains separated from the system (Raza, 2021). Research on legal literacy has been conducted among educators in Malaysia (Abdul Hamid, 2018), among Malaysian consumers (Samsudin, 2020), among enforcement officers (Khairil et al., 2017) and among human resource officers (Patrick, 2021; Abdul, 2022). The question that arises is whether company officers in Malaysia have adequate knowledge of the Companies Act 2016 to what the company anticipates they will have?

In relation to this study, it is contended that literacy of the Companies Act 2016 in Malaysia is essential for company officers while managing the company.

A research on legal literacy can be approached in a two-fold manner; firstly, in disadvantaged and oppressed group of persons and secondly, involving professions that could run into legal problems for instance, medical practitioners and teachers (Samuri & Khan, 2021, Perry-Hazan & Tal-Weibel, 2020). In the context of this study, company officers working can be categorised under the second group as they are open to legal suits while managing affairs of the company. The findings of this study fill in the gap in the discussion of legal literacy principles as it extends the analysis to a specific understanding and application of a legal document, known as the Companies Act 2016 and its understanding among the company officers. Understanding and using the law are two aspects of legal literacy. For company officers in Malaysia, the capacity to guarantee that the company complies with all applicable rules and regulations is essential. The legal knowledge of company officers in Malaysia will be covered in this paper, with particular emphasis on the function of director, auditor and company secretary.

Corporate Governance

Corporate governance refers to the system of rules, practices, and processes by which a company is directed and controlled. It encompasses the relationships among a company's management, board of directors, shareholders, and other stakeholders. Good corporate governance ensures transparency, accountability, fairness, and responsibility in an organization's operations. It serves as a framework for attaining a company's objectives, while reflecting the context of the regulatory environment, ethical standards, and market dynamics. One of the most fundamental reasons for the importance of corporate governance is the enhancement of investor confidence. Investors are more likely to commit capital to companies that demonstrate clear governance structures, ethical leadership, and proper internal controls. Transparent decision-making and the equitable treatment of shareholders help mitigate the risk of mismanagement and financial irregularities. As a result, strong corporate governance can reduce the cost of capital, improve stock performance, and attract long-term investment.

Another critical aspect of corporate governance is the promotion of accountability and ethical behavior at all levels of the organization. The board of directors plays a key role in setting the tone at the top, overseeing the strategic direction of the company, and holding management accountable for performance. Clear delineation of roles and responsibilities, combined with robust internal controls and audit mechanisms, helps prevent corporate fraud and abuse. This is particularly important in maintaining stakeholder trust and upholding the company's reputation. Corporate governance also contributes to risk management and sustainability. With increasing expectations from regulators, investors, and the public, companies are under pressure to identify and manage environmental, social, and governance (ESG) risks. Good governance practices integrate ESG considerations into corporate strategy and decision-making. This long-term perspective not only enhances financial performance but also ensures the organization is responsive to global sustainability goals, such as the United Nations Sustainable Development Goals (SDGs).

Moreover, sound corporate governance can improve operational efficiency and strategic decision-making. By establishing a framework for timely and informed decisions, companies can respond effectively to market challenges and opportunities. Boards that comprise diverse, skilled, and independent members bring varied perspectives to the table, enabling more balanced and objective judgments. This leads to better oversight, innovation, and value creation for all stakeholders. For listed companies, compliance with corporate governance codes and disclosure requirements is often mandated by law or stock exchange regulations. However, the value of corporate governance extends beyond regulatory compliance. It is a strategic tool that strengthens organizational resilience and facilitates growth. Even in small and medium enterprises (SMEs), adopting corporate governance principles can foster professional management, succession planning, and access to external financing.

Furthermore, in the wake of corporate scandals and financial crises, the need for stronger governance structures has become more evident. These events revealed how poor governance can lead to catastrophic outcomes for companies, economies, and society at large. Consequently, there is a growing emphasis on enhancing board oversight, stakeholder engagement, and ethical corporate culture. Thus, corporate governance is a vital component of modern business practice. It serves not only as a safeguard against mismanagement but also as a driver of organizational success and sustainability. By promoting transparency, integrity, and accountability, good corporate governance strengthens public trust and supports long-term value creation. As business environments evolve, the continuous development and enforcement of effective governance practices will remain essential to corporate resilience, stakeholder confidence, and sustainable development.

Director

A director is a person who sits on the board of a company and has legal status and responsibilities towards the company's business (Conmy, 2022). In Malaysia, the director of a company can be any person that fulfils the requirements of the Act (Section 198). Section 2 of the Act refers a director to include “any person occupying the position of director of a corporation by whatever name called, as well as a person in accordance with whose directions or instructions the majority of directors of a corporation are accustomed to act as an alternate or substitute director". Qualifications to become a director are firstly, he shall ordinarily reside in Malaysia by having a principal place of residence in Malaysia, a natural person and at least eighteen years of age. The director must not be a bankrupt and does not have a record convicting them of an offence relating to bribery, fraud, dishonesty, offences in the course of managing the company.

Company directors are expected to perform their fiduciary duties while overseeing the company's affairs. According to common law principles, director holds fiduciary duties which consist of; firstly, to act in good faith for the interest of the company and the duty not to exercise their powers for any collateral purpose.

Secondly, a director must avoid situations where his or her personal interests and duty to the company come into conflict and he must refrain from using his director position to his advantage. Apart from that, the director must act reasonably and with adequate skill that might reasonably be expected of a person of his knowledge and experience to handle company's affair. These fiduciary duties are embedded in the Malaysian Companies Act 2016. This can be seen in section 213, where the section states that directors must act with a proper purpose and in the best interests of the company. The test for assessing whether the director is acting in bona fide or the best interest of the company is introduced in the case of Charterbridge Corporation Ltd v Lloyds Bank Ltd [1970] Ch 62 which asks this question of "whether an intelligent and honest man in the position of a director of the company concerned, could, in the whole of the existing circumstances, have reasonably believed that the transactions were for the benefit of the company", For instance, in the case of Re Smith & Fawcett Ltd [1942] Ch 304, the court stated that the director's decision in refusing issuance of shares was considered a genuine decision made in the company's interest. While in the case of Tengku Dato' Ibrahim Petra bin Tengku Indra Petra v Petra Perdana Bhd and Wong Fook Heng [2018] 2 MLJ 177, the Court of Appeal decided that the director's action in selling the shares was not in the company's best interests, and they were therefore found to have breached their fiduciary duties.

Section 213 also states that directors are required to exercise reasonable care, skill and diligence in carrying out their duties. Directors should have the knowledge, skill, and experience that can reasonably be expected of a director in a similar position. Romer J in the case of Re City Equitable Fire Insurance Co Ltd [1925] Ch 407 explains the duty as follows, "A director need not exhibit in the performance of his duties a greater degree of skill than may reasonably be expected from a person of his knowledge and experience". It can be observed that the skill that is expected from Malaysian directors is not high.

Section 218 introduces the duty of directors and officers to avoid conflicts of interest and the misuse of company resources. This section prohibits directors and officers from utilizing company property, information, or their positions for personal gain without obtaining consent from a general meeting. It also restricts them from taking advantage of business opportunities discovered through their roles or engaging in competing business activities. A director must also disclose their interest, any position or property that could create a conflict of interest with their duties during a board of directors' meeting (Section 221). Lord Cranworth in the case of Aberdeen Railway Co v Blaikie Bros (1854) 1 Macq 461 held that a director holds fiduciary duties and should not be allowed to engage in agreements where their personal interests conflict or may conflict with the interests of the company. It is important to regulate a director's duties while managing the affairs of the company. Directors owe these duties to the company and not to individual shareholders. The director's action will affect the company's interest. A director that breaches his duties can be punishable with a maximum of five years of imprisonment and fined a maximum three million ringgit or both.

Auditor

An auditor is an individual with a licence to look through financial records, ensure their accuracy, and ensure that companies are adhering to tax laws. Auditors play an important role to prevent fraud and deception to happen in a company, highlighting the irregularities that occurs in the company's account and financial records and give consultation service on how improve the company's business. The Companies Act 2016 outlines provisions regarding the qualifications of auditors in Malaysia. Among the qualifications are certain requirements such as the person must be at least 21 years old, considered a fit and proper individual, must have successfully completed the final examination at one of the institutions specified in the Act, and it is necessary for the individual who is seeking to become an auditor to be a member of one of the designated professional bodies.

An auditor must provide a report on the company's accounting, financial statements, and other papers that relate to the financial statements to the company members (section 266(1). It is then the duty of the auditor of the company to conduct an audit under section 266(3) and decide on each of the following: whether all required disclosures and justifications have been received; whether the company maintains proper accounting records, including the registers required by this law and whether the company's branches generate sufficient income. The auditor should state in the report whether any deficiencies, inactions, or inadequacies were identified with respect to the matter. The auditor is given the authority to report in writing to the Registrar any breach or non-compliance committed by the company with respect to any provision of the Act (section 266(8)). Failure of the auditor to disclose any offences or non-compliance with the Act to the Registrar will subject the auditor to a punishment of up to five years jail, a fine of up to three million Ringgit, or both.

In the case of Re London and General Bank Ltd (1895), the directors had been informed in full of the auditor's discovery that the debts were doubtful. But instead of openly informing the shareholders that the board had failed to make provisions, the auditor only stated that 'the value of the assets is dependent upon the realization.' The auditor was held liable for some wrongly awarded dividends when it was determined that he had violated his obligation to effectively communicate the material in his report. It was held that an auditor owes shareholders a duty to provide clear information. In this case, the court determined that the auditor owed a duty of care to the shareholders and was thus found liable for the loss. Auditors should develop procedures to detect errors and irregularities in conducting audits, especially when the company's finances are complex (Pacific Acceptance Corp. Ltd. v. Forsyth (1970)).

Additionally, section 266(7) stipulates that a company's auditor, or a representative designated by him in writing or documented, shall be entitled to participate in every general meeting of the company. The auditor is also entitled to be given all information that relates to any of the general meetings, as well as to voice his opinion and be listened to on any matter affecting the members' meeting that he is invited to. Based on the case of Re Kingston Cotton Mill Co. [1896], auditors are obliged to exercise in their work, the skill, care and diligence that any reasonably competent, prudent and prudent auditors would exercise. What constitutes equitable skill, care and attention depends on the specific circumstances of each case.

In the case of PwC v. Tyco International (2009), the shareholders alleged that PwC had failed to detect a number of accounting irregularities at Tyco, including improper revenue recognition, excessive expenses and fictitious inventory. The shareholders also alleged that PwC had failed to properly investigate these irregularities, even after being alerted to them by whistleblowers. In the case of CIMB Investment Bank Bhd v Ernst & Young & Another Appeal [2014] 6 CLJ 438, it was by the court that the auditors had breached their dutiy of care to the company when they failed to catch the fraudulent activity that was going on at the company. Thus from this case it can be observed that auditors must be diligent in performing statutory audits and notify the company in case of illegal activities.

Company Secretary

It is a legal requirement that a secretary be appointed following a company's formation. The company secretary plays an important role in the management of the company. This involves assisting with the company's formation, ensuring the company complies with all relevant regulations and laws, supporting the board of directors, managing shareholder relations, keeping track of documents and paperwork, facilitating disclosure and reporting, and applying corporate governance policies into practice. The company secretary prepares meeting minutes and, as directed, follows up on any decisions taken during meetings. In the event that the board determines that a written resolution is adequate, the company secretary drafts and sends circular resolutions to the directors for signature. They are not mere clerks as they have extensive duties and responsibilities in managing the affairs of the company. Sound knowledge of the Companies Act 2016 is a qualification required to become a company secretary. This includes a person who appears to have experience to perform the company secretary tasks. As spelt out in section 235 of the Act, a person must be a member of one of the professional bodies in order to be qualified as a company secretary. The professional bodies are the Malaysian Bar, the Advocates' Association of Sarawak, and the Sabah Law Association, the Malaysian Association of Company Secretaries (MACS), the Malaysian Institute of Certified Public Accountants (MICPA), the Malaysian Institute of Accountants (MIA) and the Malaysian Institute of Chartered Secretaries and Administration (MAICSA). The listed professional bodies are according to the list by the Ministry of Domestic Trade, Cooperation and Consumerism.

Liability for Company Officers

Section 20 of the Act states that an incorporated company has a legal personality that is separate from its members. In other words, the company and its members are separate entities. A third party can make a claim against the company and not its members. This separate legal entity principle provides immunity to the company officers from any action taken against them. Lord Macnaghten in the case of Salomon v Salomon & Co Ltd [1897] AC 22 held that:

> *"The company is at law a different person altogether from the subscribers to the memorandum; and though it may be that after incorporation the business is precisely the same as it was before, and the same persons are managers, and the same hands receive the profits, the company is not in law the agent of the subscribers or trustee for them. Nor are the subscribers as members liable, in any shape or form, except in the manner provided by the Act."*

However, the concept of separate legal entity will not protect any wrongdoers under certain situations. The situations are for example, in case of agency, fraud, group enterprise, trusts, tort, tax, enemy, the companies legislation and other legislation. Therefore, company officers can be held personally liable if they commit wrongful acts through the principle of lifting the veil of incorporation. The Court of Appeal in Chin Chee Keong v. Toling Corporation (M) Sdn Bhd [2016] 4 MLRA 180 CA stated that the veil of incorporation can be lifted in the case of fraudulent trading to ensure the culprit to be accountanble and be responsible for his action.

RESULTS AND DISCUSSION

Duties of Company Officers

This theme evaluated the understanding of director, company secretary and auditor in understanding the duties and consequence of breach of duties of company officers as mentioned under the Companies Act 2016. It can be observed that respondent who hold the position of company secretary have a sound knowledge of the duties of a company secretary. For instance, when R7 is asked about the duties of a company secretary, the respondent explained:

"A company secretary is essentially an officer that is tasked with managing and overseeing a corporation. A corporation cannot be formed unless a company secretary is appointed. As a result, choosing company secretaries to set up your company is critical. The responsibility of a company secretary is to see that decisions made by higher-ups, such as the board of directors, chairman, CEOs and others are carried out. A company's successful management and administration, as well as compliance with legal and regulatory requirements, are the responsibility of the company secretary. They have to participate in general meetings, manage legal paperwork, and advise the board as needed. The company secretary's job is not secretarial in nature."

While, a respondent that hold the position as a director demonstrated that he has a fair understanding about his duties as a director. R2 shows that he is aware that a director holds the duty to declare his conflict of interest. This can be seen based on the following statements:

"When I have the board meeting the first thing that I tell in the agenda every of my board meeting, asking all the directors to declare if there is any conflict of interest in every board meeting. Activities which are connected to director must be disclosed."

R2 mentioned that during board meetings, directors are required to declare any potential conflicts of interest, emphasizing the company's commitment to maintaining transparency. The director also has demonstrated his understanding of the principle of fiduciary duty as follows:

"Fiduciary duty is something that a director cannot run away from. A director cannot say that I did not know it was happening, I did not know about it, I was not there at the meeting. Director is fully responsible for any financial transaction of the company."

R4 shows a lack of understanding of the duty of director under the Companies Act 2016. This can be seen in the statement:

"as a company governed under Bank Negara Malaysia (BNM), he has to ensure that the company follows the requirements properly before they are being penalized".

Director is not expected to have a high level of skills in managing the affairs of a company but the knowledge, skill and experience that may reasonably be expected from other directors (Re City Equitable Fire Insurance Co Ltd [1925] Ch 407).

Liability of Company Officers

This theme evaluated on the legal literacy of of company officers on the liability under the Companies Act 2016. It can be observed that R7 has a sound understanding about the liabilities of a company secretary and she is aware that a company secretary can be sued for negligence. According to R7:

"A company secretary must be honest and perform work in good faith for the corporation as a corporate secretary. After that he or she must take additional care to avoid engaging in criminal conduct while serving as a secretary. A company secretary can be sued in the court if they are negligent or commit criminal conducts."

This can also be observed through a statement of R1, where he quoted a statutory provision from the Act in explaining the liability of a company secretary.

"If you look at the Companies Act 2016, the company secretary is just like any other director or officers of the company, so if you look at Section 213, anything to do with the director, just like the director, the company officers also have the same liability. Because the company secretary regarded as the officer of the company. You can refer to the Section 2 of the Companies Act, what is company secretary all about."

Director (R4) shows a good understanding of the concept of lifting the veil of incorporation through the following statement:

"any director can be held liable if they do wrongful acts related to the company. However, if the company is in a winding up status, there's a veil to cover or protect the directors. But, if the director itself perform wrongful acts, they will be held liable"

UNDERSTANDING OF THE COMPANIES ACT 2016

The Companies Act 2016 was introduced to establish a modernised corporate legal framework in Malaysia. This theme evaluated the level of understanding of the Companies Act 2016 among company officers in Malaysia. R7 is also able to understand the effect of an amendment made to the Companies Act 2016. According to R7:

"Although some of the changes made in CA 2016 can be undone to return to CA 1965, I would argue that this is not a vulnerability. The idea of forming a firm with a single director comes first. Before, a corporation had to have at least two directors in order to be incorporated. It was safer where if a director was involved in any unlawful business might be caught by another one. However, if an organisation just has one director, that director may engage in illicit activities that could eventually have an impact on our nation, such as the sale of drugs or illegal weapons. Additionally, there are no actual AGM meetings where it can be mandated. Lack of communication with the board of directors, members, and company secretaries might result from missing meetings for at least a year."

R6 mentioned that:

"it is important to comply with the Companies Act 2016 to ensure the stakeholders of the company can assure on a business running and to provide the assurance to the public and relevant authority on a proper business running without any loopholes."

The data also shows that some directors are not familiar with the Companies Act 2016. For instance, according to R3:

"I am not really familiar with the Companies Act 2016. That is why I appointed a company secretary to get her advise on corporate governance matters. The company secretary will manage most of the company affairs."

The technical language used in the Companies Act 2016 is a challenge for the company officers. According to R1:

"Not many people understand the Companies Act. Because it is very technical and it has like 620 sections, so not many people understand it. So I think that the problem of the Companies Act is that it is quite technical, quite thick. It becomes a challenge for company secretary, director and auditors to read the Companies Act 2016."

R5 believes that the Companies Act 2016 can be improved to be more user-friendly. The Act should be more accessible and less complex for auditors to use.

According to R6:

"auditor must report to the members on the financial statements and on the company's accounting and other records relating to those financial statements."

Due to the complexity of the Companies Act 2016, training and courses are important in order to increase the literacy of company officers, especially concerning their duties and liabilities. R2 stated that his company ensures its directors and officers are adequately trained and informed about their obligations under the Companies Act 2016.

"..., their training is important and you must also ensure as a director, the senior management and the staff are always upgraded in their knowledge every time. So you must also in your company's budget have allocated a certain amount for

staff training so that you send them to various courses to upgrade their skills, upgrade their knowledge."

Our results show that the level of legal literacy among company officers in Malaysia varies. Company secretaries and auditors demonstrates high level of legal literacy on their duties, liabilities and on the overall understanding of the Act. However, respondents that hold the position as a director shows low level of legal literacy when it comes to duties, liabilities as a director of a company. This includes lack of awareness on the consequences of breaching the duties as a director. Zajac and Stearns (1997) stated that compared to a company director with practical background, one with legal expertise is more experienced in handling the affairs of the company. This is because a company director with legal literacy knows how to perform his job properly. According to Ishak, Ismail and Abdullah (2012), a company director with legal education and qualifications get better opportunities in developing their career path with higher compensation as their skills are important in managing a company. Study shows that a company with low audit quality is as a result of poor governance structures had higher occurences of fraudulent financing reporting (Hasan & Mahenthiran, 2014).

CONCLUSION

In conclusion, good corporate governance ensures transparency, accountability, fairness, and responsibility in an organization's operations. The integration of legal literacy within sustainable development frameworks is essential for ensuring compliance with the SDGs. Company officers should be aware of and understand the Companies Act 2016 while managing their companies. They are expected to know their duties and liabilities as a director, company secretary and auditor. It can be observed from the above data that respondents who hold positions as company secretaries and auditors have a good legal literacy of the Companies Act 2016 compared to the company directors. This is due to the qualification prerequisite of company secretary and auditor which requires them to be members of professional bodies. Instead, respondents who hold the position as directors lack knowledge of the Companies Act 2016 and some even depend on their company secretaries to explain the laws. These results are perhaps due to the low standard imposed to qualify as a director as stated in the Companies Act 2016. However, despite the low expectation, there is a dire need for a company director to be well-versed with the Companies Act 2016 to prevent any breach of duties while managing the company (Ali, 2017). Company officers must be willing to join conferences on company law or training on the Companies Act 2016 to improve their legal literacy as company officers and to stay up-to-date with any amendments regarding company law.

According to Zariski (2014), a proper understanding and application of law will assist an individual to solve legal issues and make proper decisions. The results of this investigation will be helpful for the government in reviewing the policies and regulatory framework relating to corporate governance in Malaysia. This research extends the legal literacy concept by adding the legal literacy theory related to the Companies Act 2016.

REFERENCES

Abdul, R. S. S., Zulkarnain, I. F., Yaacob, T. Z., & Omain, S. T. (2022). Legal literacy of human resource officers in Malaysia. *International Journal of Academic Research in Business & Social Sciences, 12*(1), 2344–2355.

Ahmed, S. (2012). *On being included: Racism and diversity in institutional life*. Duke University Press.

Ali, H. M. (2017). Liabiliti jenayah korporat di Malaysia mengikut perspektif tadbir urus korporat. *Jurnal Pengurusan, 51*, 225–234. DOI: 10.17576/pengurusan-2017-51-18

Bernama. (2023). Company director arrested for bribery with paid vacation. https://www.bernama.com/en/crime_courts/news.php?id=2160748

Brikci, N., & Green, J. (2007). *A guide to using qualitative research methodology*. London School of Hygiene and Tropical Medicine.

Brito, P. (2011). Teen conceptualization of digital technologies. *New Media & Society, 14*(3), 513–532. DOI: 10.1177/1461444811420822

Coffee, J. C. (2006). *Gatekeepers: The professions and corporate governance*. Oxford University Press. DOI: 10.1093/oso/9780199288090.001.0001

Conmy, S. (2022). What are the duties of a company director? Corporate Governance Institute. https://www.thecorporategovernanceinstitute.com/insights/guides/what-is-a-companydirector-what-does-a-company-director-do/

Cronin, C. (2014). Using case study research as a rigorous form of inquiry. *Nurse Researcher, 21*(5), 19–27. DOI: 10.7748/nr.21.5.19.e1240 PMID: 24877907

Dasgupta, M. (2015). Exploring the relevance of case study research. Vision. *The Journal of Business Perspective, 19*(2), 147–160. DOI: 10.1177/0972262915575661

Dioubate, B. M., & Daud, W. N. (2022). A review of cybersecurity risk management framework in Malaysia higher education institutions. *International Journal of Academic Research in Business & Social Sciences, 12*(5), 1031–1093. DOI: 10.6007/IJARBSS/v12-i5/12924

Hasnan, S., Rahman, R. A., & Mahenthiran, S. (2014). Determinants of fraudulent financial reporting: Evidence from Malaysia. *Jurnal Pengurusan, 42*, 103–117. DOI: 10.17576/pengurusan-2014-42-09

Healy, P. M., & Palepu, K. G. (2003). The fall of Enron. *The Journal of Economic Perspectives*, *17*(2), 3–26. DOI: 10.1257/089533003765888403

Ishak, R., Ismail, K. N. I. K., & Abdullah, S. N. (2012). Corporate performance, CEO power and CEO turnover: Evidence from Malaysian public listed companies. *Jurnal Pengurusan*, *35*, 33–41. DOI: 10.17576/pengurusan-2012-35-04

Kaur, M. (2022). Former company director charged with 64 counts of misappropriation, fraud. The Star. https://www.thestar.com.my/news/nation/2022/07/21/former-company-director-charged-with-64-counts-of-misappropriation-fraud

Khairil, M., Jeganathan, C. S., Razman, M. R., Zakaria, S. Z., & Ismail, M. S. (2017). Influence of legal literacy and communication in the enforcement of environmental laws. *International Journal of Business and Society*, *20*(10A), 7199–7208.

Mohd Zulkhairi Kamaruzaman. (2013). Company secretary pleads guilty to making false statement. The Borneo Post. https://www.pressreader.com/malaysia/the-borneopost/20131001/281848641310905

Moriarty, J. (2011). *Qualitative methods overview*. NIHR School for Social Care Research.

Nguyen, T., Carnevale, J. J., Scholer, A. A., Miele, D. B., & Fujita, K. (2019). Metamotivational knowledge of the role of high-level and low-level construal in goal-relevant task performance. *Journal of Personality and Social Psychology*, *117*(5), 879–899. DOI: 10.1037/pspa0000166 PMID: 31120290

Parliament, U. K. (2018). Carillion collapse inquiry report published. https://www.parliament.uk/business/committees/committees-a-z/commons-select/business-energy-industrial-strategy/news-parliament-2017/carillion-report-published-17-19/

Patrick, P. (2019). Core functions of human resource management and its effectiveness on organization: A study. *International Journal of Research in Economics and Social Sciences*, *9*(5), 257–266.

Perry-Hazan, L., & Tal-Weibel, E. (2020). On legal literacy and mobilization of students' rights from a disempowered professional status: The case of Israeli teachers. *Teaching and Teacher Education*, *90*, 103016. DOI: 10.1016/j.tate.2020.103016

Raza, A. (2021). Legal literacy: A key to socio-economic justice. In *Young India Fellowship* (pp. 182–191). Ashoka University.

Romig, J. M., & Burge, M. E. (2020). Legal literacy and communication skills: Working with law and lawyers. Carolina Academic Press. (Texas A&M University School of Law Legal Studies Research Paper No. 19-66). https://papers.ssrn.com/sol3/papers.cfm?abstract_id=3491498

Samsudin, N., Abu Bakar, E. M., Jusoh, Z., & Arif, M. A. M. (2020). Personal and environmental determinants of consumer legal literacy among Malaysian consumers. *Malaysian Journal of Consumer and Family Economics*, *25*(S1), 27–40.

Samuri, M. A. A., & Khan, A. S. N. (2021). Legal literacy for Muslim converts in Malaysia. *Pertanika Journal of Social Science & Humanities*, *29*(3). Advance online publication. DOI: 10.47836/pjssh.29.3.12

Soto, C. J., & John, O. P. (2017). The next big five inventory (BFI-2): Developing and assessing a hierarchical model with 15 facets to enhance bandwidth, fidelity, and predictive power. *Journal of Personality and Social Psychology*, *113*(1), 117–143. DOI: 10.1037/pspp0000096 PMID: 27055049

Suruhanjaya Syarikat Malaysia. (2015). Audit partner jailed one year, fined RM400,000 for misleading disclosure of financial information. https://www.sc.com.my/resources/media/media-release/audit-partner-jailed-one-year-fined-rm400000-for-misleading-disclosure-of-financial-information

Valukas, A. R. (2010). Lehman Brothers Holdings Inc. Chapter 11 proceedings examiner's report. Jenner & Block.

Zajac, E. J., & Westphal, J. D. (1996). Who shall succeed? How CEO/board preferences and power affect the choice of new CEOs. *Academy of Management Journal*, *39*(1), 64–90. DOI: 10.2307/256631

Zariski, A. (2014). *Legal literacy: An introduction to legal studies*. Athabasca University Press. DOI: 10.15215/aupress/9781927356449.01

KEY TERMS AND DEFINITIONS

Auditor: A qualified professional who independently examines and verifies a company's financial records to ensure accuracy, compliance with applicable standards, and financial transparency.

Company secretary: An officer responsible for ensuring a company complies with statutory and regulatory requirements, maintaining company records, and providing guidance on corporate governance practices.

Company: A legal entity formed by individuals or groups to engage in commercial or industrial activities, recognized by law with separate identity, rights, and obligations.

Director: An individual appointed to oversee the management and strategic direction of a company, entrusted with fiduciary duties to act in the company's best interests.

Legal literacy: The ability to understand, interpret, and apply basic legal concepts, rights, and obligations effectively in everyday and professional contexts.

Liability: A legal obligation or responsibility, often involving accountability for actions, debts, or obligations, which may result in penalties or sanctions if breached.

Sustainable Development Goals: A global set of 17 goals established by the United Nations aimed at addressing poverty, inequality, climate change, environmental degradation, peace, and justice by 2030.

Compilation of References

Abd Ghadas, Z. A., & Hassan, H. (2008). Good governance in Malaysian public higher learning institutions: Special reference to International Islamic University Malaysia. In *International Conference on Higher Education in Muslim World: Challenges and Prospect*, 24th-25th March 2008, Kuala Lumpur.

Abdelaaty, L. (2021). The relationship between human rights and refugee protection: An empirical analysis. *International Journal of Human Rights*, *25*(10), 1704–1723. DOI: 10.1080/13642987.2021.1874358

Abdul Rahman, M. Z., Ismail, N., & Hassan, A. (2018). Socio-economic impact of transgenic fish technology on Malaysian fisheries communities. *Aquaculture Economics & Management*, *22*(3), 210–225.

Abdul Rahman, M. Z., & Lee, S. H. (2020). Risk management and insurance obligations for developers of transgenic organisms in Malaysia. *Malaysian Journal of Biosafety and Biosecurity*, *8*(1), 15–29.

Abdul Shukor, S. F., & Ghazali, F. (2025). Embracing ESG in the Era of Remote Work: Legal Requirement and Benefits. In Implementing ESG Frameworks Through Capacity Building and Skill Development (pp 365- 380). IGI Global.

Abdul, R. S. S., Zulkarnain, I. F., Yaacob, T. Z., & Omain, S. T. (2022). Legal literacy of human resource officers in Malaysia. *International Journal of Academic Research in Business & Social Sciences*, *12*(1), 2344–2355.

ACCC (Australian Competition and Consumer Commission). (2023). Guidelines on Environmental Claims. https://www.accc.gov.au

Act, R. 2006. (2006). https://ulii.org/akn/ug/act/2006/21/eng@2006-08-04

Adeola, R., Oette, L., Lwabukuna, O., & Viljoen, F. (2021). Introduction: Refugees, Returnees and Internally Displaced Persons in Africa. *Journal of African Law*, *65*(S1), 5–8. DOI: 10.1017/S0021855321000140

Aerni, P. (2004). Risk, regulation and innovation: The case of aquaculture and transgenic fish. *Aquatic Sciences*, *66*(3). Advance online publication. DOI: 10.1007/s00027-004-0715-8

Afewerki, S., Asche, F., Misund, B., Thorvaldsen, T., & Tveteras, R. (2023). Innovation in the Norwegian aquaculture industry. *Reviews in Aquaculture*, *15*(2), 759–771. DOI: 10.1111/raq.12755

Agosto, G., & Rubinstein, F. (2022). Migration and the 2030 Agenda in Argentina. International Development Policy/Revue Internationale de Politique de Développement, 14. DOI: 10.4000/poldev.4939

Aguilar-Ortiz, J., Zamudio-García, V. M., & Simancas-Acevedo, E. (2025). Sustainable Development Goal 16 Peace and Justice Criminal Justice and Artificial Intelligence Applications for a More Efficient and Fair System. In *Machine and Deep Learning Solutions for Achieving the Sustainable Development Goals* (pp. 435-460). IGI Global Scientific Publishing.

Ahern, J. (2018). Urban landscape sustainability and resilience: The promise and challenges of integrating ecology with urban planning. *Landscape Ecology*, *33*(8), 1291–1301.

Ahmad, A. R., Farley, A., & Kim-Soon, N. (2013). Funding Reforms in Malaysian Public Universities: Transitions towards Competitive Funding. *Australian Journal of Basic and Applied Sciences*, *7*(10), 553–561.

Ahmed, S. (2012). *On being included: Racism and diversity in institutional life*. Duke University Press.

Ahmed, Z. S. (2018). The Role of SAARC and EU in Managing Refugees in South Asia and Beyond: Potential for North-South Cooperation. *Global Policy*, *9*(1), 76–84. DOI: 10.1111/1758-5899.12526

Ajuntament de Barcelona. (2024). Smart tourism regulation annual report. https://www.barcelona.cat

Akama, J. (2023). Conservation finance and community displacement in Kenyan tourism. *African Studies Review*, *66*(1), 45–67.

Akama, J. (2023). Conservation finance and corruption in African tourism. *African Studies Review*, *66*(1), 45–67.

Akhtaruzzaman, M., Banerjee, A. K., & Boubaker, S. (2025). Government intervention and green innovation in renewable energy. *Energy Economics*, *108*, 108185. DOI: 10.1016/j.eneco.2025.108185

Akhter, F., Hossain, M. R., Elrehail, H., Rehman, S. U., & Almansour, B. (2023). Environmental disclosures and corporate attributes, from the lens of legitimacy theory: A longitudinal analysis on a developing country. *European Journal of Management and Business Economics*, *32*(3), 342–369. DOI: 10.1108/EJMBE-01-2021-0008

Akhundov, A. (2025). The Role of Ethics in Modern Technology Development. *Porta Universorum*, *1*(4), 169–177. DOI: 10.69760/portuni.0104017

Al Mokdad, A. (2025). Role of Civil Society and Non-Governmental Organizations in Addressing Developmental Disparities in the Middle East: Empowering Communities for Sustainable Development. In *Unveiling Developmental Disparities in the Middle East* (pp. 93–140). IGI Global.

Albers, H., Winter, J. D., & Voeten, H. (n.d.). Inspiration guide: Integrating the SDGs into your multi-annual policy plan. *VVSG*. https://www.local2030.org/library/707/SDGs-in-policy-plan.pdf

Albluwi, T. S., Sarker, M. A. R., Abir, Z. R., & Mone, F. H. (2022). Work from Home During COVID-19 Outbreak: Problems and Remedies. *International Journal of Social Sciences and Management Review.*, *5*, 331–342. DOI: 10.37602/IJSSMR.2022.5122

Albrecht, J. (2024). Climate adaptation law: a European perspective. s*China-EU Law Journal*, 1-25.

Albrecht, R., Roberts, M., & Williams, P. (2020). *Restorative justice: Principles and practice*. Cambridge University Press.

Alessia, D. (2017). Applying GRI sustainability reporting in the water sector: Evidences from an Italian company. *International Journal of Business Administration*, *8*(3), 10–23. DOI: 10.5430/ijba.v8n3p10

Ali, I. M., Ayub, N., Husin, N. M., Alrazi, B., Mohd Ali, I., & Mat Husin, N. (2019). Water disclosure and financial performance: The CASE of CDP water a-list companies. *European Proceedings of Social and Behavioural Sciences, 100*.

Aliaziz, M., & Ab Rahman, M. A. (2018). Growth hormone effects on essential amino acid absorption, muscle amino acid profile, N-retention and nutritional requirements of striped bass hybrids. *Genetic Analysis: Biomolecular Engineering*, *15*(3–5), 107–113. PMID: 10596748

Alibašić, H. (2025). Resilience in action: Kosovo's National Development Strategy to incorporate sustainable development goals. *Sustainable Development (Bradford)*, *33*(1), 319–332. DOI: 10.1002/sd.3121

Ali, H. M. (2017). Liabiliti jenayah korporat di Malaysia mengikut perspektif tadbir urus korporat. *Jurnal Pengurusan, 51*, 225–234. DOI: 10.17576/pengurusan-2017-51-18

Alkathiri, A., Ahmad, M., & Alghamdi, A. (2023). Public-private partnerships in smart city infrastructure: Challenges and prospects. *Journal of Urban Management, 12*(1), 45–59.

Allam, Z., & Jones, D. S. (2019). On the Smart City Concept and Smart City Governance. *International Journal of Public Administration, 42*(7), 596–615.

Allam, Z., & Newman, P. (2018). Redefining the smart city: Culture, metabolism and governance. *Smart Cities, 1*(1), 4–25. DOI: 10.3390/smartcities1010002

Allen, T. D., Golden, T. D., & Shockley, K. M. (2015). How Effective Is Telecommuting? Assessing the Status of Our Scientific Findings. *Psychological Science in the Public Interest, 16*(2), 40–68. DOI: 10.1177/1529100615593273 PMID: 26403188

Allouhi, A., Rehman, S., Buker, M. S., & Said, Z. (2022). Up-to-date literature review on Solar PV systems: Technology progress, market status and R&D. *Journal of Cleaner Production, 362*, 132339. DOI: 10.1016/j.jclepro.2022.132339

Almeida, L., & Agrawal, A. A. (2020). Biosafety and bioethics of genome editing in agriculture: Lessons from natural diversity. *Trends in Biotechnology, 38*(4), 334–344.

Altman, J., & Jackson, S. (2023). Aboriginal Customary Law and National Park Management in Australia. *Journal of Legal Pluralism and Unofficial Law, 55*(1), 112–130.

Amaruzaman, S., Trong Hoan, D., Catacutan, D., Leimona, B., & Malesu, M. (2022). Polycentric Environmental Governance to Achieving SDG 16: Evidence from Southeast Asia and Eastern Africa. *Forests, 13*(1), 68. DOI: 10.3390/f13010068

Amil, A. C. (2024, December). Implementation of SDG 16:'Peace, Justice, and Strong Institutions' in The Philippines: Status, Collaborative Efforts, and Prospects. In *International Conference on Public Administration and Social Science (ICoPASS)* (Vol. 1, No. 1).

Amirul, S. R., Shaari, S. C., & Jones, S. (2024). "Advancing Workforce Sustainability: Policy Reforms for Flexible Working Arrangements in Achieving National SDGs," International Journal of Research and Innovation in Social Science [IJRISS]. *International Journal of Research and Innovation in Social Science, 8*(12), 1386–1398.

Amoh, G. (2024). *National peace infrastructure and sustainable development goal 16: a study of the national peace council of Ghana* (Doctoral dissertation, University of Cape Coast).

Andersen, E. (2025). Closing Access to Justice Gaps Globally. In *Higher Education and SDG16: Peace, Justice, and Strong Institutions* (pp. 13-36). Emerald Publishing Limited. DOI: 10.1108/978-1-80455-892-820251002

Andrades, J., Martinez-Martinez, D., Herrera, J., & Larran, M. (2024). Is water management really transparent? A comparative analysis of ESG reporting of Andalusian publicly-owned enterprises. *Public Money & Management, 44*(3), 208–215. DOI: 10.1080/09540962.2023.2171844

Angelidou, M. (2018). Smart City Policies: A Spatial Approach. *Cities (London, England), 78*, 4–13.

An, Q. (2024). Empirical analysis of trade costs and their impact on carbon emissions in RCEP countries. *Journal of Environmental Management, 365*, 121666. DOI: 10.1016/j.jenvman.2024.121666 PMID: 38968893

Ansari, M. F., Dash, B., Sharma, P., & Yathiraju, N. (2022). The impact and limitations of artificial intelligence in cybersecurity: A literature review. *International Journal of Advanced Research in Computer and Communication Engineering, 11*(9), 81–90. DOI: 10.17148/IJARCCE.2022.11912

Arajarvi, N. (2017). The Rule of Law in the 2030 Agenda. *Hague Journal on the Rule of Law, 10*(2), 187–217. Advance online publication. DOI: 10.1007/s40803-017-0068-8

Areiqat, A. Y., Zamil, A. M. A., Alheet, A. F., Ahmadd, M. M., & Abushaare, H. M. (2020). The Concept of Governance in Universities: Reality and Ambition. *International Journal of Innovation. Creativity and Change, 13*(1), 951–963.

Ari, I., & Sari, R. (2017). Developing CBDR-RC indices for fair allocation of emission reduction responsibilities and capabilities across countries†. *Cogent Environmental Science, 3*(1), 1420365. Advance online publication. DOI: 10.1080/23311843.2017.1420365

Asche, F., Bellemare, M., Roheim, C., Smith, M., & Tveterås, S. (2015). Fair enough? food security and the international trade of seafood. *World Development, 67*, 151–160. DOI: 10.1016/j.worlddev.2014.10.013

ASEAN. (2024). *ASEAN Guide on AI Governance and Ethics Contents*. https://asean.org/wp-content/uploads/2024/02/ASEAN-Guide-on-AI-Governance-and-Ethics_beautified_201223_v2.pdf

Asimirana, S., & Ismail, I. A. (2019). Exploring critical success factors in the governance of Malaysian public universities. *International Journal of Innovation. Creativity and Change*, *9*(12), 268–282.

Asmelash, H. (2023). The WTO dispute settlement system as a forum for climate litigation? *Review of European, Comparative & International Environmental Law*, *32*(2), 321–333. DOI: 10.1111/reel.12490

Asuhaimi, F. A. (2017). Waqf management and administration in Malaysian higher education institutions. *International Journal of Academic Research in Business & Social Sciences*, *7*(4), 1–10.

Aunsmo, A., Martinsen, L., Bruheim, T., Sekkelsten-Kindt, M., Sandtrø, A., Gaasø, S., Braaen, S., & Rimstad, E. (2022). Triploid atlantic salmon (salmo salar) may have increased risk of primary field outbreaks of infectious salmon anaemia. *Journal of Fish Diseases*, *45*(11), 1733–1743. DOI: 10.1111/jfd.13695 PMID: 35914108

Auslender, E. (2021). Multi-level Governance in Refugee Housing and Integration Policy: a Model of Best Practice in Leverkusen. Journal of International Migration and Integration / Revue de l Integration et de La Migration Internationale, 23(3), 949. DOI: 10.1007/s12134-021-00876-4

Avelino, F. (2021). Theories of power and social change. Power contestations and their implications for research on social change and innovation. *Journal of Political Power*, *14*(3), 425–448. DOI: 10.1080/2158379X.2021.1875307

Awang, N., & Mohd Nadzri, N. R. (2023). The Implementation of Flexible Work Arrangements (FWAS) And Its Impact for Work-Life Balance of Women's Workforce. *I-IECONS E-Proceedings*, *10*(1), 438–449. DOI: 10.33102/iiecons.v10i1.15

Azam, A. H. M., Zainuddin, M. R. K. V., & Tarmidi, T. (July, 2023). *Malaysia's Blue Economy: Position, Initiatives, and Challenges*. Economic Research Institute for ASEAN and East Asia. https://www.eria.org/uploads/Malaysia-Blue-Economy-Position-Initiatives-Challenges.pdf

Aziz, N., Muhammad, Z., Farahdilah, G., Talaat, W. I. A. W., & Saputra, J. (2019). Marine Spatial Planning: The Way Forward for Sustainable Development of Central Terengganu, Malaysia. *Journal of Southwest Jiaotong University*, *54*(4), 1–11. DOI: 10.35741/issn.0258-2724.54.4.9

Azman, N. (2020). Trends in Governance and Management of the Malaysian Academic Profession (2007-2013): Evolution or Devolution? *Higher Education Governance and Policy*, *1*(2), 109–125.

Baal, N. K. (2023). Including refugees and IDPs in national data systems. https://www.fmreview.org/issue66/krynskybaal

Badwi, E. (2023). Integration and Participation of Refugees and Migrants: Building Inclusive Societies. https://ehab-badwi.medium.com/integration-and-participation-of-refugees-and-migrants-building-inclusive-societies-9b806ef772c0

Baker, K. (2020). Health policy in correctional facilities: Current challenges. *Health Policy and Research*, *28*(4), 52–65.

Baker, L. (2020). Barriers to healthcare in correctional facilities. *Journal of Correctional Health*, *35*(2), 234–240. DOI: 10.1016/j.jch.2020.02.003

Baker, L., Kepler, B., & Reid, A. (2019). Malnutrition in prison populations. *Public Health Nutrition*, *22*(6), 1190–1197. DOI: 10.1017/S1368980019001234

Baker, L., Kepler, B., & Reid, A. (2020). The role of harm reduction programs in prisons. *Globalization and Health*, *7*(1), 22–30. PMID: 32138789

Balliu, D. (2025). The new role of supreme audit institutions in monitoring the SDGs. A comparative study between the western balkans and nordic countries.

Banchio, P. R. (2025). Introduction to human rights: An overview of principles, evolution and contemporary relevance. EVOLUTION AND CONTEMPORARY RELEVANCE Table of Contents (February 24, 2025).

Bandi, S., & Nandeshwar, J. (2024). Legal Status under Family Law of LGBT Community in India: A Review of Research on the Status of Same Sex Marriage Pre and Post Navtej Singh Johar v. Union of India (2018). Issue 4 Int'l JL Mgmt. & Human., 7, 1603.

Barkane, I. (2022). Questioning the EU proposal for an Artificial Intelligence Act: The need for prohibitions and a stricter approach to biometric surveillance. *Information Polity*, *27*(2), 147–162. DOI: 10.3233/IP-211524

Barnes, T., Junge, C., Myers, S., Taylor, M., Rogers, P., Ferguson, G., & Gillanders, B. (2016). Population structure in a wide-ranging coastal teleost (*Argyrosomus japonicus*, sciaenidae) reflects marine biogeography across Southern Australia. *Marine and Freshwater Research*, *67*(8), 1103. DOI: 10.1071/MF15044

Baroncini, E., de Stefano, C., & Rubini, L. (2025). New Institutional Architectures and Substantive Rules in International Economic Law-The EU and the UN Sustainable Development Goals.

Basheer, M., Nechifor, V., Calzadilla, A., Ringler, C., Hulme, D., & Harou, J. J. (2022). Balancing national economic policy outcomes for sustainable development. *Nature Communications, 13*(1), 5041. DOI: 10.1038/s41467-022-32415-9 PMID: 36028486

Basu, S. (2020). Cultural heritage law in India: A critical analysis of the Ancient Monuments and Archaeological Sites and Remains Act. *Journal of Heritage Tourism, 15*(3), 258–272. DOI: 10.1080/1743873X.2020.1728957

Bates, R., & Smith, T. (2020). *Prison reform in the 21st century*. Wiley.

Bates, R., & White, J. (2020). *Prison health and rehabilitation: Theories and practices*. Springer.

Bates, S., & White, M. (2020). *Prison health and well-being: A global perspective*. Springer.

Batool, A., Zowghi, D., & Bano, M. (2025). AI governance: A systematic literature review. *AI and Ethics, 2024*(3), 1–15. DOI: 10.1007/s43681-024-00653-w

Batty, M., Axhausen, K. W., Giannotti, F., Pozdnoukhov, A., Bazzani, A., Wachowicz, M., Ouzounis, G., & Portugali, Y. (2019). Smart Cities of the Future. *The European Physical Journal. Special Topics, 214*(1), 481–518. DOI: 10.1140/epjst/e2012-01703-3

Beatley, T. (2011). *Biophilic Cities: Integrating Nature into Urban Design and Planning*. Island Press. DOI: 10.5822/978-1-59726-986-5

Beatley, T. (2018). *Green cities of Europe: Global lessons on green urbanism*. Island Press.

Bedair, M., & Glenn, K. (2020). Evaluation of the use of untargeted metabolomics in the safety assessment of genetically modified crops. *Metabolomics, 16*(10), 111. DOI: 10.1007/s11306-020-01733-8 PMID: 33037482

Bellmann, C., & van der Ven, C. (2020). Greening regional trade agreements on non-tariff measures through technical barriers to trade and regulatory co-operation. *OECD Trade and Environment Working Papers, No. 2020/04*. OECD Publishing. https://doi.org/DOI: 10.1787/18166881

Benkhodja, M. T., Fromentin, V., & Ma, X. (2023). Macroeconomic effects of green subsidies. *Journal of Cleaner Production, 410*, 137166. DOI: 10.1016/j.jclepro.2023.137166

Bennett, A., Basurto, X., Virdin, J., Lin, X., Betances, S. J., Smith, M. D., & Zoubek, S. (2021). Recognize fish as food in policy discourse and development funding. *Ambio*, *50*(5), 981–989. DOI: 10.1007/s13280-020-01451-4 PMID: 33454882

Benvenuto, A., & Lloyd, P. (2019). Prison conditions and human rights. *Journal of Human Rights Law*, *9*(2), 173–185.

Bera, B. (2024). Transgenic fish and its progress., 77-86. DOI: 10.58532/V3BJBT-6P4CH2

Berezovska, N., Zahorskyi, V., Kalashnyk, N., Novak-Kalyayeva, L., Lipentsev, A., Olefirenko, O., Oliyarnyk, V., & Sushynskyi, O. (2024). Implementing an ecosystem approach in public administration: Achieving sustainable development goals in crisis and recovery. *Cadernos de Educação Tecnologia e Sociedade*, *17*(se4), 334–347. DOI: 10.14571/brajets.v17.nse4.334-347

Berke, P. R., Manta, E., & Stevens, A. (2018). Land Use Policies, Transit-Oriented Development, and Housing Affordability: A Review of Portland's Urban Growth Boundary. *Journal of Planning Education and Research*, *38*(4), 411–424.

Bernama. (2023). Company director arrested for bribery with paid vacation. https://www.bernama.com/en/crime_courts/news.php?id=2160748

Berrone, P., Rousseau, H. E., Ricart, J. E., Ruiz, E. B., & Giuliodori, A. (2023). How can Research Contribute to the Implementation of Sustainable Development Goals? An Interpretive Review of SDG Literature in Management. *International Journal of Management Reviews*, *25*(2), 318–339. DOI: 10.1111/ijmr.12331

Bertram, C., & Van Coppenolle, H. (2024). Strengthening the Paris Agreement through trade? The potential and limitations of EU preferential trade agreements for climate governance. *International Environmental Agreement: Politics, Law and Economics*, *24*(4), 589–610. DOI: 10.1007/s10784-024-09653-x

Betts, A., Omata, N., & Sterck, O. (2019). The Kalobeyei Settlement: A Self-reliance Model for Refugees? *Journal of Refugee Studies*, *33*(1), 189–223. DOI: 10.1093/jrs/fez063

Bexell, M., Hickmann, T., & Schapper, A. (2023). Strengthening the Sustainable Development Goals through integration with human rights. *International Environmental Agreement: Politics, Law and Economics*, *23*(2), 1–7. DOI: 10.1007/s10784-023-09605-x

Bhattacharjee, S. (2008). India Needs a Refugee Law. SSRN Electronic Journal. https://papers.ssrn.com/sol3/Delivery.cfm/SSRN_ID2066397_code396686.pdf?abstractid=1760460&mirid=1

Bhattacharjee, R. (2024). Public Finance for Inclusive Governance and SDG Implementation: The South Asian Perspective and India. In *Governance and Sustainable Development in South Asia: Bridging the Gap* (pp. 339–355). Springer Nature Switzerland. DOI: 10.1007/978-3-031-67616-1_18

Bhattacharya, S., & Pal, S. (2023). Inclusivity in urban development through PPPs: A sustainability perspective. *Sustainable Cities and Society*, *81*, 103868.

Bianchi, R. (2022). The political economy of tourism development: A critical review. *Tourism Geographies*, *24*(4-5), 467–489.

Bibri, S. E. (2019). The new smart city as a platform for pursuing sustainable urban development goals. *Sustainable Cities and Society*, *45*, 483–495.

Bibri, S. E. (2020). The IoT for smart sustainable cities of the future: An analytical framework for sensor-based big data applications for environmental sustainability. *Sustainable Cities and Society*, *45*, 230–253.

Bibri, S. E. (2020). The Role of Smart City Characteristics in Urban Sustainability: An Empirical Study of Cities. *Sustainable Cities and Society*, *62*, 102369.

Biermann, F., Hickmann, T., Senit, C. A., & Grob, L. (2022). The Sustainable Development Goals as a Transformative Force? *Cambridge University Press*. 204-226. https://doi.org/DOI: 10.1017/9781009082945.009

Biradar, D. (2024). Ethics and Compliance: The Foundation of Sustainable Business Practices. *CXO Today*. https://cxotoday.com/story/ethics-and-compliance-the-foundation-of-sustainable-business-practices/

Blix, T. B., & Myhr, A. I. (2023). A sustainability assessment framework for genome-edited salmon. *Aquaculture (Amsterdam, Netherlands)*, *562*, 738803. DOI: 10.1016/j.aquaculture.2022.738803

Blokker, P. (2024). Populism, human rights, and (un-) civil society. In *The Rule of Law in the EU: Challenges, Actors and Strategies* (pp. 73–90). Springer International Publishing. DOI: 10.1007/978-3-031-55322-6_5

Böhringer, C., Schneider, J., & Asane-Otoo, E. (2021). Trade in Carbon and Carbon Tariffs. *Environmental and Resource Economics*, *78*(4), 669–708. DOI: 10.1007/s10640-021-00548-y

Boley, B. B., & Johnson Gaither, C. (2020). Exploring empowerment within the framework of sustainable tourism: A multilevel analysis of the tourism empowerment scale. *Journal of Sustainable Tourism*, *28*(4), 529–549. DOI: 10.1080/09669582.2019.1707216

Borlini, L. S., & Montanaro, F. (2018). Climate change and trade: Challenges and lingering questions on the relationship between renewable energy subsidies and WTO disciplines. *China-EU Law Journal*, *6*(1), 81–101. DOI: 10.1007/s12689-017-0079-x

Boswell, C. (2017). The Ethics of Refugee Policy. DOI: 10.4324/9781315239910

Braje, N. Ivana. (2022). Chapter 5 The New Normal: Remote Work after the COVID-19 Pandemic. Available at https://doi.org/DOI: 10.24818/978-606-34-0416-0_5

Bramwell, B., & Lane, B. (2018). Sustainable tourism: A global perspective. *Tourism Management*, *68*, 450–454. DOI: 10.1016/j.tourman.2018.04.014

Branham, E. R. (2025). Ability, advocacy, and access: Pre-law students and the Americans with Disabilities Act.

Breuer, A., Leininger, J., Malerba, D., & Tosun, J. (2023). Integrated policymaking: Institutional designs for implementing the sustainable development goals (SDGs). *World Development*, *170*, 106317. Advance online publication. DOI: 10.1016/j.worlddev.2023.106317

Brikci, N., & Green, J. (2007). *A guide to using qualitative research methodology*. London School of Hygiene and Tropical Medicine.

Brito, P. (2011). Teen conceptualization of digital technologies. *New Media & Society*, *14*(3), 513–532. DOI: 10.1177/1461444811420822

Brosio, M. (2024). *Measuring women's economic empowerment at the intersection of gender, law, and development: an exploration of the UN Agenda 2030 Indicator Framework and its effects* (Doctoral dissertation, University of Birmingham).

Brücker, H., Kosyakova, Y., & Vallizadeh, E. (2020). Has there been a "refugee crisis"? New insights on the recent refugee arrivals in Germany and their integration prospects. *Soziale Welt*, *71*(1-2), 24–53. DOI: 10.5771/0038-6073-2020-1-2-24

Bryan, K. (2022). Sustainability reporting at EU level: Leading by example? *Journal of Public Budgeting, Accounting & Financial Management*, *34*(3), 488–497. DOI: 10.1108/JPBAFM-05-2021-0083

Buckley, R. (2018). *Tourism and conservation: Science, ethics, and practice*. CABI.

Buckley, R. (2019). *Tourism and biodiversity: Concepts and issues*. Channel View Publications.

Buckley, R. (2019). Tourism development and environmental protection: Definitions, concepts, and approaches. *Tourism Geographies*, *21*(5), 685–694. DOI: 10.1080/14616688.2018.1557735

Bursalı, C., & Ercis, Y. (2024). Sustainable Development Goals: The Role of Logistics in Peace, Justice, and Strong Institutions. In *Effective Logistics for Sustainable Development Goals* (pp. 234-253). IGI Global.

Buwono, I. D., Grandiosa, R., & Iskandar, I. (2021). Molecular analysis of functional domain and protein motif of endoglucanase gene in marine bacteria isolated from *Eucheuma* sp. and *Sargassum* sp. *International Journal of Fisheries and Aquatic Studies*, *9*(1), 2403. DOI: 10.22271/fish.2021.v9.i1c.2403

Buwono, I. D., Junianto, J., Iskandar, I., & Alimuddin, A. (2019a). Growth and expression level of growth hormone in transgenic mutiara catfish second generation. *Journal of Biotech Research*, *10*, 102–109.

Cai, W., Richter, J., & Zhan, Y. (2020). Blockchain Technology in Sustainable Supply Chain Management: Applications and Challenges. *Journal of Cleaner Production*, *274*, 123233. DOI: 10.1016/j.jclepro.2020.123233

Cai, X., Dan, W., Ge, D., Zhao, X., & Wang, Y. (2023). The impact of environmental regulations and government subsidies and their policy mix on clean technology innovation. *Environment, Development and Sustainability*, *27*(1), 1987–2023. Advance online publication. DOI: 10.1007/s10668-023-03953-z

Camilleri, M. A. (2015). Valuing stakeholder engagement and sustainability reporting. *Corporate Reputation Review*, *18*(3), 210–222. DOI: 10.1057/crr.2015.9

Cammalleri, C., Naumann, G., Mentaschi, L., Bisselink, B., Gelati, E., De Roo, A., & Feyen, L. (2020). Diverging hydrological drought traits over Europe with global warming. *Hydrology and Earth System Sciences*, *24*(12), 5919–5935. DOI: 10.5194/hess-24-5919-2020

Cantele, S., Tsalis, T. A., & Nikolaou, I. E. (2018). A new framework for assessing the sustainability reporting disclosure of water utilities. *Sustainability (Basel)*, *10*(2), 433. DOI: 10.3390/su10020433

Cao, Y., Li, S., Liu, Y., Yan, Z., Dai, Y., Yu, P. S., & Sun, L. (2023). *A comprehensive survey of AI-generated content (AIGC): A history of generative AI from GAN to ChatGPT*. http://arxiv.org/abs/2303.04226

Caragliu, A., Del Bo, C., & Nijkamp, P. (2019). Smart cities in Europe. *Journal of Urban Technology*, *22*(1), 65–82.

Carattini, S., Kim, G., Melkadze, G., & Pommeret, A. (2024). Carbon taxes and tariffs, financial frictions, and international spillovers. *European Economic Review*, *170*, 104883. DOI: 10.1016/j.euroecorev.2024.104883

Carlos, B. G., Díaz-Noriega, S., Elola, J. M., & Daniel, R. G. (2021, 10 mayo). *Principios ESG y cadena de Valor: del Reporting al Impacto Social.* http://hdl.handle.net/11531/55617

Cartagena Declaration on Refugees. (2005). Adopted at a colloquium entitled "Coloquio Sobre la Proteccion Internacional de los Refugiados en American Central, Mexico y Panama: Problemas Juridicos y Humanitarios" held at Cartagena, Colombia from 19-22 November 1984. *Refugee Survey Quarterly, 24*(2), 153–157. DOI: 10.1093/rsq/hdi038

Cartagena Declaration on Refugees. (2023). https://amerainternational.org/cartagena-declaration-on-refugees/

Casla, K., & Sandner, M. (2024). Solidarity as foundation for economic, social and cultural rights. *Human Rights Law Review, 24*(2), ngae011. DOI: 10.1093/hrlr/ngae011

Cath, C. (2018). Governing artificial intelligence: Ethical, legal and technical opportunities and challenges. In *Philosophical Transactions of the Royal Society A: Mathematical, Physical and Engineering Sciences* (Vol. 376, Issue 2133). Royal Society Publishing. DOI: 10.1098/rsta.2018.0080

Cebeci, A., Aydın, İ., & Goddard, A. (2020). Bigger, stronger, better: Fish transgenesis applications and methods. *Biotech Studies, 29*(2), 85–97. DOI: 10.38042/biost.2020.29.02.05

Cellini, R., & Cuccia, T. (2019). The economics of cultural tourism: International perspectives. *Tourism Economics, 25*(2), 245–259. DOI: 10.1177/1354816619829189

Chai, J., & Ma, Z. (2025). Energy governance systems and climate change in the world's major economies under the low carbon background. *Sustainable Energy Research, 12*(2), 2. Advance online publication. DOI: 10.1186/s40807-024-00145-9

Chakraborty, D., & Dey, O. (2024). Trade, environment and climate change. In Chakraborty, D., & Dey, O. (Eds.), *Influence of WTO and global dynamics on trade flows* (pp. 289–347). Springer., DOI: 10.1007/978-981-99-7375-0_4

Chakravarty, S. (2023). Enforcement of social and economic rights: South Asian judicial discourses (Doctoral dissertation, © University of Dhaka).

Chan, C. (2024). *Cyber Security Act 2024: A new era for cybersecurity in Malaysia.* https://www.pwc.com/my/en/assets/publications/2024/pwc-my-cyber-security-act-2024-new-era-for-cybersecurity-in-malaysia.pdf

Chan, C., Tran, N., Cheong, K., Sulser, T., Cohen, P., Wiebe, K., & Nasr-Allah, A. (2021). The future of fish in Africa: Employment and investment opportunities. *PLoS One*, *16*(12), e0261615. DOI: 10.1371/journal.pone.0261615 PMID: 34936682

Chan, K. (2016). Malaysia Biosafety Act 2007 and Cartagena Protocol On Biosafety: A critical comparative analysis. DOI: 10.7287/peerj.preprints.2569v1

Chapparban, S. N. (2020). Religious Identity and Politics of Citizenship in South Asia: A Reflection on Refugees and Migrants in India. *Development*, *63*(1), 52–59. DOI: 10.1057/s41301-020-00247-z

Charnovitz, S. (1991). Exploring the environmental exceptions in GATT Article XX. *Journal of World Trade*, *25*(5), 37–55. https://kluwerlawonline.com/journalarticle/Journal+of+World+Trade/25.5/TRAD1991028. DOI: 10.54648/TRAD1991028

Charnovitz, S. (2014). Green subsidies and the WTO. *Robert Schuman Centre for Advanced Studies Research Paper No. RSCAS 2014/93, GWU Law School Public Law Research Paper No. 2014-51, GWU Legal Studies Research Paper No. 2014-51*. Available at *SSRN*: https://ssrn.com/abstract=2498518 or http://dx.doi.org/DOI: 10.2139/ssrn.2498518

Cheah, Y. L. K. (2023, February 27). Transparency and Protection of Privacy Crucial for Personal Data Collected through the MySejahtera Application. *Malaysian Bar*. https://www.malaysianbar.org.my/article/news/press-statements/press-statements/press-release-transparency-and-protection-of-privacy-crucial-for-personal-data-collected-through-the-mysejahtera-application

Cheau Wei, L., & Mui Li, C. (2024). The Role of Flexible Work Arrangements in Enhancing Employee Well- Being and Productivity: A Study on SDG 8 Implementation in Tech Companies. Journal of Business and Social Sciences, 2024. Retrieved from https://iuojs.intimal.edu.my/index.php/jobss/article/view/601

Chehbouni, G. (2024). Assessing the Alignment and Implementation Challenges of the Sustainable Development Goals (SDGS) 2030 in Morocco: A Relevant Inquiry. *Journal of Sustainable Development Law and Policy (The)*, *15*(2), 186–223. DOI: 10.4314/jsdlp.v15i2.8

Cheng, X., Wang, W., Chen, X., Zhang, W., & Song, M. (2024). Carbon tariffs and energy subsidies: Synergy or antagonism? *Energy*, *306*, 132563. DOI: 10.1016/j.energy.2024.132563

Chen, H., Yang, H., Sun, Y., & Pan, C. (2016). Advances in gene editing technology and its application in aquaculture. *Frontiers in Genetics*, *7*, 141.

Chen, T. T. (1995). Growth hormone gene expression and growth enhancement in fish and shellfish. *Aquaculture Research, 26*(3), 233–239. DOI: 10.1111/j.1365-2109.1995.tb00822.x

Chen, T. T., Lin, C., Shamblott, M., Lu, J. K., & Knight, K. (1995). *Transgenic fish and aquaculture. Towards sustainable aquaculture in Southeast Asia and Japan.* SEAFDEC Aquaculture Department.

Chevalier, J. M. (2023). Legal pluralism and tourism governance at Machu Picchu. *World Development, 161*, 106132.

Choi, W. G. (2019). Asian Civil Society and Reconfiguration of Refugee Protection in Asia. *Human Rights Review (Piscataway, N.J.), 20*(2), 161–179. DOI: 10.1007/s12142-019-0548-4

Christopher & Lee. (2020). Going Remote – Challenges employers face in work from home arrangements. Rajah & Tann Asia. Available at https:// www.christopherleeong.com/media/4009/clo employment up-date_going_remote_v5.pdf2020

Cima, E. (2017). Caught between WTO rules and climate change: The economic rationale of 'green' subsidies. In Mathis, K., & Huber, B. (Eds.), *Environmental law and economics: Economic analysis of law in European legal scholarship* (Vol. 4, pp. 379–404). Springer., DOI: 10.1007/978-3-319-50932-7_15

Cima, E., & Esty, D. C. (2024). Making international trade work for sustainable development: Toward a new WTO framework for subsidies. *Journal of International Economic Law, 27*(1), 1–17. DOI: 10.1093/jiel/jgae008

City of Amsterdam. (2023). Regulation of Platform-Based Short-Term Rentals. https://www.amsterdam.nl

City of Toronto. (2019). *Digital Governance Framework.* Toronto Public Service.

Clarke, R., & Murphy, K. (2024). Bridging the digital divide: Policy and practice in equitable smart city initiatives. *Journal of Urban Technology, 31*(2), 120–138.

CLIA. (2023). *Global cruise industry environmental report.* Cruise Lines International Association.

CLIA. (2023). *State of the cruise industry report.* Cruise Lines International Association.

Cocchia, A. (2018). Smart and digital city: A systematic literature review. In Dameri, R. P., & Rosenthal-Sabroux, C. (Eds.), *Smart City: How to Create Public and Economic Value with High Technology in Urban Space* (pp. 13–43). Springer.

Codex Alimentarius Commission. (2009). Guidelines for the Conduct of Food Safety Assessment of Foods Derived from Recombinant-DNA Animals. CAC/GL 68-2008.

Coffee, J. C. (2006). *Gatekeepers: The professions and corporate governance.* Oxford University Press. DOI: 10.1093/oso/9780199288090.001.0001

Colau, A., & Martí-Costa, M. (2022). Urban tourism governance in Barcelona: From deregulation to recentralization. *Cities (London, England), 131*, 103998.

Colchester, M., & Ferrari, M. (2021). Indigenous peoples' rights and tourism: A legal perspective. *Journal of Sustainable Tourism, 29*(5), 731–748. DOI: 10.1080/09669582.2021.1879196

Commission Delegated Regulation (EU) 2023/2772 supplementing Directive 2013/34/EU of the European Parliament and of the Council as regards sustainability reporting standards. 31 July. O.J. (L)

Committee Against Torture. (2018). *Annual report 2017.* Council of Europe. https://www.coe.int/en/web/cpt/annual-reports

Comune di Venezia. (2023). Tourist Access Regulation. https://www.comune.venezia.it

Conmy, S. (2022). What are the duties of a company director? Corporate Governance Institute. https://www.thecorporategovernanceinstitute.com/insights/guides/what-is-a-companydirector-what-does-a-company-director-do/

Convention on Biological Diversity (CBD). (2000). Cartagena Protocol on Biosafety to the Convention on Biological Diversity: Text and Annexes. Secretariat of the Convention on Biological Diversity. https://www.cbd.int/doc/legal/cartagena-protocol-en.pdf

Convention Relating to the Status of Refugees. (1969). Convention Relating to the Status of Refugees. *The American Journal of International Law, 63*(2), 389–407. DOI: 10.2307/2197458

Cosma, S., Venturelli, A., Schwizer, P., & Boscia, V. (2020). Sustainable development and European banks: A non-financial disclosure analysis. *Sustainability (Basel), 12*(15), 6146. DOI: 10.3390/su12156146

Couture, T., & Gagnon, Y. (2010). An analysis of feed-in tariff remuneration models: Implications for renewable energy investment. *Energy Policy, 38*(2), 955–965. DOI: 10.1016/j.enpol.2009.10.047

Cowey, C. B. (1994). Amino acid requirements of fish: A critical appraisal of present values. *Aquaculture (Amsterdam, Netherlands), 124*(1-4), 1–11. DOI: 10.1016/0044-8486(94)90349-2

Cowx, I. G., Bolland, J. D., Nunn, A. D., & Peeler, E. J. (2010). Defining environmental risk assessment criteria for genetically modified fishes to be placed on the EU market. *Environmental Biosafety Research, 9*(4), 209–221. DOI: 10.1051/ebr/2011004

Coyle, A. (2009). *A human rights approach to prison management: Handbook for prison staff.* International Centre for Prison Studies.

Cronin, C. (2014). Using case study research as a rigorous form of inquiry. *Nurse Researcher, 21*(5), 19–27. DOI: 10.7748/nr.21.5.19.e1240 PMID: 24877907

Crowder, L. B., Osherenko, G., Young, O. R., Airamé, S., Norse, E. A., Baron, N., Day, J. C., Douvere, F., Ehler, C. N., Halpern, B. S., Langdon, S. J., McLeod, K. L., Ogden, J. C., Peach, R. E., Rosenberg, A. A., & Wilson, J. A. (2006). Resolving Mismatches in U.S. Ocean Governance. *Science, 313*(5787), 617–618. DOI: 10.1126/science.1129706 PMID: 16888124

Cullen, F. T., & Gendreau, P. (2020). *The principles of effective intervention in corrections.* Oxford University Press.

D'Rosario, M., & Zeleznikow, J. (2018). Compliance with International Soft Law: Is the Adoption of Soft Law Predictable? *International Journal of Strategic Decision Sciences, 9*(3), 1–15. DOI: 10.4018/IJSDS.2018070101

D'Silva, R. I. (2021). Rohingya Refugees in South Asia: An Exploration of Social Borders and the Margins. *Borders in Globalization Review, 3*(1), 35–45. DOI: 10.18357/bigr31202120261

Dagar, P. (2022). Evaluating and reframing vocational education and training for refugees: Insights from five refugee groups across three cities of India. *Compare: A Journal of Comparative Education, 54*(1), 110–127. DOI: 10.1080/03057925.2022.2078957

Dagar, P. (2023). Rethinking skills development and entrepreneurship for refugees: The case of five refugee communities in India. *International Journal of Educational Development, 101*, 102834. DOI: 10.1016/j.ijedudev.2023.102834

Daily, S. (2024, April 18). Mosti launches AI Sandbox Pilot Programme. *MRANTI.* https://mranti.my/happenings/news/mosti-launches-ai-sandbox-pilot-programme

Damelang, A., & Kosyakova, Y. (2021). To work or to study? Postmigration educational investments of adult refugees in Germany – Evidence from a choice experiment. *Research in Social Stratification and Mobility*, *73*, 100610. DOI: 10.1016/j.rssm.2021.100610

Dameri, R. P., & Benevolo, C. (2019). Governing smart cities: The art of balancing innovation and regulation. *Journal of Urban Technology*, *26*(2), 29–45.

Dasgupta, M. (2015). Exploring the relevance of case study research. Vision. *The Journal of Business Perspective*, *19*(2), 147–160. DOI: 10.1177/0972262915575661

Das, S. (2020). Innovations in digital banking service brand equity and millennial consumerism. In *Digital transformation and innovative services for business and learning* (pp. 62–79). IGI Global. DOI: 10.4018/978-1-7998-5175-2.ch004

Dattler, R., Barclay, H., & Marshall, A. (2016). Sustainable Development Goals and human rights. *IPPF*. https://www.ippf.org/sites/default/files/2016-11/SDG%2BHR_facts.pdf

Davis, J., Carter, R., & Collins, M. (2021). Collaborative governance in tourism: Lessons from indigenous co-management of national parks. *Journal of Sustainable Tourism*, *29*(4), 567–585. DOI: 10.1080/09669582.2021.193890

Davis, M. (2015). *Ecology of Fear: Los Angeles and the Imagination of Disaster*. Vintage Books.

De Iorio, S., Zampone, G., & Piccolo, A. (2022). Determinant factors of SDG disclosure in the university context. *Administrative Sciences*, *12*(1), 21. DOI: 10.3390/admsci12010021

De Silva, S. S., Nguyen, T. T., & Ingram, B. A. (2008). Fish reproduction in relation to aquaculture. *Fish reproduction*, 535-575.

Debbarma, M. (2024). Refugees Experience and the Host Communities: Critical Analyses on Absence of Refugee Law in India. *Journal of Asian and African Studies*, 00219096241228804. Advance online publication. DOI: 10.1177/00219096241228804

Debnath, K., & Debnath, K. (2020). Chakma Refugees in Arunachal Pradesh: Their Inclusion and Setback. Emerald Publishing Limited eBooks, 137. DOI: 10.1108/978-1-83982-190-520201015

Dechezleprêtre, A., Nachtigall, D., & Venmans, F. (2023). The joint impact of the European Union emissions trading system on carbon emissions and economic performance. *Journal of Environmental Economics and Management, 118*, 102758. DOI: 10.1016/j.jeem.2022.102758

Deem, R. (2001). Globalisation, new managerialism, academic capitalism and entrepreneurialism in universities: Is the local dimension still important? *Comparative Education, 37*(1), 7–20. DOI: 10.1080/03050060020020408

del Olmo Casalderrey, J., & Corrales, F. X. L. (2024). Las normas de elaboración de información sobre sostenibilidad, armonización internacional o enredo global. *Técnica contable y financiera*, (70), 1.

Delgado, L. (2012). Good Governance in Higher Education. The Right to Education. In *2nd World Conference on the Right to and Rights in Education.*

Delwaulle, J. C., Smith, T., & Nguyen, P. (2015). Environmental liability frameworks and biotechnology: Lessons from the European Union. *Journal of Environmental Law and Policy, 22*(4), 345–367.

Demaidi, M. N. (2023). Artificial intelligence national strategy in a developing country. *AI & Society, 40*(2), 423–435. DOI: 10.1007/s00146-023-01779-x

Demircan, M. S., & Özdestan, O. (2021). Does dietary incorporation level of pea protein isolate influence the digestive system morphology in rainbow trout (*Oncorhynchus mykiss*)? *Anatomia, Histologia, Embryologia, 50*(6), 956–964. DOI: 10.1111/ahe.12740 PMID: 34558733

Denaro, C., & Giuffré, M. (2021). UN Sustainable Development Goals and the "Refugee Gap": Leaving Refugees Behind? *Refugee Survey Quarterly, 41*(1), 79–107. DOI: 10.1093/rsq/hdab017

Department of Biosafety Malaysia. (2010). *Guidelines for the release of genetically modified organisms into the environment.* Ministry of Natural Resources and Environment.

Department of Economic and Social Affairs Sustainable Development. (2025). *The 17 Goals | Sustainable Development.* United Nations. https://sdgs.un.org/goals

Department of Economic and Social Affairs. (2015). *The 17 Sustainable Development Goals.* United Nations. https://sdgs.un.org/goals

Devlin, R. H., Yesaki, T. Y., Donaldson, E. M., & Hew, C. L. (2001). Transmission and phenotypic effects of an antifreeze/GH gene construct in coho salmon (Oncorhynchus kisutch). *Aquaculture (Amsterdam, Netherlands), 194*(1–2), 37–49.

Devos, Y., Demont, M., Dillen, K., Reheul, D., Kaiser, M., & Sanvido, O. (2009). Coexistence of genetically modified (GM) and non-GM crops in the European Union. A review. *Agronomy for Sustainable Development, 29*(1), 11–30. DOI: 10.1051/agro:2008051

Dictionary, C. (2024). Reviewed on May 2025 https://dictionary.cambridge.org/dictionary/english/remote-working

Dimitrov, D., Smith, M., & Johnson, R. (2013). Growth hormone effects on essential amino acid absorption, muscle amino acid profile, N-retention and nutritional requirements of striped bass hybrids. *Genetic Analysis, Techniques and Applications, 15*(3–5), 107–113. DOI: 10.1016/S1050-3862(99)00012-1 PMID: 10596748

Dioubate, B. M., & Daud, W. N. (2022). A review of cybersecurity risk management framework in Malaysia higher education institutions. *International Journal of Academic Research in Business & Social Sciences, 12*(5), 1031–1093. DOI: 10.6007/IJARBSS/v12-i5/12924

Directive (EU) 2020/2184 of the European Parliament and of the Council of December 16, 2020, concerning the quality of water intended for human consumption. Gazzetta Ufficiale dell'Unione European L, 435 (2).

Directive (EU) 2022/2464 of the European Parliament and of the Council amending Regulation (EU) No 537/2014, Directive 2004/109/EC, Directive 2006/43/EC and Directive 2013/34/EU, as regards corporate sustainability reporting. 14 December. O.J. (L 322), 15-80.

Dlamini, N., Nkambule, N., & Masuku, M. (2022). Community engagement in public-private partnerships for urban development: Lessons from Johannesburg. *Urban Affairs Review, 58*(4), 1011–1037.

Dobranschi, M., Nerudová, D., Solilová, V., & Stadler, K. (2024). Carbon border adjustment mechanism challenges and implications: The case of Visegrád countries. *Heliyon, 10*(10), e30976. DOI: 10.1016/j.heliyon.2024.e30976 PMID: 38770295

Do, D.-N.-M., Hoang, L.-K., Le, C.-M., & Tran, T. (2020). A human rights-based approach in implementing sustainable development goal 4 (quality education) for ethnic minorities in Vietnam. *Sustainability (Basel), 12*(10), 4179. DOI: 10.3390/su12104179

Donald, K., & Way, S. A. (2016). Accountability for the Sustainable Development Goals: A Lost Opportunity? *Ethics & International Affairs, 30*(2), 201–213. DOI: 10.1017/S0892679416000083

Dorji, T. (2023). Bhutan's GNH-based tourism policy: Lessons for regenerative tourism. *Journal of Sustainable Tourism, 31*(2), 312–330.

Dorji, T. (2023). Buddhist ecology and tourism regulation in Bhutan. *Journal of Sustainable Tourism, 31*(2), 312–330.

Dossa, K. F., & Miassi, Y. E. (2024). Impact of carbon pricing policies on economic growth and green innovation: A global analysis. *Climate Change*, 10, e5cc1031. https://doi.org/DOI: 10.1016/j.clima.2024.01.004

Doughty, L. (2006). Reconciliation and justice: Rwanda's Gacaca courts. *Journal of Peace and Justice, 12*(3), 198–205.

Dredge, D. (2023). Comparative tourism law in civil law systems. *Annals of Tourism Research, 98*, 103525.

Dredge, D., & Gyimóthy, S. (2017). *Collaborative Economy and Tourism: Perspectives, Politics, Policies and Prospects*. Springer. DOI: 10.1007/978-3-319-51799-5

Dredge, D., & Jamal, T. (2015). Progress in tourism planning and policy: A post-structural perspective on knowledge production. *Tourism Management, 51*, 285–297. DOI: 10.1016/j.tourman.2015.06.002

Dressler, W.. (2023). Indigenous tourism governance in the Cordilleras. *Journal of Sustainable Tourism, 31*(4), 567–585.

Droege, P. (2025). Beyond Paris: Emergency imperatives for global policy and local action. *Sustain Earth Reviews, 8*(1), 2. DOI: 10.1186/s42055-024-00100-y

Duan, Y., Xi, B., Xu, X., & Xuan, S. (2024). The impact of government subsidies on green innovation performance in new energy enterprises: A digital transformation perspective. *International Review of Economics & Finance, 94*, 103414. DOI: 10.1016/j.iref.2024.103414

Duffy, L. N., Kline, C., & Mowatt, R. A. (2023). Informal tourism labor and systemic exclusion in island economies. *Annals of Tourism Research, 98*, 103522. DOI: 10.1016/j.annals.2023.103522

Dugarova, E. (2015). Social Inclusion, Poverty Eradication and the 2030 Agenda for Sustainable Development. MPRA Paper. https://ideas.repec.org/p/pra/mprapa/69055.html

Dulume, W. (2019). Linking the SDGS with human rights: Opportunities and challenges of promoting goal 17. *Journal of Sustainable Development Law and Policy, 10*(1), 57–72. DOI: 10.4314/jsdlp.v10i1.3

Dunham, R. A., & Su, B. (2020). Genetically engineered fish: potential impacts on aquaculture, biodiversity, and the environment. *GMOs: Implications for Biodiversity Conservation and Ecological Processes*, 241-275.

Dunham, R. A., Smitherman, R. O., & Stocker, R. L. (2002). Genetically improved fish strains: Progress and prospects. *Aquaculture Research*, *33*(9), 793–800. DOI: 10.1046/j.1365-2109.2002.00707.x

Dunham, R. A., & Winn, R. N. (2014). Introduction to genetics in aquaculture XI: The past, present and future of aquaculture genetics. *Aquaculture (Amsterdam, Netherlands)*, *420*, S1–S3. DOI: 10.1016/j.aquaculture.2013.10.019

Dutta, H. (2022). The Environmental Aspects of Refugee Crises: Insights from South Asia, Middle East, and Sub-Saharan Africa. Journal of International Migration and Integration / Revue de l Integration et de La Migration Internationale, 24(2), 913. DOI: 10.1007/s12134-022-00986-7

Dwivedi, P., & Bhattacharjee, S. D. (2024). Emerging Partnerships of SDGs and HRM Practices During the Pandemic: A Study of the Indian IT Industry. *Vision (Basel)*, *0*(0), 09722629241258863. Advance online publication. DOI: 10.1177/09722629241258863

Economic Planning Unit. P. M. D. (2021). *National fourth industrial revolution (4IR) Policy*. Economic Planning Unit, Prime Minister's Department. https://www.mosti.gov.my/wp-content/uploads/2021/07/National-Fourth-Industrial-Revolution-4IR-Policy.pdf

Edwards, L. (2022). *The EU AI Act: A summary of its significance and scope Expert explainer*. Ada Lovelace Institute.

Ehler, C. N., & Douvere, F. (2009). *A Step-By-Step Approach Towards Ecosystem-Based Management* (IOC Manual and Guides no. 53, ICAM Dossier no. 6). Paris: UNESCO.

Ehler, C., Zaucha, J., & Gee, K. (2018). Maritime/Marine Spatial Planning at the Interface of Research and Practice. In Zaucha, J., & Gee, K. (Eds.), *Maritime Spatial Planning*. Palgrave Macmillan.

Ellis, J., & Edmonds, D. (2023). Coming to terms with the SDGs: A perspective from legal scholarship. *Leiden Journal of International Law*, *36*(2), 251–271. DOI: 10.1017/S0922156522000838

Erin, O., Bamigboye, O. A., & Oyewo, B. (2022). Sustainable development goals (SDG) reporting: An analysis of disclosure. *Journal of Accounting in Emerging Economies*, *12*(5), 761–789. DOI: 10.1108/JAEE-02-2020-0037

Escobar, O., & Guzman, A. (2019). Digital inclusion and social equity in Medellín. *Journal of Urban Technology*, *26*(2), 57–75.

European Commission, Brussels, 1.2.2018, COM 753 final 2017/0332 (COD). Proposal for a Directive of the European parliament and of the council on the quality of water intended for human consumption (recast)

European Commission. (2014). Directive 2014/95/EU of the European Parliament and of the Council. Retrieved from https://eur-lex.europa.eu

European Commission. (2018). Commission Directive (EU) 2018/350 amending Directive 2001/18/EC as regards the environmental risk assessment of genetically modified organisms. Official Journal of the European Union. https://enveurope.springeropen.com/articles/10.1186/s12302-023-00734-3

European Commission. (2020). A European Green Deal: Striving to be the first climate-neutral continent. Retrieved from https://ec.europa.eu/green-deal

European Commission. (2021). EU Emissions Trading System (EU ETS). Retrieved from https://ec.europa.eu/clima/policies/ets_en

European Commission. (2021). *Smart cities and communities.*

European Commission. (2022). *EU Biodiversity Strategy for 2030*. Publications Office.

European Commission. (2022). *The Urban Agenda for the EU: Action Plan 2020.* European Commission.

European Commission. (2022). *Tourism and Transport Package: Policy Initiatives for Sustainable*

European Commission. (2023). Directive on Green Claims. https://ec.europa.eu

European Commission. (2023). *Overview of EU Tourism Policy.*

European Commission. (2023). Questions and Answers on the Adoption of European Sustainability Reporting Standards. Retrieved from https://ec.europa.eu/commission/presscorner/detail/en/qanda_23_4043

European Commission. (2023). *Smart Specialisation Strategy for Sustainable Tourism: Policy Brief.* Retrieved from https://ec.europa.eu

European Commission. (2025). *European Commission, official website*. https://commission.europa.eu/index_en

European Court of Human Rights. (2020). *Conditions of detention: Case law and the European Court of Human Rights*. https://www.echr.coe.int

European Parliament & Council. (2001). Directive 2001/18/EC on the deliberate release into the environment of genetically modified organisms. Official Journal of the European Communities. https://eur-lex.europa.eu/legal-content/EN/TXT/?uri=CELEX%3A32001L0018

European Parliament. (2014). Directive 2014/52/EU of the European Parliament and of the Council of 16 April 2014 amending Directive 2011/92/EU on the assessment of the effects of certain public and private projects on the environment. *Official Journal of the European Union*. Retrieved from https://eur-lex.europa.eu/legal-content/EN/TXT/?uri=CELEX%3A32014L0052

EUROPEAN, ICDU (1999). Council Directive 98/83/EC of 3 November 1998 concerning the quality of water intended for human consumption. Official Journal L, 330, 5.

Evans, N., Kocher, D., Kögel, N., & Duwe, M. (2023). The landscape of national climate framework laws in Europe.

Fallah, S. N., & Judijanto, L. (2025). The influence of social economic law on social welfare: Literature review and policy implications. *International Journal of Finance & Economics*, *2*(1), 8–15.

Fam, C. (2024, August 19). The new face of online crimes: Deepfakes redefine cybercrime. *The Star*. https://www.thestar.com.my/tech/tech-news/2024/08/19/the-new-face-of-online-crimes-deepfakes-redefine-cybercrime

Familoni, B. T.Babajide Tolulope Familoni. (2024). Cybersecurity challenged in the age of AI: Theoretical approaches and practical solutions. *Computer Science & IT Research Journal*, *5*(3), 703–724. DOI: 10.51594/csitrj.v5i3.930

Fang, L., & Zhao, S. (2023). On the green subsidies in a differentiated market. *International Journal of Production Economics*, *257*, 108758. DOI: 10.1016/j.ijpe.2022.108758

FAO 2024. The State of World Fisheries and Aquaculture 2024. Blue Transformation in action. Rome. https://doi.org/DOI: 10.4060/cd0683en

FAO/WHO. (2003). *Guidelines for the Safe Use of Genetically Modified Organisms*. Food and Agriculture Organization of the United Nations / World Health Organization.

Farhan, N. M., Nizam, N. M., Mutalib, S., Darus, M. Y., Ismail, A., Mokayed, H., & Abdul-Rahman, S. (2024). International Journal of Computing and Digital Systems Text Classification on Cybercrime Cases From News Articles Using Supervised Learning. *International Journal of Computing and Digital Systems, 17*(1).

Faye, M. (2021). A forced migration from Myanmar to Bangladesh and beyond: Humanitarian response to Rohingya refugee crisis. *Journal of International Humanitarian Action, 6*(1), 1–7. DOI: 10.1186/s41018-021-00098-4

Feinstein, S., Poleacovschi, C., Drake, R., & Winters, L. (2022). States and Refugee Integration: a Comparative Analysis of France, Germany, and Switzerland. Journal of International Migration and Integration / Revue de l Integration et de La Migration Internationale, 23(4), 2167. DOI: 10.1007/s12134-021-00929-8

Felbermayr, G., Peterson, S., & Wanner, J. (2024). Trade and the environment, trade policies and environmental policies—How do they interact? *Journal of Economic Surveys*, •••, 1–37. DOI: 10.1111/joes.12628

Fernández de Gatta Sánchez, D. (2021). La ley 7/2021, de 20 de mayo, de cambio climático y transición energética (entre la expectación y una cierta decepción). Foro: Revista de Ciencias Juridicas y Sociales Nueva Epoca, 24(2).

Ferrante, L., & Fearnside, P. M. (2023). Legal protection of the Amazon for tourism. *Nature Sustainability, 6*(3), 256–269.

Ferrero-Ferrero, I., Torres, M. J. M., Rivera-Lirio, J. M., Escrig-Olmedo, E., & Izquierdo, M. Á. F. (2023). SDG reporting: An analysis of corporate sustainability leaders. *Marketing Intelligence & Planning, 41*(4), 457–472. DOI: 10.1108/MIP-07-2022-0332

FIC (Foundation for International Law). (2024). Climate litigation case tracker. https://www.fil.org

Fielden, J. (2008). Global trends in university governance. *Education Working Paper Series*, 9, 1-48.

Figueiredo, M. A., Lanes, C. F. C., Almeida, D. V., & Marins, L. F. (2007). Improving the production of transgenic fish germlines: In vivo evaluation of mosaicism in zebrafish (*Danio rerio*) using a green fluorescent protein (GFP) and growth hormone cDNA transgene co-injection strategy. *Genetics and Molecular Biology, 30*(1), 31–36. DOI: 10.1590/S1415-47572007000100008

Fiorino, M. (2020). Are companies using water disclosure toward Sustainable Development Goal 6? An analysis of two water-intensive sectors.

Fletcher, G. L., Shears, M. A., King, M. J., & Davies, P. L. (2004). Transgenic fish for aquaculture: a scientific review of the regulatory and biosafety issues associated with transgenic fish. FAO Fisheries Circular, No. 989.

Fletcher, R. (2023). Against the regenerative turn in tourism. *Annals of Tourism Research*, *98*, 103524.

FMT. (September, 2022). *Environmental laws outdated, penalties too low, says law minister.* FMT (Free Malaysia Today) Media. https://www.freemalaysiatoday.com/category/nation/2022/09/02/environmental-laws-outdated-penalties-too-low-says-law-minister/

Font, X., & McCabe, S. (2017). Sustainability and marketing in tourism: Its contexts, paradoxes, approaches, challenges, and potential. *Journal of Sustainable Tourism*, *25*(7), 869–883. DOI: 10.1080/09669582.2017.1301721

Food and Agriculture Organization (FAO). (2019). The State of Food and Agriculture 2019. Moving forward on food loss and waste reduction. FAO. https://www.fao.org/3/ca6030en/ca6030en.pdf

Fraiture, M., D'aes, J., Guiderdoni, E., Meunier, A., Delcourt, T., Hoffman, S., & Roosens, N. (2023). Targeted high-throughput sequencing enables the detection of single nucleotide variations in crispr/cas9 gene-edited organisms. *Foods*, *12*(3), 455. DOI: 10.3390/foods12030455 PMID: 36765984

Francis, J., & Jensen, S. (2020). Green infrastructure and public health: A case study of New York City's green roofs. *Urban Forestry & Urban Greening*, *53*, 126733.

Freeman, M. (2022). Human rights. John Wiley & Sons.Hamelink, C. J. (2025). International human rights. In Global Health and Human Rights (pp. 7–26). Routledge.

Frewer, L. J., Howard, C., & Shepherd, R. (1997). Public concerns in the United Kingdom about general and specific applications of genetic engineering: Risk benefit and ethics. *Science, Technology & Human Values*, *22*(1), 98–124. DOI: 10.1177/016224399702200105 PMID: 11654686

Frey, D. F., & MacNaughton, G. (2016). A Human Rights Lens on Full Employment and Decent Work in the 2030 Sustainable Development Agenda. *SAGE Open*, *6*(2), 2158244016649580. Advance online publication. DOI: 10.1177/2158244016649580

Friedman, E. A. (2016). An Independent Review and Accountability Mechanism for the Sustainable Development Goals: The Possibilities of a Framework Convention on Global Health. *Health and Human Rights*, *18*(1), 129–140. https://pmc.ncbi.nlm.nih.gov/articles/PMC5070686/ PMID: 27781005

Fulgenzi, M. (2024). Subnational Authorities as Key Global Actors. *Athena: Critical Inquiries L. Phil. & Globalization*, *4*, 92.

Fullagar, S., & Wilson, E. (2020). Slow tourism and wellbeing: The convergence of the sustainable and the restorative. *Journal of Sustainable Tourism*, *28*(6), 938–953. DOI: 10.1080/09669582.2020.1715997

Fülöp, M. T., & Topor, D. I. (2025). The digital transformation of SMEs: Opportunities and challenges for sustainability reporting in Romania. *Journal of Global Responsibility*. Advance online publication. DOI: 10.1108/JGR-10-2024-0211

Galanakis, C. M. (2020). Sustainable aquaculture: The role of genetically modified fish. In *Sustainable Food Systems from Agriculture to Industry* (pp. 243–268). Academic Press., DOI: 10.1016/B978-0-12-817576-4.00012-9

Gallagher, M. (2001). Modern university governance: A national perspective. *Journal of Higher Education Policy and Management*, *23*(1), 49–58.

Galligan, D. (2017). *Law and the judicial process*. Routledge. https://www.routledge.com/Law-and-the-Judicial-Process/Galligan/p/book/9780367335449

García-Meca, E., Martínez-Ferrero, J., y Sánchez-Ballesta, J. P. (2021). El cumplimento de los ODS y sus efectos en la rentabilidad económica en la empresa cotizada española. *Contabilidad y Tributación, CEF/Contabilidad y TributacióN, CEF*, 195-220. https://doi.org/DOI: 10.51302/rcyt.2021.7463

Garschagen, M., & Doshi, D. (2022). Does funds-based adaptation finance reach the most vulnerable countries? *Global Environmental Change*, *73*, 102450. DOI: 10.1016/j.gloenvcha.2021.102450

Geba, N. B., & Giusio, M. (2017). *Contabilidad social y ambiental: los estándares GRI 2016 y los objetivos del desarrollo sustentable*. http://sedici.unlp.edu.ar/handle/10915/72810

George, M., Sabaruddin, J. S. H., & Chong, V. C. (2016). Marine Spatial Planning: What Does It Have to Offer Malaysia? *International Journal of Marine and Coastal Law*, *31*(2), 242–278. DOI: 10.1163/15718085-12341397

Gibson, J. L. (2006). Truth and reconciliation in South Africa: At the intersection of personal and political justice. *The Journal of Politics*, *68*(1), 172–185.

Giffinger, R., & Gudrun, H. (2019). Smart governance as key factor for urban development. *Theoretical and Empirical Researches in Urban Management*, *14*(3), 5–16.

Gil, L., & Bernardo, J. (2020). An approach to energy and climate issues aiming at carbon neutrality. *Renewable Energy Focus*, *33*, 37–42. DOI: 10.1016/j.ref.2020.03.003

Gissi, E., Fraschetti, S., & Micheli, F. (2019). Incorporating change in marine spatial planning: A review. *Environmental Science & Policy*, *92*, 191–200. DOI: 10.1016/j.envsci.2018.12.002

Glass, L.-M., & Newig, J. (2019). Governance for achieving the Sustainable Development Goals: How important are participation, policy coherence, reflexivity, adaptation and democratic institutions? *Earth System Governance*, *2*, 100031. DOI: 10.1016/j.esg.2019.100031

Glasson, J., Therivel, R., & Chadwick, A. (2019). *Introduction to environmental impact assessment*. Routledge. DOI: 10.4324/9780429470738

Global Tourism Resilience Council. (2022). Advancing regenerative tourism through public-private collaboration. *Tourism and Development Review*, *36*(2), 112–126.

Glover, K., Pertoldi, C., Besnier, F., Wennevik, V., Kent, M., & Skaala, Ø. (2013). Atlantic salmon populations invaded by farmed escapees: Quantifying genetic introgression with a bayesian approach and snps. *BMC Genetics*, *14*(1), 74. DOI: 10.1186/1471-2156-14-74 PMID: 23968202

Glover, K., Quintela, M., Wennevik, V., Besnier, F., Sørvik, A., & Skaala, Ø. (2012). Three decades of farmed escapees in the wild: A spatio-temporal analysis of atlantic salmon population genetic structure throughout Norway. *PLoS One*, *7*(8), e43129. DOI: 10.1371/journal.pone.0043129 PMID: 22916215

Glover, K., Solberg, M., McGinnity, P., Hindar, K., Verspoor, E., Coulson, M., & Svåsand, T. (2017). Half a century of genetic interaction between farmed and wild Atlantic salmon: Status of knowledge and unanswered questions. *Fish and Fisheries*, *18*(5), 890–927. DOI: 10.1111/faf.12214

Goh, E. V. (2018). The status of fish in Malaysian diets and potential barriers to increasing consumption of farmed species (Doctoral dissertation, University of Nottingham). University of Nottingham, Theses Repository. https://eprints.nottingham.ac.uk/52379/

Goh, C., & Tham, A. (2016). Sustainable smart cities: How Singapore is moving towards urban sustainability. *Urban Sustainability*, *4*(2), 123–139.

Goh, K. C., & Tham, K. W. (2016). Smart water systems for smart cities: Data analytics and IoT-enabled water grids. *Water (Basel)*, *8*(6), 266.

Golden, C., Koehn, J., Shepon, A., Passarelli, S., Free, C., Viana, D., & Thilsted, S. (2021). Aquatic foods to nourish nations. *Nature*, *598*(7880), 315–320. DOI: 10.1038/s41586-021-03917-1 PMID: 34526720

Goldenziel, J. I. (2015). When Law Migrates: Refugees in Comparative International Law. SSRN Electronic Journal. DOI: 10.2139/ssrn.2435251

Goldstein, D. (2016). Human dignity and the prison system. *Oxford Journal of Legal Studies*, *36*(4), 459–477.

Goodman, R. (2024). Twenty-eight years of gm food and feed without harm: Why not accept them? *GM Crops and Food: Biotechnology in Agriculture and the Food Chain*, *15*(1), 40–50. DOI: 10.1080/21645698.2024.2305944 PMID: 38471133

Goodman, R., Ebisawa, M., Ferreira, F., Sampson, H., Ree, R., Vieths, S., & Taylor, S. (2016). Allergenonline: A peer-reviewed, curated allergen database to assess novel food proteins for potential cross-reactivity. *Molecular Nutrition & Food Research*, *60*(5), 1183–1198. DOI: 10.1002/mnfr.201500769 PMID: 26887584

Goos, H. J. T., Bain, M., & Cunningham, D. (2001). Chromosome manipulation techniques for genetic improvement in aquaculture. In M. S. K. (Ed.), Genetic Improvement of Farmed Aquatic Species (pp. 123–142). Springer.

Gopalakrishnan, M. (2019). Securitization of refugees in South Asia: Through the prism of Kautilya's Arthashastra. *Asian Journal of Comparative Politics*, *5*(4), 400–415. DOI: 10.1177/2057891119881505

Gössling, S., & Hall, C. M. (2019). *Sustainable Tourism: A Global Perspective*. Routledge.

Gössling, S., & Higham, J. (2021). *Sustainable tourism: A global perspective*. Routledge.

Gössling, S., & Peeters, P. (2015). Assessing tourism's global environmental impact 1900-2050. *Journal of Sustainable Tourism*, *23*(5), 639–659. DOI: 10.1080/09669582.2015.1008500

Government of Canada. (2021). Impact assessment process for indigenous participation in tourism. Retrieved from https://www.canada.ca

Government of Spain. (2022). PERTE de Digitalización del ciclo del Agua. https://www.prtr.miteco.gob.es/content/dam/prtr/es/perte/maquetacionperteoficialmoncloa-memoria-vertical-v1_tcm30-538587.pdf

Graham, J., & Ble, G. M., Panayotatos, D., & Leghtas, I. (2020, October 18). From Displacement to Development: How Colombia Can Transform Venezuelan Displacement into Shared Growth. https://www.cgdev.org/publication/displacement-development-how-colombia-can-transform-venezuelan-displacement-shared

Gratacap, R., Wargelius, A., Edvardsen, R., & Houston, R. (2019). Potential of genome editing to improve aquaculture breeding and production. *Trends in Genetics*, *35*(9), 672–684. DOI: 10.1016/j.tig.2019.06.006 PMID: 31331664

Great Barrier Reef Marine Park Authority [GBRMPA]. (2023). Reef 2050 Long-Term Sustainability Plan.

Green, A., & Johnson, T. (2019). *Justice and health in the United States prison system*. Oxford University Press.

Greenfield, A. (2021). *Radical Technologies: The Design of Everyday Life* (2nd ed.). Verso Books.

Green, P., & Johnson, L. (2019). *Prison overcrowding and its effects on health*. Oxford University Press.

Gretzel, U.. (2021). Smart tourism cities: Legal and governance challenges. *Journal of Sustainable Tourism*, *29*(12), 2045–2062.

Griggs, D., Smith, M. S., Rockström, J., Öhman, M. C., Gaffney, O., Glaser, G., Kanie, N., Noble, I., Steffen, W., & Shyamsundar, P. (2014). An integrated framework for sustainable development goals. *Ecology and Society*, *19*(4), art49. https://www.jstor.org/stable/26269703. DOI: 10.5751/ES-07082-190449

GSTC. (2023). *Global Sustainable Tourism Council: Reporting Tools for Sustainable Tourism*. Retrieved from https://www.gstc.org

Guan, B., Hu, W., Zhang, T., Duan, M., Li, D., Wang, Y., & Zhu, Z. (2010). Acute and chronic un-ionized ammonia toxicity to 'all-fish' growth hormone transgenic common carp (cyprinus carpio l.). *Chinese Science Bulletin*, *55*(35), 4032–4036. DOI: 10.1007/s11434-010-4165-5

Guarini, E., Mori, E., & Zuffada, E. (2022). Localizing the Sustainable Development Goals: A managerial perspective. *Journal of Public Budgeting, Accounting & Financial Management*, *34*(5), 583–601. DOI: 10.1108/JPBAFM-02-2021-0031

Guerrero-Baena, M. D., Castilla-Polo, F., & Rodríguez-Gutiérrez, P. (2024). What are the main drivers of SMEs' production of sustainability reports? *Small Business International Review*, *8*(1), e617. DOI: 10.26784/sbir.v8i1.617

Gugler, K., Haxhimusa, A., & Liebensteiner, M. (2021). Effectiveness of climate policies: Carbon pricing vs. subsidizing renewables. *Journal of Environmental Economics and Management*, *106*, 102405. DOI: 10.1016/j.jeem.2020.102405

Guiry, N. (2024). *Why Do States Adhere to the Sustainable Development Goals?* Cambridge University Press., https://www.cambridge.org/core/journals/transnational-environmental-law/article/why-do-states-adhere-to-the-sustainable-development-goals/45E55CBD8F82F0018BA52A15FB6E349F DOI: 10.1017/S2047102524000190

Gupta, A., & Falkner, R. (2006). The influence of the Cartagena Protocol on Biosafety: Comparing Mexico, China and South Africa. *Global Environmental Politics*, *6*(4), 23–55. DOI: 10.1162/glep.2006.6.4.23

Gupta, H., & Rakshit, D. (2023). Assessing the demand for carbon credits from the most polluting and hard-to-abate sectors in India. *Journal of Cleaner Production*, *425*, 138825. DOI: 10.1016/j.jclepro.2023.138825

Guttentag, D. (2023). Regulating Airbnb: How cities adapt laws to the sharing economy. *Annals of Tourism Research*, *98*, 103521.

Gutterman, A. S. (2023). Sustainability and Corporate Governance. *ResearchGate*. https://www.researchgate.net/publication/371902191_Sustainability_and_Corporate_Governance

Hagendorff, T. (2020). The ethics of AI ethics: An evaluation of guidelines. *Minds and Machines*, *30*(1), 99–120. DOI: 10.1007/s11023-020-09517-8

Hall, C. M. (2019). Tourism and sustainable development goals: The role of national tourism laws and policies. *Journal of Sustainable Tourism*, *27*(4), 492–504. DOI: 10.1080/09669582.2018.1557398

Hannafi, C., & Marouani, M. A. (2022). Social integration of Syrian refugees and their intention to stay in Germany. *Journal of Population Economics*, *36*(2), 581–607. DOI: 10.1007/s00148-022-00913-1

Han, S., Li, C., Li, M., Lenzen, M., Chen, X., Zhang, Y., Li, M., Yin, T., Li, Y., Li, J., Liu, J., & Li, Y. (2024). Prospects for global sustainable development through integrating the environmental impacts of economic activities. *Nature Communications*, *15*(1), 1–16. DOI: 10.1038/s41467-024-52854-w PMID: 39341803

Han, S., Peng, D., Guo, Y., Aslam, M. U., & Xu, R. (2025). Harnessing technological innovation and renewable energy and their impact on environmental pollution in G-20 countries. *Scientific Reports*, *15*(1), 2236. DOI: 10.1038/s41598-025-85182-0 PMID: 39824979

Hantzopoulos, M., & Bajaj, M. (2021). *Educating for peace and human rights: An introduction*. Bloomsbury Publishing. DOI: 10.5040/9781350129757

Harmsworth, G., & Awatere, S. (2023). Māori Environmental Knowledge in Tourism Policy. *New Zealand Geographer, 79*(2), 89–104.

Harris, E., & Pappalepore, I. (2021). Regenerative tourism: A new approach to sustainable tourism in the post-COVID-19 era. *Journal of Sustainable Tourism, 29*(9), 1499–1518. DOI: 10.1080/09669582.2021.1906503

Harrison, D. (2023). Customary marine tenure in Pacific Island tourism. *Oceania, 93*(1), 78–95.

Harrison, D. (2023). Fijian Vanua Law in Coastal Tourism Governance. *Pacific Studies, 46*(2), 45–68.

Harrison, D. (2023). Tourism and displacement in Pacific island communities. *Pacific Affairs, 96*(1), 23–45.

Harrison, J. (2023). Trade agreements and sustainability: Exploring the potential of global value chain (GVC) obligations. *Journal of International Economic Law, 26*(2), 199–215. DOI: 10.1093/jiel/jgac057

Harrisson, K., Beheregaray, L., Bice, C., Booth, E., Brauer, C., Butler, G., & Zampatti, B. (2025). Otolith and genomic data reveal temporal insights into stocking across a large river basin in a mobile, long-lived Australian freshwater fish species. *Molecular Ecology, 34*(7), e17714. DOI: 10.1111/mec.17714 PMID: 40040486

Hasnan, S., Rahman, R. A., & Mahenthiran, S. (2014). Determinants of fraudulent financial reporting: Evidence from Malaysia. *Jurnal Pengurusan, 42*, 103–117. DOI: 10.17576/pengurusan-2014-42-09

Hassan, H. (2023). The Roles of the National Hydrographic Centre in Harnessing the Nation's Blue Economy. In Ivan, M. A. & Nazli, A. (eds) *Malaysia A Maritime Nation Agenda: Steering the Course*. PUSMAS, TLDM.

Hathaway, J. C. (2005). The Rights of Refugees under International Law. DOI: 10.1017/CBO9780511614859

Healy, P. M., & Palepu, K. G. (2003). The fall of Enron. *The Journal of Economic Perspectives, 17*(2), 3–26. DOI: 10.1257/089533003765888403

Hegab, H., Shaban, I., Jamil, M., & Khanna, N. (2023). Toward sustainable future: Strategies, indicators, and challenges for implementing sustainable production systems. *Sustainable Materials and Technologies, 36*, e00617. DOI: 10.1016/j.susmat.2023.e00617

Hegazy, I. R., & Tohlob, A. A. (2024). Strategic environmental assessment and SDG integration: Enhancing sustainable development in Egypt. *Journal of Umm Al-Qura University for Engineering and Architecture, 15*(3), 340–354.

Henriksson, P. J. G., Troell, M., Banks, L. K., Belton, B., Beveridge, M. C. M., Klinger, D. H., Pelletier, N., Phillips, M. J., & Tran, N. (2021). Interventions for improving the productivity and environmental performance of global aquaculture for future food security. *One Earth, 4*(9), 1220–1232. DOI: 10.1016/j.oneear.2021.08.009

Heu, W. Y., & Edhan, N. H. (2023, November). *Legal Landscape of Generative AI Governance in Malaysia - Azmi & Associates*. Azmi & Associates. https://www.azmilaw.com/insights/legal-landscape-of-generative-ai-governance-in-malaysia/

Hew, C. L., & Fletcher, G. L. (1997). Techniques and applications of chromosome manipulation in fish breeding. *Aquaculture Research, 28*(6), 439–449. DOI: 10.1111/j.1365-2109.1997.tb00853.x

Hew, C. L., & Fletcher, G. L. (2001). The role of aquatic biotechnology in aquaculture. *Aquaculture (Amsterdam, Netherlands), 197*(1), 191–204. DOI: 10.1016/S0044-8486(01)00587-7

Higgins-Desbiolles, F. (2020). The Elusive Sustainable Tourism Model: The Risks of Caution and the Need for Boldness. *Tourism Geographies, 22*(4), 689–704.

Higgins-Desbiolles, F. (2020). The evolution of sustainable tourism: From economic growth to the well-being of all life. *Journal of Sustainable Tourism, 28*(3), 365–384. DOI: 10.1080/09669582.2019.1679823

Higgins-Desbiolles, F. (2023). Regenerative tourism: A deconstruction. *Tourism Recreation Research, 48*(3), 1–15.

Higher Education Sustainability Initiative. (2021). *Assessments of Higher Education's progress towards the UN Sustainable Development Goals Volume 2: for higher education institutions participating in assessments*. HESI Working Group, United Nations. https://sdgs.un.org/sites/default/files/2021-09/HEI%20assessment%20for%20the%20SDGs%20-%20Volume%202%20HEIs1.pdf

Hill, R., & Sendashonga, C. (2006). Conservation biology, genetically modified organisms, and the biosafety protocol. *Conservation Biology, 20*(6), 1620–1625. DOI: 10.1111/j.1523-1739.2006.00534.x PMID: 17181797

Hinton, E. (2020). *Mass incarceration and the global health crisis*. Harvard University Press.

Höhne, N., Gidden, M. J., den Elzen, M., Hans, F., Fyson, C., Geiges, A., Jeffery, M. L., Gonzales-Zuñiga, S., Mooldijk, S., Hare, W., & Rogelj, J. (2021). Wave of net zero emission targets opens window to meeting the Paris Agreement. *Nature Climate Change*, *11*(10), 820–822. DOI: 10.1038/s41558-021-01142-2

Hoi JAck S'ng & Tan Hooi Ping. (2024). OSHA Amendments and Their ESG Impact in Malaysia. Retrieved on May 2025 https://chambers.com/articles/osha-amendments-and-their-esg-impact-in-malaysia

Holden, A. (2019). *Environment and tourism*. Routledge.

Honey, M., & Krantz, D. (2021). *Costa Rica: A global leader in sustainable tourism*. Island Press.

Hong, B., Du, Y., Mukerji, P., Roper, J., & Appenzeller, L. (2017). Safety assessment of food and feed from gm crops in Europe: Evaluating efsa's alternative framework for the rat 90-day feeding study. *Journal of Agricultural and Food Chemistry*, *65*(27), 5545–5560. DOI: 10.1021/acs.jafc.7b01492 PMID: 28573861

Hood, C. (1991). A public management for all seasons? *Public Administration*, *69*(1), 3–19. DOI: 10.1111/j.1467-9299.1991.tb00779.x

Horbachevska, T., Zeben, J. V., & Bernaz, N. (2024). A capability approach to the sustainable development goals: Towards positive corporate human rights obligations. *Transnational Legal Theory*, *15*(3), 465–492. Advance online publication. DOI: 10.1080/20414005.2024.2434383

Horne, R., & Venables, D. (2020). Legal frameworks for sustainable tourism: Building resilience in a changing world. *Journal of Environmental Law*, *32*(2), 291–311. DOI: 10.1093/jel/eqaa006

Hossain, M. B., Miraz, M. H., & Ya'u, A. (2024). From legality to responsibility: Charting the course for AI regulation in Malaysia. *IIUM Law Journal, 32*(1), 397–429. https://journals.iium.edu.my/iiumlj/index.php/iiumlj/article/view/927/475

Hossain, A. N. M. Z. (2022). Geopolitics of Rohingya Refugee Crisis and Regional Security. *International Journal of Safety and Security Engineering*, *12*(2), 167–177. DOI: 10.18280/ijsse.120204

Hostetler, C. E., Ellis, L. R., & Zinn, S. A. (2005). Effects of dietary carbohydrate and phytate on glucose metabolism and nutrient utilization in salmonids. *Aquaculture Nutrition*, *11*(6), 407–416. DOI: 10.1111/j.1365-2095.2005.00382.x

How does IHL protect refugees and internally displaced persons? (2018). https://www.icrc.org/en/document/how-does-humanitarian-law-protect-refugees-and-internally-displaced-persons-0

Huang, J., Chen, X., & Zhao, X. (2024). How Digital Technology Reduces Carbon Emissions: From the Perspective of Green Innovation, Industry Upgrading, and Energy Transition. *Journal of the Knowledge Economy*, *15*(4), 19294–19326. Advance online publication. DOI: 10.1007/s13132-024-01895-z

Huang, M.-T., & Zhai, P.-M. (2021). Achieving Paris Agreement temperature goals requires carbon neutrality by middle century with far-reaching transitions in the whole society. *Advances in Climate Change Research*, *12*(2), 281–286. DOI: 10.1016/j.accre.2021.03.004

Huang, Y. (2021). Technology innovation and sustainability: Challenges and research needs. *Clean Technologies and Environmental Policy*, *23*(9), 1663–1664. DOI: 10.1007/s10098-021-02152-6 PMID: 34276276

Hummel, K., & Szekely, M. (2022). Disclosure on the sustainable development goals–evidence from Europe. *Accounting in Europe*, *19*(1), 152–189. DOI: 10.1080/17449480.2021.1894347

Hunjra, A. I., Bouri, E., Azam, M., Azam, R. I., & Dai, J. (2024). Economic growth and environmental sustainability in developing economies. *Research in International Business and Finance*, 70(A), 102341. https://doi.org/DOI: 10.1016/j.ribaf.2024.102341

Husainy, A. S., Mangave, S. S., Patil, C. C., & Mane, S. D. (2024). Harmonizing Responsibilities: Challenges and Opportunities in the Integration of Climate Change and Sustainable Development Goals (SDGs). *The Asian Review of Civil Engineering*, *13*(1), 30–43. DOI: 10.70112/tarce-2024.13.1.4232

Hussin, R., Kader, S. Z. S. A., Manshor, N. M., Roslim, S., & Sirat, N. I. M. (2021). Good governance practices for waqf in Malaysian higher education institutions (HEIs). *Academy of Entrepreneurship Journal*, *20*(2S), 1–13.

Idem, U. J., Olarinde, E. S., Sesan, F., Bamidele, I., Ogundele, A. T., & Olipede, D. E. (2024, November). Cyber security Institutional Frameworks in Nigeria: A Panacea for Achieving Sustainable Development Goal 16. In *2024 IEEE 5th International Conference on Electro-Computing Technologies for Humanity (NIGERCON)* (pp. 1-6). IEEE.

Ieong, M. C. A. (2024). Exploring New Judicial Models under the Sustainable Development Goals. In *SHS Web of Conferences* (Vol. 200, p. 02036). EDP Sciences. DOI: 10.1051/shsconf/202420002036

Ife, J., Soldatić, K., & Briskman, L. (2022). *Human rights and social work.* Cambridge University Press. DOI: 10.1017/9781108903868

Ijlal, T. (2022). *Artificial Intelligence (AI) governance and cybersecurity: A beginner's guide to governing and securing AI.*

ILO. (2020). *Teleworking during the COVID-19 Pandemic and Beyond: a Practical Guide.*

ILO. (2023). *Decent work in island tourism economies.* International Labour Organization.

ILO's Home Work Convention (No. 177) and Recommendation (No. 184), 1996

Immler, N. L., & Sakkers, H. (2021). The UN-Sustainable Development Goals going local: Learning from localising human rights. *International Journal of Human Rights, 26*(2), 262–284. DOI: 10.1080/13642987.2021.1913411

India, R. I. Legal Framework, Law Enforcement And Security. (2023). http://www.worldlii.org/int/journals/ISILYBIHRL/2001/7.html

Institute for Social Accountability. (2020). Judicial reforms in Kenya: Addressing corruption and improving access to justice. *The International Journal of Politics and Law, 25*(4), 342–358.

Internal Revenue Service. (2021). Energy Incentives for Businesses in the American Recovery and Reinvestment Act. Retrieved from https://www.irs.gov

International Centre for Prison Studies. (2019). *World prison population list* (12th ed.). https://www.prisonstudies.org/world-prison-brief

International Labour Organization (ILO). (2023). *Decent work in the tourism sector: Addressing informality and seasonality.* https://www.ilo.org

Ioannou, I., & Serafeim, G. (2019). The consequences of mandatory corporate sustainability reporting.

IOC-UNESCO. (2022). *State of the Ocean Report* (IOC Technical Series, 173). Paris, IOC-UNESCO.

IOC-UNESCO. (2024). *State of the Ocean Report* (IOC Technical Series, 190). Paris, IOC-UNESCO.

IOC-UNESCO/European Commission. (2022). *Updated Joint Roadmap to accelerate Marine/Maritime Spatial Planning processes worldwide –MSProadmap (2022–2027)* (IOC Technical Series, 182). Paris, UNESCO.

Irudaya Rajan, S. (2022). The Routledge Handbook of Refugees in India. In *Routledge eBooks*. Informa., DOI: 10.4324/9781003246800

Ishak, R., Ismail, K. N. I. K., & Abdullah, S. N. (2012). Corporate performance, CEO power and CEO turnover: Evidence from Malaysian public listed companies. *Jurnal Pengurusan*, *35*, 33–41. DOI: 10.17576/pengurusan-2012-35-04

Ishay, M. R. (2022). *The human rights reader: Major political essays, speeches, and documents from ancient times to the present.* Routledge. DOI: 10.4324/9781003121404

ISO. (2019). Water efficiency management systems — Requirements with guidance for use. https://www.iso.org/standard/68286.html

Izzati & Chew. (2025). Azmi & Associates. Reviewed on May 2025 https://www.azmilaw.com/insights/key-changes-to-occupational-safety-and-health-law/#:~:text=By%20broadening%20the%20scope%20of,also%20protected%20under%20the%20Act

Jackson, J. (2020). The effects of incarceration on mental health: A case study approach. *International Journal of Prison Health*, *15*(2), 78–91.

Janke, T. (2020). Indigenous intellectual property and tourism: Protecting indigenous art and culture. *Australian Indigenous Law Review*, *23*(1), 45–62.

Janssen, M., Charalabidis, Y., & Zuiderwijk, A. (2019). Benefits, Adoption Barriers and Myths of Open Data and Open Government. *Information Systems Management*, *35*(4), 293–304.

Janssen, M., Charalabidis, Y., & Zuiderwijk, A. (2021). Benefits, adoption barriers and myths of open data and open government. *Information Systems Management*, *38*(3), 239–255.

Jhingan, E., Devlin, R. H., & Iwama, G. K. (2003). Disease resistance, stress response, and effects of triploidy in growth hormone transgenic coho salmon. *Journal of Fish Biology*, *63*(3), 806–823. DOI: 10.1046/j.1095-8649.2003.00194.x

Jin, A., He, G., Ge, S., & Wu, S. (2025). The impact of government green subsidies on corporate green innovation. *Finance Research Letters*, *71*, 106378. DOI: 10.1016/j.frl.2024.106378

Jinek, M., Chylinski, K., Fonfara, I., Hauer, M., Doudna, J. A., & Charpentier, E. (2012). A programmable dual-RNA–guided DNA endonuclease in adaptive bacterial immunity. *Science, 337*(6096), 816–821. DOI: 10.1126/science.1225829 PMID: 22745249

Jones, R.. (2022). Haida Law and Marine Tourism Governance. *Coastal Management, 50*(3), 215–233.

Jones, R.. (2023). Haida Oral Law in Park Management. *Journal of Legal Anthropology, 7*(1), 112–130.

Joshi, A. (2017). Legal Empowerment and Social Accountability: Complementary Strategies Toward Rights-based Development in Health? *World Development, 99*, 160–172. DOI: 10.1016/j.worlddev.2017.07.008

Judge, B., Nitzberg, M., & Russell, S. (2025). When code isn't law: Rethinking regulation for artificial intelligence. *Policy and Society, 44*(1), 85–97. DOI: 10.1093/polsoc/puae020

Julve, V. M., & Alijarde, I. B. (2022). Hacia la divulgación de información de sostenibilidad en el sector público. *Apuntes Contables, 31*(31), 11–32. DOI: 10.18601/16577175.n31.02

Kabisch, N.. (2020). Nature-based solutions to climate change mitigation and adaptation in urban areas: Linkages between science, policy and practice. *Ecological Economics, 152*, 105–115.

Kabisch, N., & Haase, D. (2018). Green infrastructure for urban resilience: Challenges and opportunities. *Urban Ecology, 35*(3), 345–354.

Kahiluoto, H.. (2021). Community-based urban resilience planning: The case of Medellín. *Sustainability, 13*(5), 2652.

Kalfagianni, A., & Young, O. R. (2022). The politics of multilateral environmental agreements: Lessons from 20 years of INEA. *International Environmental Agreement: Politics, Law and Economics, 22*(2), 245–262. DOI: 10.1007/s10784-022-09567-6 PMID: 35228841

Kallio, T. J., Kallio, K. M., Huusko, M., Pyykkö, R., & Kivistö, J. (2022). Balancing between accountability and autonomy: The impact and relevance of public steering mechanisms within higher education. *Journal of Public Budgeting, Accounting & Financial Management, 34*(6), 46–68. DOI: 10.1108/JPBAFM-10-2020-0177

Kampourakis, I. (2022). Legal theory in search of social transformation. *European Law Open, 1*(4), 808–821. DOI: 10.1017/elo.2023.15

Kanade, M. (2024). The right to international solidarity and the right to development. In *Research Handbook on International Solidarity and the Law* (pp. 122–142). Edward Elgar Publishing. DOI: 10.4337/9781803923758.00009

Kanchiswamy, C. N. (2016). Genome editing: A new tool for crop improvement. *Plant Cell Reports*, *35*(1), 41–51. DOI: 10.1007/s00299-015-1878-5

Kandahari, S., & Wali, S. (2020). The judicial system in Afghanistan: Challenges and reforms. *International Review of Law and Policy*, *41*(2), 122–139.

Kanie, N., Griggs, D., Young, O. R., Waddell, S., Shrivastava, P., Haas, P. M., Broadgate, W., Gaffney, O., & Kőrösi, C. (2019). Rules to goals: Emergence of new governance strategies for sustainable development. *Sustainability Science*, *14*(6), 1745–1749. DOI: 10.1007/s11625-019-00729-1

Kapfudzaruwa, F. (2024). Internationalization of Higher Education and Emerging National Rationales: Comparative Analysis of the Global North and South. *Higher Education Policy*, ●●●, 1–30. DOI: 10.1057/s41307-024-00358-z

Kapuscinski, A. R., Hayes, K. R., Li, S., & Dana, G. (2007). Environmental risk assessment of genetically modified organisms. *Integrated Environmental Assessment and Management*, *3*(4), 439–450.

Kapuscinski, A., & Hallerman, E. (1990). Transgenic fish and public policy: Anticipating environmental impacts of transgenic fish. *Fisheries (Bethesda, Md.)*, *15*(1), 2–11. DOI: 10.1577/1548-8446(1990)015<0002:TFAPPA>2.0.CO;2

Karim, M. S., Deane, F., Arif, A. A., Garwood-Gowers, A., Humphries, F., Uddin, M. M., & Deagon, A. (2024). Integrating Sustainable Development Goals in the Law Curriculum: Legal Education for" People, Planet and Prosperity. *Belmont L. Rev.*, *12*, 196.

Kauffman, C. M. (2023). Ecuador's nature rights jurisprudence. *World Development*, *161*, 106132.

Kauffman, C. M., & Martin, P. L. (2021). Can Rights of Nature Make Development More Sustainable? Why Some Laws are Better than Others. *World Development*, *144*, 105452. DOI: 10.1016/j.worlddev.2021.105452

Kauffman, C. M., & Martin, P. L. (2021). Rights of nature in tourism governance. *World Development*, *144*, 105452.

Kauffman, C. M., & Martin, P. L. (2023). Global expansion of nature's rights. *Science*, *379*(6634), 654–656.

Kaur, M. (2022). Former company director charged with 64 counts of misappropriation, fraud. The Star. https://www.thestar.com.my/news/nation/2022/07/21/former-company-director-charged-with-64-counts-of-misappropriation-fraud

Kaur, N. (2013). Protection of Refugees in India: A Critical Analysis. SSRN Electronic Journal. DOI: 10.2139/ssrn.2214274

Kawarazuka, N., & Béné, C. (2010). Linking small-scale fisheries and aquaculture to household nutritional security: An overview. *Food Security*, *2*(4), 343–357. DOI: 10.1007/s12571-010-0079-y

Keller, E. J., Omwami, E. M., & Anena, C. P. (2022). The Gordian Knot. *African Review (Dar Es Salaam, Tanzania)*, *14*(2), 151–170. DOI: 10.1163/09744061-bja10002

Ketenci, S. T., & Kubar, Y. (2025). Contribution of Economic Variables to Sustainable Development Goals (SDG 16): The Case of G20 Countries. *Journal of Lifestyle and SDGs Review*, *5*(2), e03920–e03920. DOI: 10.47172/2965-730X.SDGsReview.v5.n02.pe03920

Khairil, M., Jeganathan, C. S., Razman, M. R., Zakaria, S. Z., & Ismail, M. S. (2017). Influence of legal literacy and communication in the enforcement of environmental laws. *International Journal of Business and Society*, *20*(10A), 7199–7208.

Khai, T. S. (2024). India's refugee policy dilemma and its impact on Myanmar refugees at the India–Myanmar frontier. *Discover Public Health*, *21*(1), 153. Advance online publication. DOI: 10.1186/s12982-024-00295-7

Khambali Hambali, K. M., Khalil, S. A., & Daud, M. Z. (2022). 'My Sejahtera' application as COVID-19 control mechanism from Islamic thought perspective: Malaysia experience. *Afkar*, *2022*, 245–284. DOI: 10.22452/afkar.sp2022no1.8

Khan, A. S. I. F., Amjad, S. O. H. A. I. L., & Usman, M. U. H. A. M. M. A. D. (2020). The evolution of human rights law in the age of globalization. Pakistan Journal of Law, Analysis and Wisdom.

Khan, R., Al-Ansari, T., & Saif, U. (2023). Blockchain applications for sustainability compliance in tourism. *Tourism Technology Journal*, *9*(1), 45–58. DOI: 10.1016/j.ttj.2023.100184

Khare, P. & Raghuwanshi, V. (2025). Exploring the Complexities of India-Bangladesh Relations. *IGI Global Scientific Publishing,* 209-230. https://doi.org/ DOI: 10.4018/979-8-3693-9626-1.ch009

Khatri-Chhetri, G., & Ahmad, S. (2021). Regulatory frameworks for genome editing in agriculture: A global overview. *Biotechnology Advances, 51*, 107796. DOI: 10.1016/j.biotechadv.2021.107796

Kickbusch, I., & Hanefeld, J. (2017). Role for academic institutions and think tanks in speeding progress on sustainable development goals. *BMJ (Clinical Research Ed.), j3519*, j3519. DOI: 10.1136/bmj.j3519 PMID: 28739591

Kilibarda, P. (2022). Torture and other cruel, inhuman or degrading treatment or punishment in international law: Towards a generic definition? In *Research Handbook on Human Rights and Humanitarian Law* (pp. 435–461). Edward Elgar Publishing.

Kim, S., Lee, J., & Lee, Y. (2020). Legal frameworks for smart city public-private partnerships. *Government Information Quarterly, 37*(4), 101481.

Kipuri, N. (2023). Maasai Customary Land Systems in Kenya's Tourism Sector. *The American Journal of International Law, 34*(2), 45–67.

Kipuri, N. (2023). Maasai customary law in Kenyan tourism governance. *The American Journal of International Law, 34*(2), 45–67.

Kirkfeldt, T. S., & Frazão Santos, C. (2021). A review of sustainability concepts in marine spatial planning and the potential to supporting the UN sustainable development goal 14. *Frontiers in Marine Science, 8*, 713980. DOI: 10.3389/fmars.2021.713980

Kirkpatrick, J. B., Kriwoken, L. K., & Styger, J. (2017). The reverse precautionary principle: Science, the environment and the salmon aquaculture industry in Macquarie Harbour, Tasmania, Australia. *Pacific Conservation Biology, 25*(1), 26–33. DOI: 10.1071/PC17014

Kitchin, R. (2022). The data-driven city? Big data and smart urbanism. *Geography Compass, 16*(1), e12657.

Klingelhöfer, D., Müller, R., Braun, M., Brüggmann, D., & Groneberg, D. A. (2020). Climate change: Does international research fulfill global demands and necessities? *Environmental Sciences Europe, 32*(1), 137. DOI: 10.1186/s12302-020-00419-1 PMID: 33078088

Kok, B. P., & Jones, D. A. (2004). Nutritional strategies for improving glucose metabolism and phytate utilization in salmonids. *Aquaculture Research, 35*(7), 665–673. DOI: 10.1111/j.1365-2109.2004.01072.x

Komninos, N. (2020). *Intelligent cities: Innovation, knowledge systems and digital spaces*. Routledge.

Komninos, N., Bratsas, C., Kakderi, C., & Kakderi, A. (2018). Smart Cities and the Future Internet: Innovation Ecosystems, Platforms, and the Public Interest. *Technological Forecasting and Social Change*, *142*, 1–12.

Kontogeorgopoulos, N. (2020). *Tourism and the Economy in Thailand: Challenges and Opportunities*. Oxford University Press.

Kontogeorgopoulos, N. (2023). Regulatory failure in Thai coastal tourism. *Journal of Sustainable Tourism*, *31*(2), 245–263.

Koskelainen, M. (2024). Study of the Novel European Sustainability Reporting Standards (ESRS)–changes and impact on the case company.

Koundouri, P., Aslanidis, P. S., Dellis, K., Plataniotis, A., & Feretzakis, G. (2025). Mapping human security strategies to sustainable development goals: A machine learning approach. *Discover Sustainability*, *6*(1), 96. Advance online publication. DOI: 10.1007/s43621-025-00883-w

Krawczyk, P. (2021). Non-financial reporting—Standardization options for SME sector. *Journal of Risk and Financial Management*, *14*(9), 417. DOI: 10.3390/jrfm14090417

Krayer, W. L., & Note, P. S. (2025). To make men free. *Legal Writing*, *29*, 305–306.

Kulovesi, K. (2013). Climate change and trade: At the intersection of two international legal regimes. In E. Hollo, K. Kulovesi, & M. Mehling (Eds.), *Climate Change and the Law* (Ius Gentium: Comparative Perspectives on Law and Justice, Vol. 21, pp. 273–289). Springer, Dordrecht. https://doi.org/DOI: 10.1007/978-94-007-5440-9_16

Kumar, J. (2024). Integrating CSR with Rajasthan's Policy Framework: A Strategic Approach to Achieving SDG 16 in the Context of Climate Change. *Journal of East-West Thought (JET) ISSN (O): 2168-2259 UGC CARE I, 14*(3), 341-363.

Kumar, K. B., Culbertson, S., & Constant, L. (2021). Colombia's Trailblazing Model for Refugees. https://www.rand.org/blog/2021/03/colombias-trailblazing-model-for-refugees.html

Kumari, S. (2023). Social justice through labour legislation. *National Journal of Labour and Industrial Law*, *6*(2), 14–23.

Kumar, P., Singh, R., & Sharma, P. (2021). IoT and smart grids for sustainable urban energy management. *Energy Reports*, *7*, 3437–3446.

Kunyanga, C., Mugiira, B., & Muchiri, N. (2024). Public perception of genetically modified organisms and the implementation of biosafety measures in Kenya. *Advances in Agriculture*, *2024*(1).

Kusumasari, B. (2015). Inclusion in public-private partnerships: Social equity in urban development. *Journal of Public Administration*, *49*(3), 277–292.

Kwak, S. Y., Choi, S. Y., & Park, K. (2009). Public-private partnerships for urban infrastructure development: Success factors and case studies. *Asian Journal of Public Affairs*, *2*(1), 23–37.

Kwak, S. Y., Lee, S., & Seo, M. (2019). Public-private partnerships for smart city development: A case study of Seoul. *Cities (London, England)*, *85*, 36–44.

Kyoto City Government. (2022). Digital Tourism Access Management System. https://www.city.kyoto.lg.jp

Lachapelle, U., Tanguay, G., & Neumark-Gaudet, L. (2017). Telecommuting and sustainable travel: Reduction of overall travel time, increases in non-motorised travel and congestion relief? *Urban Studies (Edinburgh, Scotland)*, *55*(10), 2226–2244. DOI: 10.1177/0042098017708985

Ladan, M. T. (2018). Achieving Sustainable Development Goals Through Effective Domestic Laws and Policies on Environment and Climate Change. *Environmental Policy and Law*, *48*(1), 42–63. DOI: 10.3233/EPL-180049

Laprévote, F.-C., & Kang, S. (2011). Subsidies issues in the WTO – An update. *European State Aid Law Quarterly, 10*(3), 445–456. https://www.jstor.org/stable/26686640

Larch, M., & Wanner, J. (2017). Carbon tariffs: An analysis of the trade, welfare, and emission effects. *Journal of International Economics*, *109*, 195–213. DOI: 10.1016/j.jinteco.2017.09.003

Larramendy, E. E., & Tiberi, S. (2019b, octubre 1). *Información Integrada – Marco teórico GRI y marco teórico de Reportes Integrados.* http://sedici.unlp.edu.ar/handle/10915/88587

Larrinaga, C., Luque-Vilchez, M., & Fernández, R. (2018). Sustainability accounting regulation in Spanish public sector organizations. *Public Money & Management*, *38*(5), 345–354. DOI: 10.1080/09540962.2018.1477669

Law 7/1985 Regulating the Bases of the Local Regime. April 2. BOE No. 80

Lazic, L. (2019). Benefit from AI in cybersecurity. *Business Information Security Conference*. https://www.researchgate.net/publication/336826190

Lee, C.-C., Hussain, J., & Abass, Q. (2025). An integrated analysis of AI-driven green financing, subsidies, and knowledge to enhance CO2 reduction efficiency. *Economic Analysis and Policy*, *85*, 675–693. DOI: 10.1016/j.eap.2024.12.021

Lee, J.. (2023). Smart water grid management through IoT and big data analytics: The Singapore model. *Journal of Cleaner Production, 379*, 134664.

Lee, J., Lee, K., & Lee, M. (2020). Smart city governance: A comparative analysis. *Government Information Quarterly, 37*(3), 101478.

Lee, O., Green, J., & Tyler, C. (2014). Transgenic fish systems and their application in ecotoxicology. *Critical Reviews in Toxicology, 45*(2), 124–141. DOI: 10.3109/10408444.2014.965805 PMID: 25394772

Lee, S., & Lee, D. (2018). Songdo International Business District: A smart city case study. *Cities (London, England), 72*, 173–185.

Leggatt, R., Hollo, T., Vandersteen, W., McFarlane, K., Goh, B., Prevost, J., & Devlin, R. (2014). Rearing in seawater mesocosms improves the spawning performance of growth hormone transgenic and wild-type coho salmon. *PLoS One, 9*(8), e105377. DOI: 10.1371/journal.pone.0105377 PMID: 25133780

Leggatt, R., Sundström, L., Woodward, K., & Devlin, R. (2017). Growth-enhanced transgenic coho salmon (oncorhynchus kisutch) strains have varied success in simulated streams: Implications for risk assessment. *PLoS One, 12*(1), e0169991. DOI: 10.1371/journal.pone.0169991 PMID: 28068416

Lenzen, M., Sun, Y.-Y., Faturay, F., Ting, Y.-P., Geschke, A., & Malik, A. (2021). The carbon footprint of global tourism. *Nature Climate Change, 8*(6), 522–528. DOI: 10.1038/s41558-018-0141-x

Lesch, M., & Reiners, N. (2023). Informal human rights law-making: How treaty bodies use 'General Comments' to develop international law. *Global Constitutionalism, 12*(2), 378–401. DOI: 10.1017/S2045381723000023

Levesque, H. M., Shears, M. A., Fletcher, G. L., & Moon, T. W. (2008). Myogenesis and muscle metabolism in juvenile Atlantic salmon (*Salmo salar*) made transgenic for growth hormone. *The Journal of Experimental Biology, 211*(1), 128–137. DOI: 10.1242/jeb.006890 PMID: 18083741

Lew, A. A., Ng, P. T., & Teng, Y. (2020). *Nature-Based Tourism: Ecology, Impacts, and Management*. Cambridge University Press.

Li, F., Li, J., & Wang, D. (2024). Policy instruments and green innovation: Evidence and implications for corporate performance. *Journal of Cleaner Production, 471*, 143443. DOI: 10.1016/j.jclepro.2024.143443

Li, H. (2006). The impacts and implications of the legal framework for sea use planning and management in China. *Ocean and Coastal Management, 49*(9–10), 717–726. DOI: 10.1016/j.ocecoaman.2006.06.015

Li, M. H., Robinson, E. H., Oberle, D. F., & Lucas, P. M. (2009). Effects of dietary protein and energy levels on growth and body composition of juvenile channel catfish, Ictalurus punctatus. *Aquaculture (Amsterdam, Netherlands), 295*(1–2), 98–101. DOI: 10.1016/j.aquaculture.2009.06.002

Lim, K. H., & Ooi, L. C. (2020). Public perception and acceptance of genetically modified fish in Malaysia. *Journal of Environmental Science and Policy, 15*(1), 23–30.

Lippert-Rasmussen, K., & Vitikainen, A. (2020). The ethics of refugee prioritization: Reframing the debate. *Ethics & Global Politics, 13*(1), 1–5. DOI: 10.1080/16544951.2020.1735019

Lisha, V., New, C., Nishibuchi, M., & Radu, S. (2017). rapid genetically modified organism (GMO) screening of various food products and animal feeds using multiplex polymerase chain reaction (pcr). *Food Research, 1*(1), 1–8. DOI: 10.26656/fr.2017.1.001

Liu, Z., Zhang, J., & Wang, L. (2021). Artificial Intelligence Applications in Sustainable Tourism Management. *Sustainability, 13*(12), 6784. DOI: 10.3390/su13126784

Li, W., Zhang, H., & Chen, J. (2023). Enhancing community participation in smart city governance. *Cities (London, England), 134*, 104102.

Li, Y.. (2021). Sustainable urban drainage systems (SuDS) and their role in flood mitigation. *Water (Basel), 13*(4), 501.

Li, Z.. (2022). Smart sensor networks for efficient water resource management. *Sensors (Basel), 22*(12), 4567. PMID: 35746349

Li, Z., Pan, Y., Yang, W., Ma, J., & Zhou, M. (2021). Effects of government subsidies on green technology investment and green marketing coordination of supply chain under the cap-and-trade mechanism. *Energy Economics, 101*, 105426. DOI: 10.1016/j.eneco.2021.105426

Lodhia, S., Kaur, A., & Kuruppu, S. C. (2023). The disclosure of sustainable development goals (SDGs) by the top 50 Australian companies: Substantive or symbolic legitimation? *Meditari Accountancy Research, 31*(6), 1578–1605. DOI: 10.1108/MEDAR-05-2021-1297

López, M. J. T., Quintana, P. J. V., Lavado-Anguera, S., & Espinosa-Elvira, M. del C. (2020). Preparing Sustainable Engineers: A Project-Based Learning Experience in Logistics with Refugee Camps. *Sustainability (Basel)*, *12*(12), 4817. DOI: 10.3390/su12124817

López-Santillán, A. (2023). Cultural zoning in Mexican tourism. *Annals of Tourism Research*, *98*, 103527.

Lovett, F. (2006). Rational Choice Theory and Explanation. *Rationality and Society*, *18*(2), 237–272. DOI: 10.1177/1043463106060155

Low, S., & Lee, C. (2023). Sustainable infrastructure development through PPPs in Singapore: Legal and institutional perspectives. *International Journal of Urban Sciences*, *27*(1), 75–90.

Lozano, R., & Huisingh, D. (2011). Inter-linking issues and dimensions in sustainability reporting. *Journal of Cleaner Production*, *19*(2-3), 99–107. DOI: 10.1016/j.jclepro.2010.01.004

Lua, W. Y., Aziz, N., Idris, I., Rahman, M. A. A., Ghazali, F. & Talaat, W. I. A. W. (2025). Marine spatial planning as a potential practical approach to manage setiu wetland as an ecologically sensitive area. *Integrated Environmental Assessment and Management, vjaf023*, 35-64. https://doi.org/DOI: 10.1093/inteam/vjaf023

Lua, W. Y., Aziz, N., Ghazali, F., Idris, I., Rasid, N. H. A., & Talat, W. I. A. W. (2021). Marine Spatial Planning and the Local Community's Awareness of Ecosystems in Setiu Wetland. *Journal of Southeast Asian Studies*, *26*(1), 97–123. DOI: 10.22452/jati.vol26no1.5

Lu, F.. (2023). Indigenous Environmental Stewardship in Amazonian Tourism. *Conservation & Society*, *21*(1), 12–25.

Lugo-Morín, D. R. (2020). Global food security in a pandemic: The case of the new coronavirus (COVID-19). *WORLD (Oakland, Calif.)*, *1*(2), 171–190. DOI: 10.3390/world1020013

Luntamo, M., Pascoe, A., & Thomas, C. (2021). Tuberculosis prevalence in prisons: A global perspective. *World Health Organization Report, 12*(4), 132–140. https://www.who.int/tb

Lyngstad, T. M., Kristoffersen, A. B., Hjortaas, M. J., Devold, M., Aspehaug, V., Larssen, R. B., & Jansen, P. A. (2012). Low virulent infectious salmon anaemia virus (ISAV-HPR0) is prevalent and geographically structured in Norwegian salmon farming. *Diseases of Aquatic Organisms*, *101*(3), 197–206. DOI: 10.3354/dao02520 PMID: 23324416

Lyu, H., Ma, C., & Arash, F. (2024). Government innovation subsidies, green technology innovation, and carbon intensity of industrial firms. *Journal of Environmental Management, 369*, 122274. DOI: 10.1016/j.jenvman.2024.122274 PMID: 39241599

M., & Xydis, G. (2023). The Inflation Reduction Act versus the 1.5 cent/kWh and 30% investment tax credit proposal for wind power. *SN Business & Economics, 3*, 68. https://doi.org/DOI: 10.1007/s43546-023-00448-x

Maclean, N. (2003). Genetically modified fish and their effects on food quality and human health and nutrition. *Trends in Food Science & Technology, 14*(5–8), 242–252. DOI: 10.1016/S0924-2244(03)00070-0

Maclean, N., & Laight, R. J. (2000). Transgenic fish: An evaluation of benefits and risks. *Fish and Fisheries, 1*(2), 146–172. DOI: 10.1046/j.1467-2979.2000.00014.x

Maclean, N., & Talwar, S. (1984). Injection of cloned genes into rainbow trout eggs. *Journal of Embryology and Experimental Morphology, 82*(Supplement), 187.

Madiega, T. (2019). EU guidelines on ethics in artificial intelligence: Context and implementation. *EPRS*. https://www.europarl.europa.eu/RegData/etudes/BRIE/2019/640163/EPRS_BRI(2019)640163_EN.pdf#:~:text=Following%20the%20call%20from%20the%20European%20Parliament%20to,that%20is%20respectful%20of%20European%20values%20and%20principles

Madiega, T. (2024). Artificial intelligence act. *EPRS, 12*. https://www.europarl.europa.eu/RegData/etudes/BRIE/2021/698792/EPRS_BRI(2021)698792_EN.pdf

Madiega, T., & Van De Pol, A. L. (2022). Artificial intelligence act and regulatory sandboxes. *European Parliamentary Research Service*. https://www.europarl.europa.eu/RegData/etudes/BRIE/2022/733544/EPRS_BRI(2022)733544_EN.pdf

Madu, K. (2024). International Law Framework for Taxation and the Sustainable Development Goals in Nigeria. *Available at SSRN* 4993714. DOI: 10.2139/ssrn.4993714

Mah, A., & Goh, C. (2021). Transnational urban networks: Knowledge sharing and smart city development. *Cities (London, England), 108*, 102969.

Mahajan, N., Kaur, N., Singh, V., Gupta, A., & Garg, N. (2023). Green trade: Transition towards a sustainable economy. *IOP Conference Series. Earth and Environmental Science, 1279*(1), 012023. DOI: 10.1088/1755-1315/1279/1/012023

Mair, J. (2019). *Community-based tourism: Principles and practices*. Channel View Publications.

Maitland, R. (2023). *Smart Cities and Tourism: The Role of Urban Law*. Routledge.

Ma, J., & Xu, J. (2024). Potential economic impacts of carbon tariffs on target countries: A systematic review. *Climate Policy*, •••, 1–17. DOI: 10.1080/14693062.2024.2407830

Majid, N. A. (2012). Review of the Issues and Governance of Genetically Modified Organisms in Malaysia. *International Journal of Biotechnology and Biochemistry, 8*(1), 1–16.

Makwara, T. (2024). Exploring the impact of Firm-Level Corporate Governance Challenges on Sustainable Development Goals (SDGs) in a Developing Economy. *International Journal of Business, Economics, and Social Development, 5*(4).

Malaysian Investment Development Authority. (2024). Revitalising the Maritime Industry Through Blue Economy. https://www.mida.gov.my/revitalising-the-maritime-industry-through-blue-economy/#:~:text=The%20maritime%20industry%20in%20Malaysia,cent%20in%20compound%20cargo%20throughput

Malaysian Science and Technology Information Centre. (2023). *Malaysia National Artificial Intelligence Roadmap 2021 - 2025 (AI-RMAP).* https://mastic.mosti.gov.my/publication/artificial-intelligence-roadmap-2021-2025/

Malaysian Science and Technology Information Centre. (2024). *"AI FOR MALAYSIA, AI FOR ALL" THE NATIONAL GUIDELINES ON AI GOVERNANCE & ETHICS.* https://mastic.mosti.gov.my/publication/the-national-guidelines-on-ai-governance-ethics/

Malaysians recognise their worth at the workplace, not willing to give up remote work (2022) https://www.pwc.com/my/en/media/press-releases/2022/20220713-malaysians-recognise-their-worth-at-the-workplace-not-willing-to-give-up-remote-work.html

Mammonas, D. (2024, May 21). Artificial intelligence (AI) act: Council gives final green light to the first worldwide rules on AI - Consilium. *European Council.* https://www.consilium.europa.eu/en/press/press-releases/2024/05/21/artificial-intelligence-ai-act-council-gives-final-green-light-to-the-first-worldwide-rules-on-ai/

Manap, N. A., & Abdullah, A. (2020). Regulating artificial intelligence in Malaysia: The two-tier approach. *UUM Journal of Legal Studies, 11*(2), 183–201. DOI: 10.32890/uumjls.11.2.2020.8779

Mang, P., & Reed, B. (2018). Designing for resilience: Regenerative tourism as a path to systemic change. *Tourism Geographies, 20*(1), 68–86. DOI: 10.1080/14616688.2017.1386968

Mansoor, S. I. U. (2022). International Environmental Law in Promoting Sustainable Development: A Critical Analysis. *Central University of Kashmir Law Review, 2*, 91–111.

Mansoor, S. I. U., & Chopra, M. (2020). Article XX Of GATT: Territoriality Of Unilateral Trade Measure And Sustainable Development. *Ilkogretim Online*, *19*(4), 7784–7792.

Månsson, J., Eriksson, L., Hodgson, I., Elmberg, J., Bunnefeld, N., Hessel, R., Johansson, M., Liljebäck, N., Nilsson, L., Olsson, C., Pärt, T., Sandström, C., Tombre, I., & Redpath, S. M. (2023). Understanding and overcoming obstacles in adaptive management. *Trends in Ecology &amp. Trends in Ecology & Evolution*, *38*(1), 55–71. DOI: 10.1016/j.tree.2022.08.009 PMID: 36202636

Mao, W., Wang, Y., Wang, W., Wu, B., Feng, J., & Zhu, Z. (2004). Enhanced resistance to *Aeromonas hydrophila* infection and enhanced phagocytic activities in human lactoferrin-transgenic grass carp (*Ctenopharyngodon idellus*). *Aquaculture (Amsterdam, Netherlands)*, *242*(1–4), 93–103. DOI: 10.1016/j.aquaculture.2004.07.020

Marceau, G. (2016). The interface between the trade rules and climate change actions. In Park, D. Y. (Ed.), *Legal issues on climate change and international trade law* (pp. 3–39). Springer., DOI: 10.1007/978-3-319-29322-6_1

Marinoni, G., & Pina Cardona, S. B. (2024). *Internationalization of Higher Education: Current Trends and Future* Scenarios. 6th IAU Global Survey Report. International Association of Universities. https://www.iau-aiu.net/IMG/pdf/2024_internationalization_survey_report_digital.pdf

Marti, E., Fuchs, M., DesJardine, M. R., Slager, R., & Gond, J. P. (2024). The impact of sustainable investing: A multidisciplinary review. *Journal of Management Studies*, *61*(5), 2181–2211. DOI: 10.1111/joms.12957

Martin, M. (2013). *Increased autonomy for universities in Asia: How to make it work? (IIEP policy brief. Policy brief on higher education*, 4(1). UNESCO International Institute for Educational Planning. https://unesdoc.unesco.org/ark:/48223/pf0000229831

Martínez, L., Garcia, P., & Torres, R. (2024). Citizen engagement in smart city PPP projects: The Barcelona model. *Journal of Urban Affairs*, *46*(1), 23–42.

Martin, M., & Godonoga, A. (2020). SDG 4-policies for flexible learning pathways in higher education. IIEP-UNESCO Working Papers, 1-52.Mensah, J. (2019). Sustainable development: Meaning, history, principles, pillars, and implications for human action: Literature review. *Cogent Social Sciences*, *5*(1), 1653531. DOI: 10.1080/23311886.2019.1653531

Matamanda, A. R., Mangara, F., Maramura, T., & Mukumba, C. P. (2024). Peace, Justice and Strong Institutions: Reflections on Health Governance and Health Inequalities in Mangaung. In *Sustainable Development Goals and Urban Health: Strides, Challenges and Way Forward for Poor Neighborhoods* (pp. 145–158). Springer Nature Switzerland. DOI: 10.1007/978-3-031-68734-1_9

Matos, S., Viardot, E., Sovacool, B. K., Geels, F. W., & Xiong, Y. (2022). Innovation and climate change: A review and introduction to the special issue. *Technovation*, *117*, 102612. DOI: 10.1016/j.technovation.2022.102612

Matsushita, M., & Associates. (2015). Environmental Protection and Trade. In *The World Trade Organization: Law, Practice, and Policy* (3rd ed.). Oxford International Law Library. https://doi.org/DOI: 10.1093/law/9780199571857.003.0020

Matuszak, Ł., Różańska, E., & Szczepankiewicz, E. I. (2025). Assessment of the Compliance of Environmental Disclosures by Energy Companies Using GRI Standards with European Sustainability Reporting Standards: A Case Study. *Sustainability (Basel)*, *17*(8), 3380. DOI: 10.3390/su17083380

Mbaiwa, J. (2023). Community-based tourism and customary law in Botswana. *Journal of Ecotourism*, *22*(1), 45–62.

Mbaiwa, J. E. (2023). Customary law in African tourism governance. *Journal of Sustainable Tourism*, *31*(3), 456–475.

McKinsey & Company. (2018). How to make public-private partnerships work for cities. McKinsey Global Institute Report.

McLennan, C. J., Becken, S., & Watt, M. (2021). Strengthening tourism laws for sustainability: A global review. *International Journal of Tourism Research*, *23*(2), 198–213. DOI: 10.1002/jtr.2412

Mclennan, C., Rudi, G., Altchenko, Y., & Ait-Mouheb, N. (2024). Will the European Regulation for water reuse for agricultural irrigation foster this practice in the European Union? *Water Reuse*, *14*(2), 115–135. DOI: 10.2166/wrd.2024.012

Meerow, S., & Newell, J. P. (2019). Urban resilience for whom, what, when, where, and why? *Urban Geography*, *40*(3), 309–329. DOI: 10.1080/02723638.2016.1206395

Meerow, S., Newell, J. P., & Stults, M. (2019). Defining urban resilience: A review. *Landscape and Urban Planning, 147*, 38–49. DOI: 10.1016/j.landurbplan.2015.11.011

Mehling, M. A., van Asselt, H., Das, K., Droege, S., & Verkuijl, C. (2019). Designing border carbon adjustments for enhanced climate action. *The American Journal of International Law, 113*(3), 433–481. DOI: 10.1017/ajil.2019.22

Mehling, M., van Asselt, H., Das, K., Droege, S., & Verkuij, C. (2017). Front matter. In *Designing border carbon adjustments for enhanced climate action* (pp. 2–3). Climate Strategies., https://www.jstor.org/stable/resrep16316.1

Mehrotra, A., & Bhardwaj, C. (2022). Need for a National Legislation on Refugees in India at 75. India Quarterly. *Journal of International Affairs, 78*(2), 297–317. DOI: 10.1177/09749284221089531

Menassa, E. (2010). Corporate social responsibility: An exploratory study of the quality and extent of social disclosures by Lebanese commercial banks. *Journal of applied accounting research*, 11(1), 4-23.

Mencütek, Z. Ş., & Nashwan, A. (2020). Perceptions About the Labor Market Integration of Refugees: Evidences from Syrian Refugees in Jordan. Journal of International Migration and Integration / Revue de l Integration et de La Migration Internationale, 22(2), 615. DOI: 10.1007/s12134-020-00756-3

Meng, H. (2024). Challenges and controversies to the European CBAM from a legal perspective. *Advances in Economics. Management and Political Sciences, 81*, 201–206.

Metzger, S. D. (1974). Governmental intervention in the international competitive process: Subsidies, countervailing duties, and "voluntary" agreements restraining imports. *Antitrust Law Journal, 43*(3), 621–630. https://www.jstor.org/stable/40842113

Michavila, F., & Martinez, J. (2018). Excellence of Universities versus Autonomy, Funding and Accountability. *European Review (Chichester, England), 26*(S1), 1–9. DOI: 10.1017/S1062798717000539

Michelon, G., Pilonato, S., & Ricceri, F. (2015). CSR reporting practices and the quality of disclosure: An empirical analysis. *Critical Perspectives on Accounting, 33*, 59–78. DOI: 10.1016/j.cpa.2014.10.003

Milano, C., Cheer, J. M., & Novelli, M. (2019). *Overtourism: Excesses, Discontents, and Measures in Travel and Tourism.* CABI. DOI: 10.1079/9781786399823.0000

Millar, K., & Tomkins, S. (2007). Ethical analysis of the use of GM fish: Emerging issues for aquaculture development. *Journal of Agricultural & Environmental Ethics, 20*(5), 437–453. DOI: 10.1007/s10806-007-9051-z

Milne, S. (2023). Neoliberal conservation and tourism displacement. *Geoforum, 138*, 103662.

Minister's Office of Malaysia Official Website. (2024, October 1). PM ANWAR UNVEILS NATIONAL CLOUD POLICY, FOCUS ON FOUR KEY AREAS. *Prime Minister's Office of Malaysia Official Website*. https://www.pmo.gov.my/2024/10/pm-anwar-unveils-national-cloud-policy-focus-on-four-key-areas/

Ministerio para la Transición Ecológica y el Reto Demográfico. (2020). Renewable energy plan. Retrieved from https://www.miteco.gob.es

Ministry of Corporate Affairs. (2013). The Companies Act, 2013. Retrieved from https://www.mca.gov.in

Ministry of Environment. Maldives. (2021). National Carbon Neutrality Strategy. https://www.environment.gov.mv

Ministry of Higher Education. (2020). *National Education Code (NEC-2020).* Ministry of Higher Education: Malaysia. https://www.mqa.gov.my/new/document/2022/Feb/National%20Education%20Code%202020%20%28NEC-2020%29.pdf

Ministry of Science. T. and I. (2024, April 18). AI Sandbox launch with NVIDIA. *MRANTI*. https://mranti.my/happenings/media-centre/press-release/ai-sandbox-launch-with-nvidia

Ministry of Social Rights and Agenda 2030 (2020). Estrategia de Desarrollo Sostenible 2030 Centro de publicaciones paseo del prado, 18-20, 28014. Madrid. https://cpage.mpr.gob.es/

Mio, C., Costantini, A., & Panfilo, S. (2022). Performance measurement tools for sustainable business: A systematic literature review on the sustainability balanced scorecard use. *Corporate Social Responsibility and Environmental Management, 29*(2), 367–384. DOI: 10.1002/csr.2206

Mishra, R. K., & Krishna, P. S. (2021). Capacity building and technical cooperation for achieving sustainable development goals. In: Leal Filho, W., Azul, A.M., Brandli, L., Lange Salvia, A., Özuyar, P.G., Wall, T. (eds) *Peace, justice and strong institutions*. Encyclopedia of the UN Sustainable Development Goals. Springer, Cham. https://doi.org/, pp 1–11.DOI: 10.1007/978-3-319-71066-2_8-1

Mizan, N. A., & Norman, H. (2024). Pre-university students' perception in using generative AI: A study at a Malaysian private university. *International Journal of Academic Research in Business & Social Sciences, 14*(8). Advance online publication. DOI: 10.6007/IJARBSS/v14-i8/22455

Mohajan, H. (2018). History of Rakhine State and the Origin of the Rohingya Muslims. *IKAT The Indonesian Journal of Southeast Asian Studies*, *2*(1), 19. DOI: 10.22146/ikat.v2i1.37391

Mohammed, N. F., Mohamed, N., Atan, R., & Said, J. (2021). Financial Transparency in Malaysian Public Universities: Are We on the Path to Achieving SDG 16? *Academy of Strategic Management Journal*, *20*(S6), 1–15.

Mohd Noor, A. R.. (2022). Application of CRISPR technology in enhancing disease resistance of freshwater fish in Malaysia. *Journal of Aquatic Biotechnology*, *10*(1), 12–20.

Mohd Zulkhairi Kamaruzaman. (2013). Company secretary pleads guilty to making false statement. The Borneo Post. https://www.pressreader.com/malaysia/the-borneopost/20131001/281848641310905

Molaba, T. I. (2025). The concept of transformative constitutionalism in post-apartheid South Africa. *Perspectives of Law and Public Administration, 14*(1).

Molnar, P. (2019). Technology on the margins: AI and global migration management from a human rights perspective. *Cambridge International Law Journal*, *8*(2), 305–330. DOI: 10.4337/cilj.2019.02.07

Mondal, A., & Islam, N. (2023). The Right to Education Act, 2009 in India after a decade: Appraising achievements and exploring unkept promises. Education 3-13, 51(1), 87–106.

Mondal, S. R. (2020). A systematic study for digital innovation in management education: An integrated approach towards problem-based learning in Vietnam. In *Digital innovations for customer engagement, management, and organizational improvement* (pp. 104–120). IGI Global., DOI: 10.4018/978-1-7998-5171-4.ch006

Mondal, S., & Sahoo, K. K. (2020). A study of green building prospects on sustainable management decision making. In *Green building management and smart automation* (pp. 220–234). IGI Global., DOI: 10.4018/978-1-5225-9754-4.ch011

Moomaw, W. R., Chmura, G. L., Davies, G. T., Finlayson, C. M., Middleton, B. A., Natali, S. M., Perry, J. E., Roulet, N., & Sutton-Grier, A. E. (2018). Wetlands in a changing climate: Science, policy and management. *Wetlands*, *38*(2), 183–205. DOI: 10.1007/s13157-018-1023-8

Mora, L., Deakin, M., & Reid, A. (2019). Strategic principles for smart city development: A multiple case study analysis. *Journal of Urban Technology*, *26*(2), 3–28.

Morales-Casetti, M., Bustos-Gutiérrez, M., Manquepillán-Calfuleo, F., & Hochstetter-Diez, J. (2024). Quality of Government, Democracy, and Well-Being as Determinants in Achieving the Sustainable Development Goals. *Sustainability (Basel)*, *16*(13), 5430. DOI: 10.3390/su16135430

Moreau, D., Fleming, I., Fletcher, G., & Brown, J. (2011). Growth hormone transgenesis does not influence territorial dominance or growth and survival of first-feeding Atlantic salmon salmo salar in food-limited stream microcosms. *Journal of Fish Biology*, *78*(3), 726–740. DOI: 10.1111/j.1095-8649.2010.02888.x PMID: 21366569

Moriarty, J. (2011). *Qualitative methods overview*. NIHR School for Social Care Research.

Morris, A., & Maxwell, G. (2018). *Restorative justice and the prison system*. Cambridge University Press.

Morshidi, S., Wan, C. D., & Norzaini, A. (2017). Governance reforms in higher education: Reflections from Malaysia. In Mihut, G., Altbach, P. G., & de Wit, H. (Eds.), *Understanding higher education internationalization: Insights from key global publications* (pp. 197–202). Sense Publishers.

Moser, L. (2020). Prison health: A fundamental human right. *Health and Human Rights Journal*, *22*(4), 234–247.

Mougenot, B., & Doussoulin, J. P. (2024). A bibliometric analysis of the Global Reporting Initiative (GRI): Global trends in developed and developing countries. *Environment, Development and Sustainability*, *26*(3), 6543–6560. DOI: 10.1007/s10668-023-02974-y PMID: 36788933

Mukheibir, P.. (2019). Integrating communities in climate resilience through legal frameworks: Johannesburg case study. *Climate Policy*, *19*(5), 598–610.

Mukheibir, P., Ziervogel, G., & Matarira, C. (2019). Inclusive urban governance through PPPs: A case study from Johannesburg. *Environment and Urbanization*, *31*(2), 557–574.

Muller, M. (2012). 11. Water accounting, corporate sustainability and the public interest. *Water Accounting*, 203.

Müller, A. (2023). *States, human rights, and distant strangers: The normative justification of extraterritorial obligations in human rights law*. Routledge. DOI: 10.4324/9781003347095

Müller, D., & Pforr, C. (2023). The implementation gap in tourism policy. *Annals of Tourism Research*, *98*, 103530.

Müller, F. (2018). Legal frameworks and smart energy management in cities. *Energy Research & Social Science*, *35*, 122–130.

Murray, R., Turner, A., & Green, J. (2021). *The intersection of public health and criminal justice systems*. Cambridge University Press.

Mwangi, W. (2023). Maasai land rights in Kenyan tourism. African Journal of International Law.

Mwangi, W. (2022). *Community Land Rights and Tourism in Kenya*. African Legal Review.

Mwangi, W., & Omwenga, M. (2021). Legal frameworks and community-led tourism in Kenya: A pathway to sustainability. *Tourism Management Perspectives*, *40*, 100827. DOI: 10.1016/j.tmp.2021.100827

Mwangi, W., & Omwenga, M. (2023). Post-colonial legal reforms in African tourism. *Third World Quarterly*, *44*(2), 234–251.

Nadanyiova, M., & Das, S. (2020). Millennials as a target segment of socially responsible communication within the business strategy. *Littera Scripta*, *13*(1), 119–134. DOI: 10.36708/Littera_Scripta2020/1/8

Nam, D. H., Maclean, N., Fu, C., Pandian, T. J., & Eguia, M. R. R. (2007). Genetic guidelines for fisheries management. *Aquatic Living Resources*, *20*(3), 241–255. DOI: 10.1051/alr:2007012

Nan Muhammad, R. R., Muhammad Hibri, N., Aiesyah, M., & Saif Aslam, L. (2024). Occupational Safety and Health (Amendment) Act 2022. Retrieved on May 2025 https://www.zulrafique.com.my/ckfinder/userfiles/files/Article/Article-Occupational-Safety-and-Health_Amendment_Act-2022.PDF

Nanda, S. K. (2021). Sustainable development and towards sustainable climate action: The way forward. 48(3).

Negi, A. (2020). The World Trade Organization and sustainability standards. In Negi, A., Pérez-Pineda, J., & Blankenbach, J. (Eds.), *Sustainability standards and global governance* (pp. 39–59). Springer., DOI: 10.1007/978-981-15-3473-7_3

Neirotti, P.. (2022). IoT and big data for crowd management in tourist cities. *Tourism Management*, *93*, 104608.

Neirotti, P., De Marco, A., Cagliano, A. C., Mangano, G., & Scorrano, F. (2020). Current Trends in Smart City Initiatives: Some Stylised Facts. *Cities (London, England)*, *38*, 25–36. DOI: 10.1016/j.cities.2013.12.010

Nelson, F. (2017). Community conservation in Tanzania: Policies and legal frameworks. *Development Policy Review*, *35*(5), 593–615. DOI: 10.1111/dpr.12245

Nelson, F. (2022). Tourism law reform in Tanzania. *Development Policy Review*, *40*(3), 412–430.

Neves, P. C., Afonso, O., Silva, D., & Sochirca, E. (2021). The link between intellectual property rights, innovation, and growth: A meta-analysis. *Economic Modelling*, *97*, 196–209. DOI: 10.1016/j.econmod.2021.01.019

New Zealand Government. (2019). Climate Change Response (Zero Carbon) Amendment Act. Retrieved from https://www.legislation.govt.nz

Ng, E., Chan, C., Cheng, A., & Singh, T. (2023). *Findings from the 2024 global digital trust insights putting security at the epicentre of innovation*. https://www.pwc.com/my/en/assets/publications/2023/pwc-malaysia-2024-digital-trust-insights-report.pdf

Nguyen, T., Carnevale, J. J., Scholer, A. A., Miele, D. B., & Fujita, K. (2019). Metamotivational knowledge of the role of high-level and low-level construal in goal-relevant task performance. *Journal of Personality and Social Psychology*, *117*(5), 879–899. DOI: 10.1037/pspa0000166 PMID: 31120290

Nguyen, T., Hoang, D., & Pham, H. (2021). Investment protection laws and their impact on smart city PPP projects in Asia. *Asian Journal of Law and Economics*, *12*(2), 245–267.

Nicolo', G., & Cervilla-Bellido, J. M. (2025). Investigating the antecedents of Sustainable Development Goals disclosure via social media: Evidence from water companies. *Corporate Social Responsibility and Environmental Management*, *32*(2), 2317–2331. DOI: 10.1002/csr.3066

Nicolo', G., Zampone, G., De Iorio, S., & Sannino, G. (2024). Does SDG disclosure reflect corporate underlying sustainability performance? Evidence from UN Global Compact participants. *Journal of International Financial Management & Accounting*, *35*(1), 214–260. DOI: 10.1111/jifm.12194

Nogueira, T., & Botelho, A. (2021). Metagenomics and other omics approaches to bacterial communities and antimicrobial resistance assessment in aquacultures. *Antibiotics (Basel, Switzerland)*, *10*(7), 787. DOI: 10.3390/antibiotics10070787 PMID: 34203511

Norwegian Correctional Service. (2021). *Rehabilitation in Norwegian prisons: A model for the world*. Norwegian Ministry of Justice.

Norwegian Directorate of Health. (2021). *Health care in Norwegian prisons*. https://www.helsedirektoratet.no

Nour, M. A. (2024). From politics to social justice: A political analysis of social policy. Politik Psikoloji Dergisi, 4(1).

Nyakabwa, A. (2023). Enforcement challenges in African conservation tourism. *Journal of Ecotourism*, *22*(1), 78–95.

Nylund, A., Brattespe, J., Plarre, H., Kambestad, M., & Karlsen, M. (2019). Wild and farmed salmon (salmo salar) as reservoirs for infectious salmon anaemia virus, and the importance of horizontal- and vertical transmission. *PLoS One*, *14*(4), e0215478. DOI: 10.1371/journal.pone.0215478 PMID: 30990853

O'Brien, W., & Aliabadi, F. (2020). Does telecommuting save energy? a critical review of quantitative studies and their research methods. *Energy and Building*, *225*, 110298. DOI: 10.1016/j.enbuild.2020.110298 PMID: 32834440

O'Hara, K., & Hall, W. (2023). Digital inclusion in smart cities: Lessons from Smart Dublin. *Information Polity*, *28*(1), 1–20.

O'Keefe, P., Caulfield, B., Brazil, W., & White, P. (2016). The impacts of telecommuting in Dublin. *Research in Transportation Economics*, *57*, 13–20. DOI: 10.1016/j.retrec.2016.06.010

Obiero, K., Meulenbroek, P., Drexler, S., Dagne, A., Akoll, P., Odong, R., Kaunda-Arara, B., & Waidbacher, H. (2019). The contribution of fish to food and nutrition security in Eastern Africa: Emerging trends and future outlooks. *Sustainability (Basel)*, *11*(6), 1636. DOI: 10.3390/su11061636

Ochoa, A. G., Khare, P., & Setia, S. (2024). Expanding Environmental Education in Honduras: A Holistic Approach for Sustainable Development. *IGI Global Scientific Publishing,* 153-170. https://doi.org/DOI: 10.4018/979-8-3693-2577-3.ch010

Odobaša, R., & Marošević, K. (2023). Expected contributions of the European corporate sustainability reporting directive (CSRD) to the sustainable development of the European union. *EU and comparative law issues and challenges series (ECLIC)*, *7*, 593-612.

OECD. (2020). *Higher education governance reforms: Patterns and trends*. OECD Publishing., DOI: 10.1787/9789264305032-

Ojo, A., Curry, E., & Janowski, T. (2022). Smart city digital inclusion: A systematic review. *Government Information Quarterly*, *39*(3), 101685.

Okedele, P. O., Aziza, O. R., Oduro, P., & Ishola, A. O. (2024). Human rights, climate justice, and environmental law: Bridging international legal standards for social equity. *Human Rights (Chicago, Ill.)*, *20*(12), 232–241.

Okoli, A. S., Blix, T., Myhr, A. I., Xu, W., & Xu, X. (2022). Sustainable use of CRISPR/Cas in fish aquaculture: The biosafety perspective. *Transgenic Research*, *31*(1), 1–21. DOI: 10.1007/s11248-021-00274-7 PMID: 34304349

Okoth, F. A. (2022). The Subaltern Can Speak: The Mobility Strategies of Forced Migrants in Kenya's Kalobeyei Integrated Settlement. Policy Press eBooks, 209. DOI: 10.1332/policypress/9781529218190.003.0013

Okwuosa, I. I. (2022). Examining disclosure of contribution towards SDG-6 and its motivation among nigeria's premium board companies. In *Environmental Sustainability and Agenda 2030: Efforts, Progress and Prospects* (pp. 135-157). Emerald Publishing Limited. DOI: 10.1108/S1479-359820220000010007

Olabi, A. G., Shehata, N., Issa, U. H., Mohamed, O. A., Mahmoud, M., Abdelkareem, M. A., & Abdelzaher, M. A. (2025). The role of green buildings in achieving the sustainable development goals. *International Journal of Thermofluids*, *25*, 101002. DOI: 10.1016/j.ijft.2024.101002

Ólafsdóttir, R., & Runnström, M. C. (2020). Managing tourism impacts on fragile ecosystems in Iceland. *Environmental Management*, *65*(3), 432–446. DOI: 10.1007/s00267-020-01282-3

Olsen, A. (2021). *Restorative justice in the modern prison system*. Routledge.

Olsen, E. (2021). *Rehabilitation and reintegration in Scandinavian prisons*. Cambridge University Press.

Olsen, E., Fluharty, D., Hoel, A. H., Hostens, K., Maes, F., & Pecceu, E. (2014). Integration at the Round Table: Marine Spatial Planning in Multi-Stakeholder Settings. *PLoS One*, *9*(10), e109964. DOI: 10.1371/journal.pone.0109964 PMID: 25299595

Osmond, A., & Colombo, S. (2019). The future of genetic engineering to provide essential dietary nutrients and improve growth performance in aquaculture: Advantages and challenges. *Journal of the World Aquaculture Society*, *50*(3), 490–509. DOI: 10.1111/jwas.12595

Ottinger, M., Clauss, K., & Kuenzer, C. (2018). Opportunities and challenges for the estimation of aquaculture production based on Earth observation data. *Remote Sensing (Basel)*, *10*(7), 1076. DOI: 10.3390/rs10071076

Ozdamirova, L., Dzhamaldinova, M., & Samatova, C. (2024). The Role of Legal Mechanisms in the Implementation of the Sustainable Development Goals (SDGs). *RT&A*, *19*(6), 1359-1367. https://gnedenko.net/Journal/2024/SI_062024/RTA_SI062024-175_56_Laura%20Ozdamirova%20Marina%20Chulpan%20The%20Role%20of%20Legal%20Mechanisms%20in%20the%20Implementation%20of%20the%20Sustainable%20Development%20Goals%20(SDGs).pdf

Padhan, L., & Bhat, S. (2023). Interrelationship between trade and environment: A bibliometric analysis of published articles from the last two decades. *Environmental Science and Pollution Research International*, *30*(7), 17051–17075. DOI: 10.1007/s11356-023-25168-5 PMID: 36626051

Palazzo, N. (2022). Comprehensive security and LGBTQ rights. *The Review of Faith & International Affairs*, *20*(4), 54–61. DOI: 10.1080/15570274.2022.2139529

Pan, J., Cross, J. L., Zou, X., & Zhang, B. (2024). To tax or to trade? A global review of carbon emissions reduction strategies. *Energy Strategy Reviews*, *55*, 101508. DOI: 10.1016/j.esr.2024.101508

Pan, X., & Liu, S. (2024). The development, changes and responses of the European Union carbon border adjustment mechanism in the context of global energy transition. *World Development Sustainability*, *4*, 100148. DOI: 10.1016/j.wds.2024.100148

Paoli, L. A. D. (2021). From Aspirational Politics to Soft Law? Exploring the International Legal Effects of Sustainable Development Goal 7 on Affordable and Clean Energy. *Melbourne Journal of International Law*, *22*(1). https://papers.ssrn.com/sol3/papers.cfm?abstract_id=3930550

Park, K. R., & Park, Y. S. (2023). *Addressing institutional challenges in sustainable development goals implementation: Lessons from the Republic of Korea*. Wiley Online Library., DOI: 10.1002/sd.2725

Parliament, U. K. (2018). Carillion collapse inquiry report published. https://www.parliament.uk/business/committees/committees-a-z/commons-select/business-energy-industrial-strategy/news-parliament-2017/carillion-report-published-17-19/

Pasquetti, S., Casati, N., & Sanyal, R. (2019). Law and Refugee Crises. *Annual Review of Law and Social Science*, *15*(1), 289–310. DOI: 10.1146/annurev-lawsocsci-101518-042609

Patel, R., & Singh, A. (2023). Accountability in smart city PPPs: Legal obligations and community engagement. *International Journal of Public Sector Management, 36*(1), 65–81.

Patrick, P. (2019). Core functions of human resource management and its effectiveness on organization: A study. *International Journal of Research in Economics and Social Sciences, 9*(5), 257–266.

Patterson, M.. (2018). Urban carbon emissions and legal frameworks for reduction. *Environmental Science & Policy, 82*, 1–8.

Pauleit, S.. (2021). Nature-based solutions for sustainable cities. *Environmental Science & Policy, 116*, 1–13.

Pauleit, S.. (2021). Urban green infrastructure and climate adaptation: Planning and implementation. *Nature-Based Solutions, 1*(1), 100001.

Păunescu, C., Nikina-Ruohonen, A., & Stukalina, Y. (2022). Fostering Research with Societal Impact in Higher Education Institutions: A Review and Conceptualization. In Păunescu, C., Lepik, K. L., & Spencer, N. (Eds.), *Social Innovation in Higher Education. Innovation, Technology, and Knowledge Management*. Springer, Cham. DOI: 10.1007/978-3-030-84044-0_8

Pauw, P., Mbeva, K., & van Asselt, H. (2019). Subtle differentiation of countries' responsibilities under the Paris Agreement. *Palgrave Communications, 5*(1), 86. DOI: 10.1057/s41599-019-0298-6

Pechlaner, H., Volgger, M., & Innerhofer, E. (2020). *Sustainable tourism and regional development: The European experience*. Edward Elgar Publishing.

Peeters, P.. (2023). Climate due diligence in tourism law. *Journal of Sustainable Tourism, 31*(8), 1789–1807.

Peeters, P., Higham, J., Kutzner, D., Cohen, S., & Gössling, S. (2018). The Paris Agreement and tourism: How can tourism contribute to the 1.5°C target? *Journal of Sustainable Tourism, 26*(7), 1093–1107. DOI: 10.1080/09669582.2018.1428391

Peretko, A. (2024). Protection of LGBTQIA+ rights in armed conflict: How (and whether) to 'queer' the crime against humanity of persecution in international criminal law? *Leiden Journal of International Law, 37*(1), 251–273. DOI: 10.1017/S0922156523000523

Permatasari, P., & Kosasih, E. (2021). Sustainability reporting guideline for small medium enterprises (SMEs): Case study from 25 SMEs in Indonesia. In *RSF Conference Series: Business, Management and Social Sciences* (Vol. 1, No. 2, pp. 10-20). DOI: 10.31098/bmss.v1i2.256

Perry-Hazan, L., & Tal-Weibel, E. (2020). On legal literacy and mobilization of students' rights from a disempowered professional status: The case of Israeli teachers. *Teaching and Teacher Education*, *90*, 103016. DOI: 10.1016/j.tate.2020.103016

Personal Data Protection Act 2010

Pettersson, R. (2023). Sami law in Scandinavian tourism. *Arctic Review*, *14*, 1–18.

Pettersson, R. (2023). Sami Reindeer Herding Law vs. Tourism Permits. *Arctic Review*, *14*, 1–18.

Pettersson, R., & Viken, A. (2023). Sami Tourism and Legal Pluralism in Scandinavia. *Arctic Review*, *14*, 1–18.

Picard, M. (2023). Balinese Hinduism and sustainable tourism. *Asian Journal of Tourism Research*, *8*(1), 112–128.

PIKOM. (2024). *Growing threat cybersecurity landscape in Malaysia 2024*. www.pikom.org.my

Postero, N. (2023). Indigenous constitutionalism and tourism in Bolivia. *Latin American Politics and Society*, *65*(1), 89–107.

Poto, M. P., & Murray, E. M. (2022). The New Horizons of Law and Science through the Lens of 2030 Sustainable Development Agenda: Some Emerging Issues. *Environmental Policy and Law*, *53*(1), 35–48. DOI: 10.3233/EPL-220039

Pradeepkiran, J. A. (2019). Aquaculture role in global food security with nutritional value: A review. *Translational Animal Science*, *3*(2), 903–910. DOI: 10.1093/tas/txz012 PMID: 32704855

Pradhan, R., Jaiswal, R., & Bhushan, V. (2024). Transgender Inclusion And Sustainable Development: Bridging Gaps For A Resilient Future. *Library of Progress-Library Science, Information Technology & Computer, 44*(2).

Prasanna, S., Ameen, A., Saurav, K., Singh, D. B., Tripathy, A., Sharma, P., & Sanjaya, K. (2023). *Empowerment and equality navigating human rights law in a complex world*. Institute of Legal Education.

Pribytkova, E. (2020). Global Obligations for Sustainable Development: Harmonizing The 2030 Agenda for Sustainable Development and International Human Rights Law. *University of Pennsylvania Journal of International Law, 41*(4), 1031–1136. https://scholarship.law.upenn.edu/cgi/viewcontent.cgi?article=2012&context=jil

Pucher, J., & Buehler, R. (2021). Sustainable urban transport in Amsterdam: Policies and outcomes. *Transport Reviews, 41*(2), 179–200.

Purkey, A. L. (2022). Vulnerability and the Quest for Protection: A Review of Canadian Migration Case Law. *Laws, 11*(2), 20. DOI: 10.3390/laws11020020

Puthucherril, T. G., Sharma, C., Shenoy, A. V., Sood, S., & Lal, S. (2024). Integrating the Sustainable Development Goals into India's Legal Education Landscape: The What, Why and How of a Reform Paradigm. *Asian Journal of Legal Education, 12*(1), 40–60. DOI: 10.1177/23220058241265614

Rabinovych, M. (2020). The Legal Status and Effects of the Agenda 2030 within the EU Legal Order. *Journal of Contemporary European Research, 16*(2), 182–199. DOI: 10.30950/jcer.v16i2.1071

Rahman, S. H., Khatri, S., & Brunner, H. P. (2012). Regional Integration and Economic Development in South Asia. *ADB*. https://www.adb.org/sites/default/files/publication/29871/regional-integration-economic-development-south-asia.pdf

Rahman, M., Hoque, M., Bhowmik, S., Ferdousi, S., Kabiraz, M., & Brakel, M. (2021). Monitoring of pesticide residues from fish feed, fish and vegetables in Bangladesh by gc-ms using the quechers method. *Heliyon, 7*(3), e06390. DOI: 10.1016/j.heliyon.2021.e06390 PMID: 33869825

Rakkannan, G., & Agarwal, D. (2025). Role of Aquaculture Biotechnology in Food Security and Nutrition. In *Food Security, Nutrition and Sustainability Through Aquaculture Technologies* (pp. 173–191). Springer Nature Switzerland. DOI: 10.1007/978-3-031-75830-0_9

Raman, R., Nair, V. K., Shivdas, A., Bhukya, R., Visvanathan, P. K., Subramaniam, N., & Nedungadi, P. (2023). *Mapping Sustainability Reporting Research with the UN's Sustainable Development Goal*. Science Direct., DOI: 10.1016/j.heliyon.2023.e18510

Rangone, N., & Megale, L. (2025). Risks Without Rights? The EU AI Act's Approach to AI in Law and Rule-Making. *European Journal of Risk Regulation*, •••, 1–16. DOI: 10.1017/err.2025.13

Rankin, M. B. (2005). Extending the Limits or Narrowing the Scope? Deconstructing the Oau Refugee Definition Thirty Years on. *South African Journal on Human Rights*, *21*(3), 406–435. DOI: 10.1080/19962126.2005.11865141

Raymond, C. M.. (2017). A framework for assessing and implementing urban nature-based solutions. *Environmental Science & Policy*, *77*, 15–24. DOI: 10.1016/j.envsci.2017.07.008

Raza, A. (2021). Legal literacy: A key to socio-economic justice. In *Young India Fellowship* (pp. 182–191). Ashoka University.

Razak, F., Lua, W. Y., Abd Rasid, N. H., Aziz, N., Repin, I. M., Xue, X. Z., & Safuan, C. D. M. (2024). Adopting Marine Spatial Planning (MSP) using coral health assessment as indicator: A case study in Pulau Redang Marine Park, Malaysia. *Ocean and Coastal Management*, *248*, 106943. DOI: 10.1016/j.ocecoaman.2023.106943

Razak, S. A., Hwang, G. L., Rahman, M. A., & Maclean, N. (1999). Growth performance and gonadal development of growth enhanced transgenic tilapia Oreochromis niloticus (L.) following heat-shock-induced triploidy. *Marine Biotechnology (New York, N.Y.)*, *1*(6), 533–544. DOI: 10.1007/PL00011808 PMID: 10612678

Reddick, C. G., & Chen, T. (2018). Smart city adoption: Looking through the lens of digital inclusion. *Government Information Quarterly*, *35*(4), 491–502.

Regnier, T., & Poropat, P. (2024a, August). *Artificial Intelligence – Q&As*. European Commission. https://ec.europa.eu/commission/presscorner/detail/en/qanda_21_1683

Regnier, T., & Poropat, P. (2024b, August 1). *European Artificial Intelligence Act comes into force*. European Commission. https://ec.europa.eu/commission/presscorner/detail/en/ip_24_4123

Regulation (EU) 2021/1119 of 30 June 2021 establishing the framework for achieving climate neutrality, OJ EU L 243, 9.7.2021, 1.

Reina, A., & Grewal, S. (2021). Digital Inclusion Policies and Social Inclusion in Barcelona's Smart City. *Journal of Urban Affairs*, *43*(3), 393–410.

Reina, A., & Grewal, S. (2021). Social inclusion in smart cities: Barcelona's approach. *Journal of Urban Affairs*, *43*(4), 556–572.

Reina, J., & Grewal, P. (2021). Smart city governance and community inclusion in Barcelona. *Urban Studies (Edinburgh, Scotland)*, *58*(7), 1449–1466.

Reina, L., & Grewal, S. (2021). Digital inclusion policies in European smart cities. *Government Information Quarterly*, *38*(4), 101583.

Reina, V., & Grewal, S. (2021). Digital inclusion and urban green space: Barcelona's legal approach. *Journal of Urban Technology*, *28*(3), 1–19.

Reiners, N. (2024). The power of interpersonal relationships: A socio-legal approach to international institutions and human rights advocacy. *Review of International Studies*, *50*(2), 252–270. DOI: 10.1017/S0260210523000438

Reis, Y., & Guedes, A. (2017). International environmental NGOs and the politics of genetically modified organisms. *Critical Perspectives on International Business*, *13*(1), 23–37. DOI: 10.1108/cpoib-03-2014-0020

Reverte, C. (2021). La importancia de las diferencias institucionales entre países en el nivel de consecución de los ODS: Un estudio empírico a escala mundial. *Revista de Fomento Social*, •••, 115–159. DOI: 10.32418/rfs.2021.299.4583

Reza, D. R. (2024, September 30). Malaysia should consider 'AI Bill of Rights', says US-based newsman | FMT. *Free Malaysia Today | FMT*. https://www.freemalaysiatoday.com/category/nation/2024/09/30/malaysia-should-consider-ai-bill-of-rights-says-us-based-newsman/

Right, H. I. (2023). Promotion and protection of all human rights, civil, political, economic, social and cultural rights, including the right to development: Written statement/submitted by Human Is Right.

Rigolon, A. (2019). Green space and health equity: A systematic review. *Environmental Research*, *174*, 86–95.

Ripple, W. J., Wolf, C., Gregg, J. W., Rockström, J., Mann, M. E., Oreskes, N., Lenton, T. M., Rahmstorf, S., Newsome, T. M., Xu, C., Svenning, J.-C., Pereira, C. C., Law, B. E., & Crowther, T. W. (2024). The 2024 state of the climate report: Perilous times on planet Earth. *Bioscience*, *74*(12), 812–824. DOI: 10.1093/biosci/biae087

Rivera-Murillo, G., Porras, I., & Barton, D. N. (2020). Lessons from Costa Rica's sustainable tourism policy. *Tourism Management*, *36*(4), 378–392. DOI: 10.1016/j.tmp.2020.100738

Roberts, A., Resh, W., Basu, R., Onyango, G., Sullivan, H., Peci, A., Kapucu, N., Schomaker, R., & Mele, V. (2024). Roundtable: How do we connect public administration and human rights? *Perspectives on Public Management and Governance*, *7*(1–2), 1–12. DOI: 10.1093/ppmgov/gvad010

Rocchi, P., Serrano, M., Roca, J., & Arto, I. (2018). Border carbon adjustments based on avoided emissions: Addressing the challenge of its design. *Ecological Economics*, *145*, 126–136. DOI: 10.1016/j.ecolecon.2017.08.003

Rochlin, J. (2023). Power, Mobility, and Space: Human Security for Venezuelan Refugees in Colombia. *Journal on Migration and Human Security*, *11*(4), 333–355. DOI: 10.1177/23315024231202492

Rodrigo, S. G. (2022, April). La política de adaptación al cambio climático en la Ley 7/2021: instrumentos generales. In *Estudios sobre cambio climático y transición energética: Estudios conmemorativos del XXV aniversario del acceso a la cátedra del profesor Íñigo del Guayo Castiella* (pp. 433–460). Ediciones Jurídicas y Sociales. DOI: 10.2307/j.ctv2zp4wzn.23

Rodríguez, D.. (2023). Legal frameworks for inclusive urban climate resilience: Lessons from Medellín. *Sustainability Science*, *18*(1), 123–138.

Rogers, C. D. F., Shi, H., & Ng, A. K. Y. (2020). Towards sustainable and smart urban development. *Sustainable Cities and Society*, *55*, 102040.

Rogers, C., Brown, D., & Carter, J. (2021). Legal frameworks for smart city inclusivity and equity. *Sustainability*, *13*(15), 8399.

Rogers, E. M., Marakas, G. M., & Henley, J. (2021). Technology adoption and social equity in smart cities. *Technological Forecasting and Social Change*, *170*, 120921.

Rogers, E. M., Singhal, A., & Quinlan, M. M. (2021). Diffusion of Innovations: A Communication Science Perspective. *The Annals of the American Academy of Political and Social Science*, *608*(1), 102–122.

Romig, J. M., & Burge, M. E. (2020). Legal literacy and communication skills: Working with law and lawyers. Carolina Academic Press. (Texas A&M University School of Law Legal Studies Research Paper No. 19-66). https://papers.ssrn.com/sol3/papers.cfm?abstract_id=3491498

Rosado, A., & Eriksson, D. (2021). Biosafety legislation and the regulatory status of the products of precision breeding in the Latin America and the Caribbean region. *Plants, People, Planet*, *4*(3), 214–231. DOI: 10.1002/ppp3.10243

Rosa, R., & Clavero, S. (2021). Gender equality in higher education and research. *Journal of Gender Studies*, *31*(1), 1–7. DOI: 10.1080/09589236.2022.2007446

Roy, A. (2025). Does carbon tax promote green trade and comparative advantages: Evidence from Panel Difference-In-Difference (DID) causal experiment. *Environmental Economics and Policy Studies*, *27*(2), 331–352. Advance online publication. DOI: 10.1007/s10018-024-00434-z

Różańska, E., Matuszak, Ł., & Dyczkowska, J. (2024). Comparative analysis of the GRI Standards and the IR Framework and their impact on the quality of disclosures. In *Research Handbook on Sustainability Reporting* (pp. 90–108). Edward Elgar Publishing. DOI: 10.4337/9781035316267.00014

Rudy, E., & Supriyadi, A. A. (2025). Security Policy Transformation to Accelerate Achievement of Sustainable Development Goals (SDGs) in Papua.

Ruhs, M. (2022). Who cares what the people think? Public attitudes and refugee protection in Europe. *Politics, Philosophy & Economics, 21*(3), 313–344. DOI: 10.1177/1470594X221085701

Ruppel, O. C., & Murray, R. (2024). The Future of the SDGs: A Comparative Constitutional Rescue Plan? One does not discover new lands without consenting to lose sight of the shore. André Gide. *Environmental Policy and Law, 54*(3), 155–187. DOI: 10.3233/EPL-239022

Saaida, M. (2024). Criticism of the liberal theory of international politics.

Sabol, W. J. (2017). *Prisoner reentry in the United States: A historical overview.* U.S. Department of Justice, National Institute of Justice.

Sadhu Singh, J. K., & Segaran, D. (2021). An AI ethical framework for Malaysia: A much-needed governance tool for reducing risks and liabilities arising from AI systems. *Malayan Law Journal, 3*, cdxiv-cdxxxvii.

Sadhu Singh, J. K., & Segaran, D. (2020). AI, law and ethics: The emergence of a new discourse in the legal thoroughfare. *Malayan Law Journal, 5*, 1–9.

Sætra, H. S. (2021). Ai in context and the sustainable development goals: Factoring in the unsustainability of the sociotechnical system. *Sustainability (Basel), 13*(4), 1–19. DOI: 10.3390/su13041738

Sætra, H. S. (2021). Ethical challenges in smart city governance. *Science and Engineering Ethics, 27*(2), 20. PMID: 33765203

Safuan, C. D. M., Ashraf, A. R. M., Tan, C. H., Jaafar, S. N., Yusop, P. A. M., Lai, R. K., & Bachok, Z. (2021). Coral Health Status Assessment in Malaysia Islands; Looking Towards Marine Spatial Planning. *Ocean and Coastal Management, 213*, 105856. DOI: 10.1016/j.ocecoaman.2021.105856

Safuan, C. D. M., Aziz, N., Repin, I. M., Xue, X. Z., Rahman, A., & Talaat, I. A. W. (2022). Assessment of Governance and Ecological Status of Terengganu Marine Park, Malaysia: Toward Marine Spatial Planning. *Sains Malaysiana, 51*(12), 3909–3922. DOI: 10.17576/jsm-2022-5112-04

Sager, T. (2018). Participatory governance in urban development: Frameworks and case studies. *Planning Theory & Practice, 19*(2), 191–211.

Sager, T. (2018). Urban resilience and community participation in planning processes. *Planning Theory & Practice, 19*(1), 43–63.

Said, F., & Nabilah, F. (2024). *Future of Malaysia's AI governance.*

Saini, M., Sengupta, E., Singh, M., Singh, H., & Singh, J. (2023). Sustainable development goal for quality education (SDG 4): A study on SDG 4 to extract the pattern of association among the indicators of SDG 4 employing a genetic algorithm. *Education and Information Technologies, 28*(2), 2031–2069. DOI: 10.1007/s10639-022-11265-4 PMID: 35975216

Sajid, M. J., Zhang, Y., & Janjua, L. R. (2024). Breaking barriers: Assessing technology transfer for climate-resilient development. *Environmental Technology & Innovation, 33*, 103471. DOI: 10.1016/j.eti.2023.103471

Salgado, M. H. A. (2024). La Transición Energética En El Contexto Constitucional Español. *Revista Direito Público, 21*(111), 176–195.

Sambo, W. (2023). Interface of Customary and State Law in Tourism. *Journal of Legal Pluralism and Unofficial Law, 55*(3), 301–320.

Samsudin, N., Abu Bakar, E. M., Jusoh, Z., & Arif, M. A. M. (2020). Personal and environmental determinants of consumer legal literacy among Malaysian consumers. *Malaysian Journal of Consumer and Family Economics, 25*(S1), 27–40.

Samuri, M. A. A., & Khan, A. S. N. (2021). Legal literacy for Muslim converts in Malaysia. *Pertanika Journal of Social Science & Humanities, 29*(3). Advance online publication. DOI: 10.47836/pjssh.29.3.12

Sanghvi, H., See, J., Ling, W., Tay, S., & Kuek, Y. (2022). Digitalisation of judiciary in Malaysia: Application of Artificial Intelligence in the sentencing process. *Proceedings of the International Conference on Law and Digitalization (ICLD 2022)*, 91–97. DOI: 10.2991/978-2-494069-59-6_9

Sanmugam, S., Sivakumar, S., Gobalakrishnan, T., Sarawanan, T., Abeweera, P., & Sandrasaigaran, P. (2021). Perception and acceptance of genetically modified foods in malaysia. *Malaysian Journal of Science and Advanced Technology*, 144-150.

Santani, S. J. (2024, January 9). *Malaysia coming up with AI governance and code of ethics*. New Straits Times. https://www.nst.com.my/business/corporate/2024/01/998905/malaysia-coming-ai-governance-and-code-ethics

Santiago, P., Tremblay, K., Basri, E., & Arnal, E. (2016). *Higher education governance and management*. OECD Education Working Papers, No. 59. OECD Publishing. https://doi.org/DOI: 10.1787/5jm3pgl7jbnr-en

Santos, C. F., Agardy, T., Andrade, F., Barange, M., Crowder, L. B., Ehler, C. N., Orbach, M. K., & Rosa, R. (2016). Ocean planning in a changing climate. *Nature Geoscience*, *9*(10), 730–730. DOI: 10.1038/ngeo2821

Santos, C. F., Ehler, C. N., Agardy, T., Andrade, F., & Orbach, M. K. (2019). Marine Spatial Planning. In Sheppard, C. (Ed.), *World Seas: An Environmental Evaluation* (2nd ed., Vol. III). Elsevier Ltd. DOI: 10.1016/B978-0-12-805052-1.00033-4

Sapre, A. A. (2023). Non-refoulment of Refugees in India- a Human Rights Perspective. *International Journal of Law and Social Sciences*, *1*, 1–16. Advance online publication. DOI: 10.60143/ijls.v5.i1.2019.28

Sarker, S. P. (2017). Protection of Refugees in India: Quest for National Refugee Law. SSRN Electronic Journal. DOI: 10.2139/ssrn.2961103

Sarkin, J. J. (2021). *The conflict in Syria and the failure of international law to protect people globally: Mass atrocities, enforced disappearances and arbitrary detentions*. Routledge. DOI: 10.4324/9781003198628

Sasmal, S., Zhang, D., Lydgate, E., & Winters, L. A. (2024). Exempting least developed countries from border carbon adjustments: Simple economically but complex legally. *World Trade Review*, *23*(3), 408–431. DOI: 10.1017/S1474745624000132

Sauter, P., Witt, J., Billig, E., & Thrän, D. (2013). Impact of the Renewable Energy Sources Act in Germany on electricity produced with solid biofuels – Lessons learned by monitoring the market development. *Biomass and Bioenergy*, *53*, 162–171. DOI: 10.1016/j.biombioe.2013.01.014

Savage, M. (2021). *The return of inequality: Social change and the weight of the past*. Harvard University Press.

Schaefer, N., & Barale, V. (2011). Maritime Spatial Planning: Opportunities & Challenges in the Framework of the EU Integrated Maritime Policy. *Journal of Coastal Conservation*, *15*(2), 237–245. DOI: 10.1007/s11852-011-0154-3

Scheyvens, R., & Biddulph, R. (2018). Inclusive tourism development. *Tourism Geographies*, *20*(4), 589–606. DOI: 10.1080/14616688.2017.1381985

Schmalz, D. (2025). Population Growth Discourse in the First Decades of the United Nations: Interpretations of Global Economic Inequality and the Struggles for a Just International Legal Order. *Max Planck Institute for Comparative Public Law & International Law (MPIL) Research Paper*, (2025-01).

Schmidt, D., Espinoza, T., Real, K., Dunlop, A., Kennard, M., & Hughes, J. (2018). Improved genetic markers for monitoring recruitment dynamics in the endangered mary river cod (maccullochella mariensis). *Journal of Applied Ichthyology, 34*(3), 633–637. DOI: 10.1111/jai.13633

Scholl, H. J., & Scholl, M. C. (2018). Smart governance: Co-creation of public value in smart cities. *Government Information Quarterly, 35*(3), 336–342.

Scholl, H. J., & Scholl, M. C. (2019). Smart city governance and the law. *Information Polity, 24*(1), 1–16. DOI: 10.3233/IP-150377

Scholl, H. J., & Scholl, M. C. (2019). Smart Governance: Concepts, Challenges, and Practices. *Communications of the Association for Information Systems, 44*, 42.

Scholz, J., Krumme, K., & Hilty, L. M. (2022). The Role of Geographic Information Systems in Sustainable Tourism. *Tourism Geographics, 24*(4), 547 563. DOI: 10.1080/14616688.2021.1983347

Schwartzman, S.. (2023). Indigenous Justice Systems and Ecotourism in the Amazon. *Conservation & Society, 21*(1), 12–25.

Scott, D., Hall, C. M., & Gössling, S. (2019). *Climate change and tourism: Impacts, adaptation, and mitigation.* Routledge.

SDSN (Sustainable Development Solutions Network). (2017). *Getting started with the SDGs in universities: A guide for universities, higher education institutions, and the academic sector.* SDSN Australia/Pacific. https://ap-unsdsn.org/regional-initiatives/universities-sdgs/

SDSN Australia/Pacific. (2017). Getting started with the SDGs in universities: A guide for universities, higher education institutions, and the academic sector. https://ap-unsdsn.org/regional-initiatives/universities-sdgs/

Selder, K. (2014). Renewable Energy Sources Act and trading of emission certificates: A national and a supranational tool to direct energy turnover to renewable electricity supply in Germany. *Energy Policy, 64*, 302–312. DOI: 10.1016/j.enpol.2013.08.030

Setyaningsih, S., Widjojo, R., & Kelle, P. (2024). Challenges and opportunities in sustainability reporting: A focus on small and medium enterprises (SMEs). *Cogent Business & Management, 11*(1), 2298215. DOI: 10.1080/23311975.2023.2298215

Sforna, G. (2019). Climate change and developing countries: From background actors to protagonists of climate negotiations. *International Environmental Agreement: Politics, Law and Economics, 19*(3), 273–295. DOI: 10.1007/s10784-019-09435-w

Shafi, M., Ramos-Meza, C. S., Jain, V., Salman, A., Kamal, M., Shabbir, M. S., & Rehman, M. (2023). The dynamic relationship between green tax incentives and environmental protection. *Environmental Science and Pollution Research International, 30*(12), 32184–32192. DOI: 10.1007/s11356-023-25482-y PMID: 36723845

Shamshad, R. (2016). Bengaliness, Hindu nationalism and Bangladeshi migrants in West Bengal, India. *Asian Ethnicity, 18*(4), 433–451. DOI: 10.1080/14631369.2016.1175918

Shamshiripour, A., Rahimi, E., Shabanpour, R., & Mohammadian, A. (2020). How is COVID-19 reshaping activity-travel behavior? evidence from a comprehensive survey in Chicago. *Transportation Research Interdisciplinary Perspectives, 7*, 100216. DOI: 10.1016/j.trip.2020.100216 PMID: 34173469

Shanker, R., & Vijayaraghavan, H. (2023). Refugee recognition challenges in India. https://www.fmreview.org/recognising-refugees/shanker-vijayaraghavan

Shanker, R., & Raghavan, P. (2020). The Invisible Crisis: Refugees and COVID-19 in India. *International Journal of Refugee Law, 32*(4), 680–684. DOI: 10.1093/ijrl/eeab011

Sharifi, A., & Yamagata, Y. (2018). Principles and criteria for assessing urban energy resilience: A comprehensive review. *Renewable & Sustainable Energy Reviews, 82*, 476–488.

Sharifi, A., & Yamagata, Y. (2020). Principles and Criteria for Assessing Smart Sustainability: A Comparative Study of Asian Smart Cities. *Sustainable Cities and Society, 45*, 383–398.

Sharma, D. (2018). Jurisdictional concerns in the settlement of environmental disputes under the WTO regime. *International Journal of Law Management & Humanities, 1*(5), 1-XX. ISSN: 2581-5369. Retrieved from https://www.ijlmh.com

Sharma, J., Srivastava, A., & Kapoor, Y. (2023). Strategic Human Resource Management. In B. K. Sarkar, R. Singh, V. Singh, S. Mishra, P. Kumar, & P. N. & Singh (eds), *Multidisciplinary International Conference on Innovations in Education Science & Technology ICIEST-2023*. USA: GEH Press.

Sharma, K., & Mishra, S. (2022). Legal stability in smart city PPPs: Challenges and opportunities. *Journal of Urban Planning and Development, 148*(4), 04022046.

Sharon, A. (2025, May 5). Malaysia: Strategic and measured approach to AI governance. *OpenGov Asia*. https://opengovasia.com/2025/05/05/malaysia-strategic-and-measured-approach-to-ai-governance/

Sharpley, R., & Telfer, D. J. (2018). *Tourism and development: Concepts and issues*. Channel View Publications.

Shayan, N. F., Mohabbati-Kalejahi, N., Alavi, S., & Zahed, M. A. (2022). Sustainable Development Goals (SDGs) as a Framework for Corporate Social Responsibility (CSR). *Sustainability (Basel)*, *14*(3), 1222. DOI: 10.3390/su14031222

Sheldon, P. J. (2020). Resilience and regenerative tourism: Facing climate change and other global challenges. *Tourism Review*, *75*(2), 243–251. DOI: 10.1108/TR-02-2020-0036

Sheng, X., Chen, L., Liu, M., Wang, Q., Ma, Q., Zuo, J., & Yuan, X. (2025). Input-output models for carbon accounting: A multi-perspective analysis. *Renewable & Sustainable Energy Reviews*, *207*, 114950. DOI: 10.1016/j.rser.2024.114950

Shi, H., & Zhou, Q. (2024). Government R&D subsidies, environmental regulation and corporate green innovation performance. *Finance Research Letters*, *69*(Part B), 106088. https://doi.org/DOI: 10.1016/j.frl.2024.106088

Shulla, K., Voigt, B. F., Cibian, S., Scandone, G., Martinez, E., Nelkovski, F., & Salehi, P. (2021). Effects of COVID-19 on the sustainable development goals (SDGs). *Discover Sustainability*, *2*(1), 1–19. DOI: 10.1007/s43621-021-00026-x PMID: 35425922

Siew, R. Y. (2015). A review of corporate sustainability reporting tools (SRTs). *Journal of Environmental Management*, *164*, 180–195. DOI: 10.1016/j.jenvman.2015.09.010 PMID: 26379255

Silva, B. N., Khan, M., & Han, K. (2020). Towards sustainable smart cities: A review of trends, architectures, components, and open challenges in smart cities. *Sustainable Cities and Society*, *38*, 697–713. DOI: 10.1016/j.scs.2018.01.053

Simms, D., Hurd, S., & Gold, A. (2020). Mental health care for incarcerated individuals. *Journal of Correctional Psychology*, *45*(3), 195–202.

Simou, S. (2022). La Ley 7/2021, de 20 de mayo, de cambio climático y transición energética en el contexto de intensificación de los esfuerzos público-privados para afrontar la emergencia climática. Anuario de la Facultad de Derecho de la Universidad Autónoma de Madrid, 215-250.

Singapore Tourism Board (STB). (2023). Smart Tourism 2025 Blueprint. https://www.stb.gov.sg

Singh, A. P. (2012). A Critique of the Foreigners Act, 1946: A Legislation de Jure or de Facto? SSRN Electronic Journal. DOI: 10.2139/ssrn.1989060

Singh, J., Jalaluddin, N., Sanan-Mishra, N., & Harikrishna, J. (2020a). Challenges to the adoption of modern crop biotechnology: Insights from Indian and Malaysian GM regulatory frameworks. *Malaysian Applied Biology*, *49*(5), 1–9. DOI: 10.55230/mabjournal.v49i5.1632

Singh, R., Ahmad, N., & Lee, K. T. (2020b). Enforcement and biosafety audits in Malaysia's GMO regulatory framework: Challenges and future directions. *Journal of Environmental Policy and Regulation*, *15*(1), 67–79. https://doi.org/10.xxxx/jer.2020.01501

Siti Hawa, J.. (2019). Genetic improvement of freshwater fish species in Malaysia using molecular techniques. *Malaysian Journal of Biotechnology*, *8*(2), 45–55.

Smith, I. D., Overland, I., & Szulecki, K. (2024). The EU's CBAM and its 'significant others': Three perspectives on the political fallout from Europe's unilateral climate policy initiative. *Journal of Common Market Studies*, *62*(3), 603–618. DOI: 10.1111/jcms.13512

Smith, L., & Hall, C. M. (2022). Policy innovation for regenerative tourism: Lessons from New Zealand. *Tourism Management Perspectives*, *43*, 101057. DOI: 10.1016/j.tmp.2022.101057

Smith, W. C., Ehren, M. C. M., & Grek, S. (2024). Global Governance of Education: The Sustainable Development Goals as a Product and Mechanism? *International Review of Education*, *70*(4), 531–545. DOI: 10.1007/s11159-024-10108-3

Soete, L. (1987). The impact of technological innovation on international trade patterns: The evidence reconsidered. *Research Policy*, *16*(2–4), 101–130. DOI: 10.1016/0048-7333(87)90026-6

Song, Y., Sahut, J.-M., Zhang, Z., Tian, Y., & Hikkerova, L. (2022). The effects of government subsidies on the sustainable innovation of university-industry collaboration. *Technological Forecasting and Social Change*, *174*, 121233. DOI: 10.1016/j.techfore.2021.121233

Soto, C. J., & John, O. P. (2017). The next big five inventory (BFI-2): Developing and assessing a hierarchical model with 15 facets to enhance bandwidth, fidelity, and predictive power. *Journal of Personality and Social Psychology*, *113*(1), 117–143. DOI: 10.1037/pspp0000096 PMID: 27055049

Spear, M., Willcock, S., Ormondroyd, G., Dimitriou, A., Roberts, G., Loxton, C., & Edwards, A. (2022). What impact have covid-19 induced changes in working practice had on greenhouse gas emissions? a rapid review. https://doi.org/DOI: 10.21203/rs.3.rs-1677535/v1

Spenceley, A. (2023). Equity in African conservation tourism. *Tourism Geographies*, *25*(1), 112–130.

Spijkers, O. (2020). The Sustainable Human Right to Water as Reflected in the Sustainable Development Goals. *Utrecht University*. https://utrechtlawreview.org/articles/10.36633/ulr.560

STB (Singapore Tourism Board). (2023). AI for sustainable visitor management. https://www.stb.gov.sg

Steiner, G., & Posch, A. (2021). *Regenerative Tourism: Challenges and Opportunities for Policy and Practice*. Springer.

Stepanyan, A. Z. (2021). European Artificial Intelligence Act: Should Russia implement the same? *Kutafin Law Review*, *8*(3), 403–422. DOI: 10.17803/2313-5395.2021.3.17.403-422

Stolowy, H., & Paugam, L. (2023). Sustainability reporting: Is convergence possible? *Accounting in Europe*, *20*(2), 139–165. DOI: 10.1080/17449480.2023.2189016

Stranadko, N. (2022). Global climate governance: Rising trend of translateral cooperation. *International Environmental Agreement: Politics, Law and Economics*, *22*(4), 639–657. DOI: 10.1007/s10784-022-09575-6 PMID: 35370522

Strutt, J., Bessarab, I., Min, J., Marican, H., & Summers, S. (2024). Rapid nanopore cloud-based monitoring and analysis of commercial aquaculture microbiomes. https://doi.org/DOI: 10.1101/2024.08.07.607111

Stryker, C., & Kavlakoglu, E. (2024, August 16). *What Is Artificial Intelligence (AI)? | IBM*. IBM. https://www.ibm.com/topics/artificial-intelligence

Stryker, C., & Scapicchio, M. (2024, March 22). *What is Generative AI? | IBM*. IBM. https://www.ibm.com/topics/generative-ai

Suárez-Rico, Y. M., Gómez-Villegas, M., & García-Benau, M. A. (2021). La utilidad de los informes de sostenibilidad en entidades públicas y privadas en Colombia: La percepción de los stakeholders. *Contaduría Universidad de Antioquia*, (79), 103–136. DOI: 10.17533/udea.rc.n79a05

Suklun, H., & Bengu, E. (2024). Raising Awareness of SDGs in Higher Education Institutions. *Research in Educational Administration & Leadership*, *9*(1), 39–72. DOI: 10.30828/real.1357661

Sulaiman, T. F., & Abd Ghadas, Z. A. (2021). Corporate governance models for higher educational institutions: An analysis. *Pertanika Journal of Social Science & Humanities*, *29*(S2), 149–168. http://www.pertanika.upm.edu.my/pjssh.php?journal=PJSSH-29-S2-11. DOI: 10.47836/pjssh.29.s2.11

Sullivan, D. (2019). *Access to justice and legal aid*. Legal Services Commission. https://www.legalservices.gov.uk/

Sullivan, M., Rosen, D., & Baker, K. (2019). Improving mental health care in prisons. *Prison Health Journal*, *11*(3), 101–109. DOI: 10.1016/j.prh.2019.06.002

Sundström, L. F., Lõhmus, M., Devlin, R. H., & Björnsson, B. T. (2007). Growth hormone transgenic salmon pay for growth potential with increased predation mortality.

Sundström, L., Vandersteen, W., Lõhmus, M., & Devlin, R. (2014). Growth-enhanced coho salmon invading other salmon species populations: Effects on early survival and growth. *Journal of Applied Ecology*, *51*(1), 82–89. DOI: 10.1111/1365-2664.12185

Sun, X., Mi, Z., Cheng, L., Coffman, D. M., & Liu, Y. (2024). The carbon border adjustment mechanism is inefficient in addressing carbon leakage and results in unfair welfare losses. *Fundamental Research (Beijing)*, *4*(3), 660–670. DOI: 10.1016/j.fmre.2023.02.026 PMID: 39659982

Suresh, B., & Sundaram, A. (2022). Cross-Embedded Relationship Nature of Human Rights-Related Treaties and Instruments with Environment-Related Sustainable Development Goals. *The Age of Human Rights Journal*, *19*(19), 205–253. DOI: 10.17561/tahrj.v19.7225

Suruhanjaya Syarikat Malaysia. (2015). Audit partner jailed one year, fined RM400,000 for misleading disclosure of financial information. https://www.sc.com.my/resources/media/media-release/audit-partner-jailed-one-year-fined-rm400000-for-misleading-disclosure-of-financial-information

Sustainable Development Goal 16 Toolkit. (2021). *Working with National Human Rights Institutions*. https://www.sdg16toolkit.org

Sustainable Development Goals. (2018). *Edward Elgar Publishing eBooks*. Edward Elgar Publishing., DOI: 10.4337/9781786438768

Suzman, J. (2023). San N!ore Systems and Community Tourism. *Journal of Southern African Studies*, *49*(4), 689–705.

Sykes, G. (2019). *The society of captives: A study of a maximum security prison.* Princeton University Press.

Taghvaee, V. M., Arani, A. A., & Agheli, L. (2022). Sustainable development spillover effects between North America and MENA: Analyzing the integrated sustainability perspective. *Environmental and Sustainability Indicators, 14*, 100182. DOI: 10.1016/j.indic.2022.100182

Talen, E. (2017). Zoning and Urban Form. *Urban Studies (Edinburgh, Scotland), 54*(6), 1383–1398.

Tamiotti, L. (2010). Trade and the Environment: Fundamental Issues in International Law, WTO Law and Legal Theory by Erich Vranes. *World Trade Review, 9*(1), 285–288. DOI: 10.1017/S147474560999022X

Tan, C. H., Singh, M., & Heng, C. H. (2021). Singapore's Green Plan 2030: Urban Sustainability Strategy. *Sustainability, 13*(3), 1234.

Tan, E., & Tan, K. (2022). Urban infrastructure governance in Singapore's smart city development. *Asia Pacific Journal of Public Administration, 44*(1), 57–73.

Tang, K. H. D. (2019). Climate change in Malaysia: Trends, contributors, impacts, mitigation and adaptations. *The Science of the Total Environment, 650*, 1858–1871. DOI: 10.1016/j.scitotenv.2018.09.316 PMID: 30290336

Tan, P. Y.. (2020). Singapore's Green Plan 2030: Legal frameworks for sustainable urban water management. *Environmental Science & Policy, 107*, 99–109.

Tan, S. B., Kankanhalli, A., & Tan, C. W. (2020). Singapore's smart nation initiative: A case study. *Information Systems Frontiers, 22*, 1407–1423.

Tanveer, A., Zeng, S., Zaman, R., & Scagnelli, S. (2024). World Trade Organization (WTO) trade policy reviews and green technology adoption: Global evidence. *International Review of Financial Analysis, 96*(B), 103715. https://doi.org/DOI: 10.1016/j.irfa.2024.103715

Tan, Y. H., Goh, W. D., & Lee, L. H. (2020). Smart Nation Singapore: A multidimensional strategy for urban innovation. *Sustainability, 12*(3), 845.

Teruel-Gutiérrez, R. (2020). Sustainability as a corporate strategy: A performance comparison of green and non-green SME hotels. [SBIR]. *Small Business International Review, 4*(2), 30–38. DOI: 10.26784/sbir.v4i2.254

The Case for Remote Work in Health Care - Sponsor Content From Siemens Healthineers. (2020, September 9). Harvard Business Review. https://hbr.org/sponsored/2020/09/the-case-for-remote-work-in-health-care

The Paris Agreement (UNFCCC, 2015).

Thelma, C. C., & Chitondo, L. (2024). Leadership for sustainable development in Africa: A comprehensive perspective. *International Journal of Research Publications*, *5*(2), 2395–2410.

Thomas, R., Kuruvilla, S., Hinton, R., Jensen, S. L. B., Magar, V., & Bustreo, F. (2015). Assessing the Impact of a Human Rights-Based Approach across a Spectrum of Change for Women's, Children's, and Adolescents' Health. *Health and Human Rights Journal*. https://www.hhrjournal.org/2015/11/22/assessing-the-impact-of-a-human-rights-based-approach-across-a-spectrum-of-change-for-womens-childrens-and-adolescents-health/

Thompson, P. B. (2019). Ethics and governance of emerging technologies in agriculture: The case of genome editing. *Agricultural Systems*, *176*, 102645. DOI: 10.1016/j.agsy.2019.102645

Toh, J., & Yee, Y. X. (2024, February 23). *An interview with Shearn Delamore & Co discussing artificial intelligence in the Malaysia - Lexology*. Lexology. https://www.lexology.com/library/detail.aspx?g=2662ef4d-0df2-44bf-87d3-7bb0048c1b48

Totlani, K. (2023). Navigating the Ethical Maze: Moral Dilemmas in the Age of AI. *International Journal for Research in Applied Science and Engineering Technology*, *11*(10), 968–972. DOI: 10.22214/ijraset.2023.56138

Tourism New Zealand. (2020). Sustainability in Tourism. Retrieved from https://www.tourismnewzealand.com

Trabelsi, M. A. (2024). The impact of artificial intelligence on economic development. *Journal of Electronic Business & Digital Economics*, *3*(2), 142–155. DOI: 10.1108/JEBDE-10-2023-0022

Transparency International. (2020). *Global corruption index 2020*. https://www.transparency.org/en/cpi/2020/index

Tripathi, K., & Gupta, R. (2016). Autonomy and Accountability in Higher Education. *Journal of Human and Work Management*, *4*, 26–31.

Troell, M., Naylor, R. L., Metian, M., Beveridge, M., Tyedmers, P. H., Folke, C., Arrow, K. J., Barrett, S., Crépin, A.-S., Ehrlich, P. R., Gren, Å., Kautsky, N., Levin, S. A., Nyborg, K., Österblom, H., Polasky, S., Scheffer, M., Walker, B. H., Xepapadeas, T., & de Zeeuw, A. (2014). Does aquaculture add resilience to the global food system? *Proceedings of the National Academy of Sciences of the United States of America*, *111*(37), 13257–13263. DOI: 10.1073/pnas.1404067111 PMID: 25136111

Twyford, E. J., Musundwa, S., Tanima, F. A., & George, S. (2024). Bridging the gap: Sustainable development goals as catalysts for change in accounting education and society. *Meditari Accountancy Research, 32*(5), 1758–1786. DOI: 10.1108/MEDAR-02-2024-2375

U.S. Environmental Protection Agency. (2020). Clean Water Act (CWA). Retrieved from https://www.epa.gov/laws-regulations/summary-clean-water-act

Uganda's approach to refugee self-reliance. (2025). https://www.fmreview.org/solutions/clements-shoffner-zamore

UN. (2015). Resolution adopted by the General Assembly on 11 September 2015. *New York: United Nations.* http://www.un.org/ga/search/view_doc.asp?symbol1/4A/RES/70/1. UNWCED. (1987). *Report of the World Commission on Environment and Development: Our Common Future.* Oxford University Press.

UNDRR. (2021). Tourism Resilience Scorecard. https://www.undrr.org

UNESCO. (1972). Convention concerning the protection of the world cultural and natural heritage. Retrieved from https://whc.unesco.org

UNESCO. (2019). Governance in higher education: A global perspective. United Nations Educational, Scientific and Cultural Organization. https://unesdoc.unesco.org/ark:/48223/pf0000371094

UNESCO. (2023). Machine learning in heritage tourism. https://whc.unesco.org

UNESCO-IOC. (2021a). *MSPglobal Policy Brief: Marine Spatial Planning and the Sustainable Blue Economy* (IOC Policy Brief no 2). Paris, UNESCO.

UNESCO-IOC. (2021b). *MSPglobal Policy Brief: Climate Change and Marine Spatial Planning* (IOC Policy Brief no 3). Paris, UNESCO.

UN-Habitat. (2018). *New Urban Agenda.* United Nations Human Settlements Programme.

UNICEF. (2019). *Guidelines on juvenile justice reform.* https://www.unicef.org/documents/guidelines-juvenile-justice-reform

United Nations Development Programme. (2020). *Strengthening the justice system for peace and security.* https://www.undp.org/peacebuilding

United Nations Development Programme. (n.d.). *Sustainable Development Goals.* https://www.undp.org/sustainable-development-goals

United Nations Economic and Social Commission for Asia and the Pacific. (2009). What is good governance? UNESCAP.https://www.unescap.org/sites/default/d8files/knowledge-products/what-is-good-governance.pdf

United Nations Goal 3: Ensure healthy lives and promote well-being for all at all ages. (n.d.). Department of Economic and Social Affairs. https://sdgs.un.org/goals/goal3

United Nations Office of Legal Affairs. (2021). *Prisoners' rights and international law*. https://legal.un.org

United Nations Office on Drugs and Crime. (2015). *Nelson Mandela Rules: United Nations standard minimum rules for the treatment of prisoners*. https://www.unodc.org/documents/justice-and-prison-reform/Nelson_Mandela_Rules-E-ebook.pdf

United Nations Office on Drugs and Crime. (2021). *Health in prisons: A global overview*. https://www.unodc.org

United Nations Office on Drugs and Crime. (2021). *Sustainable Development Goal 16: Peace, justice, and strong institutions*. https://www.un.org/sustainabledevelopment/peace-justice/

United Nations Office on Drugs and Crime. (2021). The health of prisoners: Issues and policies. *UNODC Annual Report on Prison Health, 7*, 39–50.

United Nations Office on Drugs and Crime. (2022). *Justice for all: The role of the justice system in achieving the SDGs*. https://www.unodc.org/unodc/en/about-unodc/sustainable-development-goals/sdg16_-peace-and-justice.html

United Nations Office on Drugs and Crime. (n.d.). *Sustainable Development Goal 3: Good health and well-being*. https://www.unodc.org/unodc/en/about-unodc/sustainable-development-goals/sdg3_-good-health-and-well-being.html

United Nations. (1948). *Universal Declaration of Human Rights*. https://www.un.org/en/universal-declaration-human-rights

United Nations. (1966). *International Covenant on Civil and Political Rights*. https://www.ohchr.org/en/instruments-mechanisms/instruments/international-covenant-civil-and-political-rights

United Nations. (1984). *Convention against torture and other cruel, inhuman or degrading treatment or punishment*. https://www.ohchr.org/en/instruments-mechanisms/instruments/convention-against-torture-and-other-cruel-inhuman-or-degrading

United Nations. (2007). United Nations Declaration on the Rights of Indigenous Peoples. Retrieved from https://www.un.org

United Nations. (2015). Transforming our world: The 2030 agenda for sustainable development. https://sdgs.un.org/2030agenda

United Nations. (2015). *Transforming our world: The 2030 Agenda for Sustainable Development.* https://sustainabledevelopment.un.org/post2015/transformingourworld

United Nations. (2015). Transforming our world: The 2030 Agenda for Sustainable Development. Retrieved from https://sustainabledevelopment.un.org/

United Nations. (2015). UN General Assembly. Transforming our world: the 2030 Agenda for Sustainable Development. A/RES/70/1. https://www.un.org/en/development/desa/population/migration/generalassembly/docs/globalcompact/A_RES_70_1_E.pdf

United Nations. (2015). *United Nations standard minimum rules for the treatment of prisoners (the Nelson Mandela Rules).* https://www.un.org/en/events/mandeladay/mandela_rules.shtml

United Nations. (2016). Clean Water and Sanitation: Why It Matters. https://www.un.org/sustainabledevelopment/wp-content/uploads/2016/08/6_Why-It-Matters-2020.pdf

United Nations. (2019). *United Nations Office on Drugs and Crime (UNODC) and justice system reforms.* https://www.unodc.org/unodc/en/justice-and-prison-reform/index.html

United Nations. (2020). *Access to justice and human rights.* United Nations Human Rights Office. https://www.ohchr.org/en/access-justice

United Nations. (2021). Glasgow Climate Pact. *UN Climate Change Conference 2021.* Retrieved from https://unfccc.int

United Nations. (2021). *Sustainable Development Goals report 2021.* https://unstats.un.org/sdgs/report/2021/The-Sustainable-Development-Goals-Report-2021.pdf

United Nations. (2021, November 25). *193 countries adopt first-ever global agreement on the Ethics of Artificial Intelligence | UN News.* United Nations. https://news.un.org/en/story/2021/11/1106612

United Nations. (2023). *Sustainable Development Goal 16: Peace, justice, and strong institutions.* https://www.un.org/sustainabledevelopment/peace-justice/

United Nations. (2023). The Sustainable Development Goals Report 2023: Special edition. United Nations, New York, NY. https://unstats.un.org/sdgs/report/2023/The-Sustainable-Development-Goals-Report-2023.pdf

UNWTO. (2017). *Sustainable development of tourism.* https://www.unwto.org/sustainable-development

Urhan, C. (2023). *A Critical Inquiry on Current Arrangements of Remote Work in Turkey and the Global North. In book: Remote and Hybrid Working: Variants, Determinants,Outcomes*. Peter Lang GmbH.

Valenzuela, P. (2023). Glacier rights in Andean tourism. *Mountain Research and Development*, *43*(1), R23–R31.

Valukas, A. R. (2010). Lehman Brothers Holdings Inc. Chapter 11 proceedings examiner's report. Jenner & Block.

van den Bergh, J. C. J. M., & Botzen, W. J. W. (2022). Governance of Smart Cities: Insights from Amsterdam's Approach. *Environmental Innovation and Societal Transitions*, *45*, 123–136.

van den Bergh, J., & Botzen, W. J. W. (2022). Smart city governance and social equity in Amsterdam. *Sustainable Cities and Society*, *81*, 103873.

Van der Borg, J. (2023). Platform regulation in urban tourism: The Amsterdam model. *Journal of Destination Marketing*, *27*, 100782.

Van der Meer, P. J., Angenon, G., Bergmans, H., Buhk, H. J., & Rüdelsheim, P. L. J. (2023). Environmental risk assessment of genetically modified organisms in the EU: Current practices and challenges. *Environmental Sciences Europe*, 35(1), Artikel 35. https://enveurope.springeropen.com/articles/10.1186/s12302-023-00734-3

van Wynsberghe, A. (2021). Sustainable AI: AI for sustainability and the sustainability of AI. *AI and Ethics*, *1*(3), 213–218. DOI: 10.1007/s43681-021-00043-6

Vandersteen, W., Leggatt, R., Sundström, L., & Devlin, R. (2019). Importance of experimental environmental conditions in estimating risks and associated uncertainty of transgenic fish prior to entry into nature. *Scientific Reports*, *9*(1), 406. DOI: 10.1038/s41598-018-35826-1 PMID: 30674960

Vasquez, M. (2018). International standards on the treatment of prisoners. *Human Rights Quarterly*, *40*(1), 45–68. DOI: 10.1353/hrq.2018.0020

Vázquez, C., & Orteu Berrocal, E. (2021). "Planificación Hidrológica Y Adaptación Al Cambio Climático En El Marco De La Nueva Ley De Cambio Climático Y Transición Energética". Actualidad Jurídica Ambiental, (115).

Vázquez-Burguete, J. L., Licandro, O., Ortigueira-Sánchez, L. C., & Correa, P. (2024). Do enterprises that publish sustainability reports have a better developed environmental responsibility and are they more transparent? *Sustainability (Basel), 16*(14), 5866. DOI: 10.3390/su16145866

Veel, P.-E. (2009). Carbon tariffs and the WTO: An evaluation of feasible policies. *Journal of International Economic Law, 12*(3), 749–800. DOI: 10.1093/jiel/jgp031

Velázquez Gomar, J. O. (2016). Environmental policy integration among multilateral environmental agreements: The case of biodiversity. *International Environmental Agreement: Politics, Law and Economics, 16*(4), 525–541. DOI: 10.1007/s10784-014-9263-4

Velten, E. K., Evans, N., Duwe, M., Spasova, D., de la Vega, R., & Duin, L. (2022). Charting a path to net zero: An assessment of national long-term strategies in the EU.

Venturelli, A., Ligorio, L., & de Nuccio, E. (2023). Biodiversity accountability in water utilities: A case study. *Utilities Policy, 81*, 101495. DOI: 10.1016/j.jup.2023.101495

Vieira, A. C. (2020). The WTO and the Paris Agreement: A Dialogue on Climate Change Mitigation. *Beijing Law Review, 11*(2), 399–414. DOI: 10.4236/blr.2020.112025

Vijayaraghavan, H. (2020). Gaps in India's Treatment of Refugees and Vulnerable Internal Migrants Are Exposed by the Pandemic. https://www.migrationpolicy.org/article/gaps-india-refugees-vulnerable-internal-migrants-pandemic

Vijeyarasa, R. (2021). Quantifying CEDAW: Concrete tools for enhancing accountability for women's rights. *Harvard Human Rights Journal, 34*, 37.

Vince, J. (2014). Oceans governance and marine spatial planning in Australia. *Australian Journal of Maritime and Ocean Affairs, 6*(1), 5–17. DOI: 10.1080/18366503.2014.888137

Viteri Mejía, C. (2023). Green gentrification in Costa Rican tourism. *Latin American Perspectives, 50*(3), 112–128.

Vuki, V. (2023). Traditional marine management in Fiji. *Oceania, 93*(1), 78–95.

Wahab, H. A., Wahed, H., & Razak, S. S. A. (2024). Flexible Work Arrangements and the Legal Considerations in Malaysia. Proceedings of the 12th UUM International Legal Conference 2023 (UUMILC 2023), Atlantis Highlights in Social Sciences, Education and Humanities 15,DOI: 10.2991/978-94-6463-352-8_31

Wahab, H. A., Razak, S. S. A., & Mahmod, N. A. K. N. (2022). Legal issues in working from home amid Covid-19 pandemic in Malaysia. *UUM Journal of Legal Studies, 13*(2), 163–186.

Wahab, S. A., & Ashutosh, I. (2022). Rebordering South Asia: Displaced Persons and Urbanization. *Annals of the American Association of Geographers, 112*(3), 742–752. DOI: 10.1080/24694452.2021.2023001

Walters, B. R. (2021). The measure of CEDAW: Religion, religious freedom, and the rights of women. *Annual Review of the Sociology of Religion, 12*, 241–270. DOI: 10.1163/9789004468085_013

Wan, C. D., Sirat, M., & Abdul Razak, D. (2020). Academic governance and leadership in Malaysia: Examining the national higher education strategic initiatives. *Journal of International and Comparative Education, 9*(2), 91–105. DOI: 10.14425/jice.2020.9.2.0913

Wang, Y., & Zhou, R. (2024). Can carbon emission trading policies promote the withdrawal of government subsidies and the green development of enterprises? Empirical evidence from China's A-share market. *Humanities and Social Sciences Communications, 11*(1723). https://doi.org/DOI: 10.1057/s41599-024-04255-z

Wang, J., & Cheng, Y. (2023). Enhancing aquaculture disease resistance: Antimicrobial peptides and gene editing. *Reviews in Aquaculture, 16*(1), 433–451. DOI: 10.1111/raq.12845

Wang, X., Olsen, L., Reitan, K., & Ôlsen, Y. (2012). Discharge of nutrient wastes from salmon farms: Environmental effects, and potential for integrated multi-trophic aquaculture. *Aquaculture Environment Interactions, 2*(3), 267–283. DOI: 10.3354/aei00044

Wang, Y., Hamid, N., Jia, P., & Pei, D. (2021). A comprehensive review on genetically modified fish: Key techniques, applications and future prospects. *Reviews in Aquaculture, 13*(3), 1635–1660. DOI: 10.1111/raq.12538

Wang, Y., & Hsieh, Y. (2021). Enhancing local stakeholder participation in smart city PPPs. *Sustainable Cities and Society, 65*, 102601.

Warren, C. (2023). Adat law and tourism governance in Indonesia. *Pacific Affairs, 96*(2), 245–263.

Water, U. N. (2021). Summary Progress Update 2021: SDG 6 — water and sanitation for all. https://www.unwater.org/app/uploads/2021/12/SDG-6-Summary-Progress-Update-2021_Version-July-2021a.pdf

Weale, A. (2023). *Equality and social policy*. Routledge. DOI: 10.4324/9781003369127

Weaver, D. (2023). Certification challenges in regenerative tourism. *Journal of Sustainable Tourism, 31*(4), 889–907.

Weaver, D., & Skyer, P. (2023). Namibian conservancies. *Tourism Management, 94*, 104632.

Web Sources / News Articles

Wei, W., & Wee, W. (2014). Fish consumption pattern among adults of different ethnics in Peninsular Malaysia. *Food & Nutrition Research*, 58(1), . https://doi.org/ DOI: 10.3402/fnr.v58.22697

Wei, L., Liu, Z., Cao, P., & Zhang, H. (2025). Environmental subsidies and green innovation: The role of environmental regulation and chief executive officer green background. *Clean Technologies and Environmental Policy, 27*(3), 389–402. DOI: 10.1007/s10098-024-02755-9

Werthmann, C. (2021). *Informal urbanization in Latin America: Collaborative transformations of public spaces*. Routledge. DOI: 10.4324/9781003089797

What Malaysian Companies Need to Know About SDGs and Sustainability Policies. (2024) Elite Asia Marketing, Reviewed on May 2025 https://www.eliteasia.co/what-malaysian-companies-need-to-know-about-sdgs-and-sustainability-policies/

Whyte, K. (2023). Indigenous justice in tourism development. *Environmental Ethics, 45*(1), 45–63.

Wieczorek, A. J. (2018). Sustainability transitions in developing countries: Major insights and their implications for research and policy. *Environmental Science & Policy, 84*, 204–216. DOI: 10.1016/j.envsci.2017.08.008

Wiegant, D., Dewulf, A., & Zeben, J. V. (2024). Alignment mechanisms to effectively govern the sustainable development goals. *World Development, 182*, 106721. Advance online publication. DOI: 10.1016/j.worlddev.2024.106721

WIPO. (2019). Traditional knowledge and cultural expressions: Intellectual property issues. Retrieved from https://www.wipo.int

Wojtara, M. (2023). Analyzing the efficacy and utility of the Americans with Disabilities Act of 1990 on college students with disabilities. University of Michigan Undergraduate Research Journal, 16.

Wolch, J. R.. (2018). Urban green space, public health, and environmental justice: The challenge of equity in urban ecosystem services. *Landscape and Urban Planning, 181*, 176–183.

Wolt, J. D., Keese, P., Raybould, A., Fitzpatrick, J. W., Burachik, M., Gray, A., & Wu, F. (2023). The role of the precautionary principle in EU GMO regulations. *Integrated Environmental Assessment and Management, 19*(2), 267–275. DOI: 10.1002/ieam.4278

Wong, R. (2019). Balancing Institutions for Implementing the Sustainable Development Goals Through 'Network Within Hierarchy'. *Sustainability (Basel), 11*(16), 4498. DOI: 10.3390/su11164498

Woodbridge, M. (2015). From MDGs to SDGs: What are the Sustainable Development Goals? *ILEI*. https://www.local2030.org/library/251/From-MDGs-to-SDGs-What-are-the-Sustainable-Development-Goals.pdf

World Bank. (2019). *Justice for the poor: Enhancing access to justice in developing countries*. https://www.worldbank.org/en/topic/governance/brief/justice-for-the-poor

World Bank. (2020). *Governance and higher education quality: An international perspective*. World Bank Group. https://documents.worldbank.org/en/publication/documents-reports/documentdetail/123456

World Health Organization. (2020). *Health and human rights in prison systems*. https://www.who.int/europe/health-topics/prisons-and-health

World Health Organization. (2020). *Health and prison systems: Strengthening health care in prisons*. https://www.who.int/news-room/fact-sheets

World Health Organization. (2020). *Mental health in prisons: Challenges and opportunities*. https://iris.who.int/bitstream/handle/10665/108156/E64328.pdf?sequence=1

World Health Organization. (2020). Prison health and the burden of disease in incarcerated populations. *WHO Guidelines on Prison Healthcare, 12*(2), 45–67.

World Health Organization. (2021). *Health systems strengthening in prisons*. https://www.drugsandalcohol.ie/35165/1/WHO_prison_framework.pdf

World Health Organization. (2022). *Guidelines for drinking-water quality: incorporating the first and second addenda*. World Health Organization.

World Prison Brief. (2020). *Prison healthcare systems worldwide: Access and limitations*. https://www.prisonstudies.org

World Tourism Organization. (2019). Sustainable Tourism Development: Guide for Policy Makers. Retrieved from https://www.unwto.org

Wunder, S. (2023). Payments for ecosystem services: Global lessons. *World Development, 161*, 106118.

Wu, Y., & Wan, J. (2024). The race between global economic growth and carbon emissions: Based on a comparative study of developed and developing countries. *Environmental Science and Pollution Research International, 31*(13), 19226–19243. DOI: 10.1007/s11356-024-32275-4 PMID: 38355861

WWF. (2015). First Marine Spatial Planning in Sabah Launched to Further Protect Semporna Priority Conservation Area (PCA). https://www.wwf.org.my/?19725/First-Marine-Spatial-Planning-in-Sabah-Launched-to-Further-Protect-Semporna-Priority-Conservation-Area-PCA

Xanthaki, A. (2023). Indigenous Jurisprudence in Sustainable Tourism. *International Journal of Human Rights, 27*(3), 456–475.

Xu, H.. (2023). Sustainable urban drainage systems and legal mandates: Innovations in flood prevention. *Water Research, 232*, 119619.

Yang, C., & Yan, X. (2023). Impact of carbon tariffs on price competitiveness in the era of global value chain. *Applied Energy, 336*, 120805. DOI: 10.1016/j.apenergy.2023.120805

Yang, Y., Chih, S. H., & Chiu, C. R. (2025). Association between the environmental efficiency and corruption perception index: A dynamic alternative metafrontier SBM approach. *Journal of Environmental Management, 374*, 124046. DOI: 10.1016/j.jenvman.2025.124046 PMID: 39793499

Yatani, V. G. (2023). Refugee Protection in Multi-level Governance Regimes: A Case for Kenya and Indonesia. *Lampung Journal of International Law, 5*(1), 59–72. DOI: 10.25041/lajil.v5i1.2868

Yatim, M. H. M., Omar, A. H., Abdullah, N. M., & Sarip, A. (2018). Extending the concept of institutional analysis to the marine spatial planning practice. *IOP Conference Series. Earth and Environmental Science, 169*(1), 012010. Advance online publication. DOI: 10.1088/1755-1315/169/1/012010

Yigitcanlar, T., Kamruzzaman, M., & Buys, L. (2021). Public-private partnerships for smart city sustainability. *Sustainable Cities and Society, 64*, 102557.

Yigitcanlar, T., Kamruzzaman, M., & Foth, M. (2020). The smart city approach for urban innovation and sustainability. *Sustainable Cities and Society, 61*, 102350.

York, R., & Gossard, M. H. (2004). Social support, environmental beliefs, and vegetarianism. *Rural Sociology*, *69*(3), 448–469. DOI: 10.1526/0036011041730467

Yunxia, X., & Yuqing, N. (2025). The technological advancement environmental regulations and their impact on energy efficiency and CO2 emissions. *Scientific Reports*, *15*(1), 2781. DOI: 10.1038/s41598-025-86581-z PMID: 39843519

Zagaris, B., & Plachta, M. (2023). Crimes against humanity and war crimes. *International Enforcement Law Reporter*, *39*, 405.

Zainal, A., Radzi, S. M., & Hashim, N. (2020). Challenges in sustainable tourism enforcement in Asia-Pacific. *Journal of Tourism Research*, *29*(3), 87–101.

Zajac, E. J., & Westphal, J. D. (1996). Who shall succeed? How CEO/board preferences and power affect the choice of new CEOs. *Academy of Management Journal*, *39*(1), 64–90. DOI: 10.2307/256631

Zakaria, Z., & Hassan, M. N. (2020). The effectiveness of environmental impact assessments in sustainable tourism planning in Malaysia. *Journal of Environmental Management*, *260*, 110154. DOI: 10.1016/j.jenvman.2020.110154

Zaleski, P. (2022). Prisoner rights and international law. *International Law Review*, *27*(2), 113–130. DOI: 10.1016/j.inlaw.2022.12.001

Zanten, J. A. V., & Tulder, R. V. (2018). Multinational enterprises and the Sustainable Development Goals: An institutional approach to corporate engagement. *Journal of International Business Policy*. https://doi.org/DOI: 10.1057/s42214-018-0008-x

Zariski, A. (2014). *Legal literacy: An introduction to legal studies*. Athabasca University Press. DOI: 10.15215/aupress/9781927356449.01

Zbikowska, H. M. (2003). Fish can be first—Advances in fish transgenesis for commercial applications. *Transgenic Research*, *12*(4), 379–389. DOI: 10.1023/A:1024267416522 PMID: 12885160

Zeppel, H. (2020). Indigenous ecotourism: Sustainable development and management. *Journal of Ecotourism*, *19*(3), 245–259. DOI: 10.1080/14724049.2020.1727483

Zerunyan, F. V., & Duzert, Y. (2024). *Advancing and Negotiating Sustainable Development Goals (SDGs): A Practical Toolkit*. Taylor & Francis. DOI: 10.4324/9781003497097

Zhang, S., Chan, S. L., & Abai, D. S. binti A. (2025). A Study on the Impact of Flexible Working Arrangements on Turnover Intention of Chinese Working Women: From the Perspective of SDG 8 (Decent Work). Journal of Lifestyle and SDGs Review, 5(2), e04211. https://doi.org/DOI: 10.47172/2965-730X.SDGsReview.v5.n02.pe04211

Zhang, J., & Choi, S. (2018). Legal frameworks and risk sharing in smart city PPPs. *International Journal of Project Management, 36*(5), 685–697.

Zhang, S., Kaikun, W., Yastrubskyi, M., & Huang, C. (2023). Carbon emissions from international trade and consumption: Assessing the role of cumulative risk for EU and Chinese economic development. *Energy Strategy Reviews, 50*, 101219. DOI: 10.1016/j.esr.2023.101219

Zhang, W., Li, H., & Xu, Y. (2019). Investment protection and PPP performance in smart cities. *Cities (London, England), 92*, 161–171.

Zhang, Z., Glover, K., Wennevik, V., Svåsand, T., Sørvik, A., Fiske, P., & Skaala, Ø. (2012). Genetic analysis of atlantic salmon captured in a netting station reveals multiple escapement events from commercial fish farms. *Fisheries Management and Ecology, 20*(1), 42–51. DOI: 10.1111/fme.12002

Zhao, J.. (2018). Urban forestry legal frameworks and biodiversity conservation. *Urban Forestry & Urban Greening, 31*, 125–134.

Zhao, R. (2024). Green trade barriers in global play: Legal challenges and strategic opportunities for developing countries. *Journal of Education. Humanities and Social Sciences, 39*, 48–55. DOI: 10.54097/kz926p47

Zhou, X., Zhu, Q., Xu, L., Wang, K., Yin, X., & Mangla, S. K. (2024). The effect of carbon tariffs and the associated coping strategies: A global supply chain perspective. *Omega, 122*, 102960. DOI: 10.1016/j.omega.2023.102960

Zhu, Z., Li, G., He, L., & Chen, S. (1985). Novel gene transfer into the fertilized eggs of goldfish (Carassius auratus L. 1758). *Journal of Applied Ichthyology, 1*(1), 31–34. DOI: 10.1111/j.1439-0426.1985.tb00408.x

Ziegler, J., Baumann, S., & Hofmann, S. (2020). Data governance and privacy in smart cities: Legal frameworks and best practices. *Journal of Urban Technology, 27*(4), 3–20.

Zubair, M., Khan, M. A., & Shah, M. (2019). An Analysis Of The Legal Framework Of International Refugee Protection System. *Global Political Review, 1*(I), 1–10. Advance online publication. DOI: 10.31703/gpr.2019(IV-I).01

Zubair, S. (2023). Maldivian traditional law and climate tourism. *Island Studies Journal, 18*(1), 89–104.

About the Contributors

Farahdilah Ghazali is a senior lecturer at School of Business and Economics, University of Putra Malaysia. Previously, she served University of Malaysia Terengganu (UMT) and University of Tenaga Nasional Malaysia (UNITEN). She obtained her PhD in Law from Ahmad Ibrahim Kulliyyah of Laws, International Islamic University Malaysia (IIUM). Her interest areas are Natural Resources Law and Sustainability, particularly related to renewable energy. She has been appointed as a technical member for the enactment of the Malaysian Legal Framework on Seabed Mining in 2019. Being a passionate researcher and academic, she has widely published in peer-reviewed journals and presented papers at several national and international conferences in her areas of interest.

Siti Fazilah Binti Abdul Shukor is a Lecturer for the Department of Business and Public Administration at the Faculty of Business and Finance, Universiti Tunku Abdul Rahman. She holds a Doctor of Philosophy (Law) degree, a Master of Comparative Laws from the International Islamic University Malaysia, and a Bachelor's degree in Law and Commerce (Honours) from Management and Science University (MSU). Her research areas include Law, Industrial Relations, Law of Dismissal, Employment Law, and Human Rights Law. Siti Fazilah has been a Lecturer at the Department of Business since October 16, 2013. Her teaching expertise encompasses courses such as Communication Law, Construction Law, Malaysian Legal System, Business Law, Corporate and Business Law, Company Law, Malaysian Company Secretarial Practice, and Legal Framework and Banking Law. She has received recognition for her academic excellence, having been awarded the Best Student Award (Academic) for the degree of Bachelor in Law and Commerce (Honours) at Management and Science University, Malaysia.

***

Shreya completed her LL.M. in Criminal & Security Law from SNIL, SOA University in 2024. Her legal education started at SNIL, SOA University where she finished my B.A.LL.B. (Hons.) in 2023. In the year 2024 she have registered for Ph.D in Law at KIIT University with area of research being Victimology. During her academic pursuit she have developed a passion in the area of Criminal law including Human Rights and have done researches on sentencing discrepancies and the factors that lead to such discrepancies.

Zuhairah Ariff Binti Abd Ghadas is a distinguished professor at the Faculty of Law and International Relations, Universiti Sultan Zainal Abidin (UniSZA), with a specialization in Company Law, Contract Law, Business Law, and Construction Law. She holds a Ph.D. in Business Law from Universiti Putra Malaysia, along with a Master's in Comparative Laws from the International Islamic University Malaysia, and a Bachelor's in Business Law from the University of Huddersfield. Prof. Dr. Zuhairah has extensive academic and professional experience, having worked as a lecturer, legal adviser, and administrator at various institutions, including her previous roles at the International Islamic University Malaysia (IIUM) and UniSZA. She has contributed to numerous journals and conferences, publishing articles on topics such as corporate social responsibility, online contracts, construction law, and human rights. Furthermore, she has participated in various legal and academic training programs, contributing significantly to the field of legal education and research.

Hamizah Abdul Rahman is a senior lecturer at Universiti Sultan Zainal Abidin (UniSZA) in Terengganu, Malaysia, specializing in Company Law, business Law and Corporate Governance. She obtained her Ph.D. in Law from the University of Sultan Zainal Abidin (UniSZA) in 2020. Prior to that, she completed a Master's in Comparative Law from the International Islamic University of Malaysia (IIUM) in 2013, and a Bachelor of Law and Commerce (Hons.) from Management and Science University (MSU) in 2010. She also holds a Diploma in Law from UniSZA, earned in 2007.In her academic career, Dr. Hamizah has held various teaching roles. Since February 2020, she has been a Lecturer at UiTM Kelantan, where she teaches courses such as Compan Law, Business Law for Accounting student, and Introduction to Partnership and Company Law. Previously, she served as a Lecturer at Management and Science University (MSU) from 2015 to 2017, and at YPC International College from 2014 to 2015, where she taught Business Law and Company Law to degree students. Her research focuses on legal frameworks for business entities like Limited Liability Partnerships (LLPs), with particular emphasis on governance issues and comparative legal studies between Malaysia, Singapore, and India. Her recent work explores the evolving nature of partnership business structures and sustainable development within corporate governance frameworks. Her academic contributions have earned her recognition, including a Silver Award at KILIEX 2021 for an innovative legal project.

Farihana Abdul Razak is a Law Lecturer at Universiti Teknologi MARA (UiTM), Perak Branch, Tapah Campus, where she has been serving since 2014. She earned her Bachelor of Law with Honours and Master of Commercial Law from Universiti Utara Malaysia and later attained her Doctor of Philosophy in Law from Universiti Sultan Zainal Abidin. With over a decade of academic experience, Dr. Farihana specializes in areas including contract law, company law, torts, and consumer law. Her current research focuses on the legal doctrines underpinning unfair contract terms and their application in Malaysia. Dr. Farihana's scholarly work has been published in numerous journals, significantly contributing to her field of expertise. She remains committed to advancing legal knowledge and fostering an understanding of complex legal concepts among her students and the broader academic community.

Natalia Alonso-Morales is a PhD Student in Finance and Accounting at the University of Almería (Spain) with a FPU Grant of the Spanish Ministry of Universities, Her research is concerning to online transparency of public administration; business companies and nonprofit organizations. She is author of several articles published in JCR publications including Sustainable Futures. Also, she has written some book chapters

Maria Caba-Pérez is a Full Professor in the Public Management Sector at the University of Almeria. Her research is concerning to online transparency of public administration; business companies and nonprofit organizations. She is author of several articles published in JCR publications including The American Review of Public Administration, International Review of Administrative Science, Online Information Review, Government Information Quarterly, Voluntas, Latin American Research Review or Public Administration and Development, Public Relations Review, Information Development, etc. Also, she has written more than 20 book chapters.

Saurabh Chandra is an accomplished legal scholar and currently serves as an Associate Professor & Assistant Dean at the School of Law, Bennett University, India. With a robust academic foundation, he earned his Bachelor of Arts and Bachelor of Laws (B.A. LL.B.) from the prestigious Aligarh Muslim University (A.M.U.). He further specialized in Business Laws, completing his Master of Laws (LL.M.) at the renowned National Law School of India University (NLSIU), Bangalore. Dr. Chandra's academic journey culminated in a Doctorate in Law

(Ph.D.) from the esteemed National Law University (NLU) Delhi. In addition to his impressive legal education from some of India's most prestigious institutions, Dr. Chandra also holds a master's degree in Management with specialization in Human Resources in Management and another in Journalism and Mass Communication. With more than sixteen years of teaching experience, he has numerous publications to his credit. His expertise is complemented by a robust portfolio of scholarly publications. Dr. Chandra brings a wealth of experience in Academic Administration, having successfully held various key administrative positions.

María García-González is a PhD Student in Finance and Accounting at colaborator reserarcher at the Department of Economics & Business Administration from the University of Almería (Spain).

Kyvalya Garikapati, currently working as Dean (Academics) at KIIT School of Law, KIIT Deemed to be University, Bhubaneswar.

Pedro Gil-García is a PhD Student in Finance and Accounting at the University of Almería (Spain) with a FPU Grant of Spanish University. His research is concerning to online transparency of public administration; business companies and nonprofit organizations. He has written some book chapters

J. Sudarvel working as an Assistant Professor of Management at Karpagam Academy of Higher Education. He produced five Ph.D. Scholars and four Ph.D. Scholars are under his guidance. Further, to his credit he published more than five articles in Scopus indexed journals and published more than 50 articles in international journals. He is acting as a Subject Experts in Board of studies of various autonomous colleges.

Sheikh Inam Ul Mansoor (BA.LLB Hon's, LLM, CPCT WIPO, Ph.D. International Trade Law) is a highly accomplished academician presently working as an Assistant Professor Law at the School of Law, Dayananda Sagar University in Bangalore, India. With a strong background in law and a passion for academia, Dr. Sheikh has made significant contributions to the field through his extensive research and publications. Pursued his BA. LLB (Hon's) from University of Kashmir, LLM from JNU Jaipur and Ph.D. International Trade Law from LPU Punjab. Prior to his academic career, Dr. Sheikh served as an Advocate and Solicitor at the Jammu and Kashmir High Court and other subordinate courts in Jammu and Kashmir. This experience as a legal practitioner has provided him with valuable insights into the practical application of law and enhanced his understanding of legal dynamics.

Abhinash Mohanta pursued a three-year LLB program at Ganjam Law College, Berhampur, under Berhampur University. He further advanced his academic journey by enrolling in the Master of Laws (LLM) program in Business Law at the P.G. Department of Law, Berhampur University, graduating in 2017. Currently, he is pursuing a Ph.D. in Law at KIIT Deemed to be University, with a research focus on critical areas such as refugee and human rights. In addition to his academic endeavors, Abhinash has authored several Scopus-indexed papers covering diverse topics, including AI, environment, migration, crime, intellectual property, and refugee studies.

Nurul Syazwani Mohd Noor obtained her bachelor's degree (Hons.) in Actuarial Science from the Universiti Teknologi MARA, Shah Alam, Selangor and Master of Science in Management (Finance and Banking) from the Universiti Sultan Zainal Abidin, Kuala Nerus, Terengganu. She graduated PhD Islamic Civilization (Islamic Finance) from Institut Islam Hadhari, Universiti Kebangsaan Malaysia. She is currently a senior lecturer at Universiti Sultan Zainal Abidin. She teaches and conducts research in the area related to Islamic finance, Islamic wealth management, takaful as well as risk management and modelling.

Ravindran Nadarajan is a distinguished legal scholar, educator, and researcher specializing in family law, matrimonial property law, and international business law. He holds a Ph.D. in Law from the International Islamic University Malaysia (2023), with his thesis focusing on equitable matrimonial property division. Currently a lecturer and Public Administration and Human Resource Cluster Head, Dr. Ravindran contributes to curriculum development and teaches a wide range of law courses. Known for his engaging teaching style, he emphasizes innovative and student-centered learning. Dr. Ravindran's research interests include matrimonial law, corporate governance, and ESG. A published author and former Case Analysis Legal Editor at LexisNexis, he bridges academic theory with legal practice, inspiring future legal professionals and advancing the legal field.

R. Velmurugan presently working as an Associate Professor in Commerce, Karpagam Academy of Higher Education, Coimbatore. He started his career as a Project Fellow under UGC Sponsored Major Research Project at NGM College, Pollachi. He has 18 years of teaching experience has 15 years of research experience. To his credit he produced 22 Ph.D. Scholars and 5 M.Phil. Scholars. At present 1 scholar submitter his thesis, 6 Ph.D. Scholars are under his guidance. Moreover, to his credit he published 168 articles in various International Journals, of which 58 articles are published in Scopus Indexed Journals and 15 articles in Web of Science and 76 articles in edited volumes. He also participates and presented 27 papers in various International Seminar / Conference and 54 National Seminar / Conference. He acted as an external examiner for various M.Phil. and Ph.D. Viva voce examinations. He acted as a Vice Chancellor nominee for Doctoral Committee Expert at Bharathiar University, Coimbatore and Periyar University, Salem. He acted as a Chairperson at various National Level Conferences. He also acted as an Expert for Syllabus Scrutiny Committee, Question Paper Scrutiny Committee and Expert members for Board of Studies at various reputed Colleges. Considering his meritorious contribution, he received awards like Best Paper Presenter, Best Research Supervisor and Best Faculty Awards from various research foundations and councils. He too acted as a resource person for 27 Guest Lectures, 30 Workshops and 10 faculty development programmes.

S. Senthilkumar, currently working as Assistant Professor in Finance and Management, Skyline University, Nigeria. His qualifications are MBA, M.Com, M.Phil, MS, and PhD. He has rich experience in teaching and academic of 18.2 years. He had published 58 papers Publications in National and International Journals and Proceedings. He Authored 4 books in Research Methodology, Corporate Finance, Principles of Accounting and Business Policy & Strategic management. Participated and presented 62 papers in National & International Seminars and Conferences. He acted as resource person and Guest lecture around 25 Programmemes. He guided 225 projects in M.B.A., 36 M.Phil, and 9 PhD. He got Authorized Guide ship for PhD & M.Phil from Indian Universities such as Anna University, Karpagam University, Bharathiar University, Periyar Manimai University and AMIET University and Vinayaka Mission University and Bahir Dar University, Ethiopia. He performed as Foreign examiner for evaluating PhD Thesis around 18 Thesis of Indian universities such as Bharathiar University, Visvesvaraya Technological University, University of Mumbai, MS University and Bharathidasan university.

Shivani Samanta, a dynamic legal professional, going to complete my B.A.LL.B. (H) in 2024 from the esteemed University Law College, a constituent college of Utkal University and currently pursuing LL.M. at South Asian University, New Delhi. Throughout my academic journey, I've embraced various leadership roles, shaping my collaborative and team-oriented approach. Key Attributes: Leadership: I have a proven track record in diverse leadership roles, fostering teamwork and achieving collective goals. Communication: As an extrovert and creative contributor to any conversation, I am adept at articulating ideas and perspectives. Academic Excellence: Being a dedicated and driven student, I've built a strong academic foundation, complemented by an insatiable curiosity for legal intricacies. Career Aspirations: I am passionate about research related to the legal field and academia. I am committed to acquiring a comprehensive understanding of the legal field and honing skills for a positive impact. Eager to specialise in an area of law aligning with my passion, whether it's human rights, social justice, or constitutional law, I aspire to contribute to ethical practices. Future Goals: My aim is to utilise my legal expertise to effect meaningful change in society. I embrace challenges for personal and professional growth and am keen on connecting with like-minded professionals to explore opportunities and discussions in the legal domain. Let's build a network that fosters positive change!

Seow Ai Na is an academic and researcher at Universiti Tunku Abdul Rahman (UTAR), specializing in tourism studies. Her research focuses on consumer behavior, environmental responsibility, and the business resilience of small and medium enterprises (SMEs) within the tourism sector.

Siti Tafzilmeriam binti Sheikh Abdul Kadir is a Research Officer at the Institute of Oceanography and Environment (INOS), Universiti Malaysia Terengganu. She is actively collaborating with partners, primarily government agencies such as the Fisheries Development Authority of Malaysia (LKIM), as well as other research institutions including Universiti Putra Malaysia, Universiti Teknologi MARA, and the International Islamic University Malaysia. Additionally, she is a member of various organizations, including the Malaysia Biodiversity Information System (MyBIS), Ocean Expert (A Directory of Marine and Freshwater Professionals), the Malaysian Fisheries Society, and the Asian Fisheries Society. In 2022 and 2021, she received the Anugerah Pentadbir UMT awards in three categories: Anugerah Pentadbir Terbilang UMT, Anugerah Pentadbir UMT (Scientific Writing), and Anugerah Pentadbir UMT (Research). Dr. Siti also achieved recognition with an Anugerah Pentadbir Gemilang MASTI 2020 award for Research (Skim Q), including a Bronze Medal from the Ministry of Higher Education Malaysia (MoHE).

Bhupinder Singh working as Professor at Sharda University, India. Also, Honorary Professor in University of South Wales UK and Santo Tomas University Tunja, Colombia. His areas of publications as Smart Healthcare, Medicines, fuzzy logics, artificial intelligence, robotics, machine learning, deep learning, federated learning, IoT, PV Glasses, metaverse and many more. He has 3 books, 139 paper publications, 163 paper presentations in international/national conferences and seminars, participated in more than 40 workshops/FDP's/QIP's, 25 courses from international universities of repute, organized more than 59 events with international and national academicians and industry people's, editor-in-chief and co-editor in journals, developed new courses. He has given talks at international universities, resource person in international conferences such as in Nanyang Technological University Singapore, Tashkent State University of Law Uzbekistan; KIMEP

University Kazakhstan, All'ah meh Tabatabi University Iran, the Iranian Association of International Criminal law, Iran and Hague Center for International Law and Investment, The Netherlands, Northumbria University Newcastle UK,

Anthony Tee Mooi Kwong is a scholar in the field of sustainable tourism development and currently serving as Assistant Professor in Universiti Tunku Abdul Rahman. Holding a Ph.D. in the subject, Dr. Tee has dedicated his career to advancing knowledge and practices in tourism planning and development. As an active researcher, Dr. Tee has contributed significantly to the discourse on sustainable tourism. In addition to research, Dr. Tee has served as a consultant in tourism planning and development.

Index

Symbols

A

B

C

D

E

F

Q

R

S

T

W

www.ingramcontent.com/pod-product-compliance
Lightning Source LLC
LaVergne TN
LVHW062341300926
849161LV00007B/1777